ENCYCLOPEDIA OF
GLOBAL RESOURCES

ENCYCLOPEDIA OF
GLOBAL RESOURCES

Volume 1

Abrasives - Energy storage

Editor

DISCARDED

Craig W. Allin

Cornell College

SALEM PRESS
Pasadena, California   Hackensack, New Jersey

Editor in Chief: Dawn P. Dawson

Editorial Director: Christina J. Moose *Production Editor:* Andrea E. Miller
Manuscript Editor: Christopher Rager *Page Design and Layout:* James Hutson
Acquisitions Editor: Mark Rehn *Additional Layout:* Mary Overell and
Research Supervisor: Jeffry Jensen William Zimmerman
Photo Editor: Cynthia Breslin Beres *Editorial Assistant:* Brett Weisberg

Cover photo: ©iStockphoto.com/Guillermo Perales

Library of Congress Cataloging-in-Publication Data

Encyclopedia of global resources / Craig W. Allin, editor.
  p. cm.
  Includes bibliographical references and index.
  ISBN 978-1-58765-644-6 (set : alk. paper) — ISBN 978-1-58765-645-3 (vol. 1 : alk. paper) — ISBN 978-1-58765-646-0 (vol. 2 : alk. paper) — ISBN 978-1-58765-647-7 (vol. 3 : alk. paper) — ISBN 978-1-58765-648-4 (vol. 4 : alk. paper) 1. Natural resources. I. Allin, Craig W.
  HC85.E49 2010
  333.703—dc22

                                                                    2010001984

Mixed Sources
Product group from well-managed
forests, controlled sources and
recycled wood or fiber
www.fsc.org Cert no. SGS-COC-005368
© 1996 Forest Stewardship Council

FSC

PRINTED IN THE UNITED STATES OF AMERICA

Publisher's Note

FROM NORTH AMERICA TO THE WORLD

Salem's critically acclaimed *Natural Resources*, which originally appeared in 1998 in three volumes, forms the foundation for this fully revised and expanded four-volume set, *Encyclopedia of Global Resources*. Hailed by the American Library Association in its first edition as an Outstanding Reference Source of 1999, *Encyclopedia of Global Resources* now adds 143 new articles (6 of which replace superseded entries) to the original 438 entries. All of the original articles have been revised to extend their scope to our global economy in 2010. All of the original 135 charts, graphs, and tables have been updated or replaced, and 110 new charts, tables, graphs, sidebars have been added, for a total of 235 data-laden sidebars that are easily understood at a graphic, visual level. Dozens of appendixes illustrate the text, providing students with worldwide insights into where we derive our mineral, biological, and energy resources; how they are processed; for what purposes they are used; and where they stand in our current economy.

The coverage touches not only on the economic applications and benefits of natural resources but also on their processing, their management, the environmental impact of their extraction, and trends in their availability—all in easily understood language. The expanded contents include 40 overviews of top resource nations and their significance in the global context. Specific minerals, organizations, historical events, and biographies are included as well as articles on energy and ecological resources. Appendixes provide both alphabetical and periodic tables of the elements, along with lists of Major U.S. Mineral Resources, Major U.S. Mineral Resources by State, Major Canadian Mineral Resource Production and Values, Major Worldwide Mineral Resources and Producers, Major Worldwide Resources by Country, a Time Line, a Glossary, a Bibliography, and a list of Web Sites.

CONTENT DEFINITION

The term "natural resources" has been in general use since the late nineteenth century, and for many decades discussions of natural resources have formed an important part of history, anthropology, and social studies curricula. In the most basic sense, natural resources have long been defined as naturally occurring raw materials and phenomena—timber, flowing water, and minerals such as iron and coal—that are economically useful to humans, particularly those materials important to major industries or to a nation's security. By the late 1960's, however, concerns about the world's growing human population, the finite nature of many "nonrenewable" resources, and the environmental and ecological ramifications of resource exploitation had taken hold. Viewed in a global context, resource issues rapidly became more complex. Today one is as likely to hear discussions of "global resources" as of natural resources, along with debates over issues such as "sustainable development," "renewable vs. nonrenewable resources," "ecological resources," and "energy resources." This sea change in the way we view our resources and their integration into a global marketplace and worldwide environmental concerns has prompted this complete overhaul of the original edition, its expansion to four volumes, and its new title: *Encyclopedia of Global Resources*.

CONTENTS AND SCOPE OF COVERAGE

Salem Press's four-volume *Encyclopedia of Global Resources* provides a wide variety of perspectives on both traditional and more recent views of Earth's resources. In this sense, *Encyclopedia of Global Resources* serves as a bridge connecting the domains of resource exploitation, environmentalism, ecology, geology, and biology, and it explains their interrelationships in terms that students and other nonspecialists can understand.

The 575 alphabetically arranged articles in *Encyclopedia of Global Resources* are as broad as "Agricultural products" and as specific as "Svalbard Global Seed Vault." They range in length from 500 words (about a page) to more than 3,000 words (6 pages) and cover topics as diverse as soil, fisheries, forests, aluminum, the Industrial Revolution, the U.S. Department of the Interior, the hydrologic cycle, glass, and placer mineral deposits. Top resources—119 mineral-based, 41 biologically based, and 39 energy-related (such as oil and tar sands)—are covered, as well as 40 countries; 32 ecological resources; 50 environment, conservation, and resource management; 41 geological processes and formations; 72 government and resources; 18 historical events and movements; 35 laws and conventions; 49 obtaining and using resources; 71 organizations, agencies, and programs; 37 people; 22 pollution and waste disposal; 23 products from resources;

19 scientific disciplines; and 31 social, economic, and political issues.

In the traditional view of natural resources, the core of the set is a series of more than one hundred articles on specific mineral and other nonliving resources, from aluminum to zirconium; more than twenty overviews were added to the original list of these mineral resources, while the others were updated. These articles begin with immediately accessible, informative subheads—"Where Found," "Primary Uses," "Technical [including chemical] Definition"—and continue with subsections that address "Description, Distribution, and Forms," "History," "Obtaining [the Resource]," and "Uses of [the Resource]." There are also survey articles on such resource categories as abrasives, gems, radioactive isotopes, and silicates as well as on the geologic processes and formations that produce mineral resources. Reflecting the overwhelming importance of petroleum products to the world, a cluster of articles discuss the chemistry, distribution, and formation of oil and natural gas in addition to oil exploration and drilling, the oil industry, oil shale and tar sands, and petrochemical products. Other energy resources, such as hydroenergy, nuclear energy, solar energy, and wind energy, are also covered in detail. Two other broad resource areas are discussed in a number of articles: plant and animal resources, and what we have called ecological resources, such as Earth's atmosphere, biodiversity, forests, medicinal plants, oceans, water, and even resources deriving from extraterrestrial exploration of our solar system. Articles on the former range from specific crops, such as corn, to overviews of animal breeding, agricultural products, and carbon. Articles on the latter reflect the realization that, in an increasingly populated world, natural systems such as rain forests, grasslands, lakes, and wetlands—from their genetic diversity to the global biosphere itself—must be considered crucially important resources, subject to threat and in continual need of being monitored and protected.

Because the concept of "natural resources" describes materials useful or necessary to people, this set includes entries on many aspects of the human dimension of resource exploitation, such as how various resources are obtained and processed. Also discussed are the major secondary or intermediate materials that resources are used to produce; among these articles are "Carbon fiber and carbon nanotubes," "Cement and concrete," "Fiberglass," "Gasoline and other petroleum fuels," and "Semiconductors." Economic, political, and societal ramifications of resource use are discussed in essays on energy economics and politics, the early history of mineral resource use, resource exploitation and health, and resource use in developing countries. A number of articles stress the environmental effects of human activities related to obtaining and using resources—air and water pollution, mining wastes, deforestation, desertification—as well as phenomena that can be either natural or caused by humans, such as droughts, erosion, and fires. Other articles delineate the issues and choices surrounding resource management, recycling, conservation, sustainable development, preservation, environmentalism, and waste disposal.

Another set of essays cover particularly significant pieces of legislation, international conventions, and activities of specific government agencies. Brief articles highlight organizations, historical events, and personages important in the history of resource exploitation, conservation, and environmental protection. Finally, several overviews of important fields of study—from agronomy to geographic information systems to risk assessment—round out the set.

REFERENCE FEATURES

Each article in *Encyclopedia of Global Resources* is signed, and each has summary information at the beginning and cross-references to other articles in the set at the end. All articles are organized using internal subheads, consistent by type of article, and articles that are 1,000 words in length or longer conclude with bibliographies. Of the 575 essays, 350 also contain sections that direct users to authoritative Web sites. All illustrations have been updated or replaced and significantly expanded with 235 charts, tables, and graphs, as well as 200 photos.

A useful reference feature at the beginning of each volume is a Complete List of Contents, and at the end of volume 4 are several appendixes: an Alphabetical Table of the Elements, the Periodic Table of the Elements, lists of Major U.S. Mineral Resources, Major U.S. Mineral Resources by State, Major Canadian Mineral Resource Production and Values, Major Worldwide Mineral Resources and Producers, Major Worldwide Resources by Country, a Time Line, a Glossary, a Bibliography, and a list of Web Sites. Finally, the set ends with a Category Index that groups similar essays, along with a comprehensive Subject Index.

ACKNOWLEDGMENTS

Salem Press wishes to acknowledge the editors of the original three-volume edition, Mark S. Coyne of the University of Kentucky and Craig W. Allin of Cornell College. For this expanded four-volume edition, Professor Allin was instrumental in defining the scope, coverage, and contents. We also thank the 199 scholars who contributed original essays, updated their previous work, and/or wrote new material for this edition; a list of their names and affiliations appears on the following pages.

Contributors

McCrea Adams
Independent Scholar

Bland Addison
Worcester Polytechnic Institute

Richard Adler
University of Michigan—Dearborn

Steve K. Alexander
University of Mary Hardin-Baylor

Craig W. Allin
Cornell College

Emily Alward
College of Southern Nevada

S. Ashok
Penn State University

Anita Baker-Blocker
Ann Arbor, Michigan

Grace A. Banks
Chestnut Hill College

Joshua I. Barrett
Charleston, West Virginia

Melissa A. Barton
Westminster, Colorado

Harlan H. Bengtson
Southern Illinois University, Edwardsville

Alvin K. Benson
Utah Valley University

John L. Berkley
SUNY, College at Fredonia

Milton Berman
University of Rochester

David M. Best
Northern Arizona University

Cynthia A. Bily
Adrian, Michigan

Margaret F. Boorstein
C. W. Post College of Long Island University

Richard G. Botzler
Humboldt State University

Lakhdar Boukerrou
Florida Atlantic University

Judith J. Bradshaw-Rouse
University of Wisconsin—Madison

Howard Bromberg
University of Michigan

JoEllen Broome
Georgia Southern University

Kenneth H. Brown
Northwestern Oklahoma State University

Jeffrey C. Brunskill
Bloomsburg University of Pennsylvania

Michael H. Burchett
Limestone College

Henry Campa III
Michigan State University

Gary A. Campbell
Michigan Technological University

Jennifer L. Campbell
Lycoming College

Byron D. Cannon
University of Utah

Roger V. Carlson
Jet Propulsion Laboratory

Robert E. Carver
University of Georgia

Dennis W. Cheek
Ewing Marion Kauffman Foundation

Kerry L. Cheesman
Capital University

Judy Arlis Chesen
Capital University

Jill A. Cooper
Boise, Idaho

Robert G. Corbett
Illinois State University

Charles V. Cordaro
Pasadena, California

Mark S. Coyne
University of Kentucky

Alan K. Craig
Florida Atlantic University

James R. Craig
Virginia Polytechnic Institute & State University

Richard A. Crooker
Kutztown University

Robert L. Cullers
Kansas State University

Alan C. Czarnetzki
University of Northern Iowa

Pat Dasch
National Space Society

Jennifer Davis
Kettering, Ohio

LeAnna DeAngelo
Arizona State University

René A. De Hon
University of Louisiana at Monroe

Joseph Dewey
University of Pittsburgh—Johnstown

Albert B. Dickas
University of Wisconsin

John R. Dickel
University of Illinois

David M. Diggs
Central Missouri State University

Steven L. Driever
University of Missouri—Kansas City

Colleen M. Driscoll
Villanova University

Thomas A. Eddy
Emporia State University

H. J. Eisenman
University of Missouri—Rolla

Jessica O. Ellison
Clarkson University

Robert D. Engelken
Arkansas State University

Victoria Erhart
Strayer University

Thomas R. Feller
Nashville, Tennessee

Mary C. Fields
Medical University of South Carolina

David G. Fisher
Lycoming College

Dale L. Flesher
University of Mississippi

Richard H. Fluegeman, Jr.
Ball State University

George J. Flynn
SUNY—Plattsburgh

James F. Fowler
State Fair Community College

Donald R. Franceschetti
University of Memphis

Yongli Gao
East Tennessee State University

June Lundy Gastón
City University of New York

Michael Getzner
Klagenfurt University

Soraya Ghayourmanesh
Bayside, New York

Lenela Glass-Godwin
Texas A&M University
Auburn University

James S. Godde
Monmouth College

Joelle D. Godwin
Eckerd College

Pamela J. W. Gore
Georgia Perimeter College

D. R. Gossett
Louisiana State University—Shreveport

D. Yogi Goswami
University of Florida

Jerry E. Green
Miami University

Richard Wayne Griffin
Prairie View A&M University

Clayton D. Harris
Middle Tennessee State University

Jasper L. Harris
North Carolina Central University

C. Alton Hassell
Baylor University

Craig Bond Hatfield
The University of Toledo

Robert M. Hawthorne, Jr.
Marlboro, Vermont

Charles D. Haynes
University of Alabama

Mark C. Herman
Edison State College

Stephen C. Hildreth, Jr.
Pickens, South Carolina

Robert M. Hordon
Rutgers University

Raymond Pierre Hylton
Virginia Union University

Domingo M. Jariel
Louisiana State University at Eunice

Albert C. Jensen
Central Florida Community College

Richard C. Jones
Texas Woman's University

Chand K. Jotshi
University of Florida

Karen N. Kähler
Pasadena, California

Mark Kanazawa
Carleton College

Kyle L. Kayler
Mahopac, New York

Diann S. Kiesel
University of Wisconsin Center—Baraboo/
Sauk County

Grove Koger
Boise State University

Narayanan M. Komerath
Georgia Institute of Technology

Padma P. Komerath
SCV, Inc.

Ludwik Kowalski
Montclair State University

Craig B. Lagrone
O.I. Analytical, CMS Field Products

Ralph L. Langenheim, Jr.
University of Illinois—Urbana

Eugene Larson
Los Angeles Pierce College

Vincent M. D. Lopez
Independent Scholar

Chungu Lu
NOAA Earth System Research Laboratory

R. C. Lutz
CII Group

Fai Ma
University of California, Berkeley

Roxanne McDonald
Wilmot, New Hampshire

Thomas R. MacDonald
University of San Francisco

Elizabeth A. Machunis-Masuoka
Midwestern State University

Marianne M. Madsen
University of Utah

Nancy Farm Männikkö
Centers for Disease Control & Prevention

A. M. Mannion
University of Reading

Sergei A. Markov
Austin Peay State University

W. J. Maunder
Tauranga, New Zealand

Raymond F. Mikesell
University of Oregon

Marian A. L. Miller
University of Akron

Randall L. Milstein
Oregon State University

Alice Myers
Bard College at Simon's Rock

John E. Myers
Bard College at Simon's Rock

Mysore Narayanan
Miami University

Terrence R. Nathan
University of California, Davis

Brian J. Nichelson
Pearland, Texas

Emmanuel U. Nzewi
North Carolina A&T State University

Oghenekome U. Onokpise
Florida A&M University

Robert J. Paradowski
Rochester Institute of Technology

John R. Phillips
Purdue University Calumet

Rex D. Pieper
New Mexico State University

George R. Plitnik
Frostburg State University

Aaron S. Pollak
Omaha, Nebraska

Oliver B. Pollak
University of Nebraska at Omaha
Pollak and Hicks

Victoria Price
Lamar University

Cynthia F. Racer
New York Academy of Sciences, Society for
Public Health Education

Steven J. Ramold
Eastern Michigan University

William O. Rasmussen
University of Arizona

Donald F. Reaser
The University of Texas at Arlington

David D. Reed
Michigan Technological University

Edward A. Riedinger
Ohio State University

Gina M. Robertiello
Felician College

Raymond U. Roberts
Oklahoma Department of Environmental
Quality

Gene D. Robinson
James Madison University

James L. Robinson
University of Illinois at Urbana-
Champaign

Charles W. Rogers
Southwestern Oklahoma State University

Carol A. Rolf
Rivier College

Kathryn L. Rowberg
Purdue University Calumet

Joseph R. Rudolph, Jr.
Towson University

Michael K. Rulison
Oglethorpe University

Neil E. Salisbury
University of Oklahoma

Panagiotis D. Scarlatos
Florida Atlantic University

Elizabeth D. Schafer
Loachapoka, Alabama

Harold H. Schobert
Penn State University

John Richard Schrock
Emporia State University

Steven C. Schulte
Mesa State College

Leslie J. Schwartz
St. John Fisher College

Rose Secrest
Chattanooga, Tennessee

Ronald John Shadbegian
University of Massachusetts—Dartmouth

S. A. Sherif
University of Florida

R. Baird Shuman
University of Illinois at Urbana-
Champaign

Carlos Nunes Silva
University of Lisbon

Paul P. Sipiera
William Rainey Harper College

Amy Sisson
Houston Community College

Roger Smith
Portland, Oregon

Robert J. Stern
University of Texas at Dallas

Joan C. Stevenson
Western Washington University

C. J. Stewart
Mote Marine Laboratory

Dion C. Stewart
Georgia Perimeter College

Robert J. Stewart
California Maritime Academy

William H. Stewart
University of Alabama

Theresa L. Stowell
Adrian College

Frederick M. Surowiec
Independent Scholar

Jacqueline Vaughn Switzer
Northern Arizona University

Glenn L. Swygart
Tennessee Temple University

Katrina Taylor
Northern Arizona University

John M. Theilmann
Converse College

Nicholas C. Thomas
Auburn University at Montgomery

Donald J. Thompson
California University of Pennsylvania

Leslie V. Tischauser
Prairie State College

Roger Dale Trexler
Southern Illinois University

Sarah A. Vordtriede
St. Ambrose University

William T. Walker
Chestnut Hill College

C. J. Walsh
Mote Marine Laboratory

Xingwu Wang
Alfred University

William J. Wasserman
Seattle Central Community College

John P. Watkins
Westminster College

Kevin D. Weakley
Western Michigan University

Shawncey Webb
Taylor University

Thomas W. Weber
SUNY at Buffalo

Robert J. Wells
Society for Technical Communication

Kristopher D. White
Kazakhstan Institute of Management, Economics, & Strategic Research

Edwin G. Wiggins
Webb Institute

Thomas A. Wikle
Oklahoma State University

Sam Wong
University of Leeds

William C. Wood
James Madison University

Lisa A. Wroble
Hodges University

Jay R. Yett
Orange Coast College

Ming Y. Zheng
Gordon College

Tom L. Zimmerman
The Ohio State University

Contents

Common Units of Measure

Common prefixes for metric units—which may apply in more cases than shown below—include *giga-* (1 billion times the unit), *mega-* (one million times), *kilo-* (1,000 times), *hecto-* (100 times), *deka-* (10 times), *deci-* (0.1 times, or one tenth), *centi-* (0.01, or one hundredth), *milli-* (0.001, or one thousandth), and *micro-* (0.0001, or one millionth).

Unit	Quantity	Symbol	Equivalents
Acre	Area	ac	43,560 square feet 4,840 square yards 0.405 hectare
Ampere	Electric current	A *or* amp	1.00016502722949 international ampere 0.1 biot *or* abampere
Angstrom	Length	Å	0.1 nanometer 0.0000001 millimeter 0.000000004 inch
Astronomical unit	Length	AU	92,955,807 miles 149,597,871 kilometers (mean Earth-Sun distance)
Barn	Area	b	10^{-28} meters squared (approx. cross-sectional area of 1 uranium nucleus)
Barrel (dry, for most produce)	Volume/capacity	bbl	7,056 cubic inches; 105 dry quarts; 3.281 bushels, struck measure
Barrel (liquid)	Volume/capacity	bbl	31 to 42 gallons
British thermal unit	Energy	Btu	1055.05585262 joule
Bushel (U.S., heaped)	Volume/capacity	bsh *or* bu	2,747.715 cubic inches 1.278 bushels, struck measure
Bushel (U.S., struck measure)	Volume/capacity	bsh *or* bu	2,150.42 cubic inches 35.238 liters
Candela	Luminous intensity	cd	1.09 hefner candle
Celsius	Temperature	C	1° centigrade
Centigram	Mass/weight	cg	0.15 grain
Centimeter	Length	cm	0.3937 inch
Centimeter, cubic	Volume/capacity	cm³	0.061 cubic inch
Centimeter, square	Area	cm²	0.155 square inch
Coulomb	Electric charge	C	1 ampere second

Unit	Quantity	Symbol	Equivalents
Cup	Volume/capacity	C	250 milliliters 8 fluid ounces 0.5 liquid pint
Deciliter	Volume/capacity	dl	0.21 pint
Decimeter	Length	dm	3.937 inches
Decimeter, cubic	Volume/capacity	dm^3	61.024 cubic inches
Decimeter, square	Area	dm^2	15.5 square inches
Dekaliter	Volume/capacity	dal	2.642 gallons 1.135 pecks
Dekameter	Length	dam	32.808 feet
Dram	Mass/weight	dr *or* dr avdp	0.0625 ounce 27.344 grains 1.772 grams
Electron volt	Energy	eV	$1.5185847232839 \times 10^{-22}$ Btus $1.6021917 \times 10^{-19}$ joules
Fermi	Length	fm	1 femtometer 1.0×10^{-15} meters
Foot	Length	ft *or* ′	12 inches 0.3048 meter 30.48 centimeters
Foot, cubic	Volume/capacity	ft^3	0.028 cubic meter 0.0370 cubic yard 1,728 cubic inches
Foot, square	Area	ft^2	929.030 square centimeters
Gallon (British Imperial)	Volume/capacity	gal	277.42 cubic inches 1.201 U.S. gallons 4.546 liters 160 British fluid ounces
Gallon (U.S.)	Volume/capacity	gal	231 cubic inches 3.785 liters 0.833 British gallon 128 U.S. fluid ounces
Giga-electron volt	Energy	GeV	$1.6021917 \times 10^{-10}$ joule
Gigahertz	Frequency	GHz	—
Gill	Volume/capacity	gi	7.219 cubic inches 4 fluid ounces 0.118 liter

Unit	Quantity	Symbol	Equivalents
Grain	Mass/weight	gr	0.037 dram 0.002083 ounce 0.0648 gram
Gram	Mass/weight	g	15.432 grains 0.035 avoirdupois ounce
Hectare	Area	ha	2.471 acres
Hectoliter	Volume/capacity	hl	26.418 gallons 2.838 bushels
Hertz	Frequency	Hz	$1.08782775707767 \times 10^{-10}$ cesium atom frequency
Hour	Time	h	60 minutes 3,600 seconds
Inch	Length	in or ″	2.54 centimeters
Inch, cubic	Volume/capacity	in^3	0.554 fluid ounce 4.433 fluid drams 16.387 cubic centimeters
Inch, square	Area	in^2	6.4516 square centimeters
Joule	Energy	J	$6.2414503832469 \times 10^{18}$ electron volt
Joule per kelvin	Heat capacity	J/K	$7.24311216248908 \times 10^{22}$ Boltzmann constant
Joule per second	Power	J/s	1 watt
Kelvin	Temperature	K	–272.15 Celsius
Kilo-electron volt	Energy	keV	$1.5185847232839 \times 10^{-19}$ joule
Kilogram	Mass/weight	kg	2.205 pounds
Kilogram per cubic meter	Mass/weight density	kg/m^3	$5.78036672001339 \times 10^{-4}$ ounces per cubic inch
Kilohertz	Frequency	kHz	—
Kiloliter	Volume/capacity	kl	—
Kilometer	Length	km	0.621 mile
Kilometer, square	Area	km^2	0.386 square mile 247.105 acres
Light-year (distance traveled by light in one Earth year)	Length/distance	lt-yr	5,878,499,814,275.88 miles 9.46×10^{12} kilometers
Liter	Volume/capacity	L	1.057 liquid quarts 0.908 dry quart 61.024 cubic inches

Unit	Quantity	Symbol	Equivalents
Mega-electron volt	Energy	MeV	—
Megahertz	Frequency	MHz	—
Meter	Length	m	39.37 inches
Meter, cubic	Volume/capacity	m³	1.308 cubic yards
Meter per second	Velocity	m/s	2.24 miles per hour 3.60 kilometers per hour
Meter per second per second	Acceleration	m/s²	12,960.00 kilometers per hour per hour 8,052.97 miles per hour per hour
Meter, square	Area	m²	1.196 square yards 10.764 square feet
Metric. *See* unit name			
Microgram	Mass/weight	mcg *or* μg	0.000001 gram
Microliter	Volume/capacity	μl	0.00027 fluid ounce
Micrometer	Length	μm	0.001 millimeter 0.00003937 inch
Mile (nautical international)	Length	mi	1.852 kilometers 1.151 statute miles 0.999 U.S. nautical miles
Mile (statute or land)	Length	mi	5,280 feet 1.609 kilometers
Mile, square	Area	mi²	258.999 hectares
Milligram	Mass/weight	mg	0.015 grain
Milliliter	Volume/capacity	ml	0.271 fluid dram 16.231 minims 0.061 cubic inch
Millimeter	Length	mm	0.03937 inch
Millimeter, square	Area	mm²	0.002 square inch
Minute	Time	m	60 seconds
Mole	Amount of substance	mol	6.02×10^{23} atoms or molecules of a given substance
Nanometer	Length	nm	1,000,000 fermis 10 angstroms 0.001 micrometer 0.00000003937 inch

Unit	Quantity	Symbol	Equivalents
Newton	Force	N	x 0.224808943099711 pound force 0.101971621297793 kilogram force 100,000 dynes
Newton meter	Torque	N·m	0.7375621 foot-pound
Ounce (avoirdupois)	Mass/weight	oz	28.350 grams 437.5 grains 0.911 troy or apothecaries' ounce
Ounce (troy)	Mass/weight	oz	31.103 grams 480 grains 1.097 avoirdupois ounces
Ounce (U.S., fluid or liquid)	Mass/weight	oz	1.805 cubic inch 29.574 milliliters 1.041 British fluid ounces
Parsec	Length	pc	30,856,775,876,793 kilometers 19,173,511,615,163 miles
Peck	Volume/capacity	pk	8.810 liters
Pint (dry)	Volume/capacity	pt	33.600 cubic inches 0.551 liter
Pint (liquid)	Volume/capacity	pt	28.875 cubic inches 0.473 liter
Pound (avoirdupois)	Mass/weight	lb	7,000 grains 1.215 troy or apothecaries' pounds 453.59237 grams
Pound (troy)	Mass/weight	lb	5,760 grains 0.823 avoirdupois pound 373.242 grams
Quart (British)	Volume/capacity	qt	69.354 cubic inches 1.032 U.S. dry quarts 1.201 U.S. liquid quarts
Quart (U.S., dry)	Volume/capacity	qt	67.201 cubic inches 1.101 liters 0.969 British quart
Quart (U.S., liquid)	Volume/capacity	qt	57.75 cubic inches 0.946 liter 0.833 British quart
Rod	Length	rd	5.029 meters 5.50 yards

Unit	Quantity	Symbol	Equivalents
Rod, square	Area	rd^2	25.293 square meters 30.25 square yards 0.00625 acre
Second	Time	s *or* sec	$\frac{1}{60}$ minute $\frac{1}{3600}$ hour
Tablespoon	Volume/capacity	T *or* tb	3 teaspoons 4 fluid drams
Teaspoon	Volume/capacity	t *or* tsp	0.33 tablespoon 1.33 fluid drams
Ton (gross or long)	Mass/weight	t	2,240 pounds 1.12 net tons 1.016 metric tons
Ton (metric)	Mass/weight	t	1,000 kilograms 2,204.62 pounds 0.984 gross ton 1.102 net tons
Ton (net or short)	Mass/weight	t	2,000 pounds 0.893 gross ton 0.907 metric ton
Volt	Electric potential	V	1 joule per coulomb
Watt	Power	W	1 joule per second 0.001 kilowatt $2.84345136093995 \times 10^{-4}$ ton of refrigeration
Yard	Length	yd	0.9144 meter
Yard, cubic	Volume/capacity	yd^3	0.765 cubic meter
Yard, square	Area	yd^2	0.836 square meter

Complete List of Contents

Volume 1

Volume 2

Volume 3

Volume 4

ENCYCLOPEDIA OF
GLOBAL RESOURCES

Abrasives

CATEGORY: Mineral and other nonliving resources

Abrasives comprise a large number of both naturally occurring minerals and rocks and manufactured products. In many cases these manufactured products have largely replaced their natural counterparts. Some, such as diamond, are rare; others, including sand and sandstone, are found abundantly in nature. All find uses in the home or in industry because of their characteristic hardness.

BACKGROUND

Because the abrasives category encompasses a great variety of materials, their worldwide distributions are highly varied. Some, such as garnet and emery, are obtained from only a few localities. Others, such as sand and sandstone, are found on all continents, in all geologic settings, and in rocks representing all geologic ages.

Use of all the abrasives reflects in some manner the characteristics of hardness. That property is utilized in cutting and drilling tools, surface polishing materials, and blasting media. The largest user of abrasives is the automobile industry. Abrasives, both natural and synthetic, are used to perform one of four basic functions: the removal of foreign substances from surfaces ("dressing"), cutting, drilling, and comminution (or pulverizing) of materials. Most abrasives lie toward the upper end of the Mohs hardness scale. With respect to one another, however, they can be categorized as hard, moderate (or "siliceous"), or soft.

HARD ABRASIVES

The hard abrasives are diamond, corundum, emery, and garnet. Diamond, the hardest naturally occurring substance (10 on the Mohs scale), is normally used in three size categories: stone, bort, and powder. Only a small fraction of the diamond stones produced by mining are of gem quality. All others, as well as those produced synthetically (together referred to as industrial diamonds), are used in various industrial applications, including diamond saws, rock-drilling bits, and other abrasive tools. Bort consists of fragments and small, flawed stones. Most bort, as well as synthetic diamond, is crushed to powder and mixed with water or oil to form a slurry that is used to polish gems. The United States has no exploitable diamond deposits, but it is the world's leading producer of diamond dust, easily satisfying its industrial needs.

Corundum, the second-hardest naturally occurring substance (9 on the Mohs scale), is used principally in crushed form for the polishing and finishing of optical lenses and metals. Its abrasive quality is enhanced by the fact that when broken it forms sharp edges. As it wears, it flakes, which produces new edges. Corundum occurs in contact metamorphic rocks, granite pegmatites, and placer deposits. The United States has no significant deposits of corundum.

Manufactured Abrasives: World Production Capacity, 2008		
	METRIC TONS	
NATION	FUSED ALUMINUM OXIDE	SILICON CARBIDE
U.S. & Canada	60,400	42,600
Argentina	—	5,000
Australia	50,000	—
Austria	60,000	—
Brazil	50,000	43,000
China	700,000	455,000
France	40,000	16,000
Germany	80,000	36,000
India	40,000	5,000
Japan	25,000	60,000
Mexico	—	45,000
Norway	—	80,000
Venezuela	—	30,000
Other countries	80,000	190,000

Source: Data from the U.S. Geological Survey, *Mineral Commodity Summaries, 2009.* U.S. Government Printing Office, 2009.

Emery is a natural mixture of corundum and magnetite, with minor amounts of spinel, hematite, or garnet. Its value as an abrasive is largely a function of the amount of corundum present. In the United States, commercial emery deposits occur near the town of Peekskill, New York, where it is mined from contact metamorphic deposits. Important production also comes from Greece and Turkey. The principal uses of emery are as abrasive sheets, grinding wheels, and nonskid surfaces on stairs and pavements. Both corundum and emery have been replaced in large measure by synthetic alumina (Al_2O_3).

Of the fifteen varieties of garnet that occur in nature, almandite is the one most commonly used as an abrasive. Uses of garnet include sandblasting, finishing hard woods, the hydrojet cutting of rocks, and (in powder form) the finishing of optical lenses. Garnet has been replaced in metalworking by synthetic materials because they can be made harder and less friable. The United States, which possesses the world's largest reserves of garnet (mostly in the Adirondack Mountains), accounts for half of the world's production and is also the world's largest consumer.

SILICEOUS ABRASIVES

The term "silica sand" is taken to mean sand of almost pure quartz content, and sandstone (or quartzite) is the lithified version of that sand. Both are examples of siliceous abrasives of moderate hardness. Silica sand is used for sandblasting and for glass grinding. Historically, sandstone has been shaped into grindstones, whetstones, and millstones. Because high-quality sandstones were deposited in shallow seas during virtually all the geological periods, the reserves of silica sand and sandstone of commercial quality in the United States are enormous. Nevertheless, siliceous material for polishing and pulverizing has been replaced to a large extent by steel balls. The market share of silica sand as a sandblasting medium has declined because of health concerns related to the breathing of silica dust, which can lead to a condition called silicosis.

Other siliceous abrasives include diatomite, pumice, tripoli, flint, and chert. Diatomite, or diatomaceous earth, is an accumulation of the siliceous remains of shell-secreting freshwater and marine algae (diatoms). Because it is lightweight and porous, diatomite finds its most important uses as a filtering medium in water purification and waste treatment plants and as a filler (extender) in paint and paper. As an abrasive it is used in scouring soaps and powders, toothpaste, and metal-polishing pastes. The United States possesses the world's most important reserves of diatomite. Tripoli is the weathering remains of siliceous limestones and is similar to diatomite in composition, characteristics, and uses. Pumice, porous volcanic glass, finds its principal market as building block. A small but significant amount of pumice, however, is used as an abrasive, for scouring and stonewashing. Chert and flint, two of the many varieties of quartz, have been used in pellet form in ball mills for the comminution of metallic ores.

Corundum, pictured, is one of four heavy-abrasive materials. (USGS)

SOFT ABRASIVES

The soft abrasives include feldspar, clay, dolomite, chalk, and talc. They are primarily used for the polishing and buffing of metals. Feldspar, mined from granite pegmatites, is also crushed and used in soaps and scouring powders.

SYNTHETIC ABRASIVES

Beginning in about 1900, a variety of manufactured abrasives were developed that have gradually replaced natural abrasives in the marketplace. In addition to lower cost, manufactured abrasives have the advantages of being tailored to meet specific industrial needs and of being produced in uniform quality. Among the important manufactured abrasives are synthetic diamond, cubic boron nitride, fused aluminum oxide, silicon carbide, alumina-zirconia oxide, and steel shot and grit. Synthetic diamonds were first produced in 1955, the result of a process that fuses graphite and metallic catalysts at extremely high temperature and pressure. Cubic boron nitride, first synthesized in 1957, is the next hardest substance after diamond and has challenged synthetic diamond as an abrasive in many industrial applications. Fused aluminum oxide is formed at high temperatures in an electric furnace by the fusing of either bauxite or corundum. Uses include tumbling, polishing, and blasting. It is also used in coated abrasives. Silicon carbide is fused from a mixture of quartz sand and coke; it finds its primary uses as a coated abrasive, in polishing and buffing media, and in wire saws for the cutting of stone. One of the primary uses of steel shot and grit is as a blasting medium. The automobile industry is the largest consumer of artificial abrasives, and the economic fortunes of the two industries are closely tied together.

Donald J. Thompson

FURTHER READING

Giese, Edward, and Thomas Abraham. *New Abrasives and Abrasives Products, Technologies, Markets.* Norwalk, Conn.: Business Communications, 1997.

Hayes, Teresa L., Debra A. Celinski, and Rebecca Friedman. *Abrasives Products and Markets.* Cleveland, Ohio: Freedonia Group, 2000.

Jensen, Mead Leroy, and Alan M. Bateman. *Economic Mineral Deposits.* 3d ed. New York: Wiley, 1979.

Kogel, Jessica Elzea, et al., eds. "Abrasives." In *Industrial Minerals and Rocks: Commodities, Markets, and Uses.* 7th ed. Littleton, Colo.: Society for Mining, Metallurgy, and Exploration, 2006.

WEB SITE

U.S. GEOLOGICAL SURVEY
Manufactured Abrasives: Statistics and Information.
http://minerals.usgs.gov/minerals/pubs/
    commodity/abrasives/index.html#mcs

SEE ALSO: Corundum and emery; Diamond; Diatomite; Garnet; Igneous processes, rocks, and mineral deposits; Metamorphic processes, rocks, and mineral deposits; Mohs hardness scale; Pegmatites; Placer deposits; Pumice; Quartz; Sand and gravel; Sandstone; Sedimentary processes, rocks, and mineral deposits.

Acid precipitation

CATEGORY: Pollution and waste disposal

The existence of acid precipitation became known in the late nineteenth century, but it claimed general attention beginning in the early 1960's. Precipitation whose acidity is greater than that of natural rainwater is termed acid precipitation and is connected to several environmental and health problems.

BACKGROUND

Natural, uncontaminated precipitation is somewhat acidic because of the interaction of the water droplets with carbon dioxide in the atmosphere. This interaction produces carbonic acid, which is weakly acidic and lowers the pH from neutral (7) to around 5.5. This is not considered acid precipitation, but any samples that show a pH of less than 5 are considered acidic.

FORMATION OF ACID RAIN

Three sources of acid precipitation stand out as the major contributors: combustion of coal or other fuels with a high sulfur content, the roasting of some metal sulfide ores, and the operation of internal combustion gasoline engines. In the first two cases the presence of sulfur is the problem. Sulfur, when combined with oxygen during combustion or heating processes, produces sulfur dioxide, which, in the presence of particulate matter in the atmosphere, is further oxidized to sulfur trioxide. This compound, dissolved in water, becomes sulfuric acid. In the internal combustion engine the temperature attained is high enough to allow nitrogen and oxygen, present in ordinary air,

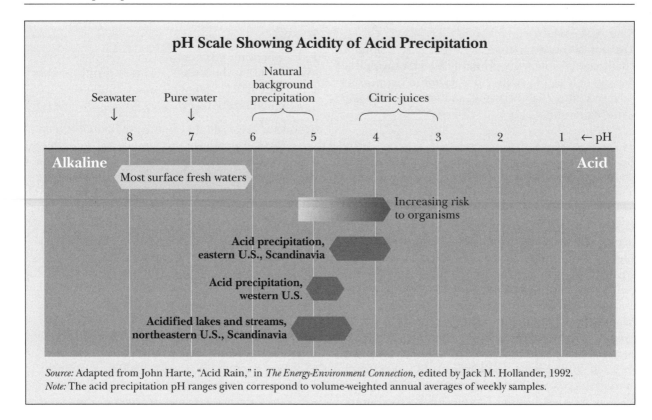

pH Scale Showing Acidity of Acid Precipitation

Source: Adapted from John Harte, "Acid Rain," in *The Energy-Environment Connection*, edited by Jack M. Hollander, 1992.
Note: The acid precipitation pH ranges given correspond to volume-weighted annual averages of weekly samples.

to react and form a complex set of nitrogen oxides. These oxides, again when dissolved in water, produce nitrous and nitric acid. Each of these acids contributes to the total acid load and causes a decrease in the pH of all forms of precipitation.

EFFECTS OF ACID PRECIPITATION

The environmental effects of acid precipitation depend on the soil on which it falls. For example, soils that are derived from the weathering of limestone have the capability of neutralizing the acidity of the precipitation, while those that have resulted from granite do not. The effects can be seen in aquatic ecosystems, in soils and their vegetative covers, and on materials of construction. Acid precipitation eventually runs off into bodies of water and, in time, can have a major impact on their acidity. Many aquatic species can tolerate only small pH changes in their environment before they are killed, and even smaller changes cause stunting and poor reproduction. Considering plants, some are directly affected by the acidity striking their leaves, while others are negatively affected by aluminum, which they take up from the soil through their roots. Aluminum in soil is usually immobilized as

an insoluble material, but acidity in the soil moisture dissolves the material and allows the aluminum to migrate to the plants. Limestone has been used as a material for much building construction as well as the material of which many statues and other decorative objects are made. However, the acidity of the precipitation causes limestone to dissolve, and the effect may be seen in the loss of definition in many outdoor monuments. Even the steel that is the backbone of much construction is corroded at a much higher rate in the presence of acids.

There are human health consequences of acid precipitation as well. The presence of fine acid droplets in the air can lead to respiratory tract irritation. For healthy people this is not a serious problem, but it is a problem for those already troubled by asthma, emphysema, or other lung conditions.

ALLEVIATION OF ACID PRECIPITATION

Abatement of the problem has been approached from two principal directions. It is possible to remove much of the sulfur from coal or liquid fuels before they are burned and therefore to greatly reduce the production of sulfur oxides. Coal liquefaction or gasification accomplishes this, but at considerable dollar cost. Internal combustion engines can be designed to operate at lower temperatures to lower the emissions of nitrogen oxides, but they are less efficient when so run. In smelting operations the ores can be preconcentrated so that a smaller amount of undesired minerals enters the smelter itself. For example, a mixed iron sulfide/nickel sulfide ore can be concentrated to minimize the iron sulfide content and take mainly the more desired nickel mineral to the smelter.

Once the oxides are formed, they can be removed from the exit gases or they can be subjected to further reaction to change them into compounds with less environmental impact. Sulfur dioxide from roasting can be trapped in the liquid form or can be converted to liquid sulfuric acid and, in each case, sold as a by-product. The sulfur dioxide in the exhaust from burning is not concentrated enough to be treated in this fashion, but it can be removed from the exhaust stream by absorbing it in a limestone slurry for later landfill disposal. The current answer for the nitrogen oxide emissions is treatment with a catalytic converter in the exhaust line of the engine. The catalyst converts the oxides back to elemental nitrogen and water at about 80 percent efficiency.

Kenneth H. Brown

FURTHER READING

Bunce, Nigel J. "Acid Rain." In *Introduction to Environmental Chemistry*. 2d ed. Winnipeg, Man.: Wuerz, 1994.

Howells, Gwyneth Parry. *Acid Rain and Acid Waters*. 2d ed. New York: E. Horwood, 1995.

Johnson, Russell W., et al., eds. *The Chemistry of Acid Rain: Sources and Atmospheric Processes*. Washington, D.C.: American Chemical Society, 1987.

Legge, Allan H., and Sagar V. Krupa, eds. *Air Pollutants and Their Effects on the Terrestrial Ecosystem*. New York: Wiley, 1986.

McCormick, John. *Acid Earth: The Politics of Acid Pollution*. 3d ed. London: Earthscan, 1997.

Manahan, Stanley E. *Environmental Chemistry*. 8th ed. Boca Raton, Fla.: CRC Press, 2005.

Somerville, Richard C. J. "Air Pollution and Acid Rain." In *The Forgiving Air: Understanding Environmental Change*. 2d ed. Boston: American Meteorological Society, 2008.

Visgilio, Gerald R., and Diana M. Whitelaw, eds. *Acid in the Environment: Lessons Learned and Future Prospects*. New York: Springer, 2007.

Whelpdale, D. M., and M. S. Kaiser, eds. *Global Acid Deposition Assessment*. Geneva, Switzerland: World Meteorological Organization, Global Atmosphere Watch, 1997.

WEB SITES

ENVIRONMENT CANADA
Acid Rain
http://www.ec.gc.ca/acidrain

U.S. ENVIRONMENTAL PROTECTION AGENCY
Acid Rain
http://www.epa.gov/acidrain

U.S. GEOLOGICAL SURVEY
Acid Rain, Atmospheric Deposition, and
    Precipitation Chemistry
http://bqs.usgs.gov/acidrain/new/
    frontpage_home.htm

SEE ALSO: Air pollution and air pollution control; Atmosphere; Coal gasification and liquefaction; Hydrology and the hydrologic cycle; Internal combustion engine; Metals and metallurgy; Nitrogen cycle; Sulfur cycle.

Aerial photography

CATEGORY: Obtaining and using resources

Aerial photography, which dates to the nineteenth century, has enabled scientists to quantify and predict changes in land use, soil erosion, agricultural development, water resources, habitat, vegetation distribution, animal and human populations, and ecosystems. Aerial photography also is used to construct thematic maps that show the distribution of a variety of global resources.

DEFINITION

Aerial photography is a form of remote sensing that relies on film or digital capture to acquire information about Earth's surface from elevated platforms. These platforms include balloons, airplanes, and satellites. The primary advantage of aerial photography over ground-based observations is the elevated vantage point, which can provide images covering vast expanses of Earth's surface.

OVERVIEW

The invention of photography was announced in 1839 at the joint meeting of the Academies of Sciences and Fine Arts in Paris, France. Nineteen years later, in 1858, Gaspard-Nadar Félix Tournachon made the first aerial photograph from a tethered balloon over Val de Bièvre, France. The oldest extant aerial photograph dates to 1860, when James Wallace Black photographed Boston, Massachusetts, from a balloon tethered above Boston Common. The first aerial photograph made from an airplane was in 1908; the first aerial photograph made from a satellite was in 1959. In the twenty-first century, aerial photography is a vital tool for documenting and managing Earth's resources.

In order to obtain quantitative information about the Earth's resources from an aerial photograph, methods must be applied to the photograph that allow for reliable estimates of spatial relationships. Obtaining such relationships falls under the broad field of photogrammetry. By applying photogrammetric methods, analysts can relate distances on the photograph to distances on the ground. Object heights and terrain elevations can be obtained by comparing photographs made from two different vantage points, each with a different line of sight. This method is based on the principle of parallax, wherein the apparent change in relative position of stationary objects is compared between the photographs. Additional information can be gleaned from aerial photographs by examining tonal changes and shadow distributions within the photograph. Tonal changes can provide information on texture, which can be used to distinguish between vegetation type, soil type, and other surface features. Because the shapes of shadows change with time of day and are unique to particular objects, such as bridges, trees, and buildings, the shadows can be used to aid in the identification of the objects. Because film can record wavelengths of radiation that are invisible to the eye, such as thermal infrared radiation, features such as plant canopy tempera-

University of Georgia researchers rely on a farm blimp to provide aerial images in their quest to detect drought stress in cotton fields. (AP/Wide World Photos)

ture can be measured and displayed on an aerial photograph.

Aerial photography has many applications, including geologic and soil mapping, agricultural crop management, forest monitoring and management, rangeland management, water pollution detection, water resource management, and urban and regional planning. In geologic mapping, for example, aerial photography can be used to identify faults and fractures in Earth's surface as well as rock and soil types. By comparing these features over time, scientists can make inferences about the forcing agents, such as wind and water, that have shaped the land. As world population grows and demand for global resources increases, aerial photography will continue to be an important tool for guiding global resource management.

Terrence R. Nathan

SEE ALSO: Conservation; Environmental engineering; Geology; Irrigation; Land management; Land-use planning; Rain forests; U.S. Geological Survey; Wind energy.

Agenda 21

CATEGORY: Laws and conventions
DATE: Adopted June, 1992

Agenda 21 is the action plan of the United Nations for the promotion of sustainable development in the twenty-first century.

BACKGROUND

Agenda 21 was approved in the United Nations Conference on Environment and Development, held in Rio de Janeiro, Brazil, from June 3 to 14, 1992, when more than one hundred heads of state met in the first Earth Summit. Sustainable development means that which "meets the needs of the present, without compromising the capacity of future generations to meet their own needs." This concept was first mentioned in the 1980 report *World Conservation Strategy*, published by the International Union for Conservation of Nature (IUCN), and defined, in 1987, in the Brundtland Report (*Our Common Future*), prepared by the U.N. World Commission on Environment and Development, created in 1983 and chaired by Gro Harlem Brundtland.

PROVISIONS

The Earth Summit adopted key documents such as the Rio Declaration on Environment and Development, the Statement of Principles for the Sustainable Management of Forests, the Convention on Climate Change, the Convention on Biological Diversity, and Agenda 21—the global plan of action on sustainable development. The monitoring of these agreements is conducted by the U.N. Commission on Sustainable Development.

Agenda 21 is a global partnership promoted by the United Nations, based on the principle that it is necessary to meet equitably the needs of present and future generations and on the idea of the indivisibility of environmental protection and economic and social development. Agenda 21 calls for ensuring the sustainable development of the environment through social and economic programs, through protection and conservation of national resources, by enabling major government and civilian groups, and by embracing education, technology, and innovation.

After 1992, the United Nations reaffirmed on several occasions that Agenda 21 remained the main program of action for achieving sustainable development, and programs for the further implementation of Agenda 21 were also adopted. In 2002, the World Summit on Sustainable Development, held in Johannesburg, South Africa, through the Johannesburg Plan of Implementation, strongly reaffirmed the U.N. commitment to the Rio principles and to the full implementation of Agenda 21 and the development goals contained in the 2000 U.N. Millennium Declaration. In 2009, the financial crisis and the global economic recession coupled with the food, energy, and climate crisis made more explicit the need for global and local approaches to sustainable development.

Chapter 28 of Agenda 21 calls for local authorities to develop their own local version of the agenda. Local Agenda 21 includes the preparation and implementation of a long-term strategic action plan for sustainable development. It is a participative, multisector, and multistakeholder process and aims to fulfill locally the objectives of Agenda 21. It is a process in which local governments, citizens, professionals, entrepreneurs, and organizations from the civil society work together to define priorities for local sustainable development in environmental, social, and economic areas. Organizations and networks of local governments have been active in the implementation of Local Agenda 21 in all continents, with such groups as

A Global Partnership

The opening paragraph of the Preamble to Agenda 21 presents an unusually stark statement of the challenges facing humanity at the beginning of the twenty-first century and the need for international cooperation to meet those challenges.

Humanity stands at a defining moment in history. We are confronted with a perpetuation of disparities between and within nations, a worsening of poverty, hunger, ill health and illiteracy, and the continuing deterioration of the ecosystems on which we depend for our well-being. However, integration of environment and development concerns and greater attention to them will lead to the fulfilment of basic needs, improved living standards for all, better protected and managed ecosystems and a safer, more prosperous future. No nation can achieve this on its own; but together we can—in a global partnership for sustainable development.

Framework Convention on Climate Change, the Convention on Biological Diversity, the Convention to Combat Desertification in Those Countries Experiencing Serious Drought and/or Desertification, and a series of agreements and conventions related to the sea and the marine environment. Progress was made through the implementation, in national and international legislation, of key principles included in the Rio Declaration on Environment and Development, such as the precautionary principle, the principle of common but differentiated responsibilities, the polluter-pays principle, and the environmental impact assessment principle.

Carlos Nunes Silva

SEE ALSO: Clays; Clean Air Act; Climate Change and Sustainable Energy Act; Earth Summit; Global 200; Greenhouse gases and global climate change; Kyoto Protocol; Stockholm Conference; United Nations climate change conferences; United Nations Environment Programme.

the International Council for Local Environmental Initiatives, an international association of local governments for sustainability; and the movement of European Cities and Towns for Sustainable Development, exemplified by the 1994 Aalborg Charter, the 2004 Aalborg Commitments, and the 2007 Spirit of Seville declaration.

IMPACT ON RESOURCE USE
In 1997, the United Nations made a five-year review of Agenda 21 and reported its findings in a resolution adopted by the General Assembly (Programme for the Further Implementation of Agenda 21). In this review, the United Nations recognized that a number of positive results had been achieved but the overall trends were considered to be worse than in 1992. Among the results the United Nations considered positive were that 150 countries had established national-level commissions or other forms of coordination designed to implement sustainable development strategies; the efforts of local authorities in the implementation of Local Agenda 21; the role of nongovernmental organizations, the scientific community, and the media in the rise of public awareness of the relationship between the environment and development; and the development of green businesses in all sectors of the economy.

Other positive developments in the implementation of Agenda 21 included the adoption of the U.N.

Aggregates

CATEGORY: Mineral and other nonliving resources

Production of rock and crushed stone is an "invisible" industry, one that exists almost everywhere but goes largely unnoticed. Only when the products of this industry are needed or when producers are in conflict with environmental or regulatory agencies is their existence given much attention. Stone and rock are available and used worldwide, primarily in the construction industry.

BACKGROUND
The crushed stone and rock industry has been in existence since time immemorial. Ancient roads throughout the world were paved with stone that was either found in the desired size or crushed by animal or human power and sized with crude sieves. As the construction industry became more sophisticated and exacting, so did requirements for engineered building products. Today the engineered aspects of manufactured stone products extend not only to physical dimensions but also to the chemical quality of the products.

The term "aggregate" represents all types of

crushed stone and rock, from sand and gravel to coarse crushed material. The aggregates industry is huge. In 2008, in the United States alone, this industry produced 2.34 billion metric tons of product valued at roughly $19 billion. Aggregate output is roughly 60 percent crushed stone and 40 percent sand and gravel. The fortunes of the industry usually follow construction conditions. In prosperous times, the aggregates industry sees growth and optimism. In recessionary times, the industry suffers accordingly. The relative abundance of construction-quality stone products lends a peculiar aspect to the industry: the widespread and numerous locations of producers. Almost fifteen hundred companies operate more than thirty-seven hundred quarries in all fifty U.S. states.

Two forces continually drive aggregate producers: low operating cost and low transportation cost. Crushed stone has a product value of approximately eight dollars per metric ton; therefore, the expense of extraction, sizing, and inventory must always be controlled. The expense of bulk transportation for relatively low-cost stone and rock products forces producers to locate near end users. Also, the drawbacks of end-user on-site storage of aggregates cause such storage to be maintained at the site of the producer, with delivery on a just-in-time basis. A common remark concerning aggregates is that they are "worn out" after a transportation distance exceeding 80 kilometers from their origin. This means that the expense of transportation overtakes the value of the product after that distance, so that a producer must find a new production site near the customer or lose market share to a competitor who will be willing to relocate near the customer.

USES OF AGGREGATES

Typical aggregates used as industrial products include sand and gravel as well as crushed sandstone, limestone, dolomite, granite, and marble. Chert, an agglomeration of minerals, is also frequently excavated and used as a "fill material." For sandstone and limestone, there is a certain "pecking order," with high-silica sandstone and high-calcium-content limestone commanding higher prices. For example, chemical-grade limestone is used in chemical reaction technology as well as in pharmaceutical manufacturing.

The bulk of aggregate production, however, goes to a "sized product" that will meet the specifications of the end user. For example, building and highway construction projects demand a certain size aggregate to meet a particular need. The mixing of concrete demands a fine-sized rock product for increasing the strength of the mixture. Gravels are also used in concrete and can be seen in the concrete matrix as small marble-shaped material. "Riprap," a name given to relatively large, football-sized rock products, is used to control erosion in areas with damaging surface water flows or to reinforce slump-prone areas such as highway embankments.

Dimension stone, a name frequently given to the largest stone products, is used for massive construction and ornamental purposes and is not considered an aggregate. Sources for dimension stone are scarce, requiring sites with very little or no disturbances in the stone deposit through faults, mud slips, cracks, or other geological irregularities. Dimension stones may include limestone and sandstone, marble and granite, and other rocks and minerals found in an undisturbed state. The Egyptian pyramids and older U.S. and state government buildings are examples of construction using dimension stone. Marble and granite are frequently used for ornamental stone because of

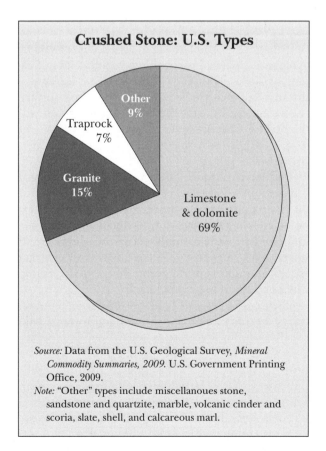

Crushed Stone: U.S. Types

Other 9%
Traprock 7%
Granite 15%
Limestone & dolomite 69%

Source: Data from the U.S. Geological Survey, *Mineral Commodity Summaries, 2009.* U.S. Government Printing Office, 2009.

Note: "Other" types include miscellanoues stone, sandstone and quartzite, marble, volcanic cinder and scoria, slate, shell, and calcareous marl.

their durability and ability to be polished to an attractive gloss finish. Examples include large building ornaments, countertops, and headstones for graves.

Sand and gravel are found in areas with past or existing streamflow. In many cases, the segregating aspects of streamflow have sized the sand and gravel so that further sizing is minimized. Crushed stone, however, is produced in mining operations, and the operator has control over the size range of the finished product. For the most part, these operations are at the surface and are known as quarries. Some stone is produced in underground mining operations, with the high quality of the stone justifying the additional expense of this type of operation. Many quarries operating in a particularly desirable deposit of stone continue to pursue it by going underground.

PREPARATIONS FOR MINING

Before any significant expense is committed to locating and developing an aggregate production site, a market study is performed to determine the amount and quality of materials needed within a certain radius of transportation. Experienced aggregate producers usually have a "sixth sense" about the need for and location of their products. After the marketing study has been completed, a quarry site is located by geological exploration techniques such as identification of surface outcrops of material or inference, through regional studies of rock type. Even surface vegetation can indicate the type of material beneath the surface. Limestone terrains, for example, do not support acidic-soil vegetation because of their high pH values.

The potential source of aggregate is identified and outlined more precisely through the digging of test pits for samples of the materials or by drilling test holes and analyzing the samples obtained. Again, the inherent size of the naturally occurring materials and the estimated expense of preparing them to market specifications are critical points that help determine whether a site is to be developed.

If an aggregate site is to be produced, mineral leases are obtained from the mineral owners, who usually own the aggregate as well as deeper minerals. Sometimes the aggregate producer purchases the property outright if the location is environmentally sensitive or if a particularly long-lived aggregate source is identified. If the property is leased, the lease is usually for a fixed term, perhaps ten years, with options to continue the lease for additional terms. A roy-

alty is paid to the owner of the minerals according to the market value of the products. The royalty usually varies from 2 percent to 10 percent of the aggregate's selling price.

After the quarry dimensions have been verified, applications to develop the site are made to the local, state, and federal agencies that will regulate all aspects of site operation. The effects of the mining operation on air, groundwater and surface water, wildlife, archaeological sites, and various natural processes must be determined. This process can be extremely expensive and consume several years. An environmental impact study and report may be necessary in certain areas. This a very detailed and comprehensive report that incorporates all the environmental factors to be considered in locating the pit or quarry.

AGGREGATE MINING OPERATIONS

When all applicable permits and releases have been obtained, mining of the aggregate begins. For sand and gravel, the products can be recovered using simple excavation equipment such as front-end loaders, pan scrapers, or dredges. The stone in quarries, however, has inherent strength such that it is usually necessary to use explosives to fragment the material and make it suitable for bulk transport from the quarry. Blasting is used to dislodge stone from the "face," or quarry wall. Almost any commercial explosive can be used for this purpose, but a mixture of ammonium nitrate and fuel oil has emerged over the past several decades as the most cost-efficient explosive. Dynamite is still used but in smaller quantities than before.

Several rows of blast holes are drilled at predetermined distances from the free quarry face. These distances are engineered to ensure efficient rock breakage without unnecessary "fly" rock, or rock that is propelled outside the desired blasting area. Explosive cord is also extensively used in blasting operations. This product, with an almost instantaneous ignition rate, is especially useful when "delay" blast rounds are used. In delay blasting, millisecond delay sequences cause the first row of blast holes to be initiated, then subsequent rows rearward from the free face to be ignited after predetermined delays. This technique, now standard in nearly all quarry blasting procedures, results in much greater blasting efficiency.

Dimension stone may also be removed by explosives, but the drill holes are very closely spaced, and the explosive is limited to the amount necessary to cut the block of dimension stone to the desired size and not fragment it further. High-pressure water jets or rock-cutting saws are also used in removing dimension stone from the quarry. Since the value of the dimension stone depends on the largest physical units minable, the stone must be gently dislodged so that it remains intact.

Blasting, while indispensable to the crushed stone industry, is also one of the predominant problems associated with it. The noise, vibration, and dust resulting from blasting operations, combined with the fact that quarries are usually located near populated areas, frequently bring ongoing conflict between producers and nearby residents. As a result, blasting is done carefully, and its side effects are measured to ensure that it is done within the guidelines set and enforced by regulatory agencies.

The sizes of sand can vary dramatically. The large-grain sand, from England, is approximately 2 millimeters in diameter. The small-grain sand is from Tunisia.

The blasted material, after it is removed from the quarry face, is loaded by front-end loaders or shovels into large trucks for transportation to the surface preparation plant. The timing of the quarry floor loading operation is a continually challenging problem involving machinery size and speed, operator efficiency, and positioning. Occasionally it is necessary to reduce the sizes of blasted fragments that are too large to be loaded and transported easily with existing equipment, and small amounts of explosives may again be necessary on the quarry floor. Transportation from the quarry floor is usually by truck, belt conveyor, or bucket conveyor, depending on the operating system in effect at the quarry. Removal of dimension stone poses a special problem because the large sizes demand gentle handling and require vehicles capable of transporting the large, heavy units of stone. Large track-mounted crawlers, rubber-tired vehicles, or cranes are frequently used for this task.

Sizing the Material

Blasted materials are transported from the quarry to be reduced in size ("comminuted") using adjustable crushers, sorted into various sizes to suit the customer's specifications, washed to remove unwanted extraneous materials such as clays, and stockpiled awaiting shipment. Typically, crushers operate by chewing on the material ("jaw crushers") or passing the material through rollers ("roll crushers"). When crushed, the material assumes sizes varying from dust-sized particles to pieces equivalent to the crusher opening. Most of these crushed products, even the fine sizes, have some value, so the sizing operation is indispensable to an efficient quarry serving multiple customers.

Sizing may be based on a number of physical principles, such as the ability to pass through or be rejected by sized openings (sieving), the tendency to drop out of a fluid stream (liquid classification), or the ability to be propelled through the air to a certain distance (air classification). If the materials have particular physical or chemical characteristics (magnetism, for example), other sizing operations can be designed to take advantage of them. Sieves (screens) frequently have a vibration device attached to them to prevent clogging and expedite the sorting process. Screening can be fully wet or dry, but merely moist materials cannot be separated in a screening operation.

The end result of sizing is having several sized products in which the size range within a sized product is quite narrow. If necessary, sized materials can be further classified by washing techniques designed to remove the fine sizes inherent in the crushing process. Practical sizes of quarry products range from dust sizes of a few microns in diameter to cubic-shaped dimension stone having dimensions exceeding 6 or 9

Crushed Stone Sold or Used in the United States, 2007

	NUMBER OF QUARRIES	METRIC TONS	TOTAL VALUE (DOLLARS)	UNIT VALUE (DOLLARS)
Calcareous marl	3	2,820,000	18,800,000	6.68
Dolomite	137	72,500,000	562,000,000	7.75
Granite	384	241,000,000	2,620,000,000	10.88
Limestone	2,123	1,020,000,000	8,280,000,000	8.13
Marble	21	7,580,000	71,100,000	9.38
Sandstone and quartzite	188	47,700,000	398,000,000	8.35
Shell	5	2,850,000	24,200,000	8.47
Slate	33	3,820,000	37,000,000	9.68
Traprock	361	105,000,000	1,030,000,000	9.82
Volcanic cinder and scoria	46	6,630,000	48,800,000	7.36
Miscellaneous stone	435	94,100,000	781,000,000	8.30

Source: Data from U.S. Bureau of Mines, *Mineral Yearbook, 2007.* U.S. Government Printing Office, 2009.

meters. For most applications, however, practical sizes include sands from 1.65 millimeters through gravels around 0.6 centimeter to 1.2 centimeters in diameter, to stone sizes 2.5 centimeters to 7.6 centimeters in diameter, to fist-sized material used for foundation bases in construction, to football-sized riprap. The ultimate goal of a stone and rock producer is to market 100 percent of the products generated in its operation. While this is a practical impossibility, the most efficient producers have been able to come remarkably close to this goal.

ENVIRONMENTAL AND CITIZENSHIP CONCERNS
Virtually all the activities of quarry operation have some undesirable side effects. Siltation problems are inherent in stream-based operations. Blasting generates noise, dust, and vibrations. Trucking activities do the same, and they present a hazard to mixed automobile traffic if public roads are used for transportation. Surface facilities are prone to emitting dust, and fluid classification equipment produces sludge that must be handled. While not toxic in themselves, these byproducts from aggregate production are objectionable and must be dealt with according to stringent regulations from municipal, state, and federal agencies. The closer an aggregate producer is to populated areas, the greater the inherent problems are (and the harder it is for the producer to be considered a good community citizen), but moving farther from these areas brings increased transportation costs and may make the producer uncompetitive. Moreover, most quarries are below the water table, which means that a constant inflow of groundwater must be pumped to a nearby creek or river. Although this water is frequently used in the crushing and sizing processes, it must still be pumped, routed, stored, and eventually disposed. Desludging equipment may also be necessary, further increasing the complexity of the operation.

Most successful aggregate producers have recognized and come to terms with the environmental consequences of their businesses. Blasting procedures are carefully engineered to minimize unwanted side effects and are scheduled at times that are least objectionable to those living or working nearby. A baghouse (a type of giant vacuum-cleaner bag) traps dusts produced by crushing operations and, in turn, frequently creates its own marketable product. Electrostatic precipitators are also used to remove and collect dust-sized material. Fines (powder or very small particles) from classification facilities are collected in sediment ponds that can be periodically "mined" to yield a marketable product. In addition to being a good environmental citizen, an aggregate producer should have a visually pleasing facility if it is located in or near populated areas. Well-kept grounds, clean equipment, and storage areas free of debris are marks of the conscientious operator.

OPERATIONAL LIFE SPAN

Although a large sand and gravel pit or stone quarry may remain open for decades, there is an ultimate life span to each location. Besides the restrictions of mining to the edges of the deposit or to the legal property limits of the miners' leases, there is a practical depth beyond which a quarry must either go underground or face significantly increased costs of lifting the material to the surface. If the decision is made to abandon the mine site, a large excavation remains that may encompass many hectares and be as much as 60 to 90 meters in depth. With the closing of the pit or quarry, the excavation quickly fills with water, and an impoundment, sometimes having very steep sides, becomes part of the landscape. Topsoil initially removed to expose the minable aggregate must be hauled away or stored nearby. Spoil that was removed and discarded during the quarrying operation may now be visually objectionable and must be remedied.

If all these remedial activities are included as a part of the overall life cycle of the pit or quarry, then a desirable residential location may be created. It is common to see upscale housing developments built around old pits and quarries, with the impoundments becoming favorite targets of sport fishermen. They are also frequented by migratory birds and other wildlife favoring large bodies of fresh water.

Charles D. Haynes

FURTHER READING

Blatt, Harvey, Robert J. Tracy, and Brent E. Owens. *Petrology: Igneous, Sedimentary, and Metamorphic.* 3d ed. New York: W. H. Freeman, 2006.

Chatterjee, Kaulir Kisor. *Uses of Industrial Minerals, Rocks, and Freshwater.* New York: Nova Science, 2009.

Grotzinger, John P., et al. *Understanding Earth.* 5th ed. New York: W. H. Freeman, 2007.

Hockensmith, Charles D. *The Millstone Industry: A Summary of Research on Quarries and Producers in the United States, Europe, and Elsewhere.* Jefferson, N.C.: McFarland, 2009.

Kogel, Jessica Elzea, et al., eds. "Stone and Rock." *Industrial Minerals and Rocks: Commodities, Markets, and Uses.* 7th ed. Littleton, Colo.: Society for Mining, Metallurgy, and Exploration, 2006.

Philpotts, Anthony R., and Jay J. Ague. *Principles of Igneous and Metamorphic Petrology.* 2d ed. New York: Cambridge University Press, 2009.

Raymond, Loren A. *Petrology: The Study of Igneous, Sedimentary, and Metamorphic Rocks.* 2d ed. Boston: McGraw-Hill, 2002.

Smith, M. R., and L. Collis, eds. *Aggregates: Sand, Gravel, and Crushed Rock Aggregates for Construction Purposes.* 3d ed. Revised by P. G. Fookes et al. London: Geological Society, 2001.

Tarbuck, Edward J., and Frederick K. Lutgens. *Earth: An Introduction to Physical Geology.* 9th ed. Illustrated by Dennis Tasa. Upper Saddle River, N.J.: Pearson Prentice Hall, 2008.

Weiss, Norman L., ed. *SME Mineral Processing Handbook.* 2 vols. New York: Society of Mining Engineers of the American Institute of Mining, Metallurgical, and Petroleum Engineers, 1985.

WEB SITES

NATURAL RESOURCES CANADA
Canadian Minerals Yearbook, Mineral and Metal Commodity Reviews
http://www.nrcan-rncan.gc.ca/mms-smm/busi-indu/cmy-amc/com-eng.htm

U.S. GEOLOGICAL SURVEY
Crushed Stone: Statistics and Information
http://minerals.usgs.gov/minerals/pubs/commodity/stone_crushed/index.html#mcs

U.S. GEOLOGICAL SURVEY
Dimension Stone: Statistics and Information
http://minerals.usgs.gov/minerals/pubs/commodity/stone_dimension/index.html#mcs

SEE ALSO: Abrasives; Cement and concrete; Dimension stone; Granite; Igneous processes, rocks, and mineral deposits; Limestone; Marble; Metamorphic processes, rocks, and mineral deposits; Quarrying; Sand and gravel; Slate.

Agricultural products

CATEGORIES: Plant and animal resources; products from resources

Agricultural products encompass all commodities derived from the production of animals and the growing of crops to be used by humans for food, fiber, shelter, medicinal applications, or aesthetic purposes.

BACKGROUND

A nation's ability to sustain an agricultural system with the capacity to feed, shelter, and clothe its population is perhaps its greatest natural resource. The human domestication of certain animals and cultivation of certain food crops predate written history. In modern society, the diversity of products that can be produced via agricultural technology is enormous. Major agricultural commodities can be divided into those that come from animals and those that are derived from plants.

AGRICULTURAL PRODUCTS FROM ANIMALS

The major animal-derived products can be divided into edible and inedible red meat products, milk and milk products, poultry and egg products, and wool and mohair. Red meat products refer primarily to those products that come from cattle (beef and veal), swine (pork), sheep (lamb and mutton), goats (chevon), and, to a lesser extent, other animals such as horses and buffalo.

Other than the meat itself, edible products from red meat animals include meat scraps used to make processed meats such as frankfurters and bologna; organ meats such as liver, tail, tongue, tripe (stomach), and sweetbread (thymus); and tallow or lard. The major inedible red meat products include rendered fat, which is used to make soap and formula animal feeds; bone meal, used in fertilizer and animal feeds; manure; and hides or skins, which are tanned and used to make leather products.

Milk and milk products, also referred to as dairy products, are major components of the human diet in many countries. Whole milk with part or all of the fat removed is sold as low-fat or skim milk. Evaporated and condensed milk refers to milk from which approximately 60 percent of the water has been removed, and dry or powdered milk has had at least 95 percent of the water removed. Cultured milk products such as buttermilk, yogurt, sour cream, and cottage cheese are produced via fermentation by the addition of appropriate bacterial cultures to fluid dairy products. Cream products are separated from liquid milk and have a milk fat content of not less than 18 percent. Butter is made by separating the butterfat from either milk or cream and contains at least 80 percent by weight milk fat. Cheese is produced through the microbial action of a variety of

bacteria and fungi on whole milk. Ice cream, ice milk, sherbet, and frozen custard are produced by freezing a variety of liquid milk products in combination with sugar and other ingredients.

Poultry products are nutritious and relatively inexpensive, and they are used by humans throughout the world. Broiler chickens provide most of the world's poultry meat, but turkeys, roaster chickens, mature laying hens (fowl), ducks, geese, pigeons, and guinea hens are also consumed and may be more important than chickens in some parts of the world. Much of the poultry meat is processed into preformed products such as poultry rolls or nuggets, canned products, or cured and ground products such as frankfurters, bologna, turkey ham, or salami. Other than meat, poultry also provides eggs. The majority of the world's eggs are now produced by chickens specifically selected to lay large numbers of eggs, but eggs from the other birds listed above are sometimes eaten. Eggs can be

Harvested corn is loaded onto a grain-hauling truck. (AP/Wide World Photos)

further processed and sold as liquid eggs or dried eggs. There is also an industry based on the meat and eggs from the ratite birds, such as the ostrich and emu.

The hair covering the skin of some farm animals is also considered an agricultural product. The two most important of these are wool from sheep and mohair from angora goats. Wool or mohair can be sheared annually from the same sheep or goat. The cleaned and processed fibers are woven into yarn, which can then be used to make carpet or cloth.

AGRICULTURAL PRODUCTS FROM PLANTS

Agricultural products that are derived from plants are also diverse. They can be subdivided into timber products, grain crops, fiber crops, fruit crops, nut crops, vegetable crops, beverage crops, spice and drug crops, ornamental crops, forage crops, and other cash crops such as sugarcane, tobacco, artichoke, and rubber. Timber products include those materials derived from the trees of renewable forests. The two major products are lumber for building and paper, but other products such as pine tar, resin, and turpentine are also extracted from trees.

More cultivated land is devoted to the production of grain crops, also known as cereal grains, and fiber crops than to any other agricultural crop. Cereal grains are the edible seed from a variety of grasses. Throughout history, these crops have been primarily responsible for sustaining large human populations and domestic animal herds. The products from the world's major grain crops include corn, wheat, oats, barley, rye, rice, and derivatives such as grain-based cereals and flours. Rice is the leading seed crop in the world and is the principal food crop of about half the world's population. Corn, barley, rye, and rice are also used to produce alcoholic beverages. Grain sorghums are also produced in large quantities in the United States, but this grain is primarily used as feed for livestock. Cotton, flax, and hemp are the principal fiber plants grown in the United States, although less important crops such as ramie, jute, and sisal are also grown. While these plants are grown primarily for their fiber, which is used to make textiles, rope, twine, and similar products, other products such as cottonseed oil and linseed oil from flax are also produced.

Fruits from a variety of perennial plants are harvested for their refreshing flavors and nourishment. Fruits can be subdivided into temperate, subtropical, and tropical crops. Grapes, a temperate fruit grown for table use, winemaking, and raisins, account for ap-

proximately 25 percent of the fruit production of the world. Examples of other temperate fruits include the pome fruits (apple and pear), stone fruits (plum, peach, apricot), kiwi fruit, and berry fruits (strawberry, raspberry, blackberry, cranberry, and blueberry). Tropical and subtropical fruit crops include banana, pineapple, mango, papaya, avocado, date, fig, olive, and citrus fruits (orange, lemon, and grapefruit). In addition to providing fresh fruit, the products from fruit crops can be canned, dried, converted to juices, and used to make jams and jellies or special products such as olive oil.

Nut crops refer to those woody plants that produce seed with firm shells that separate them from an inner kernel. Nuts are generally considered to be luxury food. They are often eaten as a delicacy (either fresh or canned) or consumed with candy or other sweets. Major temperate nut crops include walnut, almond, chestnut, pistachio, pecan, and hazelnut. Tropical nut crops include the coconut, cashew, Brazil nut, and macadamia. Nuts are characteristically rich in oil. The inedible tungnut is grown exclusively for its oil.

Vegetable crops are extremely diverse and range from starchy calorie sources (potato) to food that supplies vitamins and minerals (broccoli). Examples of the major vegetable crops include the edible legumes (beans, soybeans, peas, lentils, and peanuts); roots, tubers, and bulbs (potato, sweet potato, taro, yam, cassava, onion, sugar beet, and carrot); solanaceous fruits (tomato, eggplant, and chili pepper); salad plants (lettuce, endive, chicory, parsley, and garden cress); cole crops (cabbage, cauliflower, broccoli, brussels sprouts, and radish); and vine crops (cucumbers, watermelon, cantaloupe, pumpkin, squash, and gourd). Like fruit crops, vegetable produce can be served fresh, canned, frozen, or in an assortment of juices.

The world's three most popular nonalcoholic beverages—coffee, tea, and cocoa—are produced in the tropics. These products represent a major proportion of the tropical world's agricultural exports, and their production is the major industry in many tropical countries. Many plants or plant parts that possess strong aroma and flavor are grown for the purpose of producing spices. Because of the diverse biochemistry of plants, some crops are cultured for the production of medicinal drug compounds. There are more than two hundred spice and drug plants; some of the more common products are peppermint, nutmeg, garlic, vanilla, allspice, cinnamon, black pepper, mustard, opium, quinine, belladonna, and digitalis.

Ornamental and forage crops are not consumed by humans. Ornamental crops are grown for aesthetic purposes and are divided into florist crops (flower and foliage plants) and landscape crops (nursery plants). Common ornamental crops include rose, orchid, carnation, chrysanthemum, and a variety of shrubs. Forage crops are grown to feed livestock and include a host of small grain grasses, clover, alfalfa, and a variety of straw crops for haymaking.

D. R. Gossett

FURTHER READING

Akinyemi, Okoro M. *Agricultural Production: Organic and Conventional Systems.* Enfield, N.H.: Science Publishers, 2007.

Brody, Aaron L., and John B. Lord, eds. *Developing New Food Products for a Changing Marketplace.* 2d ed. Boca Raton, Fla.: CRC Press/Taylor & Francis, 2008.

Field, Thomas G., and Robert E. Taylor. *Scientific Farm Animal Production: An Introduction to Animal Science.* 9th ed. Upper Saddle River, N.J.: Prentice Hall, 2008.

Janick, Jules. *Horticultural Science.* 4th ed. New York: W. H. Freeman, 1986.

Ward, Janet D., and Larry T. Ward. *Principles of Food Science.* Tinley Park, Ill.: Goodheart-Willcox, 2002.

WEB SITES

AGRICULTURE AND AGRI-FOOD CANADA
Producers
http://www4.agr.gc.ca/AAFC-AAC/display-afficher.do?id=1165871799386&lang=eng

U.S. DEPARTMENT OF AGRICULTURE
Animal Production
http://www.usda.gov/wps/portal/!ut/p/_s.7_0_A/7_0_1OB?navid=ANIMAL_PRODUCTION&parentnav=AGRICULTURE&navtype=RT

U.S. DEPARTMENT OF AGRICULTURE
Crop Production
http://www.usda.gov/wps/portal/!ut/p/_s.7_0_A/7_0_1OB?navid=CROP_PRODUCTION&parentnav=AGRICULTURE&navtype=RT

SEE ALSO: Agriculture industry; Corn; Horticulture; Monoculture agriculture; Plant domestication and breeding; Plant fibers; Plants as a medical resource; Rice; Rubber, natural; Sugars; Wheat; Wood and timber.

Agriculture industry

CATEGORIES: Plant and animal resources; obtaining and using resources

The ability to produce sufficient food and fiber to feed and clothe its population is the most important natural resource a nation can have. In modern urban societies, it is also the natural resource that is most often taken for granted.

BACKGROUND

The beginnings of agriculture predate the written history of humankind. No one knows when the first crop was cultivated, but at some time in the distant past humans discovered that seeds from certain wild grasses could be collected and planted in land that could be controlled, the end product of which could later be gathered for food. Most authorities believe this occurred at about the same time in both the Old World and New World, some eight thousand to ten thousand years ago. The earliest attempts at growing crops were primarily to supplement the food supply provided by hunting and gathering. However, as the ability to produce crops increased, people began to domesticate animals, and their reliance on hunting and gathering decreased, allowing the development of permanent human settlements.

As far back as six thousand years ago, agriculture was firmly established in Asia, India, Mesopotamia, Egypt, Mexico, Central America, and South America. The earliest agricultural centers were located near large rivers that helped maintain soil fertility by the deposition of new topsoil with each annual flooding cycle. As agriculture moved into regions that lacked the annual flooding of the large rivers, people began to utilize a technique known as slash-and-burn agriculture. In this type of agriculture, a farmer clears a field, burns the trees and brush, and farms the field. After a few years, soil nutrients become depleted, so the farmer must repeat the process. This type of agriculture is still practiced in some developing countries and is one reason that the tropical rain forests are disappearing at such a fast rate.

Until the nineteenth century, most farms and ranches were family-owned, and most farmers practiced sustenance agriculture: Each farmer or rancher produced a variety of crops sufficient to feed himself and his family as well as a small excess to be sold for

A farm manager practices weed control in a soybean field as an aspect of the farm's weed-tillage system. (United States Department of Agriculture/Keith Weller)

cash or bartered for other goods or services. Agricultural tools such as plows were made of wood, and almost all agricultural activities required human or animal labor. This situation placed a premium on large families to provide the help needed to tend the fields. The Industrial Revolution changed agriculture just as it did almost all other industries. Eli Whitney invented the cotton gin in 1793. The mechanical reaper was invented by Cyrus McCormick, and John Lane and John Deere began the commercial manufacture of the steel plow in 1833 and 1837, respectively. These inventions led the way for the development of the many different types of agricultural machinery that resulted in the mechanization of most farms and ranches. By the early part of the twentieth century, most agricultural enterprises in the United States were mechanized. The Industrial Revolution produced a significant change in society. The industrialized nations were gradually transformed from agrarian societies into urban societies. People involved in agricultural produc-

tion left the farms to go to the city to work in the factories. At the same time, there was no longer a need for large numbers of people to produce crops. As a result, fewer people were required to produce more agricultural produce for an increasing number of consumers. This trend continues in developing nations with more rural dwellers, adding to the overcrowding in urban centers.

MODERN AGRICULTURE
As populations continued to grow, there was a need to select and produce crops with higher yields. The Green Revolution of the twentieth century helped to make these higher yields possible. Basic information supplied by biological scientists allowed the agricultural scientists to develop new, higher-yielding varieties of numerous crops, particularly the seed grains that supply most of the calories necessary for maintenance of the world's population. These higher-yielding crop varieties, along with improved farming

methods, resulted in tremendous increases in the world's food supply. The new crop varieties also led to an increased reliance on monoculture. While the practice of growing only one crop over a vast number of hectares has resulted in much higher yields than planting multiple crops, it has also decreased the genetic variability of many agricultural plants, increased the need for commercial fertilizers, and produced an increased susceptibility to damage from a host of biotic and abiotic factors. These latter two developments have resulted in a tremendous growth in the agricultural chemical industry. Today's modern agricultural unit requires relatively few employees, is highly mechanized, devotes large amounts of land to the production of only one crop, and is highly reliant on agricultural chemicals such as fertilizers and pesticides.

AGRICULTURAL DIVERSITY

With all the diversity that has occurred in modern agriculture, the industry is subdivided into many different specialties. On the animal side of the industry, there is the beef industry, which deals with the production of beef cattle; the dairy industry, which focuses on the production of dairy cattle, milk, and milk products; the horse industry, which produces horses for work, sport, or pleasure; the sheep and goat industry; the swine industry, which deals with the production of pigs and hogs; and the poultry industry, which is concerned with the production of commercial birds and bird products such as eggs. Those agricultural industries that deal with plants include agronomy, the production of field crops (wheat, cotton, and so on); forestry, the growth and production of trees; and horticulture. Horticulture is subdivided into pomology, the growth and production of fruit crops (oranges, apples, and so on); olericulture, the growth and production of vegetable crops (tomatoes, lettuce); landscape horticulture, the growth and production of trees and shrubs that are used in landscape design; and floriculture, the growth and production of flowering plants used in the floral industry.

The various agriculture industries produce a tremendous number of different agricultural products. Those agricultural products that are derived from plants can be subdivided into timber products (such as lumber, furniture), grain products (wheat, oats), fiber products (cotton, flax), fruit products (grapes, peaches), nut crops (pecans, hazelnuts), vegetable products (lettuce, cabbage), beverage products (tea, coffee), spice and drug crops (garlic, mustard, opium, quinine), ornamental crops (carnation, chrysanthemum), forage crops (alfalfa, clover), and other cash crops, such as sugarcane, tobacco, artichoke, and rubber.

The animal industries provide products such as red meats from cattle (beef and veal), swine (pork), sheep (lamb and mutton), and goats (chevon). Milk and milk products, also referred to as dairy products, include milk, ice cream, and cheeses. Broiler chickens provide most of the world's poultry meat, but turkeys, roaster chickens, mature laying hens (fowl), ducks, geese, pigeons, and guinea hens are also consumed and may be more important than chickens in some parts of the world. Other than meat, poultry also provides eggs. The hair covering the skin of some farm animals is also considered an agricultural product. The two most important of these are wool from sheep and mohair from angora goats.

IMPACT ON OTHER NATURAL RESOURCES

While there have been tremendous increases in agricultural productivity through the use of modern agricultural practices, these same practices have had a significant impact on some other natural resources. Soil is one of the most overlooked and misunderstood resources. Most people think of soil as an inert medium from which plants grow. In reality, topsoil—that upper 15 to 25 centimeters of the Earth's terrestrial surface in which nearly all plants grow—is a complex mixture of weathered mineral materials from rocks, partially decomposed organic molecules, and a large number of living organisms. The process of soil formation is very slow. Under ideal conditions, topsoil can form at a rate sufficient to produce a layer of about 1 millimeter thick when spread over 1 hectare per year. Under less favorable conditions, it can take thousands of years to produce this small amount of soil. With proper management, topsoil can be kept fertile and productive indefinitely. However, many agricultural techniques lead to the removal of trees and shrubs, which provide windbreaks, or to the depletion of soil fertility, which reduces the plant cover over the field. These practices have exposed the soil to increased erosion from wind and moving water, and as a result, as much as one-third of the world's current croplands are losing topsoil faster than they can be replaced.

Because plants require water in order to grow, agriculture represents the largest single global user of water. Worldwide, about 70 percent of all fresh water withdrawn from groundwater supplies, rivers, and lakes is used to irrigate crops, and almost 15 percent of the world's croplands are irrigated. Water usage varies among countries. Some countries have abundant water supplies and irrigate liberally, while water is scarce in other countries and must be used carefully. Because as much as 60 percent of the water intended for irrigation is lost through old pipes and canals or to evaporation before the water reaches the field, the efficiency of water use in some countries can be very low. There is no doubt that irrigation has dramatically increased crop production in many areas, but some irrigation practices have been detrimental. Overwatering can lead to a waterlogging of the soil. Waterlogging cuts off the supply of oxygen to the roots, and the plants die. Irrigation of crops in dry climates can often result in salinization of the soil. In these climates, the irrigation water rapidly evaporates from the soil, leaving behind the mineral salts that were dissolved in the water. As the salts accumulate, they become lethal to most plants. Some experts estimate that as much as one-third of the world's agricultural soil has been damaged by salinization. There is also an argument as to whether or not the increased usage of water for agriculture has decreased the supply of potable water fit for other human uses.

Plants require sunshine, water either from rainfall or irrigation, carbon dioxide from the atmosphere, and thirteen mineral nutrients from the soil. Of these, calcium, magnesium, nitrogen, phosphorus, and potassium are required in the greatest amounts. Calcium and magnesium are plentiful in soils located in dry climates, but in wetter climates, these nutrients are often leached through the soil. In these regions, calcium and magnesium are returned to the soil in the form of lime, which is primarily used to raise the soil pH. Nitrogen, phosphorus, and potassium are the nutrients most often depleted from agricultural soils, and these nutrients are often referred to as the fertilizer elements. Because these nutrients stimulate plant growth and usually greatly increase crop yields, it is necessary to apply them to the soil regularly in order to maintain fertility.

The amount of fertilizer applied to the soil has increased more than twentyfold in the past fifty years. While this increase in the use of fertilizers has more than tripled the worldwide crop production, it has also caused some problems. The increased production of fertilizers has required the use of energy and mineral resources that could have been used elsewhere. In many cases, farmers tend to overfertilize. Overfertilization not only wastes money but also contributes to environmental degradation. Fertilizer elements, particularly nitrogen and phosphorus, are carried away by water runoff and are eventually deposited in the rivers and lakes, where they contribute to pollution of aquatic ecosystems. In addition, nitrates can accumulate in underground water supplies. These nitrates can be harmful if ingested by newborns.

Modern agriculture, as it is practiced in the industrialized nations, consumes large amounts of energy. Farm machinery utilized in planting, cultivating, harvesting, and transporting crops to market consumes the largest supplies of liquid fossil fuels such as gasoline or diesel. The energy required to produce fertilizers, pesticides, and other agricultural chemicals is the

An agronomist cradles a box of broccoli on a farm in Salinas, California. (United States Department of Agriculture)

second largest energy cost associated with agriculture. The use of fuel-requiring pumps to irrigate crops is also a major energy consumer. Additional energy is used in food processing, distribution, storage, and cooking after the crop leaves the farm. The energy used for these activities may be five times as much as that used to produce the crop.

CURRENT TRENDS IN AGRICULTURE

The development of biofuels, fuels produced from plants, such as corn and soy ethanol and cellulosic ethanol (produced from inedible portions of plants), has been encouraged by the need to find a substitute for expensive and environmentally harmful fossil fuels. However, the fluctuating price of oil has caused this industry to advance in fits and starts. Critics point out that biofuels use cropland that otherwise would be producing food, and the rise of the electric car could speed the decline in the use of fossil fuels, making biofuels obsolete.

The next major development in agriculture will be the biotechnical revolution, in which scientists will be able to use molecular biological techniques to produce exotic new crop varieties. In the future, perhaps agricultural scientists will be able to use these techniques to develop crop plants that can be produced, processed, and distributed with less impact on other resources. Many scientists feel nanotechnology, the ability to restructure matter at the level of molecules and atoms, could meet the need for growth in agriculture through improving the production of both plants and animals and improving both the safety and quality of food. A wide range of developed and developing countries, from the United Kingdom to Iran to India, are providing funding to scientific laboratories to develop nanotechnology products. The potential products range from antibacterial agents to technology that signals when a product is near the end of its shelf life. There remains concern that including nanoparticles in food may pose a health risk, and consumer advocates are encouraging more research, consumer awareness, and governance.

The trend toward globalization in agriculture has been good for the developed countries, but it poses a threat to developing nations. For example, countries in Africa do not benefit from the advances in global agriculture. Rural dwellers have neither the money nor the natural resources to take advantage of modern agricultural methods. At the same time, the agricultural practices in the developed world bring with

them many negative consequences for the environment. Water pollution from fertilizers and pesticides; global warming from increasing land under cultivation and decreasing forests; and decreased diversity of agricultural products in specific regions, which results in increased energy use to get these products to their global markets. Interest in organic farming, which is practiced in more than one hundred countries, offers opportunities for organic farmers from developing countries. However, if organic farming follows the pattern of commercial agriculture, with the growth of large farms, specialized products, and need for increasing capital, the benefit to the small, local farmer will disappear and the environmental impact will turn negative.

COMMERCIAL IMPACT OF THE AGRICULTURE INDUSTRY

Worldwide, some 45 percent of the population makes a living through agriculture, both subsistence and commercial. This also includes those people hired by the agriculture chemical companies, those companies that produce or sell agriculture implements and machinery, processing and canning plants, and wholesale and retail marketing firms, such as grocery stores. There are some eight thousand different agricultural products on the market, and while agriculture is big business, it amounts to less than 5 percent of the gross domestic product of all nations. Approximately one-third of the land worldwide is used for agriculture.

D. R. Gossett

FURTHER READING

Akinyemi, Okoro M. *Agricultural Production: Organic and Conventional Systems.* Enfield, N.H.: Science Publishers, 2007.

Brody, Aaron L., and John B. Lord, eds. *Developing New Food Products for a Changing Marketplace.* 2d ed. Boca Raton, Fla.: CRC Press/Taylor & Francis, 2008.

Field, Thomas G., and Robert E. Taylor. *Scientific Farm Animal Production: An Introduction to Animal Science.* 9th ed. Upper Saddle River, N.J.: Prentice Hall, 2008.

Janick, Jules. *Horticultural Science.* 4th ed. New York: W. H. Freeman, 1986.

Kipps, M. S. *Production of Field Crops: A Textbook of Agronomy.* 6th ed. New York: McGraw-Hill, 1970.

Metcalfe, Darrel S., and Donald M. Elkins. *Crop Production: Principles and Practices.* 4th ed. New York: Macmillan, 1980.

Southgate, Douglas, Douglas H. Graham, and Luther Tweeten. *The World Food Economy*. Malden, Mass.: Blackwell, 2007.

Weis, Tony. *The Global Food Economy: The Battle for the Future of Farming*. New York: Zed Books, 2007.

Wojtkowski, Paul A. *Agroecological Economics: Sustainability and Biodiversity*. Boston: Elsevier/Academic Press, 2008.

WEB SITES

AGRICULTURE AND AGRI-FOOD CANADA
Agri-Industries
http://www4.agr.gc.ca/AAFC-AAC/display-afficher.do?id=1166532974345&lang=eng

U.S. DEPARTMENT OF AGRICULTURE
Agriculture
http://www.usda.gov/wps/portal/!ut/p/_s.7_0_A/7_0_1OB?navtype=SU&navid=AGRICULTURE

SEE ALSO: Agricultural products; Animal breeding; Animal domestication; Biofuels; Corn; Cotton; Flax; Forestry; Forests; Genetic prospecting; Global Strategy for Plant Conservation; Green Revolution; Hemp; Horticulture; Land ethic; Monoculture agriculture; Plant domestication and breeding; Plant fibers; Rice; Rubber, natural; Seed Savers Exchange; Slash-and-burn agriculture; Soil; Svalbard Global Seed Vault; United Nations Food and Agriculture Organization; Wheat; Wood and timber.

Agronomy

CATEGORIES: Scientific disciplines; environment, conservation, and resource management

Agronomy comprises a group of applied-science disciplines concerned with land and soil management and crop production. Agronomists' areas of interest range from soil chemistry to soil-plant relationships to land reclamation.

DEFINITION

There are multiple definitions of agronomy, as befits a discipline with many different facets. The *Oxford Universal Dictionary* defines agronomy as "the study of land management or rural economy"; *Merriam-Webster's Collegiate Dictionary* calls it "a branch of agriculture dealing with field-crop production and soil management." The word derives from the ancient Greek *agros* (field) and *nemein* (manage): field management. Thus the American Society of Agronomy defines agronomy as "the theory and practice of crop production and soil management."

OVERVIEW

Agronomy is essentially the discipline or disciplines that investigate the production of crops supplying food, forage, and fiber for human and animal use and that study the stewardship of the soil from which those crops are grown. Agronomy covers all aspects of the agricultural environment, from agroclimatology to soil-plant relationships; crop science; soil science; weed science; biometry (the statistics of living things); crop, soil, pasture, and range management; crop, forage, and pasture production and utilization; turfgrass; and agronomic modeling. Within each area are subdisciplines. For example, within soil science are traditional disciplines such as soil fertility, soil chemistry, soil physics, soil microbiology, soil taxonomy and classification, and pedogenesis (the science of how soils form). Newer disciplines within soil science include such studies as bioremediation, or the study of how living organisms can be used to clean up toxic wastes in the environment, and land reclamation, the study of how to reconstruct landscapes disturbed by human activities such as surface mining.

Agronomy treats the agricultural environment as humankind's greatest natural resource: It is the source of our food, the source of our clothing, the source of our building materials, and the environment that purifies the air we breathe and the water we drink. Agronomists, whatever their specific field, utilize the soil resources and plant resources around them to benefit society. Crop breeders, for example, use the genetic diversity of wild varieties of domesticated plants to obtain the genetic information needed to breed plants for greater productivity or pest resistance. Soil scientists study landscapes to determine how best to manage the soil resource by integrating agricultural practices with the environment in terms of maintaining soil fertility and in terms of keeping soil in place so that erosion does not reduce the quality of the surrounding environment.

Poor field management leads to reduced productivity and reduced environmental quality. Historical examples abound, ranging from the 1930's Dust Bowl in the United States to the deforestation on the island of Madagascar in the late twentieth century. It is the role of agronomy to manage soil and crop resources as effectively as possible so that the twin goals of productivity and environmental quality are preserved.

Mark S. Coyne

SEE ALSO: Dust Bowl; Erosion and erosion control; Farmland; Fertilizers; Monoculture agriculture; Rangeland; Slash-and-burn agriculture; Soil; Soil testing and analysis; Wheat.

Air pollution and air pollution control

CATEGORY: Pollution and waste disposal

An air pollutant is any substance added to the atmosphere by human activities that affects humans, animals, or the environment adversely. Many pollutants are toxic, while seemingly benign emissions such as carbon dioxide, a major contributor to global warming, and chlorofluorocarbons, which decimate the stratospheric ozone layer, are dangerous in less obvious ways. Significant worldwide resources have been committed to reducing all such hazardous emissions.

BACKGROUND

Air pollution, occurring in gaseous, particulate, or aerosol form, has been problematic since humans began living in large cities and burning carbon-based fuels. The first known air pollution ordinance was passed in London in 1273, in an attempt to alleviate the soot-blackened skies from excessive combustion of wood. From the mid-eighteenth century through the mid-twentieth century, the increasingly heavy use of coal for heat, electricity, and transportation resulted in filthy air and an escalation of respiratory diseases. In the latter half of the twentieth century, governments began attacking the problem with legislation to control noxious emissions at their source.

Earth's atmosphere consists primarily of nitrogen, oxygen, water vapor, and trace amounts of many other substances. Emissions from human activities can alter the concentrations of these substances or release noxious chemicals with serious implications—including smog, acid rain, the greenhouse effect, and holes in the ozone layer—for both human and planetary health.

The major air pollutants are carbon oxides, sulfur oxides, nitrogen oxides, hydrocarbons, and particulate matter. Each year the United States adds more than 5.5 billion metric tons of carbon dioxide (CO_2) to the air; China adds approximately 6 billion metric tons. Worldwide, the amount of CO_2 inserted into the atmosphere exceeds 28 billion metric tons annually, contributed in roughly equal proportions by fossil-fuel electric power plants, industry, transportation, and homes and businesses.

AIR POLLUTANTS

CO_2 results whenever a carbon-containing fuel—such as coal, oil, or gasoline—is burned. When combustion is incomplete carbon monoxide (CO) is also produced. Although CO_2 is a relatively benign compound, the vast amount of fossil fuels (coal, oil, and natural gas) burned since the Industrial Revolution has increased the atmospheric amount by about 40 percent and continues to increase at an escalating rate. Carbon dioxide molecules, while transparent in visible light from the Sun, reflect infrared radiation emitted by Earth and reradiate it as heat. Eventually, this will likely raise Earth's average temperature in proportion to the amount of atmospheric CO_2. This "greenhouse effect" poses a long-term risk because a warming trend could increase sea levels, change rainfall patterns, disrupt grain belts, cause storms of greater intensity, and shift climate zones. Carbon monoxide is a toxic compound that causes death by suffocation by replacing oxygen in the bloodstream, thus depriving cells of their necessary oxygen.

Sulfur oxides are created whenever fossil fuels, particularly coal containing sulfur, are burned. Inhaling even relatively small concentrations of these gases can damage the upper respiratory tract and lung tissue. Another problem is that they react with water vapor in the atmosphere to produce sulfuric acid, a major component in acid rain.

Nitrogen oxides are synthesized whenever air is rapidly heated under pressure, followed by quick cooling, such as occurs in internal combustion engines and thermoelectric power plants. These compounds play a major role in the formation of acid rain, photochemical smog, and ozone (O_3), a potent reactive compound that attacks the lungs. Combustion-caused ozone is dangerous to living organisms near Earth's surface, but in the stratosphere it occurs naturally. This "ozone layer" prevents most of the Sun's ultraviolet light from reaching Earth's surface. Therefore, it can cause skin cancer in humans as well as affect plants and wildlife adversely.

Particulates are minuscule solid or liquid particles suspended in the air. They occur from combustion, dry grinding processes, and spraying. The human respiratory system has evolved a mechanism to prevent certain sizes of particulates from reaching the lungs, but there is no protection against the smaller particles of coal dust and the larger particulates in tobacco smoke. Coal dust settling in the lungs leads to black lung disease, while the particulates from tobacco smoke are a leading cause of lung cancer.

The United States emits millions of metric tons of suspended particulate matter each year, chiefly from fossil-fuel electric power plants and industrial smelting plants. Even particulates that do not reach the lower regions of the respiratory tract can affect breathing, cause emphysema, aggravate an existing cardiovascular disorder, or damage the immune system.

SMOG

The word "smog" is a melding of "smoke" and "fog" to describe fog polluted by smoke. When a local atmosphere becomes stagnant, smog pollution levels can create "killer fogs." Three times in recent history these killer fogs have caused statistically significant increases in the death rate, particularly among those with respiratory problems. The first instance occurred in 1948 in Donora, Pennsylvania, when a stagnated fog became progressively more contaminated with the smoky effluents from local steel mills. The second case occurred in 1952 in London when a stagnant fog mixed with the smoke from thousands of coal-burning homes caused many with respiratory ailments to die. Finally, during Thanksgiving of 1966, New York City experienced an increased death rate because of choking smog.

A second, completely different type of smog is "photochemical smog," a noxious mixture of reactive chemicals created when sunlight catalyzes reactions of residual hydrocarbons and nitrogen oxides from automotive exhaust. The first occurrence of such was in the late 1940's in Los Angeles, where the abundant sunlight and the dramatic increase of vehicular traffic created ideal conditions for photochemical smog. This smog contains, among other things, powerful eye irritants, noisome odors, and dangerous reactive compounds. Although first observed in Los Angeles, photochemical smog later became prevalent in most other large cities.

CHLOROFLUOROCARBONS

When first synthesized in the 1930's, chlorofluorocarbon (CFC) was hailed as an ideal refrigerant

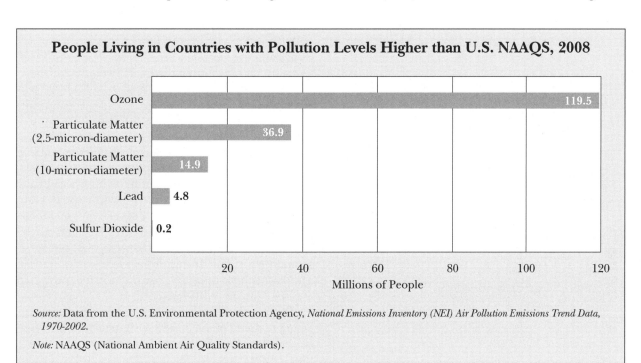

People Living in Countries with Pollution Levels Higher than U.S. NAAQS, 2008

Pollutant	Millions of People
Ozone	119.5
Particulate Matter (2.5-micron-diameter)	36.9
Particulate Matter (10-micron-diameter)	14.9
Lead	4.8
Sulfur Dioxide	0.2

Source: Data from the U.S. Environmental Protection Agency, *National Emissions Inventory (NEI) Air Pollution Emissions Trend Data, 1970-2002.*

Note: NAAQS (National Ambient Air Quality Standards).

(Freon) because it was nontoxic, noncorrosive, non-flammable, and inexpensive to produce. Later, pressurized CFCs were used as aerosol propellants and as the working fluid for air conditioners and refrigerators. By 1970 scientists realized that the huge quantities of CFCs released into the atmosphere from aerosol cans and discarded refrigerant units were migrating to the stratosphere, where they were decomposed by highly energetic ultraviolet radiation from the Sun, releasing large quantities of ozone-destroying chlorine. The reduction of ozone was most pronounced over Antarctica, where an "ozone hole," first detected in the early 1970's, was increasing in size annually. In 1978, pressured by environmentalists and consumer boycotts, the U.S. government banned aerosol cans and refrigeration units utilizing CFC propellant, forcing the chemical industry to develop alternatives. By 1987 the depletion of the ozone layer had become so problematic that most industrial nations met in Montreal to ratify an international treaty calling for immediate reductions in all CFC use with a complete phase-out by the year 2000. By 2001 the Montreal Protocol had limited the damage to the ozone layer to about 10 percent of what it would have been had the agreement not been ratified.

AIR POLLUTION CONTROL IN THE UNITED STATES
In the United States, the first attempts to control the smog or black smoke prevalent in industrial cities were the Clean Air Act of 1963 and the Motor Vehicle

Pollution Act of 1965. The 1963 act was too weak to be effective; in 1967, the stronger Air Quality Act was enacted. The Clean Air Act Amendments of 1970 mandated national air quality standards set by the Environmental Protection Agency (EPA) to be met by 1975. Standards for six major air pollutants (sulfur oxides, nitrogen oxides, particulates, ozone, carbon monoxide, and lead) were legislated. When the pollution concentration exceeded these limits, control devices were obligatory, regardless of the cost.

Although most forms of air pollution were reduced after enactment of the Clean Air Act Amendments, mounting public concern over the continuing deterioration of air quality in major cities resulted in several important revisions in 1990. New legislation mandated that coal-burning power plants reduce sulfur oxide emissions by 9 million metric tons per year from 1980 levels by the year 2000. The revisions also required that industry reduce several hundred carcinogenic airborne substances by up to 90 percent by the year 2000. Because of its smog problem, California set even more stringent standards by legislating that 2 percent of all new vehicles must emit zero emissions by 1998, a rate that was to increase to 10 percent by 2003. In October, 2006, the EPA's scientific advisers recommended that the allowable levels of surface ozone be substantially reduced, but industrial lobbying and the conservative political climate prevented any substantial change.

During the decades following the Clean Air Act Amendments, particulate emissions decreased by 80 percent, carbon monoxide by 55 percent, hydrocarbon emissions by 40 percent, sulfur oxides by 27 percent, and atmospheric lead by 98 percent. The particulate emission reduction is attributed to control equipment installed on utility plant and industrial smokestacks, a decreased use of coal, and less burning of solid wastes. Carbon monoxide and hydrocarbon emissions have decreased, despite an increase in automotive traffic, because of federal automotive emission standards. The drop in sulfur oxides is directly attributable to a switch to low-sulfur coal and the removal of sulfur from the discharged gases at electric power plants. The drastic drop of lead compounds in the atmosphere resulted from the switch to unleaded gasoline during the 1970's.

During the first decade of the twenty-first century, concern about global warming caused by CO_2 created a consensus that drastic action was needed to reduce this threat. Early in 2009, the EPA declared CO_2 an air

Percentage Change in U.S. Emissions (millions of tons per year)	
	1980 vs. 2008
Carbon monoxide	−56
Lead	−99
Nitrogen oxides	−40
Volatile organic compounds	−47
Direct particulate matter (10-micron-diameter)	−68
Direct particulate matter (2.5-micron-diameter)	—
Sulfur dioxide	−56

Source: Data from U.S. Environmental Protection Agency, *Air Quality Trends,* 2009.

pollutant, thus empowering the Clean Air Act to establish national emission standards for new automobiles and new coal-fired electric power plants, the two largest contributors to global warming emissions.

GLOBAL AIR QUALITY CONTROL

Air pollution, an ongoing problem in industrialized nations, has also become problematic in virtually all undeveloped countries undergoing rapid industrialization. The countries of the European Union have taken collective action because pollution generated in one country affects air quality in neighboring countries. Because road transportation is Europe's largest air polluter, beginning in the 1970's motor vehicles manufactured on the Continent have had required exhaust-emission controls. Fossil-fuel emissions from power plants and factories are also stringently regulated.

In Bangladesh, workers in a brick field stand adjacent to a chimney emitting black smoke. (AP/Wide World Photos)

In the United Kingdom, national air quality objectives were instituted in 2000 in association with an air quality network to monitor levels of major pollutants in various locations and a daily warning system to indicate potentially dangerous air pollution levels. In the summer of 2006, a directive on emission ceilings for cleaner air in Europe was passed by the European Parliament.

The environmental crisis in the former Soviet republics of Eastern Europe is a direct result of the policies pursued under the communist regime, when rapid industrialization ignored local conditions. Air pollution controls were deemed unnecessary because the biosphere was assumed to be self-purifying. With the advent of glasnost, a state committee on environmental protection was instituted in 1988; this became a state ministry in 1991 but was abolished nine years later. No significant change in ecological concerns occurred after the fall of the communist regime and the transition to capitalism. Because agencies responsible for environmental matters are either nonexistent or severely underfunded, internationally funded pollution abatement projects are abandoned when the funds expire.

The country with the greatest number of premature deaths because of air pollution is India, where rapid industrialization and urbanization combined with unregulated vehicular emissions and uncontrolled industrial effluents have exacerbated a preexisting problem. Legislation to alleviate the crisis in cities such as New Delhi, one of the top-ten most polluted cities in the world, has been extremely difficult to implement. Auto emissions account for approximately 70 percent of urban air pollution, and regulations required all public transportation vehicles in New Delhi to switch to compressed natural gas engines by April 1, 2001. However, the statute had to be rescinded when it removed about fifteen thousand taxis and ten thousand buses from service, creating commuter chaos and public riots. India's high air pollution has not happened because of a lack of legislation but because of insufficient enforcement at the local level.

China's growing economy has removed millions of people from poverty, to the detriment of the environment. The increase of urban automotive traffic, the dependence on coal, and a weak environmental protection system have left China with sixteen of the world's twenty most polluted cities. Both urban and rural dwellers suffer from air pollution, which annually causes approximately 400,000 premature deaths and 75 million asthma attacks. In 2005, to help alleviate the problem, the government proposed that strict fuel efficiency standards and emission controls be required on all vehicles. China's excessive air pollution is not contained within its borders. Unregulated airborne effluents from the numerous coal-burning plants reach Japan and become a major contributor to acid rain. In addition, sulfate-encrusted dust, carbon particulates, and nitrates cross the Pacific Ocean, where they are responsible for almost one-third of the polluted air over Los Angeles and San Francisco.

Arguably, Japan is the Asian country that has taken air pollution abatement and control most seriously. Laws regulating the emission of sulfur dioxide and nitrogen oxides are among the strictest in the world, but polluted air from China keeps the rain acidic. The huge increase in automotive traffic in recent decades is a major contributor to urban air pollution as well as severe congestion. Several stringent laws regulate automotive emissions in an attempt to control these related problems. In addition, the Japanese environment agency promotes low-emission vehicles and continues to strengthen measures to reduce factory emissions. In June, 2001, the Japanese legislature passed a law strengthening controls on diesel vehicle emissions; two years later, diesel-powered commercial vehicles were banned from Tokyo if these limits were exceeded.

CONTEXT

More than three million premature deaths in the world occur annually because of air pollution, the greatest number of these occurring in India. In both developed and developing nations, air pollution from the escalating number of vehicles, as well as consumer preference for larger, more powerful vehicles, continues as a major challenge despite gains since the 1980's. Controlling air pollution is not inexpensive. Pollution control devices increase costs to factories and to automobiles, costs that are passed to the consumer. Unless a radical change away from conspicuous consumption and the overreliance on fossil fuels occurs, air quality will not improve substantially.

The issue of whether global warming is caused by humans may not be completely resolved, but strong measures to control carbon dioxide as well as noxious gaseous and particulate air pollutants began during the last decades of the twentieth century. Because the preponderance of scientific evidence suggests that global warming is due to humanity's excessive use of fossil fuels, it would seem prudent to curtail the disproportionate dependence on nonrenewable resources. When it was discovered that the ozone layer was being depleted by CFCs, the Montreal Protocol was ratified by most industrial nations. This precedent indicates that strong, effective action and international cooperation are possible when the threat to the environment are grave enough.

George R. Plitnik

FURTHER READING

Ayres, Jon, Robert Maynard, and Roy Richards, eds. *Air Pollution and Health.* London: Imperial College Press, 2006.

Calhoun, Yael, ed. *Air Quality.* Philadelphia: Chelsea House, 2005.

Gribbin, John. *Hothouse Earth: The Greenhouse Effect and GAIA.* New York: Grove Weidenfeld, 1990.

Jacobson, Mark Z. *Atmospheric Pollution: History, Science, and Regulation.* New York: Cambridge University Press, 2002.

Metcalfe, Sarah, and Dick Derwent. *Atmospheric Pollution and Environmental Change.* London: Hodder Arnold, 2005.

Miller, G. Tyler, Jr. *Living in the Environment: Principles, Connections, and Solutions.* 15th ed. Pacific Grove, Calif.: Brooks/Cole, 2007.

Seinfeld, John H., and Spyros N. Pandis. *Atmospheric Chemistry and Physics: From Air Pollution to Climate Change.* New York: John Wiley & Sons, 2006.

Somerville, Richard C. J. *The Forgiving Air: Understanding Environmental Change.* 2d ed. Boston: American Meteorological Society, 2008.

Vallero, Daniel. *Fundamentals of Air Pollution.* 4th ed. Burlington, Mass.: Academic Press, 2008.

WEB SITES

ENVIRONMENT CANADA
Clean Air Online
http://www.ec.gc.ca/cleanair-airpur/Home-WS8C3F7D55-1_En.htm

U.S. ENVIRONMENTAL PROTECTION AGENCY
Clean Air Act
http://www.epa.gov/air/caa

U.S. ENVIRONMENTAL PROTECTION AGENCY
Air Pollution Effects
http://www.epa.gov/ebtpages/airairpollutioneffects.html

SEE ALSO: Acid precipitation; Atmosphere; Carbon; Clean Air Act; Electrical power; Environmental Protection Agency; Greenhouse gases and global climate change; Internal combustion engine; Ozone layer and ozone hole debate.

Alaska pipeline

CATEGORIES: Historical events and movements; obtaining and using resources

DATE: Congress authorized construction in November, 1973; construction began April, 1974; pipeline completed in 1977

The plan to construct a trans-Alaskan oil pipeline network generated considerable controversy. After completion, the pipeline, a triumph of engineering, helped lower U.S. dependency on imported oil during the 1980's.

BACKGROUND

The Naval Petroleum Reserve was created on the north slope of Alaska in 1923, but for two decades, the exploratory wells drilled there came up dry. Moreover, the cost of commercial drilling in Alaska appeared prohibitive. From the 1930's to the 1950's, oil was cheap, and interest in Alaska's unproven reserves plummeted.

During the 1960's, the increasing price of oil and the possibility of a decline in the security of oil supplied from abroad combined to revive interest in Alaska's oil possibilities. The Atlantic Richfield Company (later ARCO) obtained the majority of the government leases granted for exploratory and developmental activity in Alaska. On December 26, 1967, in temperatures 30° Celsius below zero, ARCO struck oil and discovered the largest oil field ever found in North America.

Huge technological challenges had to be overcome, including obtaining the oil in volume in the subzero temperatures of Alaska's north slope and

This portion of the Alaska pipeline was designed to trace the path of the Denali fault. (USGS)

transporting it safely to the port of Valdez in the south of Alaska for shipment by tankers to California. Construction of a mammoth, nearly 1,300-kilometer pipeline seemed to be the only way to transport the oil across the frozen tundra.

The political obstacles to transporting the oil proved even more challenging. Environmentalists feared that the pipeline would do irrevocable damage to Alaska's ecological systems. The National Environmental Policy Act (NEPA), which was passed after the Santa Barbara oil spill of 1969, gave environmentalists the leverage they needed to oppose the pipeline's construction. When the Department of the Interior tried to satisfy the NEPA requirements by filing a slight eight-page environmental impact statement, the Friends of the Earth and the Environmental Defense Fund obtained a court injunction on April 13, 1970, which halted construction of the pipeline until a definitive court ruling on compliance with NEPA could be obtained.

Work on the pipeline was suspended for nearly four years as proponents and opponents battled in the bureaucracy and the courts. Then came the October, 1973, Yom Kippur War, the Arab oil embargo on Western countries assisting Israel, and the quadrupling of the price of imported oil to nearly twelve dollars per barrel. A month later, on November 16, 1973, Congress relieved the Department of the Interior of further obligations under NEPA and approved the construction of a nearly ten-billion-dollar trans-Alaska pipeline from Prudhoe Bay to Valdez. In April, 1974, the monumental task of constructing a pipeline that would not be environmentally disruptive began.

IMPACT ON RESOURCE USE
The pipeline was completed in 1977 and within a year was carrying one million barrels of oil per day to Valdez. By the early 1980's, the amount being transported had doubled, reducing the U.S. appetite for imported oil. The opening of the Alaska pipeline came too late to prevent a second oil crisis in 1979 from driving the price of imported oil to more than thirty-six dollars per barrel but not too late to contribute to the general decline in Western demand for Organization of Petroleum Exporting Countries (OPEC) oil during the 1980's. During that decade OPEC lost control over the production rates of member states and was unable to prevent the price of oil from plummeting before restabilizing in the 1990's at approximately twenty dollars per barrel. In 2006, oil prices

spiked again when the Department of Transportation insisted the Alaska pipeline be examined after an oil spill that leaked nearly 6,290 barrels. Upon inspection conducted by British Petroleum (BP), the pipeline was found to have a high level of corrosion, forcing BP to replace nearly 26 kilometers of pipeline and causing a temporary shutdown of service.

Joseph R. Rudolph, Jr.

SEE ALSO: Energy economics; Energy politics; *Exxon Valdez* oil spill; Oil and natural gas drilling and wells; Oil and natural gas exploration; Organization of Petroleum Exporting Countries.

Alloys

CATEGORIES: Mineral and other nonliving resources; products from resources

Alloys are solid combinations of metals or of metals and nonmetallic elements that have technologically desirable properties. The discoveries of various alloys have marked significant turning points in human history.

BACKGROUND
Alloys are mixtures of metal—such as iron, coal, copper, tin, and lead—with other metals or with nonmetallic elements developed to add desirable properties to those possessed by the metallic elements. These properties include strength, hardness, resistance to corrosion, and the ability to withstand high temperatures. The properties of alloys depend not only on their chemical composition but also on the way they have been prepared. Steel, a family of alloys based on the addition of carbon and other elements to iron, is perhaps the most familiar example in modern technology, but alloys based on aluminum, cobalt, gold, nickel, mercury, titanium, and many other elements are also of great practical importance. In many cases the role they play in alloy formation is the determining factor in the importance attached to these elements as natural resources. The metals used in alloys must be extracted from their ores, a process that often leaves environmentally troublesome by-products such as sulfur oxides. The manufacture of alloys generally requires sustained high temperatures, creating a demand for fossil fuels and raising concern about thermal pollution.

HISTORY

Archaeologists and historians have named the stages of early civilization after the principal materials used for tools in each of them. Thus at various times in different parts of the world, civilization progressed from the Stone Age to a Bronze Age, and then to an Iron Age. Bronze, a mixture of copper and tin, was the first alloy to receive extensive use. Bronze artifacts dated as early as 3500 B.C.E. have been found in both Asia Minor and China. The Hittites are believed to have been the first peoples, in about 1500 B.C.E., to have discovered how to extract metallic iron from its ores. The superior strength of iron led to the replacement of bronze by iron in armor, weaponry, and knives. The iron used by early civilizations was undoubtedly an alloy, though it was not understood as such. Steel, formed by the addition of carbon to iron, was made in India by 1000 B.C.E. Brass, a mixture of copper and zinc, appears to have been known to the Romans.

MODERN ALLOYS

Alloys are generally grouped into ferrous alloys, those containing iron, and nonferrous alloys. Bronze and brass remain among the most common nonferrous alloys. Bronze is used in numerous industrial applications and as a durable material for sculptures. Brass is readily machined and widely used in hardware, electrical fixtures, and decorations. Aluminum, extracted from bauxite ore by high-temperature electrolysis, is alloyed with manganese, magnesium, or other elements to produce a lightweight rigid material.

Ferrous alloys include steels and cast iron. Cast irons are alloys of iron with 2 to 4 percent carbon and up to 3 percent silicon. Steels are alloys of iron that contain a smaller amount of carbon as well as other elements. The manufacture of steel requires extremely high temperatures. Numerous forms of steel exist. Chromium steel has increased hardness and rust resistance. Stainless steel is a special form of chromium steel with admixtures of manganese, silicon, and nickel. Molybdenum, titanium, phosphorus, and selenium may also be added. Manganese is added to steel to increase strength and durability. Tungsten steels are stronger at high temperatures. Vanadium steel has greater elasticity and is suited to parts that must bend and regain their shape.

Alloys of gold and silver are important in coinage and for decorative purposes. Gold is alloyed with silver and copper for jewelry. Sterling silver is an alloy of silver with copper.

Certain alloys are employed in dentistry and medicine. Throughout most of the twentieth century dentists made liberal use of mercury amalgam, a moldable mixture of mercury, silver, and other elements, as a filling material for dental caries (cavities). Concern about mercury toxicity led to a reduction in use of this material. Orthopedic surgeons frequently use stainless steel screws, pins, and rods to hold fractured bones in place so that they can heal properly. Alloys also play a role in a variety of orthopedic implants used to replace badly worn or damaged joints.

Another important group of alloys is those used for permanent magnets. These include alnico, a combination of aluminum, nickel, and cobalt. Other magnetic materials include iron-nickel and iron-aluminum combinations. The rare earth elements also play a role in some magnetic materials.

Superalloys are materials based on nickel, cobalt, or an iron-nickel mixture and contain carefully controlled amounts of trace elements designed to exhibit high strength at temperatures above 1,000° Celsius. These materials are used in jet engines, in heat exchangers, and in chemical production plants.

IMPACT OF ALLOYS ON NATURAL RESOURCES

The development and refinement of alloy technology have had a dual effect on natural resource utilization. By making a larger variety of consumer goods available, the development of new alloys has tended to accelerate the use of mineral ores and energy sources. However, the emergence of alloys that are lighter, more corrosion resistant, and amenable to recycling, as well as the replacement of some alloys by polymer-based materials and other alloys, slowed the rate of resource use somewhat after its peak in the 1970's.

Donald R. Franceschetti

FURTHER READING

Askeland, Donald R., and Pradeep P. Phulé. *The Science and Engineering of Materials.* 5th ed. Toronto: Nelson, 2006.

Campbell, F. C., ed. *Elements of Metallurgy and Engineering Alloys.* Materials Park, Ohio: ASM International, 2008.

Kranzberg, Melvin, and Cyril Stanley Smith. "Materials in History and Society." In *The Materials Revolution,* edited by Tom Forester. Cambridge, Mass.: MIT Press, 1988.

Plowden, David. *Steel.* New York: Viking Press, 1981.

Raymond, Robert. *Out of the Fiery Furnace: The Impact of*

Metals on the History of Mankind. University Park: Pennsylvania State University Press, 1986.

Shackelford, James F. *Introduction to Materials Science for Engineers.* 7th ed. Upper Saddle River, N.J.: Pearson Prentice Hall, 2009.

Simons, Eric N. *An Outline of Metallurgy.* New York: Hart, 1969.

Street, Arthur, and William Alexander. *Metals in the Service of Man.* 10th ed. London: Penguin, 1994.

SEE ALSO: Aluminum; Brass; Bronze; Cobalt; Copper; Manganese; Metals and metallurgy; Nickel; Rare earth elements; Steel.

Aluminum

CATEGORY: Mineral and other nonliving resources

WHERE FOUND

Aluminum is the most abundant metallic element in the Earth's crust, comprising 8.3 percent of the mass in the crust by weight. As an element it is exceeded in crustal abundance only by oxygen and silicon. Commercially, the most important aluminum ore is bauxite, a mixed aluminum oxide hydroxide with a composition that varies with climate. Large reserves of this mineral exist, typically found in thick layers with little topsoil or overburden so that it can be easily mined. Worldwide reserves are tremendously large, notably in Australia, Africa, Brazil, and countries in Central America.

PRIMARY USES

By far the main use of aluminum in its metallic form is as a structural material in the construction and transportation (particularly aircraft) industries. Another major use is as a container material, of which the soft drink can is the most widely recognizable example. Aluminum is a more effective conductor per unit of mass than copper, so it is a more versatile material for power lines. Electrical transmission lines thus account for a sizable fraction of total world production as well.

TECHNICAL DEFINITION

Aluminum (atomic number 13) is a member of the boron group (Group III) of the periodic table of the elements. In terms of chemical and physical proper-

ties, the metallic element aluminum is more like boron than the other elements in the group. There is only one stable, naturally occurring isotope of aluminum, with an atomic weight of 26.98154. The pure solid exists in a single crystalline form in which every aluminum atom in the solid-state lattice is surrounded by twelve others at equal distances. Aluminum has a density of 2.699 grams per cubic centimeter. It has a melting point of 660.37° Celsius and a boiling point of 2,467° Celsius.

DESCRIPTION, DISTRIBUTION, AND FORMS

Aluminum is the most abundant metallic element accessible in the Earth's crust. Of the other metallic elements, only iron and copper display abundances approaching that of aluminum. Aluminum is a constituent of igneous minerals such as feldspar and mica. When these ores weather, they tend to generate clays such as kaolinite and vermiculite. These materials are widespread in the Earth's crust. In addition, aluminum may be found in rarer minerals such as cryolite, spinel, beryl, turquoise, and corundum. Aluminum compounds are important as precious minerals as well. The presence of a slight trace of a transition metal impurity in the aluminum oxide crystalline lattice typically imparts color to the solid. The ore of central commercial importance in the primary extraction of aluminum is bauxite, a mixed aluminum oxide and hydroxide first discovered in 1821. It is generated when silica and other materials are leached by weathering from silicates of aluminum.

An aluminum compound of some importance is lithium aluminum hydride. This compound is an effective reducing agent and functions as a hydrogenating agent. It was a mainstay in organic synthesis until supplanted by organometallic hydrides that are less expensive to produce and easier to manipulate. Commercial production of lithium aluminum hydride dates from around 1950. Within twenty years the compound had displayed reactivity with more than sixty types of organic functional groups (the part of an organic molecule that gives it a characteristic reactivity, such as a hydroxyl group).

Total annual worldwide production of aluminum from its ores is almost 38 million metric tons, and there are large-scale production plants in many locations around the world. The largest producer of primary aluminum is China with approximately 13 million metric tons, which accounts for 33 percent of the world total. Russia and Canada account for another

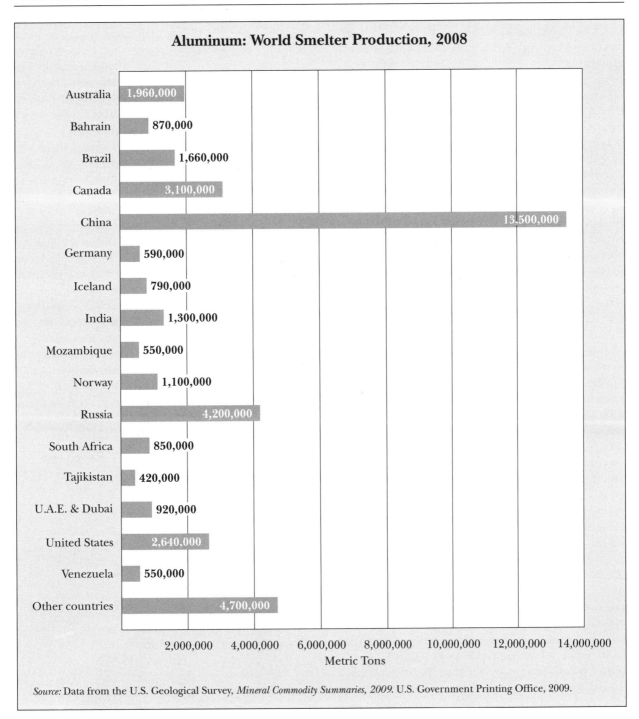

Aluminum: World Smelter Production, 2008

Country	Metric Tons
Australia	1,960,000
Bahrain	870,000
Brazil	1,660,000
Canada	3,100,000
China	13,500,000
Germany	590,000
Iceland	790,000
India	1,300,000
Mozambique	550,000
Norway	1,100,000
Russia	4,200,000
South Africa	850,000
Tajikistan	420,000
U.A.E. & Dubai	920,000
United States	2,640,000
Venezuela	550,000
Other countries	4,700,000

Source: Data from the U.S. Geological Survey, *Mineral Commodity Summaries, 2009.* U.S. Government Printing Office, 2009.

20 percent of the world's production. The United States, Australia, and Brazil are also major producers of primary aluminum.

The need for primary extraction of aluminum from its ores is somewhat alleviated because of the ease with which metallic aluminum can be recycled. Recycling requires a fraction of the energy cost of primary extraction. Primary extraction consumes almost two metric tons of ore for every metric ton of aluminum produced; it also consumes approximately one-half of a metric ton of carbon, one-tenth of a metric ton of cryolite, and fifteen thousand kilowatt-hours of electrical energy. The air pollution one might expect from such a large energy output is moderated by the fact that aluminum production plants typically are run by hydroelectric power. This means that often the location in which the ore is mined and the location in which the metal is extracted are widely separated. (For most metals, the refining plant is situated as close as possible to the material source to minimize transportation costs.)

Aluminum and most aluminum compounds are relatively benign in the environment. Primary environmental impact results from the direct electrochemical extraction of aluminum from its ores. The process requires a tremendous amount of electrical energy, an applied potential of about 4 volts and a current of 105 amperes, and a reaction vessel heated to about 900° Celsius. These power requirements place tremendous demand on resources, but the availability of hydroelectric power has minimized the air and thermal pollution produced by these plants.

Aluminum also provides a means of determining acid rain effects. When lakes become acidic, aluminum can be leached from the soil and dissolved in the water. A water sample can be treated with appropriate agents that bind with the metal to form brightly colored species. The concentration of aluminum can be determined by measuring the amount of light these materials absorb. This in turn provides information about the extent of acid contamination by determining the amount of aluminum leached into the water.

HISTORY

Although aluminum is the most abundant metallic element accessible on Earth, it was not isolated in its elemental form until the early 1800's. Even then, for most of the nineteenth century, its rarity made it a precious metal with an expensive price tag and uses centering on decorative rather than practical applications. Chemical thermodynamics, the study of energy relationships in chemical reactions, provides a basis for understanding why isolating aluminum was so difficult and why a pyrometallurgical technique could not be used.

Most metallic elements, with the exception of gold, silver, and a few others, tend to react with oxygen in the atmosphere or with other elements and form compounds rather than remain in their elemental,

metallic state. To isolate the metal from the compound in its elemental form, the metal must receive electrons in a process called reduction. Typically this process requires heat energy, so the reduction (or smelting) must be done at elevated temperatures. Some elements, such as copper and lead, can be reduced at a relatively low, easily attainable temperature. Because of their ease of extraction, these elements have been known for a long time. Other elements, such as iron, require a much higher temperature for the reduction reaction to proceed at an appreciable rate. These higher temperatures are much more difficult to obtain, requiring a higher level of technology, especially in terms of furnace development. Elemental iron could not be produced until this higher technological level was reached. Still other elements, such as aluminum, can be made to undergo chemical reduction only at temperatures so high that they are not commercially attainable or physically containable. Rather than being reduced at high temperatures, they are reduced by utilizing an electrochemical reaction that requires application of an electrical potential high enough to overcome the energy barrier to the reaction. This procedure elimi-

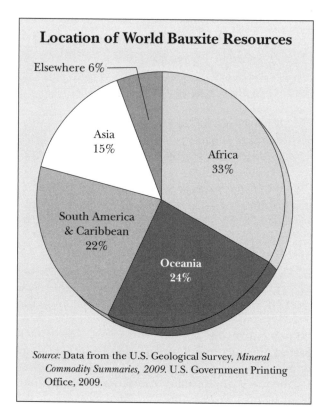

Location of World Bauxite Resources

Elsewhere 6%

Asia 15%

Africa 33%

South America & Caribbean 22%

Oceania 24%

Source: Data from the U.S. Geological Survey, *Mineral Commodity Summaries, 2009.* U.S. Government Printing Office, 2009.

nates the need for the extremely high temperatures of a pyrometallurgical reduction, but it requires the existence of a large, reliable source of electricity for industrial-scale production to be feasible. Such an electrical source did not exist until the nineteenth century, when the dynamo was invented. Availability of the dynamo and hydroelectric power provided the massive amounts of electrical energy needed to produce large quantities of metallic aluminum.

While the elemental form of aluminum was rare and even unknown prior to the technological advances of the 1800's, compounds containing aluminum have been known since the days of ancient Greece and Rome. The very name "aluminum" is derived from "alum," the common name for the hydrate of aluminum potassium sulfate. In the Greek and Roman civilizations, alum was known as an astringent (a substance that causes muscles to contract) and a mordant (a substance that causes dye molecules to adhere to cloth). Sir Humphry Davy, a pioneer of electrochemical methods, attempted to isolate the metal but was unsuccessful. He proposed the name alumium, a name consistent in form with such names as sodium and potassium, elements that Davy had discovered in 1807 and named in terms of their historical sources (soda ash and potash). This was changed soon after to aluminum and was still further modified to aluminium. The United States is one of the few countries still preferring the use of the name aluminum.

The discovery of aluminum was facilitated by Davy's isolation of sodium and potassium in their elemental forms. These elements are effective reducing agents, meaning they have a strong tendency to force electrons onto other materials, thereby reducing their charge. In the early 1800's, Hans Christian Ørsted used sodium amalgamated with mercury to chemically reduce aluminum from aluminum chloride. While he was able to isolate and identify aluminum in this process, the reaction was inefficient, yielding small amounts of impure aluminum. In 1845, Friedrich Wöhler prepared samples of aluminum that were large enough to allow preliminary determination of the elusive element's chemical and physical properties. The results of these studies stimulated a great deal of academic interest in the metal, although little interest in commercial utilization of the metal arose.

The first commercial production method was developed in 1854 by Henri-Étienne Sainte-Claire De-Ville. This method used sodium as a reducing agent.

Its introduction caused the price of aluminum to drop dramatically. Aluminum had cost about twelve hundred dollars per kilogram; with the introduction of the improved synthetic method, the price dropped to less than five hundred dollars per kilogram in the mid-nineteenth century. Even then, the element was perceived more as a curiosity than as a useful natural resource. At the time of the Paris exposition in 1855, the samples of aluminum displayed were billed as "silver from clay," a term evocative of both the perceived value of the element and the typical source from which it was derived.

By the year 1880, construction of a plant capable of producing almost fifty thousand kilograms of aluminum per year using the Sainte-Claire DeVille process was begun. By the time the plant had been built and gone into full-scale production, the cost of aluminum had dropped to about twenty dollars per kilogram. During this same time period, the first serious attempt to produce aluminum in the United States was made by William Frishmuth. Among the more notable items produced was a three-kilogram pyramid of aluminum that was used to cap the Washington Monument as a functional part of its lightning rod system. Prior to its installation, this oddity was placed on public display.

OBTAINING ALUMINUM
The difficulty in extracting aluminum from its ores, coupled with the interesting properties of the metal, made the quest for an economical means of production a target of many prospective inventors. The key discoveries needed to realize large-scale production were made almost simultaneously in 1886 by two young men, Charles Martin Hall in the United States and Paul Héroult in France. Both men were in their early twenties. The key to the success of these individuals lay in the extractive technique they utilized (an electrochemical method) and critical experimental modifications that they made. Hall correctly deduced that, at the high operating temperatures of his apparatus, impurities from the clay container he was using as a reaction vessel may have been causing undesired side reactions to take place, thus preventing aluminum formation. He eliminated the clay vessel and instead used one lined with graphite, a form of elemental carbon. The graphite also served as one of the electrodes in the electrochemical cell. With these modifications, Hall was able to produce large pieces of aluminum. These pieces were kept by the company Hall founded and dubbed the "crown jewels." Com-

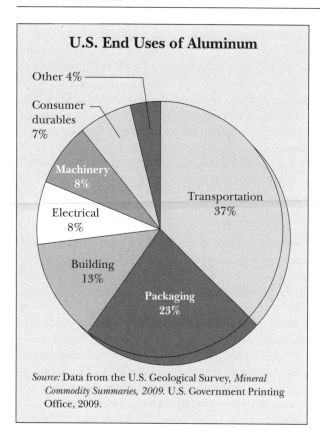

U.S. End Uses of Aluminum

Other 4%
Consumer durables 7%
Machinery 8%
Electrical 8%
Building 13%
Packaging 23%
Transportation 37%

Source: Data from the U.S. Geological Survey, *Mineral Commodity Summaries, 2009.* U.S. Government Printing Office, 2009.

mercial production escalated rapidly, resulting in another tremendous downward shift in price, from around twelve dollars per kilogram to about seventy-five cents per kilogram only fifteen years later.

Uses of Aluminum

Aluminum is of great importance in modern society. Many of the engineering accomplishments of the twentieth century would have been impossible without the availability of aluminum. Modern airliners would be impossible to construct without it. The importance of aluminum is based on its great strength, light weight, and resistance to corrosion. This resistance occurs because typically a thin film of chemically inert aluminum oxide forms on the surface of the metal, shielding it from further corrosion. This protective layer can be artificially produced through an anodization process. Production of differing oxide layer thicknesses provides a variety of appearances and properties in the anodized materials. An oxide layer on the order of 15 micrometers in thickness gives sufficient corrosion protection for exterior structural use. Aluminum's appearance makes it a de-

sirable external feature. The first skyscraper to be clad with aluminum was built in the 1950's. The limited tensile strength of aluminum means that alloys typically offer better service as structural components. There is no doubt that, after the construction industry, the aviation industry is the greatest beneficiary of aluminum's benefits. Aluminum and aluminum alloys make possible strong, lightweight airframes.

In addition to their major applications when in the metallic state, aluminum compounds are utilized in industrial processes and to make materials ranging from cements to chemical reaction catalysts. Aluminum compounds are important in the production of portland cement, first patented in 1824. This strong cement does not dissolve in water. John Smeaton found aluminum silicates to be an important ingredient of this cement. Portland cement contains approximately 11 percent by mass tricalcium aluminate. Although it was known to be an important component, the chemical structure of this compound was not known until 1975. The aluminate ion is a cyclic ion, with a key structural feature of individual aluminum and oxygen atoms linked alternately into a twelve-member ring. The reaction of this material with water is a key step and must be properly controlled to facilitate the setting of the cement. After the production process, the finished cement contains about 5 percent aluminum oxide. The portland cement industry is an important one, with production in the United States on the order of 85 million metric tons per year. Another versatile cement, ciment fondu, is useful in marine environments and contains up to 40 percent aluminum oxide.

While aluminum itself is light and strong, its properties can typically be enhanced by an alloying process. Typically, aluminum is alloyed with copper, manganese, zinc, or silicon. Each of these alloying agents produces alloys with certain desired properties. The strength-to-weight factor is enhanced in copper alloys. Silicon alloys have low melting points and do not expand much when heated. This property makes these materials particularly useful as welding filler and for the production of castings. The corrosion resistance of aluminum is enhanced by alloying with magnesium. These alloy types are widely used in ship construction, especially as external fittings. Perhaps the most widely seen examples of aluminum alloys are the manganese alloys, used in cookware, storage tanks, furniture, and highway signs.

One of the more spectacular uses of aluminum is based on its strong affinity for oxygen and its tendency to lose electrons (to be oxidized) in chemical reactions. This is well demonstrated by the thermite reaction, in which aluminum reacts with another metal oxide to reduce the other metal to its elemental form and generate aluminum oxide. This type of reaction tends to liberate considerable thermal energy and proceed very rapidly. This rapid heat evolution causes the other metal to be generated in a molten form. Thermite reactions are used in welding operations.

While there is only one stable isotope of aluminum, a short-lived radioactive isotope, aluminum 26, it is of potential use in dating the universe. There is evidence from ancient rock samples that this isotope was common in the early solar system, and this isotope decays to a magnesium isotope. Measurement of the ratio of this decay product to the remaining aluminum 26 allows determination of the age of the object, in much the same way that the ratio of isotopes is used in carbon dating. From these measurements, estimating the length of time it took the solar system to develop becomes possible.

Craig B. Lagrone

FURTHER READING

Altenpohl, Dietrich. *Aluminum—Technology, Applications, and Environment, a Profile of a Modern Metal: Aluminum from Within.* 6th ed. Washington, D.C.: Aluminum Association, 1998.

Büchel, Karl Heinz, Hans-Heinrich Moretto, and Peter Woditsch. *Industrial Inorganic Chemistry.* 2d rev. ed. Translated by David R. Terrell. New York: Wiley-VCH, 2000.

Geller, Tom. "Aluminum." *Chemical Heritage* 25, no. 4 (Winter, 2007/2008): 32-36.

Greenwood, N. N., and A. Earnshaw. "Aluminium, Gallium, Indium, and Thallium." In *Chemistry of the Elements.* 2d ed. Boston: Butterworth-Heinemann, 1997.

Krebs, Robert E. *The History and Use of Our Earth's Chemical Elements: A Reference Guide.* Illustrations by Rae Déjur. 2d ed. Westport, Conn.: Greenwood Press, 2006.

Massey, A. G. "Group 13: Boron, Aluminum, Gallium, Indium, and Thallium." In *Main Group Chemistry.* 2d ed. New York: Wiley, 2000.

Totten, George E., and D. Scott MacKenzie, eds. *Handbook of Aluminum.* New York: M. Dekker, 2003.

Walker, Jearl. "Retracing the Steps by Which Aluminum Metal Was Initially Purified Back in 1886." *Scientific American* 255, no. 2 (August, 1986): 116.

WEB SITES

NATURAL RESOURCES CANADA
Canadian Minerals Yearbook, Mineral and Metal Commodity Reviews
http://www.nrcan-rncan.gc.ca/mms-smm/busi-indu/cmy-amc/com-eng.htm

U.S. GEOLOGICAL SURVEY
Aluminum: Statistics and Information
http://minerals.usgs.gov/minerals/pubs/commodity/aluminum

SEE ALSO: Abrasives; Alloys; Brazil; Canada; Cement and concrete; China; Clays; Gems; Hydroenergy; Metals and metallurgy; Oxides; Russia; United States.

American Chemistry Council

CATEGORY: Organizations, agencies, and programs
DATE: Established 1872

The American Chemistry Council plays a vital role in ensuring that necessary natural resources are used responsibly and economically in the production of useful chemicals and that manufactured chemical products are safe for humans, wildlife, and the environment and pose no threat to national security.

BACKGROUND

The Manufacturing Chemists Association was formed in 1872 to represent the interests of the chemical industries to state and federal governments. The name was changed to the Chemical Manufacturers Association. The name American Chemistry Council (ACC) was adopted at the membership meeting held in June, 2000.

The ACC is an industry trade association that represents approximately two hundred American chemical manufacturers. Members apply the science of chemistry to produce innovative products and services that help make human lives better, healthier, and safer. ACC moved its headquarters from Rosslyn, Virginia, to Washington, D.C., in 2010.

IMPACT ON RESOURCE USE

The ACC establishes and implements goals and guidelines on health, safety, security, and environmental issues that are related to the use of global resources by chemical companies before, during, and after the manufacturing of chemical products. In 1988, the ACC adopted the Responsible Care® program to reduce harmful chemical emissions and increase safety. Since then emissions have been reduced by 78 percent and safety has become five times better than the average for the manufacturing industry in the United States. The Responsible Care® initiative was adopted globally and practiced in many countries with the commitment to increase the safety and secure management of chemical processes and products. Implementation is managed at the global level by the International Council of Chemical Associations. Practices vary from country to country as dictated by the laws and national industry association of each country.

In 2002, the American Plastics Council merged with the ACC. The plastics division of the ACC represents plastic resin manufacturers, which produce versatile plastic products that seek to make life better, healthier, and safer. Innovative use of plastics contribute to a more efficient use of global resources. In addition to the plastics industries, the ACC represents the producers and distributers of chlorine.

As part of the global warming and climate change debate, the ACC is a strong proponent for development of alternative energy sources and greater energy production in the United States. Because chemical manufacturers rely heavily on natural gas as an affordable supply of energy to produce chemical products necessary in making medicines, packaging, computers, cell phones, automobile parts, antifreeze, and health and personal care products, the ACC lobbies for reduced natural gas prices and increased natural gas exploration.

In 2005, the ACC launched its "essential2" campaign to improve its public image and reputation by promoting the chemical industry as a vital part of the economy and growth of the United States. It has worked with the U.S. Environmental Protection Agency to make available data related to the hazards associated with manufacturing high-production-volume chemicals. The top priorities of the ACC are energy and climate change, chemical regulations and manufacturer-site security, support for more railway competition for transporting chemical products, and the education of the general public about the risks associated with chemicals.

Alvin K. Benson

WEB SITE

AMERICAN CHEMISTRY COUNCIL
American Chemistry
http://www.americanchemistry.com/s_acc/
  index.asp

SEE ALSO: Chlorites; Oil and natural gas chemistry; Petrochemical products.

American Farm Bureau Federation

CATEGORY: Organizations, agencies, and programs
DATE: Established 1919

The American Farm Bureau Federation, comprising nearly three thousand county farm bureaus, is the largest farm organization in the United States and claims to be the "voice of agriculture." It is concerned with many issues that affect the profitability of farming and resists those efforts to protect natural resources and safeguard the environment that it regards as extreme.

BACKGROUND
The first local group to be known as a "farm bureau" was established as a subdivision of the Chamber of Commerce of Binghamton, New York, in 1911. Over the next several years many additional local farm bureaus were created, primarily at the county level. The main impetus for the organization of these new units came from the county farm agents funded by the Smith-Lever Act of 1914, which established the Agricultural Extension Service. The county agents set up many new farm bureau units to help farmers obtain higher yields in the areas in which the agents worked. This official relationship between a government agency and an interest group did not end until the 1950's.

IMPACT ON RESOURCE USE
In addition to the local units, the agricultural extension agents promoted the formation of state associations of farm bureaus. The American Farm Bureau Federation was created at a meeting in Chicago in 1919. While the federation gave early and strong support to the New Deal agricultural program, it gradually assumed a more conservative stance and advocated more free-market-oriented policies. The Ameri-

President Dwight Eisenhower speaks to representatives of the American Farm Bureau Federation at the White House in 1959. (AP/Wide World Photos)

can Farm Bureau Federation describes itself as an "independent, nongovernmental, voluntary organization." In addition to strictly farm-related programs, many state farm bureaus are heavily involved in the sale of casualty and property insurance.

William H. Stewart

WEB SITE

AMERICAN FARM BUREAU FEDERATION
The Voice of Agriculture: American Farm Bureau
http://www.fb.org/

SEE ALSO: Agricultural products; Agriculture industry; Farmland; Rangeland.

American Forest and Paper Association

CATEGORY: Organizations, agencies, and programs
DATE: Established 1992

The American Forest and Paper Association is the U.S. national trade association of the forest, pulp, paper, paperboard, and wood products industry.

BACKGROUND
The American Forest and Paper Association was formed in 1992 by the merger of the American Forest Council, established in 1932; the American Paper Institute, established in 1964; and the National Forest Products Association, established in 1902. The association publishes trade-related information for both members and nonmembers. *American Tree Farmer: The Official Magazine of the American Tree Farm System* is published bimonthly, and two annual statistical summaries provide information on recovered paper utilization and on paper, paperboard, and wood pulp. A comprehensive annual study of every mill in the United States gives capacity estimates for major grades of paper, paperboard, and wood pulp. When the association believes that sound forestry practices are being misrepresented, it responds in print, as in its 1994 publication *Closer Look: An On-the-Ground Investigation of the Sierra Club's Book, "Clearcut."*

IMPACT ON RESOURCE USE
Member companies grow, harvest, and process wood and wood fiber; manufacture pulp, paper, and paperboard from both virgin and recycled fiber; and produce solid wood products.

Annual awards recognize companies that make the best use of recycled wood products, that demonstrate wood's versatility, and that are innovative in addressing environmental concerns. An annual monetary award is also made to a young scientist or engineer for original research.

Jill A. Cooper

WEB SITE

AMERICAN FOREST AND PAPER ASSOCIATION
http://www.afandpa.org/

SEE ALSO: Forestry; Forests; Timber industry; Western Wood Products Association; Wood and timber.

American Gas Association

CATEGORY: Organizations, agencies, and programs
DATE: Established 1918

The American Gas Association is a multinational association of more than twenty-five hundred corporations. It works with the companies in conducting infor-

mational, training, and public relations activities regarding the storage, transport, distribution, and sales of natural gas and gas-related products.

BACKGROUND

In 1918, the Gas Institute and the National Commercial Gas Association merged to form the American Gas Association (AGA). The AGA is headquartered in Washington, D.C. Corporate members include the major utilities and pipeline companies that deal with the storage and transport of natural gas; utilities that distribute and sell natural gas; and many companies that produce, test, and sell gas-related appliances.

The AGA provides information to members and the general public through its publications. The *AGA Gas Energy Review* is a monthly journal devoted to issues such as future supplies of gas, demand, prices, consumption, and marketing strategies. A monthly magazine entitled *American Gas* provides gas company profiles and discusses new technologies, marketing programs, and trends in the gas industry.

IMPACT ON RESOURCE USE

The AGA provides its membership with important information on gas utilization, sales, finance, research management, safety, and all phases of gas transmission. Further, it compiles for its membership and the general public a wide variety of national and regional statistics as well as financial, economic, and marketing studies. The association has developed operating practices and rate schedules for each type of gas service available for virtually all gas companies. The AGA established the Gas Appliance Improvement Network (GAIN) in cooperation with the Gas Appliance Manufacturers Association to improve appliance design and performance.

Dion C. Stewart

WEB SITE

AMERICAN GAS ASSOCIATION
http://www.aga.org/

SEE ALSO: Oil and natural gas drilling and wells; Oil and natural gas exploration; Oil and natural gas reservoirs.

American Mining Congress

CATEGORY: Organizations, agencies, and programs
DATE: Established 1897

The American Mining Congress, an industry association, was created to promote the interests of the U.S. mining industry on a national level. In 1995, it joined with the National Coal Association to form the National Mining Association.

BACKGROUND

The American Mining Congress (AMC) was created in 1897 to represent the U.S. mining industry on national issues of concern for the industry. Member companies represent mineral producers, equipment producers, and consulting and financial services providers. The AMC patterned its initial organizational structure after that of the U.S. Congress. The first permanent office was established in Denver, Colorado, in 1904. AMC's Washington, D.C., office became the official headquarters in 1919. In April, 1995, the AMC joined with the National Coal Association to form the broader-based National Mining Association (NMA) to act as a single lobbying voice for the mining industry.

IMPACT ON RESOURCE USE

The AMC was (and the NMA is) concerned with issues such as health and safety, access to public lands, the environment, taxation, and international competitiveness. The AMC had a role in the creation of the U.S. Bureau of Mines in 1910 and was involved with the implementation of federal safety requirements and the establishment of industry standards. The AMC was involved in lobbying Congress, working with government agencies that regulate mining activities, distributing information and educational materials through its own publications and the news media, pursuing litigation initiatives, organizing trade shows and conferences, and supporting research.

Gary A. Campbell

WEB SITE

AMERICAN MINING CONGRESS
http://www.nma.org/

SEE ALSO: Bureau of Mines, U.S.; Mining safety and health issues; National Mining Association; Public lands; Underground mining.

American Petroleum Institute

CATEGORY: Organizations, agencies, and programs

DATE: Established 1919

The American Petroleum Institute is the leading organization in the United States for establishing standards on oil-field drilling and oil-producing equipment. It is a clearinghouse of oil industry opinion.

BACKGROUND

Impressed by the success of intra-industry cooperation during World War I, oil industry leaders created the American Petroleum Institute (API) in 1919. The API seeks to coordinate an industry noted for its individualism, and thus to avert government regulation as much as possible. The API gathers and periodically publishes statistics on the industry's operations, promotes the standardization of oil industry equipment, and represents the industry before the public and the government. It establishes standard units of measurement—such as the API gravity unit, used to measure the density of petroleum—and it assigns a unique number to each oil well drilled in the United States, known as the API well number.

IMPACT ON RESOURCE USE

The API is the principal lobbying group of the oil industry as a whole and is its center of analytical studies. It establishes committees to investigate and publish information about such problems as hydrocarbon reservoir mechanics, petroleum production methods, American dependence on foreign oil, and conservation practices. The API has been successful in most of its endeavors, including securing favorable tax treatment for the oil industry and helping the oil industry through many difficult situations involving public skepticism, oil-company scandals, and oil-price fluctuations. The API maintains departments of transportation, refining, and marketing in Washington, D.C., and a department of production in Texas.

Alvin K. Benson

WEB SITE

AMERICAN PETROLEUM INSTITUTE
Energy API
http://www.api.org/

SEE ALSO: Oil and natural gas drilling and wells; Oil and natural gas exploration; Oil industry; Petroleum refining and processing.

Ammonia. *See* Nitrogen and ammonia

Animal breeding

CATEGORY: Plant and animal resources

Animal breeding is the practice of selecting and mating domesticated animals to enhance their contributions to humans.

BACKGROUND

Animal breeding has been used to produce animals more useful to humankind since animals were first domesticated. Traditionally it involved selecting individual animals for desired traits and mating them, with the intent of producing improved offspring. In the second half of the twentieth century, extensive performance records and computer-aided analysis permitted superior animals to be identified more accurately and, via reproductive technologies, to be utilized more rapidly for improving the major livestock species. In the future, molecular biology and biotechnology promise to expedite this process by identifying desirable genes from the same or different species and incorporating them into domesticated animals. Animal breeding will continue to augment the value of domesticated animals as a renewable resource.

GENETIC INHERITANCE AND DETERMINANCE

Animal breeding is predicated on two principles: that the genes of an animal are inherited from its parents and that its genes are an important determinant of its appearance, structure, behavior, and productivity. In animal species, almost all genes are located in the nucleus of an organism's cells; these nuclear genes are inherited from both parents. A few genes, located outside the nucleus in subcellular structures called mitochondria, are derived only from the mother. The full complement of genes, known as the genome, directs the development of an individual animal, the synthesis of all body tissues, including metabolic machinery, and to a large extent the characteristics or traits exhibited. Different forms of genes, referred to as alleles, are responsible for the individuality of living things.

Some characteristics are determined by alleles of one gene—for instance, the absence of horns or the occurrence of a metabolic disease. In such cases a single mutation can lead to a deleterious condition. However, most traits of significance involve alleles of more than one gene. Superior characteristics for growth rate or milk yield, so-called polygenic traits, result from the combination of alleles of many genes. Animal breeding seeks to improve genetically the future population of a particular species by increasing the proportion of desirable alleles or the appropriate combination of such alleles. Genetic improvement re-

quires selection of appropriate breeding animals and a mating plan for such animals.

SELECTION AND MATING SYSTEMS

Selection is the process of determining which animals are to be used as breeding stock. The simplest form of selection considers only traits of the individual, whereas more complex selection takes account of additional information on relatives, such as siblings, parents, and offspring. The accuracy of predicting genetic progress is improved by considering relatives. This process requires reliable measures for desired traits, acquisition of records from numerous animals, and analysis of the records, which has been aided by advances in statistical theory and computational

Since the 1940's, dairy cows in the United States, such as these in Sacramento, California, have been intensively bred for milk production, which has tripled since that time. (Photo courtesy of USDA NRCS)

power. The result is a ranking of animals based on their genetic merit for single or multiple traits.

Several systems have been used for mating selected animals. One involves complementarity, whereby individuals with high genetic merit for different traits are mated. It has been used to improve livestock in developing countries by mating animals adapted to local conditions with highly productive ones from developed countries. The beef cattle, swine, and poultry industries make heavy use of crossbreeding, in which animals from different breeds are mated. One of its advantages is the "hybrid vigor" that results. Another system is mating the best to the best. One of its hazards is inbreeding, or the mating of relatives, which often results in decreased fertility and viability.

ENVIRONMENTAL FACTORS

Performance or productivity is determined not only by genetics but also by environmental factors. Climate, nutrition, and management can affect the extent to which the genetic potential of an animal is realized. Because the productivity of an animal can be affected deleteriously by heat and disease, climate and other environmental factors can influence animals' performance. Similarly, the management system used, whether intensive or extensive, can also affect productivity. Accordingly, the most productive animal under one set of conditions may not necessarily be the most productive under another. Interactions between genetics and the environment must be considered in animal breeding.

POST-1940'S DEVELOPMENTS

Beginning in the mid-twentieth century, reproductive technologies, most notably artificial insemination, contributed to rapid improvement in animal performance. These technologies permit animals with the best genetics to be used widely, resulting in numerous offspring from which to select the best breeding stock for the next generation. As a result of intensive selection and management in the United States beginning in the 1940's, milk production per cow has more than tripled. The growth rate of chickens has more than doubled, as has egg production. Such increases have occurred concurrently with a higher efficiency in raising animals for human food.

Molecular biology and biotechnology hold the potential to alter animal breeding processes significantly in the early twenty-first century. Further understanding of the genomes of livestock species should permit identification of specific genes that will increase the productivity of these animals. One approach, known as marker-assisted selection, would use genetic markers associated with desirable production characteristics to enhance genetic improvement. If such markers prove to be accurate predictors, they will allow selection of desirable animals long before performance records are available. Transfer of desirable genes, within or between species, may also expedite the generation of superior animals. The goal of animal breeding can be expected to remain similar to that of the past—namely the improvement of animal species to better meet human needs—but the precise nature of the improvements desired and the methodologies used to achieve them could be vastly different.

James L. Robinson

FURTHER READING

Bourdon, Richard M. *Understanding Animal Breeding.* 2d ed. Upper Saddle River, N.J.: Prentice Hall, 2000.

Falconer, D. S., and Trudy F. C. Mackay. *Introduction to Quantitative Genetics.* 4th ed. New York: Longman, 1996.

Field, Thomas G., and Robert E. Taylor. *Scientific Farm Animal Production: An Introduction to Animal Science.* 9th ed. Upper Saddle River, N.J.: Prentice Hall, 2008.

Sandøe, Peter, and Stine B. Christiansen. *Ethics of Animal Use.* Oxford, England: Blackwell, 2008.

Schatten, Heide, and Gheorghe M. Constantinescu, eds. *Comparative Reproductive Biology.* Ames, Iowa: Blackwell, 2007.

Van der Werf, Julius, Hans-Ulrich Graser, Richard Frankham, and Cedric Gondro, eds. *Adaptation and Fitness in Animal Populations: Evolutionary and Breeding Perspectives on Genetic Resource Management.* London: Springer, 2009.

Weaver, Robert F., and Philip W. Hedrick. *Genetics.* 3d ed. Dubuque, Iowa: W. C. Brown, 1997.

WEB SITE

U.S. DEPARTMENT OF AGRICULTURE
Animal Breeding, Genetics, and Genomics
http://www.csrees.usda.gov/
    animalbreedinggeneticsgenomics.cfm

SEE ALSO: Animal domestication; Animals as a medical resource; Biotechnology; Livestock and animal husbandry.

Animal domestication

CATEGORY: Plant and animal resources

The domestication of animals began long before recorded history and has been integral to the development of human societies. Domesticated species are renewable resources that provide humans with food, fiber, fuel, power, implements, and other benefits.

BACKGROUND

Domestication is the process of bringing a species under control of humans and gradually changing it through careful selection, mating, and handling so that it is more useful. Domestication of plants and animals led to the development of agriculture, permitting people to abandon a hunter-gatherer existence. Instead of following available game and edible wild plants, people were able to establish permanent settlements. Agriculture gave them more time to develop other skills and arts, eventually leading to complex societies and civilizations.

A critical aspect of domesticating animals is directing breeding toward a specific function. Although taming is probably a first step, domestication is more than accustoming animals to the presence of people. Domestication does not apply to captive wild animals in zoos or circuses, for example; although humans control such animals and their breeding, the latter is not directed toward a useful goal (although one could argue that breeding in captivity helps propagate the animal and perhaps helps maintain genetic diversity). Wild animals are those that have not been domesticated, and feral animals are previously domesticated animals that are no longer under human control. Wild relatives of domesticated species are relatively easily domesticated, and feral animals can be readily redomesticated.

CHARACTERISTICS THAT FAVOR DOMESTICATION

In 1865, the English naturalist Francis Galton suggested the following six physiological and behavioral characteristics that make some animals good candidates for domestication: hardiness, "dominance" social behavior, herd behavior, utility to humans, facile reproduction, and facile husbandry. First, hardiness refers to the ability of the young to tolerate removal from the mother and the presence of humans. The guinea pig is perhaps an extreme example of tolerat-

ing removal from its mother; it is born ready to eat solid food. Most mammals, on the other hand, depend on their dams' milk. Primates are poor subjects for domestication because of their helplessness at birth and their relatively long dependence on their mothers for food and nurturing.

Second, dominance social behavior, in contrast to territorial behavior, refers to one animal assuming leadership, with the rest of the group acquiescing to it. In domestication, humans co-opt the function of the leader, and animals remain submissive even as adults. Third, herd animals are contrasted to those that are solitary or disperse in response to danger. Domesticated animals are penned or otherwise restricted at various times. If they remain together in herds, they are easier to manage. Fourth, utility to humans includes their use for food, fiber, traction, companionship, and even worship. Humans would not make the effort to domesticate an animal unless it had some perceived value. However, the purpose for domestication may change with time. It is likely that the initial motivation for domesticating cattle was for worship—to capture the strength and aura of these animals, which were revered. Traction became a subsequent goal, while contemporary utility in Western societies involves meat and milk production.

The fifth characteristic is facile reproduction under confined conditions: Animals with finicky reproductive behavior and/or elaborate courtship rituals make poor candidates for domestication. Sixth, facile husbandry refers to placid behavior and versatility in terms of nutrition. Poor candidates for domestication are those animals that are very high strung or dependent on a unique feedstuff. Koalas, which eat leaves from only certain eucalyptus trees, are poor candidates for domestication. On the other hand, pigs and goats are excellent candidates because they are not fastidious in their eating habits. These six characteristics, enunciated more than a century ago, apply strongly to livestock species and somewhat less well to dogs and cats; some argue that cats are not so much domesticated as they are tolerant of humans.

HISTORY OF ANIMAL DOMESTICATION

Evidence from archaeology suggests that agriculture developed at least ten thousand years ago, after the last ice age. That agricultural development occurred at that point, when the climate was warmer and more stable than it had been, was probably not coincidence. Predictability of the weather is particularly crucial for

Sheep were one of the first animals to be domesticated. (USDA)

plant agriculture. Plant and animal domestication apparently developed together, suggesting a synergy between the two.

Domestication of any animal did not occur at once, but rather over a substantial period of time, perhaps hundreds of years. Accordingly, the dates for domestication have a substantial margin of error. Further, they may be modified as new information becomes available. For some species, domestication occurred independently at more than one location. In the beginning, the process may have been almost accidental, as by raising a captured young animal after its mother had been killed and observing its behavior and its responses to various treatments. The domestication of an animal then spread from the site of origin through trade or war.

Animal domestication occurred in various parts of the world. The Middle East, the so-called Fertile Crescent, stretching from Palestine to southern Turkey

and down the valley of the Tigris and Euphrates rivers, was an important site. There sheep, goats, cattle, and pigs were domesticated by around 8000 B.P. The Indian subcontinent and east Asia were independent sites for domesticating cattle and pigs, respectively. Llamas, alpacas, and guinea pigs were domesticated in the Andes Mountains of South America. Domestication of cats occurred in Egypt, and rabbits were domesticated in Europe. No native animal has been domesticated in Australia, with the possible exception of the emu. Interestingly, few successful domestications occurred after 1000 B.P.

Archaeology, coupled with the natural history of domesticated animals and their wild relatives, has been essential in reconstructing the history of domestication. Examining the skeletal remains at archaeological sites for changes in morphology and distributions by age and sex has helped researchers deduce the extent of domestication. Lately, traditional archaeology has been supplemented by the methods of molecular biology. Examining extant breeds for their degrees of genetic relationship has been particularly useful in distinguishing single versus dual sites of domestication.

EARLY DOMESTICATES: DOGS AND REINDEER

Dogs (*Canis familiaris*) were the earliest known domesticated animals. They were widespread across the Northern Hemisphere before other animals were domesticated. They derive from wolves (*Canis lupus*), with whom they are completely interfertile. The earliest known dog is in a burial site in northern Iraq that dates from 12,000 to 14,000 B.P. Other sites, dating from 9000 to 12,000 B.P., have been documented in England, Palestine, Japan, and Idaho. While the original domestication may have occurred in China (the Chinese wolf has some of the detailed physical features of domesticated dogs), domestication probably occurred at a number of separate sites. Domesticated dogs accompanied the American Indians when they occupied the Americas in several waves prior to the end of the last ice age. Dingoes were brought to Australia by trade from Asia long after the Aborigines settled Australia 40,000 years ago. While dogs were considered a food animal, they have long been known as companions and guards. Subsequently, they were developed for hunting and herding.

Reindeer (*Rangifer tarandus*) were another early domesticate, dating from around 14,000 B.P. in northern Scandinavia and Russia. Herding reindeer continues as a principal occupation of the Laplanders of Finland, Sweden, and Norway. Reindeer are used to pull loads and for clothing and shelter (skins), tools (antlers), and food (meat and milk). They are well suited to their environment and, contrary to other domesticated animals, their range has not been extended by domestication. Attempts to establish reindeer industries in Canada and Alaska have not been successful. In contrast, the farming of several other deer species (such as *Cervus dama* and *Cervus elaphus*) has recently gained in importance in New Zealand and Western Europe. They are raised for meat (venison) and "velvet," the new growth of antlers, which is the basis for traditional medicines in Asia.

SHEEP, PIGS, AND CATTLE

Sheep (*Ovis aries*) were the first of the common food animals to be domesticated. They were derived from wild sheep (*Ovis orientalis*) and were first domesticated in the western Fertile Crescent around 9000 B.P. Goats (*Capra hircus*), derived from Persian wild goats (*Capra aegarus*), were domesticated in the central Fertile Crescent slightly later, 8000-9000 B.P. Sheep and goats have been used for food, skins, and, in the case of sheep, wool. Both were later selected for milk production.

Pigs (*Sus domesticus*) probably originated at two separate sites, the central Fertile Crescent around 8000 B.P. and in eastern Asia around 7000 B.P. Derived from wild pigs, they were primarily raised for meat.

Despite Islamic and Judaic restrictions against eating pork, it has long been the principal meat consumed in the world. The most populous country, China, has approximately 50 percent of the world's pigs.

Cattle (*Bos taurus* and *Bos indicus*) are derived from now-extinct wild cattle (aurochs, *Bos primigenius*) that ranged over much of Europe and Asia. They were probably domesticated independently at two locations, the western Fertile Crescent around 8000 B.P. for *Bos taurus* and the Indian subcontinent around 7000 B.P. for *Bos indicus*. Initially, the animals were worshiped and used in religious ceremonies. Reverence for cattle is still practiced by Hindus in India. Subsequently, cattle were developed for draft (pulling loads), meat, and milk. Their hides are made into leather. Traditional cattle in Africa are derived from initial importations of *Bos taurus* and subsequent importations of male *Bos indicus*.

OTHER DOMESTICATED ANIMALS

Asiatic buffaloes (*Bubalus bubalus*) were domesticated as the water buffalo in India (5000 B.P.) and as the swamp buffalo in Southeast Asia and southern China (4000 B.P.). While both were developed as draft animals, the water buffalo has also been selected as a dairy animal. In 2008, almost 60 percent of the milk production in India was from buffaloes. In spite of its tropical origin, the Asiatic buffalo is not very heat tolerant and compensates by wallowing in water or mud. Neither the African buffalo (*Syncerus caffer*) nor the

Eight Major Domesticated Animal Species Worldwide

	MILLIONS	LEADING COUNTRIES	PRIMARY USES
Ruminants			
Buffalo	174	India, China, Pakistan	Draft, milk, meat, hides
Cattle	1,355	India, Brazil, China, United States, Argentina	Meat, milk, hides
Goats	808	China, India, Pakistan, Sudan	Milk, meat, hair, hides
Sheep	1,081	China, Australia, India, Iran	Wool, meat, milk, hides
Nonruminants			
Chickens	16,740	China, United States, Indonesia, Brazil	Meat, eggs, feathers
Ducks	1,046	China, Vietnam, Indonesia	Meat, eggs, feathers
Swine	960	China, European Union, United States	Meat
Turkeys	280	United States, France, Italy, Chile	Meat, eggs, feathers

Source: Data from Thomas G. Field and Robert E. Taylor, *Scientific Farm Animal Production*, 9th ed., 2008.

American buffalo (more properly, bison, *Bison bison*) have been domesticated. Yaks (*Bos [Poephagus] grunniens*) were domesticated at an unknown time in Tibet or surrounding areas, where they are used as pack animals and as sources of milk, hair, and hides.

Horses (*Equus caballus*) originated from wild horses in the Caucasus Mountains around 6000 B.P. Originally used for food and skins, they were also developed for draft and, much later, for riding. Because they arrived in the Middle East after the development of written language, their arrival is documented in writing, so scholars do not need to rely only on the archaeological record. Donkeys (*Equus asinus*) were domesticated in the Middle East or Northern Africa (5000 B.P.). They are used as pack animals and for riding, as is the mule, an infertile cross between a horse and donkey.

Llamas (*Lama glama*) and alpacas (*Lama pacos*) were domesticated in Peru by Incas around 6000 B.P. Llamas are from wild guanaco and alpaca from wild vicuña, found at higher elevations. Llamas are used as pack animals, alpacas are valued for their fine wool, and both serve as sources of meat. Camels, the one-humped dromedary (*Camelus dromedarius*) and two-humped Bactrian (*Camelus bactrianus*), were domesticated in Arabia (4000 B.P.) and Central Asia (3500 B.P.), respectively. Both are pack animals, and the dromedary is also used for meat.

The largest animal to be domesticated, at 4.5 metric tons, was the Asian elephant (*Elephas maximus*); the African elephant has not been domesticated. Domesticated elephants have been used for draft and riding for more than 2,000 years. In 2007, Asian elephants numbered less than 40,000 and were approaching endangered status. A substantial fraction were working elephants. Burma (also known as Myanmar) alone had 5,700 working elephants, primarily used for selective logging of teak forests. They drag logs weighing more than a metric ton, making use of trails, rather than the roads needed by mechanized log skidders. Elephants are less destructive of the environment than mechanized equipment. However, because elephants are susceptible to heat stroke, they can work only during the cooler parts of the day (early morning and late afternoon) and not at all during the hottest three months of the year. Thus, they are not as efficient as mechanical equipment. Nevertheless, the survival of Asian elephants may depend on their continued use as working elephants.

Guinea pigs (*Cavia porcellus*) were domesticated in Peru around 5000 B.P. They continue to be used as a meat animal in parts of South America. Rabbits (*Oryctlagus cuniculus*) were domesticated between 600 and 1000 C.E. in France. They are primarily raised for meat and fur, with Angora rabbits producing a valued wool.

Cats (*Felis catus*) are the animals least changed, morphologically, by domestication. In addition, they are quite capable of surviving without human intervention. Their domestication occurred relatively late, around 4000 B.P., in Egypt, the home of the African wild cat (*Felis catus libyca*), which is difficult to distinguish from domestic tabby cats. The early Egyptians adopted cats enthusiastically, deifying them and prohibiting their export. After conversion to Christianity, Egyptians ceased worshiping cats, which were carried to all parts of the Roman Empire and thence to the rest of the world. Cats have been used for companions and for rodent pest control.

Chickens (*Gallus gallus*), along with turkeys (from North America), ducks and geese, ostriches (from Africa), and emus (from Australia), are nonmammals that have been domesticated. Chickens were probably derived from wild Red Junglefowl in Southeast Asia before 4,000 B.P. Cockfighting was an initial purpose for their domestication. The fowls acquired religious significance and were also used for meat and feathers. Their selection for egg production has been a relatively recent development.

Two insects have also been domesticated: honeybees and silkworms. Honeybees were domesticated shortly after the last ice age and were the principal source of dietary sweetener until two hundred years ago. Also valuable were their wax and venom, the latter used for medicinal purposes. One of ten varieties of silk-producing insects, silkworms were domesticated around 5000 B.P. in China, producing fiber used in apparel.

UTILITY OF DOMESTICATED ANIMALS

As noted in the foregoing section, domesticated animals provide for various basic human needs: food, shelter, clothing, fuel, and emotional well-being. Clearly, their predominant use has been as a source of food in the form of meat, milk, and eggs. As omnivores, humans included animal products in their diets long before they domesticated animals. Animal products are good sources of high-quality protein, minerals, and vitamins, particularly vitamin B_{12}, which is not available in plant materials. Humans have an appetite for foods of animal origin, and as economic circumstances permit, the consumption of animal foods increases.

Domesticated animals have long provided shelter and clothing from their hides, hair, wool, and feathers. Their bones, horns, and antlers have been used as implements. Animal tissues and blood were the original sources of many pharmaceuticals that are now manufactured. For example, before the development of synthetic insulin, porcine (pig) insulin was provided to diabetics. Animal hearts, kidneys, and livers have been transplanted into humans. Although these transplants are eventually rejected by the human body, it seems possible that the development of transgenic pigs with human tissue factors could provide a source of permanent transplantable organs. Animals are also used as research subjects, for testing new devices and drugs before they are applied to humans. Although such uses of animals have become somewhat controversial, much of the development of modern medicine has depended on domesticated animals and on laboratory animals maintained expressly for research, primarily rats and mice.

The wastes generated by animals are used to fertilize crops. They also provide fuel; dried manure is burned for warmth and to cook food in many countries of the developing world. The development of biogas generators, in which animal wastes are converted to methane gas, is a more efficient way to generate fuel. It has the added advantage that the residue can be used as fertilizer for crops.

Domesticated animals provide power to cultivate crops, pull carts or carry loads, lift water, and skid logs. In the last decades of the twentieth century, use of draft animals increased around the world. This slightly reduced the need for petroleum. Nevertheless, a return to heavy use of animal power is unlikely.

Domesticated animals also serve as insurance and bank, particularly in developing countries, areas subject to drought, flooding, and pests, and where inflation is rampant. In some areas, animals are the currency of exchange. Animals are used as a walking larder, especially when refrigeration and other means of preserving food are unavailable. Because storage of crops for more than a year is difficult and results in large losses, having animals may buffer a bad crop year. Risk management favors more small animals over fewer large animals, although this may not be most efficient from a resource management perspective; minimizing risk also favors a variety over similar-

ity of animals. Until other forms of insurance and banking are fully reliable, animals will continue to be used to alleviate risk.

Finally, animals contribute to human well-being by providing companionship and recreation. Animals such as dogs and cats are companions to humans, providing emotional support particularly important for the young, elderly, and infirm. The use of animal companions to promote recovery from illness has been demonstrated to be effective. Guide dogs contribute to an independent lifestyle for blind persons, and monkeys have been trained to provide help to paraplegics and quadriplegics. Animals also provide recreation for humans, as in the form of rodeos, polo playing, riding, backpacking, and racing. Nonconsumptive uses of animals for companionship and recreation make definitive contributions to the quality of human life.

NUMBERS OF DOMESTICATED ANIMALS

In the early twenty-first century, according to the ninth edition of *Scientific Farm Animal Production* (2008), by Thomas G. Field and Robert E. Taylor, world estimates for the major domesticated animal species were 16.7 billion chickens, 1.4 billion cattle, 1.1 billion sheep, 1 billion pigs, 0.8 billion goats, 1 billion ducks, 280 million turkeys, 174 million buffaloes, 55 million horses, 41 million donkeys, 19 million camels, and 12 million mules. (For comparison, human beings number about 7 billion.) Domestication brought these animals under human control and vastly increased their numbers and range. Domesticated animals represent a renewable resource that contributes substantially to the well-being of humans.

James L. Robinson

FURTHER READING

Budiansky, Stephen. *The Covenant of the Wild: Why Animals Chose Domestication.* New York: W. Morrow, 1992. Reprint. New Haven, Conn.: Yale University Press, 1999.

Clutton-Brock, Juliet. *A Natural History of Domesticated Mammals.* 2d ed. New York: Cambridge University Press, Natural History Museum, 1999.

Diamond, Jared. "Why Is a Cow Like a Pyramid?" *Natural History* 104, no. 7 (July, 1995): 10.

Field, Thomas G., and Robert E. Taylor. *Scientific Farm Animal Production: An Introduction to Animal Science.* 9th ed. Upper Saddle River, N.J.: Prentice Hall, 2008.

Price, Edward O. *Animal Domestication and Behavior.* New York: CABI, 2002.

Roots, Clive. *Domestication.* Westport, Conn.: Greenwood Press, 2007.

Smith, Bruce D. *The Emergence of Agriculture.* 1995. Reprint. New York: Scientific American Library, 1998.

WEB SITE

FOOD AND AGRICULTURE ORGANIZATION OF THE UNITED NATIONS
Agricultural Statistics
http://faostat.fao.org/site/573/default.aspx#ancor

SEE ALSO: Agricultural products; Animal breeding; Animal power; Animals as a medical resource; Livestock and animal husbandry.

Animal husbandry. *See* Livestock and animal husbandry

Animal power

CATEGORIES: Energy resources; plant and animal resources

By using animals' muscle power for traction and transport, humans expanded the efficiency of these processes immensely. Animal power, essential for heavy hauling or rapid travel until the mid-1800's, remains important to much of the world's agriculture.

BACKGROUND

The dog was the first animal domesticated, tamed and bred from wolf ancestors. Archaeological sites showing this development date back approximately eleven thousand years in both northern Europe and North America. The first dogs may have helped Stone Age hunters chase and exhaust game. They also may have pulled snow sleds and hauled loads via travois, as they did for American Indians in later centuries. If dogs were so employed in this era—and it has not been proved that they were—these would be the first intentional uses of animal power as an energy resource. Other important tasks using their senses and group instincts to help humans—tracking, scavenging, and

guarding—probably meant that dogs were seldom kept primarily for their muscle power.

The next successfully domesticated animals were sheep, goats, pigs, and cattle. This process is shown in remains and artifacts from Jericho that document the origins of agriculture. Centuries after grain was first cultivated, people began to keep livestock. At first the animals were probably loosely controlled and were seen as "walking meat larders" and occasionally providers of milk, fiber, and leather. Once the process was under way, around 8000-7000 B.C.E., people must have experimented with riding and other ways to use the animals in their farming.

Of these anciently domesticated species, only cattle proved to have the combination of strength and malleability to do useful work under human direction. Shifting from a plow pushed by a man or woman to one pulled by an ox multiplied the traction enormously and enabled much more food to be produced with the same investment of human time. This was a major step in the ongoing "agricultural revolution" that created a growing population, town life, and a material surplus to support specialized trades. Using cattle in the fields also called forth other innovations. Harnesses and/or yokes had to be created to control the animals, implements had to become larger, and castration of young male animals had to be practiced to produce oxen that were both strong and docile. Later (sometime around 3000 B.C.E.), the wheel was invented. Hitching such animals to wheeled carts and wagons, humans could travel farther and more easily and could move bulkier goods. Draft animals (animals used for hauling) thus served not only as a direct resource in agriculture and transportation but also as a source of synergy, expanding their owners' geographic and trade horizons and inspiring further inventions.

While most of the evidence for this sequence of events exists in the ancient Near East, some of the same steps took place independently, perhaps several times, elsewhere in Eurasia. For example, the working cattle native to Asia—water buffaloes and yaks—were bred from wild species different from European domestic cattle's ancestors.

HORSES AND RELATED SPECIES
Horses and their kin, the most versatile of hauling and riding animals, were domesticated later. Wild horses roamed much of the world during the last ice age but had become extinct in the Americas by 10,000 B.C.E.

An Indian family sits atop a cart pulled by two bulls. People throughout the world have relied on draft power for centuries. (AFP/Getty Images)

and rare in Western Europe and the Mediterranean region about the same time. How much this disappearance was due to climate change and how much to humans' overhunting is uncertain.

Many prehistorians believe that horses were first tamed and trained for riding north of the Black Sea, where they survived in large numbers. Hence they were reintroduced into Europe and western Asia, between 3000 and 2000 B.C.E., by successive invasions of mounted tribesmen from the central Asian steppes. However, as with much of prehistory, the evidence is unclear. Horses never disappeared completely in Europe, and they may have been domesticated in several places from local stock.

The donkey or ass, which is native to North Africa, was brought into use in the same millennium. Donkeys loaded with packs or wearing saddlecloths are shown in Egyptian friezes from 2500 B.C.E.; they also appear in early Sumerian and Assyrian records.

Horses and asses were already being interbred at this time to produce vigorous offspring, notably the mule, with the traits of both species. From then until the end of the nineteenth century, the equids were the most widely used animals in the world for transporting people and goods. They also became immensely important in agricultural processes.

Because of their gait, asses cannot be ridden at high speeds, but their adaptability to harsh conditions makes them good pack animals and beasts-of-all-trades on small farms. Mules, hybrids from mare mothers and donkey sires, combine the horse's strength with the ass's stamina. Mules have been known to carry 450 kilograms each, going as far as 80 kilometers between water stops.

Horses' special qualities include speed, herd hierarchical instincts that dispose them to follow human leadership, and relative intelligence. Horses have been bred to strengthen various traits: the Arabian and the modern thoroughbred for speed; the medieval war horse and the modern shire and Clydesdale for strength and stamina; the Shetland pony for multiple tasks in damp and ferocious weather. As an example of the speed gained from using horses, over short distances (up to 5 kilometers) a horse can travel in the range of 48 kilometers per hour. A horse carrying rider and saddle might make a trip of 480 kilometers in sixty hours, and the time can be shortened by frequent changes of mount. A person in top condition—for example, a soldier accustomed to long marches—typically can walk around 65 kilometers a day.

Horse-related technology also developed continuously over time, adding to the effectiveness of horse and rider, and horse and vehicle. Bit and reins, stirrups (not adopted in Europe until the early Middle Ages), horseshoes, saddle and carriage designs, and modern veterinary medicine, all brought new capacities to the horse power on which humankind relied.

Not only was the horse an essential energy resource, but its presence also repeatedly changed history and society. The rise of cavalry as a mobile force in warfare and the change to a horse-based economy and culture by North American Plains Indians when horses were reintroduced by Spanish invaders are only two of the many transformations wrought by horse power.

OTHER ANIMALS AS ENERGY SOURCES

Humans have attempted to put many kinds of large animals to work, but only a few other species have proved useful. Of these, the most important have been those already adapted to extreme climates and terrains.

The camel is called the "ship of the desert" because of its ability to travel for long distances between water holes. Some desert nomad tribes organize their way of life around the use of camels. Normally employed as pack and riding animals, camels were also occasionally used in war in the ancient world, partly to frighten the enemy's men and horses. Llamas, members of the camelid family native to South America, serve as pack animals in the Andes mountain region.

Reindeer, adapted to living in an Arctic environment, can find forage on the barren tundra and survive temperatures of −50° Celsius. Laplanders who live in far northern areas have used them in the roles filled by cattle and horses in warmer climates, including riding, pulling carts, and carrying loads as pack animals.

Elephants, native to the Indian subcontinent and to Africa, have been trained in both regions to lift and carry extremely heavy objects, although their use as riding beasts has been largely confined to ceremonial occasions and entertainment.

ANIMAL POWER TODAY

From prehistory through the nineteenth century, much of the work of civilization depended upon animal power. With the coming of steam power and the internal combustion engine, animals gradually became less essential for transport and traction, at least in the developed world. Yet as late as the 1930's, horses or mule teams, rather than tractors, were used by many American farmers.

In Asia and Africa, most of the farmland is still worked with draft animals. For a small farmer of limited means or in an isolated area, animal power has several advantages. Unlike machines, animals do not need complex networks to supply their fuel or parts for repair. They produce their own replacements, and their malfunctions sometimes heal themselves without special knowledge or tools on the owner's part. Their by-products can be recycled into agricultural use.

For these reasons, and because they bring less devastation to land and air, some members of "back to the Earth" movements in the United States choose animal power. Heavy horses are also used in selected logging operations to avoid the clear-cutting and other environmental damage that machines bring.

Emily Alward

FURTHER READING

Ableman, Michael. *From the Good Earth: A Celebration of Growing Food Around the World.* New York: H. N. Abrams, 1993.

Chamberlin, J. Edward. *Horse: How the Horse Has Shaped Civilizations.* New York: BlueBridge, 2006.

Chenevix Trench, Charles. *A History of Horsemanship.* Garden City, N.Y.: Doubleday, 1970.

Clutton-Brock, Juliet. *Domesticated Animals from Early Times.* Austin: University of Texas Press, 1981.

_____. *Horse Power: A History of the Horse and the Donkey in Human Societies.* Cambridge, Mass.: Harvard University Press, 1992.

_____. *A Natural History of Domesticated Mammals.* 2d ed. New York: Cambridge University Press, Natural History Museum, 1999.

Greene, Ann Norton. *Horses at Work: Harnessing Power*

in Industrial America. Cambridge, Mass.: Harvard University Press, 2008.

Kalof, Linda, and Brigitte Resl, eds. *A Cultural History of Animals.* 6 vols. New York: Berg, 2007.

Pynn, Larry. "Logging with Horse Power." *Canadian Geographic* 111, no. 4 (August/September, 1991): 30.

Schmidt, Michael J., and Richard Ross. "Working Elephants: They Earn Their Keep in Asia by Providing an Ecologically Benign Way to Harvest Forests." *Scientific American* 274, no. 1 (January, 1996): 82.

Tiwari, G. N., and M. K. Ghosal. "Draught Animal Power." In *Renewable Energy Resources: Basic Principles and Applications.* Harrow, England: Alpha Science International, 2005.

Watts, Martin. *Working Oxen.* Princes Risborough, England: Shire, 1999.

SEE ALSO: Animal breeding; Animal domestication; Livestock and animal husbandry; Transportation, energy use in.

Animals as a medical resource

CATEGORY: Plant and animal resources

The use of animals has been a critical component of both human medical research and veterinary research. Although animal research has become a source of controversy among the public, nearly all modern medical advances have been based on some form of animal research.

BACKGROUND

Animals have served purposes related to medicine for centuries. They provided medical products for apothecaries in medieval Europe and for traditional Chinese medicine. Most applications, such as the use of ground rhinoceros horn as an aphrodisiac, were based on nonscientific concepts that have been discarded by modern medicine. However, some techniques, such as the use of spiderweb to stop bleeding, functioned until more effective products became available.

More recently, insulin used to treat diabetes was first harvested from the pancreatic glands of cattle or pigs used in the meat industry; however, the foreign animal proteins sometimes caused allergic reactions.

Today, genetically engineered bacteria can provide many hormone products that previously were extracted from animals. Animals have also provided transplant organs. Tissue rejection has been a major problem, but medications can reduce rejection dramatically.

Through genetic engineering, genes that code for pharmaceutical proteins can be incorporated into animals, and medicinal drugs can then be produced from the animal's milk. Clinical trials are under way for animal production of anti-blood-clotting agents. Transgenic animals have also been proposed for the production of drugs to treat cystic fibrosis, cancer, and other disorders. The uses of animals for products and tissues, however, have been minor compared with the use of animals as test subjects in medical research.

ANIMAL MEDICAL RESEARCH

Phenomenal advances in the treatment of human diseases occurred in the century following the Civil War. The development of germ theory by Louis Pasteur and Robert Koch, as well as the conquest of most major infectious diseases, was based on extensive animal research. Pasteur's studies of chicken cholera formed a basis for his work, and Koch's breakthrough work with anthrax involved studies with sheep. Most Nobel Prizes in Physiology or Medicine (first awarded in 1901) have involved some form of animal research. The first half of the twentieth century was an era of widespread public support for medical and scientific research. Animal research underlay basic studies in the development of penicillin and other major antibiotics as well as insulin, surgical techniques, and vaccinations. Partly because people had recent memories of the severity of such major diseases as smallpox and polio, animal research engendered little protest or controversy.

Not all animals are equally useful or appropriate in medical research, because some have systems that differ significantly from human physiology. The closer an animal is to humans evolutionarily, the more likely it is that it will respond to drugs and medical interventions in the same manner that humans will. Most new drugs are first screened on laboratory rats or mice; those drugs that show promise and have no toxic effects may then be tested on primates. Approximately 95 percent of medical research uses mice and other rodents, and nearly all the mice and rats used are "purpose bred" for research. (Cats, dogs, and nonhuman primates make up less than 1 percent of animals used in research.) The protocols for Federal Drug Administration approval of new drugs, as well as agricultural and environmental standards, are based on substantial animal testing to ensure the safety and effectiveness of new medications.

OPPOSITION AND CONTROVERSY

Beginning in the late 1970's, opposition to animal research began to gain national attention. The books *Animal Liberation*, by Peter Singer (1977), and *The Case for Animal Rights*, by Tom Regan (1983), provided a rationale to activists who questioned humans' use of other animals for medical research as well as for food, fur, and educational uses. Organizations opposed to some or all animal use in research range from radical groups allegedly responsible for vandalism of research laboratories (the Animal Liberation Front is among the most radical groups) to milder animal protectionist organizations. Probably the best-known animal-rights group is People for the Ethical Treatment of Animals (PETA). Well-known defenders of animal research for medical science include the National Association for Biomedical Research (NABR), the Incurably Ill for Animal Research, and Putting People First.

Some anti-animal-research activists have contended that all animal research can be replaced with alternatives such as research involving tissue culture and computer simulation. Activists also object to the use of animals taken from animal shelters and complain that current animal care regulations, particularly under the Animal Welfare Act, are not rigorously enforced by the U.S. Department of Agriculture.

The scientific community has defended animal research for a number of reasons. Biological systems are much more complex than any computer model devised, so at present computer simulation has severe limitations. New drugs rarely respond in tissue culture exactly as they do in a whole living organism. Researchers point out that, although animals are taken from shelters for research use, they constitute a minuscule amount of the dogs and cats that are euthanized annually. By far, most of the animals used in research and teaching are mice and rats. Research facilities are inspected by agencies such as the United States Department of Agriculture's Animal and Plant Health Inspection Service, which enforces Animal Welfare Act criteria. The Food and Drug Administration and the Environmental Protection Agency also have laboratory practice regulations. The research community also states that approximately 95 percent of laboratory animals are never subjected to pain and that the remaining animals are provided pain-relieving drugs or anesthetics as soon as the study permits.

John Richard Schrock

This mouse was genetically engineered by researchers at the University of California, Davis, to use in the study of breast cancer. (AP/ Wide World Photos)

FURTHER READING

Birke, Lynda, Arnold Arluke, and Mike Michael. *The Sacrifice: How Scientific Experiments Transform Animals and People.* West Lafayette, Ind.: Purdue University Press, 2007.

Carbone, Larry. *What Animals Want: Expertise and Advocacy in Laboratory Animal Welfare Policy.* New York: Oxford University Press, 2004.

Haugen, David M., ed. *Animal Experimentation.* Detroit: Greenhaven Press, 2007.

Monamy, Vaughan. *Animal Experimentation: A Guide to the Issues.* 2d ed. New York: Cambridge University Press, 2009.

National Research Council of the National Academies. *Science, Medicine, and Animals: A Circle of Discovery.* Washington, D.C.: National Research Council, National Academies Press, 2004.

Paul, Ellen Frankel, and Jeffrey Paul, eds. *Why Animal Experimentation Matters: The Use of Animals in Medical Research.* Edison, N.J.: Transaction, 2001.

Regan, Tom. *The Case for Animal Rights.* 1983. Reprint. Berkeley: University of California Press, 2004.

Rudacille, Deborah. *The Scalpel and the Butterfly: The Conflict Between Animal Research and Animal Protection.* Berkeley: University of California Press, 2001.

Singer, Peter. *Animal Liberation.* 2d ed. New York: New York Review of Books, 1990.

Verhetsel, Ernest. *They Threaten Your Health: A Critique of the Antivivisection/Animal Rights Movement.* Tucson, Ariz.: People for Ethical Animal Research, 1986.

WEB SITES

HUMANE SOCIETY OF THE UNITED STATES
Animal Testing
http://www.hsus.org/animals_in_research/
animal_testing

NATIONAL ACADEMIES PRESS
Science, Medicine, and Animals
http://www.nap.edu/
catalog.php?record_id=10733#toc

U.S. FOOD AND DRUG ADMINISTRATION
Animal Testing
http://www.cfsan.fda.gov/~dms/cos-205.html

SEE ALSO: Animal breeding; Animal domestication; Biotechnology; Livestock and animal husbandry; Plants as a medical resource; Wildlife.

Antarctic treaties

CATEGORY: Laws and conventions
DATE: Final draft presented on December 1, 1959; became effective on June 23, 1961

The Antarctic Treaty of 1959, created and endorsed by representatives of the twelve signatory nations and endorsed by many other nations since, designates Antarctica as a demilitarized zone and bans commercial mineral and oil exploration there until 2041, when the treaty's provisions will be reviewed and possibly altered. It also bans the disposal of radioactive waste in the area.

BACKGROUND

Exploration of Antarctica began early in the twentieth century when sailors hunting whales and seals penetrated the waters surrounding this forbidding continent. As early as 1940, seven countries—Argentina, Australia, Chile, France, New Zealand, Norway, and the United Kingdom—had laid claim to various parts of Antarctica. Some such claims overlapped, increasing the potential for conflict.

Antarctica is unique among Earth's seven continents because it has no permanent residents and no established government. Its harsh climate makes it more suitable for scientists than for soldiers and entrepreneurs. During the International Geophysical Year (IGY), which ran from July 1, 1957, until December 31, 1958, twelve nations built thirty-five scientific research stations on the continent and fifteen on the nearby Antarctic islands. As of 2009, there were sixty-five research stations in Antarctica, many of which operated only during the Antarctic summer, which runs from mid-October until early March.

When the IGY ended, representatives from the twelve nations involved in that project gathered in Washington, D.C., and produced the Antarctic Treaty, whose sixteen articles spelled out how the continent would be devoted to scientific research. Representatives of the twelve signatory nations presented the treaty on December 1, 1959. It went into effect on June 23, 1961.

Among other documents that compose the Antarctic Treaty System are the Conservation of Antarctic Fauna and Flora, the Convention for the Conservation of Antarctic Seals, and the Convention on the Conservation of Antarctic Marine Living Resources.

The Antarctic Treaty was expanded in 1991, when twenty-four countries signed the Madrid Protocol, which banned commercial development, mining, and exploration for oil on the continent for fifty years. This provision will be reconsidered in 2041.

By 2010, forty-five nations, representing more than 80 percent of the world's population, had endorsed the Antarctic treaties, which are the most effective such international treaties ever entered into by such a broad spectrum of nations. Antarctica remains the most peaceful of Earth's seven continents, with representatives of nearly one hundred nations working cooperatively on their scientific pursuits and sharing their findings with their fellow scientists.

PROVISIONS

The provisions of the Antarctic treaties were not accepted merely on the basis of a majority vote. They were, instead, passed by consensus, which explains, at least partially, their overwhelming success and broad acceptance.

As the IGY neared its termination in 1958, considerable concern existed that the seven nations that had laid claim to parts of Antarctica would begin to have disputes about their claims. It was these concerns that led the U.S. State Department to inaugurate meetings in Washington, D.C., with eleven other nations that had vested interests in Antarctica.

Representatives of these nations met for more than a year in an attempt to reach an accord that would protect Antarctica from widespread incursions from a host of nations. Through these meetings the Antarctic Treaty was forged. It was signed on December 1, 1959, by representatives of the twelve nations that participated in the IGY, after which it was ratified and went into effect on June 23, 1961.

Perhaps the most important provision of the treaty is its stipulation that all of the signatories agree to abandon all territorial claims on this frozen continent. This provision alleviated the fear that the seven nations that had previously laid claim to parts of Antarctica, all of which were involved in drafting the treaty, would exercise what they considered their proprietary rights and could conceivably enter into dangerous conflicts to protect such rights.

Once this caveat was overcome, the rest of the provisions of the treaty fell into place. Cognizant of the importance of keeping Antarctica a peaceful continent, the initial Antarctic Treaty banned all military activity on the continent. It also forbade the testing of weapons, nuclear testing, and the disposal of nuclear waste on the continent. These provisions set aside 10 percent of the Earth's surface as nuclear-free and demilitarized zones.

Among the protective stipulations of the Antarctic Treaty produced in 1959 is the prohibition of the importation of soil into the continent. The fear is that imported soil will carry with it unknown biohazards such as fungi, bacteria, and insects that might pollute the pristine atmosphere of Antarctica.

Openness is a major theme of the treaty's provisions, which call for the free exchange of scientific information among the disparate groups of scientists who are involved in polar research. Scientists from the signatory nations covered by the treaty are expected to share information with one another and to make their research plans and scientific outcomes available. The provisions of the treaty permit personnel from any of the research stations to visit and inspect without prior notice any of the research facilities in Antarctica.

Realizing that disputes arise inevitably in multinational situations, those who drafted the treaty provided for conflict resolution. Efforts must be made to settle disputes through arbitration or negotiation. If such efforts fail, however, the problem is referred to the International Court of Justice for a resolution that is considered binding. Those who drafted the treaty were conscious of the need to make it sufficiently flexible to deal with new issues or problems as they arise in rapidly changing contexts.

The official languages of the treaty are English, French, Russian, and Spanish. The documents associated with the treaty are held by the government of the United States, which is responsible for preserving them and distributing them as required.

There are two levels of membership in the Antarctic Treaty System, consultative and nonconsultative. In order to be consultative members, nations must maintain at least one research station in Antarctica. Consultative members have voting rights that are not available to nonconsultative members. In some instances, consultative members close their research stations, as India did its Dakshin Gangotri Station in 1981, but as long as they maintain one station—India continues to maintain the Maitre Station as a permanent facility—they retain consultative membership.

Since the enactment of the treaty, society has become increasingly sensitive to environmental problems that received less attention in the 1960's than they did in the 1990's and beyond. As a result of this change in outlook, the Madrid Protocol was enacted in 1991. It bans exploration for oil and other minerals in Antarctica for fifty years. In 2041, this provision will be revisited and possibly reconsidered.

IMPACT ON RESOURCE USE

Antarctica is a mineral-rich continent, but its harsh climate and the thick ice sheets—some more than 3 kilometers deep—that cover it make the retrieval of minerals expensive and hazardous. Many parts of the continent never reach temperatures above freezing, and even those areas, such as the Antarctic Peninsula, that have more moderate climates are too cold to sustain much plant and animal life. Nevertheless, as mining equipment becomes increasingly sophisticated, the recovery of oil and other minerals from Antarctica will undoubtedly become feasible.

The enactment of the Antarctic Treaty System has been aimed at the preservation of a frozen wilderness that has considerable potential as a source of natural resources, although this potential remains underdeveloped. Among the other natural resources of which the continent boasts are stores of fresh water, estimated to constitute 80 percent of the fresh water on Earth. As water shortages become commonplace in many parts of the developed world, means will be explored for transporting some of Antarctica's abundant water to water-starved regions.

Some Middle Eastern countries have already explored the possibility of hauling huge icebergs into areas that are parched and of using the fresh water in them for irrigation and other purposes, including drinking water. Most of the ice in icebergs is composed of fresh water. Future additions to the Antarctica Treaties will likely deal with the preservation and transportation of huge masses of ice into the populated parts of the world that are much in need of water. At the same time, future amendments may need to address the consequences of global climate change as well.

R. Baird Shuman

FURTHER READING

Bocknek, Jonathan. *Antarctica: The Last Wilderness.* North Mankato, Minn.: Smart Apple Media, 2004.

Currie, Stephen. *Antarctica.* New York: Lucent Books, 2004.

Karner, Julie. *Roald Amundsen: The Conquest of the South Pole.* New York: Crabtree, 2007.

Myers, Walter Dean. *Antarctica: Journeys to the South Pole.* New York: Scholastic Press, 2004.

Rubin, Jeff. *Antarctica.* 4th ed. London: Lonely Planet, 2008.

Shackleton, Ernest. *The Heart of the Antarctic: Being the Story of the British Antarctic Expedition, 1907-1909.* New ed. London: Carroll and Graff, 1999.

Stonehouse, Bernard. *North Pole, South Pole: A Guide to the Ecology and Resources of the Arctic and Antarctic.* London: Prion, 1990.

SEE ALSO: Climate and resources; Oil and natural gas distribution; Oil and natural gas exploration; Ozone layer and ozone hole debate; Population growth; Resources as a source of international conflict.

Antimony

CATEGORY: Mineral and other nonliving resources

WHERE FOUND

While antimony does not often occur free in nature, its ores are widely distributed. The antimony ore of greatest commercial importance is stibnite (Sb_2S_3), most of which is supplied by China, Germany, Peru, and Japan, among other countries.

PRIMARY USES

Antimony is a strategic resource with many uses. It is a key component in many alloys, and its compounds are employed in the manufacture of such products as ceramics and glass, batteries, paints and pigments, chemicals, matches, explosives, fireworks, flame retardants, and medicines.

TECHNICAL DEFINITION

Antimony (abbreviated Sb), atomic number 51, is a metalloid belonging to Group VA of the periodic table of the elements. It has two naturally occurring isotopes and an average molecular weight of 121.75. Pure antimony has rhombohedral crystals and is silvery blue-white in color. It is brittle, can be easily powdered, and conducts heat and electricity poorly. Its specific gravity is 6.69 at 20° Celsius; its melting point is 630.5° Celsius, and its boiling point is 1,380° Celsius.

DESCRIPTION, DISTRIBUTION, AND FORMS

Antimony is a metalloid with a lithospheric concentration of 0.2 gram per metric ton. When used in metallurgical combinations antimony forms hard, brittle materials that melt at relatively low temperatures, characteristics that make this element an important component in many alloys.

The most economically important antimony ore is antimony sulfide, or stibnite. In the United States the element is usually obtained only as a by-product of smelting the copper ore tetrahedrite, $(Cu, Fe)_{12}Sb_4S_{13}$, or other sulfide ores of base metals. While recycling scrap metal and storage batteries was once a significant secondary source of antimony for the United

States, the development of low-maintenance lead-acid automobile batteries that use lead alloys with less or no antimony has decreased this supply. In 2007, for example, the United States consumed 9,590 metric tons of antimony, and total world production was estimated at 170,000 metric tons.

Antimony ores are widely distributed; China, Bolivia, South Africa, Russia, Tajikistan, and Australia are the chief producers. China is believed to have the world's greatest reserves of the element; extensive deposits of stibnite are found in the southern province of Hunan. Antimony-bearing rocks can be found in soils, groundwater, and surface waters. Most antimony deposits are associated with igneous activity and are believed to have been precipitated from watery fluids at relatively shallow depths and low temperatures.

Antimony is rarely found free in nature. Stibnite, the predominant antimony ore, is a silvery gray sulfide mineral that occurs in masses or prismatic crystals. Frequently it is found in association with quartz and economic minerals such as ores of mercury, tungsten, tin, lead, copper, silver, and gold. Stibnite deposits are often in the form of veins, seams, pockets, or lenses.

Antimony can enter groundwater and surface water through the natural weathering of rock or through industrial pollution. It can cause disorders of the human respiratory and cardiovascular systems, skin, and eyes, and it is a suspected cancer-causing agent. The 1974 Safe Drinking Water Act set the maximum allowable concentration for total antimony in drinking water in the United States at 6 micrograms per liter.

HISTORY

Antimony has been used since biblical times as an ingredient in medicines and in kohl, an eye cosmetic made up of powdered stibnite mixed with soot and other materials. In Tello, Chaldea, a vase from approximately 4000 B.C.E. was found that had been cast in elemental antimony; antimony was also reportedly used by the early Egyptians to coat copper items. By the sixteenth century, the element was recognized as an alloy ingredient that could improve the tone of bell metal; as a source of yellow pigment for painting earthenware, enamels, and glass; and as an ulcer medicine. The earliest known description of the extraction of antimony from stibnite was written by Basilius Valentinus around 1600. The increasing industrialization of the late nineteenth and early twentieth centuries was accompanied by a rapid rise in antimony consumption. The need for ammunition, arms, and

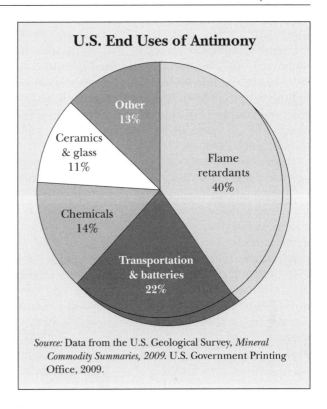

U.S. End Uses of Antimony

Other 13%
Ceramics & glass 11%
Flame retardants 40%
Chemicals 14%
Transportation & batteries 22%

Source: Data from the U.S. Geological Survey, *Mineral Commodity Summaries, 2009.* U.S. Government Printing Office, 2009.

flame-retardant items during World Wars I and II further increased the demand for antimony. In the 1930's, consumption of the element also rose with the expansion of the automobile industry, which used lead-antimony alloys in storage batteries.

OBTAINING ANTIMONY

Antimony ore is roasted with iron in a blast furnace; the roasting produces antimony oxide, from which the iron removes the oxygen to free the antimony. A flux of sodium sulfate or sodium carbonate may be used to prevent the loss of molten antimony through evaporation. Complex ores, those with base metals present, are treated by leaching and electrolysis.

USES OF ANTIMONY

Antimony is an important element in many alloys. Britannia metal, an alloy of tin with antimony, copper, and sometimes bismuth and zinc, resembles pewter in appearance and is used in the manufacture of tableware. Antimony is sometimes added to pewter, an alloy composed largely of tin, to increase whiteness and hardness. Babbitt metal, an antifriction alloy used in bearings, is composed chiefly of tin, copper, and antimony. Type metal, named for its use in the manufacture of printing type, is an alloy of lead with antimony, tin, and sometimes copper; this alloy is also used in metal parts for some musical instruments. Various alloys of antimony and lead are used in solder, starting-lighting-ignition batteries (particularly plates, terminals, and connectors), ammunition, communication equipment, corrosion-resistant pumps and pipes, tank linings, and roofing sheets.

Antimony is used as a decolorizing and refining agent in television screens, fluorescent tubes, and optical glass. Small amounts of the element are used in some medicines. Antimony oxides serve as stabilizers and flame retardants in plastics. They are also used to make adhesives, rubber, textiles, paints, and other combustibles flame resistant. Antimony sulfides are employed as a component of fireworks and ammunition. Antimony compounds are used in the manufacture of matches, explosives, vulcanized rubber, paints and pigments, chemicals, semiconductors, batteries, glass, and ceramics. Its military applications make antimony a strategic mineral.

Karen N. Kähler

FURTHER READING

Greenwood, N. N., and A. Earnshaw. "Arsenic, Antimony, and Bismuth." In *Chemistry of the Elements*. 2d ed. Boston: Butterworth-Heinemann, 1997.

Henderson, William. "The Group 15 (Pnictogen) Elements: Nitrogen, Phosphorus, Arsenic, Antimony, and Bismuth." In *Main Group Chemistry*. Cambridge, England: Royal Society of Chemistry, 2000.

Krebs, Robert E. *The History and Use of Our Earth's Chemical Elements: A Reference Guide*. Illustrations by Rae Déjur. 2d ed. Westport, Conn.: Greenwood Press, 2006.

Massey, A. G. "Group 15: The Pnictides—Nitrogen, Phosphorus, Arsenic, Antimony, and Bismuth." In *Main Group Chemistry*. 2d ed. New York: Wiley, 2000.

WEB SITES

NATURAL RESOURCES CANADA
Canadian Minerals Yearbook, Mineral and Metal Commodity Reviews
http://www.nrcan-rncan.gc.ca/mms-smm/busi-indu/cmy-amc/com-eng.htm

U.S. GEOLOGICAL SURVEY
Antimony: Statistics and Information
http://minerals.usgs.gov/minerals/pubs/commodity/antimony

SEE ALSO: Alloys; China; Germany; Hydrothermal solutions and mineralization; Japan; Metals and metallurgy; Peru; Russia; South Africa; Strategic resources.

Antiquities Act

CATEGORIES: Laws and conventions; government and resources
DATE: Signed into law June 8, 1906

By designating sites of historic importance for special protection and preservation, the Act for the Preservation of American Antiquities, commonly known as the Antiquities Act, pioneered the use of government power to defend both the environmental and cultural resources of nations.

BACKGROUND

As the population and economy of the United States expanded throughout the late nineteenth and early twentieth centuries, various groups became concerned about the survival of important elements of American culture and environment. Expanding urban centers threatened wilderness areas, unrestrained tourism damaged natural wonders, and archaeological sites were vulnerable to unregulated pillaging.

The destruction of American Indian archaeological sites by commercial relic hunters was a particular concern, as archaeologists feared the loss or destruction of vital cultural artifacts. Their concerns reached the desk of Iowa congressman John F. Lacy, chairman of the House Committee on Public Lands (later the Committee on Natural Resources). Concerned about protecting properties in the public interest, Lacy introduced the Antiquities Act as a means of preserving properties of national importance even if the properties were in private hands. The act passed easily through Congress, and became law when signed by pro-conservation president Theodore Roosevelt.

The Antiquities Act represented a move toward greater federal responsibility for preservation. Recognizing that state and local governments lacked either the will or the authority to protect sites of importance to the national heritage, the U.S. federal government used its power of eminent domain to place sites under government care. This marked a major philosophical shift away from government indifference to environmental issues and toward federal participation in preservation efforts.

PROVISIONS

The Antiquities Act authorized the president of the United States to designate an area of historic, cultural, or environmental importance a "national monument" under the ownership and stewardship of the federal government, specifically the Department of the Interior. If the federal government did not already own the property, the president could use the power of eminent domain to acquire private property. The act provided for the "proper care and management" of the site to ensure its preservation but did allow archaeological excavation by qualified researchers under the supervision of the government. In an attempt to curb the pillaging of artifacts, the unauthorized removal of historical artifacts became a federal offense.

IMPACT ON RESOURCE USE

Although intended to protect archaeological sites, the Antiquities Act also ensured the survival of a number of environmentally important areas. President Roosevelt took a broad interpretation of the legislation and designated a wide range of sites for protection. Roosevelt designated Devils Tower in Wyoming as the first national monument, followed by a number of American Indian sites in the Southwest. Since 1906, the government has created more than one hundred monuments in both rural areas, such as Muir Woods in California, and urban areas, such as the Statue of Liberty in New York. Between 2006 and 2008, President George W. Bush created the first underwater monuments when he designated the Papahānaumokuākea Marine National Monument near Hawaii, Marianas Trench Marine in the central Pacific, and the Pacific Remote Islands and Rose Atoll Marines in the U.S.-owned islands of the South Pacific.

Steven J. Ramold

SEE ALSO: National Park Service; National Parks Act, Canadian; National parks and nature reserves; Resource Conservation and Recovery Act; Takings law and eminent domain.

Appliances. *See* Buildings and appliances, energy-efficient

Aquifers

CATEGORY: Geological processes and formations

An aquifer is a body of earth material that can store and transmit economically significant amounts of water. The earth material can be in either consolidated or unconsolidated form as long as it has sufficient permeability for the movement of water. In terms of groundwater occurrence, all the rocks found on and below the Earth's surface are associated with either aquifers or confining beds.

BACKGROUND

An aquifer is a rock unit that is permeable enough to yield water in usable amounts to a well or a spring. In geologic usage, the term "rock" includes unconsolidated sediments such as sand, silt, and clay, as well as what is commonly considered to be rock. A confining bed is a rock unit that has such low hydraulic conductivity (poor permeability) that it restricts or severely impedes the flow of groundwater into or out of nearby aquifers.

UNCONFINED AND ARTESIAN AQUIFERS

There are two major types of groundwater occurrence in aquifers. The first type pertains to those aquifers that are only partially filled with water. In those cases, the upper surface (or water table) of the saturated zone can rise or decline in response to variations in precipitation, evaporation, and pumping from wells. The water in these aquifers is classified as unconfined, and such aquifers are called unconfined, or water-table, aquifers.

The second type occurs when water completely fills an aquifer that is overlain by a confining bed. In this case, the water in such an aquifer is classified as confined and the aquifers are called confined, or artesian, aquifers. In some fractured rock formations, such as those that occur in the west-central portions of New Jersey and eastern Pennsylvania, local geologic conditions result in semiconfined aquifers that, as one might expect, have hydrogeologic characteristics of both unconfined and confined aquifers.

Wells that are drilled in unconfined, water-table aquifers are simply called water-table wells. The water level in these unconfined wells indicates the depth below the surface of the water table, which is the top of the saturated zone. Wells that are drilled into confined aquifers are called artesian wells. The water level in an artesian well is generally located at a height above the top of the confined aquifer but not necessarily above the land surface. Flowing artesian wells occur when the water level in an artesian well stands above the land surface. The water level in tightly cased wells in unconfined or artesian aquifers is called the potentiometric surface of the aquifer.

AQUIFER PERMEABILITY

Water flows (very slowly) in aquifers from recharge areas in interstream areas at higher elevations to dis-

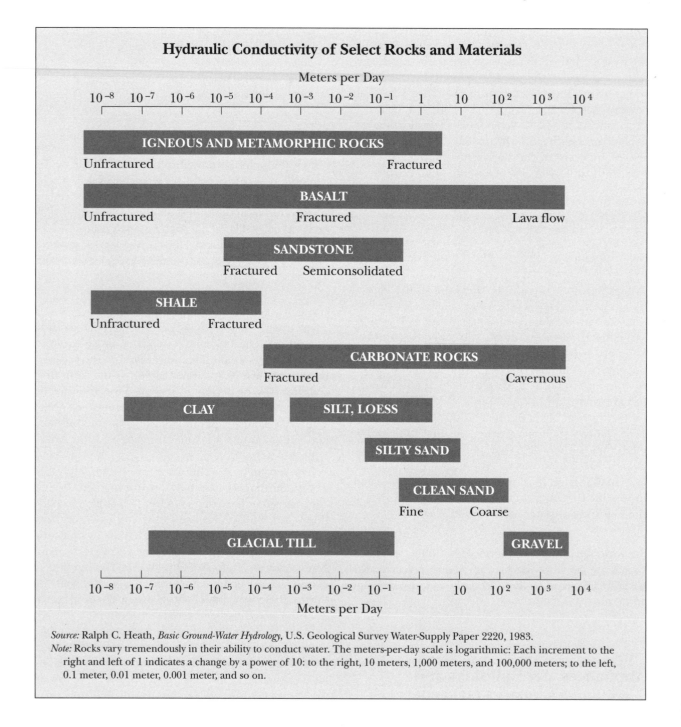

Hydraulic Conductivity of Select Rocks and Materials

Meters per Day

Source: Ralph C. Heath, *Basic Ground-Water Hydrology*, U.S. Geological Survey Water-Supply Paper 2220, 1983.

Note: Rocks vary tremendously in their ability to conduct water. The meters-per-day scale is logarithmic: Each increment to the right and left of 1 indicates a change by a power of 10: to the right, 10 meters, 1,000 meters, and 100,000 meters; to the left, 0.1 meter, 0.01 meter, 0.001 meter, and so on.

charge areas along streams and adjacent floodplains at lower elevations. Thus, aquifers function as "pipelines" filled with various types of earth material. Darcy's law governing groundwater flow was developed by Henry Darcy, a French engineer, in 1856. In brief, Darcy's law states that the amount of water moving through an aquifer per unit of time is dependent on the hydraulic conductivity (or permeability) of the aquifer, the cross-sectional area that is at a right angle to the direction of flow, and the hydraulic gradient. The hydraulic conductivity depends upon the size and interconnectedness of the pores and fractures in an aquifer. It ranges through an astonishing twelve orders of magnitude. There are few other physical parameters that have such a wide range of values. For example, the hydraulic conductivity ranges from an extremely low 10^{-7} and 10^{-8} meters per day in unfractured igneous rock such as diabase and basalt to as much as 10^3 and 10^4 meters per day in cavernous limestone and coarse gravel. Typical low-permeability earth materials include unfractured shale, clay, and glacial till. High-permeability earth materials include lava flows and coarse sand.

In addition to this wide range of values, hydraulic conductivity varies widely in place and in directionality within the same aquifer. Aquifers are isotropic if the hydraulic conductivity is about the same in all directions, and anisotropic if it is different in different directions. As a result of all of these factors, groundwater yield is extremely variable both within the same aquifer and from one aquifer to another when they are composed of different rocks.

AQUIFER TESTS

In order to determine the groundwater yield and contaminant transport characteristics of an aquifer, it is necessary to obtain sufficient geologic and hydrologic information. One of the most important hydrologic investigations in such a study is the analysis of the change over time of the water levels in an aquifer as a consequence of well pumpage. This type of study is called an aquifer test and usually involves pumping a well at a constant rate for several hours to several days while changes in the water levels of one or more observation wells located at different distances from the pumped well are measured. The test provides invaluable information about the ability of an aquifer to yield sufficient water under the stress of constant pumping.

Robert M. Hordon

FURTHER READING

Appelo, C. A. J., and D. Postma. *Geochemistry, Groundwater, and Pollution.* 2d ed. New York: Balkema, 2005.

Fetter, C. W. *Applied Hydrogeology.* 4th ed. Upper Saddle River, N.J.: Prentice Hall, 2001.

Price, Michael. *Introducing Groundwater.* 2d ed. New York: Chapman & Hall, 1996.

Todd, David Keith, and Larry W. Mays. *Groundwater Hydrology.* 3d ed. Hoboken, N.J.: Wiley, 2005.

Younger, Paul L. *Groundwater in the Environment: An Introduction.* Malden, Mass.: Blackwell, 2007.

Zektser, Igor S., and Lorne G. Everett, eds. *Ground Water Resources of the World and Their Use.* Paris: UNESCO, 2004. Reprint. Westerville, Ohio: National Ground Water Association Press, 2006.

WEB SITES

NATURAL RESOURCES CANADA
Groundwater
http://atlas.nrcan.gc.ca/site/english/maps/freshwater/distribution/groundwater/1

U.S. GEOLOGICAL SURVEY
Aquifer Basics
http://water.usgs.gov/ogw/aquiferbasics

SEE ALSO: Environmental engineering; Glaciation; Groundwater; Hydrology and the hydrologic cycle; Land-use planning; U.S. Geological Survey; Water pollution and water pollution control; Water supply systems.

Argentina

CATEGORIES: Countries; government and resources

Argentina's greatest primary natural resource is its agricultural land. Owing to its size, Argentina has a variety of climates and soils in which to grow crops and raise livestock. As a result, the country is a top-ten exporter of a variety of crop and meat products. Moreover, a complex geology endows Argentina with deposits of petroleum, natural gas, copper, gold, and other minerals that make the country a significant exporter of these materials to its neighbors and other countries around the globe.

THE COUNTRY

Argentina is a wedge-shaped country at the tip of South America. Physically, the nation has the largest territory and fourth largest population—after Mexico, Colombia, and Spain—of all Spanish-speaking countries in the world. In total area, it is four times the size of Texas and is the eighth largest country in the world. Its capital, Buenos Aires, is the largest city in the Southern Cone, which includes Argentina, Chile, Paraguay, and Uruguay. Argentina's annual gross domestic product is consistently second in South America. Brazil, the largest country in the region, is always first. Argentina clearly has great wealth and greater economic potential owing to its natural resource base. However, the top 1 percent of the people have nearly all of the wealth and the bulk of the land, and the national debt is high. Additionally, growing crops for export and simultaneously producing food crops for domestic consumption constitute a challenge for Argentina. As world food prices have escalated, export critics have worried about Argentina's ability to feed its own people at affordable prices. Thus, Argentina has natural resource problems for which the country's diverse and educated people must eventually find solutions.

AGRICULTURAL LAND OF THE PAMPAS

Agricultural land composes 47 percent of Argentina's total area, and agricultural products account for about one-half the annual value of the country's exports to the global economy. The bulk of Argentina's agricultural exports come from the Pampas, which is the wealthiest rural area in South America. The region's vast, open plains, deep, rich soil, and moderate climate are the physical bases for the wealth. The plains topography is conducive to raising large fields of fodder crops for livestock yards and for open field grazing. The climate of the Pampas area is much like that of the Middle Atlantic states of the East Coast of the United States. The Pampas has year-round precipitation, a relatively long growing season, and mild winter temperatures. The region's best-known agricultural exports are hides (for leather), beef, wool, and wheat. However, its two most valuable commodities are animal feed (including unmilled cereals) and vegetable fats, oils, and oil seeds, which come mostly from soybeans and sunflower seeds. Argentina's main trading partners for these products are China, India, Brazil, and Chile.

In addition to the land's natural resources, outside influences were important in the development of Argentina's export trade. During the late 1800's, in addition to capital and business methods, the British transplanted technology that was especially suitable to the Pampas' windswept, grassy plains; the windmill and barbed wire spurred the grazing and breeding of high-quality beef cattle. Additionally, the British and other foreign interests introduced refrigeration technology, an efficient railroad network, seaport facilities in Buenos Aires, and swift iron-hulled ships. As a result, Argentina was one of the leading agricultural exporters in the world by the close of the nineteenth century.

In the twenty-first century, the country ranks among the top-ten exporters in more than one dozen agricultural categories. The "Wet Pampa," the more humid eastern part of the region, is more productive than the "Dry Pampa" to the west. The Wet Pampa produces most of the nation's exports, serving as the granary of South America, with soybeans, alfalfa, corn, sunflowers, and flax as the principal crops. Nevertheless, experts have expressed concern about degradation of the soil in the Wet Pampa because of overuse and abuse. The main crop in the Dry Pampa is wheat. Cattle and sheep ranches exist throughout the Pampas, especially in the southeast and north. The region produces most of the beef and mutton that are exported from the country. Dairy products and vegetables, which are destined primarily for Argentine consumers, are important near Buenos Aires.

AGRICULTURAL LAND OF THE INTERIOR

Argentines often describe their population as composed of two groups, *porteños* and people of the interior. *Porteños* live in greater Buenos Aires, which corresponds to the city of Buenos Aires and its intertwining connections of highways, railroads, and cities in the Pampas region. People of the interior live outside the Pampas and are much more rural in their outlook and economy.

The climate and soils of Argentina's interior lands vary from humid tropical and subtropical to desert and mountain. The Paraná Plateau, which is north of Buenos Aires, is the warmest and wettest part of the country. Coffee, tea, and yerba maté, a popular variety of tea in Argentina and adjoining areas, are the region's chief export crops.

The Mesopotamia lowland is just west of the plateau, where the Paraná and Uruguay rivers flow parallel to each other. The lowland has a subtropical cli-

Argentina: Resources at a Glance

Official name: Argentine Republic
Government: Republic
Capital city: Buenos Aires
Area: 1,073,596 mi^2; 2,780,400 km^2
Population (2009 est.): 40,913,584
Language: Spanish
Monetary unit: Argentine peso (ARS)

ECONOMIC SUMMARY:

GDP composition by sector (2008 est.): agriculture, 9.9%; industry, 32.7%; services, 57.4%
Natural resources: fertile plains of the Pampas, lead, zinc, tin, copper, iron ore, manganese, petroleum, uranium, boron, bauxite, precious metals, lithium
Land use (2005): arable land, 10.03%; permanent crops, 0.36%; other, 89.61%
Industries: food processing, motor vehicles, consumer durables, textiles, chemicals and petrochemicals, printing, metallurgy, steel
Agricultural products: sunflower seeds, lemons, soybeans, grapes, corn, tobacco, peanuts, tea, wheat, livestock
Exports (2008 est.): $70.59 billion
Commodities exported: soybeans and derivatives, petroleum and gas, boron, vehicles, corn, wheat
Imports (2008 est.): $54.55 billion
Commodities imported: machinery, motor vehicles, petroleum and natural gas, organic chemicals, plastics
Labor force (2008 est.): 16.27 million (urban areas only)
Labor force by occupation (2008 est.): agriculture, 1%; industry, 23%; services, 76%

ENERGY RESOURCES:

Electricity production (2006 est.): 109.4 billion kWh
Electricity consumption (2006 est.): 97.72 billion kWh
Electricity exports (2007 est.): 2.628 billion kWh
Electricity imports (2007 est.): 10.27 billion kWh

Natural gas production (2007 est.): 44.8 billion m^3
Natural gas consumption (2007 est.): 44.1 billion m^3
Natural gas exports (2007 est.): 2.6 billion m^3
Natural gas imports (2007 est.): 1.9 billion m^3
Natural gas proved reserves (Jan. 2008 est.): 446 billion m^3

Oil production (2007 est.): 790,800 bbl/day
Oil imports (2005): 23,380 bbl/day
Oil proved reserves (Jan. 2008 est.): 2.186 billion bbl

Source: Data from *The World Factbook 2009.* Washington, D.C.: Central Intelligence Agency, 2009.
Notes: Data are the most recent tracked by the CIA. Values are given in U.S. dollars. Abbreviations: bbl/day = barrels per day; GDP = gross domestic product; km^2 = square kilometers; kWh = kilowatt-hours; m^3 = cubic meters; mi^2 = square miles.

A soybean farmer in the Pampas region of Argentina inspects his harvest. (Andres Stapff/Reuters/Landov)

mate and exports spices (pepper, cumin, turmeric, nutmeg, cinnamon, and ginger), tobacco, citrus, and cattle.

The semiarid Gran Chaco, which sits immediately west of Mesopotamia, exports some live cattle, cotton, and oil crops, especially peanuts and sunflower seeds. Still farther west is the Dry Chaco, which is truly a desert because it is in the rain shadow of high summits of the Andes Mountains. Nevertheless, the Gran Chaco's fertile valley oases in the states of Jujuy, Salta, Tucumán, San Juan, and Mendoza export several products, including sugar, grape juice, fruits, and corn. Wine from these valleys, in particular, has gained popularity in the U.S. market. Livestock husbandry, especially of cattle and sheep, has been important also.

Patagonia is the final agricultural region that contributes to the nation's export economy. Sheep ranching (chiefly for wool) is a principal product of the region. The poor soils of Patagonia and its cool and dry climate limit crop production.

PETROLEUM AND NATURAL GAS

Oil and petroleum-related products and natural gas make up Argentina's second most valuable category of exports. Together, they amount to about 15 percent of the total value of the country's exports. The main recipients are Chile, the United States, Brazil, and China, in that order. Most of Argentina's produc-

tion of these two products takes place in Patagonia, the country's largest state, in the Neuquén and the Astral basins at the base of the Andes. Neuquén accounts for the bulk of the national production. Other long-standing producing basins are the Cuyo, San Jorge, and Magallenes. From 1980 to 2010, national gas production more than quadrupled.

Argentina is not a world leader in oil and gas exports, but it plays a relatively significant role supplying these products to its South American neighbors. The country was the second largest exporter of natural gas in South America in 2008. Only Bolivia exported more. In that year, Argentina ranked fourth in the exportation of petroleum in the South America region, behind Venezuela, Brazil, and Ecuador, in decreasing order. Argentina's natural gas and petroleum exports are relatively important to the region, but Venezuela and Bolivia exceed Argentina by far in terms of totals for both resources in production and proved reserves. In 2008, the leading producing company in the country was YPF S.A., followed by Pan American Energy LLC, Petrobrás Energía S.A., and Chevron Argentina S.R.L., in decreasing order.

COPPER, GOLD, AND SILVER

Economists and geologists classify gold and silver as precious metals because of their relatively high value per unit of weight. In contrast, owing to the bulk of impurities of copper ore, copper is considered an industrial mineral or nonprecious metal. Argentina's production of copper, gold, and silver has increased rapidly. Ores of all three metals can form in similar geological environments. For example, all three are hidden beneath the dry hills of the Puna region in the country's northwest corner. The Puna also produces small amounts of tin, lead, zinc, and ferrous minerals. The grassy knolls of Argentina's north-central region have gold and porphyry copper, but also small amounts of nickel-platinum and manganese. One-third of the mining is done in Patagonia, which makes up the southern third of the country. Scattered in the region are large epithermal gold and silver deposits as well as polymetallic lead-zinc deposits. The last setting is the magnificent Andes Mountains region, which has deposits of porphyry copper and gold as well as chromium. The Andes region is where most of Argentina's mining takes place, although explorations by mining companies have indicated that great potential exists for expanded mining in the other three regions. Mineral exploration has increased because of direct foreign investment ventures by Canadian, Chinese, U.S., and British companies, in decreasing order of investment.

Together, copper and gold accounted for about 75 percent of the annual value of all mining in the country in 2006, but copper is by far the more important of the two minerals. Copper accounted for 98 percent of value of all nonprecious metal ores that were mined and exported from the country that year. However, gold exports rose rapidly after the opening of the Veladero Mine in 2006. Catamarca is the leading producing province for gold, most of which comes from the Bajo de la Alumbrera Mine. San Juan Province, where the Veladero Mine is located, is the number-two producer. Other producing provinces are Santa Cruz and La Rioja. Most of the gold produced in Santa Cruz is from the Cerro Vanguardia Mine. A small amount of gold is from the Martha Mine in La Rioja. Argentina is the fourth-largest producer of silver in Latin America. In 2006, the leading recipients of Argentina's metallic ores were Germany, Spain, South Korea, India, and Brazil.

ALUMINUM AND WATER POWER

The manufacture of aluminum requires the raw material alumina and massive amounts of electricity. Argentina's alumina comes from smelting bauxite (alumina ore), which the country imports. Hydroelectricity is a necessary power source because it can

be produced more cheaply than electricity generated by burning expensive fossil fuels. The refining of alumina is the last step in aluminum production, which begins with exploratory drilling to locate the ore, then removing overburden through blasting and the use of giant earthmoving equipment.

Aluar Aluminio Argentino S.A.I.C., or Aluar, is Argentina's only producer of aluminum. The company is a privately owned stock-trading company that controls every aspect of the aluminum business. It converts alumina to primary aluminum and aluminum products for use in transportation, construction, electrical, medical, water treatment, and packaging industries. Aluar generates its own electricity at its dam on the Futaleufú River in the Andes Mountains. The company transfers the electricity via its own power lines to its aluminum factory near Puerto Madryn in Chubut Province. The company's energy consumption has exceeded its capacity for generating hydroelectricity, so it has supplemented its needs with electricity from burning natural gas, an abundant and a relatively low-cost power source in Argentina. More than 80 percent of Aluar's production is exported to other countries. The products include aluminum bars, tubes, and profiles (flat-angle shapes) in a variety of sizes and forms. Other products include sheet metal and rolls in a wide range of alloys for multiple uses, including foil for disposable food containers and for packaging tobacco, pills, food, and other consumer items. The primary importers are the United States, Japan, Chile, Brazil, and Mexico.

BORON

Argentina was the world's third largest exporter of boron in 2006. Turkey and the United States were first and second, respectively. In that year, the country produced 15 percent of the total world supply. Boron is processed from borate ore, which formed in ancient lake beds at different times. The Puna region, which includes the northwestern corner of Argentina and adjoining areas in Bolivia and Chile, is the main area of borate deposits in South America. The oldest deposits in Argentina formed from 6 to 1.5 million years ago. The Puna is in the high desert of Salta Province, about 4,000 meters above sea level. The main producer of boron in this area is Salta Mining and Energy Resources, an Argentine company. Borax, an American company, mines boron in the Loma Blanca area southeast of the Puna region. Most of Argentina's production is exported to South American customers.

Boron-based compounds are used in the manufacture of such items as boric acid, cosmetics, soaps and detergents, flame retardants, glazes on ceramics, fiberglass, and glass fibers.

LITHIUM

In 2006, Argentina produced 12 percent of the total world production of lithium. Lithium is a rare earth mineral that forms during mountain building, when igneous activities enrich lithium-bearing ores in silicic and pegmatite rocks. The weathered products of these rocks are the most economical sources of lithium; they appear as lithium carbonate and lithium chloride in rare brine deposits of ancient lake beds. Lithium-bearing deposits are in northwestern Argentina, in the Puna, Loma Blanca, and Salar de Hombre Muerto areas. The lithium division of the FMC Corporation, an international and publicly traded company, established the first and largest commercially viable lithium-mining operation at Salar de Hombre Muerto. That mine produces lithium chloride from the brine of the *salar* (salt flat) using a patented ionic exchange process.

Refined lithium is used in the manufacture of ceramics, glass, batteries, lubricating greases, pharmaceuticals and polymers, air-conditioning, and primary aluminum production. Lithium use in batteries has expanded significantly because such batteries have a much longer lifetime than ordinary batteries do. As a result, lithium batteries have been used increasingly in portable electronic devices, such as laptop computers, and in home fire alarms and electrical tools. The greatest potential market is in batteries for plug-in hybrid vehicles. The potential market in the United States expanded significantly when General Motors announced it would introduce a line of hybrid vehicles in late 2009. Argentina's northwest could see greater mining of lithium, as the mineral has increasingly become a strategic material for its projected role in helping alleviate the automobile's reliance on fossil fuels.

OTHER RESOURCES

Argentina is one of six Latin American exporters of lead and zinc, ranking second to Mexico in lead. Other metallic ores that are mined commercially include nickel, manganese, chromium, titanium, and molybdenum. The country's marine resources also enter the global economy, as Argentine fishing companies catch crustaceans and shellfish that they export primarily to Spain, Italy, Brazil, and France, in descending order. A fair amount of agricultural land, which is a natural resource that depends on local climate and soil fertility, is planted with feed crops that support the production of dairy products and eggs to Algeria, Venezuela, Brazil, and Chile. Additional Argentine exports are timber products (logs, lumber, and pulpwood), mainly to Brazil, South Africa, and France.

Richard A. Crooker

FURTHER READING

Arnold, Guy. *The Resources of the Third World.* New York: Cassell, 1997.

Crooker, Richard A. *Argentina.* Edgemont, Pa.: Chelsea House, 2004.

Foster, David William, Melissa Fitch Lockhart, and Darrell B. Lockhart. *Culture and Customs of Argentina.* Westport, Conn.: Greenwood Press, 1998.

Garrett, Donald E. *Borates: Handbook of Deposits, Processing, Properties, and Use.* San Diego: Academic Press, 1998.

Kogel, Jessica Elzea, et al., eds. *Industrial Minerals and Rocks: Commodities, Markets, and Uses.* 7th ed. Littleton, Colo.: Society for Mining, Metallurgy, and Exploration, 2006.

Lewis, Daniel K. *The History of Argentina.* Westport, Conn.: Greenwood Press, 2001.

Rotolo, G. C., et al. "Energy Evaluation of Grazing Cattle in Argentina's Pampas." *Agriculture, Ecosystems, and Environment* 119, no. 3 (March, 2007): 383-395.

WEB SITES

CENTRAL INTELLIGENCE AGENCY
The World Fact Book
https://www.cia.gov/library/publications/the-world-factbook/index.html

FOOD AND AGRICULTURE ORGANIZATION OF THE UNITED NATIONS
Country Profiles
http://faostat.fao.org/site/342/default.aspx

INTERNATIONAL TRADE CENTRE
Countries
http://www.intracen.org/menus/countries.htm

U.S. GEOLOGICAL SURVEY
Aluminum
http://minerals.usgs.gov/minerals/pubs/commodity/aluminum/myb1-2006-alumi.pdf

U.S. GEOLOGICAL SURVEY
Boron
http://minerals.usgs.gov/minerals/pubs/
     commodity/boron/boronmcs07.pdf

U.S. GEOLOGICAL SURVEY
Lithium
http://minerals.usgs.gov/minerals/pubs/
     commodity/lithium/lithimcs07.pdf

U.S. GEOLOGICAL SURVEY
2006 Minerals Yearbook, Argentina
http://minerals.usgs.gov/minerals/pubs/country/
     2006/myb3-2006-ar.pdf

WORLD BANK
http://www.worldbank.org/

SEE ALSO: Agricultural products; Agriculture industry; Aluminum; Boron; Farmland; Forests; Lithium;
Oil and natural gas distribution.

Army Corps of Engineers, U.S.

CATEGORY: Organizations, agencies, and programs
DATE: Established 1802

> *The U.S. Army Corps of Engineers has historically
> been one of the most important government agencies
> affecting the development, use, and conservation of
> natural resources, especially water resources. Since its
> founding in 1802, the organization has engaged in a
> multitude of civil and military activities. It has some-
> times been in conflict with other agencies with overlap-
> ping responsibilities.*

BACKGROUND
The U.S. Army Corps of Engineers was established by
an act of Congress on March 16, 1802. This legislation
stationed the group at West Point, New York, where, in
addition to performing work on coastal defenses, it
was to operate a military academy that would train
critically needed engineers.

IMPACT ON RESOURCE USE
The U.S. Army Corps of Engineers' relationship to
natural resources, particularly water resources, came
into focus gradually. One important statement of national responsibility concerning water came in 1824
when the Supreme Court ruled that the federal gov-

ernment had broad interstate commerce regulatory
power, covering river navigation. Following this Court
decision, Congress gave the Corps of Engineers important responsibilities relating to the development
of civil works. During this period, and for a long time
thereafter, natural resources were seen as virtually inexhaustible, and the emphasis was overwhelmingly
on development, not on conservation.

The General Survey Act of 1824 seemed to represent a commitment to engage in professional and systematic national planning for resource development.
However, this was not to be the case. Congress, operating according to procedures that encouraged individual congressional members to promote localized
projects of benefit to their particular constituencies,
essentially converted the Corps of Engineers into a
tool for spending sizable amounts of federal money in
congressional members' own states and districts. The
funds were spent on river and harbor improvements
and on roads. Sometimes the engineers lobbied Congress for permission to participate in projects in which
they were especially interested. Corps activities related to canal-building were most visible. Construction of large and increasingly controversial waterways
continued until the late twentieth century.

By the late twentieth century, support for costly
public works projects was far less than it had once
been. For fiscal as well as environmental reasons, approval for such projects became more difficult than
had been the case previously. An important piece of
legislation bearing on the missions of the U.S. Army
Corps of Engineers was the Water Resources Development Act of 1986. It states explicitly that environmental factors are crucial in all planning related to water
resources. All projects are subject to modification to
produce environmental benefits. The Corps became
committed to an enlightened handling of environmental concerns and to safeguarding as well as developing natural resources. When the problem of water
pollution first began to be perceived as an important
area of government concern, the Army Corps of Engineers' position typically was that the problem should
be handled at state and local levels. Later, however,
the Corps considered its antipollution activities to be
among its most important responsibilities.

The Corps started promoting flood control in the
years following the Civil War. Not until 1936 did Congress officially state that flood control was a legitimate
federal function. The Corps played an important role
in the building of levees affecting the hurricane-

ravaged coastal regions of the states adjacent to the Gulf of Mexico. The Corps has also developed ways for many areas throughout the country to obtain water, and many communities draw their water from Corps projects.

William H. Stewart

WEB SITE

U.S. ARMY CORPS OF ENGINEERS
http://www.usace.army.mil/Pages/default.aspx

SEE ALSO: Bureau of Land Management, U.S.; Bureau of Reclamation, U.S.; Dams; Environmental movement; Floods and flood control.

Arsenic

CATEGORY: Mineral and other nonliving resources

WHERE FOUND
Elemental arsenic is occasionally found in minerals, but more frequently it is combined chemically with sulfur, either alone or with metals such as copper, nickel, cobalt, or iron. China is the world's largest producer of elemental arsenic. Because of the health risks of arsenic, there has been no U.S. production of arsenic trioxide or arsenic metal since 1985.

PRIMARY USES
Wood preservatives, herbicides, and insecticides are major uses of arsenic chemicals. Arsenic is used to harden lead alloys for battery plates, solder, and lead shot, while arsenides of gallium and indium have uses in lasers, light-emitting diodes, and transistors. In the United States, approximately 4 percent of arsenic (measured in metric tons of arsenic content) goes to agricultural chemicals, 3 percent to glass products, 3 percent to nonferrous alloys and electronics, and 90 percent to pressure-treated wood. The electronics industry uses a very pure form of arsenic in gallium-arsenide semiconductors for solar cells, space research, and telecommunications.

TECHNICAL DEFINITION
Arsenic (abbreviated As), atomic number 33, belongs to Group V of the periodic table of the elements and is classified as a metalloid, rather than a metal or nonmetal. There is only one naturally occurring isotope, with an atomic weight of 74.93. Elemental arsenic exhibits gray, yellow, and black forms with densities of 5.73, 1.97, and 4.73 grams per cubic centimeter. The common gray form sublimes when heated to 613° Celsius and melts under a pressure of 28 atmospheres (2.8 million pascals) at 817° Celsius.

DESCRIPTION, DISTRIBUTION, AND FORMS
Arsenic is widely distributed and is found in soils and seawater in trace amounts: 1 to 40 parts per million in soil, and 2 to 5 parts per billion in seawater. It averages about 1.8 parts per million by weight. The most abundant arsenic mineral is arsenical pyrite (also called arsenopyrite or mispickel), a sulfide of iron and arsenic. Other significant ores are arsenolite (arsenious oxide), orpiment (As_2S_3), and realgar (As_4S_4). Seawater averages 0.5 to 2 parts per billion of arsenate, but lakes and streams often have higher concentrations; these vary from one body of water to another. Lake Michigan, for example, has levels of 0.5 to 2.4 parts per billion. Fish and shellfish have arsenic levels about one thousand times greater than seawater and much higher than federal drinking water standards (0.05 part per million). Arsenobetaine, with a formula of $(+)(CH_3)3As\text{-}CH_2\text{-}CO_2(-)$, is common in fish, and many other methylated compounds are found in marine organisms.

Arsenic toxicity is highly dependent on the state of chemical combination of the element. Elemental arsenic is less toxic than combined forms; the most dangerous forms are arsine, arsenites, and arsenious oxide. Ingestion of as little as 0.1 gram of arsenious oxide has caused death. Methylated compounds such as arsenobetaine are much less toxic.

Arsenic intoxication symptoms include skin rashes, anemia, gastrointestinal distress, internal bleeding, and shock. Chronic poisoning can result in a gangrenous condition of the feet ("blackfoot disease"), and the action of arsenic as a carcinogen and teratogen has been established. Paradoxically, arsenic, like selenium, is an essential trace nutrient for some species. The toxicity of arsenic is only partly understood, particularly its carcenogenicity. Arsenate, $AsO_4(3-)$, because of its similarity to phosphate, can react with adenosine, leading to uncoupling of oxidative phosphorylation, an important energy-producing system in plants and animals. Arsenite, $AsO_3(3-)$, inhibits many enzymes by binding to thiol (−SH) groups that exist, for example, in pyruvate oxidase. The vital tricarboxylic acid cycle is thereby disrupted. Admin-

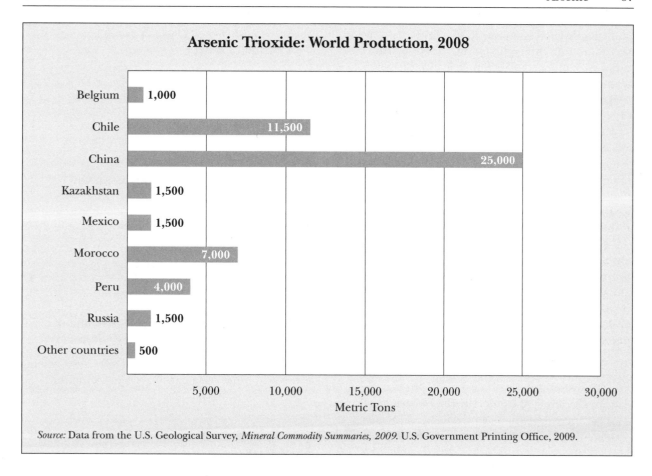

Arsenic Trioxide: World Production, 2008

Country	Metric Tons
Belgium	1,000
Chile	11,500
China	25,000
Kazakhstan	1,500
Mexico	1,500
Morocco	7,000
Peru	4,000
Russia	1,500
Other countries	500

Source: Data from the U.S. Geological Survey, *Mineral Commodity Summaries, 2009.* U.S. Government Printing Office, 2009.

istration of antidotes such as penicillamine or dimer-captopropanol that contain –SH groups will bind preferentially to the arsenite and keep it from the enzymes. Ingested arsenic tends to accumulate in the hair and can be detected by neutron activation analysis. Atomic absorption spectroscopy can also detect and measure trace amounts of arsenic.

HISTORY

Arsenic was known in early times in India, Persia, and Mesopotamia, and it is mentioned in the writings of Aristotle, Hippocrates, and Pliny the Elder. These ancient writings are often vague and do not allow the modern reader to decide exactly whether elemental arsenic or some compound such as an oxide or sulfide is described. European alchemists such as Albertus Magnus (thirteenth century) and Johannes Schröder (seventeenth century) published procedures for preparing arsenic from orpiment (As_2S_3) or arsenious oxide (As_2O_3), but priority in discovery is considered uncertain.

The toxic characteristics of arsenious oxide were noticed long ago, and the substance became notorious in various homicidal poisoning cases. The Roman emperor Nero, for example, poisoned his own brother. Accidental arsenic poisoning is exemplified by the events reported in 1973 in Pelham, Minnesota, where a well had been drilled on land that had received heavy dosages of arsenic insecticides.

In spite of the danger, pigments containing arsenic were still used in cakes and candy in the nineteenth century, and arsenic-containing medicines of dubious value were used in the early twentieth century. Arsenicals are still occasionally used to treat stubborn parasitic diseases (trypanosomiasis, amoebiasis).

OBTAINING ARSENIC

There are more than two hundred recognized arsenic-containing minerals. Arsenic is leached into water by weathering of rocks and is distributed by volcanic action. In the soil, microorganisms can metabolize arsenate or arsenite, producing a variety of organic methylated compounds that find their way into water and into the bodies of all sorts of marine creatures. An estimated 40,000 metric tons of arsenic are added to the world's oceans annually by weathering of rocks, as compared with world industrial production of 55,000 to 70,000 metric tons per year.

Human activity accounts for significant releases of arsenic into the air, water, and soil. Smelters emit arsenic oxide dust, and herbicides and insecticides remain in the soil. One of the large smelters in the United States (no longer operating) emitted 181 metric tons of arsenious oxide per year into the area surrounding Tacoma, Washington.

USES OF ARSENIC

Production of arsenic has ceased in the United States, and uses are subject to increasingly severe regulation. Nevertheless, the United States still imports about several thousand metric tons per year, mainly for wood preservation and pesticide uses.

John R. Phillips

FURTHER READING

Adriano, Domy C. "Arsenic." In *Trace Elements in Terrestrial Environments: Biogeochemistry, Bioavailability, and Risks of Metals*. 2d ed. New York: Springer, 2001.

Fowler, Bruce A., ed. *Biological and Environmental Effects of Arsenic*. New York: Elsevier, 1983.

Greenwood, N. N., and A. Earnshaw. "Arsenic, Antimony, and Bismuth." In *Chemistry of the Elements*. 2d ed. Boston: Butterworth-Heinemann, 1997.

Henderson, William. "The Group 15 (Pnictogen) Elements: Nitrogen, Phosphorus, Arsenic, Antimony, and Bismuth." In *Main Group Chemistry*. Cambridge, England: Royal Society of Chemistry, 2000.

Massey, A. G. "Group 15: The Pnictides—Nitrogen, Phosphorus, Arsenic, Antimony, and Bismuth." In *Main Group Chemistry*. 2d ed. New York: Wiley, 2000.

Naidu, Ravi, et al., eds. *Managing Arsenic in the Environment: From Soil to Human Health*. Enfield, N.H.: Science Publishers, 2006.

Ng, J., ed. *Arsenic and Arsenic Compounds*. 2d ed. Geneva, Switzerland: World Health Organization, 2001.

Nriagu, Jerome O., ed. *Arsenic in the Environment*. 2 vols. New York: Wiley, 1994.

Ravenscroft, Peter, Hugh Brammer, and Keith Richards. *Arsenic Pollution: A Global Synthesis*. Malden, Mass.: Wiley-Blackwell, 2009.

Thayer, John S. *Environmental Chemistry of the Heavy El-*

ements: Hydrido and Organo Compounds. New York: VCH, 1995.

WEB SITES

HEALTH CANADA
Healthy Living: Arsenic in Drinking Water
http://www.hc-sc.gc.ca/hl-vs/iyh-vsv/environ/
    arsenic-eng.php

U.S. ENVIRONMENTAL PROTECTION AGENCY
Arsenic in Drinking Water
http://www.epa.gov/safewater/arsenic/index.html

U.S. GEOLOGICAL SURVEY
Arsenic: Statistics and Information
http://minerals.usgs.gov/minerals/pubs/
    commodity/arsenic

U.S. GEOLOGICAL SURVEY
Arsenic in Ground Water of the United States
http://water.usgs.gov/nawqa/trace/arsenic

SEE ALSO: Bronze; China; Gallium; Herbicides; Mining wastes and mine reclamation; Native elements.

Asbestos

CATEGORY: Mineral and other nonliving resources

WHERE FOUND

Asbestos-form minerals are common in metamorphic rocks all over the world, but the great majority of the world's production has come from only two types of deposits. The most important of these, represented by major deposits in Canada and Russia, are produced by metamorphic alteration of alpine-type ultramafic rocks—dark-colored, high-density igneous rocks low in silica and high in iron and magnesium. The second major type of deposit, much less important than the first, is produced by the metamorphism of layered ultramafic intrusions. Important deposits of this type occur in Africa.

PRIMARY USES

The major use in the world market is in the manufacturing of asbestos-cement products. Other important uses are in friction products, such as clutch facings and brake linings, and in roofing products. Asbestos with particularly long fibers is spun into cloth and used to manufacture fire-resistant conveyor belts, safety clothing, and other types of fireproof textiles, such as curtains and blankets.

TECHNICAL DEFINITION

There are six different minerals that have been produced as asbestos. By far the most important one, accounting for approximately 95 percent of the world production and consumption, is chrysotile, or "white asbestos," a fibrous form of the serpentine group of minerals. The serpentines are hydrous magnesium silicates with a layered structure. Commercial deposits of chrysotile occur in ultramafic rocks, particularly peridotite, that have undergone metamorphism. The five other forms of asbestos are members of the amphibole group of minerals. In order of importance, these are crocidolite ("blue asbestos"), amosite ("brown asbestos"), anthophyllite, tremolite, and actinolite. The amphiboles are silicates with a chainlike structure and an extremely variable composition.

DESCRIPTION, DISTRIBUTION, AND FORMS

Asbestos is not a mineral or a rock; rather, it is an industrial term used to refer to a few minerals that sometimes occur in a fibrous form. Asbestos refers to a few types of minerals that sometimes occur as long, slender fibers. It is this fibrous nature that accounts for both the usefulness and hazards of asbestos. Asbestos minerals differ from one another in many ways, but they share great resistance to heat, chemical attack, and friction. These properties make asbestos an important industrial commodity. The major asbestos deposits of the world are located in Canada, China, Russia, Kazakhstan, and some African countries. The Thetford District in the eastern townships of Quebec, Canada, and the Bazhenov area in the Ural Mountains of south-central Russia and Kazakhstan have been the most productive sites for asbestos. Thetford production has been continuous since 1878. The deposits in the Urals have not operated as long but are thought to have the greatest reserves in the world. The geology of both of these two great districts is similar. Chrysotile occurs as veins and fissures in ultramafic rock that has undergone metamorphism during mountain-building events. The Ural deposits have the greater tonnage of production, but the Thetford deposits are of a higher grade and produce more long-fiber asbestos. African production includes both chrysotile and amphibole asbestos (amosite and crocidolite) and comes from Zimbabwe, South Africa,

and Swaziland. Zimbabwean production is minor compared to those of Russia, China, and Kazakhstan, whose combined output accounted for approximately 73 percent of the world's total production of approximately 2.2 million metric tons in 2007. This figure represents a decline of about one-third from the early 1970's. The rate of decline has leveled off from the late 1980's but is projected to continue because of opposition to the use of asbestos in building and consumer products. Decline in production in the United States was sharper, falling by more than 90 percent from the early 1970's to the end of the 1990's. The United States ceased production of asbestos in 2002.

HISTORY

The ancient Romans were the first to use asbestos. They wove it into a cloth and used it in cremations and for permanent lamp wicks. Knowledge of asbestos seems to have been lost after the Romans until it was rediscovered in Italy in 1868. The development of asbestos as an important industrial mineral began with the opening of the world's first great deposit in eastern Quebec, Canada, in 1878.

OBTAINING ASBESTOS

Fibers with a length-to-width ratio greater than 50 to 1 command the highest price because they can be mixed

Anthophyllite is one of six minerals that are classified as asbestos. (USGS)

with other fibers and spun or milled into cloth. The shorter, or "nonspinning," fibers are generally made into compressed, molded, or cast products, such as asbestos pipe and sheet, in which the fibers are added to a binder such as portland cement or plastic. Such products account for most of the asbestos produced each year. Of the six different minerals that have been produced as asbestos, only crocidolite and amosite have been produced in important quantities. Production of anthophyllite, tremolite, and actinolite has been extremely limited and was nonexistent by the end of the twentieth century.

USES OF ASBESTOS

Although the individual properties of asbestos minerals differ from one another, they share to varying degrees several properties that make them useful and cost-effective. These include nonflammability, great resistance to heat and acid attack, high tensile strength and flexibility, low electrical conductivity, resistance to friction, and a fibrous habit.

Over a span of only a few years, the public's view of asbestos changed dramatically: Once considered a useful commodity, asbestos became known as an extremely dangerous material. The change began with

U.S. End Uses of Asbestos, 1977 vs. 2003

END USE	METRIC TONS	
	1977	2003
Cement pipe	145,000	—
Cement sheet	139,500	—
Coatings & compounds	32,500	1,170
Flooring products	140,000	—
Friction products	83,100	—
Insulation: electrical	3,360	—
Insulation: thermal	15,000	—
Packing & gaskets	25,100	—
Paper products	22,100	—
Plastics	7,260	—
Roofing products	57,500	2,800
Textiles	8,800	—
Other	30,200	677

Source: Data from the U.S. Geological Survey.
Note: U.S. mining of asbestos ended in 2002.

passage of the Clean Air Act (1972), which classified asbestos as a carcinogenic material because studies of workers exposed to high concentrations of asbestos dust for many years showed a high incidence of asbestosis, a lung disease that decreases the ability to breathe, and mesothelioma, a cancer of the lungs. Then, in 1973, a lawsuit against a number of asbestos manufacturers on behalf of an asbestos worker was decided against the companies. Litigation mounted, and, in 1982, manufacturer Johns-Manville filed for bankruptcy in the face of overwhelming litigation; eventually, as a compromise measure, the company established a $2.5 billion fund to pay future asbestos claims.

Widespread publicity concerning asbestos hazards led to a near hysteria among the general public; many people were afraid to send their children to a school unless asbestos insulation had been removed. People brought lawsuits demanding that asbestos be removed from public buildings. The courts awarded large damage rewards based on the argument that low-level exposure to asbestos should be considered dangerous because a safe level of exposure had not been scientifically established. This led to the "single fiber" concept—that exposure to only one fiber of asbestos may be deadly—in keeping with a widely held public perception that there should be no exposure to carcinogenic materials in the environment. The "asbestos scare" was largely the result of mass media sensationalism and resultant political and legal pressure rather than the result of scientific investigation. For example, very few people realized that, according to scientific estimates, a person breathing normal outdoor air inhales nearly 4,000 asbestos fibers per day, or more than 100 million over a lifetime.

Asbestos can be a health hazard, but the seriousness depends on the length of exposure, the amount of asbestos in the air, and the type of asbestos involved. The danger to miners and others working with asbestos in unprotected conditions is demonstrable, but the danger to the general public from minimal exposure has been greatly exaggerated. Some researchers believe that the danger is so small as to be virtually nonexistent. Melvin Benarde in *Asbestos: The Hazardous Fiber* (1990) outlined the statistical risks (the number of deaths expected per 100,000 people) for a number of potential hazards. The risk of dying from nonoccupational exposure to asbestos is one-third the risk of being killed by lightning and nearly five thousand times less than the chance of dying in a car

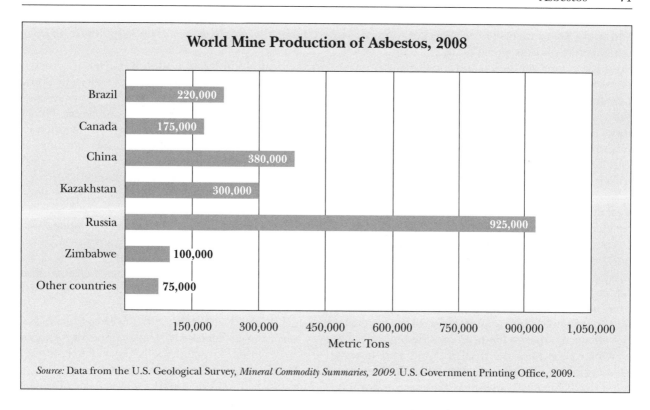

World Mine Production of Asbestos, 2008

Country	Metric Tons
Brazil	220,000
Canada	175,000
China	380,000
Kazakhstan	300,000
Russia	925,000
Zimbabwe	100,000
Other countries	75,000

Metric Tons

Source: Data from the U.S. Geological Survey, *Mineral Commodity Summaries, 2009.* U.S. Government Printing Office, 2009.

accident. Nevertheless, by the mid-1990's more than $35 billion had been spent on asbestos abatement in rental, commercial, and public buildings. Most common uses of asbestos—applications such as pipeline insulation, clothing, and roofing felt—were banned in the United States in 1990, and virtually all asbestos products were banned in the country by 1996.

It has been estimated that in the time period from 1965 to 2029 there will be 432,465 asbestos-related cancers in the United States. Although this figure has been disputed by some epidemiologists and other experts, it is enough to indicate the misery that many will suffer because of their exposure to asbestos. Nevertheless, the litigation-centered approach to asbestos issues in the United States has been criticized. In a 2003 report, the Manhattan Institute's Center for Legal Policy described asbestos litigation as the longest-running mass tort in the history of the nation and arguably the most unjust. Some critics have claimed that the massive asbestos tort litigation is more likely to enrich lawyers than relieve victims. The Manhattan Institute estimated that of the $70 billion paid out by companies for asbestos claims, $40 billion has gone to plaintiffs and defense lawyers. Numerous companies have been driven into bankruptcy by asbestos lawsuits,

some of which had only a tangential connection to the original asbestos exposure. Of the twenty-nine companies that filed for bankruptcy in the years from 2000 to 2002 because of asbestos litigation, six were valued at more than $1 billion. These included such industrial giants as Owens Corning, W. R. Grace, and U.S. Gypsum. As the companies that directly produced asbestos have gone under, plaintiffs' lawyers have increasingly sued companies outside the asbestos and building products industry. Companies in more than one-half of all industries in the United States have been sued over asbestos. With the total eventual cost of asbestos litigation estimated at $200 billion, Congress has considered several proposals to establish a compensation fund in place of litigation. In 2004, industrial states such as Michigan and Ohio enacted measures to implement some form of asbestos tort reform.

Although asbestos use has become rare in developed countries, the same cannot be said of developing economies. In most of Europe and North America, use of asbestos is strictly limited or banned by law. However, emerging nations have continued and even increased the use of asbestos in manufacturing and building. Countries such as China, India, Brazil, Iran, and South Korea are major consumers of asbestos. Asbestos mining is widespread in Africa. Many developing nations consider the low cost and the effectiveness of asbestos as an industrial material to outweigh the health risks. The adverse effects of asbestos as an industrial pollutant are below the surface and long-term. Many of these nations face a more obvious health risk from such epidemics as HIV/AIDS, cholera, tuberculosis, and malaria, which have been linked to poverty or inadequate infrastructure. Likewise, many developing nations have accepted a great deal of air, water, and ground pollution as the price of accelerating the growth of fragile economies. Asbestos has apparently been accepted as another pollutant. Certainly these countries lack the extensive and ubiquitous legal and regulatory system of the United States that has focused attention on asbestos. However, in some African nations, such as South Africa and Swaziland, compensation for workers suffering the effects of asbestos has been provided.

China is perhaps the most dynamic and fastest-growing of all emerging markets. Many have speculated that China will emerge as the most important economy of the twenty-first century. It is worth noting, therefore, some facts about asbestos consumption in China. China continues to make extensive use of asbestos. Production of asbestos in China has remained steady since 1995. China is one of the five leading producers of asbestos but is perhaps its leading consumer. Imports of asbestos to China rose from 1,083 metric tons in 1990 to 145,425 metric tons in 2003, an increase nearly 150-fold. Estimates indicate that more than 100,000 workers in China are exposed to asbestos. Although the Chinese government has official policies against pollutants, they are often not enforced.

With the United States and China taking such different approaches to the use of asbestos, it is not yet possible to speak of a unified world approach to this industrial product. Certainly its use, associated health risks, and remediation represent one of the most important confluences of industry, medical concerns, and law in the world economy.

Gene D. Robinson, updated by Howard Bromberg

FURTHER READING

Carroll, Stephen, et al. *Asbestos Litigation.* Santa Monica, Calif.: Rand Corporation, 2005.

Castleman, Barry. *Asbestos: Medical and Legal Aspects.* 5th ed. New York: Aspen, 2005.

Chatterjee, Kaulir Kisor. "Asbestos." In *Uses of Industrial Minerals, Rocks, and Freshwater.* New York: Nova Science, 2009.

Craighead, John E., and Allen R. Gibbs, ed. *Asbestos and Its Diseases.* New York: Oxford University Press, 2008.

Deffeyes, Kenneth S. "Asbestos." In *Nanoscale: Visualizing an Invisible World.* Illustrations by Stephen E. Deffeyes. Cambridge: Massachusetts Institute of Technology Press, 2009.

Dodson, Ronald, and Samuel Hammar, eds. *Asbestos: Assessment, Epidemiology, and Health Effects.* Boca Raton, Fla.: CRC Press, 2005.

Guthrie, George D., Jr., and Brooke T. Mossman, eds. *Health Effects of Mineral Dusts.* Washington, D.C.: Mineralogical Society of America, 1993.

Harben, Peter W., and Robert L. Bates. *Industrial Minerals: Geology and World Deposits.* London: Industrial Minerals Division, Metal Bulletin, 1990.

Kogel, Jessica Elzea, et al., eds. "Asbestos." In *Industrial Minerals and Rocks: Commodities, Markets, and Uses.* 7th ed. Littleton, Colo.: Society for Mining, Metallurgy, and Exploration, 2006.

McCulloch, Jock, and Geoffrey Tweedale. *Defending the Indefensible: The Global Asbestos Industry and Its Fight for Survival.* New York: Oxford University Press, 2008.

McDonald, J. C., et al. "The Health of Chrysotile Asbestos Mine and Mill Workers of Quebec." *Archives of Environmental Health* 28 (1974).

Maines, Rachel. *Asbestos and Fire: Technological Trade-offs and the Body at Risk.* New Brunswick, N.J.: Rutgers University Press, 2005.

Skinner, H. Catherine W., Malcolm Ross, and Clifford Frondel. *Asbestos and Other Fibrous Materials: Mineralogy, Crystal Chemistry, and Health Effects.* New York: Oxford University Press, 1988.

WEB SITES

MANHATTAN INSTITUTE CENTER FOR LEGAL POLICY
Trial Lawyers Inc.: Asbestos
http://www.triallawyersinc.com/asbestos/asb01.html

U.S. GEOLOGICAL SURVEY
Asbestos: Statistics and Information
http://minerals.usgs.gov/minerals/pubs/
commodity/asbestos

U.S. GEOLOGICAL SURVEY
Mineral Commodities Profiles—Asbestos
http://pubs.usgs.gov/circ/2005/1255/kk

SEE ALSO: Clean Air Act; Health, resource exploitation and; Hydrothermal solutions and mineralization; Metamorphic processes, rocks, and mineral deposits; Silicates.

Asphalt

CATEGORY: Products from resources

WHERE FOUND
Before the growth of the petroleum industry in the early twentieth century, when asphalt began to be mass-produced, naturally occurring asphalt was found in pools of petroleum-heavy deposits, most notably Trinidad's 46-hectare Pitch Lake (off the coast of Venezuela), the 4,000-hectare Bermudez Lake in Venezuela, and areas around the Dead Sea basin in Israel and Jordan.

PRIMARY USES
Asphalt is most associated with road-surface paving. Apart from highway construction and repairs, asphalt is used for airport runways, running tracks, and driveways. In addition, asphalt is a waterproofing agent in fabrics, irrigation systems, roofing shingles, jetties and sea walls designed to combat beach erosion, and insulation. More than 60 billion metric tons of manufactured asphalt are used annually in the United States alone.

TECHNICAL DEFINITION
Asphalt is a by-product of petroleum refining, either occurring naturally over geologic eras or processed industrially in the controlled refining process called fractional distillation that occurs once naphtha, gasoline, and kerosene have all been extracted from the crude. It is difficult to define a single chemical profile because asphalt varies depending on the grade of crude petroleum and the type of refining production used. Generally, asphalts contain saturated and unsaturated aliphatic compounds (organic compounds whose carbon atoms configure in open branches rather than closed rings) and aromatic compounds (organic compounds whose carbon atoms configure in closed rings) with up to 150 carbon atoms. Asphalt contains about 80 percent carbon, 10 percent hydrogen, and 6 percent sulfur with trace amounts of oxygen and nitrogen. Molecular weight varies. These compounds are further classified by their solubility—more insoluble compounds are called asphaltenes and less soluble compounds maltenes.

DESCRIPTION, DISTRIBUTION, AND FORMS
Asphalt is a dark (brown or black), cementitious (highly adhesive) material. Its predominant elements are bitumens, solid and/or semisolid high-molecular-weight hydrocarbons. Because more than 80 percent of commercially produced asphalt is used for paving, the properties of asphalt are graded according to its performance as a pavement adhesive, particularly how well it holds up over time, specifically in the areas of aging, stiffening, and cracking.

Only 5 percent of the asphalt used today is naturally occurring. Its most prominent naturally occurring site is Pitch Lake in the petroleum-rich southwest corner of the island of Trinidad, near the town of La Brea. Although difficult to determine dimensions with any accuracy because it grows and shrinks, this "lake"—it is more accurately a sludgy 40-plus-hectare mineral deposit created by a slow underground seepage of asphalt, or pitch—is estimated to be more than 35 meters across and 107 meters deep at its deepest point (the edges of the lake are crusty and support weight, but toward the center of the lake, the pitch becomes characteristically sticky and far more hazardous, easily swallowing entire objects). Given its dimensions, the lake has provided an apparently inexhaustible supply of asphalt for centuries—large holes left by removing asphalt are quickly filled in as the lake maintains a kind of fluid dynamic. Western explorers were fascinated by the phenomena of this vast tar lake, not merely for the usefulness of the asphalt (they immediately used it to upgrade the waterproofing on their ships) but because the lake also preserved the remains of prehistoric mammals and birds.

Commercially produced asphalt is primarily a taffylike binder known as asphaltic concrete. Asphaltic concrete, a tacky, ductile resin suspended in an oily medium, maintains the integrity of aggregate particles. Because asphaltic concrete is highly sticky, it must be heated into liquid to be used for pavement construction. It is most often sprayed on a graded roadbed. It is then compacted into the proper density, usually 25 to 30 centimeters. Because it solidifies into a tough and flexible surface able to maintain its integrity against both the weight and frequency of traffic and the deformations from weather conditions (notably ice and extreme heat), asphalt remains the pri-

Russian workers repave an asphalt road on the outskirts of Abakan. (Kolbasov Alexander/ITAR-TASS/Landov)

mary roadway surface. Given the diminishing supply of fossil fuel and concerns over the depletion of that resource, asphaltic concrete is attractive because more than 80 percent of removed asphalt can be recycled for new road projects.

HISTORY

Asphalt was used as early at 3600 B.C.E. by the Sumerians as a mortar adhesive for paving and building and as a waterproofing agent in canal construction and public pools (records indicate it also was used for medical treatments, statuary enhancement, and mummification throughout the Middle East). Pitch is mentioned early in the Bible: It binds Noah's ark and later makes waterproof the bulrush basket in which the baby Moses is set adrift on the Nile.

Following the discovery of huge natural deposits of pitch in South America in the fifteenth and sixteenth centuries (notably by Sir Walter Ralegh), asphalt became a commercially viable waterproofing agent for the burgeoning shipbuilding industry. Not until 1870, however, was asphalt first tested for paving. The idea came from accounts discovered among Incan archives dating back to the twelfth century. A stretch of streets

in Newark, New Jersey, was made of Trinidad asphalt. Its appeal was evident—it was cheap to import, easy to apply, flexible, and once hardened made for a smooth ride. Within six years, asphalt was selected for a most ambitious—and prestigious—paving project: Pennsylvania Avenue in Washington, D.C. By the turn of the century, more than 35 million square meters of streets in America were asphalt. With the rise of the oil industry, however, commercially produced asphalt became more profitable.

OBTAINING ASPHALT

Asphalt may be obtained directly from sludgy beds near petroleum fields. However, far more asphalt is obtained as a small fraction of residue distilled during the refining process of crude oil. Heavy crude oil is heated to nearly 370° Celsius in large furnaces. As the crude is processed, lighter components vaporize and are released into the atmosphere through refinery towers (in the early 1980's, facing pressure from environmental groups, the petroleum industry overhauled the distillation towers to minimize pollution). To render the remaining asphalt into asphaltic cement, the residue is distilled further through a vacuum process designed to prevent the residue from cracking, and then it is mixed with the appropriate aggregate materials, most commonly crushed rock, slag, sand, and/or cement stone. In turn, the asphalt must be stored (and transported) at a constant 65.55° Celsius to ensure liquidity. If the asphalt must be transported a considerable way, kerosene or diesel oil can be temporarily added and then separated before the asphalt is applied to the roadbed.

USES OF ASPHALT

Long before the automobile made highway construction a pressing concern, as thousands of kilometers of roadway needed to be laid quickly and economically, asphalt was valued because it was waterproof. It revolutionized the shipping industry because of its caulking ability. Even in modern society, asphalt helps solidify sea walls to protect against the effects of tides, waves, and harsh weather. In addition, asphalt lines the retaining tanks in industrial fish hatcheries, preserves the integrity of irrigation systems (before asphalt, up to one-third of water transported would be lost in transit), and maintains holdings by providing underlining for reservoirs. Furthermore, asphalt has become a primary liner for the disposal of hazardous waste and a liner at landfill sites.

In addition, because it is waterproof and fire retardant, asphalt can be used, when combined with felt and mineral granules, to produce the familiar rectangular roofing shingles. This asphalt is slightly harder than paving asphalt (it is typically heated at a much higher temperature to make it less flexible). Asphalt shingles are remarkably adaptable to a variety of roofing needs and styles; shingles can be adjusted for the slope of the roof, climate conditions, and even house design.

However, asphalt is best known as a paving agent. It is durable, tough, and flexible enough to provide a comfortable riding surface. Industry standards measure durability of standard asphalt roadways at fifteen to twenty years. That longevity is most often compromised by cracks from water seeping into the surface during the winter, freezing, and then cracking the upper layers or by ruts that appear during hot summers when the asphalt softens. However, asphalt provides for relatively easy repairs. The durability of asphalt, particularly its capacity to hold up under constant traffic and enormous weights, has made it the primary coating for airplane runways. For much the same reason, asphalt is also used for railroad beds and

even subway system track beds. Finally, asphalt is used for smaller, high-volume traffic surfaces such as walking trails, tennis courts, biking paths, running tracks, basketball courts, golf-cart paths, and playgrounds. Users of these recreational surfaces appreciate the give in asphalt, as compared to concrete surfaces. In 1986, the National Center for Asphalt Technology (NCAT) was established at Auburn University to develop asphalt production quality.

Joseph Dewey

FURTHER READING

Karnes, Thomas L. *Asphalt Politics: A History of the American Highway System.* Jefferson, N.C.: McFarland, 2009.

Lavin, Patrick. *Asphalt Pavements: A Practical Guide to Design, Production, and Maintenance for Engineers and Architects.* London: Spon Press, 2003.

Nicholls, Cliff. *Asphalt Surfacing: A Guide to Asphalt Surfacings and Treatments Used for the Surface Course of Road Pavements.* London: Spon Press, 1998.

O'Flaherty, C. A. *Highways: The Location, Design, Construction, and Maintenance of Road Pavements.* 4th ed. Oxford: Butterworth-Heinemann, 2002.

WEB SITE

NATIONAL CENTER FOR ASPHALT TECHNOLOGY
http://www.eng.auburn.edu/center/ncat

SEE ALSO: Petroleum refining and processing; Renewable and nonrenewable resources; Transportation, energy use in.

Aspinall, Wayne

CATEGORY: People
BORN: April 3, 1896; Middleburg, Ohio
DIED: October 9, 1983; Palisade, Colorado

Aspinall, a Colorado Democrat, served in the U.S. Congress from 1948 to 1972. From 1958 to 1972, he chaired the House Interior and Insular Affairs Committee, shaping some of the most important natural resource legislation in American history.

BIOGRAPHICAL BACKGROUND

Wayne Norviel Aspinall's shadow looms large over the modern American West. After growing up near Palisade, Colorado, on the Grand (now Colorado) River, Aspinall attended Denver University, served in World War I, became a schoolteacher, obtained a law degree, and ran a peach orchard business. Always active in local Democratic Party politics, he served as a state representative and senator for sixteen years before he was elected to Congress in 1948.

Aspinall quickly made a name for himself as an expert on public land and federal reclamation issues. In 1958, he began chairing the House Interior and Insular Affairs Committee, a post he did not relinquish until after his defeat in the 1972 Colorado primary. During Aspinall's twenty-four-year congressional career, his name became synonymous with some of the most notable legislation that shaped the landscape of the American West, including the Upper Colorado River Storage Act (1956), the Wilderness Act (1964), and the Colorado River Basin Act (1968). From 1964 until 1970, he chaired the Public Land Law Review Commission, which made dozens of recommendations for reforming the management of the nation's federal lands.

IMPACT ON RESOURCE USE

By the mid-1960's, Aspinall's strict adherence to a multiple-use philosophy of resource management had made him a target for environmentalist criticism. In 1970, political columnist Jack Anderson labeled Aspinall the environmentalists' "most durable foe" and accused him of defending timber, oil, cattle, and chemical interests "against the beauty of American nature." To Aspinall, nature had been placed in the stewardship of humankind, and while he appreciated the American West's beauty, he always favored the controlled use of its resources over what he saw as the program of "extreme" environmentalists who, in his view, wanted to "lock up" the region's resources.

Steven C. Schulte

SEE ALSO: Bureau of Reclamation, U.S.; Dams; Energy politics; Irrigation; Public lands; Wilderness Act.

Astor, John Jacob

CATEGORY: People
BORN: July 17, 1763; Waldorf, near Heidelberg, Germany
DIED: March 29, 1848; New York, New York

Astor, a leader in early American capitalism, founded the American Fur Company, considered the first American business monopoly. Astor's astounding financial success, although atypical, pointed to the fortunes that could be made from the exploitation of resources in the young and resource-rich United States.

BIOGRAPHICAL BACKGROUND

As a young man aboard a ship from Germany, John Jacob Astor learned about the lucrative fur trade in North America. In 1786, three years after arriving in New York City, he opened a fur-goods store and began dealing directly with American Indians to secure his furs. In 1796, as his area of activity expanded, Astor secured a charter from the British East India Company. This charter opened foreign markets, especially the rich fur market of China.

John Jacob Astor earned most of his multimillion-dollar fortune in the fur trade. (Library of Congress)

IMPACT ON RESOURCE USE

Astor established the American Fur Company in 1808. In 1811, in an attempt to gain control of fur trade in the Northwest, he founded the town of Astoria in Oregon. However, this plan failed when the British captured Astoria during the War of 1812. The setback was temporary, and by 1827, Astor had obtained his monopoly of the American fur trade.

Astor's trading empire benefited from his friendship with U.S. presidents such as Thomas Jefferson, who appointed Astor executive agent in the Northwest. An Astor ship was also allowed to go to China during the Embargo Act of 1807, producing a profit of $200,000. Exploitation of human and natural resources was the inevitable result of Astor's activities. American Indians, to whom the profit motive was hitherto unknown, were exploited because of their skill in obtaining animal furs. The tremendous popularity of furs led to exploitation of the animals from which furs were obtained.

In 1834, Astor retired from the fur-trading business to concentrate on investments in New York City. His estate, worth $20 million when he died, made him the wealthiest person in the United States. He left $400,000 to establish the Astor Library, now part of New York City Public Library.

Glenn L. Swygart

SEE ALSO: Capitalism and resource exploitation; Endangered Species Act; Forests; United States; Wildlife.

Athabasca oil sands

CATEGORY: Energy resources

WHERE FOUND

The Athabasca oil sands are located in the Athabascan basin of northeastern Alberta, Canada, near the Saskatchewan border. The Athabasca River runs through the region—hence its name. With two smaller oil sand deposits located elsewhere in the province, Alberta has a total of about 140,200 square kilometers of oil sands, the largest quantity in the world. There are also oil sands located outside Canada, primarily in Venezuela.

PRIMARY USES

With industrial processes, bitumen can be extracted from the oil sands and upgraded into light crude oil. Although the First Nations (Canadian aborigines) used the tarlike substance to waterproof and patch their boats, in modern times the oil sands have one commercial use: the production of crude oil. To produce crude oil, an energy-intensive process is required to extract the bitumen from the thick, sludgy, sandy substance. Bitumen is a heavy, viscous oil that can be industrially upgraded into synthetic crude oil, which in turn is refined into gasoline and diesel fuels.

TECHNICAL DEFINITION

The Athabasca oil sands consist of a tarlike mixture of about 80 to 85 percent sand and rich mineral clays, 10 to 12 percent bitumen, and 4 to 6 percent water. The valuable resource in this mixture is the bitumen. Bitumen is a heavy, black, asphaltlike substance that has been pressurized underground for millions of years but not long enough to be concentrated into coal or light sweet crude oil. Nonetheless, it is a form of crude oil that can be processed for commercial use. Technically, bitumen is a mix of petroleum hydrocarbons with a density greater than 960 kilograms per cubic meter.

DESCRIPTION, DISTRIBUTION, AND FORMS

Oil sands are a viscous mix of hydrocarbons and can be found throughout the world but most prevalently in Alberta, Canada. While the Athabasca region has the largest quantity of oil sands, and the only surface quantities, there are also deposits buried in the Peace River and Cold Lake regions of Alberta. (Although the United States has some oil sand deposits, it also has massive quantities of oil shale, rocklike formations containing crude oil that can also be refined at high industrial cost.) The oil sands contain a mix of sands, clays, water, and bitumen, but the bitumen, a form of heavy crude oil, is what gives oil sands their distinctive properties. Many ancient cultures made use of bitumen for its sticky, adhesive qualities. It was used as a sealant for boats, a building mortar, and an ingredient for mummification. In modern times, bitumen is valuable as a crude oil that can be refined into commercial petroleum. The Athabasca basin has the largest reserves of naturally occurring bitumen in the world. Semisolid at normal temperatures, the bitumen must be heated or diluted with hydrocarbons to make it flow through supply pipelines. The bitumen is extracted through a steam separation process. Hot water is injected into the mined oil sands, causing the bitumen to float to the surface, where it can be recovered. The bitumen is then upgraded into synthetic oil and petroleum products.

HISTORY

The First Nations knew about the oil sands deposits from ancient times and used the tarlike material to bind their canoes. Early Canadian explorers such as Peter Pond and Alexander Mackenzie wrote of the fluid bitumen pooling near the Athabasca River. In 1882, geologist Robert Bell surveyed the basin and oil fields. However, oil production did not become possible until Karl Clark first developed a process for separating the bitumen from the sands. Clark's process, developed between 1922 and 1929, relied on hot water and steam to turn the sand into a soupy substance from which the bitumen could be extracted. In 1930, the Canadian government leased a large portion of the Athabasca basin for development to petroleum engineer Max Ball and his Abasand Oils company. Abasand's separation process was primitive, however, and even by the 1940's Abasand processed less than 20,000 metric tons of sand per year.

The technological challenges of extraction remained daunting, but in the 1960's the Great Canadian Oil Sands (GCOS) company built the first large-scale oil sands production plant, capable of producing about 24,000 barrels of synthetic crude oil per day. GCOS eventually became the Suncor Oil Company, which remains the leading oil producer in the Athabasca region. In 1978, prompted by the oil embargoes of the 1970's, the Syncrude consortium of oil companies built a second major oil sands plant, followed by Imperial Oil's Cold Lake plant in 1987, Alsands Project Group's facility in 1988, and Shell's Albian Sands mine in 2003. In the twenty-first century, oil production increased, with new technologies reducing the cost of bitumen extraction. Dozens of oil companies and industrial consortiums opened plants and increased supply. The proven feasibility of oil sands production led the U.S. Department of Energy to tabulate 32 trillion liters of oil reserves in the basin, second only to the reserves of Saudi Arabia.

OBTAINING OIL SANDS

The bulk of the oil sands are located near the surface and can be obtained through massive open-pit mining operations. Because of the heavy mineral clays that make up most of the sand, the operations use the largest shovels and trucks in the world to dig up and move the sands. Deposits that are located deeper—below 75 meters—are recovered by in situ methods, which include cyclic steam stimulation and steam-assisted gravity drainage. About 75 percent of the valuable resource, the bitumen, is obtained during the recovery. After the sand is processed and the bitumen removed, Canadian environmental laws require the processed sand to be returned to the pit and the site restored to its original condition.

USES OF OIL SANDS

The Athabasca oil sands represent one of the great oil reservoirs in the world. Containing a potential 300 billion barrels of crude oil, the oil sands of Alberta, representing 15 percent of the world's oil, are second only to Saudi Arabia as potential oil reserves. There are currently four thousand agreements in Alberta between Canadian governments and oil companies for production of oil. More than 1 million barrels of oil are produced a day. Because of the thickness of the oil sands, it takes a tremendous amount of energy to produce oil flow. In the winter, temperatures in the Athabasca region fall to as low as −40° Celsius and the extraction machinery can easily freeze up and break down. Massive amounts of surface material are moved, sifted, and heated. Thus, two major issues must be addressed for the world to exploit this resource: first, the high cost of extraction and, second, the impact on the environment.

The profitability of the oil sands depends directly on the price of oil. While light crude oil flows easily from conventional oil wells, oil sand producers must expend fixed costs for mining and extracting the bitumen and converting it to liquid crude. Thus the oil sands may be profitable if the price of oil is more than fifty dollars per barrel, for example, but noncompetitive below fifty dollars per barrel and completely unfeasible below thirty dollars. With new technology, production costs have been lowered to about thirty-three to thirty-seven dollars per barrel, spurring an oil sands boom. As to the environment, the massive processing of oil sands is bound to leave a certain scarring of the earth, despite Canadian restoration legislation. Oil sands production releases carbon dioxide, which is believed to contribute to the greenhouse effect. The recovery of bitumen itself requires the consumption of tremendous amounts of resources, mostly in the form of natural gas and water.

In 2003, with the rise of oil prices, the oil sands operation became consistently profitable for the first time, and the three major mines—Suncor, Syncrude Consortium, and Shell Canada—began producing about 1.2 million barrels of synthetic crude oil per day. It was estimated that production could grow within a decade to more than 3 million barrels per day, making Canada one of the world's leading oil-producing countries in the world. The oil companies engaged in the major production of oil from the Athabasca region include Suncor, Imperial Oil, Petro Canada, Marathon, Chevron, Occidental Petroleum, Canadian Natural Resources, Shell Canada, EnCana, British Petroleum, Husky, Total, UTS, Teck, Conoco Philips, Japan Canada Oil, Devon Energy, and various joint ventures. Cumulative investment in oil sands production in the first decade of the twenty-first century was estimated to be about $70 billion, resulting in about 275,000 jobs. As of 2009, royalties to the Canadian government were close to $3 billion a year and oil sands production accounted for about 44 percent of Canada's total output of crude oil.

Howard Bromberg

FURTHER READING

Breen, David. *Alberta's Petroleum Industry and the Conservation Board.* Edmonton: University of Alberta Press, 1993.

Chastko, Paul. *Developing Alberta's Oil Sands: From Karl Clark to Kyoto.* Calgary: University of Calgary Press, 2004.

Comfort, Darlene. *The Abasand Fiasco: The Rise and Fall of a Brave Pioneer Oil Sands Extraction Plant.* Fort McMurray, Alta.: Jubilee Committee, 1980.

Ferguson, Barry Glen. *Athabasca Oil Sands: Northern Resource Exploration, 1875-1951.* Edmonton: Alberta Culture, 1985.

Hicks, Brian, and Chris Nelder. *Profit from the Peak: The End of Oil and the Greatest Investment Event of the Century.* New York: John Wiley & Sons, 2008.

Nikiforuk, Andrew. *The Tar Sands: Dirty Oil and the Future of a Continent.* Vancouver: Greystone, 2009.

Tertzakian, Peter. *A Thousand Barrels a Second: The Coming Oil Break Point and the Challenges Facing an Energy Dependent World.* New York: McGraw-Hill, 2006.

WEB SITE

ATHABASCA OIL SANDS CORP.
http://www.aosc.com/

SEE ALSO: Canada; Oil and natural gas distribution; Oil and natural gas drilling and wells; Oil shale and tar sands; Petroleum refining and processing.

Atmosphere

CATEGORY: Ecological resources

The atmosphere is the envelope of gases that surrounds Earth. Held in place by the attractive force of gravity, Earth's atmosphere pervades all facets of the environment. Almost every aspect of Earth's system is dependent upon or markedly influenced by the behavior of weather systems spawned within the atmosphere. The atmosphere provides resources in the form of individual gases, which can be separated industrially; it also directly affects other resources, most notably food resources.

BACKGROUND

The composition of the atmosphere (excluding water vapor) below 80 kilometers is about 78 percent nitrogen and 21 percent oxygen by volume (76 percent nitrogen, 23 percent oxygen by mass). The remaining 1 percent includes all other dry gases, chiefly argon, carbon dioxide, neon, helium, krypton, hydrogen, and ozone. Water vapor, the most variable constituent of the atmosphere, typically occupies between 0 percent and 4 percent of the atmospheric volume. This mixture of gases is commonly referred to as "air."

The two principal constituents of air are greatly dissimilar in their chemical properties. While oxygen is an extremely active chemical, reacting with many substances, nitrogen reacts only under limited conditions. The inert nature of nitrogen is believed to be the reason it came to be the atmosphere's most abundant constituent. Volcanic outgassing in Earth's early history is the likely source of its present atmosphere. Though nitrogen is a minor component of volcanic emissions, the lack of chemical reactions able to remove it from the atmosphere allowed its concentration to grow dramatically over time. Photosynthesis and, to a lesser degree, photodissociation of water by sunlight are believed to account for atmospheric oxygen.

Carbon dioxide, a principal constituent of volcanic emissions, is also released into the atmosphere by the oceans, respiration, and fossil fuel combustion. Argon, far more abundant in Earth's atmosphere than any of the other noble (inert) gases, is a by-product of the radioactive decay of an isotope of potassium. Helium is also mainly a by-product of radioactive decay.

VERTICAL STRUCTURE

The atmosphere has a well-defined lower boundary but extends indefinitely away from the Earth; at 30,000 kilometers molecules are no longer effectively held in orbit by gravity. The atmosphere can be thought of as a series of layers. However, the layering is far subtler than what may be found in, for example, a geologic formation. The most common method of demarcating layers is to examine the average change of temperature as a function of elevation. Earth's surface, warmed by the absorption of solar radiation, conducts heat into the lowest portion of the atmosphere. This lowest layer, known as the troposphere, extends to about 10 kilometers above the surface and is characterized by temperatures that decrease with height. Virtually all the phenomena that are commonly referred to as "weather" occur in the troposphere. The average density of air at sea level is about 1.225 kilograms per cubic meter. Because air is a compressible fluid, air density decreases logarithmically with height. Half the mass of the atmosphere lies below about 5.5 kilometers. Approximately 80 percent of the atmosphere's mass is found in the troposphere.

Between 10 and 50 kilometers, temperatures increase with increasing altitude in the layer known as the stratosphere. The warming of air in this layer is accounted for by the heat released as ozone molecules absorb ultraviolet wavelengths of solar radiation. Ozone concentration is at a maximum in this layer. Historically, it was thought that there was little exchange of air between the troposphere and stratosphere, except during volcanic and atomic explosions, because temperature profiles such as that found in the stratosphere typically suppress mixing. However, the occurrence of human-made chlorofluorocarbons (CFCs) in the stratosphere is evidence that exchange does take place. The presence of CFCs in the stratosphere is detrimental to ozone and serves as an ozone sink that has no compensating source.

Temperatures once again decrease with increasing height between 50 and 80 kilometers in the mesosphere. The troposphere and stratosphere together account for about 99.9 percent of the atmosphere's mass. The mesosphere contains about 99 percent of the remaining mass.

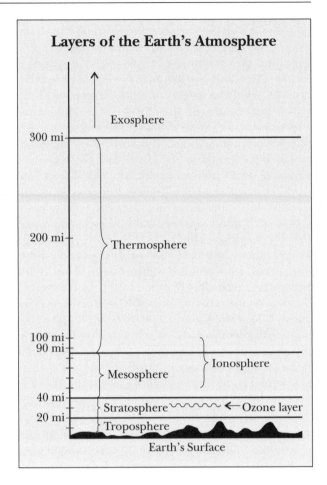

Layers of the Earth's Atmosphere

The thermosphere is situated above the mesosphere and extends indefinitely away from the Earth. Temperatures once again increase with height in this layer and can reach 500 to 2,000 Kelvin depending upon the amount of solar activity. However, temperatures begin to take on a different meaning at these altitudes owing to the relatively small number of molecules and the relatively large mean free path between collisions.

The tops of these four layers are known as the tropopause, stratopause, mesopause, and thermopause, respectively. Temperatures typically remain constant for a few kilometers at the interface of the layers. A feature of note at the tropopause is the jet stream, an especially swift current of air.

The atmosphere can also be partitioned vertically based on how uniformly mixed its constituents are. Turbulent processes in the atmosphere below about 80 kilometers keep the constituents in the lower atmosphere well mixed. This region is known as the homosphere. Air sampled near both the top and bottom of the homosphere will contain nearly equal percentages of each constituent gas, although the densities of the samples will be markedly different. Above 80 kilometers, the vertical mixing of constituents is controlled by molecular diffusion, allowing them to separate by mass, with the lightest gases (hydrogen and helium) present at the highest levels. This region is known as the heterosphere. Sunlight in the heterosphere is more intense than sunlight that penetrates to the homosphere because little filtering has taken place. As a result, ionization occurs in the heterosphere, and this ionization affects the transmittable range of commercially broadcast radio signals that are redirected by the ionized molecules.

BALANCE OF ENERGY

The Sun is the source of nearly all of the energy the atmosphere receives. Minor amounts of energy are contributed by lightning and Earth's internal heat sources. There is a global balance between the solar radiation that heats the atmosphere and the terrestrial radiation emitted to space. However, the balance does not hold for individual latitudes. The complex geometry of a spherical planet having its rotational axis tilted with respect to an elliptical orbit about the Sun results in an imbalance between absorbed and emitted radiation. Over the course of a typical year, the tropical region of the Earth between about 37° north and 37° south latitude receives more energy from the Sun than what is regionally emitted back to space. Poleward of this region, Earth radiates to space more than it receives from the Sun.

As a result of the regional imbalance of energy, there is a continuous transport of energy in the atmosphere and the oceans from the tropical latitudes, where there is a surplus of energy, to the polar latitudes, where there is a deficit. If this transport did not occur, the tropics would continually warm while the polar latitudes would grow colder year after year. The transport of energy by winds and weather systems is most apparent in the middle latitudes of the planet across the interface between the regions of surplus and deficit. In the lower atmosphere the principal forms of the energy are internal energy (associated with the temperature of the air) and latent energy (associated with the phase of water). In the case of the latter, the evaporation of ocean water in the tropics transforms internal energy into latent energy. Water vapor, being a gas and thus highly mobile, is trans-

ported away from the tropics and may subsequently condense to form clouds or dew. Condensation releases an amount of energy equal to that used in evaporation. Evaporation and condensation are first-order processes in Earth's heat budget. In addition, they play key roles in Earth's hydrologic cycle. This cycle purifies and redistributes the planet's single most important compound and the resource without which life would not exist.

THE HYDROLOGIC CYCLE

Though there are approximately 1.3 billion cubic kilometers of water on Earth, about 97 percent of this is ocean water rather than fresh water. Evaporation of ocean water into the atmosphere, its transport by weather systems, and the subsequent condensation in clouds provide life's most precious resource, fresh water, to the continents. The evaporation of water from the oceans and evapotranspiration over land, the transport of water in the atmosphere, and its eventual return to the oceans are collectively known as the hydrologic cycle.

Over the continents, precipitation exceeds evaporation, while the reverse is true over the oceans. Some of the water vapor added to the atmosphere by evaporation from the oceans is transported to the continents, where it combines with water vapor from evapotranspiration, condenses, and falls as precipitation. Some of this precipitation percolates into and becomes part of underground aquifers, or groundwater. Some of the precipitation is returned to the ocean by runoff in rivers. Water vapor is also transported from over the continents to over the oceans in the atmosphere. Generally, water evaporated in one location is not the same water that precipitates on that location. Water vapor is usually transported hundreds or even thousands of kilometers from its source. For example, the majority of water that falls as precipitation on the portion of the United States east of the Rocky Mountains is evaporated off the Gulf of Mexico. Evaporation off the Indian Ocean is the source of the precipitation for the wet Indian monsoon. The hydrologic cycle is rarely completed on a local scale.

Observations indicate that rain and snowfall on the continents is well in excess of the runoff from these same areas. Only about 20 percent of the precipitation that falls on land is returned to the ocean by runoff. While some of the remaining precipitation is stored underground in permeable rock, the majority of the excess is transported back to the oceans by air masses. Cold, dry air masses moving equatorward over land areas are warmed and moistened by evapotranspiration from the surfaces over which they pass. Studies of the change in moisture content of continental polar air moving equatorward over the Mississippi River drainage basin in the United States indicate that these air masses can remove, by evapotranspiration, a quantity of water equal to nine times the average discharge of the Mississippi River. The hydrologic cycle is subject to great disruptions under conditions of short-term or long-term climate change. Examples of such disruptions include floods and droughts.

Resources from the Atmosphere

The atmosphere is a ready source of several gases used in industry and other applications. The industrial use of gases obtained from the atmosphere began in the early years of the twentieth century. The separation of the constituents of air is basically a three-step process. First, impurities are removed. Second, the purified air is liquefied by compression and refrigeration. Third, the individual components are separated by distillation, making use of the fact that each component boils at a different temperature.

Air separation plants produce oxygen, nitrogen, and argon for delivery in both the gaseous and liquid phases. The total mass of the atmosphere is about 5.27×10^{18} kilograms. Given the percentage, by mass, of nitrogen (76 percent) and oxygen (23 percent) in the atmosphere, there are about 1.2×10^{18} kilograms of oxygen and 4.0×10^{18} kilograms of nitrogen available for separation and use.

Gases from the atmosphere are used by the steel industry in the cutting and welding of metals. Other user communities include the aerospace industry, chemical companies, and the medical industry. Liquid nitrogen is used in applications requiring extreme cold. The inert nature of gaseous nitrogen makes it ideal for flushing air out of systems when one also needs to prevent chemical reactions from occurring. The atmosphere also provides a source of argon, neon, krypton, and xenon and is the only known source of several of the rare gases.

The Atmosphere and Human Health

In addition to being a resource itself, the atmosphere has direct and indirect effects on many other resources and on human health. Examples of aspects dependent on atmospheric conditions include the resistance of crops to disease and insects; the health and productivity of forests; milk, wool, and egg production; and meat quality. Biometeorology, also known as bioclimatology, is the branch of atmospheric science concerned with the effects of weather and climate on the health and activity of human beings.

Deaths from heart attacks and heart disease increase when the human body experiences great thermal stress, as in extreme heat or cold or when temperature changes abruptly. Deaths tend to peak in winter in colder climates and in summer in warmer climates.

An example of the devastating effect high temperature can have on human health is the European heat wave of 2003. Temperatures varied from country to country, but France reported seven days that exceeded 40° Celsius. More than 50,000 people died throughout Europe as a result of the aberrant climate. In Switzerland, where temperatures reached 41° Celsius, flash floods occurred because of melting glaciers. The European agricultural industry suffered extensive losses because of this heat wave: In the wake of severe climate, wheat production fell by 20 percent in France and grapes ripened prematurely. The heat wave was caused by an anticyclone, which inhibited precipitation.

Alan C. Czarnetzki

Further Reading

Brimblecombe, Peter. *Air Composition and Chemistry.* 2d ed. New York: Cambridge University Press, 1996.

Frederick, John E. *Principles of Atmospheric Science.* Sudbury, Mass.: Jones and Bartlett 2008.

Griffiths, John F., ed. *Handbook of Agricultural Meteorology.* New York: Oxford University Press, 1994.

Lutgens, Frederick K., and Edward J. Tarbuck. *The Atmosphere: An Introduction to Meteorology.* 11th ed. Upper Saddle River, N.J.: Prentice Hall, 2009.

McElroy, Michael B. *The Atmospheric Environment: Effects of Human Activity.* Princeton, N.J.: Princeton University Press, 2002.

Möller, Detlev, ed. *Atmospheric Environmental Research: Critical Decisions Between Technological Progress and Preservation of Nature.* New York: Springer, 1999.

Simpson, Charles H. *Chemicals from the Atmosphere.* Garden City, N.Y.: Doubleday, 1969.

Somerville, Richard C. J. *The Forgiving Air: Understanding Environmental Change.* 2d ed. Boston: American Meteorological Society, 2008.

Stull, Roland B. *An Introduction to Boundary Layer Meteorology.* Boston: Kluwer Academic 1988.

NATIONAL WEATHER SERVICE, NATIONAL OCEANIC
AND ATMOSPHERIC ADMINISTRATION
The Atmosphere
http://www.srh.noaa.gov/srh/jetstream/atmos/
atmos_intro.htm

SEE ALSO: Air pollution and air pollution control;
Drought; Floods and flood control; Gases, inert or noble; National Oceanic and Atmospheric Administration; Solar energy; Weather and resources; Wind energy.

Atomic energy. *See* Nuclear energy

Atomic Energy Acts

CATEGORIES: Laws and conventions; government
and resources
DATE: Signed August 1, 1946, and August 30, 1954

*The Atomic Energy Acts provided for control of all
atomic research and nuclear material, including the
production of nuclear weapons, by a civilian panel,
the Atomic Energy Commission.*

BACKGROUND
The Atomic Energy Act of 1946 was signed by President Harry S. Truman on August 1, 1946. Prior to this
act, the Manhattan Engineering District, the military-
controlled organization that developed and produced
the atomic bombs used in World War II, controlled all
nuclear research and production in the United States.
The Atomic Energy Act replaced the Manhattan Engineering District with a civilian-controlled agency, the
Atomic Energy Commission, consisting of a chairper-
son and four commissioners appointed by the president and confirmed by the Senate.

PROVISIONS
The Atomic Energy Act of 1946 gave the commission
broad authority over atomic research and the production and use of fissionable materials, effectively transferring control over the development and production
of nuclear weapons from the military to a civilian
agency. The Atomic Energy Commission supervised
the development of the "hydrogen bomb," the high-

powered successor to the atomic bomb.
The act restricted sharing of information on nuclear research with foreign governments and made
no provision for private ownership of nuclear facilities in the United States. By the early 1950's, important civilian uses of atomic energy were recognized.
Nuclear power plants capable of generating large
amounts of electric power were envisioned, medical
uses of radioactive isotopes had been developed, and
American industry was eager to play a role in the commercialization of nuclear technology. On an international level, in 1953, President Dwight D. Eisenhower
proposed his Atoms for Peace program to the United
Nations General Assembly. Under this program the
United States would share its knowledge regarding
the civilian applications of nuclear technology with
the rest of the world.
To implement this program, Eisenhower proposed
revisions to the Atomic Energy Act. The new Atomic
Energy Act, signed by the president on August 30,
1954, allowed, for the first time, private ownership of
atomic facilities under licenses from the Atomic Energy Commission. It also permitted the release of
information, previously kept secret, on the design of
nuclear power reactors. These provisions allowed electric power companies to own and operate nuclear
power generating plants. The first such plant went
into operation at Shippingport, Pennsylvania, in 1957,
producing 60,000 kilowatts of power. By 1985, the
electric power industry in the United States was operating ninety-three nuclear power plants, more than
any other nation in the world.

IMPACT ON RESOURCE USE
United States participation in the Atoms for Peace
program resulted in the use of atomic materials in industry, agriculture, and medicine around the world.
By the mid-1960's, fifteen nuclear power reactors had
been constructed in other nations, and an information exchange between the United States and Canada
resulted in the development of the heavy water nuclear reactor, a design that operates on natural uranium rather than uranium enriched in the uranium-
235 isotope, which is used in atomic bombs.

George J. Flynn

SEE ALSO: Atomic Energy Commission; Edison Electric Institute; Manhattan Project; Nuclear energy; Nuclear Energy Institute; Plutonium; Three Mile Island
nuclear accident; Uranium.

Atomic Energy Commission

CATEGORY: Organizations, agencies, and programs
DATE: Established 1946

The Atomic Energy Commission was a civilian agency of the United States government responsible for administration and regulation of all aspects of the production and use of atomic and nuclear power from 1946 to 1974.

BACKGROUND

In July, 1945, an interim committee formed by President Harry S. Truman drafted legislation to establish a peacetime organization similar to the Manhattan Project. This proposed legislation, the May-Johnson bill, proposed a nine-member part-time board of commissioners that included a significant military contingent and continued government control over atomic research and development. The bill was opposed by most U.S. atomic scientists because it established military control over research and would thereby stifle the free exchange of ideas. In late 1945, as support for the May-Johnson bill collapsed, Senator Brien McMahon introduced substitute legislation with reduced security requirements and diminished military involvement. This bill was signed into law by President Truman on August 1, 1946. The McMahon Act, officially the Atomic Energy Act (AEA) of 1946, transferred control over atomic research and development from the Army to the Atomic Energy Commission (AEC), which consisted of a five-member full-time civilian board assisted by general advisory and military liaison committees.

IMPACT ON RESOURCE USE

While the main mission of the AEC was to ensure national defense and security, the Atomic Energy Act also called for the development of atomic energy for improving the public welfare, increasing the standard of living, strengthening free enterprise, and promoting world peace. The commission was also authorized to establish health and safety regulations for possessing and using fissionable materials and their by-products.

In 1953, President Dwight Eisenhower's famous "atoms for peace" speech to the United Nations called for the development of peaceful applications of atomic energy, and in particular for nuclear reactors that would produce power. This goal required eliminating the AEC's monopoly on nuclear research; Congress passed the Atomic Energy Act of 1954, which continued the AEC's role as sole regulator of nuclear activities, allowed licensing of privately owned facilities for production of fissionable materials, and imposed several safety and health requirements. To transfer technology from government to private industry, the AEC established the Power Demonstration Reactor Program, under which industries designed, constructed, owned, and operated power reactors with financial and other assistance from the AEC.

As the nuclear power industry grew during the 1960's, the Atomic Energy Commission came under increasing criticism for an inherent conflict of interest in its roles as promoter of nuclear power and regulator of environmental and reactor safety. At the end of the decade, the growing environmental movement charged that AEC regulations, which addressed only potential radiological hazards to public health and safety, were not consistent with the National Environmental Policy Act (NEPA) of 1970. In 1971, courts ruled that the commission was required to assess environmental hazards beyond radiation effects, such as thermal pollution. More stringent licensing requirements increased the costs associated with new reactor construction. The commission was simultaneously faced with the growing problem of disposal of high-level radioactive waste.

Under the Energy Reorganization Act of 1974, the AEC was abolished. The Nuclear Regulatory Commission (NRC) was created to handle commercial aspects of nuclear energy, while responsibility for research and development and the production of fissionable materials was transferred to the Energy Research and Development Administration.

Michael K. Rulison

WEB SITES

U.S. DEPARTMENT OF ENERGY
About the Department of Energy: Origins and
    Evolution of the Department of Energy
http://www.energy.gov/about/origins.htm

U.S. DEPARTMENT OF ENERGY
Office of Science: The Atomic Energy Commissions
    (AEC), 1947
http://www.ch.doe.gov/html/site_info/
    atomic_energy.htm

SEE ALSO: Atomic Energy Acts; Energy economics; Manhattan Project; Nuclear energy; Nuclear Regulatory Commission; Nuclear waste and its disposal; Plutonium; Thermal pollution and thermal pollution control; Uranium.

Australia

CATEGORIES: Countries; government and resources

Australia is the world's largest net exporter of coal, accounting for 29 percent of global coal exports. In addition, Australia's other mineral resources, climatic resources, and hence the resources provided by the soils and the associated agricultural products are significant in the global economy. These include wool (mainly from sheep); meat products from beef, sheep, and lamb; crops such as cotton, pineapples, sugarcane, wheat, corn, and oats; and a flourishing wine industry.

THE COUNTRY

Australia, in the area called Oceania, is a continent between the Indian Ocean and the South Pacific Ocean. Its Aboriginal people are thought to have arrived from Southeast Asia during the last ice age, at least fifty thousand years ago. At the time of European discovery and settlement, up to one million Aboriginal people lived across the continent as hunters and gatherers. They were scattered in 300 clans and spoke 250 languages and 700 dialects. Each clan had a spiritual connection with a specific piece of land but also traveled widely to trade, find water and seasonal produce, and conduct ritual and totemic gatherings. Despite the diversity of their homelands—from Outback deserts and tropical rain forests to snow-capped mountains—Aboriginal people all shared a belief in the timeless, magical realm of the "Dreamtime." These spirit ancestors continue to connect natural phenomena—as well as past, present, and future—through every aspect of Aboriginal culture and resources.

European settlers arrived in 1788. These settlers took advantage of the continent's natural resources to develop agricultural and the manufacturing industries. Australia transformed itself into an internationally competitive, advanced market economy based on the vast quantities of natural resources, particularly mineral resources. Described in 1964 by author Donald Horne as "The Lucky Country," Australia is ranked about twentieth in the world in terms of gross domestic product, twenty-ninth in terms of oil production, twenty-fifth in terms of exports, and sixteenth in terms of electricity production. Australia's economic demonstrated resources (EDRs) of zinc, lead, nickel, mineral sands (ilmenite, rutile, zircon), tantalum, and uranium remain the world's largest. In addition, bauxite, black coal, brown coal, copper, gold, iron ore, lithium, manganese ore, niobium, silver, and industrial diamond rank in the top six worldwide.

Long-term concerns include climate-change issues, such as the depletion of the ozone layer, more frequent droughts, and management and conservation of coastal areas, especially the Great Barrier Reef. Only 6 percent of the land is arable, including 27 million hectares of cultivated grassland. Permanent crops occupy only 0.04 percent of the total land area. Australia is the world's smallest continent but its sixth-largest country in terms of population, which is concentrated along the eastern and southeastern coasts. The city of Perth, on the west coast of Australia, is one of the most isolated cities in the world. Of the total population of Australia, 89 percent is urban.

MINERALS

Minerals have had a tremendous impact on Australia's human history and patterns of settlement. Alluvial gold (gold sediments deposited by rivers and streams) spurred several gold rushes in the 1850's and set the stage for Australia's present demographic patterns. Beginning around the time of World War II, there has been almost a continuous run of mineral discoveries, including gold, bauxite, iron, and manganese reserves as well as opals, sapphires, and other precious stones.

The Australian minerals industry is an industry of considerable size and economic and social significance, benefiting all Australians both directly and indirectly. The mining and minerals-processing sectors underpin vitally important supply-and-demand relationships with the Australian manufacturing, construction, banking and financial, process engineering, property, and transport sectors.

Australia is the world's largest exporter of black coal, iron ore, and gold. It also holds the status of the leading producer of bauxite and alumina (the oxide

Australia: Resources at a Glance

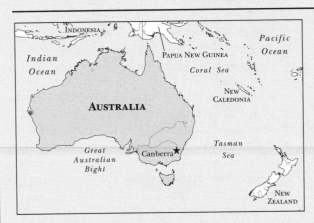

Official name: Commonwealth of Australia
Government: Federal parliamentary democracy and Commonwealth realm
Capital city: Canberra
Area: 2,989,119 mi^2; 7,741,220 km^2
Population (2009 est.): 21,262,641
Language: English
Monetary unit: Australian dollar (AUD)

ECONOMIC SUMMARY:

GDP composition by sector (2008 est.): agriculture, 3.4%; industry, 26.8%; services, 69.8%
Natural resources: bauxite, coal, iron ore, copper, tin, gold, silver, uranium, nickel, tungsten, mineral sands, lead, zinc, diamonds, natural gas, petroleum (largest net exporter of coal, accounting for 29% of global coal exports)
Land use (2005): arable land, 6.15% (includes about 27 million hectares of cultivated grassland); permanent crops, 0.04%; other, 93.81%
Industries: mining, industrial and transportation equipment, food processing, chemicals, steel
Agricultural products: wheat, barley, sugarcane, fruits, cattle, sheep, poultry
Exports (2008 est.): $190.2 billion
Commodities exported: coal, iron ore, gold, meat, wool, alumina, wheat, machinery and transport equipment
Imports (2008 est.): $193.3 billion
Commodities imported: machinery and transport equipment, computers and office machines, telecommunication equipment and parts, crude oil and petroleum products
Labor force (2008 est.): 11.25 million
Labor force by occupation (2005 est.): agriculture, 3.6%; industry, 21.1%; services, 75%

ENERGY RESOURCES:

Electricity production (2007 est.): 244.2 billion kWh
Electricity consumption (2006 est.): 220 billion kWh
Electricity exports (2007 est.): 0 kWh
Electricity imports (2007 est.): 0 kWh

Natural gas production (2007 est.): 43.62 billion m^3
Natural gas consumption (2007 est.): 29.4 billion m^3
Natural gas exports (2007 est.): 19.91 billion m^3
Natural gas imports (2007 est.): 5.689 billion m^3
Natural gas proved reserves (Jan. 2008 est.): 849.5 billion m^3

Oil production (2008 est.): 600,000 bbl/day
Oil imports (2005): 615,000 bbl/day
Oil proved reserves (Jan. 2008 est.): 1.5 billion bbl

Source: Data from *The World Factbook 2009.* Washington, D.C.: Central Intelligence Agency, 2009.
Notes: Data are the most recent tracked by the CIA. Values are given in U.S. dollars. Abbreviations: bbl/day = barrels per day; GDP = gross domestic product; km^2 = square kilometers; kWh = kilowatt-hours; m^3 = cubic meters; mi^2 = square miles.

form of aluminum, Al_2O_3); the second largest producer of uranium, lead, and zinc; the third largest producer of iron ore, nickel, manganese, and gold; the fourth largest producer of black coal, silver, and copper; and the fifth largest producer of aluminum. However, only a handful of major discoveries were made in the late twentieth century. In an attempt to reverse this trend, mining companies stepped up exploration efforts both in existing areas of mineralization and in areas that had attracted limited exploration investment. Mineral exploration expenditure in 2006-2007 was $1.7 billion Australian (about $1.4 billion U.S.).

In addition, the mining industry directly and indirectly employs some 320,000 Australians (many of whom are in sparsely populated, remote regions of Australia) and is responsible for significant infrastructure development. For example, starting in 1967, the mineral industry built twenty-six towns, established twelve ports, created additional port bulk-handling infrastructure at many existing ports, built twenty-five airfields, and laid more than 2,000 kilometers of railway line.

The Australian government, through the agency Geoscience Australia, has helped to limit the risk associated with mineral exploration by developing a greater understanding of the geological makeup of the continent. The agency has begun a program to look below the surface at the geological architecture of the Earth's crust far beneath some of Australia's most significant mineral provinces and in areas that geologists believe hold the potential for major mineral deposits. This approach, which uses techniques such as deep seismic surveys, gravity surveys, and airborne electromagnetic surveys, can be expected to increase the opportunities for new mineral discoveries significantly. This heightened interest, combined with the continuing passion among Australian miners and the dedication of geologists and other scientists in the various geosciences, will ensure that Australia has a mining heritage for many years to come.

COAL

Mining in Australia dates back thousands of years, but the country's first truly commercial mining venture was at Newcastle in 1799, when coal (discovered by a convict, William Bryant) was exported to Bengal. This coal resource led to the establishment of a penal settlement at what was then known as "Coal River" in 1801. From those humble beginnings, Newcastle developed into a major metropolitan center and Australia became one of the largest coal producers in the world. Production of raw black coal reached a total of 398 million metric tons in 2006 and created exports worth around $23 billion Australian (about $19 billion U.S.).

Coal has become Australia's major mineral export and accounts for nearly 25 percent of Australia's export earnings. Australia is the world's fourth largest coal producer, producing 391 million metric tons of coal in 2007. Australia is also the world's largest net exporter of coking and steaming coal. According to the 2008 British Petroleum (BP) Statistical Energy Survey, Australia had, at the end of 2007, coal reserves of 76,600 million metric tons—9.03 percent of the world total.

Almost all of Australia's export production coal deposits are located in Permian-age sediments (250 million years old) in the Bowen basin in Queensland and the Hunter Valley basins in New South Wales. Western Australia has some producing mines south of Perth. Australia also has reserves of lower-grade lignite coal, located in Victoria. Coal is exported from nine terminals at seven ports along the east coast.

Australia's coal industry is dominated by four companies: BHP Billiton, Anglo American (UK), Rio Tinto (Australia-UK), and Xstrata (Switzerland). BHP Billiton is the world's largest supplier of seaborne-traded hard coking coal from its predominantly open-cut mines at its low-cost asset base in Queensland and New South Wales. BHP's Mt Arthur coal, located in the Upper Hunter region of New South Wales, produces about 20 million metric tons of raw energy coal per annum at full production.

The company Xstrata, which is the world's largest exporter of thermal coal, exports around 80 percent of its Australian thermal coal production to major power companies in the Pacific region, including companies in Japan, South Korea, Taiwan, and Mexico. Coal properties owned by Rio Tinto produce low-sulfur steam coal for electricity generating stations, metallurgical coking coal for iron and steel mills, and coal for international trade from nine properties mainly located in Queensland and New South Wales. Anglo Coal Australia is one of Australia's leading coal producers, with extensive coal-mining interests and prospects. Anglo Coal Australia operates five mines in Queensland and one in New South Wales.

NICKEL

The Western Australian shield is rich in nickel deposits. They were first discovered near Kalgoorlie in south Western Australia in 1964. Small quantities of platinum and palladium have been extracted side-by-side with nickel reserves. About 99 percent of Australia's nickel is produced in Western Australia, supplying about 13 percent of world production. The state produces more than 140,000 metric tons of nickel, valued at $1 billion Australian (about $830,000 U.S.).

Until 1998, only sulfide ores were used for nickel extraction. These are deep and associated with volcanic rock. New projects use laterite ores (oxides), which are cheaper to mine because of new technologies, including high-temperature and high-pressure acid leaching, ion exchange, and electrowinning to produce an almost pure (99.8 percent) nickel at one site. These developments shifted the center of world production away from Canada to Australia.

URANIUM

Beginning in the 1930's, the Australian uranium industry has developed substantially, making Australia one of the world's major producers and exporters of uranium. Australia's vast, low-cost uranium resources make the country the top-ranked nation in the world with more than 1.3 million metric tons of known recoverable resources. In fact, Australia has 1.4 times the uranium resources, and 2.6 times the quantity of recoverable resources, of Kazakhstan. Australia's uranium resources are also known for having a relatively low cost of extraction compared to that of other nations.

The resources are distributed in a fairly clustered manner throughout Australia, with three-quarters of the known and inferred resources found in South Australia and more specifically at the Olympic Dam, the world's largest deposit. Other significant resources have been found in Northern Territory, Queensland, and Western Australia. Australia's uranium is exported only to countries that have committed to nuclear safeguard agreements.

GOLD

Gold production in Australia, which was very important in the past, has declined from a peak production of 4 million fine ounces in 1904 to several hundred thousand fine ounces today. Most of the gold is extracted from the Kalgoorlie-Norseman area of Western Australia.

OPALS AND OTHER PRECIOUS STONES

Australia is well known for its precious stones, particularly white and black opals from South Australia and western New South Wales. Sapphires and topaz are mined in Queensland and in the New England District of northeastern New South Wales. The state of South Australia has earned an international reputation as the largest producer of precious opal in the world, and opal was adopted as that state's mineral emblem in September, 1985. The Burra copper mine was once a significant source of gem-quality malachite, and chrysoprase has been produced from Mount Davies. However, only opal and jade are mined commercially, the latter from extensive deposits near Cowell.

Gem-quality or precious opal is distinguished from common opal by a characteristic play of spectral colors. Precious opal is classified according to the body or background colors of the gem and the color pattern. South Australia produces about half of the Australian output of gem opal; the major production fields are Coober Pedy, Mintabie, and Andamooka. Since 1915, the major opal-producing center has been Coober Pedy. The opal workings comprise numerous large fields extending 30 kilometers northwest and 40 kilometers southeast of the town. Mining is carried out by individuals and small syndicates generally equipped with bulldozers, or underground tunneling or bogging machines, in conjunction with pneumatic jackpicks and explosives.

OIL AND NATURAL GAS

The oil and gas industry is an important contributor to the Australian economy and employs around fifteen thousand people. Liquid natural gas (LNG) production and exports have been valued at $5.8 billion Australian (about $4.8 billion U.S.). Australia is the world's twentieth largest producer of natural gas and the sixth largest exporter of LNG. Australia supplies much of its oil consumption needs domestically. The first Australian oil discoveries were in southern Queensland. Australian oil production amounts to about 25 million barrels per year and includes pumping from oil fields off northwestern Australia near Barrow Island, in the southern part of the Northern Territory, and fields in the Bass Strait.

IRON ORE

Australia has billions of metric tons of iron ore reserves. Most of Australia's substantial iron ore re-

Australia's Gladstone Great Barrier Reef at low tide. (De Agostini/Getty Images)

Farming is nevertheless an economically and culturally important part of life in Australia. Many Australians are directly or indirectly involved in farming, and for those not directly involved with farming, the country's rural and agricultural history still has strong links to the heritage and culture of Australia. In the first few decades after Europeans arrived in Australia, farms developed around the early settlements, and farmers grew wheat crops and raised sheep that had originally been imported from Europe.

Government-sponsored exploration during the 1800's opened up new tracts of land, and farmers gradually moved inland and occupied huge areas of pasture. The creation of railways, beginning in the 1850's, began to connect more remote farmers with their markets, making it possible to transport produce to cities and ports more easily and quickly.

The dry climate and infertile soil of Australia presented challenges to farmers from the start, but they quickly determined that the country was well suited for production of high-quality wool. Wool became the cornerstone of Australian agriculture, and Australia is often said to have "ridden on the sheep's back" through the early days of its economic development.

By the early part of the twentieth century, Australia's agricultural production had rapidly increased and output expanded well beyond the needs of the Australian population. This increased production led Australia to become one of the world's major food exporters. Across much of the early twentieth century, the Australian government provided assistance to farmers and primary producers in the form of bounties, to encourage production, employment, and export. The government also placed tariffs on some goods to discourage imports.

The relative importance of farming to the Australian economy decreased in the second half of the twentieth century; at the beginning of the twenty-first century only 3 percent of the country's population was employed in farming. Government assistance has been reduced, and wool is no longer such a significant and valuable commodity. Nevertheless, agriculture remains an important sector for the Australian econ-

serves are in Western Australia, which accounts for 97 percent of the nation's total production. The Pilbara region of Western Australia is particularly significant, with 85 percent of Australia's total identified resources and 92 percent of its production. Locally significant iron-ore mines also operate in the Northern Territory, South Australia, Tasmania, and New South Wales. In 2007, Australia's iron ore production was 299 metric tons, and 267 metric tons were exported. Australia produces about 13 percent of world iron ore and ranks fourth in the world.

AGRICULTURE

Australia's climate can rightly be regarded as a real resource, although in times of drought the climate can be regarded as having a distinctly negative impact on agricultural resources. Rainfall patterns across Australia are highly seasonal and vary considerably from year to year and decade to decade. Compared to the other continental landmasses, Australia is very dry; more than 80 percent of Australia has an annual rainfall of less than 600 millimeters. Because of this aridity, Australia suffers from leached, sandy, and salty soils. The continent's largely arid land and marginal water resources represent challenges for conservation and prudent environmental management. The challenge is to maximize the use of these resources for human beings while preserving ecosystems for animal and plant life.

omy, generating up to $5 billion Australian (about $4 billion U.S.) in gross value each year and employing around 370,000 people across Australia. Farms in Australia have traditionally been family businesses, passed on from generation to generation. However, beginning in the 1950's, international economic factors and changes in farming methods led to larger farms being more economically viable than small ones. The number of farming families in Australia has steadily decreased and the average size of farms has increased.

Different types of farming are concentrated mainly in the areas that suit them best, depending on water availability and climatic conditions. The grazing of livestock (mainly sheep and cattle) takes up the most land in Australian agriculture. Sheep are found primarily in New South Wales, Western Australia, and Victoria. About 90 percent of all cattle are used for beef. Queensland and New South Wales are Australia's main beef cattle producers, with the Northern Territory contributing about 10 percent of the beef cattle market. Dairying occurs mainly in the southern states, predominantly in Victoria.

Crop growing contributes to more than 50 percent of the value of Australian agriculture every year. Wheat and other grain crops are spread fairly evenly across New South Wales, South Australia, Victoria, Western Australia, and Queensland, and sugarcane is a major crop in Queensland and New South Wales. Fruit growing and vegetable growing occur in all states.

OTHER RESOURCES

Australia is also extremely rich in zinc reserves, the principal sources for which are Mount Isa and Mount Morgan in Queensland. The Northern Territory also has lead and zinc mines and vast reserves of bauxite (aluminium ore), near Weipa on the Gulf of Carpenteria and at Gove in Arnhem Land.

W. J. Maunder

FURTHER READING

Browne, G. S. *Australia, a General Account: History, Resources, Production, Social Conditions.* Whitefish, Mont.: Kessinger, 2007.

Halliday, James. *James Halliday's Wine Atlas of Australia.* Prahran, Vic.: Hardie Grant Books, 2009.

Horne, Donald. *The Lucky Country: Australia in the Sixties.* 2d rev. ed. Sydney: Angus & Robertson, 1978.

Malcolm, Bill, et al. *Agriculture in Australia: An Introduction.* New York: Oxford University Press, 2009.

Turner, Lynne, et al. *Where River Meets Sea: Exploring Australia's Estuaries.* Canberra, A.C.T.: CSIRO, 2006.

SEE ALSO: Agricultural products; Agriculture industry; Coal; Copper; Tungsten; Uranium.

Austria

CATEGORIES: Countries; government and resources

While Austria is known for its cultural heritage in terms of classical music, it is also one of the most economically rich countries in Europe and the world. Austria has limited natural resources in terms of fossil fuels, metals, ores, and other raw materials, and many of the resources used for production and consumption have to be imported. However, Austria is rich in renewable resources such as timber and hydropower. Austria is also home to the largest Alpine national park, with many natural habitats and species.

THE COUNTRY

Austria is a small, land-locked country in central Europe, covering the eastern half of the Alps. The country's gross domestic product (GDP) is about 270 billion euros (about $385 billion), with a per-capita income that averages 32,570 euros (about $46,000). Austrian per-capita income therefore ranks among those of the ten richest countries in the world. The Austrian population is concentrated mostly in the eastern lowlands of the country and in some inner-Alpine valleys and basins, with the eastern Alps covering more than two-thirds of the country's area. Of the nation's total area, 47 percent is covered by forests, arable land amounts to about 17 percent, and high alpine mountains and rocks cover more than 10 percent. About 38 percent of the land is permanent settlement area.

LAND USE

Forests are the most important land cover in Austria, occupying 47 percent. Forest growth has been on the rise, because marginal soils have been covered again by trees, while in densely populated areas forests have been increasingly pushed back. Dense agriculture can be found in about one-third of the land area. Of Austria's total area, about 3 percent (2,300 square kilome-

Austria: Resources at a Glance

Official name: Republic of Austria
Government: Federal republic
Capital city: Vienna
Area: 31,999 mi²; 82,871 km²
Population (2009 est.): 8,210,281
Language: German
Monetary unit: euro (EUR)

ECONOMIC SUMMARY:

GDP composition by sector (2008 est.): agriculture, 1.9%; industry, 30.7%; services, 67.4%
Natural resources: oil, coal, lignite, timber, iron ore, copper, zinc, antimony, magnesite, tungsten, graphite, salt, hydropower
Land use (2005): arable land, 16.59%; permanent crops, 0.85%; other, 82.56%
Industries: construction, machinery, vehicles and parts, food, metals, chemicals, lumber and wood processing, paper and paperboard, communications equipment, tourism
Agricultural products: grains, potatoes, sugar beets, wine, fruit, dairy products, cattle, pigs, poultry, lumber
Exports (2008 est.): $163.6 billion
Commodities exported: machinery and equipment, motor vehicles and parts, paper and paperboard, metal goods, chemicals, iron and steel, textiles, foodstuffs
Imports (2008 est.): $168.9 billion
Commodities imported: machinery and equipment, motor vehicles, chemicals, metal goods, oil and oil products, foodstuffs
Labor force (2008 est.): 3.633 million
Labor force by occupation (2005 est.): agriculture, 5.5%; industry, 27.5%; services, 67%

ENERGY RESOURCES:

Electricity production (2007 est.): 59.31 billion kWh
Electricity consumption (2006 est.): 62.35 billion kWh
Electricity exports (2007 est.): 18.47 billion kWh
Electricity imports (2007 est.): 28.5 billion kWh

Natural gas production (2007 est.): 1.848 billion m³
Natural gas consumption (2007 est.): 8.436 billion m³
Natural gas exports (2007 est.): 2.767 billion m³
Natural gas imports (2007 est.): 9.658 billion m³
Natural gas proved reserves (Jan. 2008 est.): 16.14 billion m³

Oil production (2007 est.): 24,920 bbl/day
Oil imports (2005): 313,500 bbl/day
Oil proved reserves (Jan. 2008 est.): 50 million bbl

Source: Data from *The World Factbook 2009.* Washington, D.C.: Central Intelligence Agency, 2009.
Notes: Data are the most recent tracked by the CIA. Values are given in U.S. dollars. Abbreviations: bbl/day = barrels per day; GDP = gross domestic product; km² = square kilometers; kWh = kilowatt-hours; m³ = cubic meters; mi² = square miles.

ters) is sealed for buildings, of which 70 percent are for residential and 30 percent for commercial purposes. In total, 4,400 square kilometers are sealed for construction and transportation purposes.

Additionally, 12 to 15 hectares per day are currently sealed for residential and transportation purposes, totaling more than 50 square kilometers per year. New industrial zones, residential areas, and transport infrastructure in particular (roads) are the main causes for sealing the land. There has been an increasing conflict between newly developed areas and areas valuable for nature conservation (habitats for fauna and flora).

The Austrian Sustainability Strategy presented by the Austrian government in 2002 aimed at reducing the "consumption" of areas to 1 hectare per day. The main reasons for area consumption are expansion of construction and transportation due to changing lifestyles, income growth, large shopping malls and commercial areas at the outskirts of the cities, and lack of consistent zoning and spatial planning. Together with other area-consuming or -using activities—such as agriculture, forestry, and sports (golf and skiing)—only small patches of Austrian mountains and forests have remained undeveloped. With the sealing of large areas, the ecological functions of soil are reduced. While the quality of Austrian soils is generally good, there is some environmental pressure in terms of pollution and erosion.

MATERIALS EXTRACTION AND CONSUMPTION

While domestic extraction is significant in the sector of nonmetallic minerals such as sand, gravel, and other construction materials—about 83 million metric tons annually—imports are low, at about 9.6 percent, because of the high transport costs relative to the price of the product. Domestic production of fossil fuels is also low compared to total consumption. Therefore, Austria has to import much of its fossil fuel. About 2.7 million metric tons are extracted domestically, while imports amount to more than 36 million metric tons.

Austria's materials consumption increased in the first decade of the twenty-first century. In terms of the direct material input (DMI), the Austrian economy used 200 million metric tons of materials in 2006. Measured by the domestic materials consumption (DMC), Austria consumes 158 million metric tons of materials. Minerals and construction materials amount to about 83 million metric tons, while fossil fuels account for around 41 million metric tons. Around 36 million metric tons of biomass are consumed by the Austrian economy. These figures correspond to an annual per-capita consumption of materials of roughly 19 million metric tons, representing a significant increase from 14.5 million metric tons in 1970. While most of the construction materials and biomass are extracted domestically at a mostly constant level, the major share of fossil fuels is imported. Relative to GDP, around 1 kilogram of materials is consumed per euro of GDP, meaning resource productivity in terms of GDP per kilogram of material inputs is also about 1 euro per kilogram. While the use of biomass stays about constant, the growth of materials consumption can be attributed to the large increase in the use of fossil fuels and construction materials. Beginning in 1970, Austrian materials consumption rose annually by 1.5 to 2.1 percent. While the DMC increased to a smaller extent, the growth in material inputs (DMI) was mainly the result of importing materials for producing export goods, especially in the metal-producing sectors. The growth of materials consumption is mainly determined by increases in income (GDP). For most material groups, especially fossil fuels and construction materials, income growth in general and the growth of the production of energy- and material-intensive export sectors are the main driving forces. After the oil price shock in the mid-1970's, material intensity decreased by roughly 20 percent but stayed rather constant beginning in the mid-1990's. Policies focusing on reducing material inputs and consumption are included in the Austrian Sustainability Strategy aiming at stabilizing materials consumption in the short run and increasing resource productivity by a factor of 4 in the long run.

BIODIVERSITY

Biodiversity as defined by the United Nations Convention on Biological Diversity comprises diversity within and between species and ecosystems (habitats, landscapes). In Austria, species (fauna and flora) as well as habitats are protected by provincial, national, and international (especially European Union) law. On a national scale, 33 percent of plant species are threatened, while an additional 21 percent are locally endangered. Of particular concern are lichen species; more than 60 percent are threatened. About 10 percent of vertebrate species are threatened. Only about one-third of mammals, birds, and fish are listed on the International Union for Conservation of Nature (IUCN) Red List of Threatened Species, category "least concern." More than 60 percent of reptile species are threatened. Species loss is mainly because of habitat loss, devaluation, and fragmentation. For instance, 83 percent of wetlands and 57 percent of forest ecosystems are endangered.

Protected areas are established on an area of 31,019 square kilometers, corresponding to 37 percent of the Austrian territory. This area includes 6 national parks (according to the IUCN's category II definition), 403 nature conservation areas, 248 protected landscapes, and 111 European conservation zones. More than 200 of these protected areas are also part of the European Union's network of protected areas. Austria supported the European Union's goal of reducing biodiversity loss by 2010.

Timber
About 47 percent of Austrian territory is covered with forests (39,600 square kilometers out of 83,872

square kilometers). Therefore, timber is a significant natural resource in Austria. However, because of the mountainous regions of the eastern Alps and the partially cold climate, not all forests can be economically managed for timber production. Timber production is generally an important use of forests. Equally important is erosion control and protection of settlements from landslides and avalanches on the steep slopes of the Alps. Furthermore, forests provide important functions in terms of water purification and storage, micro- and meso-climate regulation, and recreation. The Austrian Forest Program presented by the Austrian government in 2006 aims at achieving a sustainable and multifunctional use of forests.

Only 3 percent of Austrian forests are categorized as "pristine," while another 22 percent are described as "natural." Forty-four percent are "moderately modified," while another 22 percent are classified as "heavily modified." Forests are generally important for conserving biodiversity. Less that 1 percent of Aus-

Forest workers load timber onto a railroad car in this 1910 photograph. Timber is one of Austria's primary resources. (Getty Images)

trian forests are categorized as "minimum intervention," while another 2.7 percent are managed under some regime for biodiversity conservation. Twenty-three percent of Austrian forests are part of protected areas.

According to the Austrian Forest Inventory, about one-half of the annual increase in biomass is harvested. Out of 9.3 cubic meters of biomass increase per hectare, 5.6 cubic meters are in use. In the first decade of the twenty-first century, forest areas grew by roughly 1 percent with an increasing trend. In 2007, 21.3 million cubic meters of timber were harvested in Austrian forests, corresponding to an increase of 11.4 percent over the previous year. Value added in the forestry sector amounted to about 1.5 billion euros (about $2.1 billion); the total annual production value was estimated to be 2.7 billion euros (about $3.8 billion) per year. The actual quantity of timber harvested is lower than the potential sustainable yield of about 24.8 million cubic meters per year. About one-third of timber is used as biofuels, the rest for commercial purposes such as furniture. Compared to the production of all European Union countries of 426 million cubic meters, Austria's share in Europe's timber production is larger than the country's size (area) might suggest. Austria produces about 3 cubic meters of timber per capita and therefore ranks fifth of all European countries. Only Sweden, Finland, Latvia, and Estonia produce more timber per capita. This also leads to an above-average paper and paperboard production, estimated at 0.54 metric ton per capita. Only in Finland and Sweden is per-capita production of paper higher than in Austria.

Climate change is one of the threats to functioning forest ecosystems. Beginning in the early 1990's, natural events such as hurricanes increased in frequency and intensity. Timber stocks in Austrian forests amount to about 1,094 billion cubic meters. In 2007, Hurricane Kyrill affected 3.3 million cubic meters of timber, which had to be extracted from the forests. This natural disaster led to a significant price decline of forest products, especially for low-quality timber. On the other hand, periods of drought such as in the summer of 2003 additionally weakened the resilience of forest ecosystems. Furthermore, the bark beetle has negatively affected large patches of forests.

Austrian forests are also considered important in terms of climate change policies. Austrian forests serve as a carbon sink because of the increase in timber stocks. Austrian forests are a major supplier of biofuels and therefore contribute to reducing greenhouse gases.

WATER RESOURCES AND USE

Austria is a country rich in water resources. As the Alps form a barrier for clouds, annual precipitation amounts to about 1,100 millimeters per square meter. Tributaries from abroad account for an additional influx of 320 millimeters per square meter. Evaporation leads to a reduction in water resources of 500 millimeters per square meter, and the outflow of surface water and groundwater amounts to 920 millimeters per square meter. The annual average of renewable water resources totals 84 billion cubic meters, with a total water consumption by the Austrian economy of 2.6 billion cubic meters. That means that around 3 percent of renewable water resources are used, mainly in the agricultural and industrial sectors. From a quantitative viewpoint, water use and diversion are most prominent in hydropower stations, as around 60 percent of Austrian rivers are significantly impacted. Austrian households receive about one-half of their drinking water from springs, while the other half comes from groundwater. Ninety percent of Austrian households are connected to the public sewage system.

More than 93 percent of groundwater bodies are in a good chemical state. The majority of surface waters have good or very good water quality. Water quality is reduced to moderate quality only in single "hot spots" such as downstream of large cities. The main threats to water resources in Austria are nonpoint pollution sources from the agricultural sector and the modification of surface waters for hydropower plants and ship transport on the main river of Austria, the Danube.

While agricultural, commercial, and residential consumption of water is important, probably the most important use of water resources, in quantitative terms, is in electricity production. About 65 percent of Austrian electricity is produced in hydropower plants along the large Austrian rivers such as the Danube. This also leads to a comparatively high share of renewable energy sources, which account for about 24 percent of total energy consumption. Some of this electricity is also traded on European energy markets.

The good state of water resources in Austria is the result of the strict regulatory framework of the Austrian Clean Water Act, which prescribes the "state of the art in pollution control technology" for all water uses and wastewater discharges, and to the extensive use of environmental subsidies for municipalities and water-polluting industries. More over, the European Union's Water Framework Directive (WFD) has been implemented in Austria, aiming at a good ecological state of all water resources and at the incorporation of all environmental and resource costs and benefits in the pricing of water services.

OTHER RESOURCES

About 40 percent of Austrian territory is used for agriculture. The share of domestic food production compared to total food consumption in Austria is 95 percent for cereals, 93 percent for sugar, 88 percent for potatoes, 66 percent for fruits, and 31 percent for vegetable oil. The production value of the agricultural sector amounts to about 8.1 billion euros (11.5 $billion) with a share of total production value of about 1.8 percent.

One resource that is plentiful in Austria is tungsten (wolfram); Austria has one of the largest deposits worldwide. Tungsten has the highest melting point of all nonalloyed metals. Therefore, it is used in filaments for lightbulbs, cathode-ray tubes, vacuum tubes, and other high-temperature applications in the electrical, heating, and welding industries.

Michael Getzner

FURTHER READING

Austrian Environmental Protection Agency. *The State of the Environment in Austria. 8th Environmental Control Report.* Vienna: Umweltbundesamt, 2008.

Köck, J., U. Schubert, and S. Sedlacek. "Environmental Policy and Environment-Oriented Technology Policy in Austria." *Environment and Policy* 38 (2003): 25-58.

Organization for Economic Cooperation and Development. *Environmental Performance Review: Austria.* Paris: Author, 2003.

Wurzel, Rüdiger K. W., et al. "Struggling to Leave Behind a Regulatory Past? 'New' Environmental Policy Instruments in Austria." In *"New" Instruments of Environmental Governance?* edited by Andrew Jordan, Rüdiger K. W. Wurzel, and Anthony R. Zito. London: Frank Cass, 2007.

WEB SITES

AUSTRIAN CENTRAL BUREAU OF STATISTICS
Statistics Austria
http://www.statistik.at/web_en/

UMWELTBUNDESAMT (AUSTRIAN FEDERAL ENVIRONMENTAL PROTECTION AGENCY)
http://www.umweltbundesamt.at/en/

SEE ALSO: Forests; Hydroenergy; Tungsten.

B

Barite

CATEGORY: Mineral and other nonliving resources

WHERE FOUND
Rich vein deposits of barite are in Mexico, Algeria, and Morocco. Residual deposits left by the weathering away of barite-bearing limestones and dolomites exist in Georgia, Missouri, and Tennessee. There are major bedded deposits in Arkansas and Nevada; important bedded deposits also exist in Germany, France, Ireland, and other European countries.

PRIMARY USES
Most of the barite produced is used in petroleum and natural gas exploration to increase the density of drilling fluid. It also has uses in the manufacture of glass, rubber, and some plastics.

TECHNICAL DEFINITION
Barite, the most common barium mineral, is barium sulfate, $BaSO_4$. It occurs as white, gray, or black tabular crystals with three good cleavages and a Mohs scale hardness of 2.5 to 3.5. Its most notable property is its high specific gravity of 4.5 (its density is 4.5 times that of water).

DESCRIPTION, DISTRIBUTION, AND FORMS
Barite occurs as vein fillings, commonly accompanied by metal sulfides; as residual deposits; and as bedded deposits. Rich vein deposits in Mexico, Algeria, and Morocco have been important sources of barite. Barite is highly insoluble, relative to limestone and dolomite, and the weathering away of barite-bearing limestones and dolomites has left sig-

nificant and easily mined residual deposits in Georgia, Missouri, and Tennessee. Bedded deposits of barite are fairly common worldwide.

HISTORY
A bedded deposit in Arkansas was the leading source of barite from 1942 to 1982. In the late 1970's, enor-

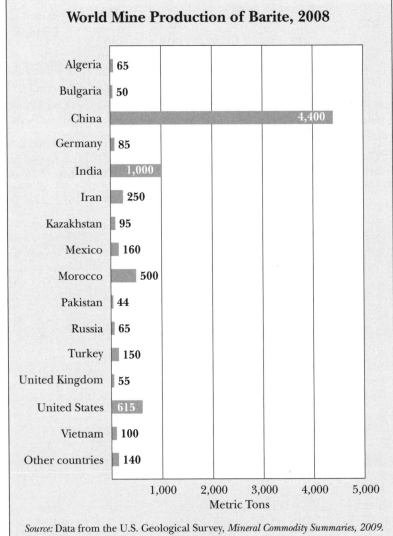

World Mine Production of Barite, 2008

Country	Metric Tons
Algeria	65
Bulgaria	50
China	4,400
Germany	85
India	1,000
Iran	250
Kazakhstan	95
Mexico	160
Morocco	500
Pakistan	44
Russia	65
Turkey	150
United Kingdom	55
United States	615
Vietnam	100
Other countries	140

Source: Data from the U.S. Geological Survey, *Mineral Commodity Summaries, 2009.* U.S. Government Printing Office, 2009.

mous reserves of bedded barite were discovered in Nevada. Important bedded deposits also occur in Germany, France, Ireland, and other European countries.

OBTAINING BARITE

Vein deposits of barite are thought to be of low-temperature hydrothermal origin and associated with igneous intrusion. Residual deposits probably are closely related to vein deposits in that barite is initially deposited in fractures in limestone and dolomite (carbonate rocks) by hydrothermal processes or deposited on the seafloor, where carbonates are accumulating as volcanic exhalations react with sulfate-rich seawater. Later uplift, followed by weathering and solution of the carbonate rocks, leaves rich deposits of barite in the carbonate rock residuum.

The origin of bedded deposits is less obvious, but research has indicated that they may occur where oxygen-depleted, and therefore sulfate-poor, barium-bearing seawater has mixed with and reacted with normal, sulfate-rich seawater, a process that may occur where deep ocean waters are forced to the surface, by strong deep water currents impinging on continental margins, to mix with shallow waters.

USES OF BARITE

Most of the barite produced is used in the petroleum and natural gas exploration industry. It is used to increase the density of drilling fluid to counteract the high pressures encountered in petroleum reservoir rocks, thus preventing disastrous blowouts. There are many other important uses for barite, however. It is used in glass manufacture to homogenize the melt and impart brilliance to the final product. Barite is also an important additive in many rubber and plastic products. Raw rubber and some plastics tend to be soft and gummy. Fillers, fine granular materials with appropriate physical properties, add firmness, wear resistance, mechanical toughness, and weight to the final products. In all, there are more than two thousand uses for barite and barite-based chemicals in industrial processes and products.

Barium is an effective gamma-ray absorber, and a mixture of barium sulfate and water has been used to render the human intestinal tract opaque to X rays and thus visible on radiographs. Barite compounds, largely derived from barite, are also used to produce a brilliant green color in fireworks.

Robert E. Carver

WEB SITES

NATURAL RESOURCES CANADA
Mineral and Metal Commodity Reviews: Barite and Witherite
http://www.nrcan-rncan.gc.ca/mms-smm/busi-indu/cmy-amc/content/2007/73.pdf

U.S. GEOLOGICAL SURVEY
Minerals Information: Barite Statistics and Information
http://minerals.usgs.gov/minerals/pubs/commodity/barite/

SEE ALSO: Hydrothermal solutions and mineralization; Oil and natural gas drilling and wells; Residual mineral deposits.

Belgium

CATEGORIES: Countries; government and resources

With few natural resources of its own, Belgium has profited from its location at the center of a highly industrialized area in Europe with several port cities that have made it one of the world's largest trading nations.

THE COUNTRY

Belgium is located in Western Europe and borders France, the Netherlands, Germany, Luxembourg, and the North Sea. Along with the Netherlands and Luxembourg, Belgium has been historically part of the "Low Countries." In some economic circles, these small countries are still connected and reported together, as they have formed a sort of union referred to as Benelux nations. Belgium is a small country, about the size of the state of Maryland, but it boasts 66.5 kilometers of coastline. It is centrally located, at the heart of the European Union, with the majority of European capitals within 1,000 kilometers of Brussels, the Belgian capital city, which is the headquarters of the European Union and North Atlantic Treaty Organization (NATO).

Belgium's geography is varied for a small country, with flat coastal plains in the northwest near the North Sea that stretch into the rugged mountains of the Ardennes forest in the southeast near its borders with France. In 2006, Belgium's gross domestic product (GDP) was ranked eighteenth in the world. Ser-

Belgium: Resources at a Glance

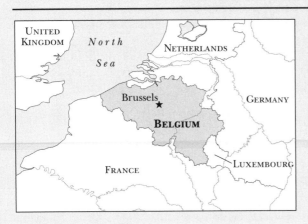

Official name: Kingdom of Belgium
Government: Federal parliamentary democracy
   under a constitutional monarchy
Capital city: Brussels
Area: 11,788 mi²; 30,528 km²
Population (2009 est.): 10,414,336
Languages: Dutch, French, and German
Monetary unit: euro (EUR)

ECONOMIC SUMMARY:

GDP composition by sector (2008 est.): agriculture, 0.8%; industry, 23.2%; services, 76.1%
Natural resources: construction materials, silica sand, carbonates
Land use (including Luxembourg, 2005): arable land, 27.42%; permanent crops, 0.69%; other, 71.89%
Industries: engineering and metal products, motor vehicle assembly, transportation equipment, scientific
   instruments, processed food and beverages, chemicals, basic metals, textiles, glass, petroleum, pharmaceuticals
Agricultural products: sugar beets, fresh vegetables, fruits, grain, tobacco, beef, veal, pork, milk
Exports (2008 est.): $371.5 billion
Commodities exported: machinery and equipment, chemicals, finished diamonds, metals and metal products,
   foodstuffs, pharmaceuticals
Imports (2008 est.): $387.7 billion
Commodities imported: raw materials, machinery and equipment, chemicals, raw diamonds, pharmaceuticals,
   foodstuffs, transportation equipment, oil products
Labor force (2008): 4.99 million
Labor force by occupation (2007 est.): agriculture, 2%; industry, 25%; services, 73%

ENERGY RESOURCES:

Electricity production (2007 est.): 82.94 billion kWh
Electricity consumption (2006 est.): 85.54 billion kWh
Electricity exports (2007 est.): 9.035 billion kWh
Electricity imports (2007 est.): 15.78 billion kWh

Natural gas production (2007 est.): 0 m³
Natural gas consumption (2007 est.): 17.39 billion m³
Natural gas exports (2007 est.): 0 m³
Natural gas imports (2007 est.): 17.34 billion m³
Natural gas proved reserves (Jan. 2006): 0 m³

Oil production (2007 est.): 8,671 bbl/day
Oil imports (2005): 1.119 million bbl/day
Oil proved reserves (Jan. 2006 est.): 0 bbl

Source: Data from *The World Factbook 2009.* Washington, D.C.: Central Intelligence Agency, 2009.
Notes: Data are the most recent tracked by the CIA. Values are given in U.S. dollars. Abbreviations: bbl/day = barrels per day;
   GDP = gross domestic product; km² = square kilometers; kWh = kilowatt-hours; m³ = cubic meters; mi² = square miles.

vices account for about 75 percent of Belgium's GDP, a surprisingly high number somewhat related to its place as the headquarters of the European Union, NATO, and other major organizations based in Europe. Its workforce is highly educated and multilingual. The capital, Brussels, is home to more than one million people and about fifty-four thousand businesses. On its own, Brussels produces about 20 percent of Belgium's GDP.

Although Belgium has few natural resources of its own, its location at the center of a highly industrialized area in Europe with several port cities means that it functions as a trading center for many goods. Its paucity of natural resources was supplemented historically by its colonial possessions in the Belgian Congo (now Democratic Republic of the Congo), which provided raw materials such as cobalt, copper, diamonds, cacao, and zinc. Belgium's economy depends heavily on importing raw materials or other goods that are finished or further processed and then exported. Historically, its most prominent natural resource was coal, but in 1992, its coal mines closed permanently, and, unless the price of coal increases to the point of making it worthwhile to extract the deeply embedded seams, the mines are unlikely to reopen. Belgium ranks fifteenth on the list of world's largest trading nations with about three-quarters of its trading done with its European Union neighbors, particularly Germany, the Netherlands, France, and the United Kingdom. Because of Belgium's economic reliance on trading and processing rough goods, its economy is dependent on world markets and their stability to a much higher degree than countries with their own natural resources and independent economies.

Coal

Historically, Belgium was a major producer and exporter of coal. Coal in Belgian coal mines, especially in the Kempen and Sambre-Meuse Valley, was easy to extract, and mining was a booming business. In the heyday of its coal-mining industry, Belgium imported workers from other countries to keep the coal mines operating. However, after the easily accessible coal had been extracted and the seams of coal ran farther underground and into harder materials, continuing to extract coal from these mines became economically inefficient. Between 1957 and 1992, Belgium shut down more than 120 coal mines, and unless the price of coal rises to the point of making this coal eco-

nomically feasible to extract and export, it is unlikely that these mines will return to operation.

Construction Materials

Belgium is a source of construction materials such as silica sand, chalk, stone, and carbonates. Chalk and limestone are mined in the regions surrounding Tournai, Mons, and Liège, where there is a cement industry of some significance. The glass manufacturing industry is also supported by sands from the Kempenland area. Pottery products and bricks are made from clays from the Borinage region. Quarries also produce stones such as specialty marble, dolomite, granite, and sandstone.

Diamonds

Belgium is the leading country in the diamond trading market. Its port city of Antwerp is the diamond capital of the world, housing the leading diamond market in the world. Rough diamonds are imported and then processed into finished diamonds in Antwerp, where they are then traded and exported. This city is also the leading diamond cutting area of the world, where, the traditional story says, the first diamond was cut in 1476. The diamond cutting and trading center called "the Diamond Quarter" near Central Station (the train station near the port) has been a growing, thriving entity since the sixteenth century. Though the diamond processing arm of the trade is diminishing, diamond exports still account for about one-tenth of all exports from Belgium. Nearly 85 percent of the world's rough diamonds and about 50 percent of the finished (polished) diamonds in the world pass through this city. In 2006, the United States accounted for about $2.8 billion of Belgium's diamond exports, which amounts to about 20 percent of all Belgian exports to the United States. Overall, about $39 billion of diamonds are traded through the city, which accounts for about 8 percent of all Belgium's exports. This diamond trade accounts for nearly 70 percent of the country's positive trade balance and represents about 15 percent of Belgium's trade with non-European Union countries. This prosperous business employs, directly or indirectly, nearly thirty-five thousand people.

Sugar

One of Belgium's fastest-growing exports is sugar from sugar beets. In 2006, the exports of sugar from Belgium to the United States rose more than 5,000 percent for a total of about $10.7 million. This industry began in Belgium in 1807 when the British started a blockade of cane sugar from the Caribbean during the Napoleonic Wars. With cane sugar unavailable, beet sugar began to be the sugar of choice throughout Napoleonic Europe. The sugar production capital of Belgium is Tienen, which hosts a large sugar-beet processing factory that was founded in 1836. This factory and related sugar production facilities owned by the Raffinerie Tirlemontoise Group employ nearly two thousand people. This company owns three other Belgian sugar factories, in Brugelette, Genappe, and Wanze.

BEER

Monks in Belgium began brewing beer sometime during the Middle Ages. There are more than one hundred breweries scattered throughout Belgium, with about eight hundred standard types of beer produced. These range from light through dark types of beer; Belgians brew and export nearly every type of beer possible. Often, each type of beer is served in its own distinctive glass, which is said to enhance the flavor of that particular type of beer. Though Belgium is famous for many kinds of beer, it is possibly most famous for lambic beer, which is made in an ancient brewing style. This style depends on a spontaneous natural fermentation process after ingredients are exposed to the wild yeasts and bacteria native to the Senne Valley, located south of Brussels. This unusual fermentation process produces a drink that is naturally effervescent or sparkling, which is then aged, up to two or three years, to improve its taste. Much like champagne (only produced in a certain region in France) or Madeira (only produced on a certain island owned by Portugal), the title of "lambic beer" can only be given to this type of beer brewed in the small Pajottenland region of Belgium. Nearly half of the beer brewed in Belgium is exported, mostly to Canada, France, Germany, Italy, Spain, the United States, and the United Kingdom.

CHOCOLATE

During the seventeenth century, when the Low Countries were ruled by Spain, Spanish conquistadores brought cacao beans back from the New World to the region that is now Belgium. By 1840, the Berwaerts Company had begun to sell Belgian chocolates that were quite popular. However, not until the nineteenth century, when King Leopold II colonized the Belgian

Congo in 1885 and discovered cacao tree fields there, did Belgian chocolatiers begin to manufacture Belgian chocolates on a large scale. At the beginning of the 1900's, there were at least fifty chocolate makers in Belgium. In 1912, Jean Neuhaus created a process for making a chocolate shell that could be filled with any number of fillings, something he called a "praline," making Belgian chocolates even more popular. Belgium produces more than 156,000 metric tons of chocolate each year, has more than two thousand chocolate shops throughout the country, and hosts about three hundred different chocolate companies. Many of the original chocolate-making companies—such as Godiva, Leonidas, Neuhaus, and Nirvana—are still in operation today, and many of them still make chocolates by hand, using original equipment, high-quality ingredients, and Old World manufacturing techniques. Chocolate shops in Belgium offer tastings, much like wineries, and host chocolate festivals, workshops, tours, and demonstrations. There is a museum dedicated to chocolate, the Musée du Cacao et du Chocolat, near the Grand Place, the town square in Brussels. Belgium's European Union neighbors (particularly France, Germany, and the United Kingdom) are the biggest importers of Belgian chocolate.

PHARMACEUTICALS

Belgium has become a world leader in the pharmaceutical industry, employing nearly thirty thousand people and accounting for about 10 percent of all Belgian exports. Major pharmaceutical companies headquartered in Belgium include UCB, Solvay, Janssen Pharmaceutica, Omega Pharma, Oystershell NV, and Recherche et Industries Thérapeutiques. Private investment in research and development in the pharmaceutical industry is at about 40 percent, which is nearly twice the average of other European companies. The pharmaceutical industry is also heavily supported by the Belgian government, which offers tax incentives for pharmaceutical research and development. The United States has imported about $2.3 billion annually in medicinal, dental, and pharmaceutical products from Belgium, which accounts for about 16 percent of all exports from Belgium to the United States.

TEXTILES

Since the thirteenth century, Belgium has been known as the home of master textile producers. The famous Unicorn Tapestries or "The Hunt of the Unicorn" series on display at The Cloisters, a part of the Metropolitan Museum of Art in New York, is thought to have been woven in Brussels sometime around 1495-1505 (when that area was still part of the Netherlands). The Flanders, or Flemish, region of Belgium is still home to many lace-making artists, particularly in the area of Bruges, which is the home of bobbin lace; however, lace is also still produced in Brussels and Mechelen. This industry can be traced back to the fifteenth century, when Charles V decreed that lace making was to be taught in the schools and convents of the Belgian provinces to provide girls with a source of income, as lace was popular on collars and cuffs for clothing of both sexes at that time. Lace is still produced in Belgium by lace artisans in their homes, one piece at a time, and, thus, is a source of artistic lace rather than high-production lace. There is even a museum dedicated solely to lace, the Musée du Costume et de la Dentelle, located near the Grand Place. Other textile production, including cotton, linen, wool, and synthetic fibers, is concentrated in Ghent, Kortrijk, Tournai, and Verviers, where carpets and blankets are manufactured.

OTHER RESOURCES

As mentioned above, Belgium has few natural resources, and its economy depends on importing raw materials, processing those materials, manufacturing, and exporting a finished product. However, in addition to sugar processing, there are a few agricultural resources grown and exported by Belgian farmers. These include fruits, vegetables, grains (wheat, oats, rye, barley, and flax), tobacco, beef, veal, pork, and milk.

Other industries in which Belgian workers are involved in processing imported goods that are then exported are motor vehicles and other metal products, scientific instruments, chemicals (fertilizers, dyes, plastics), glass, petroleum, textiles, electronics, and processed foods and beverages, such as the beer and chocolate described above.

Marianne M. Madsen

FURTHER READING

Binneweg, Herbert. *Antwerp, the Diamond Capital of the World*. Antwerp: Federation of Belgian Diamond Bourses, 1993.

Blom, J. H. C., and Emiel Lamberts. *History of the Low Countries*. New York: Berghahn Books, 2006.

Hieronymus, Stan. *Brew Like a Monk: Trappist, Abbey,*

and Strong Belgian Ales and How to Brew Them. Boulder, Colo.: Brewers, 2005.

Kockelbergh, Iris, Eddy Vleeschdrager, and Jan Walgrave. *The Brilliant Story of Antwerp Diamonds*. Antwerp: MIM, 1992.

Mommen, Andre. *The Belgian Economy in the Twentieth Century*. New York: Routledge, 1994.

Parker, Philip M. *The 2007 Import and Export Market for Unagglomerated Bituminous Coal in Belgium*. San Diego, Calif.: ICON Group International, 2006.

Sparrow, Jeff. *Wild Brews: Culture and Craftsmanship in the Belgian Tradition*. Boulder, Colo.: Brewers, 2005.

Wingfield, George. *Belgium*. Edgemont, Pa.: Chelsea House, 2008.

Witte, Els, Jan Craeybeckx, and Alain Maynen. *Political History of Belgium: From 1830 Onwards*. Brussels: Free University of Brussels Press, 2008.

WEB SITES

BELGIUM: A FEDERAL STATE
http://www.diplomatie.be/en/belgium

U.S. DEPARTMENT OF STATE
Background Note: Belgium
http://www.state.gov/r/pa/ei/bgn/2874.htm

SEE ALSO: Coal; Diamond; Sugars; Textiles and fabrics.

Beryllium

CATEGORY: Mineral and other nonliving resources

WHERE FOUND

The element beryllium is believed to occur in the Earth's igneous rocks to the extent of 0.0006 percent. It does not occur in its free state in nature; it is found only in minerals. The leading producers are the United States, China, and some African countries.

PRIMARY USES

Beryllium has a number of important industrial and structural applications. Its widest use is in the preparation of alloys used in the manufacture of watch springs, welding electrodes, hypodermic needles, dentures, and molds for casting plastics. Metallic beryllium is used to make windows in X-ray tubes because of its high degree of transparency. Finally, beryllium compounds have various uses in glass manufacture, in aircraft spark plugs, and as ultra-high-frequency radar insulators.

TECHNICAL DEFINITION

Beryllium (abbreviated Be), atomic number 4, belongs to Group II of the periodic table of the elements and is one of the rarest and lightest structural metals. It has four naturally occurring isotopes and an average atomic weight of 9.0122.

DESCRIPTION, DISTRIBUTION, AND FORMS

Pure beryllium is a steel-gray, light, hard, and brittle metal that becomes ductile at higher temperatures and may be rolled into a sheet. Beryllium burns with a brilliant flame, but it becomes oxidized easily and forms a protective coating of the oxide. Beryllium has a density of 1.85 grams per cubic centimeter, a melting point of 1,285° Celsius, and a boiling point of 2,970° Celsius.

Among the elements, beryllium ranks thirty-second in order of abundance. Like lithium, it is usually isolated from silicate minerals. It is believed that its nucleus, like the nucleus of lithium and boron, is destroyed by high-energy protons in the Sun and other stars. As a result it cannot survive the hot, dense interiors of the stars, where elements are formed, which accounts for its low abundance. At least fifty beryllium-containing minerals are known, but only beryl and bertrandite—which contain up to 15 percent beryllium oxide and whose clear varieties are the gems aquamarine and emerald—are the major producers of the metal. The richest beryllium-containing ore deposits are pegmatite varieties of granite rocks. Many beryllium compounds have properties that resemble those of aluminum compounds. Beryllium oxide absorbs carbon dioxide readily and is moisture sensitive. Beryllium hydroxide is a gelatinous precipitate that is easily soluble in acid. All beryllium halides are easily hydrolyzed by water and emit hydrogen halides.

HISTORY

Beryllium was discovered as an oxide by Louis-Nicolas Vauquelin during an analysis of emerald in 1798 and was originally named glucinum because of the sweet taste of its salts. It was first isolated as a free metal by Friedrich Wöhler and Antoine Bussy, who reduced beryllium chloride with potassium metal.

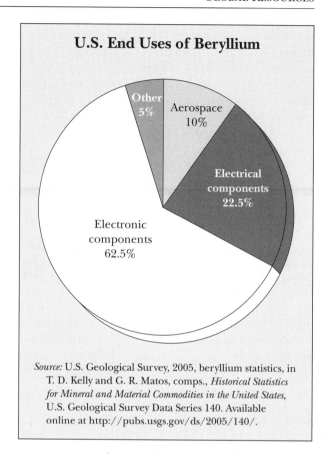

U.S. End Uses of Beryllium

Other 5%
Aerospace 10%
Electrical components 22.5%
Electronic components 62.5%

Source: U.S. Geological Survey, 2005, beryllium statistics, in T. D. Kelly and G. R. Matos, comps., *Historical Statistics for Mineral and Material Commodities in the United States*, U.S. Geological Survey Data Series 140. Available online at http://pubs.usgs.gov/ds/2005/140/.

OBTAINING BERYLLIUM

Beryllium ore is usually converted to a more reactive compound, such as beryllium fluoride, which is then electrolyzed with magnesium. The element is inert with respect to water.

Beryllium exists in the atmosphere of urban and coal-burning neighborhoods in much greater quantities than in rural areas. Dry dust, fumes, and aqueous solutions of the metal compounds are toxic, creating dermatitis, and inhaling them produces the effects of phosgene gas. Its toxicity is believed to result from the substitution of the smaller beryllium atoms for magnesium atoms in enzymes, which are the biochemical catalysts.

USES OF BERYLLIUM

As a result of beryllium's unusual physical properties, such as its high melting point, high electrical conductivity, high heat capacity, and oxidation resistance, beryllium serves as a component in alloys of elements such as copper, where it adds a high tensile strength to the metal. The added beryllium is no more than 3 percent of the alloy. Beryllium's ability to transmit X rays seventeen times more effectively than aluminum makes it useful in cases where high-intensity X-ray beams are needed.

Soraya Ghayourmanesh

WEB SITES

U.S. DEPARTMENT OF LABOR: OCCUPATIONAL
      SAFETY AND HEALTH ADMINISTRATION
Safety and Health Topics: Beryllium
http://www.osha.gov/SLTC/beryllium/

U.S. GEOLOGICAL SURVEY
Minerals Information: Beryllium Statistics and
      Information
http://minerals.usgs.gov/minerals/pubs/
      commodity/beryllium/

SEE ALSO: Alloys; Boron; China; Lithium; Nuclear energy; United States.

Bessemer process

CATEGORY: Obtaining and using resources

The Bessemer process was the first method for producing large quantities of inexpensive steel.

DEFINITION
In the 1850's, Henry Bessemer, looking for a way to improve cast iron, stumbled upon a way to make a new kind of steel. By blowing air through molten iron in a crucible, he was able to burn off the carbon and many harmful impurities, and then the iron was heated to the point that it could be poured into molds.

Bessemer eventually learned to add Spiegeleisen, a manganese-rich cast iron, to the molten iron after the carbon and impurities were burned off. The manganese countered the effects of the remaining traces of oxygen and sulfur, while the carbon (always present in cast iron) helped create the properties of steel.

The Bessemer converter, on display at England's Science Museum, was used for steel production and is recognized as an important invention of the Industrial Revolution. (SSPL via Getty Images)

OVERVIEW

Prior to the late 1850's, there were two common iron-based construction materials. One was cast iron, an impure, brittle, high-carbon material used in columns, piers, and other load-bearing members. The other was wrought iron, a workable, low-carbon material used in girders, rails, and other spans. The word "steel" usually referred to a custom material produced in very small quantities by adding carbon to high-quality wrought iron.

Bessemer's resulting product, which came to be known as "mild steel," proved to be reliable and durable. Because of these qualities, and because it could be produced in large quantities, mild steel quickly found widespread use in rails, ship plates, girders, and many other applications, often replacing wrought iron.

Brian J. Nichelson

SEE ALSO: Iron; Manganese; Metals and metallurgy; Steel.

Biodiversity

CATEGORY: Ecological resources

Scientist Walter G. Rosen coined the term "biodiversity" in 1986 for the National Forum on Biodiversity; the term was popularized later by the biologist Edward O. Wilson. Biodiversity includes the variations and associated processes within and among organisms. It is linked to the stability and predictability of ecosystems and can be measured through the numbers and composition of species.

BACKGROUND

Conservation was a priority in the United States in the late 1800's and early 1900's, but efforts were driven by the mistaken beliefs that there were regions untouched by humanity and that humans were not part of nature. Intensified use of lands leading up to and during World War II hastened the loss of species and wilderness areas. The science of ecology was emerging but "natural" ecosystems were hard to identify. Thus, conservation efforts in the 1960's and 1970's focused on the preservation of particular species in order to preserve biodiversity and led to passage of the Endangered Species Preservation Act in 1966. Political support for protecting the environment and biodiversity spread globally, leading to the 1992 Earth Summit, in which representatives of 175 nations met in Rio de Janeiro, Brazil. As of 2009, all countries present at the summit, except the United States, had ratified the agreements. All participating countries were expected to identify, monitor, and report on various aspects of biodiversity within their borders; help deteriorating regions recover; include indigenous peoples in discussions of biodiversity; and educate citizens about the importance of biodiversity. Preservation of original habitats was preferred over off-site recovery efforts.

RECOGNIZING AND MEASURING BIODIVERSITY

Biodiversity can be subdivided for analysis into a nested hierarchy of four levels (genetic, population or species, community or ecosystem, and landscape or region) or it can be studied in terms of composition (genetic constituency, species and relative proportions in a community, and kinds and distribution of habitats and communities), structure (patterns, sequence, and organization of constituents), and function (evolutionary, ecological, hydrological, geological, and climatic processes responsible for the patterns of biodiversity). Diversity likely enhances stability of the ecosystem, defined as the physiochemical setting associated with a community of living organisms in complex, multifaceted interactions. Biodiversity is one characteristic of an ecosystem, and the simplest measure of diversity is the number of types of organisms (usually species or another group of organisms in the Linnaean classification system). Alpha diversity is the number of types of organisms relative to abundance, and beta diversity is a relative measure of how much an ecosystem adds to a region.

Species richness measures are typically favored in conservation planning as a proxy for overall level of biodiversity. However, there are many definitions of species, and species can be hard to identify no matter what one's theoretical biases (whether one prefers to explain species change by differing contributions of the evolutionary mechanisms of natural selection, mutation, genetic drift, and gene flow operating slowly and gradually over time or by relatively rapid means during more dramatic environmental shifts). Species exist as ecological mosaics and include a variety of phenotypes that evolve as local environments change. The variety of phenotypes within a species is another kind of diversity, named disparity; species

Rain forests such as El Yunque Caribbean Recreation Area in Puerto Rico are some of the most biodiverse places on Earth. (AP/Wide World Photos)

number and species disparity are not necessarily correlated. Phenotypes are altered or transformed as a function of phenotypic plasticity, adaptation, and migration, but there is no standard means of measuring and comparing morphological difference within or between species. Which aspects of phenotype are of interest will again depend on the aims of the researcher.

About 2 million species have been described, and counts of the total number of species range from 5 million to 30 million. However, monitored species indicate that there have been dramatic declines. About 6,200 vertebrate species, 2,700 invertebrate species, and at least 8,500 species of plants from around the globe were identified as "threatened" in 2009 in the International Union for Conservation of Nature (IUCN) Red List of Threatened Species. There is particularly intense interest in identifying regions, called "hot spots," where a large concentration

of species are experiencing especially high levels of extinctions. About 44 percent of vascular plants and 35 percent of vertebrates except fish are found in twenty-five hot spots, representing only 1.4 percent of the Earth's land surface. Most are found in the tropics. Habitats vary in their distribution of biodiversity, but the environments richest in species are tropical rain forests (primarily because of the impressive numbers of insects), coral reefs, large tropical lakes, and maybe the deep sea. Terrestrial habitats tend to be richest in species at lower elevations and in regions with plenty of rainfall. In general, geologically and topographically complicated areas are also likely to have more species.

All threatened species are at high risk for becoming extinct in their natural settings because of human impacts that lead to fragmentation and devastation of habitats as well as the spread of nonnative species, the impact of big-business agriculture and forestry, pollution, direct use of species, global climate change, and destructive interference with ecosystem processes. Conserved areas are not enough to stop or reverse the declines. Selection of areas to conserve has been haphazard, and most represent limited ecologies with the poorest soils, steepest slopes, and highest elevations.

VALUING BIODIVERSITY
In the 1950's, biologists assumed that increasing biological diversity stabilized ecosystems because any single aspect of an ecosystem, if changed, should be less disruptive the greater the level of complexity. In the 1970's, mathematical modeling of complex systems confirmed that instability increased with biological complexity, a view that was favored until the models proved inadequate to describe all the varying aspects of living ecosystems. Nonequilibrium (unpredictable) processes also affected species diversity. Thus, interest continued in the relationship between measures of biodiversity and productivity, which was the focus of much experimental research in artificial and natural settings in the 1990's. However, few simple associations were found, making the outcome of a disruption to a particular ecosystem difficult to predict.

Some diversity is not evident. For example, biodiversity is partly determined by genes that may be somewhat or fully expressed, depending on the selective demands of local conditions. Gene expression is also sensitive to developmental context as well as selection pressures as the organism survives to reproduce. The prior history of a lineage (phylogeny) is also relevant. Precipitous population declines can reduce genetic variability in a lineage, likely lowering its flexibility in surviving environmental disturbances. Larger populations are more likely to inhabit more diverse settings and to accumulate more genetic and phenotypic diversity. Longer-lived (older) systems seem to accumulate more diversity and are better able to maintain their integrity.

Biological diversity can be assessed in terms of diversity among species within an ecosystem, their varying roles in food chains (trophic) networks, their biogeochemical cycles, and the accumulation and production of energy. Low species diversity can mean low productivity when, for example, one compares deserts and tundra to tropical forests, or high productivity when evaluating energy subsidized agricultural systems. In addition, greater redundancy of species with similar roles or functions produces a more stable system that responds more adaptively to disruptions.

The difficulty is that the "roles" and functions of various organisms within a particular local setting are hard to identify and measure, making the outcomes of any specific disruptions challenging for planners to predict. The stability of a system may mean stability of processes rather than continuity of the same grouping of species.

The Organization for Economic Co-operation and Development advocates the use of marketing strategies for increasing the types and levels of biodiversity worldwide. There are five economically useful kinds of biodiversity: direct extractive uses such as foods, plants, and animals of commercial value; direct nonextractive uses, including ecotourism, education, recreation, and extracting and making commercially useful plant products for new medications; indirect uses, as in the case of ecosystems that cleanse air and water, provide flood control, or maintain soil systems; option values or utility for future generations; and existence or bequest values, or how much people are willing to pay to preserve biodiversity. Support for biodiversity will occur if benefits are made explicit and marketable in the global economy.

MANAGING BIODIVERSITY
Humans are part of an evolving lineage and are also part of global biodiversity. Human population growth and the integration of rural, formerly isolated peoples into the global economic system have led to extensive losses of human languages, worldviews, and knowledge about local ecologies and biodiversity. No human group should be forced to live on the brink of starvation with high rates of mortality and be excluded from discussions about their region's biodiversity. In addition, humans scrambling to survive also have suppressed immune systems and are vulnerable to epidemic disease.

Protection and adequate management of biodiversity require that humanity give up the typical short-term, immediate-needs perspective dominated by the most wealthy and politically influential interests and move in the direction of collaboration among diverse interests, including all levels of government, nongovernmental organizations, the public, industry, property owners, developers, and scientists representing academia, government, and industry. The planning and associated decision making must include focus on both public and private lands.

Contemporary agricultural systems influence and are influenced by surrounding ecologies less affected by human activities. Genetically modified plants may introduce traits that can alter their "wilder" cousins. Agricultural biodiversity has also been declining at precipitous rates because of reliance on fewer species as large corporations homogenize and simplify industrial agriculture with reliance on one (monocrop) or just a few domesticated species. All regions are reporting declines in mammal, bird, and insect pollinators. This loss of biodiversity in "wild" and "domestic" ecologies increases the susceptibility of these plants and animals to virulent diseases that do not stop at agricultural or natural boundaries, threatening both economic and political stability in affected regions.

CONSERVATION

Preservation of species in their natural (in situ) settings involves legislation to protect species, setting aside protected areas, and devising effective management plans, all of which are expectations of the agreement made at the Earth Summit. A reserve may include a less disturbed core surrounded by buffer zones that differ in the intensity of human use. The designs of reserves are influenced by the research and theory of the discipline of ecology. Larger protected regions are better than smaller; closely placed blocks of habitats are better than widely spaced blocks; and interconnected zones are better than isolated ones. All planning must involve the local peoples living in or adjacent to the protected regions.

Many situations exist in which there is too much disturbance by humans or the remnant population is too small to survive under current conditions. Thus, the maintenance of these species in artificial ex situ (off-site) conditions—such as zoos, aquariums, botanical gardens, and arboretums—under human supervision becomes necessary. Sometimes captive colonies can be used to introduce species into the wild. Seed banks and sperm preservation are other ways to conserve genetic diversity, an idea initially pushed by Nikolai Ivanovich Vavilov in the early twentieth century. Gary P. Nabhan advocates a means of increasing the biodiversity of local plants and the resulting foods in a sustainable manner by creating markets patronized by restaurant chefs as well as home cooks for locally grown, traditional foods. Many creative strategies will be required to stop the declines in biodiversity, which, over time, will most likely increase the stability and predictability of the Earth's living resources.

Joan C. Stevenson

FURTHER READING

Chivian, Eric, and Andrew Bernstein. *Sustaining Life: How Human Health Depends on Biodiversity.* New York: Oxford University Press, 2008.

Cockburn, Andrew. *An Introduction to Evolutionary Ecology.* Illustrated by Karina Hansen. Boston: Blackwell Scientific, 1991.

Farnham, Timothy J. *Saving Nature's Legacy: Origins of the Idea of Biological Diversity.* New Haven, Conn.: Yale University Press, 2007.

Groves, Craig R. *Drafting a Conservation Blueprint: A Practitioner's Guide to Planning for Biodiversity.* Washington, D.C.: Island Press, 2003.

Jarvis, Devra I., Christine Padoch, and H. David Cooper, eds. *Managing Biodiversity in Agricultural Ecosystems.* New York: Columbia University Press, 2007.

Jeffries, Michael J. *Biodiversity and Conservation.* 2d ed. New York: Routledge, 2006.

Ladle, Richard J., ed. *Biodiversity and Conservation: Critical Concepts in the Environment.* 5 vols. New York: Routledge, 2009.

Lévêque, Christian, and Jean-Claude Mounolou. *Biodiversity.* New York: John Wiley and Sons, 2003.

Louka, Elli. *Biodiversity and Human Rights: The International Rules for the Protection of Biodiversity.* Ardsley, N.Y.: Transnational, 2002.

Lovejoy, Thomas E., and Lee Jay Hannah, eds. *Climate Change and Biodiversity.* New Haven, Conn.: Yale University Press, 2005.

Maclaurin, James, and Kim Sterelny. *What Is Biodiversity?* Chicago: University of Chicago Press, 2008.

Mann, Charles C. *Noah's Choice: The Future of Endangered Species.* New York: Knopf, 1995.

Nabhan, Gary Paul. *Where Our Food Comes From: Retracing Nikolay Vavilov's Quest to End Famine.* Washington, D.C.: Island Press, 2009.

Organization for Economic Co-operation and Development. *Harnessing Markets for Biodiversity: Towards Conservation and Sustainable Use.* Paris: Author, 2003.

Primack, Richard B. *Essentials of Conservation Biology.* 4th ed. Sunderland, Mass.: Sinauer Associates, 2006.

Wilson, Edward O. *The Diversity of Life.* Cambridge, Mass.: Belknap Press of Harvard University Press, 1992. Reprint. New York: W. W. Norton, 1999.

Zeigler, David. *Understanding Biodiversity.* Westport, Conn.: Praeger, 2007.

WEB SITES

HERITAGE CANADA
The Canadian Biodiversity Web Site
http://canadianbiodiversity.mcgill.ca/english/
    index.htm

U.S. GEOLOGICAL SURVEY
Biodiversity
http://www.usgs.gov/science/science.php?term=92

SEE ALSO: Animals as a medical resource; Biosphere reserves; Conservation; Environmental degradation, resource exploitation and; Genetic diversity; Land management; Land-use planning; Nature Conservancy; Plants as a medical resource; Population growth; Species loss.

Biofuels

CATEGORY: Energy resources

WHERE FOUND
Biofuels are made mainly from plant material such as corn, sugarcane, or rapeseed. Theoretically, biofuels can be generated anywhere on Earth where living organisms can grow.

PRIMARY USES
Biofuels such as ethanol and biodiesel are excellent transportation fuels that are used as substitutes or supplements for gasoline and diesel fuels. Biofuels can also be burned in electrical generators to produce electricity. Two biofuels are used in vehicles: ethanol and biodiesel. Biogas and methane are used mainly to generate electricity. Biomass was used traditionally to heat houses.

TECHNICAL DEFINITION
Biofuels are renewable fuels generated from or by organisms. They can be manufactured from this organic matter and, unlike fossil fuels, do not require millennia to be produced. Since they are renewable, biofuels are considered by many as potential future substitutes for fossil fuels, which are nonrenewable and dwindling. Moreover, pollution from fossil fuels affects public health and has been associated with global climate change, because burning them in engines releases carbon dioxide (CO_2) into the atmosphere.

Using biofuels as an energy source generates fewer pollutants and little or no carbon dioxide. In addition, the utilization of biofuels reduces U.S. dependence on foreign oil.

DESCRIPTION, DISTRIBUTION, AND FORMS
Over millions of years, dead organic matter—both plant and animal organisms—played a crucial role in the formation of fossil fuels such as oil, natural gas, and coal. Since the nineteenth century, humans have increasingly depended on fossil fuels to meet energy needs. As the supply of fossil fuels has diminished, humankind has begun looking for alternative energy sources. Thus, the use of biofuels—including ethanol, biodiesel, methane, biogas, biomass, biohydrogen, and butanol—is increasing.

Ethanol is a colorless liquid with the chemical formula C_2H_5OH. Another name for ethanol is ethyl alcohol, grain alcohol, or simply alcohol.

Biodiesel is a diesel substitute obtained mainly from vegetable oils, such as soybean oil or restaurant greases. It is produced by the transesterification of oils, a simple chemical reaction with alcohol (ethanol or methanol), catalyzed by acids or bases (such as sodium hydroxide). Transesterification produces alkyl esters of fatty acids that are biodiesel and glycerol (also known as glycerin).

Methane is a colorless, odorless, nontoxic gas with

Biofuel Energy Balances

The following table lists several crops that have been considered as viable biofuel sources and several types of ethanol, as well as each substance's energy input/output ratio (that is, the amount of energy released by burning biomass or ethanol, for each equivalent unit of energy expended to create the substance).

BIOMASS/BIOFUEL	ENERGY OUTPUT PER UNIT INPUT
Switchgrass	14.52
Wheat	12.88
Oilseed rape (with straw)	9.21
Cellulosic ethanol	1.98
Corn ethanol	~1.13-1.34

Source: Data from the British Institute of Science in Society.

the molecular formula CH_4. It is the main chemical component (70 to 90 percent) of natural gas, which accounts for about 20 percent of the U.S. energy supply. Methane was discovered by the Italian scientist Alessandro Volta, who collected it from marsh sediments and showed that it was flammable. He called it "combustible air."

Biogas is a gas produced by the metabolism of microorganisms. There are different types of biogas. One type contains a mixture of methane (50 to 75 percent) and carbon dioxide. Another type comprises primarily nitrogen, hydrogen, and carbon monoxide (CO) with trace amounts of methane.

Biomass is a mass of organisms, mainly plants, that can be used as an energy source. Plants and algae convert the energy of the Sun and carbon dioxide into energy that is stored in their biomass. Biomass, burning in the form of wood, is the oldest form of energy used by humans. Using biomass as a fuel source does not result in net CO_2 emissions, because biomass burning will release only the amount of CO_2 it has absorbed during plant growth (provided its production and harvesting are sustainable).

Molecular hydrogen (H_2) is a colorless, odorless, and tasteless gas. It is an ideal alternative fuel to be used for transportation because the energy content of hydrogen is three times greater than in gasoline. Also, it is virtually nonpolluting and a renewable fuel. Using H_2 as an energy source produces only water; H_2 can be made from water again. A great number of microorganisms produce H_2 from inorganic materials, such as water, or from organic materials, such as sugar, in reactions catalyzed by enzymes. Hydrogen produced by microorganisms is called biohydrogen.

Butanol (butyl alcohol) is a four-carbon alcohol with the molecular formula C_4H_9OH. Among other types of biofuels, butanol has been the most promising in terms of commercialization. It is another alcohol fuel but has higher energy content than ethanol. It does not pick up water as ethanol does and is not as corrosive as ethanol but is more suitable for distribution through existing pipelines for gasoline. However, compared to ethanol, butanol is considered toxic. It can cause severe eye and skin irritation and suppression of the nervous system.

HISTORY

The concept of biofuels is not new. People have been using biomass such as plant material to heat their houses for thousands of years. The idea of using hydrogen as fuel was expressed by Jules Verne in his novel *L'Île mystérieuse* (1874-1875; *The Mysterious Island*, 1875). In 1900, Rudolf Diesel, the inventor of the diesel engine, used peanut oil for his engine during the World Exhibition in Paris, France. Henry Ford's first (1908) car, the Model T, was made to run on pure ethanol. Later, the popularity of biofuels as a fuel source followed the "oil trouble times." For example, biofuels were considered during the 1970's oil embargo. Early in the twenty-first century, concerns about global warming and oil-price increases reignited interest in biofuels. In 2005, the U.S. Congress passed the Energy Policy Act, which included several sections related to biofuels. In particular, this energy bill required more research on biofuels, mixing ethanol with gasoline, and an increase in the production of cellulosic biofuels.

OBTAINING BIOFUELS

Ethanol is produced mainly by the microbial fermentation of starch crops (such as corn, wheat, and barley) or sugarcane. In the United States, most of the ethanol is produced by the yeast (fungal) fermentation of sugar from cornstarch. Ethanol can be produced from cellulose, the most plentiful biological material on Earth; however, current methods of converting cellulosic material into ethanol are inefficient and require intensive research and development efforts. Ethanol can also be produced by chemical means from petroleum. Therefore, ethanol that is produced by microbial fermentation is commonly referred to as "bioethanol."

In the United States, biodiesel comes mainly from soybean plants; in Europe, the world's top producer of biodiesel, it comes from canola oil. Other vegetative oils that have been used in biodiesel production are corn, sunflower, cottonseed, jatropha, palm oil, and rapeseed. Another possible source for biodiesel production is microscopic algae (microalgae), the microorganisms similar to plants.

Methane is produced by microorganisms and is an integral part of their metabolism. Biogas is produced during the anaerobic fermentation of organic matter by a community of microorganisms (bacteria and archaea). For practical use, methane and biogas are generated from wastewater, animal waste, and "gas wells" in landfills. Biomass is produced naturally, in the forest, and agriculturally, from agricultural residues and dung.

No commercial biohydrogen production process

exists. The most attractive for industrial applications is H_2 production by photosynthetic microbes. These microorganisms, such as microscopic algae, cyanobacteria, and photosynthetic bacteria, use sunlight as an energy source and water to generate hydrogen.

Butanol can be produced by the fermentation of sugars similar to the ethanol production. The most well-known pathway of butanol generation is fermentation by bacterium *Clostridium acetobutylicum*. Substrates utilized for butanol production—starch, molasses, cheese whey, and lignocellulosic materials—are exactly the same as for ethanol fermentation. The biological production by fermentation is not economically attractive because of low levels of product concentrations and high cost of product recovery compared to the chemical process.

This Volvo car runs on bioethanol, a biofuel manufactured from common household trash. (AP/Wide World Photos)

USES OF BIOFUELS

With increasing energy demands and oil prices, ethanol has become a valuable option as an alternative transportation fuel. The Energy Policy Act of 2005 included a requirement to increase the production of ethanol from 15 to 28 billion liters by 2012. Beginning in 2008, a majority of fuel stations in the United States were selling gasoline with 10 percent ethanol in it. Nearly all cars can use E10, fuel that is 10 percent ethanol. Blending ethanol with gasoline oxygenates the fuel mixture, which burns more completely and produces fewer harmful CO emissions. Another environmental benefit of ethanol is that it degrades in the soil, whereas petroleum-based fuels are more resistant to degradation and have many damaging effects when accidentally discharged into the environment. However, a liter of ethanol has significantly less energy content than a liter of gasoline, so vehicles must be refueled more often. Ethanol is also more expensive than gasoline, although rising prices of gasoline could cancel that disadvantage. In addition, carcinogenic aldehydes, such as formaldehyde, are produced when ethanol is burned in internal combustion engines. Carbon dioxide, a major greenhouse gas, forms as well. Moreover, the widely used fuel mix that is 85 percent ethanol and 15 percent gasoline (the E85 blend) requires specially equipped "flexible fuel" engines. In the United States, only a fraction of all cars are considered "flex fuel" vehicles. By comparison, however, most cars in Brazil have flex engines. Beginning in 1977, the Brazilian government made using ethanol as a fuel for cars mandatory. Brazil has the largest and most successful "ethanol for fuel" program in the world. As a result of this successful program, the country reached complete self-sufficiency in energy supply in 2006.

Biodiesel performs similarly to diesel and can be used in unmodified diesel engines of trucks, tractors, and other vehicles, and it is better for the environment. Burning biodiesel produces fewer emissions than petroleum-based diesel; it is essentially free of sulfur and aromatics and emits less CO. Additionally, biodiesel is less toxic to the soil. Biodiesel is often blended with petroleum diesel in different ratios of 2, 5, or 20 percent. The most common blend is B20, or 20 percent biodiesel to 80 percent diesel fuel. Biodiesel can be used as a pure fuel (100 percent or B100), but pure fuel is not suitable for winter because it thickens in cold temperatures. In addition, B100 is a solvent that degrades engines' rubber hoses and gaskets. Moreover, biodiesel energy content is less than in diesel. In general, biodiesel is not used as widely as ethanol. However, biodiesel users include the United States Postal Service; the U.S. Departments of Defense, Energy, and Agriculture; national parks; school districts; transit authorities; and public-utilities, waste-management, and recycling companies across the United States. In January, 2009, Continental Airlines successfully demonstrated the use of a biodiesel mixture from plants and algae (50 percent to 50 percent) to fly its Boeing 737-800.

In the 1985 Mel Gibson movie *Mad Max Beyond Thunderdome*, a futuristic city was run on methane that was generated by pig manure. In reality, methane can be a very good alternative fuel. It has a number of advantages over other fuels produced by microorganisms. First, it is easy to make and can be generated locally, which does not require distribution. Extensive natural gas infrastructure is already in place to be utilized. Second, the utilization of methane as a fuel is an attractive way to reduce wastes such as manure, wastewater, or municipal and industrial wastes. In local farms, manure is fed into digesters (bioreactors) where microorganisms metabolize it into methane. Methane can be used to fuel electrical generators to produce electricity. In China, millions of small farms have simple small underground digesters near the farm houses. There are several landfill gas facilities in the United States that generate electricity using methane. San Francisco has extended its recycling program to include conversion of dog waste into methane to produce electricity and to heat homes. With a dog population of 120,000 this initiative promises to generate a significant amount of fuel with a huge reduction of waste at the same time. Methane was used as a fuel for vehicles for a number of years. Several Volvo car models with bi-fuel engines were made to run on compressed methane with gasoline as a backup. Biogas can also be compressed, like methane, and used to power motor vehicles.

In many countries, millions of small farms maintain a simple digester for biogas production to generate energy. Currently, there are more than five million household digesters in China, used by people mainly for cooking and lighting, and there are more than one million biogas plants of various capacities in India.

Utilization of methane and biogas as an energy source in place of fossil fuels is providing significant environmental and economic benefits. Biofuels are essentially nonpolluting, although their utilization results in production of CO_2 and contributes to global warming, though with less impact on Earth's climate than methane itself as a greenhouse gas. Even though the use of methane and biogas as energy sources releases CO_2, the process as a whole can be considered "CO_2 neutral" in that the released CO_2 can be assimilated by their producers, archaea and bacteria.

Some examples of biomass use as an alternative energy source include burning wood or agricultural residue to heat homes. This is an inefficient use of energy—typically only 5-15 percent of the biomass energy is actually utilized. Using biomass that way produces harmful indoor air pollutants such as carbon monoxide. Yet biomass is an almost "free" resource costing only labor to collect. Biomass supplies more than 15 percent of the world's energy consumption. Biomass is the top source of energy in developing countries; in some countries it provides more than 90 percent of the energy used.

Hydrogen powered U.S. rockets for many years. Today, a growing number of automobile manufacturers around the world are making prototype hydrogen-powered vehicles. Only water is emitted from the tailpipe—no greenhouse gases. The car is moved by a motor that runs on electricity generated in the fuel cell via a chemical reaction between H_2 and O_2. Hydrogen vehicles offer quiet operation, rapid acceleration, and low maintenance costs. During peak time, when electricity is expensive, fuel-cell hydrogen cars could provide power for homes and offices. Hydrogen for these applications is obtained mainly from natural gas (methane and propane) via steam reforming. Biohydrogen is used in experimental applications only. Many problems need to be overcome before biohydrogen can be easily available. One of the reasons for the delayed acceptance of biohydrogen is the difficulty of its production on a cost-effective basis. For biohydrogen power to become a reality, tremendous research and investment efforts are necessary.

Butanol can be used as transportation fuel. It contains almost as much energy as gasoline and more energy than ethanol for a particular volume. Unlike 85 percent ethanol, a butanol/gasoline mix (E85 blend) can be used in cars designed for gasoline without making any changes to the engine.

Sergei A. Markov

FURTHER READING

Chisti, Yusuf. "Biodiesel from Microalgae." *Biotechnology Advances* 25, no. 3 (2007): 294-306.

Glazer, Alexander N., and Hiroshi Nikaido. *Microbial Biotechnology: Fundamentals of Applied Microbiology.* New York: W. H. Freeman, 2007.

Service, Robert F. "The Hydrogen Backlash." *Science* 305, no. 5686 (August 13, 2004): 958-961.

Wald, Matthew L. "Is Ethanol for the Long Haul?" *Scientific American* 296, no. 1 (January, 2007): 42-49.

Wright, Richard T. *Environmental Science: Towards a Sustainable Future.* 9th ed. Englewood Cliffs, N.J.: Prentice Hall, 2004.

WEB SITE

AE BIOFUELS
http://www.alternative-energy-news.info/technology/biofuels/

SEE ALSO: Brazil; Energy economics; Ethanol; Methane; Sugars; Sustainable development.

Biogeochemical cycles. *See* Carbon cycle; Geochemical cycles; Hydrology and the hydrologic cycle; Nitrogen cycle; Phosphorus cycle; Sulfur cycle

Biogeographic realms. *See* Ecozones and biogeographic realms

Biological invasions

CATEGORIES: Environment, conservation, and resource management; pollution and waste disposal

A biological invasion is an enormous increase in the numbers of a type of organism entering an ecosystem that the organism previously was not inhabiting. The "invading" organism may be an infectious virus, a bacterium, a plant, or an animal.

BACKGROUND

Species introduced to an area from somewhere outside that area are referred to as alien or exotic species or as invaders. Because the exotic species is not native to the new area, it is often unsuccessful in establishing a viable population and disappears. The fossil record, as well as historical documentation, indicates that this is the fate of many exotic species as they move from their native habitats to invade new environments. Oc-

casionally, however, an invading species finds the new environment to its liking; in this case the invader may become so successful in exploiting its new habitat that it can completely alter the ecological balance of an ecosystem, destroying biodiversity and altering the local biological hierarchy. Because of this ability to alter ecosystems, exotic invaders are considered major agents in driving native species to extinction and are thought to be responsible for an estimated 40 percent of all known extinctions of land animals beginning in the year 1600.

Biological invasions by notorious species constitute a significant component of Earth's history. In general, large-scale climatic changes and geological crises are at the origin of massive exchanges of flora and fauna. On a geologic timescale, invasions of species from one continent to another are true evolutionary processes, just as speciation and extinction are. On a smaller scale, physical barriers such as oceans, mountains, and deserts can be overcome by many organisms as their populations expand. Organisms can be carried by water in rivers or ocean currents, transported by wind, or carried by other species as they migrate seasonally or to escape environmental pressures. However, the geological and historical records of the Earth also show that specific biological invasions by exotic species have altered the course of world history. The extinction of genetically distinct populations is the least reversible of all global changes, and evidence suggests that biological invasions contribute substantially to an increase in the rate of extinction within ecosystems.

Humans have transplanted species throughout history, to the point where most people are not aware of the distinction between native and exotic species living in their region. Recent increases in intercontinental invasion rates by exotic species, brought about primarily by human activity, create important ecological problems for the recipient lands. Among animals, the most notorious recent invaders of North America have been the house mouse and the Norway rat; others include the wild boar, donkey, horse, nutria, Pierid butterfly, house sparrow, starling, Africanized ("killer") bee, tiger mosquito, and red fox. One of the most destructive invaders is the house cat. More than seventy million domestic and feral cats live in the United States, and they are efficient at hunting small mammals and birds. Domestic cats are credited with killing twenty million birds annually in Great Britain.

It would seem logical to assume that invading species might add to the biodiversity of a region, but many invaders have the opposite effect. The new species are often opportunistic and successful predators that eliminate native species not adapted to their presence. For example, the brown tree snake was accidentally introduced to Guam during World War II as a stowaway on military cargo ships, and the snakes have eliminated most of the island's birds. The snakes are credited with the extinction of one-third of the island's native bird species, and the surviving bird population is so decimated that birds are rarely seen or heard. The invasion of the brown tree snake has unalterably reduced the biological diversity of Guam.

ECOSYSTEM ALTERATION

The invasion of an ecosystem by an exotic species can effectively alter ecosystem processes. An invading species does not simply consume or compete with native species but can actually change the rules of existence within the ecosystem by altering processes such as primary productivity, decomposition, hydrology, geomorphology, nutrient cycling, and natural disturbance regimes. Invading exotic species may also drive

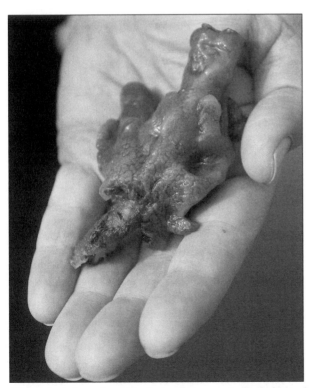

The tunicate is an invasive species that grows in the habitat of anemones and sea cucumbers. (AP/Wide World Photos)

out native species by competing with them for resources. One of the exotic invaders of the North American continent is the zebra mussel, which came to the United States in 1986 in the ballast water of oceangoing vessels; it was carried from the Elbe or Rhine River in Europe and released into the water of the St. Clair River near Detroit, Michigan. The mussel larvae found biological conditions in the Great Lakes ideal. The mussel now exists in all the Great Lakes, and after the catastrophic flood of 1993 the mussels were sighted in the Mississippi River Basin. Mussel density in certain locations of the Great Lakes is known to be astonishing—greater than 94,000 individuals per square meter. In 1990, the Detroit Edison power plant discovered a water intake pipe blocked by a mussel population density of 700,000 mussels per square meter. When they reach high population densities, the mussels are able to filter virtually all the larger plankton from the water. The planktonic food chain of the Great Lakes, which supports Great Lakes fisheries, may decline so much that higher trophic species will be deprived of their vital plankton food sources. The mussels also cause a demise of native bivalves through competition for food and because they attach themselves to the shells of other bivalves.

FORESTS

The invasion of native forests by non-native insects and microorganisms has been devastating on many continents. The white pine blister rust and the balsam woolly adelgid have invaded both commercial and preserved forestlands in North America. Both exotics were brought to North America in the late 1800's on nursery stock from Europe. The balsam woolly adelgid attacks fir trees and causes death within two to seven years by causing chemical damage and by feeding on the tree's vascular tissue. The adelgid has killed nearly every adult cone-bearing fir tree in the southern Appalachian Mountains. The white pine blister rust attacks five-needle pines; in the western United States fewer than 10 pine trees in 100,000 are resistant, and since white pine seeds are an essential food source for bears and other animals, the loss of the trees has had severe consequences across the forest food chain.

Beginning in the 1800's the deciduous forests of eastern North America were attacked numerous times by waves of invading exotic species and diseases. One of the most notable invaders is the gypsy moth, which consumes a variety of tree species. Other invaders of eastern forests have virtually eliminated the once dominant American chestnut and the American elm. Other tree species that continue to decline because of new invaders include the American beech, mountain ash, white birch, butternut, sugar maple, flowering dogwood, and eastern hemlock. It is widely accepted that the invasion of exotic species is the single greatest threat to the diversity of deciduous forests in North America.

EFFECTS ON HUMANS, AND HUMANS AS INVADERS

Some introduced exotic species are beneficial to humanity. It would be impossible to support the present world human population entirely on species native to their regions. However, many invading species degrade human health and wealth, and others affect the structure of ecosystems or the ability to maintain native biodiversity. Many invading species can act as vectors of disease: Examples include bubonic plague, vectored by rats; a host of diseases transmitted between human populations during first contacts, including smallpox, polio, influenza, and venereal infections; and malaria, dengue fever, Ross River fever, and eastern equine encephalitis, carried by mosquitoes. Mosquitoes alone are thought to account for half of all human deaths throughout history.

Humans, the ultimate biological invaders, have been responsible for the extinction of many species and will continue to be in the future. Like other animal invaders, humans tend to have a broad diet. Humans are also able to adapt culturally to diverse habitats, an ability that complements an ability to breed all year round. These attributes give humans a distinct advantage over less aggressive and less destructive species.

Randall L. Milstein

FURTHER READING

Burdick, Alan. *Out of Eden: An Odyssey of Ecological Invasion.* New York: Farrar, Straus and Giroux, 2005.

Cartwright, Frederick F., and Michael Biddiss. *Disease and History.* 2d ed. Stroud, England: Sutton, 2000.

Crosby, Alfred W. *Ecological Imperialism: The Biological Expansion of Europe, 900-1900.* 2d ed. New York: Cambridge University Press, 2004.

Elton, Charles S. *The Ecology of Invasions by Animals and Plants.* London: Methuen, 1958. Reprint. Chicago: University of Chicago Press, 2000.

Hengeveld, Rob. *Dynamics of Biological Invasions.* New York: Chapman and Hall, 1989.

Lockwood, Julie L., Martha F. Hoopes, and Michael P. Marchetti. *Invasion Ecology.* Malden, Mass.: Blackwell, 2007.

Mooney, Harold A., and James A. Drake, eds. *Ecology of Biological Invasions of North America and Hawaii.* New York: Springer, 1986.

Mooney, Harold A., and Richard J. Hobbs, eds. *Invasive Species in a Changing World.* Washington, D.C.: Island Press, 2000.

Nentwig, Wolfgang, ed. *Biological Invasions.* New York: Springer, 2007.

Pimentel, David, ed. *Biological Invasions: Economic and Environmental Costs of Alien Plant, Animal, and Microbe Species.* Boca Raton, Fla.: CRC Press, 2002.

WEB SITE

UNIVERSITY OF TENNESSEE, DEPARTMENT OF ECOLOGY AND ENVIRONMENTAL BIOLOGY
Institute for Biological Invasions
http://invasions.bio.utk.edu

SEE ALSO: Genetic diversity; Pesticides and pest control; Species loss.

Biomes

CATEGORY: Ecological resources

Biomes (terrestrial and aquatic ecosystems) are distributed throughout the Earth's surface. Terrestrial biomes occupy the landmass from North Pole to South Pole. Aquatic biomes occupy the bodies of water on Earth.

BACKGROUND

Biomes are natural habitats for bacteria, protists, fungi, plants, and animals. Biomes maintain the natural life cycle of these organisms and preserve the products of geological processes on Earth. A biome is a source of shelter, rocks and minerals, and food and fiber for human needs.

TECHNICAL DEFINITION

A terrestrial biome is a large ecosystem characterized by a particular type of climate and soils with defined groups of highly adapted living organisms. Biome formation is influenced by warm temperature and heavy precipitation in the tropics and extreme cold and low precipitation near the poles. Most ecologists do not consider aquatic ecosystems as biomes and refer to them as "aquatic biomes," which are classified based on the concentration of dissolved salts: less than 0.1 percent in freshwater biomes, 0.1 to 1.0 percent in estuaries, and more than 1.0 percent in marine biomes.

CLIMATE AND BIOMES

Climate shapes terrestrial biomes. Climate is predominantly driven by the solar energy and atmospheric circulation. Air circulation is initiated at the equator, because the equator receives the greatest solar energy with the warmest air near the ground. Because of different air densities, warm air in the troposphere rises into the stratosphere and cools. Cool air in the stratosphere descends into troposphere and warms. This rise and fall pattern of circulating air starts at 0° (equator) to 30° latitude, then continues at 30° to 60° latitude, and ends at 60° to 90° latitude (poles).

There are six major atmospheric circulations: Three move from the equator to the North Pole; the other three move from the equator to the South Pole. At 0° latitude, the ascending warm, humid air from the troposphere cools and condenses as it reaches the stratosphere, releasing heavy rain to or near the equator. That the dominant biomes formed at the equator are the tropical rain forests is no accident. After releasing rain, the cool, dry air moves poleward and descends at 30° latitude. The descending cool, dry air becomes warm as it reaches the troposphere and then absorbs all the available moisture. Not surprisingly, the dominant biomes at 30° latitude are the deserts, where the warm, humid air splits. One air mass moves equatorward to recirculate at 0° latitude. The other moves poleward and rises at 60° latitude, releasing rain or snow while at the stratosphere. As a result, the dominant biomes at 60° latitude are the temperate forests and temperate grasslands. The cool, dry air at the stratosphere divides again 60° latitude. One air mass moves toward 30° latitude to descend and recirculate in the desert. The other moves poleward, then descends and releases the remaining moisture near the poles, where the arctic tundra biomes are formed.

TERRESTRIAL BIOMES

The are nine major terrestrial biomes.

ARCTIC TUNDRA. Arctic tundra is located in the Northern Hemisphere near the North Pole and covers 20 percent of Earth's landmass. It has extremely long, freezing, and harsh winters, with very short (six- to eight-week) summers. It is considered "cold desert,"

because it receives 20 centimeters of precipitation per year. Melting snow creates bogs in summer, but there are frozen layers of subsoil (permafrost) at least a meter deep that exist throughout the year. Soil is nutrient-poor. Only the low-growing grasses and dwarf woody shrubs adapted to extreme cold and a short growing season are found. No trees survive. Their roots cannot penetrate the permafrost. Few animal species live in tundra. In winters, ptarmigans, musk oxen, snowy owls, lynxes, arctic foxes, and snowshoe hares are found. Polar bears are common in the coastal regions. In summers, few migrating animals from taiga move to tundra. No reptiles are found, but mosquitoes survive.

TAIGA. Taiga, also called boreal coniferous forest, exists south of tundra and covers 11 percent of the Earth's land surface. It is found in the northern parts of North America and Eurasia and along the Pacific coast of northern North America to Northern California. It has patchy and shallower permafrost than tundra, and has acidic, nutrient-poor soil. It has short summers and long, cold winters and receives 50 centimeters precipitation per year. Evergreen conifers are adapted to these conditions, with low-lying mosses and lichens beneath the forest canopy. Seeds of conifers attract birds. Bears, deer, moose, beavers, muskrats, wolves, mountain lions, and wolverines inhabit the taiga.

TEMPERATE RAIN FOREST. Temperate rain forest, a coniferous forest, stretches along the west coast of Canada and the United States, the southeast of Australia, and the south of South America. It has dense fog, mild winters, cool summers, and high annual precipitation of 250 centimeters. With abundant rain and nutrient-rich soil, the temperate rain forests have retained some of the tallest conifers (such as coastal redwoods) and oldest trees, some as old as eight hundred years. Moisture-loving plants (mosses and ferns) grow on the tree trunks of evergreen conifers. Temperate rain forest is a habitat for squirrels, lynxes, and several species of amphibians, reptiles, and birds (such as the spotted owl).

TEMPERATE DECIDUOUS FOREST. Temperate deciduous forest is located south of the taiga in eastern North America, eastern Asia, and much of Europe. Temperate deciduous forests have a moderate climate, with occasional hot summers and cold winters and high annual precipitation of 75 to 150 centimeters. They have long growing seasons ranging from 140 to 300 days. The soil is rich in minerals. The dominant trees are deciduous (oak, beech, sycamore, and maple), which shed their broad leaves in the fall and grow them in the spring. Under the forest's canopy, understory trees and shrubs are found. Layers of growth in the forest are home for several insects and birds. Ground animals include rabbits, squirrels, woodchucks, chipmunks, turkeys, beavers, and muskrats.

TEMPERATE GRASSLANDS. Temperate grasslands include the South American pampas, the Russian steppes, and the North American prairies. Tall-grass prairies are found between Illinois and Indiana, whereas short-grass prairies extend from Texas to Montana and North Dakota. They have hot and dry summers and bitterly cold winters, with annual precipitation of 25 to 75 centimeters. Grasses in these biomes produce a deep, dark, mineral-rich soil. Herbivore mammals (bison, pronghorn antelope, mice, prairie dogs, and rabbits) dominate the temperate grasslands. Hawks, snakes, badgers, coyotes, and foxes are the predators in this biome.

SHRUBLAND. Shrubland, or chaparral, is composed of thickets of small-leaf evergreen shrubs (shorter than trees and without main trunks). Shrublands, with frequent fires in dry summers and winters of 25 to 75 centimeters of rain annually, are found along the cape of South Africa, the western coast of North America, the southwestern and southern shores of Australia, around the Mediterranean Sea, and in central Chile. The shrubland in California is called chaparral, because it lacks understory. Shrubs are fire-adapted and highly flammable. The seeds of many species require the scarring action of fire to induce germination. Other shrubs resprout from the roots after fire. Mule deer, rodents, scrub jays, and lizards inhabit the shrublands.

DESERTS. Deserts exist near or at 30° north and south latitudes and cover approximately 30 percent of the Earth's land surface. The dry air that descends in this region absorbs most of the available moisture, then moves away to the equator and to 60° latitude. Deserts receive less than 25 centimeters of rain annually. The Sahara Desert of Africa and the Arabian Peninsula and the deserts of North America (Mojave, Chihuahuan, and Sonoran) have little or no vegetation. Organisms with specialized water-conserving adaptations survive, including cactus, agave, Joshua trees, and sagebrush plants. Hawks prey on lizards, snakes, roadrunners, and kangaroo rats.

TROPICAL GRASSLANDS. Tropical grasslands, or savannas (such as African savannas), characterized by widespread growth of grasses with few interspersed trees, are found in areas with seasonal low rainfall and prolonged dry periods. Other savannas occur in South America and northern Australia. Savanna has an annual precipitation of 25 to 75 centimeters. Savanna soil is nutrient-poor. Acacia trees survive the severe dry season. Hoofed herbivore mammals (giraffes, elephants, zebras, and rhinoceroses) feed on tree vegetation and on grasses. Carnivores such as hyenas, lions, cheetahs, and leopards prey on herbivores.

TROPICAL RAIN FORESTS. Tropical rain forests are located in South America, Africa, Southeast Asia, and the Indo-Malayan region on or near the equator. Wet and dry seasons are warm year-round. Annual rainfall is 200 to 450 centimeters. Tropical rain forest soil is typically nutrient-poor, but plentiful rain supports the growth of diverse groups of woody and herbaceous plants. Some of the rains come from recycled water released by forest trees by transpiration. Of all the biomes, tropical rain forest is the richest, based on species diversity, productivity, and abundance of all organisms. Tropical rain forest has three levels: the canopy (the highest layer of the forest), the understory (middle layers of small trees and shrubs), and forest floor (ground layers of herbaceous plants). Epiphyte plants (such as bromeliads, orchids, ferns, and Spanish moss) gain access to sunlight by growing on trunks and branches of tall trees. Lemurs, sloths, and monkeys are tree-dwelling primates that feed on fruits. The largest carnivores in the tropical rain forest are the jaguars in South America and the leopards in Africa and Asia.

AQUATIC BIOMES

All aquatic biomes share three ecological groups of organisms: the plankton, nekton, and benthos. Plankton are classified into microscopic phytoplankton and large zooplankton. Phytoplankton are producers and include photosynthetic cyanobacteria and free-floating algae, which provide oxygen and food for heterotrophic organisms. Zooplankton are consumers, heterotrophic, nonphotosynthetic organisms that include protozoa, small crustaceans, and larvae of aquatic animals. Nekton are larger swimming animals such as turtles, fishes, and whales. Benthos are bottom-dwelling animals that attach themselves to a substratum (sponges, oysters, and barnacles), burrow themselves into soil (clams, worms, and echinoderms) or simply swim or walk on the bottom (crayfish, crabs, lobsters, insect larvae, and brittle stars).

Based on salt contents, the three major aquatic ecosystems are the freshwater, estuary, and marine ecosystems. Freshwater ecosystems, which contain less than 0.1 percent dissolved salts and occupy about 2 percent of the Earth's surface, include flowing waters (streams and rivers), standing waters (ponds and lakes), and freshwater wetlands (marshes and swamps). While all freshwater habitats provide homes for animal species, greater vegetations are found in marshes (grasslike plants) and in swamps (trees and shrubs) than in flowing- and standing-water ecosystems. Estuaries occur where fresh water and salt water meet, with salt concentrations of 0.1 to 1.0 percent. Temperate estuaries called salt marshes are dominated by salt-tolerant grasses. Tropical estuaries are called mangrove forests. Marine ecosystems, which contain more than 1.0 percent dissolved salts, dominate, occupying about 70 percent of the Earth's surface. Marine biomes have three zones: the intertidal, pelagic, and benthic zones. The intertidal zone is the shoreline area between low and high tide. The pelagic zone is the ocean water (shallow or deep), where plankton and swimming marine organisms are found. The benthic zone is the ocean floor, where marine animals burrow. Coral reefs, kelp forests, and seagrass beds are part of the benthic zone.

History
The existence of aquatic and terrestrial ecosystems was discovered through fossil records. Aquatic biomes emerged before the terrestrial biomes. Approximately 542 million years ago, during the Cambrian period, organisms in marine biomes became diversified and included bacteria, cyanobacteria, algae, fungi, marine invertebrates, and first chordates. The first terrestrial biome existed when the first forest and gymnosperm appeared about 416 million years ago, during the Denovian period. About 359 million years ago, during the Carboniferous period, the formation of much more diversified forest occurred, which consisted of ferns, clubmosses, horsetails, and gymnosperms and which housed many insects, amphibians, and first reptiles. Flowering plants (angiosperms) later evolved and became the dominant organisms of most major biomes.

Domingo M. Jariel

Further Reading
Kirchner, Renee. *Biomes.* Detroit: KidHaven Press/ Thomson Gale, 2006.

Roth, Richard A. *Freshwater Aquatic Biomes.* Westport, Conn.: Greenwood Press, 2009.
Solomon, Eldra Pearl, Linda R. Berg, and Diana W. Martin. "Ecology and the Geography of Life." In *Biology.* 8th ed. Monterey, Calif.: Brooks/Cole, 2008.
Woodward, Susan L. *Marine Biomes.* Westport, Conn.: Greenwood Press, 2008.

Web Site

University of California Museum of Paleontology
http://www.ucmp.berkeley.edu/exhibits/biomes/index.php

See also: Biodiversity; Biosphere; Biosphere reserves.

Biopyriboles

Category: Mineral and other nonliving resources

Biopyriboles are minerals composed of linked silicate groups. Some hard biopyriboles are used as gemstones. Fibrous biopyriboles are used to manufacture asbestos. Micas are used in electrical components and as fillers, absorbents, and lubricants. Clays are used in bricks, pottery, and fillers.

Definition
Biopyriboles are a large and varied group of minerals in which silicate groups (one silicon atom bonded to four oxygen atoms) are linked together in one-dimensional chains (either single chains or two chains linked together) or two-dimensional sheets. Those with chains are usually hard, while those with sheets are usually soft. Hard biopyriboles are usually found as separate minerals within igneous and metamorphic rocks. Soft biopyriboles are usually found as flakes of mica within rocks or as particles of clay in soils and freshwater sediments.

Overview
There are three broad categories of biopyriboles, depending on whether the silicate groups are linked together into single chains, double chains, or sheets. Single-chain biopyriboles are known as pyroxenes. Double-chain biopyriboles are known as amphiboles. Together these two subgroups are known as pyriboles or inosilicates. Sheet biopyriboles are known as

phyllosilicates. The word "biopyribole" is a combination of "biotite" (a common phyllosilicate), "pyroxene," and "amphibole."

Pyroxenes are composed of chains of silicate groups combined with a wide variety of other atoms, including sodium, magnesium, calcium, iron, and aluminum. They are generally fairly hard minerals with a density between three and four grams per cubic centimeter. Pyroxenes are usually dark green or black, but other colors also exist. The most common pyroxene is augite, a green or black mineral sometimes used as a gemstone. Spodumene is a white, light gray, or light yellow pyroxene that contains lithium. It is the most important source of that element. Jadeite, a type of jade, is a green pyroxene used as a gemstone.

Amphiboles are composed of two linked chains of silicate groups combined with the same variety of atoms as those found in pyroxenes. They also contain hydroxyl groups (one oxygen atom bonded to one hydrogen atom), which cause them to release water when heated. At high temperatures the double chains

Augite is the most common pyroxene, a type of biopyribole. (USGS)

break down into single chains to form pyroxenes. Amphiboles are fairly hard minerals with a density between 2.9 and 3.6 grams per cubic centimeter. The most common amphibole is hornblende, a dark green or black mineral. Nephrite, a green amphibole, is a form of jade.

Phyllosilicates are composed of sheets of silicate groups combined with the same kinds of atoms as those

Biopyribole Categories

	EXAMPLES			EXAMPLES
Sheet silicates			Monoclinic calcic pyroxenes	Diopside, augite
Brittle mica group	—		Orthorhombic pyroxenes	Enstatite, hypersthene
Chlorite	—			
Clays	Kaolinite, smectite, illite		Pyroxenoids	Wollastonite
Serpentine	Antigorite, chrysotile asbestos		*Double silica tetrahedra chains:*	
Talc	Talc, pyrophyllite		Monoclinic alkali amphiboles	Glaucophane, riebeckite
Mica	Biotite, moscovite		Monoclinic calcic amphiboles	Tremolite, hornblende
Chain silicates			Monoclinic magnesium-iron amphiboles	Cummingtonite
Single silica tetrahedron chains:			Orthorhobmic amphiboles	Anthophyllite
Monoclinic alkali pyroxenes	Jadeite			

found in pyriboles. Most phyllosilicates are soft minerals with a density between 2 and 3 grams per cubic centimeter. Talc, a light-colored, very soft phyllosilicate, is used in paint, ceramics, and talcum powder. Serpentine, a green, fibrous mineral, is used to make asbestos. Many phyllosilicates exist as clays, used in ceramics and fillers, or as micas, used in electrical components.

Rose Secrest

SEE ALSO: Asbestos; Clays; Gems; Mica; Silicates; Talc.

Biosphere

CATEGORY: Ecological resources

The biosphere is the relatively thin layer around the Earth's surface where life is naturally possible. The concept is important in ecology for the calculation of energy and mineral resource budgets, in space exploration for the establishment and maintenance of livable environments for space travelers, and perhaps for understanding the possibilities for life on other planets.

BACKGROUND

The first use of the term "biosphere" dates to 1875, when geologist Eduard Suess described layers of the Earth in his book on the origin of the Alps. The Russian geologist Vladimir Vernadsky popularized the term in his lectures, published in French in 1929 as *La Biosphere*. Vernadsky noted that the concept, although not the term, had originated much earlier with the French biologist Jean-Baptiste Lamarck (1744-1829).

EXTENT OF THE BIOSPHERE

Although most people would think nothing of traveling 50 kilometers to a nearby town, journeying upward far less than this distance would mean certain death without a special support system. As altitude increases, decreases in pressure, vital gases, and temperature prevent active metabolism. However, dormant bacterial and fungal spores can apparently drift upward indefinitely in this "parabiosphere." Most jet plane passengers are aware that artificial cabin pressure is required to sustain them in the thinning atmosphere when they are only a few kilometers high. Chlorophyll plants cannot live above about 6,200 meters because all water freezes at that altitude and the carbon dioxide available for photosynthesis is at less than half that available at sea level. The few spiders and springtails that live on top of Mount Everest survive on plant and animal debris blown up there by wind currents.

Life also extends downward into the deepest ocean trenches, although the density of organisms is drastically less in the dark zones beneath the thin top layer, where sunlight feeds algae and the resultant food chains. Most deep-ocean organisms must feed on the rain of organic matter that sinks from the surface or feed in the detritus food chain. Many organisms live on the surface of the ocean bottom, and sampling studies have shown that life extends deep into these bottom muds. Not all organisms here derive their energy indirectly from plant photosynthesis; some thrive on food chains originating with sulfur bacteria. Organisms that have evolved to live under the tremendous water pressure of the lower oceans burst open if pulled to the surface; conversely, humans would be crushed at these depths, so exploration requires heavy protective equipment. Like deep-ocean fish brought to the surface, humans decompress when exposed at high altitudes. Therefore, much of the biosphere is beyond humans' day-to-day reach.

BIOMES

The terrestrial part of the biosphere can be subdivided into such categories as hot and wet tropical rain forests, frozen arctic tundra, cold mountaintop meadows, and prairie grasslands. These natural communities with similar plants and animals are called "biomes." For example, conifer forests stretch around the upper latitudes of Canada, Europe, and Russia. Although the species of conifer trees, large grazers, and predators differ, the ecology is very similar. The same is true for the grassland biome that occurs in the U.S. plains states, Russia, Argentina, and South Africa, and the temperate deciduous forests of the eastern United States, Europe, and China. Other biomes include taiga, savanna, thornbush, chaparral, and various tropical rain forest types.

The first breakdown of biotic communities was made by C. Hart Merriam, working in 1890 in California and Arizona; his "vegetative life zones" were based on temperature and ignored rainfall. Victor E. Shelford added detailed descriptions of animal associations but did not try to correlate communities with climate. While Shelford's followers consider biomes to be distinct entities, other ecologists view them as human concepts that hide the fact that communities gradually blend into one another. The biome concept finds use in the biosphere reserve program, which is based on environmental planning aimed at saving substantial portions of each unique biome.

Energy Entering the Biosphere

The biosphere concept serves an accounting function by placing all living systems on one enclosed "spaceship Earth"—a concept that became far easier for the public to visualize when the space program provided actual photographs of Earth as a planet. It became obvious that energy input was limited and that nutrients must be recycled. The Earth intercepts about 2.5 billion billion horsepower of energy per year as sunlight. Most reflects back into space or temporarily heats surfaces. Because photosynthetic leaves and algae intercept less than 1 percent of this light, there is a limit on the amount of plant life that can be supported and on the amount of animal life and decomposers that can be fed. Ecologists have estimated that the maximum amount of living tissue (both animals and plants) that can be supported in the biosphere each year is about 370 billion metric tons, consisting of about 260 billion metric tons of plants and 110 billion metric tons of consumers.

Cycles in the Biosphere

Water in the biosphere is stable at about 1.5 billion cubic kilometers, all but 3 percent of which is salt water in oceans. Three-quarters of fresh water has been estimated to be frozen in glaciers and polar ice caps. The Earth's water cycle (hydrologic cycle), then, involves less than 1 percent of the total water, which evaporates from ocean surfaces or transpires through plant leaves and then precipitates back down as rain, snow, and so on. While water is involved in the photosynthesis reaction, water is far more important in plant transpiration, where on average a hundred units of water must flow through a plant to produce one unit of plant tissue. More than any other factor, the pace of the water cycle and the uneven distribution of water account for the variation in vegetation zones on the Earth's land surfaces.

In addition to the hydrogen and oxygen in water, all organisms use carbon, nitrogen, phosphorus, sulfur, sodium, potassium, and many other elements. Whereas water may evaporate and condense back down in an average of ten days, carbon may take a decade to cycle. In the atmosphere, 635 billion metric tons of carbon exist as carbon dioxide. Green plants

convert a portion into carbon in plant tissues on land (408 billion metric tons) or in phytoplankton (4.5 billion metric tons) each year. Decomposition returns some carbon in dead organic matter (408 billion metric tons) to the atmosphere as carbon dioxide, while some dead organic matter sinks to become part of a huge sediment repository (18 million billion metric tons). Coal and oil represent stored carbon from earlier photosynthesis that is rapidly released into the atmosphere when fossil fuels are burned. With about 5 billion metric tons of fossil carbon released into the atmosphere each year, a dramatic increase in atmospheric carbon dioxide would be expected. However, the ocean appears to be a sink that can absorb excess carbon dioxide and buffer these fluctuations.

Oxygen is a vital element that cycles through many complex molecules. In general, however, atmospheric oxygen gas molecules find themselves cycled through plants by photosynthesis about every two thousand years. Oxygen in atmospheric carbon dioxide is respired by plants about once every three hundred years. Nitrogen makes up 70 percent of the atmosphere, but it must be combined with hydrogen or oxygen before it can be incorporated into plants. By cultivating legumes (beans and related plants) and industrially "fixing" nitrogen, humans have boosted the amount of nitrogen fixation in the nitrogen cycle by 10 percent. The amount of fixed nitrogen introduced to the biosphere each year exceeds that which is denitrified, with the difference likely building up in groundwater, rivers, lakes, and oceans.

The biosphere concept is too broad to be useful in most modern ecological research, with ecologists specializing in detailing specific ecosystems, refining energy flow budgets, or calculating biogeochemical cycles. However, the concept still finds use in biology textbooks for defining the limits where life is physically possible. Combining the studies of the large-scale cycles allows scientists to assemble the "big picture" of the biosphere.

John Richard Schrock

Further Reading

Huggett, Richard John. *The Natural History of the Earth: Debating Long-Term Change in the Geosphere and Biosphere.* New York: Routledge, 2006.

Lovelock, James. *Gaia: A New Look at Life on Earth.* New York: Oxford University Press, 2000.

_____. *The Vanishing Face of Gaia: A Final Warning.* New York: Basic Books, 2009.

Rambler, Mitchell B., Lynn Margulis, and René Fester, eds. *Global Ecology: Towards a Science of the Biosphere.* Boston: Academic Press, 1989.

Samson, Paul R., and David Pitt, eds. *The Biosphere and Noosphere Reader: Global Environment, Society, and Change.* New York: Routledge, 1999.

Smil, Vaclav. *The Earth's Biosphere: Evolution, Dynamics, and Change.* Cambridge, Mass.: MIT Press, 2002.

Trudgill, Stephen. *The Terrestrial Biosphere: Environmental Change, Ecosystem Science, Attitudes, and Values.* New York: Prentice Hall, 2001.

SEE ALSO: Atmosphere; Biosphere reserves; Ecosystems; Geochemical cycles; Greenhouse gases and global climate change; Lithosphere; Nitrogen cycle; Oceans; Oxygen; Soil; Water.

Biosphere reserves

CATEGORY: Ecological resources
DATE: Developed 1974; revised 1995

The biosphere reserve network is an international conservation initiative under the United Nations Educational, Scientific and Cultural Organization's (UNESCO's) program on Man and the Biosphere (MAB). It designates legally protected mosaics of ecological systems.

BACKGROUND

Although the original concept of biosphere reserves was first discussed in 1968 at UNESCO's Biosphere Conference, it did not become a formal designation until 1974, when UNESCO developed the biosphere reserve designation under the MAB program. The biosphere reserve designation was intended to set aside combinations of terrestrial, coastal, and marine ecosystems for conversation and management to maintain biodiversity. Unlike many conservation systems, the biosphere reserve system is specifically intended to encourage research into and implementation of sustainable human use of resources. The biosphere reserve network was launched in 1976 and grew rapidly. In 1983, the First International Biosphere Reserve Congress in Minsk, Belarus, gave rise in 1984 to an Action Plan for Biosphere Reserves.

The program was significantly revised in 1995 at the International Conference on Biosphere Reserves in Seville, Spain, when the World Network of Biosphere Reserves (WNBR) was established. The Madrid Action Plan agreed upon at the Third World Congress of Biosphere Reserves in 2008 built further upon the Seville Strategy.

The WNBR consists of more than five hundred sites in more than 105 countries. Biosphere reserves consist of a core, conservation-only zone, a buffer zone that allows certain ecologically sound practices, and a transition zone where sustainable resource use is permitted within the parameters of international agreements such as Agenda 21 and the Convention on Biological Diversity.

Reserves are nominated to the WNBR by national governments according to a set of criteria and conditions. Many biosphere reserves overlap with other types of protected areas, such as national parks and UNESCO World Heritage sites. In the United States, for example, many biosphere reserves are under the management of the U.S. National Park Service. These include Big Bend National Park, Denali National Park, Glacier National Park, Rocky Mountain National Park, Virgin Islands National Park, and Isle Royale National Park, among others.

The United States, China, Russia, and Spain have the largest number of biosphere reserves. Some reserves cross international borders. While nearly all reserves follow the three-zone scheme, they are managed in a wide variety of ways and with varying conformation to the guidelines set out by UNESCO.

PROVISIONS

The MAB has three main objectives: to contribute to minimizing biodiversity loss, to promote environmental sustainability through the WNBR, and to enhance linkages between cultural and biological diversity. Under the first objective, the program focuses on a broad interdisciplinary research agenda examining the ecological, social, and economic impacts of biodiversity loss. Along with this, a network of learning centers for integrated ecosystem management was developed.

In specific biosphere reserve contexts, emphasis is placed on linkages between biodiversity conservation and socioeconomic development. These strengthen knowledge of environmental sustainability, including the sustainable use of natural resources for local communities.

Finally, the program provides special attention to cultural landscapes and sacred sites, particularly biosphere reserves and World Heritage sites. It seeks to

A ship navigates Chile's Northern Patagonia Ice Field, a UNESCO World Biosphere Reserve. (AFP/Getty Images)

establish a knowledge base on cultural practices and traditions that involve local-level sustainable use of biodiversity in biosphere reserves.

Biosphere reserves are used to test new approaches to managing nature and human activities, connecting conservation, development, research, monitoring, and education. The core area or areas are traditional conservation areas for preserving biodiversity, monitoring minimally disturbed ecosystems, conducting nondestructive research, and other low-impact uses. The core areas are surrounded by a buffer zone, which is used more extensively for environmental education, ecotourism, and a wider range of research. Finally, this is surrounded by a flexible transition area, which may include settlements and agricultural activities. In the transition area, local communities work with management agencies, scientists, and others to develop and manage resources with the intention of sustainability.

The Seville Strategy for Biosphere Reserves, outlined in 1995, has as its objectives to improve the coverage of natural and cultural biodiversity (I.1), to integrate biosphere reserves into conservation planning (I.2), to secure the support and involvement of local people (II.1), to ensure better harmonization and interaction among different biosphere reserve zones (II.2), to integrate biosphere reserves into regional planning (II.3), to improve knowledge of interactions between humans and the biosphere (III.1), to improve monitoring activities (III.2), to improve education, public awareness, and involvement (III.3), to improve training for specialists and managers (III.4), to integrate the functions of biosphere reserves (IV.1), and to strengthen the WNBR (IV.2). The three goals of the Convention on Biological Diversity are to conserve biodiversity, to use its components sustainably, and to share equitably the benefits related to genetic resources.

IMPACT ON RESOURCE USE

The WNBR has played a major role in encouraging and supporting sustainable development and agriculture initiatives as well as in encouraging conservation projects that protect natural resources. The Madrid Action Plan of 2008 aims to make biosphere reserves the principal internationally designated areas dedicated to sustainable development. Socioeconomic development is a key function of transition areas.

At the Fourth World Congress on National Parks and Protected Areas, held in 1992 in Caracas, Venezuela, many managers of protected areas adopted practices similar to those used for the biosphere reserve network. Biosphere reserve use ranges from sustainable agriculture and subsistence hunting to tourism, and conservation practices can enhance those uses. For example, the Hawaiian Islands biosphere reserve (which encompasses Haleakala and Hawaii Volcanoes National Parks) has been a key part of initiatives to remove nonnative species such as feral pigs and the extremely invasive velvet tree (*Miconia calvescens*). Protecting Hawaii's unique and fragile ecosystem is important not only for science and biodiversity but also for Hawaii's tourism industry.

Another example of common biosphere reserve activities can be found in the North Norfolk Coast Biosphere Reserve in the United Kingdom. In addition to tourism, environmental education, and scientific research, this reserve supports cultivation of cereals and sugar beets, harvesting of shellfish, and some commercial shore-netting. Sarali Lands Between Rivers Biosphere Reserve in Russia allows traditional activities such as plant gathering, fishing, and haymaking and a variety of sustainable forestry and agriculture activities in the buffer zone, including beekeeping and hunting. More than sixteen hundred people live in this region.

Most biosphere reserves have not achieved the ideal goals of sustainable resource use, but are viewed as a tool to encourage sustainable resource use and development in the future. Managers hope that through sustainable resource use, ecotourism, and ecologically based industries, local living standards can be raised while preserving ecological biodiversity. In some reserves, efforts have already made significant change. For example, the Seaflower Biosphere Reserve in the San Andrés archipelago was developed by local communities to emphasize ecotourism and revive traditional subsistence agriculture and artisanal fishing. These efforts help protect the fragile coral reefs from threats from poorly planned urban development, mass tourism, and other issues.

However, not all biosphere reserves have been successful in protecting the core areas from illegal activities such as poaching. This is a particular concern in countries facing political instability and widespread poverty. For example, Volcans Biosphere Reserve in Rwanda faces expanding agricultural areas, poaching of gorillas, illegal wood and bamboo cutting, and overgrazing.

Also, application of the biosphere reserve framework has not been equally successful in all countries. For example, the biosphere reserve designation in Russia is largely a formality, and Russian biosphere reserves function very similarly to regular scientific nature reserves (*zapovedniks*) in that there is very little human use of resources.

Because of the international nature of the biosphere reserves and the variance in local management, the biosphere reserve designation forms a loose guideline or goal implemented in many different ways and with differing degrees of success. However, its focus on integrating conservation, science, education, and sustainable resource use is notable and has produced a valuable knowledge base for future efforts toward sustainable development.

Melissa A. Barton

FURTHER READING

Hadley, Malcolm, et al. *Biosphere Reserves: Special Places for People and Nature.* Paris: UNESCO, 2002.

Mose, Ingo. *Protected Areas and Regional Development in Europe: Towards a New Model for the Twenty-first Century.* Burlington, Vt.: Ashgate, 2007.

Peine, John D. *Ecosystem Management for Sustainability: Principles and Practices Illustrated by a Regional Biosphere Reserve Cooperative.* Boca Raton, Fla.: Lewis, 1999.

United Nations Educational, Scientific and Cultural Organization. *Man and the Biosphere Series.* Park Ridge, N.J.: Parthenon, 1989-   .

U.S. National Committee for Man and the Biosphere. *Biosphere Reserves in Action: Case Studies of the American Experience.* [Washington, D.C.]: The Program, [1995].

SEE ALSO: Biomes; Biosphere; Ecology; Ecosystems; Ecozones and biogeographic realms; Endangered species.

Biotechnology

CATEGORY: Scientific disciplines

Biotechnology is the use of living organisms, or substances obtained from these organisms, to produce products or processes of value to humanity.

BACKGROUND

Modern biotechnological advances have provided the ability to tap into a natural resource, the world gene pool, with such great potential that its full magnitude is only beginning to be appreciated. Theoretically, it should be possible to transfer one or more genes from any organism in the world into any other organism. Because genes ultimately control how any organism functions, gene transfer can have a dramatic impact on agricultural resources and human health in the future.

Although the term "biotechnology" is relatively new, the practice of biotechnology, according to the foregoing definition, is at least as old as civilization. Civilization did not evolve until humankind learned to produce food crops and domesticate livestock through the controlled breeding of selected plants and animals. Eventually humans began to utilize microorganisms in the production of foods such as cheese and alcoholic beverages. During the twentieth century, the pace of human modification of various organisms accelerated. Because both the speed and scope of this form of biotechnology are so different from what has been historically practiced, it is sometimes referred to as modern biotechnology to discriminate it from traditional biotechnology. Through carefully controlled breeding programs, plant architecture and fruit characteristics of crops have been modified to facilitate mechanical harvesting. Plants have been developed to produce specific drugs or spices, and microorganisms have been selected to produce antibiotics such as penicillin and other useful medicinal or food products.

DEVELOPMENTS IN BIOTECHNOLOGY

For many years, the methods for selecting desirable traits in living organisms remained unchanged. In the early 1900's, even with the realization that specific traits are linked with packets of deoxyribonucleic acid (DNA) called genes (the amount of DNA required to encode a single protein), scientists remained constrained to the methods of artificial selection in use throughout history. This changed in the 1970's, when techniques were developed both to determine the order of the four possible DNA "bases" (which spell out the information found in a gene)—a process called DNA sequencing—and to transfer this gene into another organism. The use of modern biotechnology in crops, livestock, and medicine can be divided into three major stages: identifying a gene of interest, transferring this gene into the organism of interest, and mass-producing the "transgenic" organisms that have taken up this foreign DNA.

IDENTIFICATION OF GENES OF INTEREST

As DNA-sequencing technology progressed, it soon became possible not only to sequence the DNA found in individual genes but also to determine the entire DNA complement of an organism, including its entire set of genes, referred to as its genome. Genome sequencing, in conjunction with traditional genetic techniques that allowed traits to be mapped to particular regions on a chromosome, soon led to a wealth of information concerning which genes controlled particular traits. Eventually, by comparing the DNA sequences of many different organisms, the role of a given gene could often be surmised, even if no direct genetic evidence was available for that particular gene. In this way genes could be targeted for experimental manipulation based on their similarity to known genes. Techniques were then developed in the late twentieth century that allowed for entire genomes to be screened for their response to given conditions, even if the function of individual genes could not be guessed from existing genetic data. Here, the genome of an organism is broken into roughly gene-sized fragments, which are in turn covalently attached to a glass slide to create a DNA microarray, or gene chip. These chips can then be probed with the ribonucleic acid (RNA) produced by organisms that have been exposed to certain conditions, RNA being the intermediate chemical produced by genes prior to the manufacture of protein in the cell.

It is ultimately these proteins, in the form of enzymes with specific desired activities, or, alternately, the small organic compounds produced by a specific enzymatic/metabolic activity, that are the target of those involved in the pharmaceutical or chemical industries. The latter are often referred to as secondary metabolites to denote the fact that they are not strictly required for the life of a cell but are produced by certain types of organisms in order to better adapt to given situations. Because it remains beyond the scope of modern DNA-sequencing technology to determine the genomic sequence of every possible organism which may be of interest to researchers, or even to create DNA microarrays from every such organism, many have turned to high-throughput screening techniques to identify proteins or secondary metabolites of biotechnological interest. Here, many separate cellular extracts are screened for a desired chemical activity at the same time, with further research and characterization carried out on only the positive samples. Robotic microtiter plate readers have been designed to read the results of many colorimetric screening assays at once, significantly increasing the speed and ease of high-throughput screening. Once a positive sample is identified, the techniques described above can then be used to characterize the gene of interest.

RECOMBINANT DNA TECHNOLOGY

Because the DNA of all cells—whether from bacteria, plants, lower animals, or humans—is very similar, when DNA from a foreign species is transferred into a different cell, it functions exactly as the native DNA functions; that is, it "codes" for protein. The simplest protocol for this transfer involves the use of a vector, usually a piece of circular DNA called a plasmid, which is removed from a microorganism such as bacteria and cut open by an enzyme called a restriction endonuclease or restriction enzyme. A section of DNA from the donor cell that contains a previously identified gene of interest is cut out from the donor cell DNA by the same restriction endonuclease. The section of donor cell DNA with the gene of interest is then combined with the open plasmid DNA, and the plasmid closes with the new gene as part of its structure. This process is referred to as "cloning" the gene. The recombinant plasmid (DNA from two sources) is placed back into the bacteria, where it will replicate and code for protein just as it did in the donor cell. The bacteria can be cultured and the gene product (protein) harvested, or the bacteria can be used as a vector to transfer the gene to another species, where it will also be expressed, creating a "transgenic" organism. This transfer of genes (and therefore of inherited traits between very different species) has revolutionized biotechnology and provides the potential for genetic changes in plants and animals that have not yet been envisioned.

The basic methodology for recombinant DNA

technology was developed in the 1970's, when restriction enzymes were first isolated and began to be used for this process, but the ease by which the cloning of genes could take place was greatly increased a decade later with the development of the polymerase chain reaction (PCR). DNA polymerase is an enzyme that can be used to artificially create DNA in the laboratory from a given DNA template that has been isolated from an organism of interest. In the 1980's, scientists realized that DNA polymerase isolated from certain thermophilic organisms—microbes that could exist at very high temperatures—could be used again and again in a "chain reaction" to create DNA without being broken down in the process. Soon, minute quantities of DNA taken from any given source could be amplified using PCR before being treated with restriction enzymes. Prior to this, relatively large quantities of the DNA of interest had been required.

MASS PRODUCTION OF DESIRED ORGANISMS

Once an organism has been transformed using recombinant DNA technology, or even if an organism that has all of the desired characteristics has been isolated from nature for a particular application, the next step in biotechnology is to produce as many exact copies of that organism as possible. Beginning in the mid-twentieth century, the ability to utilize artificial media to propagate plants led to the development of a technology called tissue culture. The earliest form of tissue culture involved using the culture of meristem tissue to produce numerous tiny shoots that can be grown into full-size plants, referred to as whole organism clones because each plant is genetically identical. More than one thousand plant species have been propagated by tissue culture techniques. Plants have been propagated via the culture of other tissues, including the stems and roots. In some of these techniques, the plant tissue is treated with the proper plant hormones to produce callus tissue, masses of undifferentiated cells. The callus tissue can be separated into single cells to establish a cell suspension culture. Callus tissue and cell suspensions can be used to produce specific drugs and other chemicals; entire plants can also be regenerated from the callus tissue or from single cells.

Numerous advances in animal biotechnology have also occurred. Artificial insemination, the process in which semen is collected from the male animal and deposited into the female reproductive tract by artificial techniques rather than natural mating techniques, has been in use for more than one hundred years. With this technique, males in species such as cattle can sire hundreds of thousands of offspring, whereas only thirty to fifty could be sired through natural means. Embryo transfer, a procedure in which an embryo in its early stage of development is removed from its own mother's reproductive tract and transferred to another female's reproductive tract, is a technique used to increase the number of offspring that can be produced by a superior female. Superovulation and embryo splitting have increased the feasibility of routine embryo transfers. Superovulation is the process in which females that are to serve as embryo donors are injected with hormones to stimulate increased egg production. Embryo splitting is the mechanical division of an embryo into identical twins, quadruplets, sextuplets, and so on. Through a combination of artificial insemination, superovulation, embryo splitting, and embryo transfer, it is possible for the sperm from a superior male to be used to fertilize several ovules (each of which can then be split into several offspring) from a superior female. All the resulting embryos can then be transferred to the reproductive tracts of inferior surrogate females.

As noted previously, clones of plants have been produced through the use of meristem tissue for some time. The far more complex cloning of plants and animals from the DNA of a single cell is a more recent development. Producing copies of organisms by this method has long been viewed as a prospective method of improving agricultural stock. Proponents have also suggested that cloning technology might be used to regenerate endangered species. Even such apparently benign ideas have had their detractors, however, as critics have noted the potential dangers of narrowing a species' genetic pool. The July, 1996, birth in Scotland of Dolly the sheep, the first cloned mammal, demonstrated that the cloning of animals had left the realm of science fiction and become a matter of scientific fact. However, Dolly's premature death at age six, about half the life expectancy of a normal sheep, signaled the scientific community that there was still much to be learned about the aging process. Dolly had contracted a progressive lung disease, along with arthritis. Both maladies are typically associated with much older sheep.

BIOTECHNOLOGY IN CROP PRODUCTION

Biotechnology will undoubtedly continue to have a tremendous impact on agriculture in the future. Experts who study human populations predict that the number of human inhabitants on Earth will reach alarming proportions by the mid-twenty-first century. The only way in which civilization can continue to advance, or even maintain a steady state, in the face of this potential disaster will be to increase food production, and biotechnology will most likely play an important role in producing this increase. Increased food production has been dependent on developments such as crop plants that produce higher yields under normal conditions and crops that produce higher yields when grown in marginal environments.

Even under the best of situations, there is a limited amount of land available for crop production, and while the number of people that have to be fed will continue to increase, the amount of good agricultural land will remain the same or decrease. If mass starvation is to be avoided, crops with higher yields will have to be developed and grown on the available land. As human populations con-

OriginOil cofounder Nicholas Eckelberry stands beside containers of algae that he and his company hope can be used as a biofuel source. (Reuters/Landov)

tinue to grow, good agricultural lands are taken over for industry, housing developments, and parking lots. As nonrenewable sources of energy—notably fossil fuels—are depleted, more land will be diverted to produce cellulosic material devoted to fuel production (the diversion of corn crops for ethanol production in the early twenty-first century is one example). The continuation of this trend will require that crops be grown on marginal lands where soil and growth conditions are less than ideal. The only way to increase crop production is to develop stress-tolerant plants that produce higher yields when grown under these marginal conditions. While the development of these higher-yielding crops could probably be accomplished though traditional breeding programs, the traditional methods are too slow to keep pace with the rapidly increasing population growth. Biotechnology provides a means of developing these higher-yielding crops in a fraction of the time it takes to develop them though traditional plant breeding programs because the genes for the desired characteristics can be inserted directly into the plant without having to go through several generations to establish the trait.

Economically, there is often a need or desire to diversify agricultural production in a given area. In many cases, soil and/or climate conditions may severely limit the amount of diversification that can take place. A producer might wish to grow a particular high-value cash crop, but environmental conditions may prevent the producer from doing so. Biotechnology can provide the tools to help facilitate a solution to these types of problems. For example, high-cash-value crops can be developed to grow in areas that heretofore would not have supported such crops. Another approach would be to increase the cash value of a crop by developing plants that can produce novel products such as antibiotics, drugs, hormones, and other pharmaceuticals. Progress toward the production of specific proteins in transgenic plants provides opportunities to produce large quantities of complex pharmaceuticals and other valuable products in traditional farm environments rather than in laboratories. These novel strategies open up routes for production of a broad array of natural or nature-based products, ranging from foodstuffs with enhanced nutritive value to the production of biopharmaceuticals, monoclonal antibodies, industrial proteins, and specialist oils. Crop plants that have been bioengineered to produce novel products may have a much higher cash value than the crop in its natural state.

BIOTECHNOLOGY AND THE ENVIRONMENT

While there will be a growing pressure for agriculture to produce more food in the future, there will also be increased pressure for crop production to be more friendly to the environment. Biotechnology plays a major role in the development of a long-term, sustainable, environmentally friendly agricultural system. For example, one of the major biotechnical goals is the development of crops with improved resistance to pests such as insects, fungi, and nematodes. The availability of crop varieties with improved pest resistance in turn reduces the reliance on pesticides. In conjunction with the improvements made through biotechnology, improved methods of crop production and harvest with less environmental impact will also have to be developed. Regardless of the technological advancements made in pest resistance, crop production, and harvest, agriculture will continue to have an impact on the environment. Agricultural pollutants will still be present, though perhaps in reduced amounts, and the need to remediate these polluting agents will continue to exist. Hence, biotechnology will play an important role in the development of bioremediation systems for agriculture as well as other industrial pollutants.

BIOTECHNOLOGY IN LIVESTOCK PRODUCTION

Biotechnology also plays an important role in livestock production. A gene product called bovine somatotropin, or BST, a hormone that stimulates growth in cattle, was one of the first proteins to be harvested from recombinant bacteria and given to dairy cattle to enhance milk production. The application of biotechnology to living organisms, especially to animals, has not been without controversy, however. Critics of the use of BST in cattle raised concerns about the health and well-being of the cows that had to be subjected to repeated injections in order to boost milk production and pointed to the presence of small quantities of this hormone, as well as a related hormone called IGF-1, in the milk produced by these cows. Despite a wealth of scientific evidence that these hormones posed no threat to humans and were in fact destroyed during the process of digestion, public concern led a majority of companies to eventually discontinue the use of BST treatment. Assuming that public concerns are sufficiently addressed, future experimentation may lead to increased productivity and, at the same time, a reduction in the cost of production of animal products. As with plants, disease-resistant animals are being genetically engineered, and parasites are being controlled by genetic manipulation of their physiology and biochemistry. Animals, like plants, have been genetically engineered to produce novel and interesting products such as pharmaceuticals.

BIOTECHNOLOGY IN MEDICINE

While recombinant technology has already had an indirect influence on human well-being through its effects on plants and livestock, it will probably also have a dramatic, direct impact on human health. Recombinant DNA technology can be used to produce a variety of gene products that are utilized in the clinical treatment of diseases. A number of human hormones produced by this methodology have been in use for some time. Human growth hormone (HGH), marketed under the name Protropin, was one of the first recombinant proteins to be approved by the U.S. Food and Drug Administration, in this case to treat a disease called hyposomatotropism. People suffering from this disease do not produce enough growth hormone and without treatment with HGH will not reach normal height. Insulin, a hormone used to treat insulin-dependent diabetics, was the first major success in using a product of recombinant technology. Beginning in 1982, recombinant DNA-produced insulin, marketed under the name Humalin, has been used to treat thousands of diabetic patients. A pituitary hormone, called somatostatin, was another early success of recombinant DNA techniques. This hormone controls the release of insulin and human growth hormone. Some of the interferons, small proteins produced by a cell to combat viral infections, have also been produced using recombinant DNA methodology. The technology could thus be used to produce vaccines against viral diseases. The first of these vaccines, marketed under the name Recombivax HB, was successfully used to vaccinate against hepatitis B, an incurable and sometimes fatal liver disease. A number of other antiviral vaccines were soon developed.

Advances in biotechnology have also enhanced the potential for the future application of gene therapy. Genetic therapy is often defined as any procedure that prevents, reduces, or cures a genetic disease, but for this discussion the term gene therapy will apply only to those procedures that involve the direct manipulation of human genes. The following forms of gene therapy are in development: gene surgery, in which a mutant gene (which may or may not be replaced by its normal counterpart) is excised from the DNA; gene repair, in which the defective DNA is repaired within the cell to restore the genetic code; and gene insertion, in which a normal gene complement is inserted in cells that carry a defective gene.

Although both gene repair and gene surgery have been performed in viruses, bacteria, and yeast, the techniques remain too complex to be used on humans, at least in the near future. Gene insertion, however, has been attempted in a variety of human cells. This process can potentially be done in germ-line cells (such as the egg or sperm), the fertilized ovum or zygote, the fetus, or the somatic cells (a nonreproductive cell) of children or adults. Of these categories, germ-line therapy remains the most controversial because it has potential to alter permanently the genetic makeup of future generations. Zygote therapy holds perhaps the most promise because through it completely normal individuals could potentially be produced, but gene insertion in zygotes is still a very complex undertaking and will likely not be practiced in the near future. Somatic gene therapy, however, has been applied in humans to a limited extent for many years. A decade after the 1990 success of human gene therapy to treat severe combined immunodeficiency (SCID), sometimes called "bubble boy" disease, the death of Jesse Gelsinger, an eighteen-year-old who was undergoing an experimental procedure to treat a non-life-threatening liver condition, put additional gene therapy trials on hold. Early in the twenty-first century, human gene therapy trials cautiously resumed, with most trials targeting the insertion of a gene into the cells of a tissue that is most influenced by a defective gene, followed by tests to determine whether the inserted gene was able to code for sufficient gene product to alleviate the symptoms of the disease.

OWNERSHIP ISSUES

Many difficult ethical and economic issues surrounding the use of modern biotechnology remain. One of the major questions concerns ownership. The U.S. patent laws currently read that ownership of an organism can be granted if the organism has been intentionally genetically altered through the use of recombinant DNA techniques. In addition, processes that utilize genetically altered organisms can be patented. Therefore one biotechnology firm may own the patent to an engineered organism, but another firm may own the rights to the process used to produce it.

D. R. Gossett, updated by James S. Godde

FURTHER READING

Campbell, Neil A., and Jane B. Reece. *Biology.* 8th ed. San Francisco: Pearson/Benjamin Cummings, 2008.

Chrispeels, Maarten J., and David E. Sadava. *Plants, Genes, and Crop Biotechnology.* 2d ed. Boston: Jones and Bartlett, 2003.

Field, Thomas G., and Robert E. Taylor. *Scientific Farm Animal Production: An Introduction to Animal Science.* 9th ed. Upper Saddle River, N.J.: Prentice Hall, 2008.

Holdrege, Craig, and Steve Talbott. *Beyond Biotechnology: The Barren Promise of Genetic Engineering.* Lexington: University Press of Kentucky, 2008.

Kreuzer, Helen, and Adrianne Massey. *Molecular Biology and Biotechnology: A Guide for Students.* 3d ed. Washington, D.C.: ASM Press, 2008.

Lewis, Ricki. *Human Genetics: Concepts and Applications.* 7th ed. Boston: McGraw-Hill Higher Education, 2007.

Mousdale, David M. *Biofuels: Biotechnology, Chemistry, and Sustainable Development.* Boca Raton, Fla.: CRC Press, 2008.

Reiss, Michael J., and Roger Straughan. *Improving Nature? The Science and Ethics of Genetic Engineering.* Cambridge, England: Cambridge University Press, 2001.

Renneberg, Reinhard. *Biotechnology for Beginners.* Edited by Arnold L. Demain. Berlin: Springer, 2008.

Taylor, Robert E., and Thomas G. Field. *Scientific Farm Animal Production.* 9th ed. Upper Saddle River, N.J.: Pearson Prentice Hall, 2008.

Thieman, William J., and Michael A. Palladino. *Introduction to Biotechnology.* 2d ed. San Francisco: Pearson/Benjamin Cummings, 2009.

Yount, Lisa. *Biotechnology and Genetic Engineering.* 3d ed. New York: Facts On File, 2008.

SEE ALSO: Agricultural products; Agriculture industry; Animal breeding; Animal domestication; Animals as a medical resource; Genetic diversity; Plant domestication and breeding; Plants as a medical resource.

Bismuth

CATEGORY: Mineral and other nonliving resources

WHERE FOUND

Bismuth is a rare element in the Earth's crust, with an abundance roughly equal to that of silver. It is also one of the few metallic elements that can be found in nature in its elemental form. As such it is often found in the same areas as lead, zinc, or tin deposits in locations such as Bolivia, Canada, and Germany. In addition, it occurs in ores as an oxide, sulfide, or carbonate. Rather than being mined and refined directly, bismuth is obtained commercially as a by-product of copper, lead, and zinc refining operations. Leading producers are China, Mexico, and Belgium.

PRIMARY USES

Bismuth and its compounds are used in pharmaceutical applications as well as in several commercial chemical syntheses. By far the main commercial use of bismuth is as an alloying agent.

TECHNICAL DEFINITION

Bismuth (atomic symbol Bi) has an atomic number of 83 and is found in the nitrogen group (main Group V) of the periodic table. It is similar to antimony in its chemical properties but has significantly greater metallic behavior than the other elements in

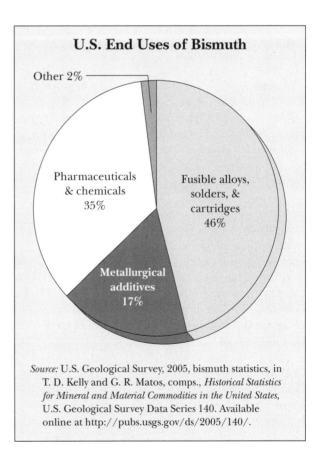

U.S. End Uses of Bismuth

Other 2%

Pharmaceuticals & chemicals 35%

Fusible alloys, solders, & cartridges 46%

Metallurgical additives 17%

Source: U.S. Geological Survey, 2005, bismuth statistics, in T. D. Kelly and G. R. Matos, comps., *Historical Statistics for Mineral and Material Commodities in the United States,* U.S. Geological Survey Data Series 140. Available online at http://pubs.usgs.gov/ds/2005/140/.

the group. There is only one naturally occurring isotope, so the atomic weight of bismuth, 208.980, is
known very precisely. The element is brittle and white
in appearance, with a pink tinge. It occurs in a variety
of crystalline structures. The metal has a high resistiv-
ity and melts at 271.4° Celsius with a boiling point of
1,564° Celsius. Bismuth is unusual in that its volume
expands by about 3 percent when it solidifies from the
liquid. The solid has a density of 9.9 grams per cubic
centimeter.

DESCRIPTION, DISTRIBUTION, AND FORMS
With a rarity akin to that of silver, bismuth is a relatively minor component of the Earth's crust. It possesses some unique credentials: For example, all elements with an atomic number higher than bismuth
are radioactive. It is one of three elements that is less
dense in the solid phase than in the liquid. It is also
one of only a handful of metals that can be found in
nature in their elemental, or native, form. Elemental
bismuth is not particularly toxic, an unusual property
in heavy metals. However, inorganic bismuth compounds are often extremely poisonous. The relative
rarity of bismuth has minimized its environmental impact.

HISTORY
The earliest recorded use of bismuth was in the mid-
1400's as an alloying material in casting type. German
scientist Georgius Agricola stated that bismuth was a
metal in the same family of metals as tin and lead. In
1753, French chemist Claude François Geoffroy identified bismuth as a chemical element, confirming
Agricola's postulation.

OBTAINING BISMUTH
In addition to the native state, bismuth occurs in ores
as an oxide, sulfide, and carbonate. Because of the
scarcity of bismuth ores in the Earth's crust, it is not
mined directly but is typically produced commercially
by extracting and refining it from the anode sludge
generated during the electrochemical production of
other metals. Annual world production of bismuth is
on the order of 6,000 metric tons.

USES OF BISMUTH
Functioning as a metallurgical additive remains one
of the major uses of bismuth. In particular, fusible alloys, which have low melting points and are particularly useful in fire detection, often incorporate bis-

muth. The other major use of bismuth is in the
pharmaceutical industry, where it is used to treat indi-
gestion and as an antisyphilitic agent.

Craig B. Lagrone

WEB SITES

NATURAL RESOURCES CANADA
Canadian Minerals Yearbook, 2005: Bismuth
http://www.nrcan-rncan.gc.ca/mms-smm/busi-
  indu/cmy-amc/content/2005/14.pdf

U.S. GEOLOGICAL SURVEY
Minerals Information: Bismuth Statistics and
  Information
http://minerals.usgs.gov/minerals/pubs/
  commodity/bismuth/

SEE ALSO: Alloys; Antimony; Belgium; Canada; China;
Germany; Metals and metallurgy; Mexico; Native elements.

Borax

CATEGORY: Mineral and other nonliving resources

WHERE FOUND
Borax, the most widespread of the borate minerals, is
found in the muds of alkaline lakes along with minerals such as rock salt, sulfates, carbonates, and other
borates. Large deposits are found in the western
United States, South America, Turkey, and Tibet.

PRIMARY USES
Borax is essential to many industrial processes, notably the manufacture of glass and enamel. Other major
users include the ceramics, agricultural, chemical,
cleanser, and pharmaceutical industries.

TECHNICAL DEFINITION
Borax (also known as sodium borate decahydrate, sodium pyroborate, birax, sodium tetraborate decahydrate, and sodium biborate) is an ore of boron with
the chemical formula $Na_2(B_4O_5)(OH)4 \cdot 8(H_2O)$. Its
average molecular weight is 381.4, composed of 12.06
percent sodium, 11.34 percent boron, 5.29 percent
hydrogen, and 71.32 percent oxygen. Borax may be
colorless, white, yellowish, or gray. Its hardness on the
Mohs scale is 2 to 2.5. Borax occurs as prismatic crys-

The mineral borax. (USGS)

tals or as a white powder. Its specific gravity is 1.69 to 1.72. It is slightly soluble in cold water, very soluble in hot water, and insoluble in acids. It has a melting point of 75° Celsius and a boiling point of 320° Celsius. When heated above 740° Celsius, it fuses to form a "borax bead."

DESCRIPTION, DISTRIBUTION, AND FORMS
Borax is a member of a group of compounds known as borates, minerals that contain the element boron. Borax is an evaporite found in dried-up lakes and playas (desert basins). A sedimentary deposit that forms in arid regions, borax derives its name from *būraq,* an Arabic word meaning "white" that was used to refer to the substance. This widespread borate mineral is found in association with other evaporites, including rock salt, sulfates, carbonates, and other borates. Borax occurs as a white powder on the soil surface or in masses of short, prismatic crystals embedded in the muds of alkaline lakes. Borax is also present in many mineral waters and salt lakes. It commonly loses water to form tincalconite ($Na_2B_4O_7 \cdot 5H_2O$).

The most widespread of the borate minerals, borax is notably found in arid regions near the sites of Pliocene lakes, where hot springs and volcanic activity are believed to be the source of the boron-rich brines that fed these lakes. Upon evaporation (hence its classification as an "evaporite"), deposits of borax and other borates formed. Buried accumulations of borax are often found in the centers of dried-up alkaline lakes,

with outcrops of calcium and calcium-sodium boron minerals marking the periphery of the lake area.

In the United States, there are large deposits of borax in California, Nevada, and Oregon. Almost half the world's refined borates come from Southern California. In California's Mojave Desert, Searles Lake in San Bernardino County and Kramer in Kern County are two major borax deposits. At Searles Lake, borax is the most abundant of the four borate-bearing minerals found there. Borax is also the most abundant mineral in the Kramer borate deposit, the largest known reserve of boron compounds in the world. Other major deposits are located in Tibet, Argentina, and Turkey. In Argentina, for example, borax is mined at Salt Province (more than 4,000 meters above sea level) and at Tincalayu, Sijes, and the lakebeds at Salar Cauchari and Salar Diablillos.

HISTORY
Borax has been used commercially for thousands of years, with the earliest confirmed use in ceramic glazes traced to the tenth century C.E. The early Chinese, Persians, Arabs, and Babylonians knew of the mineral and its properties. It was introduced to Europe by Marco Polo about 1275 C.E. Europe's earliest source for the mineral was Tibet, where tincal (crude borax) was used for making glazes and soldering gold. By the 1800's, borax had gained widespread use in glassblowing and gold refining.

Italy, Tibet, and Chile were the principal world suppliers of borate minerals until extensive borate deposits were discovered in California and Nevada. An 1864 report on borax crystals found in the muds of Borax Lake in Lake County, California, was the first to publish the discovery of the mineral in the western United States. In the early 1880's, borax was also found in Death Valley. The twenty-mule teams that hauled the material mined from Death Valley across the California desert to the railroad junction at Mojave became a widely recognized symbol for the borax industry in the United States.

OBTAINING BORAX

Borax may be obtained directly from dry lake beds on which the evaporite has formed, from open-pit borate mines, or from drilling for underground mines. At Searles Lake, borax is recovered by fractional crystallization from lake brine. Borax may also be made from other borate ores, including as kernite ($Na_2B_4O_7 \cdot 4H_2O$), colemanite ($Ca_2B_6O_{11} \cdot 5H_2O$), and ulexite ($NaCaB_5O_9 \cdot 8H_2O$), or by the reaction of boric acid with soda. Crystalline borax readily effloresces— that is, it loses its water of crystallization to form a white powder—particularly upon heating.

Deposits of borate ores are found underground by drilling and then blasting to remove the sandstone that overlies the ore deposit. (Eventually such sites will turn into open-pit mining operations.) Huge shovels remove the rubble to get at the ore, which is then crushed and refined by mixing the crushed ore with hot water. Borates dissolve in the water, leaving the unwanted debris in solid form; the debris-free solution can then be pumped into tanks, which cool the solution so that the borates can crystallize and then be removed for drying, storage, and further processing.

USES OF BORAX

The uses of borax are based on its many functional properties, which include metabolizing effects, bleaching effects, buffering effects, dispersing effects, vitrifying effects, inhibiting effects, flame-proofing effects, and neutron-absorbing effects. Borax has been used for centuries in making glass and enamels, and it has become an essential part of many other industrial processes. It is used in the manufacture of glass (notably heat-resistant and optical varieties), porcelain enamels, ceramics, shellacs, and glazes. It is a component of agricultural chemicals such as fertilizers and herbicides. It is used in the manufacture of chemicals, soaps, starches, adhesives, cosmetics, phar-

maceuticals, insulation material, and fire retardants. In the textile industry, borax is used in fixing mordants on textiles, tanning leather, and spinning silk. It is effective as a mild antiseptic, a water softener, and a food preservative, although it is toxic if consumed in large doses. It is added to antifreeze to inhibit corrosion and used as a flux for soldering and welding. Borax is also a source of elemental boron, which is used as a deoxidizer and alloy in nonferrous metals, a neutron absorber in shields for atomic reactors, and a component of motor fuel and rocket fuel.

Borax also plays an important role in chemical analysis. Borax fused by heating is used in the "bead test," a form of chemical analysis used in the identification of certain metals. Powdered borax is heated in a platinum-wire loop over a flame until the mineral fuses to form a clear glassy bead. The borax bead is then dipped into a small quantity of the metallic oxide to be identified. Upon reheating over the flame, the bead reacts chemically with the metallic oxide to form a metal borate, which gives the bead a characteristic color that helps identify the metal. For example, cobalt compounds yield a deep blue bead, and manganese compounds produce a violet one.

Perhaps the most familiar use of borax is as a cleansing agent. Borax combined with hot water will create hydrogen peroxide; it lowers the acidity of water, which facilitates the bleaching action of other cleansers. Borax also acts as both a disinfectant and a pesticide by blocking the biochemistry of both macro- and microorganisms, such as bacteria, fungi, fleas, roaches, ants, and other pests. These same properties, however, mean that people must avoid overexposure to borax lest it prove toxic to the kidneys and other organs (a typical symptom is red and peeling skin). Finally, borates such as borax enhance the power of other cleansing chemicals by bonding with other compounds in such a way that it maintains the even dispersal of these cleansing agents in solution, thereby maximizing their surface area and hence their effectiveness.

Karen N. Kähler

FURTHER READING

Chatterjee, Kaulir Kisor. "Borax and Related Minerals." In *Uses of Industrial Minerals, Rocks, and Freshwater.* New York: Nova Science, 2009.

Garrett, Donald E. "Borax." In *Borates: Handbook of Deposits, Processing, Properties, and Use.* San Diego, Calif.: Academic Press, 1998.

Grew, E. S., and L. M. Anovitz, eds. *Boron: Mineralogy, Petrology, and Geochemistry.* Washington, D.C.: Mineralogical Society of America, 1996.

Spears, John Randolph. *Illustrated Sketches of Death Valley and Other Borax Deserts of the Pacific Coast.* Edited by Douglas Steeples. Chicago: Rand McNally, 1892. Reprint. Baltimore: Johns Hopkins University Press, 2001.

Travis, N. J., and E. J. Cocks. *The Tincal Trail: A History of Borax.* London: Harrap, 1984.

U.S. Borax and Chemical Corporation. *The Story of Borax.* 2d ed. Los Angeles: Author, 1979.

WEB SITES

U.S. GEOLOGICAL SURVEY
Boron: Statistics and Information
http://minerals.usgs.gov/minerals/pubs/
    commodity/boron/index.html#myb

U.S. GEOLOGICAL SURVEY
Death Valley Geology Field Trip: All About Death
    Valley Borax
http://geomaps.wr.usgs.gov/parks/deva/
    fthar4.html#basics

U.S. GEOLOGICAL SURVEY
Death Valley Geology Field Trip: Harmony Borax
    Works
http://geomaps.wr.usgs.gov/parks/deva/
    fthar1.html

SEE ALSO: Boron; Ceramics; Evaporites; Fertilizers; Glass; Sedimentary processes, rocks, and mineral deposits.

Boron

CATEGORY: Mineral and other nonliving resources

WHERE FOUND
Boron is not abundant. There are about 9 parts per million of boron in the Earth's crust, which makes boron the thirty-eighth element in abundance. Commercially valuable deposits are rare, but the deposits in California and Turkey are very large.

PRIMARY USES
The main uses of boron are in heat-resistant glasses, glass wool, fiberglass, and porcelain enamels. It is also used in detergents, soaps, cleaners and cosmetics, and synthetic herbicides and fertilizers.

TECHNICAL DEFINITION
Boron (abbreviated B), atomic number 5, belongs to Group III of the periodic table of the elements and resembles silicon in many of its chemical properties. It has two naturally occurring isotopes: boron 10 (19.8 percent) and boron 11 (80.2 percent). Boron exists in several allotropic forms. The crystalline forms are a dark red color, and the powdered forms are black. The most stable form has a melting point of 2,180° Celsius, a boiling point of 3,650° Celsius, and a density of 2.35 grams per cubic centimeter.

DESCRIPTION, DISTRIBUTION, AND FORMS
Boron is found primarily in dried lake beds in California and Turkey. Isolated deposits also occur in China and numerous South American countries. The major deposits of borate minerals occur in areas of former volcanic activity and in association with the waters of former hot springs. Searles Lake in southeastern California has layers that are 1.6 percent and 2.0 percent borax. Boron is found naturally only as borate minerals such as ulexite $[B_5O_6(OH)_6]\cdot5H_2O$ and borax $Na_2[B_4O_5(OH)_4]\cdot8H_2O$ or as borosilicates. Boron is more concentrated in plants than in animal tissue.

The use of borax laundry detergents, the burning of coal, and mining have filled the atmosphere and irrigation waters in some areas with boron compounds. Although there have been some reports of damage to grazing animals, boron is not considered a danger unless it is in the form of a pesticide, an herbicide, or fiberglass, which is carcinogenic.

Boron is an essential element only for higher plants. The amount needed by those plants and the amount that is toxic are only a few parts per million apart, so toxicity effects can easily occur. Boron is not known to be necessary to animal life, and it is quickly excreted in urine. In high concentrations toxicity effects can occur, especially in the brain, before all the boron is excreted.

HISTORY
Borax was used in ancient times to make glazes and hard glass and was traded by the Babylonians four thousand years ago. However it was not isolated in pure enough form to be characterized as an element until 1808. The isolation was achieved by Joseph-Louis Gay-Lussac and Louis-Jacques Thénard and in-

dependently by Sir Humphry Davy. Boron was isolated from boric acid through a heated reaction with potassium. The first pure (95 to 98 percent) boron was isolated by Henri Moissan in 1892.

OBTAINING BORON

The four main methods of isolating boron are reduction by metals at high temperature, electrolytic reduction of fused borates or tetrafluoroborates, reduction by hydrogen of volatile compounds, and thermal decomposition of hydrides or halides. About 3.8 million metric tons are produced annually. Boron will form compounds with almost every element except the noble gases and a few of the heavier metals. It is said to have the most diverse chemistry next to carbon and is characterized as a metalloid by some properties and as a nonmetal by others. This rich chemistry leads to a wide range of uses.

USES OF BORON

One of the most common uses of boron is in the production of borosilicate glass (Pyrex glass). Borosilicate glass does not expand or contract as much as regular glass, so it does not break with temperature changes as easily as regular glass. Pyrex cooking vessels and most laboratory glassware are made of borosilicate glass. Boron improves the tempering of steel better than other alloying elements. Boron carbide is one of the hardest substances known and is used in both abrasive and abrasion-resistant applications as well as in nuclear shielding. Lighter elements are better shields for neutrons than are heavy elements such as lead. Boron-10 neutron capture therapy is one of the few ways to treat a nonoperable brain tumor. The boron-10 isotope collects in the tumor. When a neutron hits the boron, a reaction produces radiation to kill the cancer cells.

Borate is used in the production of glass fiber thermal insulation, the principal insulating material used in construction. Another glass application is as a thin, glassy coating fused onto ceramics and metals. Examples include wall and floor tiles, tableware, bone china, porcelain, washing machines, pots, and architectural

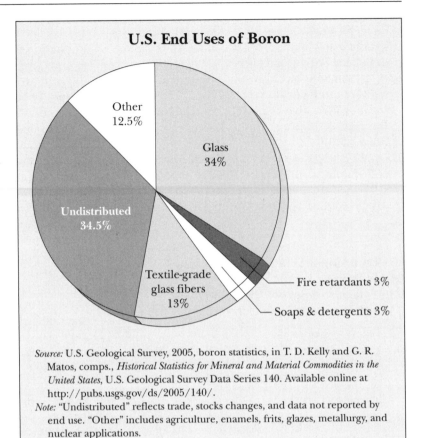

U.S. End Uses of Boron

Other 12.5%

Glass 34%

Undistributed 34.5%

Textile-grade glass fibers 13%

Fire retardants 3%

Soaps & detergents 3%

Source: U.S. Geological Survey, 2005, boron statistics, in T. D. Kelly and G. R. Matos, comps., *Historical Statistics for Mineral and Material Commodities in the United States*, U.S. Geological Survey Data Series 140. Available online at http://pubs.usgs.gov/ds/2005/140/.

Note: "Undistributed" reflects trade, stocks changes, and data not reported by end use. "Other" includes agriculture, enamels, frits, glazes, metallurgy, and nuclear applications.

paneling. Boron is also used in algicides, fertilizers, herbicides, insecticides, and water treatments. Sodium polyborate can be used to control fleas, and boric acid has been used in the control of cockroaches. Fire retardants include zinc borate, ammonium pentaborate, and boric oxide. These are used in chipboard, cellulose insulation, and cotton mattresses. Boron compounds are also used in metallurgical processes such as fluxes and shielding slags and in electroplating baths. Borax is a water-softening agent, while boron is used as a bleaching agent. Perborates in water form hydrogen peroxide to act as a bleach. Boron is also used in cosmetics, pharmaceutical and hygienic products, pH adjusters, emulsifiers, stabilizers, and buffers.

C. Alton Hassell

FURTHER READING

Adriano, Domy C. "Boron." In *Trace Elements in Terrestrial Environments: Biogeochemistry, Bioavailability, and Risks of Metals.* 2d ed. New York: Springer, 2001.

Greenwood, N. N., and A. Earnshaw. "Boron." In *Chemistry of the Elements*. 2d ed. Boston: Butterworth-Heinemann, 1997.

Grew, E. S., and L. M. Anovitz, eds. *Boron: Mineralogy, Petrology, and Geochemistry*. Washington, D.C.: Mineralogical Society of America, 1996.

Housecroft, Catherine E. *Cluster Molecules of the P-Block Elements*. New York: Oxford University Press, 1994.

Kogel, Jessica Elzea, et al., eds. "Boron and Borates." In *Industrial Minerals and Rocks: Commodities, Markets, and Uses*. 7th ed. Littleton, Colo.: Society for Mining, Metallurgy, and Exploration, 2006.

Krebs, Robert E. *The History and Use of Our Earth's Chemical Elements: A Reference Guide*. Illustrations by Rae Déjur. 2d ed. Westport, Conn.: Greenwood Press, 2006.

Massey, A. G. "Group 13: Boron, Aluminum, Gallium, Indium, and Thallium." In *Main Group Chemistry*. 2d ed. New York: Wiley, 2000.

Smallwood, C. *Boron*. Geneva, Switzerland: World Health Organization, 1998.

Weeks, Mary Elvira. *Discovery of the Elements: Collected Reprints of a Series of Articles Published in the "Journal of Chemical Education."* Kila, Mont.: Kessinger, 2003.

WEB SITE

U.S. GEOLOGICAL SURVEY
Boron: Statistics and Information
http://minerals.usgs.gov/minerals/pubs/
    commodity/boron/index.html#myb

SEE ALSO: Borax; China; Fiberglass; Glass; Herbicides; Pesticides and pest control; Turkey.

Botany

CATEGORY: Scientific disciplines

Any topic dealing with plants, from the level of their cellular biology to the level of their economic production, is considered part of the field of botany.

DEFINITION

Botany is an old branch of science that began with early humankind's interest in the plants around them. In modern society, plant science extends beyond that interest to cutting-edge biotechnology.

OVERVIEW

The origins of botany, beginning around 5000 B.C.E., are rooted in human attempts to improve their lot by raising better food crops. This practical effort developed into intellectual curiosity about plants in general, and the science of botany was born. Some of the earliest botanical records are included with the writings of Greek philosophers, who were often physicians and who used plant materials as curative agents. In the second century B.C.E., Aristotle had a botanical garden and an associated library.

As more details became known about plants and their function, particularly after the discovery of the microscope, the growing body of knowledge became too great for general understanding, so a number of subdisciplines arose. Plant anatomy is concerned chiefly with the internal structure of plants. Plant physiology delves into the living functions of plants. Plant taxonomy has as its interest the discovery and systematic classification of plants. Plant geography deals with the global distribution of plants. Plant ecology studies the interactions between plants and their surroundings. Plant morphology studies the form and structure of plants. Plant genetics attempts to understand and work with the way that plant traits are inherited. Plant cytology, often called cell biology, is the science of cell structure and function. Economic botany, which traces its interest back to the origins of botany, studies those plants that play important economic roles (these include major crops such as wheat, rice, corn, and cotton). Ethnobotany is a rapidly developing subarea in which scientists communicate with indigenous peoples to explore the knowledge that exists as a part of their folk medicine. Several new drugs and the promise of others have developed from this search.

At the forefront of modern botany is the field of genetic engineering, including the cloning of organisms. New or better crops have long been developed by the technique of cross-breeding, but genetic engineering offers a much more direct course. Using its techniques scientists can introduce a gene carrying a desirable trait directly from one organism to another. In this way scientists hope to protect crops from frost damage, to inhibit the growth of weeds, to provide insect repulsion as a part of the plant's own system, and to increase the yield of food and fiber crops.

The role that plants play in the energy system of the Earth (and may someday play in space stations or other closed systems) is also a major area of study. Plants, through photosynthesis, convert sunlight into other useful forms of energy upon which humans have become dependent. During the same process carbon dioxide is removed from the air, and oxygen is delivered. Optimization of this process and discovering new applications for it are goals for botanists.

Kenneth H. Brown

SEE ALSO: Agricultural products; Agriculture industry; Biotechnology; Farmland; Grasslands; Green Revolution; Horticulture; Plant domestication and breeding; Plants as a medical resource; Rain forests.

Brass

CATEGORY: Products from resources

Brass, a metal alloy, has numerous practical applications because of its ease of fabrication, corrosion resistance, and attractive appearance. It is used in hardware items, electrical fixtures, inexpensive jewelry, and metal decorations.

DEFINITION

Brass is a copper-based alloy consisting mainly of copper and zinc. It can also be mixed with lead, tin, nickel, aluminum, iron, manganese, arsenic, antimony, and phosphorus.

OVERVIEW

The first brass was probably made accidentally by melting copper ore that contained a small amount of zinc. The earliest known brass object was made by the Romans about 20 B.C.E. By the eleventh century, brass was made on a large scale throughout Western Europe, and brass coins, kettles, and ornaments were manufactured. In the United States, the brass industry developed mainly in Connecticut; at first it was devoted primarily to making buttons.

The color and composition of brass vary with the amount of copper, which ranges from 55 percent to 95 percent. When the alloy contains about 70 percent copper, it has a golden-yellow color (such brass is called yellow brass or cartridge brass). When it contains 80 percent or more copper, it has a reddish copper color (red brass). When zinc is added, brass becomes stronger and tougher. The ductility (ability to be stretched) improves with increasing amounts of zinc up to about 30 percent. The best combination of

strength and ductility occurs in yellow brass.

Lead is added to improve machinability (ease of cutting). Tin and nickel are often added to increase the alloy's resistance to corrosion and wear. Nickel may be added to obtain a silvery-white color that makes the alloy a more suitable base for silver plating. Aluminum is useful in improving the corrosion resistance of brass in turbulent or fast-moving water. The strength of brass is also improved with the addition of iron, manganese, nickel, and aluminum.

The first step in making brass is to melt copper in an electric furnace. Solid pieces of zinc are then added to the melted copper, and the zinc melts rapidly. After the copper and zinc have been melted and thoroughly mixed, the brass is ready for pouring. It is typically made into blocklike forms (ingots) or small bars (billets), making it easy to work with the brass or to store it. When it is time to make a particular piece, the bars are placed in a furnace, and after they have been reheated to the proper temperature for working, the brass can be rolled and formed into the desired shape. A milling machine removes surface imperfections, and the brass is then cold rolled.

Brass is used in making automobile components, ship propellers, refrigeration and air-conditioning equipment (condenser tubes), decorative elements (architectural trim), plumbing hardware, camera parts, valves, screws, buttons, keys, watch and clock parts, and coins. Some brasses, mainly containing tin and manganese, are called bronzes, which are used to make statues, bells, vases, cups, and a variety of ornaments.

Alvin K. Benson

SEE ALSO: Alloys; Bronze; Copper; Metals and metallurgy; Tin; Zinc.

Brazil

CATEGORIES: Countries; government and resources

Brazil's metallic mineral resources, especially iron and aluminum, underpin a strong industrial sector and are high-value exports. Brazil is the second most important producer of iron ore in the world after China and is a significant gold-producing nation. It ranks tenth as a diamond producer and has the second largest crude oil reserves in South America after Venezuela.

Brazil's forest industry contributes about 4 percent to the nation's gross domestic product (GDP) and accounts for 7 percent of its exports, providing employment for two million people. Brazil is in the top five among world nations in relation to area of land used for agriculture and ranks in the top three as an exporter of agricultural produce.

THE COUNTRY

Brazil is the fifth largest country in the world, with an area of 8.5 million square kilometers. It is the largest and most geographically diverse country in South America, occupying most of the northeast of the continent, and has a coastline of about 7,490 kilometers along the Atlantic Ocean. The country has a tropical or semitropical climate, with diverse natural vegetation dominated by tropical rain forests, dry forests, and savannas. Brazil is generally low lying, with elevations between 200 and 800 meters. Higher elevations, of about 1,200 meters, are limited to the south. Brazil has a drainage system dominated by the Amazon River, which originates in the Andes Mountains and has created an extensive lowland floodplain area in the northern part of the country.

Brazil's economy is growing rapidly. It is the largest in South America and the eighth largest in the world. Its resource base has not been fully ascertained, but key resources so far exploited include iron ore, in the states of Minas Gerais (in the south-central region) and Pará (in the north); oil, mostly in offshore fields; timber, from extensive natural forests and plantations; and precious stones in various locations. Agriculture is most important in the south, where most of Brazil's commercial crops are produced and where most cattle ranches are located. In the northeast and in the Amazon basin, agriculture tends to be subsistent and may involve shifting cultivation.

METALS

Brazil's iron ore accounts for about 5 percent of its total exports, with approximately half going to China, Japan, and Germany. Reserves of iron ore are estimated at almost 20 billion metric tons, about 7 percent of the world total, ranking Brazil sixth in the world. However, in terms of iron content the reserves are the best in the world. Iron ore accounts for almost 58 percent of the value of Brazil's mineral production. There are thirty-seven companies extracting iron and fifty-nine mines, all of which are open cast. The Brazilian mining company Vale S.A. (formerly Companhia

Vale do Rio Doce) produces more than 60 percent of the iron ore in Brazil and about 15 percent of world iron ore, making it the world's largest producer of iron ore. It is also the world's second largest producer of nickel and is involved in the mining of bauxite, manganese, copper, kaolin, and potash.

Approximately 70 percent of Brazil's iron reserves are in the state of Minas Gerais and 25 percent are in Pará. The ores occur as hematite (ferric oxide), and, in 2007, more than 300 million metric tons were produced. The Carajás Mine in Pará is the world's largest iron-ore mine. Owned by Vale S.A., it is an open-cast mine with reserves of 1.4 billion metric tons, plus deposits of manganese, copper, tin, cobalt, and aluminum. In general, the Carajás District is exceptionally rich in minerals and has iron-ore reserves estimated at 16 billion metric tons. Other base metals produced in substantial quantities include manganese and aluminum, of which Brazil accounts for 25 percent and 12.4 percent, respectively, of world production.

Gold, tantalum, and niobium are also produced in Brazil. The late 1980's were the period of peak gold production for Brazil. Reserves comprise almost 2 percent of the world total and are found mainly in Minas Gerais and Pará. In 2006, Brazil produced 40 metric tons; the chief mining company was Anglogold Ashanti Mineração Ltda., which contributed about 7.7 metric tons. Most was used by the jewelry industry. About 32 metric tons were exported; Japan was the major recipient.

Tantalum and niobium are relatively rare metals, but Brazil is a major source of both. Tantalum is extracted from tantalite and colombite mined from one site, Pitinga/Mineração Taboca, in the state of Amazonas. It is used for the manufacture of electrolytic capacitors. Brazil provides roughly 20 percent of the world total, making it the second largest producer behind Australia. This mine also produces tin, uranium, and niobium. The latter is used in forensic science and to make alloys with iron to improve the strength of piping, among other uses. It is found in four states, of which Minas Gerais contains 73 percent of the reserves, and is extracted from pyrochlore (niobium oxide). Brazil produces most of the world's niobium, which amounted to about 57,000 metric tons in 2008.

FOSSIL FUELS

Brazil has substantial reserves of coal, oil, and natural gas. Brazil's energy production is as follows: 38 per-

Brazil: Resources at a Glance

Official name: Federative Republic of Brazil
Government: Federal republic
Capital city: Brasília
Area: 3,287,851 mi²; 8,514,877 km²
Population (2009 est.): 198,739,269
Language: Portuguese
Monetary unit: real (BRL)

ECONOMIC SUMMARY:

GDP composition by sector (2008 est.): agriculture, 6.7%; industry, 28%; services, 65.3%
Natural resources: bauxite, gold, iron ore, manganese, nickel, niobium, phosphates, platinum, tin, tantalum, uranium, petroleum, hydropower, timber, precious and semiprecious stones, graphite
Land use (2005): arable land, 6.93%; permanent crops, 0.89%; other, 92.18%
Industries: textiles, shoes, chemicals, cement, lumber, iron ore, tin, steel, aircraft, motor vehicles and parts, other machinery and equipment
Agricultural products: coffee, soybeans, wheat, rice, corn, sugarcane, cocoa, citrus, beef
Exports (2008 est.): $197.9 billion
Commodities exported: transport equipment, iron ore, soybeans, footwear, coffee, automobiles
Imports (2008 est.): $173.1 billion
Commodities imported: machinery, electrical and transport equipment, chemical products, oil, automotive parts, electronics
Labor force (2008 est.): 93.65 million
Labor force by occupation (2003 est.): agriculture, 20%; industry, 14%; services, 66%

ENERGY RESOURCES:

Electricity production (2007 est.): 437.3 billion kWh
Electricity consumption (2007 est.): 402.2 billion kWh
Electricity exports (2007 est.): 2.034 billion kWh
Electricity imports (2007 est.): 40.47 billion kWh (supplied by Paraguay)

Natural gas production (2007 est.): 9.8 billion m³
Natural gas consumption (2007 est.): 19.8 billion m³
Natural gas exports (2007 est.): 0 m³
Natural gas imports (2007 est.): 10 billion m³
Natural gas proved reserves (Jan. 2008 est.): 347.7 billion m³

Oil production (2007 est.): 2.277 million bbl/day
Oil imports (2005): 648,800 bbl/day
Oil proved reserves (Jan. 2008 est.): 12.35 billion bbl

Source: Data from *The World Factbook 2009.* Washington, D.C.: Central Intelligence Agency, 2009.
Notes: Data are the most recent tracked by the CIA. Values are given in U.S. dollars. Abbreviations: bbl/day = barrels per day; GDP = gross domestic product; km² = square kilometers; kWh = kilowatt-hours; m³ = cubic meters; mi² = square miles.

cent from oil, 9.6 percent from natural gas, 6 percent from coal, and the remainder comprising hydroelectric power, ethanol from sugarcane, and nuclear power. Globally, its coal reserves are not extensive (930 million metric tons compared to 271,000 million metric tons produced by the United States). More than 50 percent of Brazil's coal comes from the state of Rio Grande do Sul, while 46 percent comes from Santa Catarina and 1.3 percent comes from Paraná, Brazil's southernmost states. This coal is used within Brazil.

In relation to global oil reserves and production, Brazil is ranked sixteenth and fourteenth, respectively, and has about 1 percent of estimated global reserves. In 2006, production was about 90 million metric tons, an annual increase of more than 5 percent that was mainly due to raised output from offshore oil fields, notably the Campos and Santos basins located off the southeast coast of the state of Rio de Janeiro. These fields contain the vast majority of Brazil's proven reserves. Such increases have made Brazil almost self sufficient in oil, though light crude is still imported because of refinery capacity. The state-owned company Petrobras controls about 95 percent of crude oil production, which amounts to about 2.277 million barrels per day. Brazil ranks fortieth for natural gas reserves and thirty-third for production. It produced about 9.8 billion cubic meters in 2007, mostly from offshore fields, all of which is consumed within Brazil.

OTHER ENERGY RESOURCES

Most of Brazil's remaining energy needs are met by hydroelectric power and ethanol, a biofuel made from sugarcane. Brazil is the third largest producer of hydropower in the world. Approximately 27 percent of its potential could be exploited economically. Although just less than half has been realized, it provides about 84 percent of Brazil's electricity. Much of this has been made possible by the vast Itaipu Dam constructed in the late 1980's, which Brazil shares with neighboring Paraguay. Other large-scale schemes include the Tucurui Dam on the Tocantins River in Pará and Boa Esperança on the Parnaíba River near the city of Guadalupe. Another dam, the Belo Monte, is proposed on the Xingu River, also in the state of Pará. However, this project is controversial because of the adverse environmental and social impacts associated with such large-scale projects. Many small-scale dams also contribute to Brazil's hydropower capacity.

Although Brazil is not the only nation to develop biofuels, it is unique insofar as ethanol became available as a fuel in the 1920's. Ethanol rose to prominence in the mid-1970's, when world oil crises prompted the Brazilian government to decree that all automobiles had to operate on a fuel that contained at least 10 percent ethanol. Brazil is a leading producer of ethanol and user of ethanol as a fuel; it has been described as having the world's first sustainable biofuel economy. In 2006, Brazil was responsible for 33 percent of the global production of ethanol and for 42 percent of the ethanol used as fuel. Ethanol is produced by the fermentation of sugarcane, one of Brazil's major crops, which was introduced by Europeans in the sixteenth century. In 2007, Brazil produced 514 million metric tons of sugarcane from 6.7 million hectares, mostly in the central/southern region. Between 40 and 50 percent is used for ethanol fuel and the rest for sugar, which is a major export. The sucrose content is the raw material for ethanol, which is produced at more than 370 processing plants, mostly in Brazil's southern and coastal states. Brazil has automobiles that can run on any combination of petroleum/ethanol-based fuels, though environmental implications remain because sugarcane plantations rely on irrigation, mechanization, and other techniques that affect the environment.

AGRICULTURAL RESOURCES

Brazil is a world leader in the export of agricultural products, and the agricultural sector contributes more than 5 percent to the nation's gross domestic product (GDP). Of Brazil's total land area (almost 8.5 million square kilometers), about 2.6 million square kilometers are used for crop production. Apart from sugarcane, soybeans, maize, rice, coffee, wheat, and cotton are significant economic crops. Beef production is also important in Brazil; the country has extensive cattle ranches in the hinterland of São Paulo. According to statistics compiled by the Food and Agriculture Organization, soybeans and maize are grown on 20.6 and 13.8 million hectares, respectively, crops that produce about 58 and 50 million metric tons, respectively. Soybean cultivation has increased significantly but is no longer dominant in São Paulo's hinterland, having expanded into central western and northeastern regions (where its and sugarcane's spread occurs at the expense of savanna and forest ecosystems). This expansion is partly associated with increased demand for biofuels. Brazil is the world's biggest exporter of soybeans, sending 25 million metric tons to markets in Asia and Europe.

Rice is produced on about 3 million hectares, though the 11 million metric tons produced are mainly consumed within Brazil. Similarly, the 3.9 million metric tons of cotton grown on 1.1 million hectares of land support Brazil's significant textile industry. In 2005, approval was given for cotton farmers to use genetically modified strains. Brazil is one of the top-ten producers of textiles.

Two other major Brazilian exports include coffee and orange juice. In 2007, coffee was grown on 2.3 million hectares, mainly in the states of São Paulo and Minas Gerais, with a production of 2.2 million metric tons. Oranges were cultivated on 0.8 million hectare, mostly in the state of São Paulo, from which 18.2 million metric tons were produced. Brazil is the world's largest producer of coffee and is responsible for about one-third of world production. It is also a leading exporter, mainly to the United States and Europe; in 2007, exports comprised twenty-eight million 60-

kilogram bags, which earned $3.4 billion. Brazil is also the world's biggest producer of orange juice; production in 2005 amounted to 1.4 million metric tons out of a world total of 2.4 million metric tons. Only about 2 percent is consumed internally, while the other 98 percent is exported.

Cattle meat (notably beef and veal), pork, and chickens/chicken meat are important components of Brazil's agriculture and export earnings. Cattle ranches are prevalent in the west-central region, though ranching has expanded north, and illegal grazing is now a major cause of Amazon deforestation. Brazil has the largest cattle industry in the world, with more than 200 million head of cattle. It is also a leading exporter of beef, mainly to Europe and Chile, with exports amounting to 80 million metric tons per month, and the industry continues to expand. Pig rearing is also important in Brazil's agricultural sector, with about 34 million head. The three southern

The Brazilian Amazon jungle is a source of numerous natural resources but has suffered from major deforestation. (©Paura/Dreamstime.com)

states dominate production, but pig rearing has spread to the center-west region, especially in the state of Mato Grosso. Russia and Eastern Europe constitute the major overseas markets; domestic demand is also high. Chicken meat is another significant export, notably to Asia. In 2007, Brazil had almost 1 billion chickens and is second to the United States as an exporter of chicken meat. The value of its exports was $5 billion in 2007. It produces 12 million metric tons annually.

WOOD AND WOOD PRODUCTS

As well as being home to the world's largest extent of tropical forest in the Amazon basin, Brazil has 6.2 million hectares of plantation forests, comprising fast-growing pine and eucalyptus. These were planted mainly between 1967 and 1987, a process stimulated by tax incentives, as some 70 percent of the land used is publicly owned. The plantations produce all of Brazil's pulp and paper, which generated about $3 billion, or 40 percent of the total GDP earned by the forest sector. Most sawn wood is produced from natural forests, of which Brazil has lost an area the size of France.

A conflict of interest between conservation and forestry has arisen, especially in relation to the serious problem of illegal felling. Approximately 30 percent of the Amazon forest has protected status, and most wood is removed from the 25 percent that is privately owned. Prior to extraction, landowners must have a management plan and a permit from Brazil's environment agency. Only 5 percent of wood is approved by the international Forest Stewardship Council. Amazonian forests, especially those in the states of Pará, Mato Grosso, and Rondônia, generate more timber than any other forests in the world. Most of this wood is used within Brazil itself. Many other forest products are significant resources, including charcoal, fuelwood, nuts, fruits, oil plants, and rubber.

OTHER RESOURCES

Brazil produces a range of precious and semiprecious stones, including diamond, emerald, topaz, tourmaline, beryl, and amethyst. These come mainly from the states of Minas Gerais, Rio Grande do Sul, Bahia, Goiás, Pará, Tocantins, Paraíba, and Piauí. Both raw and cut stones are exported, especially to the United States, and they also support an internal jewelry industry.

Brazil is a significant producer of graphite, magnesite, and potash and has abundant sand and gravel deposits. It has almost 30 percent of the world's graphite reserves, which are widely distributed. The richest deposits are in Minas Gerais, Ceará, and Bahia. About 22 percent is exported, and the remainder is used domestically in the steel industry and for battery production. Reserves of magnesite are also extensive, ranking Brazil fourth in the world. The deposits occur in the Serra das Éguas, in the state of Bahia. About 30 percent is exported and 70 percent is used in a variety of Brazil's industries, especially steel manufacture. In 2005, some 403 metric tons of potash were produced from Sergipe and Amazonas, where deposits of silvinite are located. This makes Brazil the world's ninth largest producer, though it continues to import most of its potassium fertilizer. Phosphate deposits also supply fertilizer, and in 2006, Brazil's production comprised almost 6 million metric tons, making it the twelfth largest producer in the world. It contributes substantially to crop production, as Brazil is the world's fourth largest consumer of fertilizers, and is also used for manufacturing detergents.

A. M. Mannion

FURTHER READING

Brazilian Development Bank and Center for Strategic Studies and Management Science, Technology, and Innovation. *Sugarcane Bioethanol: Energy for Sustainable Development.* Rio de Janeiro: Author, 2008.

Goulding, Michael, Ronaldo Barthem, and Efrem Jorge Gondim Ferreira. *Smithsonian Atlas of the Amazon.* Washington, D.C.: Smithsonian Books, 2003.

Lusty, Paul. *South America Mineral Production, 1997-2006: A Product of the World Mineral Statistics Database.* Nottingham, Nottinghamshire, England: British Geological Survey, 2008.

WEB SITES

ENERGY INFORMATION ADMINISTRATION
Country Analysis Briefs: Brazil
http://www.eia.doe.gov/emeu/cabs/Brazil/
    Oil.html

INFOMINE
Brazil: Great Potential
http://www.infomine.com/publications/docs/
    InternationalMining/IMMay2006a.pdf

SEE ALSO: Agricultural products; Agriculture industry; Biofuels; Ethanol; Timber industry.

Brick

CATEGORY: Products from resources

Brick as a building material has a long history. Its qualities of durability and ease of manufacture—as well as the fact that suitable clay is widely available—have made it desirable.

DEFINITION

Brick has been used as a building material since before the advent of written history. Bricks are durable, fireproof, and decorative. They also have high heat- and sound-insulating qualities. The clay from which bricks may be made is widespread on the Earth's surface. Clay can be used directly if it is relatively free of impurities. In such cases the clay is formed, dried, and fired. Clays that are suitable but contain some undesirable elements, such as roots or pebbles, can be refined through removal of the unwanted material.

OVERVIEW

Clay resources for brick making are usually mined by open-pit or strip mining. In small mining operations, hand labor may serve to remove the overlying earth material (overburden). In larger operations, a combination of mechanical devices is used. Graders and drag lines may be used to remove the overburden and expose the clay. Once the clay has been removed, it is ready for preparation.

The complexity of clay preparation depends on the quality of the clay. Primary preparation involves crushing the raw material, removing stones, and blending different clays if desired. Secondary preparation grinds the crushed lumps to the desired fineness. At this stage, more blending may occur; storage of the milled clay follows.

The manufacture of bricks begins when the processed clay is moistened enough to permit formation of bricks. In some instances hand molding is used; in other cases the brick material may be extruded and cut into lengths of the desired size. Once the bricks have been produced, they must be dried prior to firing. The preliminary drying is necessary to reduce the water content, because too much water could cause problems resulting from expansion during the firing process. Drying is done by placing the bricks either in a protected place to allow natural drying or in an artificially heated dryer.

Following the drying process, the bricks are ready for firing. Firing removes the remaining moisture from the bricks and, as the intensity of the heating increases, renders the brick stable and able to resist weathering. The firing itself can be done in the open, with the fuel and prepared bricks intermixed. More controlled firing takes place with the use of kilns, in which the firing occurs under closed, controlled conditions. Following firing, the bricks are allowed to cool slowly to prevent damage and are then ready for use.

Jerry E. Green

SEE ALSO: Cement and concrete; Clays; Open-pit mining; Strip mining.

Bromine

CATEGORY: Mineral and other nonliving resources

WHERE FOUND

Bromine is widely distributed in small quantities in the Earth's crust. The oceans contain most of the world's bromine, and it is also found in inland evaporitic (salt) lakes. Recovered from underground brines in Arkansas, bromine became that state's most important mineral commodity and made the United States the producer of one-third of the world's bromine. In descending order, Israel, China, Jordan, and Japan account for most of the balance.

PRIMARY USES

The use of bromine in flame retardants is a quickly expanding industry. Bromine is also used in agricultural applications, water treatment and sanitizing, petroleum additives, well-drilling fluids, dyes, photographic compounds, and pharmaceuticals.

TECHNICAL DEFINITION

Bromine (abbreviated Br), atomic number 35, belongs to Group VII (the halogens) of the periodic table of the elements and resembles chlorine and iodine in its chemical properties. It has two naturally occurring isotopes: bromine 79 (50.69 percent) and bromine 81 (49.31 percent). Bromine is the only nonmetal that is liquid at room temperature. A volatile liquid, it is deep red in color with a density of 3.14 grams per cubic centimeter, a freezing point of $-7.3°$ Celsius, and a boiling point of $58.8°$ Celsius. A diatomic element, bromine exists as paired bromine atoms in its elemental form.

DESCRIPTION, DISTRIBUTION, AND FORMS

Bromine has an abundance of 2.5 parts per million in the Earth's crust, ranking it forty-sixth in order of abundance of the elements. It is more prevalent in the oceans, at 65 parts per million. In salt lakes such as the Dead Sea, at 4,000 parts per million, and Searles Lake in California, at 85 parts per million, bromine is more abundant than in the oceans. The most concentrated sources of bromine are brine wells; one in Arkansas has 5,000 parts per million.

As a halogen, bromine needs one electron to achieve filled "s" (sharp) and "p" (principal) shells. Thus, bromine exists in nature as a bromide ion with a negative 1 charge. High concentrations of bromine in plants have not been noted. However, marine plants do have a relatively higher concentration than land plants.

Bromine, along with chlorine, tops the list of elements suspected of causing ozone depletion in the stratosphere. Because of this, the Environmental Protection Agency has listed methyl bromide and hydrobromofluorocarbons as a class I ozone-depleting substances. This classification means a limit to the production of these compounds in the United States.

Because availability has become more common because of pesticides and gasoline additives, the human intake of bromine has increased. There have not been toxicity problems, however, as bromine is retained for only short periods before it is excreted in urine. Plant and animals alike show little toxic reaction to bromine.

HISTORY

Antoine-Jérôme Balard first established bromine as an element. He had extracted bromine from brine by saturating it with chlorine and distilling. When attempts to decompose the new substance failed, he

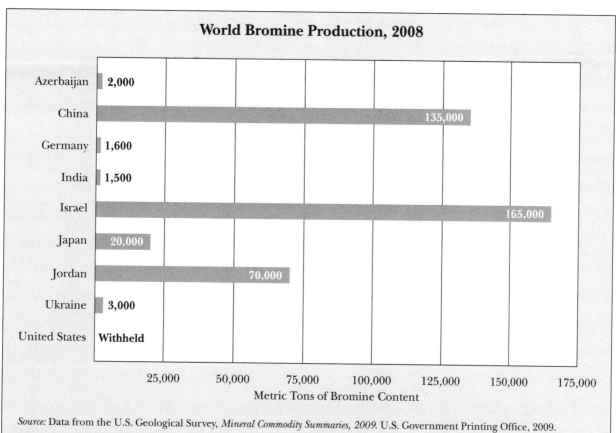

World Bromine Production, 2008

Country	Metric Tons of Bromine Content
Azerbaijan	2,000
China	135,000
Germany	1,600
India	1,500
Israel	165,000
Japan	20,000
Jordan	70,000
Ukraine	3,000
United States	Withheld

Source: Data from the U.S. Geological Survey, *Mineral Commodity Summaries, 2009.* U.S. Government Printing Office, 2009.

Note: U.S. data were withheld to avoid disclosure of company proprietary data.

correctly deduced that bromine was an element and published his results in 1826. Balard wanted to call the new element "muride," but the French Academy did not like the name. Bromine, from the Greek *bromos*, for stink or bad odor, was chosen instead. The first mineral of bromine found was bromyrite (silver bromide), found in Mexico in 1941. Silver bromide was used as the light-sensitive material in early photographic emulsions from about 1840, and potassium bromide began to be used in 1857 as a sedative and an anticonvulsant. The purple pigment known as Tyrian purple and referred to in Ezekiel in the Old Testament of the Bible is a bromine compound. Originally the dye was obtained from the small purple snail *Murex brandaris.*

Obtaining Bromine

Acidified solutions of bromine (either brines or seawater) are pumped into the top of a ceramic-filled tower. As the solution falls through the tower, the bromine reacts with chlorine. The chlorine becomes chloride ions dissolved in solution. The bromide ions in solution become bromine molecules. The bromine is then steamed out (collected in steam) or blown out (collected in air) by the steam or air passing through the tower. The bromine condenses and is separated from the gases at the top of the tower. It then can be purified or reacted with other substances to form bromine compounds. In Israel, the brine comes from the production of chemicals such as sodium chloride or potash and contains about 14,000 parts per million. Yearly world production of bromine in 2008 was about 400,000 metric tons (excluding U.S. production).

Uses of Bromine

Flame retardants use the highest percentage of the bromine produced, about 45. These products are used in circuit boards, television cabinets, wire, cable, textile coverings, wood treatments, fabric treatments, polyurethane foam insulation, and polyester resins. Bromine compounds are used in portable fire extinguishers as well as in closed spaces such as computer rooms. Use of bromine in agriculture as pesticides such as ethylene bromide, dibromochloropropane, or methyl bromide accounts for 10 percent of the total produced. Methyl bromide is a very effective nematocide (worm killer) as well as herbicide, fungicide, and insecticide. Bromine is also used in treating water and sanitizing water equipment such as swimming pools, hot tubs, water cooling towers, and food

washing appliances. Bromine is more efficient than other materials because it has a higher biocidal activity.

In the 1970's, the principal use of bromine was in ethylene dibromide, a scavenger for lead. With the decreased use of leaded gasoline, less ethylene dibromide is needed. High-density drilling fluids made with bromine compounds account for another 20 percent. Dyes and photography usage account for 5 percent. Silver bromide is still the main light-sensitive compound used in film. The pharmaceutical industry uses about 4 percent of the bromine produced. Because bromine is very reactive, forming compounds with every group except the noble gases, new uses for bromine will undoubtedly be found.

C. Alton Hassell

Further Reading

Greenwood, N. N., and A. Earnshaw. "The Halogens: Fluorine, Chloride, Bromine, Iodine, and Astatine." In *Chemistry of the Elements.* 2d ed. Boston: Butterworth-Heinemann, 1997.

Henderson, William. "The Group 17 (Halogen) Elements: Fluorine, Chlorine, Bromine, Iodine, and Astatine." In *Main Group Chemistry.* Cambridge, England: Royal Society of Chemistry, 2000.

Jacobson, Mark Z. "Effects of Bromine on Global Ozone Reduction." In *Atmospheric Pollution: History, Science, and Regulation.* New York: Cambridge University Press, 2002.

Kogel, Jessica Elzea, et al., eds. "Bromine." In *Industrial Minerals and Rocks: Commodities, Markets, and Uses.* 7th ed. Littleton, Colo.: Society for Mining, Metallurgy, and Exploration, 2006.

Krebs, Robert E. *The History and Use of Our Earth's Chemical Elements: A Reference Guide.* Illustrations by Rae Déjur. 2d ed. Westport, Conn.: Greenwood Press, 2006.

Massey, A. G. "Group 17: The Halogens: Fluorine, Chlorine, Bromine, Iodine, and Astatine." In *Main Group Chemistry.* 2d ed. New York: Wiley, 2000.

Weeks, Mary Elvira. *Discovery of the Elements: Collected Reprints of a Series of Articles Published in the "Journal of Chemical Education."* Kila, Mont.: Kessinger, 2003.

Web Site

U.S. Geological Survey
Bromine: Statistics and Information
http://minerals.usgs.gov/minerals/pubs/
    commodity/bromine/index.html#myb

SEE ALSO: Agriculture industry; Air pollution and air pollution control; Atmosphere; Clean Air Act; Environmental Protection Agency; Herbicides; Oceans; Ozone layer and ozone hole debate; Pesticides and pest control.

Bronze

CATEGORY: Products from resources

Bronze is a term applied to a variety of alloys that contain copper; the oldest of these, which was the first metallic alloy produced, is an alloy of copper and tin. Other alloying elements include tin, nickel, phosphorus, zinc, and lead.

BACKGROUND

A variety of related alloys are called bronze. The one with the longest history is an alloy composed primarily of copper, with a smaller percentage of tin. Various forms of bronze have been smelted for thousands of years; in fact, bronze was the first true metallic alloy developed. Bronze replaced the use of copper as the material of choice for tools, weapons, jewelry, and other items in the ancient Near East and other early centers of civilization. Although eventually it was largely replaced by iron and finally by various steel alloys, bronze still is employed extensively for a variety of industrial uses worldwide.

HISTORY

The first metal used by ancient metallurgists was copper, because surface deposits of this metallic element in its native, or naturally pure, form were once relatively plentiful in certain areas. However, objects produced from pure or nearly pure copper possess several drawbacks, chief among them are softness and lack of resistance to damage. Archaeological finds from the Near East dating back at least to around 3000 B.C.E. indicate that early metalworkers discovered that by adding other metals in small percentages, they could produce a new, stronger metal that also boasted several other favorable characteristics: a lower melting point (950° Celsius instead of the 1,084° Celsius required for copper), greater ease of flowage into molds in the casting process, and elimination of the troublesome bubbles that plagued the casting of pure copper.

Through experimentation, early metallurgists discovered that the ideal metal proportions for bronze were about 10 percent tin and 90 percent copper. The invention of bronze led to a veritable explosion of metal-casting industries that produced elaborate and intricate bronze artifacts and ushered in a period of flourishing mining and trading networks linking far-flung areas for bronze production. Some bronze-producing centers, such as sites in ancient China, experimented with bronze using other admixtures, such as lead. Eventually, with the development of hotter smelting furnaces and other techniques, bronze was replaced for most of its applications by a still harder metal, iron, and then by the various alloys of steel.

Various bronze alloys, however, have always been employed for some uses even while other metals became the primary choice for most metal applications. Statuary made from bronze, for example, has always enjoyed popularity. In addition, the modern industrial world uses various types of bronze for cast products such as pumps, gears, nuts, tubes, rods, and machine or motor bearings. Modern bronze alloys typically do not have a tin content in excess of 12 percent, as percentages above that ratio produce alloys with declining ductility (the capaciity for being easily shaped or molded), and they tend to become very brittle.

SPECIALIZED BRONZES

Some specialized modern bronze alloys are produced with small percentages of lead, nickel, phosphorus, zinc, and even aluminum. Copper-tin-lead bronzes, for example, are used for machine bearings that must withstand both a heavy load and frictional heat. The lead is added to produce a desired degree of elasticity. A bronze combining copper, tin, and phosphorus is smelted with a percentage of phosphorus in the range of 0.1 to 0.5 percent. The phosphorus in this alloy allows the molten metal to flow more freely and makes casting easier. It also helps deoxidize the melt during the smelting process and produces a bronze with great resistance to wear. Phosphor bronzes, as they are termed, are used in machine gear wheels, an application where hardness and wear resistance are desired. Another type of bronze that is similarly employed is zinc bronze. The zinc typically makes up 2 to 6 percent of the alloy, which also includes copper and tin. Another term for zinc bronze is "gunmetal" bronze, and if the alloy has the specific formula 88 percent copper, 10 percent tin, and 2 percent zinc it is termed "admiralty gunmetal" bronze.

Yet another type of bronze is copper-tin-nickel bronze, in which the proportion of nickel is usually 1 to 2 percent of the alloy. Nickel bronze is designed to withstand high temperatures and strongly resist corrosion. It possesses a microstructure that is more closely grained than most bronzes, while having both added toughness and strength. Other types of bronze alloys include aluminum bronzes, which typically are 1 to 14 percent aluminum and usually have smaller percentages of other metals, such as iron, nickel, and manganese. Aluminum bronzes are used in the production of special wires, strips, tubings, and sheets for which ductile strength is desirable.

A by-product of exposure to the elements of bronze alloys that are less resistant to corrosion is the production of a thin greenish or greenish-blue crust or patina called "verdigris." This crust, often seen on outdoor statuary, fixtures, and fountains, is composed typically of either copper sulfide or copper chloride.

Frederick M. Surowiec

FURTHER READING

Callister, William D. "Nonferrous Alloys." In *Materials Science and Engineering: An Introduction.* 7th ed. New York: John Wiley & Sons, 2007.

Cverna, Fran, ed. "Bronzes." In *Worldwide Guide to Equivalent Nonferrous Metals and Alloys.* 4th ed. Materials Park, Ohio: ASM International, 2001.

Hummel, Rolf E. *Understanding Materials Science: History, Properties, Applications.* 2d ed. New York: Springer, 2004.

Raymond, Robert. *Out of the Fiery Furnace: The Impact of Metals on the History of Mankind.* University Park: Pennsylvania State University Press, 1986.

Simons, Eric N. *An Outline of Metallurgy.* New York: Hart, 1969.

SEE ALSO: Alloys; Aluminum; Brass; Copper; Iron; Manganese; Nickel; Oxides; Steel; Tin.

Buildings and appliances, energy-efficient

CATEGORY: Environment, conservation, and resource management

Before the 1970's, buildings and appliances were designed without thought to efficient energy usage or their environmental impact. Then came a growing awareness that the burning of fossil fuels for energy releases gases that pollute the environment, causes acid rain, and contributes to global warming. Environmental and health concerns and energy costs led to the increased development of renewable, or "clean energy," resources: solar, wind, hydro, geothermal, and biomass. Movements toward "green buildings," energy management systems (EMS's), and intelligent control systems developed.

BACKGROUND

In 1990, the energy used in American buildings for heating, cooling, lighting, and operating appliances amounted to roughly 36 percent of U.S. energy use and cost nearly $200 billion. About two-thirds of this amount was fuel energy, including the fuel energy lost in generating and delivering electricity. Electricity is considered worth the extra cost because it is quiet, convenient, and available in small units. Because of continuing improvements in space conditioning, appliances, and the controls for both, building and appliance energy use could be cut by half or even three-quarters.

INSULATION

"Space conditioning" is the warming and cooling of rooms and buildings. Ways to make it more efficient include improving insulation, siting, heat storage, heaters, and coolers. Structures gain and lose heat in three ways: air movement, conduction, and radiation. Insulating a building requires isolating it from these processes. The most important consideration is reducing a building's air flow, and walls and ceilings are the primary reducers. The space-conditioning load of a structure may be construed as the number of "air changes" per hour. The next level of consideration is heat conduction through walls, windows, ceilings, and floors. Heat conduction can be slowed by constructing a building with thicker walls or by using insulating materials that conduct heat more slowly. A material's insulating ability is measured by its resistance to conduction, called its R value. A major innovation during the 1970's was the practice of framing houses with 5-by-15-centimeter (2-by-6-inch) studs instead of the standard two-by-fours. That design allowed insulation to be 50 percent thicker.

Windows are a major heat conductor. One window can conduct as much heat as an entire wall. During the 1980's in the United States, the amount of heat lost through windows was estimated to have equaled half the energy that was obtained from Alaskan oil fields. Double-paned and even triple-paned windows (with air space between the panes) to reduce this loss became more common. To reduce conduction further, the air between panes can be partially evacuated, or the space can be filled with a less conductive gas, such as xenon. Finally, windows can also have coatings that reflect infrared (heat) radiation, thereby keeping summer heat out and holding heat inside during winter.

Beginning in the 1970's, Canadian researchers worked to develop "superinsulated" houses: structures so well insulated that they hardly required furnaces, even in the severe winter climates characteristic of much of Canada. The costs were an additional two thousand to seven thousand dollars in construction and an ongoing expense of running an air exchanger. In the winter, the exchanger warms incoming fresh air with the heat from air being exhausted; in the summer it cools incoming air. Because such a building is so well sealed, without the air exchanger one could smell yesterday's bacon and coffee (as well as more noxious lingering odors).

SITING

The importance of the siting of a structure—that is, the direction it "faces," including where windows and doors are placed and where there are solid walls—has been known since ancient times. In the developed nations of the twentieth century, as energy sources became widely and cheaply available, designers and architects often ignored this aspect of building design. For example, they often did not consider the importance of catching sunlight on south-facing sides, protection from the cold on the north side, hardwood trees (which can supply summer shade and then drop their leaves to allow more sunlight to pass through in winter), and overhangs to shade against the high summer Sun. These design elements alone can reduce the need for heating and cooling energy significantly.

The energy crises of 1973 and 1979 reminded builders of the drawbacks of old, energy-intensive approaches to building design and led to renewed consideration of natural heat flow. The awareness that oil is a limited resource also gave credence to a more radical siting idea known as terratecture: A structure can be made more energy-efficient by locating it partially underground. Terratecture is particularly efficient when used to shield a north-facing wall. Insulation

and thermal inertia reduce heating and cooling loads, while windows facing south and opening into courtyards allow as much window space as conventional structures. For a slight increase in construction costs, terratectural houses have significant energy advantages, allow more vegetation, and require less maintenance. They are quite different from conventional houses, however, and have not been widely adapted.

HEATING AND COOLING

During the mid-1700's, the British colonies in North America faced an energy crisis: a declining amount of firewood. Traditional large fireplaces sent most heat up the chimney. Benjamin Franklin studied more efficient fireplaces in Europe, and he invented a metal stove that radiated more of the fire's heat into the room. The Franklin stove (1742) provided more heat by increasing "end-use efficiency" rather than by increasing energy use. Two hundred years later, the energy crises of the late twentieth century led to the application of burner advances that had been developed or proposed earlier. Studies of flame dynamics and catalysts led to more complete fuel combustion, and better radiators captured more heat from the burner.

Hot climates and commercial buildings that produce excess heat require air-conditioning. Air-conditioning is based on heat pumping, which cools the hot internal air by moving the heat elsewhere. Most heat pumps compress a gas on the hot side and allow it to decompress on the cold side.

Electronic controls have helped reduce energy waste in space conditioning. For instance, in winter, computerized thermostats can maintain lower temperatures while people are not in a building and then automatically change the settings to a higher, more comfortable level at times when people are scheduled to return. For gas appliances, the replacement of pilot lights with electric igniters has helped reduce unnecessary fuel use. (Electric igniters are even more important for intermittently used burners, such as those used in stoves.)

Another way of decreasing energy input is storing heat or cold from different times of the day, or even different seasons of the year. Thick stone on walls and floors, such as those made of adobe bricks in the Southwest, have been used for centuries in desert climates; they remain relatively cool during the afternoon heat and then slowly give off the day's heat during cold nights. Higher-technology variants of storage use less material per unit of heat. Office complexes that are designed to store cool air can use smaller air-conditioners and cheaper, off-peak power.

LIGHTING AND MOTORS

Until the mid-nineteenth century, people rose at dawn and retired at sundown because there was no form of artificial lighting that could provide sufficient light for most work or leisure activities after dark. Improved oil lamps and then incandescent electric lights (first widely marketed by Thomas Edison in 1879) started a revolution that eventually consumed roughly a quarter of U.S. electricity directly and, in addition, contributed to building cooling loads.

Incandescent lights use resistance heating to make a wire filament glow, so they generate significant heat in addition to light. Fluorescent lights, with a glow of current flowing through gases under partial vacuum, are more efficient and last longer. Fluorescent lighting was invented in 1867 by Antoine-Edmond Becquerel but not widely marketed until the 1940's. In the 1980's, compact fluorescents for small lamps were developed, followed by light-emitting diode technology; such low-energy forms of lighting have begun to supplant incandescent lighting, especially in new building projects. Moreover, controllers can improve efficiency by switching off lights when people are gone; they can also be programmed to reduce lighting when sunlight is available.

Electric motors range from tiny shaver motors to power drives for elevators and large air conditioners. A number of methods have been developed to make motors more efficient. The use of additional motor windings (costing more copper wire) has always been an option. Electronic controls that match power used to the actual load rather than based on a constant high load were developed after the 1970's energy crises. Amorphous metals (produced by rapid cooling from the molten state) have been developed to allow electromagnets in motors to switch off faster, reducing drag; they also make more efficient transformers for fluorescent lights.

Most improvements to appliance efficiency involve some combination of better motors and better space conditioning. The electrical loads from refrigerators—among the largest in most homes in industrialized nations—dropped by half in average energy demand in the United States between 1972 and 1992. More efficient motors and better insulation were responsible for the improvement.

THE ENERGY STAR PROGRAM

In 1992, the U.S. Environmental Protection Agency established Energy Star, a voluntary labeling program that identifies products meeting strict standards of energy efficiency. The program set the standard for commercial buildings, homes, heating and cooling devices, major appliances, and other products. The Energy Star concept eventually expanded to other countries, including members of the European Union, Japan, Taiwan, Canada, China, Australia, South Africa, and New Zealand.

In 1992, the first labeled product line included personal computers and monitors. In 1995, the label was expanded to include residential heating and cooling products, including central air conditioners, furnaces, programmable thermostats, and air-source heat pumps. Energy Star for buildings and qualified new homes was also launched. In 1996, the U.S. Department of Energy became a partner in the program, and the label expanded to include insulation and appliances, such as dishwashers, refrigerators, and room air conditioners. By March, 2006, Americans had purchased more than two billion products that qualified for the Energy Star rating, and by December of that year, there were almost 750,000 Energy Star qualified homes nationally.

In 2008, energy cost savings to consumers, businesses, and organizations totaled approximately $19 billion. The average house can produce twice the greenhouse-gas emissions as the average car. The amount of energy saved in 2008 helped prevent greenhouse-gas emissions equal to those from 29 million cars. By 2009, Energy Star had partnerships with more than 15,000 public and private sector organizations, and had labels on more than sixty product categories, including thousands of models for home and office use.

Compared to conventional products, those approved by Energy Star are more energy-efficient, save on costs, and feature the latest technology. By using less energy, they help reduce the negative impact on the environment.

In the average home, heating and cooling are the largest energy expenditures, accounting for about one-half of the total energy bill. Energy Star compliant heating and cooling equipment can cut yearly energy bills by 30 percent, or more than six hundred dollars per year. A qualified furnace, when properly sized and installed, along with sealed ducts and a programmable thermostat, uses about 15 percent less energy than a standard model and saves up to 20 percent on heating bills. An Energy Star room air conditioner use at least 10 percent less energy than conventional models, and they often include timers for better temperature control. To keep heating, ventilating, and air-conditioning (HVAC) systems running efficiently, Energy Star recommends changing air filters regularly, installing a programmable thermostat, and sealing heating and cooling ducts.

The second largest energy expenditure is water heating, which costs the typical household four hundred to six hundred dollars per year. A new Energy Star water heater would cut water heating bills by half.

Energy Star refrigerators use 20 percent less energy than other models, thus cutting energy bills by $165 over its lifetime. They also have precise temperature controls and advanced food compartments to keep food fresher for a longer time. Because they use much less water than conventional models, Energy Star dishwashers help ease the demand on the country's water supplies. Energy Star also recommends running the dishwasher with a full load and that the air-dry option be used instead of the heat-dry.

Using the most innovative technology, Energy Star clothes washers cut energy and water consumption by more than 40 percent, compared to conventional models. Most do not have a central agitator and use a reduced amount of hot water in the wash cycle. Instead of rubbing laundry against an agitator in a full tub, front-load washers tumble laundry through a small amount of water. Modern top loaders flip or spin clothes through a reduced stream of water. Sophisticated motors spin clothes two to three times faster during the spin cycle to extract more water, thus requiring less time in the dryer.

Lighting accounts for 20 percent of the electric bill in the average U.S. home, and 7 percent of all energy consumed in the United States is used in lighting for homes and businesses. An Energy Star qualified compact fluorescent light bulb (CFL) uses 75 percent less energy and lasts ten times longer than an incandescent bulb. It pays for itself in six months, and the savings are about thirty dollars over its lifetime.

THE GREEN BUILDING MOVEMENT

After the rise of environmental consciousness in the 1960's, and the 1973 and 1979 oil shortages, concerned groups around the world began to look for ways to conserve energy and preserve natural resources. One of the most important applications for this cul-

tural shift was the transformation of human dwellings and workplaces, resulting in the green building movement. Starting with heat from the Sun, architects incorporated active photovoltaic systems and passive designs that cleverly positioned windows, walls, and rooftops to capture and retain heat. Another factor was an increased attention to heat exchange as affected by materials and construction techniques. Building materials were also reexamined in terms of toxicity; pollution and energy consumption in factory processing; durability; interaction with soil, bedrock, water; and other factors.

Contemporary green building looks at all of these issues and more, because a narrow approach could actually do more harm than good. A building sealed too tightly, for example, could have excellent heat retention, but might not have enough internal air circulation. Recycled materials might lower resource consumption, but could actually be more toxic. Therefore cross-disciplinary collaboration is necessary in order to achieve effective green building design. In the United States, the Office of the Federal Environmental Executive (OFEE) recognizes the complexity of green building, and organizes the effort around two primary goals: limiting the consumption of basic resources such as materials, water, and energy and protecting the environment and people's health.

One of the most important elements in a green building is its use of green energy. Although some governments have established precise technical definitions of green energy for purposes of incentive programs, the term is generally associated with environmentalism; conveys the idea of safe, nonpolluting energy; and often means renewable energy. Although not all consumers are able to construct a new green building, many achieve these goals by transforming existing structures. A key element in both new and existing buildings is the use of Energy Star compliant appliances.

RENEWABLE ENERGY SOURCES

The energy crises of the 1970's and environmental concerns led to interest in alternative, renewable energy resources. Renewable energy is "clean" energy from a source that is inexhaustible and easily replenished. Nonrenewable energy comes from sources not easily replaced, such as fossil fuels and nuclear energy. Renewable energy does not pollute air or require waste cleanups like nonrenewable energy generation.

This solar-powered building in Athens, Greece, opened in 2007 and is expected to generate enough energy not only to power the building but also to sell the government its surplus. (AP/Wide World Photos)

Solar panels, or modules, are one of the most promising sources of inexpensive and environmentally safe energy. Although earlier efforts to harness solar energy utilized steam from solar-heated water, modern solar panels are photovoltaic: They produce electricity from sunlight. The phenomenon was discovered in the eighteenth century and studied by Albert Einstein in the 1920's. After the widespread adoption of silicon for circuitry in the twentieth century, photovoltaic cells became less expensive to produce and more efficient in power output. The most common forms of silicon used for the cells are crystalline, which became available in the 1950's, and amorphous silicon, which is more frequently used now.

Typically, the cells are joined together in panels, which may also be connected together in an array. The units are produced in a great variety of forms. In home applications, they may be placed on rooftops, or in independent structures at some distance from the dwelling. Some units are also designed so that they are able to move over time to capture the most sunlight, like the solar arrays on the International Space Station. For homes and other buildings, they may also be disguised visually as shingles or other kinds of roofing material, so that they are more seamlessly integrated with the design. The most desirable locations are unshaded or thinly-shaded areas. On roof installations in the Northern Hemisphere, southern exposures are preferred.

Solar panels may be connected to a grid or self-contained, depending on their function. Owners may earn credit by giving energy to the grid during times when their consumption is lower than their own unit's production. The energy may also be stored in batteries. Solar power is a key element in the zero energy building concept. A zero energy building is defined as one which creates more energy than it uses. Combined with other elements such as energy-saving building design and the use of Energy Star qualified appliances, the building's photovoltaic system, which contributes to the grid, earns energy credit equal to or in excess of its consumption.

Wind was an energy resource as early as the fourth century B.C.E., when the Egyptians used wind to move sailboats. Windmills appeared as early as 500 C.E. in Persia. In 1890, in Denmark, Poul La Cour built the first wind turbine, a large windmill capable of generating electricity. From 1956 to 1957, also in Denmark, Johannes Juul developed the Gedser wind turbine, which was the world's first alternating current (AC) wind turbine. Typically, large wind plants are connected to the local electric utility transmission network. Energy Star recommends small wind electric systems as a highly effective home-based system, which could lower electricity bills by 50 to 90 percent. The world's ten largest producers of wind power, as of 2008, were the United States, Germany, Spain, China, India, Italy, France, the United Kingdom, Denmark, and Portugal.

Centuries before electricity was harnessed, hydropower was a significant source of energy, largely in the form of water wheels, in which water moved wooden paddles attached to mechanical devices for grinding grains, pumping, and other functions. While displaced in industrialized regions, these mechanical forms of renewable energy technology are still used in rural areas. Typically, modern hydropower comes from large power plants attached to dams and connected to the grid. In the United States, for example, hydropower contributes roughly 70 percent of the electricity from renewable sources and 6 percent of the nation's total electricity. Other countries—especially Norway, Switzerland, and Canada—derive a much higher portion of their electricity from hydropower. A less common use of hydropower, to generate electricity, is provided by micro hydro water turbines, which may be used when a home or other building is next to or over a stream or river. These may be self-contained, or used in conjunction with other systems, including renewable systems such as solar arrays.

The American Recovery and Reinvestment Act of 2009 (ARRA) provided measures benefiting renewable energy and tax incentives for energy efficiency. It includes a Treasury Department grant program for renewable energy developers and a manufacturing tax credit. The Act also allows individual taxpayers a federal tax credit of 30 percent of the cost of residential alternative energy equipment, such as geothermal heat pumps, wind turbines, and solar hot-water heaters. There are also tax credits for homeowners to make energy efficient improvements such as adding insulation, energy-efficient heating and air-conditioning systems, and energy efficient exterior windows.

EMERGING TECHNOLOGY

Energy Star appliances have become commonplace. An emerging technology is the "smart appliance," which promises even greater energy efficiency and lower energy costs. Smart appliances can have a computer chip or "smart meter" which communicates with a central system, such as the local electrical grid. They can sense when the system is overloaded, such as during peak hours. The appliance can be programmed to turn off partially or to wait for convenient times when the system is less stressed. For instance, a refrigerator can delay running its automatic defrost cycle until the local grid signals that it is an off-peak time. Smart appliances can shut off their own power when they sense an electrical surge. They can be part of smart homes

or buildings, where all electrical appliances or devices are connected to a computer system and function automatically or operate by remote control.

There are numerous benefits of smart appliances. They reduce electrical demand upon grids during peak hours and help avoid huge power failures, such as the large-scale blackouts in the western United States in 1996 and in the Northeast in 2003. With the rise in electric plug-in vehicles, decreasing peak energy demand nationally becomes even more important. Under a real-time pricing structure, consumers would receive price signals from the grid, indicating higher prices during peak hours and lower prices when demand is less. Consumers would see cost savings by managing their energy usage. Because utility companies have to build more generating plants to meet the huge stress on the system during peak hours, less demand would mean fewer plants and carbon emissions. Estimations indicate that this technology could eliminate the need to build thirty coal-fired power plants over twenty years.

General Electric has been testing "energy management-enabled appliances" such as washers and dryers, microwaves, ranges, and dishwashers. These smart appliances are able to time themselves to operate during off-peak periods. Consumers can override the program if they want to use the appliance during peak hours. Whirlpool plans for all its appliances worldwide to be smart appliances by 2015.

The ARRA of 2009 provided billions of dollars to modernize the aging U.S. electrical grid and create a "smart grid," a high-tech electricity distribution and transmission system. A digital communications system and networking technology would be applied to the existing grid. Wireless devices, controls, smart meters, and sensors would be installed along the whole grid, thus providing more services for consumers and giving utilities more control of power production and delivery. More renewable energy sources would be able to come online. The result would be improved electricity efficiency and reliability. A standardized system with a common language understood by all smart appliances when communicating with their grids is in development. A hacker could break into the system, so security issues would have be resolved. In 2009, U.S. commerce secretary Gary Locke and U.S. energy secretary Steven Chu announced the first set of technical standards for the interoperability and security of the "smart grid."

Roger V. Carlson, updated by Alice Myers

FURTHER READING

Amann, Jennifer Thorne, Alex Wilson, and Katie Ackerly. *Consumer Guide to Home Energy Savings.* 9th ed. Washington, D.C.: American Council for an Energy-Efficient Economy, 2007.

Beggs, Clive. *Energy: Management, Supply, and Conservation.* Oxford, England: Butterworth-Heinemann, 2002.

Bonta, Dave, and Stephen Snyder. *New Green Home Solutions: Renewable Household Energy and Sustainable Living.* Layton, Utah: Gibbs Smith, 2008.

Bridgewater, Alan, and Gill Bridgewater. *Renewable Energy for Your Home: Using Off-Grid Energy to Reduce Your Footprint, Lower Your Bills, and Be More Self-Sufficient.* Berkeley, Calif.: Ulysses Press, 2009.

Federal Trade Commission. *How to Buy an Energy-Efficient Home Appliance.* Washington, D.C.: Federal Trade Commission, Bureau of Consumer Protection, Office of Consumer and Business Education, 2000.

Fickett, Arnold P., Clark W. Gellings, and Amory B. Lovins. "Efficient Use of Electricity." *Scientific American* 263, no. 3 (September, 1990): 64.

Flavin, Christopher, and Nicholas Lenssen. *Power Surge: Guide to the Coming Energy Revolution.* New York: W. W. Norton, 1994.

Gipe, Paul. *Wind Energy Basics: A Guide to Home- and Community-Scale Wind-Energy Systems.* White River Junction, Vt.: Chelsea Green, 2009.

Johnston, David, and Scott Gibson. *Green from the Ground Up, a Builder's Guide: Sustainable, Healthy, and Energy-Efficient Home Construction.* Newtown, Conn.: Taunton Press, 2008.

McKay, Kim, and Jenny Bonnin. *True Green Home: One Hundred Inspirational Ideas for Creating a Green Environment at Home.* Washington, D.C.: National Geographic Society, 2009.

Moss, Keith J. *Energy Management in Buildings.* 2d ed. New York: Taylor & Francis, 2006.

Rosenfeld, Arthur H., and David Hafemesiter. "Energy-Efficient Buildings." *Scientific American* 258, no. 4 (April, 1988): 78.

Smith, Colin. *This Cold House: The Simple Science of Energy Efficiency.* Baltimore: Johns Hopkins University Press, 2007.

Woodside, Christine. *Energy Independence: Your Everyday Guide to Reducing Fuel Consumption.* Guilford, Conn.: Lyons Press, 2009.

Yudelson, Jerry. *The Green Building Revolution.* Washington, D.C.: Island Press, 2008.

WEB SITES

FEDERAL TRADE COMMISSION
Energy
http://www.ftc.gov/bcp/menus/consumer/energy/energy.shtm

NATURAL RESOURCES CANADA
Office of Energy Efficiency
http://oee.nrcan.gc.ca/english

U.S. ENVIRONMENTAL PROTECTION AGENCY
Energy Star
http://www.energystar.gov

SEE ALSO: Energy storage; Geothermal and hydrothermal energy; Solar chimneys; Solar energy.

Bureau of Land Management, U.S.

CATEGORY: Organizations, agencies, and programs
DATE: Established 1946

The Bureau of Land Management has the responsibility for land-use management on U.S. national unreserved public lands.

BACKGROUND

The way land is used and the management choices that direct such use are important resource issues. Often such land-use decisions are made by individuals in the context of private land ownership. However, the federal government also has a variety of agencies whose responsibilities include making appropriate land-use management decisions.

One of these agencies is the Bureau of Land Management, a part of the U.S. Department of the Interior. According to bureau literature, the Bureau of Land Management's responsibility is to administer those public lands that are in federal ownership but are not a part of any other established management agency such as the National Park Service. The Bureau of Land Management oversees the use of 104 million surface hectares and 283 million hectares of subsurface mineral estate, comprising 13 percent of the total land in the United States.

The Bureau of Land Management was formed in 1946 when the General Land Office and the Grazing Service were merged. The Bureau of Land Management's authorization included such diverse areas of concern as mineral leasing, public land sales, and grazing regulation.

In 1964, Congress created the Public Land Law Review Commission to review policies regarding public land management. The work of this commission was followed in 1976 by the passage of the Federal Land Policy and Management Act. This act clarified the position that the remainder of public lands would not be widely transferred to private ownership but would be held in trust for all to enjoy. The management of these lands was to be undertaken using the principles of sustained yield and multiple use, related concepts that were embodied in law with passage of the Multiple-Use Sustained-Yield Act of 1960.

IMPACT ON RESOURCE USE

Management practices on public lands must meet a wide range of land-use needs. Resource needs in such categories as mineral production, timber provision, and grazing must be balanced with such needs as public recreation, archaeological preservation, American Indian land rights, and general conservation practices. Land-use planning that uses input from citizen groups and is applied in the context of multiple-use sustained-yield principles has provided a framework for balancing this wide variety of needs and concerns.

The complexity of managing such diverse land-use issues is complicated by the diversity of geography under Bureau of Land Management authority. Most of the land under its authority is in the western United States. However, concerns about mineral leasing on federal land east of the Mississippi led to the establishment of an eastern office in 1954. Thus the bureau operates in areas ranging from highly populated eastern areas to the virtually empty wilderness areas of Alaska. In order to oversee such a diverse landscape, the bureau has a variety of management programs. Some of these programs are land disposition and use, range management, resource conservation and development, forest management, outdoor recreation, and wilderness resources.

Jerry E. Green

WEB SITE

U.S. BUREAU OF LAND MANAGEMENT
http://www.blm.gov/wo/st/en.html

SEE ALSO: Bureau of Mines, U.S.; Department of the Interior, U.S.; Land management; Land-use planning; Multiple-use approach; National parks and nature reserves; Public lands; Rangeland; Wilderness.

Bureau of Mines, U.S.

CATEGORY: Organizations, agencies, and programs
DATE: Established 1910; abolished February, 1996

The U.S. Bureau of Mines focused on mine safety, mining efficiency, and minerals and materials research.

BACKGROUND

In December, 1907, explosions killed more than eight hundred coal miners in West Virginia, Pennsylvania, and Alabama. Before these events, between 1890 and 1906, many thousands of coal miners had been killed in the United States. The tremendous loss of life was caused by unsafe working conditions and a lack of inspection by any governmental authority. States refused to interfere in mining operations run by large corporations. Finally, as a result of a huge outpouring of public concern following the disastrous events of 1907, the U.S. Congress gave the technological branch of the U.S. Geological Survey authority to investigate the causes of mine explosions. In 1910, this branch became the Bureau of Mines in the Department of the Interior. Its responsibilities included mine safety, improvement of working conditions, and training in the proper use of electricity and explosives.

Because of opposition from mine owners, however, the bureau was unable to study conditions outside the coal industry, and metal mines in Western states remained extremely dangerous. Congress responded to industry pressure by reducing the bureau's budget and restricting its authority to conduct inspections.

IMPACT ON RESOURCE USE

In 1913, Congress extended the agency's powers but insisted that it spend as much effort on reducing waste and inefficiency in mining as it did on worker safety. Mine-safety inspections did not become a responsibility of the bureau until 1941. Inspectors could search mines looking for health and safety violations but could do little more than publish inspection reports.

In 1952, President Harry S. Truman signed a bill

creating the Federal Mine Safety Board of Review. This agency could send inspectors into mines once a year unless the mine owners had submitted an approved safety program. If unsafe practices were discovered or unsafe areas of mines were being worked, the board could order an immediate shutdown of the unsafe area. Fines and other penalties could also be assessed, subject to review by a federal judge. The next major change in mine safety enforcement came after a huge explosion killed seventy-eight miners near Farmington, West Virginia, in November of 1968. After this disaster even the coal industry pushed for tougher regulations, inspections, and enforcement. The Federal Coal Mine Health and Safety Act of 1969 gave the federal government more power than it had ever had regarding mine safety. It covered almost every coal mine in the United States and authorized

more rigorous and frequent inspections, along with heavy fines and penalties for violators. Coal mines were required to reduce the amount of dust in the air; to prohibit smoking; and to take action to reduce black lung disease, or pneumoconiosis, a deadly disease contracted by many miners. Enforcement of these provisions went to the Department of Health, Education, and Welfare, however, not the Bureau of Mines.

The bureau saw a constant reduction of its responsibilities in the area of safety in the 1970's and 1980's. Instead, it became the primary agency for mineral research. This had become the primary job of the agency by the 1990's, with major emphasis placed on the availability of basic resources and restoration of abandoned mines and mining properties. Bureau of Mines scientists worked with industry in developing

Nurses tend to injured miners during a rescue drill in this 1917 U.S. Bureau of Mines photograph. (Library of Congress)

mining technology that could leave the surface of the land virtually untouched. They also did valuable work in the areas of materials research, conservation, and extraction and separation, with the long-term goal of addressing U.S. materials supply in the twenty-first century. The bureau was a leader in developing recycling technology. The Bureau of Mines also regularly published a number of informative works on mining and minerals, including annual reports such as the *Minerals Yearbook*.

In the fall of 1995, a conference committee in the U.S. Congress recommended abolishing the Bureau of Mines and transferring some of its functions to other agencies; the bureau was closed in 1996. Its health and safety research and materials research programs were transferred to the Department of Energy, the land and mineral resources program went to the Bureau of Land Management, and the minerals information section went to the U.S. Geological Survey, which continued the Bureau of Mines' publishing activities.

Leslie V. Tischauser

WEB SITES

NATIONAL ARCHIVES
Records of the U.S. Bureau of Mines
http://www.archives.gov/research/guide-fed-
    records/groups/070.html

U.S. GEOLOGICAL SURVEY
Bureau of Mines Minerals Yearbook (1932-1993)
http://minerals.usgs.gov/minerals/pubs/
    usbmmyb.html

SEE ALSO: Bureau of Land Management, U.S.; Department of Energy, U.S.; Mining safety and health issues; Mining wastes and mine reclamation; Recycling; U.S. Geological Survey.

Bureau of Reclamation, U.S.

CATEGORY: Organizations, agencies, and programs
DATE: Established as the Reclamation Service in 1902; renamed 1923

The Bureau of Reclamation is the federal agency that has been chiefly responsible for the development of federal irrigation water projects in the American West.

BACKGROUND
The Bureau of Reclamation is an agency within the U.S. Department of the Interior whose chief mandate is to develop and manage irrigation water supplies in the western United States. Toward this end, the bureau surveys potential project sites; acquires water rights; constructs dams, reservoirs, and diversion facilities; and in many cases subsequently manages reclamation projects. Together with its predecessor agency, the Reclamation Service, the bureau has constructed hundreds of reclamation projects and provides water to a vast number of Western farms. Some of the largest and most famous dam projects in the West, including Hoover Dam, Glen Canyon Dam, and Grand Coulee Dam, are projects of the Bureau of Reclamation.

Under reclamation law, farmers receiving bureau water enter into a long-term (typically forty-year, but sometimes much longer) contract with the bureau that fixes the terms under which repayment is to occur. These terms include the maximum quantity of water that farmers are entitled to receive in a given year and the price that they are required to pay over the term of the contract. Farmers lucky enough to contract with the bureau are exempted from paying interest on the cost of construction of the project. In multiple-purpose projects, the bureau has on occasion reduced the payment burden to farmers still further by levying heavier fees on other user groups, such as urban recipients and hydropower. The overall subsidy to farmers is believed to be considerable, in some cases exceeding 90 percent of the actual cost of water development.

IMPACT ON RESOURCE USE
The policies of the Bureau of Reclamation have been highly controversial. Supporters of federal reclamation argue that the bureau has provided considerable income to western farmers and has greatly expanded agricultural production. Opponents point out that many reclamation projects have not been economically justified and question whether western farmers should receive the massive subsidies given them under reclamation law. Furthermore, it is likely that a considerable fraction of these subsidies has gone to large farming operations, a situation that goes directly against the intent of the original federal reclamation program, which targeted small farmers. The Reclamation Reform Act, passed by Congress in 1982, went some way toward reducing the magnitude of the average subsidy while expanding the size of the farm

eligible to receive bureau water. The latter provision had the effect of making actual bureau policy more consistent with reclamation law.

Since the 1980's, bureau policies have increasingly deemphasized water development in favor of a stronger focus on water management, mainly through water conservation and reallocation. This changed emphasis reflects the fact that few economically feasible water projects remain to be undertaken in the West. Consequently, additional demands for water are unlikely to be met through expansion of supply but rather through improved management of existing supplies.

Mark Kanazawa

WEB SITE

U.S. BUREAU OF RECLAMATION
Reclamation: Managing Water in the West
http://www.usbr.gov/

SEE ALSO: Department of the Interior, U.S.; Irrigation; Reclamation Act; Water.

Cadmium

CATEGORY: Mineral and other nonliving resources

WHERE FOUND

Cadmium, a rare element, does not occur in nature in its elemental form. Its ore deposits are of insufficient concentration to permit direct mining. Cadmium is found in sulfides of zinc, lead, and copper and is typically obtained as a by-product of zinc. Main producers are China, South Korea, Canada, Kazakhstan, and Japan.

PRIMARY USES

Cadmium is used principally in batteries and in alloys. It is also used in coatings and plating, pigments, and stabilizers for plastics and similar synthetic products.

TECHNICAL DEFINITION

Cadmium (abbreviated Cd), atomic number 48, belongs to Group IIB of the periodic table of the elements and resembles zinc in its chemical and physical properties. It has eight stable isotopes and an average molecular weight of 112.40. Pure cadmium is a lustrous, silver-white, malleable metal. Its specific gravity is 8.65, its melting point is 321° Celsius, and its boiling point is 765° Celsius.

DESCRIPTION, DISTRIBUTION, AND FORMS

Cadmium is a rare element that is chemically and physically similar to zinc. Its concentration in the lithosphere is 0.1 to 0.2 gram per metric ton, making it the sixty-seventh most abundant element. The few known cadmium minerals include greenockite, hawleyite, cadmoselite, monteponite, otavite, and saukovite, none of which occurs in commercial deposits. Cadmium is concentrated principally in sulfide deposits. It frequently substitutes for zinc in zinc minerals, where it occurs as an impurity or a surface coating; it is found to a much lesser extent with lead and copper.

Cadmium is softer than zinc, is capable of taking a high polish, and alloys readily with other metals. Its characteristics make it particularly useful to the alloy, plating, and coating industries, some of its chief consumers. The United States produced approximately 750 metric tons of cadmium in 2008, and total world refinery production was about 21,000 metric tons. Cadmium is a toxic element; its toxicity has led to a search for alternative industrial materials and has heightened efforts to recycle cadmium-containing products.

Cadmium-containing zinc deposits occur in many diverse geological settings. Commercially, stratabound deposits are the most important source of cadmium. Internationally, chief producers of cadmium are China, South Korea, Canada, Kazakhstan, and Mexico.

The most common cadmium minerals are the sulfides hawleyite and greenockite. Typically these occur only as impurities or surface incrustations in zinc ores. Zinc sulfide ores such as sphalerite and wurtzite are the main commercial source of cadmium.

HISTORY

Cadmium was isolated and identified in 1817 by Friedrich Stromeyer. One of the earliest uses of cadmium sulfides was as a paint pigment. Commercial production of cadmium as a by-product of zinc smelting began in the nineteenth century. Cadmium was first produced in the United States on a pilot-plant scale; during World War I, production increased rapidly, and it continued to rise in the following decades.

Cadmium is toxic to almost all human body systems and plays no known part as a trace element in human metabolism. Cadmium elimination proceeds slowly enough that the element can accumulate in the body over time, with storage primarily in the kidneys and liver. Chronic exposure can lead to irreversible kidney disease and fluid in the lungs as well as to osteomalacia, an extremely painful softening of the bones. Cadmium can also induce hypertension and can cross the placenta to cause fetal damage. Victims of acute exposure may exhibit symptoms similar to those of food poisoning.

Industrial pollution has introduced cadmium into surface water, groundwater, and the air. Zinc mine tailings can be a source of environmental cadmium in regions where transporting waters are acidic. In Western Europe, where landfilling is less common than in

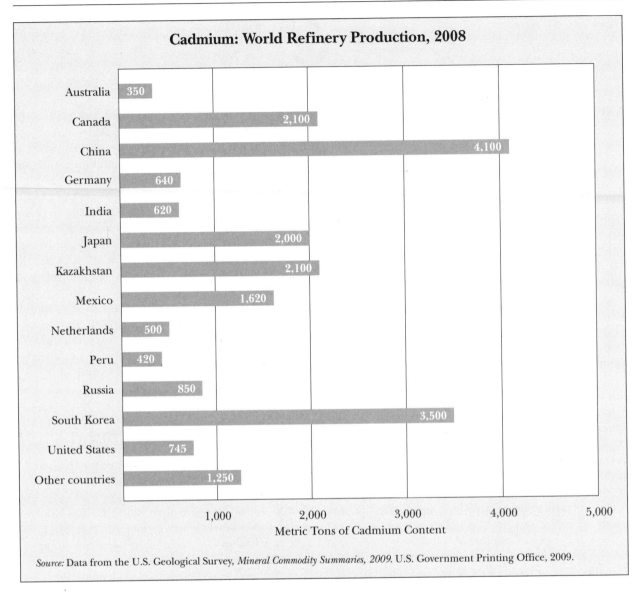

Cadmium: World Refinery Production, 2008

Country	Metric Tons of Cadmium Content
Australia	350
Canada	2,100
China	4,100
Germany	640
India	620
Japan	2,000
Kazakhstan	2,100
Mexico	1,620
Netherlands	500
Peru	420
Russia	850
South Korea	3,500
United States	745
Other countries	1,250

Source: Data from the U.S. Geological Survey, *Mineral Commodity Summaries, 2009.* U.S. Government Printing Office, 2009.

the United States, incineration of plastics is a potential source of cadmium release to the atmosphere.

In the late 1960's, *itai-itai* (literally "ouch-ouch") disease was diagnosed in several localities in Japan. The disease, characterized by osteomalacia, multiple bone fractures, and kidney dysfunction, was linked to elevated levels of cadmium in body tissues and bone. High concentrations of cadmium derived from mine tailings, metal smelters, and other industrial sources were found in soil and drinking water.

In the United States, the 1974 Safe Drinking Water Act set the maximum allowable concentration for cadmium in drinking water at 10 micrograms per liter. Regulatory criteria have also been established for aquatic environments: 5.0 micrograms per liter for salt water, and between 0.4 to 12.0 micrograms per liter for fresh water, depending on water's hardness and the sensitivity of resident fish species.

Environmental regulations based on cadmium's toxicity have led to a search for alternative materials. Cadmium plating is still necessary where surface characteristics of the coating are critical, notably in aircraft parts. Recycling cadmium-containing products and recovering the element for reuse can diminish its release into the environment through landfilling or incineration.

OBTAINING CADMIUM

Cadmium is entirely a by-product metal. It is obtained principally from the smelting and refining of sulfide ores of zinc, lead, and copper. Cadmium can be volatilized from the ores, recovered from the dust and fumes produced during ore roasting and sintering, or precipitated from electrolytic refining slimes.

USES OF CADMIUM

Cadmium is a key component of alkaline nickel-cadmium batteries, accounting for 83 percent of world consumption. Although its use in consumer electronics has been declining as a result of the more popular lithium ion technologies, nickel-cadmium batteries are seeing new industrial applications, including electric vehicles and photovoltaic (solar-energy) systems.

Cadmium is also an important element in alloys. When alloyed with nickel or with silver and copper, it forms a high-pressure antifriction metal for automobile bearings. It hardens copper and makes silver resistant to tarnish. Cadmium plating forms a thin, rustless surface alloy, especially on iron and steel; it is electroplated onto vehicle and aircraft parts such as bolts, nuts, and locks to make them corrosion-resistant. It also provides an adhering bond between iron and other plating metals. Cadmium compounds are used in chemicals, photographic materials, television picture tubes, rubber, soaps, textile printing, and fireworks. Cadmium serves as a stabilizer for plastics and similar synthetic products. Cadmium sulfide forms a durable yellow pigment used in paints, glass, and enamels.

Karen N. Kähler

FURTHER READING

Adriano, Domy C. "Cadmium." In *Trace Elements in Terrestrial Environments: Biogeochemistry, Bioavailability, and Risks of Metals*. 2d ed. New York: Springer, 2001.

Bhattacharyya, M. H., et al. "Biochemical Pathways in Cadmium Toxicity." In *Molecular Biology and Toxicology of Metals*, edited by Rudolfs K. Zalups and James Koropatnick. New York: Taylor & Francis, 2000.

Dobson, S. *Cadmium: Environmental Aspects*. Geneva, Switzerland: World Health Organization, 1992.

Greenwood, N. N., and A. Earnshaw. "Zinc, Cadmium, and Mercury." In *Chemistry of the Elements*. 2d ed. Boston: Butterworth-Heinemann, 1997.

Khan, Nafees A., and Samiullah, eds. *Cadmium Toxicity and Tolerance in Plants*. Oxford, England: Alpha Science, 2006.

Massey, A. G. "Group 12: Zinc, Cadmium, and Mercury." In *Main Group Chemistry*. 2d ed. New York: Wiley, 2000.

Nordberg, G. F., R. F. M. Herber, and L. Alessio, eds. *Cadmium in the Human Environment: Toxicity and Carcinogenicity*. New York: Oxford University Press, 1992.

Scoullos, Michael J., ed. *Mercury, Cadmium, Lead: Handbook for Sustainable Heavy Metals Policy and Regulation*. Boston: Kluwer Academic, 2001.

WEB SITES

NATURAL RESOURCES CANADA
Canadian Minerals Yearbook, Mineral and Metal Commodity Reviews
http://www.nrcan-rncan.gc.ca/mms-smm/busiindu/cmy-amc/com-eng.htm

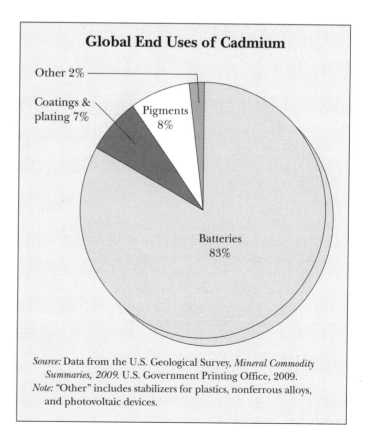

Global End Uses of Cadmium

Other 2%
Coatings & plating 7%
Pigments 8%
Batteries 83%

Source: Data from the U.S. Geological Survey, *Mineral Commodity Summaries, 2009*. U.S. Government Printing Office, 2009.
Note: "Other" includes stabilizers for plastics, nonferrous alloys, and photovoltaic devices.

SEE ALSO: Alloys; Canada; China; Kazakhstan; Metals and metallurgy; Mexico; South Korea; Steel; United States; Zinc.

Calcium compounds

CATEGORY: Mineral and other nonliving resources

WHERE FOUND

Calcium compounds are widely distributed. Naturally occurring calcareous materials include calcite, aragonite, chalk, marble, shell, and coral, all of which are predominantly calcium carbonate ($CaCO_3$); other common calcium-bearing minerals include fluorite (CaF_2) and apatite ($Ca[PO_4, CO_3]_3[F, OH, Cl]$). Principal calcium ores are limestone (predominantly calcite), dolostone (chiefly dolomite, $MgCa(CO_3)_2$), and gypsum rock (mostly the mineral gypsum, or calcium sulfate, $CaSO_4$), all widespread sedimentary rocks. Calcium is present in all soil, most water, and all plant and animal life.

PRIMARY USES

Calcium compounds are used for a variety of applications, including chemical manufacture, construction, and agriculture. Uses for elemental calcium include metal refining, alloy manufacture, and uranium and plutonium processing.

TECHNICAL DEFINITION

Calcium (abbreviated Ca), atomic number 20, is a metallic element belonging to Group IIA of the periodic table of the elements (alkaline-earth metals). It is chemically similar to strontium and barium. Its average molecular weight is 40.08. Its specific gravity is 1.55 at 20° Celsius, its melting point is approximately 850° Celsius, and its boiling point is 1,480° Celsius.

DESCRIPTION, DISTRIBUTION, AND FORMS

Calcium has a cubic crystalline structure and is silver-white in color. It is relatively soft, ductile, and malleable. A chemically active element, it occurs in nature only in combination with other elements. It tarnishes readily in air, reacts with water to form a hydroxide, and combines with oxygen, carbon, hydrogen, chlorine, fluorine, phosphorus, sulfur, and other elements to form many compounds.

Calcium is the fifth most abundant element in the Earth's crust, of which it makes up roughly 3.6 percent. Calcium is not found uncombined in nature, but it is widely distributed in its many naturally occurring compounds. Calcium is found in all soil and most water, as well as in all plant and animal life. Bones and teeth are composed mostly of calcium and phosphorus, with calcium predominant.

Calcium is widely distributed in its naturally occurring compounds, which are found in many deposits throughout the world in rocks of varying geologic age. The chief ores of calcium—limestone, dolostone, and gypsum—are sedimentary in origin and can be found in thick, extensive beds. Limestone, largely or entirely composed of calcium carbonate, is generally formed by the deposition and consolidation of the skeletons of invertebrate marine organisms, although some limestones are the result of chemical precipitation from solution. Dolostone, composed chiefly of the mineral dolomite, originates from the partial replacement of the calcium in limestone with magnesium. The mineral gypsum, or calcium sulfate, precipitates to form deposits as seawater evaporates. Calcium in carbonate form is found not only in limestone and dolostone but also in chalk, marble, shell, and coral. Fluorite is a calcium fluoride mineral found in igneous deposits. Phosphate rock, which contains calcium in the form of the mineral apatite, occurs in both igneous and sedimentary deposits. Calcium is also naturally present in soil and most water.

Calcium combines with other elements to form a wide variety of natural compounds, including calcium carbonate, calcium sulfate, fluorite, and apatite. Some of these compounds may take several forms: Calcium carbonate, for instance, may exist as calcite (the predominant mineral in limestone, chalk, and most marble), Iceland spar, aragonite, shell, or coral, while calcium sulfate occurs in nature as gypsum rock, gypsite, alabaster, satin spar, and selenite.

HISTORY

In general, the earliest known uses of calcium compounds were as construction materials. From calcareous substances such as limestone, dolostone, marble, gypsum, and lime (calcium oxide, CaO, made by heating limestone or other calcium-rich materials), ancient peoples and the civilizations to follow made mortar, plaster, cement, stucco, building stone, and ornamental carvings. Limestone, lime, gypsum, and other calcareous materials also have been used for centuries as soil conditioners. Beginning in the late eighteenth century, calcium compounds were increasingly employed in industrial processes and chemical manufacture: Limestone, for example, found use as a key ingredient in the Leblanc and Solvay processes, two early commercial processes for manufacturing soda ash from salt. Elemental calcium was not isolated until 1808, when English chemist Sir Humphry Davy produced it as a mercury amalgam by electrolysis of calcium chloride in the presence of a mercury cathode. By 1904 calcium was obtained commercially by electrolysis of molten calcium chloride in the presence of an iron cathode. The advent of World War II necessitated greater quantities of calcium. To meet the increased demand, an aluminothermic reduction process was developed for commercial use.

Obtaining Calcium

Calcium is obtained from lime through the aluminothermic reduction process. Limestone or a similar calcareous material is heated to produce lime and carbon dioxide. After lime is ground finely, it is heated with finely divided aluminum in a retort under a high vacuum to produce calcium metal.

Uses of Calcium

Natural and manufactured calcium compounds are used for a variety of applications. Limestone serves as a flux in iron smelting, a key component in portland cement, a building stone, and a raw material for lime production. Lime, an essential industrial compound, is used in chemical manufacture, construction, water softening, industrial waste treatment, and soil deacidification. Gypsum is widely used in agriculture as a soil conditioner and in the construction industry in plaster, wallboard, cement, and tiles. Calcium chloride is employed as a filler in rubber, plastics, and ceramics. Calcium hypochlorite is a disinfectant used in swimming pools and in municipal and industrial bleaching and sanitation processes. Calcium nitrate is used as a concrete additive to reduce setting time and minimize the corrosion of steel reinforcement bars. Calcium carbide is used in the production of acetylene gas and calcium cyanamide, a fertilizer. Arsenate and cyanide compounds of calcium are used as insecticides. Elemental calcium is a component of alloys used in maintenance-free batteries. It is used in lead refining to remove bismuth and in steel refining to remove sulfur and oxygen. Its role in uranium and plutonium processing makes calcium a strategic resource. Elemental calcium is also used in the preparation of vitamin B and chelated calcium supplements.

Karen N. Kähler

Further Reading

Boynton, Robert S. *Chemistry and Technology of Lime and Limestone*. 2d ed. New York: Wiley, 1980.

Greenwood, N. N., and A. Earnshaw. "Beryllium, Magnesium, Calcium, Strontium, Barium, and Radium." In *Chemistry of the Elements*. 2d ed. Boston: Butterworth-Heinemann, 1997.

Henderson, William. "The Group 2 Elements: Beryllium, Magnesium, Calcium, Strontium, Barium, and Radium." In *Main Group Chemistry*. Cambridge, England: Royal Society of Chemistry, 2000.

Jensen, Mead L., and Alan M. Bateman. *Economic Mineral Deposits*. 3d ed. New York: Wiley, 1979.

Krebs, Robert E. *The History and Use of Our Earth's Chemical Elements: A Reference Guide*. Illustrations by Rae Déjur. 2d ed. Westport, Conn.: Greenwood Press, 2006.

Myers, Richard L. *The One Hundred Most Important Chemical Compounds: A Reference Guide*. Westport, Conn.: Greenwood Press, 2007.

Web Sites

Natural Resources Canada
Canadian Minerals Yearbook, Mineral and Metal Commodity Reviews
http://www.nrcan-rncan.gc.ca/mms-smm/busi-indu/cmy-amc/com-eng.htm

U.S. Geological Survey
Fluorspar: Statistics and Information
http://minerals.usgs.gov/minerals/pubs/commodity/fluorspar/index.html#myb

U.S. Geological Survey
Gypsum: Statistics and Information
http://minerals.usgs.gov/minerals/pubs/commodity/gypsum/index.html#myb

U.S. Geological Survey
Lime: Statistics and Information
http://minerals.usgs.gov/minerals/pubs/commodity/lime/index.html#myb

U.S. GEOLOGICAL SURVEY
Phosphate Rock: Statistics and Information
http://minerals.usgs.gov/minerals/pubs/
    commodity/phosphate_rock/index.html#myb

SEE ALSO: Cement and concrete; Feldspars; Fluorite;
Gypsum; Lime; Limestone; Marble; Phosphate.

Canada

CATEGORIES: Countries; government and resources

*Canada is one of the most important countries in the
world in terms of resources. Ranking third in reserves of
both oil and uranium, Canada stands in a position of
prime importance as a supplier of energy. Its vast hydropower resources add even greater importance to its
role as an energy supplier. Canada's forest resources, particularly in combination with its hydropower resources,
make the country a major source of clean, renewable energy for the future. Canada is also a significant producer of metals, including nickel and copper, which are
essential in the manufacturing of goods worldwide.*

THE COUNTRY

Canada is located in the northernmost part of the
North American continent. The country is primarily
bordered by water, with the north Atlantic Ocean to
the east, the north Pacific Ocean to the west, and the
Arctic Ocean to the north. It shares its southern border with the United States and a portion of its western
border with the state of Alaska. Canada primarily
comprises plains but does have mountain ranges in
the west and lowlands in the south. Canada's key resources are oil, natural gas, potash, uranium, zinc,
hydropower, and forests. Canada ranks fifteenth in
purchasing power parity and tenth in competitiveness
in the global economy. The country is the fifteenth
richest country in the world based on gross domestic
product (GDP) per capita.

OIL

Oil is a form of petroleum composed of hydrogen and
carbon compounds. It is a liquid form of fossilized
biomass contained in underground reservoirs in sedimentary basins both on land areas and in seabeds.
Crude oil is refined and used for fuel, lubricants, and
various petrochemical feedstocks.

Oil is an abundant resource in Canada. Approximately 47 percent of Canada's land is covered by sedimentary basins. Only a small number of these land
basins are exploited. The major basin is the Western
Canadian Sedimentary Basin, which has an area of
181.6 million hectares. The major oil fields of the basin—including the LeDuc oil field, Norman Wells,
and Redwater—are all located in the province of Alberta. However, Canada's greatest resources for oil
production in the future are located in basins in the
Beaufort Sea and in the waters off the east coast. The
Hibernia oil field in the Atlantic Ocean is a major producer of oil. The Canadian government, in cooperation with private companies, is developing many of
these basins, including those under the Beaufort Sea.
All leases to explore and extract oil and the manner in
which it is extracted are regulated by the Canadian
government.

The oil sands located in the Athabasca basin in Alberta constitute another rich source of oil for Canada.
However, oil sands require unconventional means of
extraction and processing that threaten the environment with increased greenhouse-gas emissions. The
oil in oil sands is bitumen, a heavy, viscous crude oil. It
is encased in sand and water and requires considerable processing to be converted into gasoline and jet
fuel.

Oil is important to the Canadian economy both domestically and globally. Canada has ranked tenth in
the world in the consumption of oil and eighth in the
production of oil. In 2005, Canada was the ninth largest exporter of oil in the world and ranked fourteenth
in oil imports. Estimates of proven oil reserves for
2008 placed Canada third in the world. Thus, Canada
is an important source for the production of oil in the
global economy of the future.

NATURAL GAS

Natural gas, a highly combustible odorless and colorless liquid, is found with crude oil and in separate deposits. Natural gas is composed of methane, butane,
ethane, and propane and, like oil, is a form of petroleum. Natural gas is extracted from wells dug deep
into the Earth and also from coal-bed methane and
from tight sandstone and shale. The methane extracted from the last two sources is referred to as tight
gas.

Natural gas is found in various areas in Canada.
The extraction of natural gas by drilling wells is the
conventional means of retrieval but is expected to de-

Canada: Resources at a Glance

Official name: Canada
Government: Parliamentary democracy, federation, and
    Commonwealth realm
Capital city: Ottawa
Area: 3,855,383 mi²; 9,984,670 km²
Population (2009 est.): 33,487,208
Languages: English and French
Monetary unit: Canadian dollar (CAD)

ECONOMIC SUMMARY:

GDP composition by sector (2008 est.): agriculture, 2%; industry, 28.4%; services, 69.6%
Natural resources: iron ore, nickel, zinc, copper, gold, lead, molybdenum, potash, diamonds, silver, fish, timber,
    wildlife, coal, petroleum, natural gas, hydropower, uranium
Land use (2005): arable land, 4.57%; permanent crops, 0.65%; other, 94.78%
Industries: transportation equipment, chemicals, processed and unprocessed minerals, food products, wood and
    paper products, fish products, petroleum and natural gas
Agricultural products: wheat, barley, oilseed, tobacco, fruits, vegetables, dairy products, forest products, fish
Exports (2008 est.): $459.1 billion
Commodities exported: motor vehicles/parts, industrial machinery, aircraft, telecommunications equipment,
    chemicals, plastics, fertilizers, wood pulp, timber, petroleum, natural gas, electricity, aluminum, uranium,
    hydropower
Imports (2008 est.): $415.2 billion
Commodities imported: machinery and equipment, motor vehicles and parts, crude oil, chemicals, electricity, durable
    consumer goods
Labor force (2008 est.): 18.22 million
Labor force by occupation (2006): agriculture, 2%; manufacturing,13%; construction, 6%; services, 76%; other, 3%

ENERGY RESOURCES:

Electricity production (2007 est.): 612.6 billion kWh
Electricity consumption (2006 est.): 530 billion kWh
Electricity exports (2007 est.): 50.12 billion kWh
Electricity imports (2007 est.): 19.66 billion kWh

    Natural gas production (2007 est.): 187 billion m³
    Natural gas consumption (2007 est.): 92.9 billion m³
    Natural gas exports (2007 est.): 107.3 billion m³
    Natural gas imports (2007 est.): 13.2 billion m³
    Natural gas proved reserves (Jan. 2008 est.): 1.648 trillion m³

        Oil production (2007 est.): 3.425 million bbl/day
        Oil imports (2005): 1.229 million bbl/day
        Oil proved reserves (Jan. 2008 est.): 178.6 billion bbl

Source: Data from *The World Factbook 2009.* Washington, D.C.: Central Intelligence Agency, 2009.
Notes: Data are the most recent tracked by the CIA. Values are given in U.S. dollars. Abbreviations: bbl/day = barrels per day;
  GDP = gross domestic product; km² = square kilometers; kWh = kilowatt-hours; m³ = cubic meters; mi² = square miles.

cline as unconventional methods of extraction (from coal-bed methane and from shale and tight sandstone) increase. The Western Sedimentary basin located in southwestern Canada contains the majority of the estimated Canadian natural gas reserves. There are also known reserves off the east coast near Nova Scotia and in Ontario. The Arctic Ocean is believed to contain a large amount of gas hydrates, methane enclosed in frozen water on the ocean floor and under areas of permafrost. These potential reserves are not included in the estimated Canadian reserves because the technology necessary to extract them has not been developed.

Natural gas plays an important role in the economy in both the domestic and global markets. In Canada, natural gas is an important resource because it is used by all sectors: residential, commercial, industrial, and power-generation. In 2007, Canada ranked fifth in the world in the production of natural gas and eighth in consumption. The United States, Canada's major trading partner, plays a significant role in the Canadian natural gas industry. The two nations participate in an integrated marketplace that unifies the two countries' regulation of the industry at all stages. In 2007, Canada exported more than one-half of the natural gas that it produced to the United States and earned $28 billion in revenues. In global trade, Canada ranked third as an exporter of natural gas and fifteenth as an importer. The country's proved reserves of natural gas placed it twenty-first in the world.

POTASH

Potash, the seventh most abundant element in the Earth's crust, includes potassium compounds and any material containing potassium. The major use of potash is in the making of fertilizer. Potash was first discovered in Canada in 1943 in the province of Saskatchewan by workers drilling oil wells. In 1951, exploration for potash deposits began. The major potash deposits are in the Middle Devonian Prairie Evaporite, which is located in central and south-central Saskatchewan and extends south into Manitoba and into the United States. Canada possesses approximately 68 billion metric tons of potash reserves. The first company to produce potash in Canada was the Potash Company of America; the firm was founded in 1958 with underground mines at Patience Lake. From 1960 to 1985, extensive development of potash mining took place in Saskatchewan and New Brunswick. In 1964, Kalium Chemical Ltd. established a potash

solution mine near Regina, Saskatchewan. This was the world's first mine of this type. The Canadian potash industry is composed of nine underground mines located in Saskatchewan and three solution mines, two in Saskatchewan and one in New Brunswick. In the 1990's, Canada became the largest exporter of potash in the world and has 43 percent of the world trade in potash. Canada exports potash to forty different countries. The United States, China, and Brazil are its greatest markets for potash.

URANIUM

Canada is the world's leading producer of uranium, a radioactive metal. The exploited deposits of uranium are all in Saskatchewan Province; the largest deposits of high-grade uranium are located in the Athabasca basin. The major operating uranium mines, all located in Saskatchewan, are at Rabbit Lake, McClean Lake, and McArthur Lake. The major use of uranium is in commercial nuclear power plants in the production of electricity. Canada exports 85 percent of its uranium for this purpose. The majority of the exported uranium is sent to the United States, Japan, and Western Europe. The remaining 15 percent is used domestically in Canada's CANDU reactors to produce approximately 15 percent of Canada's electricity. Canada produces almost one-third of the uranium produced in the world and ranks third in reserves of uranium. The country is expected to maintain its position as the leader in uranium production.

HYDROPOWER

Hydropower, a renewable resource, first became an important source of energy in Canada in the late 1800's. Hydroelectric plants were constructed at Niagara Falls in Ontario and at Shawinigan Falls in Quebec. Afterward, hydropower continued to play an important role in Canada's economic development. The number of hydroelectric plants in Canada has grown to 475, and hydropower furnishes approximately two-thirds of Canada's electricity. Although the number of facilities using hydropower throughout Canada has increased dramatically, the country has not begun to utilize fully its resources of potential hydropower. Globally, Canada is a leader both in the production of hydropower-generated electricity and in the development of hydroelectric power-plant technology. France is the only country that exports more electricity than Canada. The United States, Canada's major trading partner, imports about $2.5 billion of electricity from Canada every year. The majority of this electricity is generated with hydropower. As global concerns about greenhouse-gas emissions and air pollution become ever greater, Canada's role as a developer of clean, renewable energy resources and technology continues to grow in importance.

ALUMINUM

Aluminum is not a metal native to Canada; nevertheless, as the major refiner of aluminum, Canada plays an importent role in supplying aluminum to the world. The metal is shipped from all over the world to Canada's refineries in Quebec, where a vast amount of hydroelectric power is available for processing. The refined aluminum is exported globally.

FORESTS

Ten percent of the world's forests are in Canada, covering 901 million hectares. Canada's forest area also accounts for 30 percent of the boreal forest of the world. Forests play a key role in Canada's economy. Globally, Canada is the largest exporter of forest products. The United States, the European Union, and China are the major markets for Canadian forest products. In 2008, the housing crisis in the United States caused a decline in both the quantity and the dollar value of soft-wood lumber exports. The popularity of electronic media throughout the world has brought about a decline in the amount of newsprint exported. However, the demand for pulp has become greater, with a significant increase in pulp export to Asia. Canada exports a wide variety of forest

Glacier Park in British Columbia, Canada, houses a wide array of wildlife and highlights the striking beauty of the country. (©Jay Beiler/ Dreamstime.com)

products, both wood and nontimber products. Christmas trees and maple products account for the majority of nontimber products. Logs, paper products, and pulp constitute the largest dollar value of timber product exports; however, Canada also exports a substantial amount of wood-fabricated products such as fiberboard, both soft- and hard-wood lumber, and plywood. Although Canada imports some forest products, the country is primarily an exporter of forest products, with exports far exceeding imports.

The forest-products industry accounts for approximately 3 percent of Canada's GDP. Forest-based food products, such as wild mushrooms and berries, and secondary manufacturing of wood products from residues of timber harvesting make a significant contribution to Canada's economy. Both are also important in that they contribute to the economy without increasing the number of trees harvested. Canada is not only the world leader in forest products but also one of the nations most concerned with forest conservation and renewal. The annual forest harvest is less than 1 percent of the total Canadian forest. Canada has a number of programs to protect its forestlands and assure their regeneration. Approximately 40 percent of the forest is covered by various programs of land-use planning or is designated as certified forest. Legislation provides protection to approximately 8 percent of the forest. Canada is actively working to increase the economic benefits derived from its forest area and, at the same time, preserve and renew this resource. In 2008, Canada enacted its sixth program of strategies to manage its forests in a responsible manner. *A Vision for Canadian Forests: 2008 and Beyond* provides guidelines through 2018. One of the major components of the plan is to increase the number of forest-derived products and of forest uses without increasing actual tree harvest. Innovations in bioenergy, bioplastics, and biochemicals are being developed to accomplish this goal.

FISHERIES

Fisheries as a resource have experienced considerable difficulties throughout the world because of climate changes. Coupled with the decline in numbers in various species of fish because of climate changes, specifically warming ocean temperatures, the overexploitation of this resource has resulted in the collapse of some segments of the industry. Canada's fishing industry has not escaped this problem. While fisheries have played a less important role in the Canadian economy than forests, they have been a major part of the economies of the coastal provinces, especially those of the Atlantic coast. The first major decline in Canada's fisheries occurred in 1992 with the collapse of the Atlantic cod fisheries. This decline came about because of colder water temperatures in the Labrador Sea and overfishing of the species. Atlantic cod had played a significant role in Canada's fish exports. Canada shifted its focus to salmon, halibut, and haddock. Shellfish—especially lobster, shrimp, and crab—account for approximately 50 percent of the dollar value of Canadian fish exports. Of the remaining 50 percent of export dollar value, 15 percent is dominated by the export of salmon. Two-thirds of the salmon exported comes from the Atlantic. However, sockeye salmon, which has a higher dollar value, is a Pacific fish and is threatened by warming in the Pacific Ocean. This is causing the salmon to move toward the Bering Sea, resulting in a reduction in the number of sockeye found in Canadian waters.

Consequently, Canada's fishing industry is shifting from reliance on a natural resource to dependency on farm-raised and ocean-cultured fish. Aquaculture, much of which is mariculture (aquaculture done in the ocean), has played an ever-greater role in the industry. Both finfish and shellfish are cultured. From 1998 to 2000, aquaculture increased steadily at a rate of 14 percent per year. This change in much of the base of fisheries has created new supply sectors in Canada's domestic economy, including the manufacturing of cages and the production of feed supplies for the captive-raised fish and shellfish.

ZINC

Zinc is a bluish white metal found in the Earth's crust. It has a large variety of uses ranging from the galvanizing of steel against corrosion to the creation of alloys such as brass to use in roofing and in paint. Zinc deposits are located in the Appalachian region of Canada and are mined in both open and underground mines. There are a large number of zinc mines operating in Canada, including mines in British Columbia, Manitoba, Saskatchewan, Ontario, Quebec, and the Northwest Territories. Canada is the world's largest producer of zinc and exports about 90 percent of its zinc production. Zinc is exported both as refined metal and as concentrate. The refined metal that is exported has been subjected to an electrolytic process and is therefore an almost pure product. Canada exports zinc worldwide. The major markets for zinc as refined metal are the United States and Taiwan. For zinc concentrate, the majority of markets are in Europe, especially in Belgium, Germany, Spain, and Italy. South Korea is also an important market for zinc concentrate.

NICKEL

Nickel is a grayish white metal and ranks twenty-fourth in abundance among metals found in the Earth's crust. It is used primarily as an alloying agent and is found in about three thousand different alloys, including stainless steel. Nickel was first discovered in Canada near Sudbury, Ontario, where a number of companies run integrated operations in mining, milling, smelting, and refining the nickel. In 1993, another large deposit of nickel was discovered at Voisey Bay. Canada is the second largest producer of nickel worldwide; only Russia produces more. Canada's domestic market uses only 2 percent of the nickel produced in the country; the remainder is exported to major markets such as the United States, Western Europe, and Japan.

OTHER RESOURCES

Canada's other resources include salt, copper, gold, and molybdenum as well as numerous others. Salt is found in both eastern Canada, where it is abundant in the Atlantic basin, and western Canada, from Manitoba to Alberta. Canada is the world's fourth largest producer of salt. All but 1 percent of Canada's trade in salt is done with its major trading partner, the United States. However, Canada imports more salt than it exports.

In Canada, copper, a reddish metal, is usually found in combination with sulfite minerals. The copper sulfides often contain gold and molybdenum as well. Canada is the fifth largest mine producer of copper globally. Its two major copper-producing provinces are Ontario and British Columbia. The copper mined in Ontario is processed there, but the copper mined in British Columbia is exported to Asia for processing.

Shawncey Webb

FURTHER READING

Barnes, Michael. *More than Free Gold: Mineral Exploration in Canada Since World War II.* Renfrew, Ont.: General Store, 2008.

Førsund, Finn R. *Hydropower Economics.* New York: Springer, 2007.

McKay, David L. *Why Mining?* Victoria, B.C.: Trafford, 2002.

Martin, Raymond, and William L. Leffler. *Oil and Gas Production in Nontechnical Language.* Tulsa, Okla.: PennWell, 2006.

Wetzel, Suzanne, Luc C. Duchesne, and Michael F. Laporte. *Bioproducts from Canada's Forests: New Partnerships in the Bioeconomy.* New York: Springer, 2006.

Zoellner, Tom. *Uranium: War, Energy, and the Rock That Shaped the World.* New York: Viking, 2009.

SEE ALSO: Aluminum; Athabasca oil sands; Canadian Environmental Protection Act; Forests; Oil and natural gas distribution; Potash; Zinc.

Canadian Environmental Protection Act

CATEGORIES: Laws and conventions; government and resources

DATE: Became law June 30, 1988

The Canadian Environmental Protection Act outlined environmental quality standards for Canada and established regulations on the manufacture, emission, and discharge of toxic substances to achieve those standards.

BACKGROUND

During the 1960's and 1970's the Canadian federal government and the governments of the Canadian provinces passed several laws intended to regulate pollution and clean up the environment. The Clean Water Act, passed in 1970, provided for cooperation between the federal and provincial governments on water resource management issues, particularly the cleanup of pollution in the Great Lakes. The Clean Air Act, passed in 1971, provided for similar cooperation to manage air quality. These acts were superseded by the Environmental Protection Act, passed in 1988, which established broad environmental quality objectives and gave the government the authority to regulate emissions of hazardous materials.

Unlike in the United States, where federal laws generally supersede local or state laws, in Canada constitutional jurisdiction to pass laws regulating the environment is shared by the federal and provincial governments. As a result, the provisions of Canada's Environmental Protection Act did not apply in any province that had enacted, and enforced, equivalent provincial laws. Canadian industry as well as the provincial governments had lobbied for this provision so that the industries would not have to deal with two different sets of laws and both provincial and federal law enforcement authorities.

PROVISIONS

The Canadian Environmental Protection Act allowed regulation of air pollution where the emissions constituted a health threat. Emissions of lead (including lead in gasoline), mercury, and other toxic substances were restricted. The act also allowed the government to control the emissions responsible for acid rain. Water quality management, provided under the act, had two objectives: to maintain the supply of safe drinking water and to minimize pollution of the fisheries. Dumping of materials into the oceans was also controlled. The act provided for the cleanup of any unauthorized releases of toxic or hazardous materials and authorized fines or jail terms for convicted polluters.

The act allowed the minister of the environment or the minister of national health and welfare to issue a temporary ban on the importation or manufacture of any new substance thought to be an environmental hazard while its toxicity could be studied. In addition, the act included a list of forty-four substances already in use that were to be tested for toxicity within five years of passage of the act.

IMPACT ON RESOURCE USE

Environment Canada is the agency of the Canadian federal government responsible for overseeing the country's environment and for the prevention of pollution of the air, land, and water across Canada. The Canadian Environmental Protection Assessment Agency, a division of Environment Canada, develops and manages the federal environmental review process and develops the national standards required to manage the toxic substances regulated by the Canadian Environmental Protection Act.

George J. Flynn

SEE ALSO: Acid precipitation; Air pollution and air pollution control; Environmental law in the United States; Environmental Protection Agency; Greenhouse gases and global climate change; United Nations Environment Programme; Water pollution and water pollution control.

Canning and refrigeration of food

CATEGORY: Obtaining and using resources

Two of the most important methods for preserving food are canning and refrigeration.

DEFINITION

Canning is the technique of preserving food in airtight containers through the use of heat, while refrigeration is the process of preservation through the use of low temperatures. Canning inactivates enzymes and kills microorganisms that would cause food to spoil during storage, while refrigeration stops the growth and activity of most microorganisms that cause food spoilage.

OVERVIEW

Canning and refrigeration are processes that preserve food by slowing down its normal decay. Without these food storage processes, most people would have to grow their own food, and large cities could not exist. Food could not be transported from rural areas to urban areas without being spoiled or destroyed by pests. Famines would be more frequent and widespread, since surpluses of food could not be stored to guard against emergencies.

Canning is the most common method of food preservation in developed countries, and it is the basis of a large segment of the commercial food industry. In this process, fruits, vegetables, fish, meat, poultry, soups, and other foods are sealed in airtight containers and then heated to destroy microorganisms that may cause spoilage. The airtight packaging protects the food from contamination and permits storage at room temperatures for many months. One disadvantage of canning is that the heat required for sterilization changes the food's texture, color, and flavor.

The canning process was developed by a French chef, Nicolas Appert, in the early 1800's. He worked out a process of packing food in glass jars, which were then tightly corked and heated in boiling water. Glass or tin-coated sheet steel containers are used in the commercial canning of many foods, and beginning in the early 1960's aluminum cans were used for canned liquids. Virtually all types of food are canned commercially, and the products are available in cans of all sizes.

Refrigeration, or cold storage, keeps food fresh at

Workers at a factory in the Philippines stuff sardines into cans. (AFP/Getty Images)

temperatures somewhat above 0° Celsius. Refrigeration takes place when heat flows to a receiver colder than its surroundings. Low temperatures do not sterilize food, but they do slow down the growth of microorganisms and decrease enzymes that cause food to deteriorate. Refrigeration produces few changes in food, and the original color, flavor, texture, and nutrients of the food are retained.

Cold storage has been used for hundreds—or thousands—of years to preserve foods, dating back to when people stored food inside cool caves. Ice was a valuable cargo for nineteenth century ships, but it was expensive and difficult to transport. In 1851, the first commercial machine for making ice was patented by John Gorrie, an American physician. This development led to the large-scale use of refrigeration for shipping and storing foods. After World War I, the domestic refrigerator began to displace the icebox, and with the widespread dissemination of mechanical refrigeration in homes, the development of a frozen-food industry became possible. Soon a large fleet of refrigerated trucks was transporting the products.

Alvin K. Benson

SEE ALSO: Agricultural products; Aluminum; Food chain; Food shortages; Freeze-drying of food; Population growth; Tin.

Capitalism and resource exploitation

CATEGORY: Social, economic, and political issues

Originating in Western Europe in the sixteenth century, capitalism is a socioeconomic system that channels individual efforts toward increasing economic growth. Historically, economic growth is associated with an increasing human population and the increasing exploitation of natural resources.

BACKGROUND

Capitalism has a number of characteristics that differentiate it from traditional economies and command economies. First, as Karl Polanyi observes in *The Great Transformation* (1964), capitalism is characterized by a market economy. A market economy means subjecting human beings, means of production, and nature to "market forces." A market economy allocates labor, capital, and resources to their most profitable uses. While markets do exist in traditional economies, they play a limited role, serving as a means of disposing of surplus products. In command economies, markets are subordinated to the authority of the state. Second, capitalism is characterized by the production of commodities. Commodities are anything produced for sale. As Vandana Shiva points out in *Staying Alive: Women, Ecology, and Development* (1989), the transformation of natural resources into commodities requires separating resources from their natural environment. From a market perspective forests, wildlife, and other natural resources have value only as commodities.

Third, capitalism is characterized by private property. Private property conveys to the owners of capital and resources the right to use their property regardless of the impact on society or nature. More recently, property refers not to the use of the property but rather to its value. Fourth, capitalism is characterized by the accumulation of capital. Accumulation begins with the capitalist who invests money to purchase inputs: capital, labor, and resources. These inputs are then converted into finished products, which are sold for money exceeding that originally invested. The resulting profit is subsequently reinvested. This implies that the accumulation of capital is self-expanding, requiring increasing quantities of resources and other inputs.

The quest for profits makes capitalism an inherently dynamic system. As Joseph Schumpeter observes in *Capitalism, Socialism, and Democracy* (1942), "Capitalism . . . is by nature a form or method of economic change and not only never is but never can be stationary." Economic change results from the introduction of innovations—that is, from opening new markets, developing new products, introducing new technologies, and so on.

Competition for profit compels capitalists to innovate. Innovations in turn alter how humans relate to one another and to nature. First, innovations alter the mix of inputs required. In turn, this alters the distribution of income by eliminating or reducing the demand for one input and increasing the demand for other inputs. Second, innovations alter the form of cooperation both within the business and among individuals in society. Television, for example, reduced the degree of human interaction. Third, innovations expand the types and quantities of resources required. From a historical point of view, this expansion is associated with the expansion of capitalism itself.

MERCANTILISM: 1600-1800

Mercantilism is the first stage of capitalism, representing a symbiotic relationship between government and business. Business provided governments with a source of tax revenue; governments provided business opportunities for profit. Governments offered business protection, established monopolies, obtained colonies, and created national markets.

Creating a national market required reducing transportation costs. Clearing waterways and digging canals reduced the costs of the two most important resources in transporting goods: wind and water. Industries spread along the rivers and into the forests. In many places the spread of industry led to widespread deforestation. European countries established colonies to provide resources, especially gold and silver, in order to fuel the expansion. In general, this meant seizing the land and labor of the traditional peoples of the world.

LAISSEZ-FAIRE OR MARKET CAPITALISM: 1800-1930's

Market capitalism is the second stage of capitalism, ushered in by the innovations introduced by the Industrial Revolution. Beginning in the last decade of the eighteenth century and the first decades of the nineteenth century in England, the Industrial Revolution introduced machines into the workplace.

The Industrial Revolution had a number of profound implications for society. First, machines (epitomized by the steam engine) freed industry from its dependence on water and wind; industries could locate anywhere. Second, the introduction of railroads reduced the price of coal relative to wood. Coal freed society from its dependence on renewable resources, enabling individuals to tap into the energy accumulated over eons. The result was an explosion in economic growth. As Jean-Claude Debeir, Jean-Paul Déléage, and Daniel Hémery state in *In the Servitude of Power* (1991, originally published in French in 1986), coal enabled "the European economies to by-pass the natural limitations of organic energy, [and] this new system set them on the path to mass production." In the United States, the railroad aided the descendants of Europeans in subjugating American Indians and taking their lands.

Third, the Industrial Revolution altered the institutions of capitalism. The Industrial Revolution introduced the factory system, depersonalizing relations between capitalists and workers. Furthermore, the dramatic increase in economic growth necessitated a change in the role of government. Government adopted a policy of laissez-faire, agreeing not to interfere with business activities.

THE CORPORATE WELFARE STATE

The corporate welfare state is the third stage of capitalism, associated with the development of new technologies. First, new technologies in railroads, steel production, oil, and so on enabled businesses to reduce their unit costs by expanding output. Corporations emerged as a means of reducing competition by controlling output. Second, many of the new technologies proved expensive. Few businesses could raise the necessary financing. Corporations provided a new means of financing, namely stocks.

Third, the new technologies expanded the resource base. Oil, for example, became increasingly important. Standard Oil Company's effort to monopolize the sources, production, and refinement of oil in the late nineteenth century fueled the public's mistrust of corporations. In response, the U.S. government passed the Sherman Antitrust Act in 1890 specifically preventing monopolies.

Fourth, the severe economic depressions of the nineteenth and early twentieth centuries became politically unacceptable. People demanded that governments provide a degree of economic security, a demand that manifested itself in the social legislation of the 1930's and the 1960's. Further threats to economic security stemmed from the West's dependence on fossil fuels. Some of the events surrounding the oil embargo of the 1970's, the Gulf War of 1990, and the War in Afghanistan beginning in 2001 show the willingness on the part of the industrialized countries of the West to intervene in those countries considered vital to ensure the flow of oil.

RESOURCE CONSUMPTION AND THE FUTURE OF CAPITALISM

The question of whether or not humankind can continue to consume the resources of the world at present rates has evoked two different perspectives regarding the future of capitalism. A tradition within British political economy since the work of economist David Ricardo in the early nineteenth century contends that the exploitation of limited resources will in time cause economic growth to decline.

Ricardo asserted that economic growth confronted with limited land would eventually raise rents, thereby squeezing profits. Eventually the rate of profit falls to zero, resulting in the stationary state. William Stanley Jevons, writing in the late nineteenth century, agreed with Ricardo except that Jevons believed that declining growth would result from limited coal deposits. More recently, Nicholas Georgescu-Roegen expressed a similar view in *The Entropy Law and the Economic Process* (1971). Georgescu-Roegen asserted that growth is ultimately limited by the finite supply of low-entropic resources.

In 1972, the Club of Rome, a group of distinguished scientists, published *The Limits to Growth*, predicting the depletion of many resources within forty years. Their time predictions proved incorrect, but their central point, concerning limitations on the rate of growth could, and can, continue, remains.

The alternative viewpoint asserts that resources are sufficiently abundant. This argument rests on the assumption that changes in prices will elicit the discovery of alternative resources. For example, as oil supplies decline, the price of oil rises. Higher oil prices provide incentives either to find additional oil or to find alternatives to oil. This concept assumes that markets "work" and that substitutes can and will be found (this has been called the assumption of infinite substitutability). Whether economic growth is sustainable ultimately turns on the human ability to substitute renewable resources for nonrenewable resources.

John P. Watkins

FURTHER READING

Daly, Herman E., and John B. Cobb, Jr. *For the Common Good: Redirecting the Economy Toward Community, the Environment, and a Sustainable Future.* 2d ed., updated and expanded. Boston: Beacon Press, 1994.

Debeir, Jean-Claude, Jean-Paul Deléage, and Daniel Hémery. *In the Servitude of Power: Energy and Civilisation Through the Ages.* Translated by John Barzman. London: Zed Books, 1991.

Georgescu-Roegen, Nicholas. *The Entropy Law and the Economic Process.* Cambridge, Mass.: Harvard University Press, 1971.

Hawken, Paul, Amory Lovins, and L. Hunter Lovins. *Natural Capitalism: Creating the Next Industrial Revolution.* London: Earthscan, 1999.

Heilbroner, Robert L. *The Nature and Logic of Capitalism.* New York: Norton, 1985.

Kovel, Joel. *The Enemy of Nature: The End of Capitalism or the End of the World?* 2d ed. London: Zed Books, 2007.

McPherson, Natalie. *Machines and Economic Growth: The Implications for Growth Theory of the History of the Industrial Revolution.* Westport, Conn.: Greenwood Press, 1994.

Porritt, Jonathon. *Capitalism: As If the World Matters.* Updated and rev. ed. London: Earthscan, 2007.

Schumpeter, Joseph A. *Capitalism, Socialism, and Democracy.* 5th ed. London: Allen and Unwin, 1976.

Speth, James Gustave. *The Bridge at the Edge of the World: Capitalism, the Environment, and Crossing from Crisis to Sustainability.* New Haven, Conn.: Yale University Press, 2008.

SEE ALSO: Coal; Developing countries; Energy economics; Environmental ethics; Industrial Revolution and industrialization; Mineral resource ownership; Oil industry; Sustainable development.

Carbon

CATEGORY: Plant and animal resources

WHERE FOUND
Diamond, graphite, and amorphous carbon (charcoal and soot) are the main minerals containing carbon only. Diamond formed in igneous rocks that formed at very great depths in the Earth; graphite formed in some metamorphic rocks. Petroleum, natural gas, and coal are composed of hydrocarbon compounds that formed from plants or animals during burial in sediment.

PRIMARY USES
Diamond is used as a gem or as an abrasive. Graphite is mixed with clays to make pencils and is used as a lubricant. Petroleum products, natural gas, and coal can be burned to provide heat or to drive engines. Plants and animals are composed of a vast number of hydrocarbon compounds. There are a large number of compounds that have special properties such as silicon carbides that are harder than diamond.

TECHNICAL DEFINITION
Carbon has an atomic number of 6, and it has three isotopes. The isotope C^{12} composes 99 percent of natural carbon, and C^{13} makes up about 1 percent of natural carbon. The isotope C^{14} is radioactive, and it constitutes only a tiny amount of natural carbon. Diamond has a hardness (resistance to scratching by another mineral) of ten, which makes it the hardest of all minerals; graphite has a hardness of two, which makes it one of the softest of all minerals. The density of diamond is 3.52 grams per milliliter, and the density of graphite is 2.27 grams per milliliter. The melting points and boiling points for graphite are high, 3,527° Celsius and 4,027° Celsius, respectively. Diamond does not conduct electricity; graphite does. Diamond is often transparent and colorless, but graphite is opaque and often dark gray. Carbon atoms combine with other atoms of carbon and with hydrogen, sulfur, nitrogen, or oxygen to form the vast number of hydrocarbon compounds found in plants and animals.

DESCRIPTION, DISTRIBUTION, AND FORMS
Graphite has been found in metamorphic rocks that have been raised to moderately high temperatures and pressures so that any of the original hydrocarbon compounds present were destroyed. Graphite has been mined in Greenland, Mexico, Russia, and the United States (New York). Diamond has been found in igneous rocks such as kimberlite and lamproite that have been formed at high pressure in the upper mantle of the Earth and in sediment formed by weathering of the diamond-bearing igneous rocks. Abundant diamonds have been found in South Africa, northern Russia, Australia, Canada, and Botswana. Some graphite and diamonds have been produced artificially.

Plants in forests may be buried out of contact with the Earth's atmosphere so that they are not oxidized. Thus, with gradually increased burial with other sediment they form peat, lignite coal, bituminous coal, and anthracite coal at gradually higher temperatures, respectively. Peat has lots of volatiles, such as water, so it does not burn well. With increasing burial the volatiles are removed and the carbon content gradually increases. Therefore, anthracite coal burns with a clear, hot flame. Coal is found worldwide. The leading coal producers are the United States, Russia, China, India, Australia, and South Africa.

Petroleum and natural gas form from small animals, such as zooplankton and algae, that have settled out of water, in muds without much oxygen, so that they were not oxidized. Petroleum forms with gradual burial of the animals in the sediment to depths of around 4 to 6 kilometers below the surface at temperatures that range from about 60° Celsius up to 200° Celsius. At temperatures much above 200° the organic constituents in petroleum decompose to natural gas (mostly methane). If the petroleum and methane collect in certain geologic traps, then drilling can potentially extract much of the two substances. Saudi Arabia, Russia, the United States, Iran, China, Mexico, and Canada, in descending order, are the leading producers of petroleum products.

HISTORY

The word "carbon" was derived from the Latin word meaning charcoal. Diamonds and charcoal have been known for thousands of years. In the eighteenth century, impure iron was changed to steel by using carbon. During that century, charcoal, diamond, and graphite were shown to be the same substance, and some people listed carbon as an elemental substance.

In the early nineteenth century, Michael Faraday and Sir Humphry Davy showed that electricity and chemical changes were linked. Jöns Jacob Berzelius used symbols, like C for carbon, for elemental materials, and he classified elements based on their chemical properties. Faraday lectured on how a candle worked by burning carbon from a candle with air to form "carbonic acid." He related the carbonic acid (now know to be carbon dioxide) to the gas that animals gave off to the atmosphere.

Later in the nineteenth century, Svante August Arrhenius determined the carbonic acid content of the atmosphere, and he related the carbonic acid content of the atmosphere to the temperature. Also in the nineteenth century, the atomic theory began to be more precisely developed by John Dalton, which led to a better explanation of chemical reactions. Dmitry Ivanovich Mendeleyev organized the known elements into the periodic table, in which the elements with similar chemical properties were ordered into columns. Thus, he put carbon and silicon in the same columns.

OBTAINING CARBON

Diamonds exist in such low concentrations in igneous rock ores that the ore must first be crushed so that the diamonds are not destroyed. Then, density separations are made to form a diamond-rich fraction, and certain instruments are used to confirm the location of this fraction. Grease belts have been used in the past to concentrate the diamonds, because diamonds stick to the grease. Finally, people carefully look through the diamond-rich fractions to pick out any missed diamonds.

Metamorphic rocks containing graphite are also usually first crushed by grinders. Graphite is less dense than most of the other minerals in the rock, so it is concentrated by floating it to the top of liquids with the right density.

Coal forms in layers in sedimentary rocks. Thus, if the coal is at or close to the surface, the top layers of sediment not containing coal may be stripped off (this procedure is used in Wyoming). The coal is broken up by large pieces of equipment like power shovels, and it is carried off in large vehicles. Underground mines are much more expensive to operate as shafts must be drilled into the coal layer and supports must be installed to keep the open spaces from collapsing.

Petroleum forms in some mudstones, and it must migrate into permeable beds like sandstones. The petroleum has to move into geologic traps, such as at the top of upward folded sedimentary structures like anticlines. Geologists attempt to find such sedimentary structures so that drilling can penetrate the structures to see if petroleum or natural gas is present. Only a small percentage of wells actually tap into petroleum or gas.

USES OF CARBON

Carbon has a vast number of uses both as an element and in compounds. Diamond can be cut in various ways to make jewelry. Those that are not of jewelry quality, such as artificial diamonds, can be used as abrasives. Powdered graphite is used as a lubricant and, mixed with clays, in pencils.

Coke is a form of carbon that can be burned with a very hot flame to reduce iron ores into iron. Some carbon may be added to the iron to produce carbon steel. Wood, coal, petroleum, and natural gas may be burned as fuels to produce heat or drive engines. Petroleum, for instance, may be refined into gasoline or kerosene.

Carbon compounds compose all living tissue, so they are essential for life. Plant and animal products like cotton, linen, wool, and silk are composed of hydrocarbons. Carbon dioxide is given off to the atmosphere by animals; plants remove the carbon dioxide. Petroleum may be refined to produce plastics.

Charcoal and carbon black are used in oil paint, in watercolors, and in toners for lasers. Activated charcoal is used in gas masks and in water filters to remove poisons. Carbon has been combined with silicon to produce silicon carbides that are harder than diamond.

Fullerenes consist of groups of carbon atoms arranged in hexagonal and pentagonal forms as spheres or cylinders. The spheres can trap other elements within them, and some are superconductors. Some of the fullerene cylinders are exceptionally strong, so they may have applications in products like bullet-proof vests.

The radioactive isotope carbon 14 has a half-life of 5,730 years. The atmosphere has a constant supply of carbon 14 that is taken up by growing organisms. If the organisms die, the isotope gradually decays. Thus, that material associated with an archaeological site may be dated based on the remaining carbon 14.

Robert L. Cullers

FURTHER READING

Homer-Dixon, Thomas, and Nick Garrison. *Carbon Shift: How the Twin Crises of Oil Depletion and Climate Change Will Define the Future.* Toronto: Random House, 2009.

Janse, A. J. A. "Global Rough Diamond Production Since 1870." *Gems and Gemology* 43, no. 2 (2007): 98-119.

Labett, Sonia, and Rodney R. White. *Carbon Finance: The Financial Implications of Climate Change.* New York: John Wiley and Sons, 2007.

Roston, Eric. *The Carbon Age: How Life's Core Element Has Become Civilization's Greatest Threat.* New York: Walker, 2008.

Saito, R., G. Dresselhaus, and Mildred Dresselhaus. *Physical Properties of Carbon Nanotubes.* London: Imperial College Press, 1999.

WEB SITE

WEBELEMENTS
Carbon: The Essentials
http://www.webelements.com/carbon/

SEE ALSO: Carbon cycle; Carbon fiber and carbon nanotubes; Carbonate minerals; Coal; Diamond.

Carbon cycle

CATEGORY: Geological processes and formations

The carbon cycle is the movement of the element carbon through the Earth's rock and sediment, the aquatic environment, land environments, and the atmosphere. Large amounts of organic carbon can be found in both living organisms and dead organic material.

BACKGROUND

An enormous reservoir of carbon may be found on the surface of the Earth. Most of this reservoir is in rock and sediment. Since the "turnover" time of such forms of carbon is so long (on the order of thousands of years), the entrance of this material into the carbon cycle is insignificant on the human scale. The carbon cycle represents the movement of this element through the biosphere in a process mediated by photosynthetic plants on land and in the sea. The process involves the fixation of carbon dioxide (CO_2) into organic molecules, a process called photosynthesis. Energy utilized in the process is stored in chemical form, such as that in carbohydrates (sugars such as glucose). The organic material is eventually oxidized, as occurs when a photosynthetic organism dies; through the process of respiration, the carbon is returned to the atmosphere in the form of carbon dioxide.

PHOTOSYNTHESIS

Organisms that use carbon dioxide as their source of carbon are known as autotrophs. Many of these organisms also use sunlight as the source of energy for reduction of carbon dioxide; hence, they are frequently referred to as photoautotrophs. This process of carbon dioxide fixation is carried out by phytoplankton in the seas, by land plants, particularly trees, and by many microorganisms. Most of the process is carried out by the land plants.

The process of photosynthesis can be summarized by the following equation: CO_2 + water + energy → carbohydrates + oxygen. The process requires energy from sunlight, which is then stored in the form of the chemical energy in carbohydrates. While most plants produce oxygen in the process—the source of the oxygen in the Earth's atmosphere—some bacteria may produce products other than oxygen. Organisms that carry out carbon dioxide fixation, using photosynthesis to synthesize carbohydrates, are often referred to as producers. Approximately 18 to 27 billion metric tons of carbon are fixed each year by the process—clearly a large amount, but only a small proportion of the total carbon found on the Earth. Approximately 410 billion metric tons of carbon are contained within the Earth's forests; some 635 billion metric tons exist in the form of atmospheric carbon dioxide.

Much of the organic carbon on the Earth is found in the form of land plants, including forests and grasslands. When these plants or plant materials die, as when leaves fall to the Earth in autumn, the dead organic material becomes known as humus. Much of the carbon initially bound during photosynthesis is in the form of humus. Degradation of humus is a slow process, on the order of decades. However, it is the decomposition of humus, particularly through the process called respiration, that returns much of the carbon dioxide to the atmosphere. Thus the carbon cycle represents a dynamic equilibrium between the carbon in the atmosphere and carbon fixed in the form of organic material.

RESPIRATION

Respiration represents the reverse of photosynthesis. All organisms that utilize oxygen, including humans, carry out the process. However, it is primarily humic decomposition by microorganisms that returns most of the carbon to the atmosphere. Depending on the particular microorganism, the carbon is in the form of either carbon dioxide or methane (CH_4). Respiration is generally represented by the equation carbohydrate + oxygen → carbon dioxide + water + energy. Energy released by the reaction is utilized by the organism (that is, the consumer) to carry out its own metabolic processes.

CARBON SEDIMENT

Despite the enormous levels of carbon cycled between the atmosphere and living organisms, most carbon is found within carbonate deposits on land and in ocean sediments. Some of this originates in marine ecosystems, where organisms utilize dissolved carbon dioxide to produce carbonate shells (calcium carbonate). As these organisms die, the shells sink and become part of the ocean sediment. Other organic deposits, such as oil and coal, originate from fossil deposits of dead organic material. The recycling time for such sediments and deposits is generally on the order of thousands of years; hence their contribution to the carbon cycle is negligible on a human timescale. Some of the sediment is recycled naturally, as when sediment dissolves or when acid rain falls on carbonate rock (limestone), releasing carbon dioxide. However, when such deposits are burned as fossil fuels, the levels of carbon dioxide in the atmosphere may increase at a rapid rate.

ENVIRONMENTAL IMPACT OF HUMAN ACTIVITIES

Carbon dioxide gas is only a small proportion (0.036 percent) of the volume of the atmosphere. However,

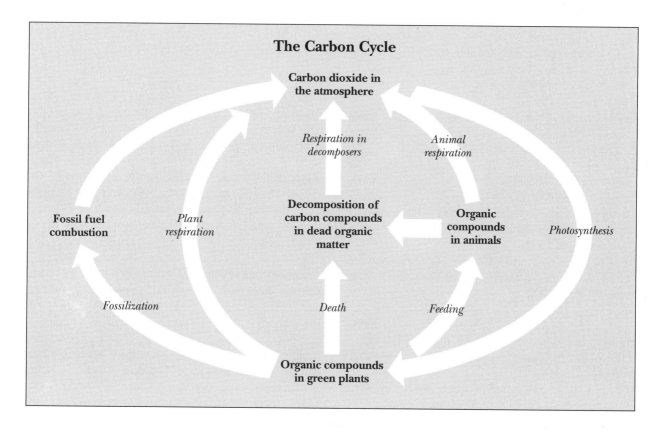

The Carbon Cycle

because of its ability to trap heat from the Earth, carbon dioxide acts much like a thermostat, and even small changes in levels of this gas can significantly alter environmental temperatures. Around 1850, humans began burning large quantities of fossil fuels; the use of such fuels accelerated significantly with the invention of the automobile. Between five and six billion metric tons of carbon are released into the atmosphere every year from the burning of fossil carbon. Some of the released carbon probably returns to the Earth through biological carbon fixation, with possible increase in the land biomass of trees or other plants. (Whether this is so remains a matter of dispute.) Indeed, large-scale deforestation could potentially remove this means by which levels of atmospheric carbon dioxide could be controlled naturally.

Richard Adler

FURTHER READING

Berner, Robert A. *The Phanerozoic Carbon Cycle: CO₂ and O₂.* New York: Oxford University Press, 2004.

Field, Christopher B., and Michael R. Raupach, eds. *The Global Carbon Cycle: Integrating Humans, Climate, and the Natural World.* Washington, D.C.: Island Press, 2004.

Harvey, L. D. Danny. *Global Warming: The Hard Science.* New York: Prentice Hall, 2000.

Houghton, R. A. "The Contemporary Carbon Cycle." In *Biogeochemistry*, edited by W. H. Schlesinger. Boston: Elsevier, 2005.

Kelly, Robert C. *The Carbon Conundrum: Global Warming and Energy Policy in the Third Millennium.* Houston, Tex.: CountryWatch, 2002.

Kondratyev, Kirill Ya., Vladimir F. Krapivin, and Costas A. Varotsos. *Global Carbon Cycle and Climate Change.* New York: Springer, 2003.

Madigan, Michael, et al., eds. *Brock Biology of Microorganisms.* 12th ed. San Francisco: Pearson/Benjamin Cummings, 2009.

Roston, Eric. *The Carbon Age: How Life's Core Element Has Become Civilization's Greatest Threat.* New York: Macmillan, 2008.

Volk, Tyler. *CO₂ Rising: The World's Greatest Environmental Challenge.* Cambridge, Mass.: MIT Press, 2008.

Wallace, Robert A., Gerald P. Sanders, and Robert J. Ferl. *Biology: The Science of Life.* 3d ed. New York: HarperCollins, 1991.

Wigley, T. M. L., and D. S. Schimel, eds. *The Carbon Cycle.* New York: Cambridge University Press, 2000.

WEB SITES

NATIONAL OCEANIC AND ATMOSPHERIC ADMINISTRATION, CLIMATE PROGRAM OFFICE
The Global Climate Cycle
http://www.climate.noaa.gov/index.jsp?pg=./ about_climate/about_index.jsp&about=physical

U.S. GEOLOGICAL SURVEY
USGS Carbon Cycle Research
http://geochange.er.usgs.gov/carbon

SEE ALSO: Carbon; Carbonate minerals; Coal; Earth's crust; Geochemical cycles; Geology; Greenhouse gases and global climate change.

Carbon fiber and carbon nanotubes

CATEGORY: Products from resources

WHERE FOUND

Produced in industrialized nations, carbon fiber and related substances are made from plastics and materials derived from fossil fuels, such as petroleum (in the form of petroleum pitch) and coal. Efforts have been made to reclaim carbon-rich waste material from ash ponds produced by industrial plants.

PRIMARY USES

First used commercially in aircraft engines manufactured in England during the 1960's, carbon fiber—which appears most frequently as a key, strength-providing component in composites with plastic—is used for vehicle parts, safety products, sports equipment, construction, and many other applications. Increasingly, smaller variants, including vapor-grown carbon fibers and carbon nanotubes, have become available, leading to further diverse applications such as microcircuitry and nano-engineering.

TECHNICAL DEFINITION

Carbon fibers are composed primarily of bonded carbon atoms that form long crystals aligned along their lengths. The atoms are bonded in hexagonal patterns, and, in both carbon fibers and carbon nanotubes, the grids formed by these bonded atoms wrap around to form the walls of long tubes. In carbon fibers, these tubes are wound together to form extremely thin strands, less than 0.010 millimeter thick.

Kevin Ausman, a scientist from Rice University, displays a bottle of carbon nanotubes, key components in the present and future of nanotechnology. (AP/Wide World Photos)

For common applications, thousands of fibers are twisted together into yarn, which is then combined with other materials to make composites. Carbon nanotubes are found at the molecular level, and because they are less than 2 nanometers thick, are exponentially smaller than carbon fibers.

DESCRIPTION, DISTRIBUTION, AND FORMS

While the variants of carbon fiber share general properties such as strength, resistance to static and corrosion, and heat and electrical conductivity, specific qualities are associated with the materials from which the fiber is made. Fiber made from coal pitch is generally good at conducting heat, but relatively brittle, while fiber made from polyacrylonitrile (PAN) can

handle more tension without breaking. Fiber made from petroleum pitch is flexible but cannot stand as much pressure.

Carbon nanotubes are molecules that can be either multi-walled or single-walled, and both forms consist of sheets of bonded carbon atoms. They are closely related to buckyballs, which are the spherical forms of the fullerene molecule.

HISTORY

Inventor Thomas Edison, in conjunction with his work on the lightbulb in the late 1800's, carbonized cotton and bamboo to make filaments for the bulbs. During World War II, contractors for the U.S. military gained experience in the use of fiber-reinforced composites in the manufacture of light-but-strong and corrosion-resistant aircraft, boats, and other vehicles. Although fiberglass was the most common material at this time, production techniques were similar to those that would be used for carbon-fiber composites.

The basic technique of heating polymers to make carbon fibers was established in the late 1950's by Roger Bacon, working at Union Carbide's Parma Technical Center near Cleveland, Ohio. While the earliest manufacture of carbon fibers was achieved by carbonizing rayon, the advantages of PAN as a precursor were soon discovered. In 1961, Akio Shindo of the Government Industrial Research Institute in Japan published findings that the use of PAN as a precursor yielded the strongest fibers. Although observations of the structures had also been made independently by others, Sumio Iijima of Japan, who published his findings in 1991, is credited with disseminating knowledge about carbon nanotubes to the global community.

OBTAINING CARBON FIBER AND CARBON NANOTUBES

Carbon fibers are processed from their precursors (PAN, rayon, pitch, and petroleum) using intense heat, often with the aid of catalytic chemicals. Usually, the precursors are first spun or extruded into fibers, which are then treated with chemicals so that they can be heated (between 1,000° and 3,000° Celsius), thus carbonizing the material. Both the raw materials used and the processes of production influence the properties of the resultant fibers. PAN, which is also used to make acrylic clothing, sails, and other products, is the most popular precursor material. Originally produced in England, Japan, and the United States, the fibers and their composite materials are now produced in most industrialized countries. As the desired sizes become smaller, isolating the particles and controlling the processes become increasingly difficult. In order to be seen and studied, carbon nanotubes require electron microscopes. Vapor-grown carbon fibers also require high heat and a catalytic vapor. Nanotubes can be obtained through laser ablation and arc discharge as well as with vapor deposition. Cost-effective mass-production techniques remain in development for carbon nanotubes.

USES OF CARBON FIBER

In England during the 1960's, Rolls-Royce and two other companies utilized processing research done by the British government and established carbon fiber production, primarily focusing on making blades for jet engines. Although many useful techniques were learned, the pioneering enterprise was not successful economically. In 1971, the Toray company in Japan began making large volumes of PAN-derived carbon-fiber yarn, which was used in many products. When the Cold War ended, emphasis shifted from military to commercial uses. However, defense applications continued to evolve, eventually to include parts for remote-controlled and stealth aircraft. In addition to the aircraft industry—which welcomed the weight-reduction advantages of carbon fiber-reinforced materials, which came in response to rising oil prices in the 1970's—carbon fiber started to appear in sports equipment such as golf-club shafts and fishing rods. Union Carbide, sometimes working with Toray, continued to develop PAN-based products.

Because of the ability of carbon fiber epoxy composites to withstand extreme conditions, both government agencies and private companies used them extensively in space vehicles and apparatuses. Carbon fiber can also conduct electricity and has been used in the construction of electrodes and many kinds of batteries and fuel cells. Because oxidized PAN fiber is fire-resistant, it has been used in protective clothing for firefighters and industry workers, for insulating cables, and as a safety measure to insulate flammable seat cushions in airplanes and other vehicles. Activated carbon fibers are useful in the design of many kinds of air filters, with applications ranging from poison chemical absorption to odor control.

In customized high-performance vehicles, cost is not a major concern, and racing bikes, cars, motorbikes, and boats have frequently used carbon fiber-reinforced materials. Graham Hawkes Ocean Technologies has developed carbon fiber electric submersible vehicles capable of diving to depths as great as 122 meters. In the field of music, these materials have made innovative new designs possible for guitars, cellos, and other stringed instruments and more durable classical guitar strings. Carbon fiber composite materials are used in medical and veterinary prosthesis products, including artificial limbs, and are also used in X-ray tables and other equipment.

In constructing support frames for concrete, the corrosion-resistant properties and relatively light weight of carbon fiber-reinforced material make it an attractive replacement for steel and welded wire. It has been used for repairing bridges, especially in England. Over time, the replacement of metal in so many industries could have a long-range impact on reductions in global resource consumption, not only of metals but also of fossil fuels, as a result of significantly lighter vehicles.

USES OF CARBON NANOTUBES

While less commercially established than carbon fiber, carbon nanotubes are even stronger and are unmatched by any other substance in terms of strength-to-weight. Like carbon fiber, they can conduct electricity and heat, and their strength, conductivity, and microscopic dimensions make them ideal candidates for applications in nanotechnology.

Carbon nanotubes are used to provide greater strength in composites with carbon fibers, as well as other materials, with applications in many of the same areas as carbon fibers. Nanotechnology research focuses on medical uses of carbon nanotubes, because the nanotubes have the potential to work on the cellular level, delivering medicine and targeting cancer cells with heat. Carbon nanotubes have also been examined as an alternative to silicon in microcircuitry for computers and other devices. International Business Machines Corporation (IBM) has constructed logic gates using the nanotubes. Nantero, Inc., has used nanotubes to develop memory chips. Other teams are working on nano-engineering, using nanotubes to construct tiny machines.

John E. Myers

FURTHER READING

Biró, L. P. *Carbon Filaments and Nanotubes: Common Origins, Differing Applications?* Boston: Kluwer Academic, 2001.

Delhaes, Pierre, ed. *Fibers and Composites.* London: Taylor & Francis, 2003.

Dresselhaus, Mildred, et al. *Carbon Nanotubes: Synthesis, Structure, Properties, and Applications.* New York: Springer, 2001.

Ebbesen, Thomas W., ed. *Carbon Nanotubes: Preparation and Properties.* Boca Raton, Fla.: CRC Press, 1997.

Kar, Kamal K., et al. "Synthesis of Carbon Nanotubes on the Surface of Carbon Fiber/Fabric by Catalytic Chemical Vapor Deposition and Their Characterization." *Fullerenes, Nanotubes, and Carbon Nanostructures* 17, no. 3 (May 3, 2009): 209-229.

Morgan, Peter. *Carbon Fibers and Their Composites.* Boca Raton, Fla.: Taylor & Francis, 2005.

Zhang, Q., et al. "Hierarchical Composites of Carbon Nanotubes on Carbon Fiber: Influence of Growth Condition on Fiber Tensile Properties." *Composites Science and Technology* 69, no. 5 (April, 2009): 594-601.

WEB SITE

THE NANOTUBE SITE
http://www.pa.msu.edu/cmp/csc/nanotube.html

SEE ALSO: Biotechnology; Carbon; Silicates; Silicon.

Carbonate minerals

CATEGORY: Mineral and other nonliving resources

WHERE FOUND

Calcite, a common carbonate mineral, dominates the metamorphic rock marble and the sedimentary rock limestone. It also occurs in cave and hot spring deposits, some dry lake deposits (including oolitic sands of Great Salt Lake, Utah), and modern marine sediment in some tropical areas such as the Great Bahama Bank, Florida, Mexico, the Persian Gulf, and Australia. Shells of many marine invertebrates are made of calcium carbonate (including corals, molluscs such as bivalves and snails, echinoderms such as sand dollars and sea urchins, and planktonic organisms whose microscopic shells accumulate to form chalk). In arid climates calcium carbonate accumulates in soil to form calcrete or caliche (hardpan). Carbonates other than calcium carbonate occur in sedimentary deposits and in association with ore veins.

PRIMARY USES

Calcite has been used in building (cement, structural and ornamental stone), as a flux in smelting various types of metal ores, in agriculture, in the chemical industry for the manufacture of various products, for polishing, and as a filler in paint and rubber. Other carbonate minerals are used as ores of various metals, in manufacturing, as ornamental stone, or in jewelry.

TECHNICAL DEFINITION

Carbonate minerals contain the carbonate anion, $(CO_3)^{-2}$, in their chemical formula. There are approximately sixty carbonate minerals, but many are rare. Among the more common carbonates are calcite and aragonite (both $CaCO_3$), dolomite ($CaMg(CO3)2$), magnesite ($MgCO_3$), and siderite ($FeCO_3$). Carbonate minerals effervesce in hydrochloric acid, but with some carbonates, the acid must be hot or the mineral must be powdered to obtain the reaction. Most carbonates are soft, and rhombohedral cleavage is common.

DESCRIPTION, DISTRIBUTION, AND FORMS

Carbonate minerals may be divided into three groups, each of which has a similar crystal structure: the calcite group, the dolomite group, and the aragonite group. Some carbonate minerals are "polymorphs" of one another, with identical chemical formulas but different crystal structures. An example is $CaCO_3$, which exists in nature as three different crystal structures: calcite (hexagonal system), aragonite (orthorhombic system), and vaterite (hexagonal, also called μ-calcite).

The calcite group belongs to the hexagonal crystal system, hexagonal-scalenohedral class. This group includes calcite ($CaCO_3$), magnesite ($MgCO_3$), siderite ($FeCO_3$), rhodochrosite ($MnCO_3$), and smithsonite ($ZnCO_3$). The dolomite group belongs to the hexagonal crystal system, rhombohedral class. This group includes dolomite ($CaMg(CO_3)_2$) and ankerite ($CaFe(CO_3)_2$). The aragonite group belongs to the orthorhombic crystal system, rhombic-dipyramidal class. This group includes aragonite ($CaCO_3$), witherite ($BaCO_3$), strontianite ($SrCO_3$), and cerussite ($PbCO_3$).

The basic copper carbonates, malachite ($Cu_2CO_3(OH)_2$) and azurite ($Cu_3(CO_3)_2(OH)_2$), belong to the monoclinic crystal system, prismatic class. Other monoclinic carbonates are trona ($NaHCO_3$

$\cdot Na_2CO_3\cdot2H_2O$), hydromagnesite ($Mg_5(CO_3)_4(OH)_2$ $\cdot4H_2O$), and artinite ($Mg_2(CO_3)(OH)_2\cdot3H_2O$).

The most abundant carbonate mineral is calcite ($CaCO_3$), which comprises limestone, chalk, travertine, tufa (sedimentary rocks), and marble (metamorphic rock). Most limestone forms in warm, shallow seas, far from sources of land-derived sediment. Chalk is made of the shells of microscopic floating organisms which once lived in the sea. Spring deposits are travertine or tufa, and cave deposits (stalactites and stalagmites) are travertine. These deposits form from the evaporation of groundwater carrying dissolved calcium carbonate. Marble is limestone which has been changed by heat and pressure. Malachite and azurite are associated with the oxidized portions of copper deposits and with copper veins through limestone deposits.

Sodium carbonate minerals are present in association with dry salt lake deposits in some parts of the world. These include trona, natron ($Na_2CO_3\cdot10H_2O$), thermonatrite ($NaCO_3\cdot H_2O$), nahcolite ($NaHCO_3$), gaylussite ($CaCO_3\cdot Na_2CO_3\cdot5H_2O$), pirssonite ($CaCO_3$ $\cdot Na_2CO_3\cdot2H_2O$), and shortite ($2CaCO_3\cdot Na_2CO_3$).

HISTORY

Calcite, because of its abundance, has a rich history. Because calcite can preserve fossil records, its presence helps date cultural artifacts. Chalk has been used for writing for thousands of years.

OBTAINING CARBONATE MINERALS

The most important use of calcite is in the production of cements and lime. When limestone is heated to about 900° Celsius, it loses CO_2 and is converted to quicklime or lime (CaO). Mixed with sand, quicklime forms mortar. When mixed with water, it hardens or "sets," swelling and releasing heat. The most widely produced cement is portland cement (used in concrete), which is generally made from limestone and silica- and alumina-bearing material such as clay or shale. The raw materials are ground together, and the mixture is heated in a kiln until it fuses into a "clinker," which is then crushed to a powder.

USES OF CARBONATE MINERALS

Lime (CaO) is also used in agriculture to neutralize acid in soils, in the manufacture of paper, glass, and whitewash, and in tanning leather. It is used in refining sugar, as a water softener, and as a flux for smelting various types of ores. Fine-grained limestone has been used in lithography (printing). Blocks of cut limestone and marble are used as building stone and ornamental stone and may be polished. Crushed limestone is used as aggregate in concrete and as road metal. Dolomite has uses similar to those of calcite.

Several carbonates are metal ores: dolomite and magnesite (ores of magnesium), rhodochrosite (manganese), siderite (iron), smithsonite (zinc), strontianite (strontium), witherite (barium), cerrusite (lead), malachite and azurite (copper), and trona (sodium).

Magnesite is used in the manufacture of refractory materials capable of withstanding high temperatures, for special types of cements, and in the paper, rubber, and pharmaceutical industries. Strontianite is also used in the manufacture of fireworks, producing a purplish-red flame. Malachite (green) and azurite (blue) are used as pigments. Sodium carbonate and sodium bicarbonate are important in the manufacture of washing soda (or sal soda) and are used as cleaning agents and water softeners. They are used in the manufacture of glass, ceramics, paper, soap, and sodium-containing compounds (such as sodium hydroxide) as well as in petroleum refining. Sodium bicarbonate, also known as baking soda, is an important part of baking powder, is a source of carbon dioxide in fire extinguishers and is used medicinally to neutralize excess stomach acid. Several carbonates are used as ornamental stone and in jewelry, including malachite, azurite, aragonite (alabaster), rhodochrosite, and smithsonite.

Pamela J. W. Gore

FURTHER READING

Klein, Cornelis, and Barbara Dutrow. *The Twenty-third Edition of the Manual of Mineral Science.* 23d ed. Hoboken, N.J.: J. Wiley, 2008.

Pellant, Chris. *Rocks and Minerals.* 2d American ed. New York: Dorling Kindersley, 2002.

Pough, Frederick H. *A Field Guide to Rocks and Minerals.* Photographs by Jeffrey Scovil. 5th ed. Boston: Houghton Mifflin, 1996.

Tegethoff, F. Wolfgang, Johannes Rohleder, and Evelyn Kroker, eds. *Calcium Carbonate: From the Cretaceous Period into the Twenty-first Century.* Boston: Birkhäuser Verlag, 2001.

Tucker, Maurice E., and V. Paul Wright. *Carbonate Sedimentology.* Boston: Blackwell Scientific, 1990.

Warren, John K. *Evaporite Sedimentology: Importance in Hydrocarbon Accumulation.* Englewood Cliffs, N.J.: Prentice Hall, 1989.

WEB SITE

CARBONATE-HYDROXYLAPATITE MINERAL DATA
http://webmineral.com/data/Carbonate-
hydroxylapatite.shtml

SEE ALSO: Carbon cycle; Crystals; Evaporites; Lime; Limestone; Minerals, structure and physical properties of; Sedimentary processes, rocks, and mineral deposits.

Carnegie, Andrew

CATEGORY: People

BORN: November 25, 1835; Dunfermline, Scotland
DIED: August 11, 1919; Lenox, Massachusetts

Carnegie established the Carnegie Steel Company, which he eventually sold for $250 million. The explosive growth of the steel industry that Carnegie's success exemplified initiated the final phase of the Industrial Revolution; it ultimately led, for example, to the mass production of automobiles and the exploitation of a variety of resources worldwide.

BIOGRAPHICAL BACKGROUND

In 1848, Andrew Carnegie moved from Scotland to the United States. He began working in an Allegheny, Pennsylvania, cotton mill for $1.20 per week. Later, he moved to Pittsburgh, becoming involved in the rapidly growing railroad business. Carnegie soon became the superintendent of the Pittsburgh division of the Pennsylvania Railroad. By investing wisely in what became the Pullman Company and in oil lands, Carnegie established the foundation for his fortune.

IMPACT ON RESOURCE USE

Following service in the War Department during the Civil War, Carnegie left the Pennsylvania Railroad and formed a company to build iron railroad bridges. This led to the next step: the production of steel. He founded a steel mill and began using the new Bessemer process of making steel. The extensive use of steel that resulted from Carnegie's work led to a greater exploitation of iron ore deposits in the United States and abroad. The need for oil and rubber, which grew alongside the booming steel industry, also accelerated resource exploitation and had profound effects on succeeding generations.

By 1899, the Carnegie Steel Company controlled 25 percent of steel production in the United States. Two years later, Carnegie sold the company to J. P. Morgan, who organized it into the U.S. Steel Corporation, the first billion-dollar corporation in the United States.

When Carnegie was thirty-three years old, with an annual income of fifty thousand dollars, he declared that a person should never seek to build a fortune unless intending to give the surplus for benevolent purposes. Although he did not always follow his own advice, he did eventually give more than $350 million to philanthropic projects, including the endowment of seventeen hundred libraries, the Tuskegee Institute, and the Peace Palace at The Hague in the Netherlands.

Glenn L. Swygart

SEE ALSO: Bessemer process; Capitalism and resource exploitation; Iron; Steel; Steel industry.

Andrew Carnegie was the leading figure in the steel industry at the end of the nineteenth century. (Library of Congress)

Carson, Rachel

CATEGORY: People
BORN: May 27, 1907; Springdale, Pennsylvania
DIED: April 14, 1964; Silver Spring, Maryland

Carson made a major contribution to the environmental movement in the United States by educating the public about the natural geological evolution of the Earth and the dangers associated with the widespread use of chemicals. Her book Silent Spring *was published in 1962.*

BIOGRAPHICAL BACKGROUND

Rachel Carson was educated at the Pennsylvania College for Women in Pittsburgh and Johns Hopkins University in Baltimore, Maryland. She did research at the Woods Hole Marine Biological Laboratory and subsequently worked for the U.S. Fish and Wildlife Service in Washington, D.C.

Rachel Carson's seminal text Silent Spring *helped spearhead the modern environmental movement. (Library of Congress)*

IMPACT ON RESOURCE USE

Carson published *Under the Sea-Wind* (1941); *The Sea Around Us* (1951), which received the National Book Award for nonfiction; *The Edge of the Sea* (1955); and her most famous work, *Silent Spring* (1962). Her writings took a naturalist's approach to explaining the ocean environment and the origin of the Earth, and they were praised for their clear explanations in lay terms. *The Edge of the Sea* revealed Carson's growing interests in the interrelationships of Earth's systems and a holistic approach to human interaction with nature. In *Silent Spring* Carson warned of the environmental contamination that results from widespread use of pesticides, particularly dichloro-diphenyl-trichloroethane (DDT). She described how the ecology of the soil had been largely ignored in the rush to apply chemicals, drew attention to the effects on wildlife where chemical mixing in runoff channels turned streams into lethal cauldrons of chemical soup, and accused the chemical companies of aggressive marketing policies that ignored the impact on the environment. The first Earth Day (April 22, 1970) and the creation of the Environmental Protection Agency in 1970 can both be attributed in part to Carson's role in changing the way Americans thought about their surroundings.

Pat Dasch

SEE ALSO: Environmental movement; Food chain; Pesticides and pest control.

Carter, Jimmy

CATEGORY: People
BORN: October 1, 1924; Plains, Georgia

As the thirty-ninth president of the United States, James Earl "Jimmy" Carter deregulated domestic crude oil prices and established the Department of Energy.

BIOGRAPHICAL BACKGROUND

Jimmy Carter graduated from the United States Naval Academy and served in the Navy until his father's death. Assuming his father's business responsibilities, Carter expanded the family business and ran for political offices. He was elected governor of Georgia in 1970. At the end of his term as governor, Carter began a campaign for the presidency. He ran against incumbent Gerald Ford in 1976 and won by a narrow margin.

Jimmy Carter, the thirty-ninth president of the United States, was an early advocate of alternative energy use. (Library of Congress)

IMPACT ON RESOURCE USE

The years before and during President Carter's term were times of instability in the world economy. World petroleum demand was increasing, and Congress had capped domestic crude oil prices, discouraging domestic petroleum exploration. In 1979, the Organization of Petroleum Exporting Countries (OPEC) raised crude oil prices by 50 percent. Because most goods were moved to market by gasoline- or diesel-powered transport, the increase in world petroleum prices contributed significantly to inflation, which reached an annual rate of 12 percent. Interest rates tracked inflation and rose 20 percent, a level unprecedented in the twentieth century.

In response to these problems, President Carter proposed an energy program that included creation of a Department of Energy, deregulation of domestic crude oil prices, and promotion of conservation and alternative energy sources. An advocate of environmentalism, President Carter was also successful in obtaining congressional action that preserved vast wilderness areas in Alaska.

Robert E. Carver

SEE ALSO: Department of Energy, U.S.; Energy economics; Oil embargo and energy crises of 1973 and 1979; Synthetic Fuels Corporation.

Carver, George Washington

CATEGORY: People
BORN: July 12, 1861?; near Diamond Grove (now Diamond), Missouri
DIED: January 5, 1943; Tuskegee, Alabama

A pioneering African American agricultural scientist, Carver is best known for popularizing and promoting the economic potential of peanuts and sweet potatoes as alternative crops for southern farmers.

BIOGRAPHICAL BACKGROUND

George Washington Carver was born into slavery near the end of the Civil War near Diamond Grove (now Diamond), Missouri. His early education was sporadic, though he did attend high school in Minneapolis, Kansas. He was briefly a homesteader in Ness County, Kansas, before he returned to school, first at Simpson College in Indianola, Iowa, where he studied fine arts, then at Iowa State University in Ames, Iowa, where he studied agriculture. After Carver completed his bachelor of agriculture degree in 1894, he was appointed to the faculty at Iowa State and received a master of agriculture degree in 1896.

IMPACT ON RESOURCE USE

Carver immediately began working as director of agriculture and director of the agricultural experiment station at Tuskegee University in Alabama. Carver won international acclaim for the educational efforts he began in the early 1900's to promote sound conservation practices and sustainable agricultural activity in the rural South, which had previously been dependent on cotton production. He is best known, however, for popularizing and promoting the economic potential of peanuts and sweet potatoes as alternative crops for southern farmers. He was instrumental in persuading Congress to protect the peanut industry from foreign competition shortly after World War I.

Scientist George Washington Carver is best known for his work with agricultural crops such as peanuts. (National Archives)

In the later stages of his career, he investigated the potential uses of peanuts and sweet potatoes, which included uses in dyes, milk substitutes, and cosmetics.

Mark S. Coyne

SEE ALSO: Agricultural products; Agriculture industry; Agronomy.

Cement and concrete

CATEGORY: Products from resources

Cement and concrete have played crucial roles in shaping humankind's physical environment. Of all manufactured construction materials worldwide, concrete is the most widely used.

BACKGROUND

Cement is an important construction material because of the ready availability of its raw materials, its capacity to be shaped prior to setting, and its durability after hardening. When combined with an aggregate (such as sand, gravel, or crushed rock), cement becomes concrete—a durable, load-bearing construction material.

Cements with the ability to set and harden underwater are called hydraulic cements. The most common of these is portland cement, consisting of compounds of lime mixed with silica, alumina, and iron oxide. Gypsum is also added to retard the setting time. When water is added, these ingredients react to form hydrated calcium silicates that will set into a hardened product.

HISTORY

Cement has been used for construction purposes for the past six thousand years. The Egyptians are known to have used a simple cement, and the Greeks and Romans advanced the technology by creating hydraulic cements from various volcanic materials and lime. Many examples of their concrete structures remain today—some underwater, where they were used in harbors.

The quality of cementing materials declined greatly during the Middle Ages but began to improve again in the late eighteenth century. In 1756, the famed British engineer John Smeaton was commissioned to rebuild the Eddystone Lighthouse near Cornwall, England. He undertook a search for lime mortars that would resist the action of the water and discovered that the best limestone contains a high proportion of clayey material. For his project he used lime mixed with pozzolana from Italy (the same volcanic material the Romans had used). Smeaton was followed by a number of researchers, including Joseph Aspdin, a Leeds builder, who patented "portland" cement, named for the high-quality building stone quarried at Portland, England.

MANUFACTURING CEMENT

Cement is a manufactured product, made from raw materials that are found relatively easily in nature. Cement manufacturers have a number of sources for lime, but the most common are limestone and chalk. Coral and marine shell deposits are also used as sources of lime, when available. Silica, alumina, and iron oxide are found in clays, shales, slates, and certain muds. Some raw materials contain almost all the ingredients of cement, especially marl (a compact clay), cement rock, and blast-furnace slag. Industrial

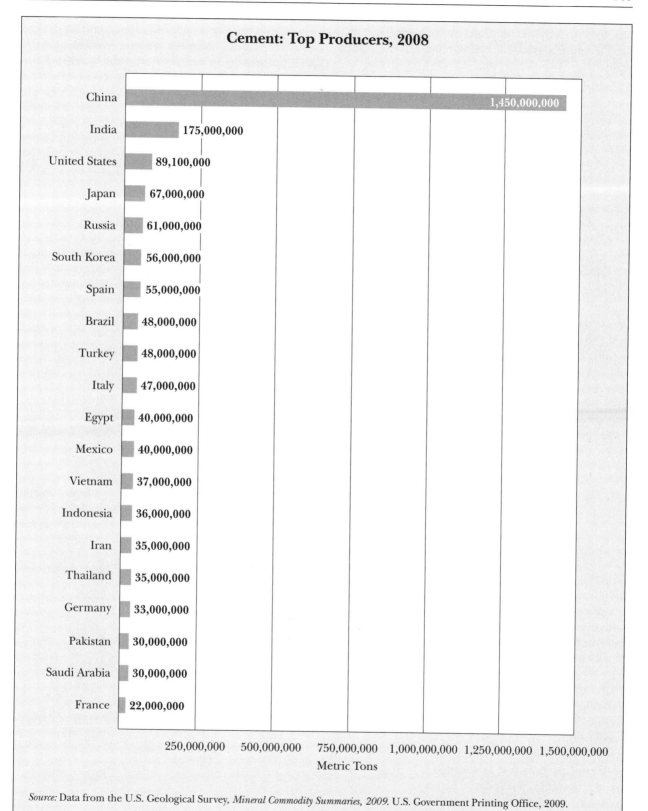

Cement: Top Producers, 2008

Country	Metric Tons
China	1,450,000,000
India	175,000,000
United States	89,100,000
Japan	67,000,000
Russia	61,000,000
South Korea	56,000,000
Spain	55,000,000
Brazil	48,000,000
Turkey	48,000,000
Italy	47,000,000
Egypt	40,000,000
Mexico	40,000,000
Vietnam	37,000,000
Indonesia	36,000,000
Iran	35,000,000
Thailand	35,000,000
Germany	33,000,000
Pakistan	30,000,000
Saudi Arabia	30,000,000
France	22,000,000

Source: Data from the U.S. Geological Survey, *Mineral Commodity Summaries, 2009.* U.S. Government Printing Office, 2009.

wastes such as fly ash and calcium carbonate are also used as raw materials for cement, but not on a large scale.

Raw materials in the form of hard rock—such as limestone, slate, and some shales—are usually quarried, but they may also be mined. If the limestone is of low quality, it may need to go through a concentrating process. Softer materials such as chalk, clay, and mud can be dug by various types of machinery, depending on the physical setting and type of material. Once extracted, the raw materials are transported to the cement manufacturing plant by truck, rail, conveyor belt, or pipeline (when in a slurry).

At the plant, the raw materials are ground into a fine powder and then mixed in predetermined ratios. The mixing can be done wet, semidry, or dry. In the wet process the materials are ground wet and mixed into a slurry. In the semidry process they are ground dry, then moistened for adhesion; and in the dry process the raw materials remain dry throughout.

After mixing, the raw materials are burned in a large rotating kiln. Kilns are usually from four to eight meters in diameter and from 90 to 200 meters long, and they consist of a steel cylindrical shell inclined slightly from the horizontal. The mixture is introduced at the upper end of the kiln, and as it flows down the incline (with the help of gravity and the kiln's steady rotation), it reaches a maximum temperature between 1,300° Celsius and 1,500° Celsius, at which point the raw materials interact to form calcium silicates. The heated material exits the kiln in the form of rough lumps or pellets—called clinker—no larger than 5 centimeters in diameter. After the clinker cools, the manufacturer adds gypsum and grinds the mixture into the fine powder known as portland cement.

USES OF CONCRETE

Concrete is generally used in four common forms: ready-mixed, precast, reinforced, and prestressed. Ready-mixed concrete is transported to a construction site as a cement paste and is then poured into forms to make roadways, foundations, driveways, floor slabs, and much more. Precast concrete—cast at a plant and then transported to the site—is used for everything from lawn ornaments to major structural elements. Reinforced concrete is created by adding steel mesh, reinforcing bars, or any other stiffening member to the concrete before it sets. Prestressed concrete, the most recently developed form, increases the strength of a beam by using reinforcing steel to keep the entire beam under compression. Concrete is much stronger under compression (pushed in on itself) than under tension (pulled apart).

Brian J. Nichelson

FURTHER READING

Gani, M. S. J. *Cement and Concrete.* New York: Chapman & Hall, 1997.

Lea, F. M. *Lea's Chemistry of Cement and Concrete.* 4th ed. Edited by Peter C. Hewlett. New York: J. Wiley, 1998.

Mehta, P. K., and Paulo J. M. Monteiro. *Concrete: Microstructure, Properties, and Materials.* 3d ed. New York: McGraw-Hill, 2005.

Mindess, Sidney, J. Francis Young, and David Darwin. *Concrete.* 2d ed. Upper Saddle River, N.J.: Prentice Hall, 2003.

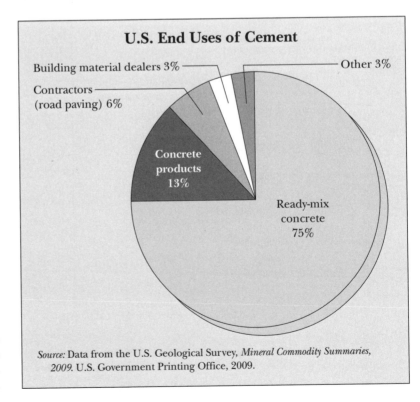

U.S. End Uses of Cement

Building material dealers 3%

Contractors (road paving) 6%

Other 3%

Concrete products 13%

Ready-mix concrete 75%

Source: Data from the U.S. Geological Survey, *Mineral Commodity Summaries, 2009.* U.S. Government Printing Office, 2009.

Neville, A. M. *Properties of Concrete.* 4th ed. Harlow, Essex, England: Longman Group, 1995.

WEB SITES

NATURAL RESOURCES CANADA
Canadian Minerals Yearbook, Mineral and Metal Commodity Reviews
http://www.nrcan-rncan.gc.ca/mms-smm/busi-indu/cmy-amc/com-eng.htm

PORTLAND CEMENT ASSOCIATION
Cement and Concrete Basics
http://www.cement.org/basics

U.S. GEOLOGICAL SURVEY
Cement: Statistics and Information
http://minerals.usgs.gov/minerals/pubs/commodity/cement/index.html#mcs

SEE ALSO: Clays; Gypsum; Lime; Limestone; Sand and gravel; Shale; Silicates; Slate.

Central Arizona Project

CATEGORY: Organizations, agencies, and programs
DATE: Established September 30, 1968; substantially completed 1993

The Central Arizona Project (CAP), a series of pumping plants, dams, aqueducts, and pipelines stretching more than 540 kilometers, is the largest water transfer project in the United States. Drawing water from Lake Havasu has supported agriculture in southwest Arizona and made possible the growth of major cities, while harming several species of fish and animals downstream.

BACKGROUND
As the area that makes up the southwestern United States was settled and populated by Europeans in the nineteenth century, the need for more water became apparent. In the early 1900's, the Southwest looked to the Colorado River basin as a source of water, and a series of laws and court decisions called the "Law of the River" were established to ensure that each state was treated equitably. Decades of court cases attempted to determine the amount of the water to which Arizona was entitled. Through the 1950's Arizona lobbied for authorization of a Central Arizona Project, and the

U.S. secretary of the interior called for a comprehensive Colorado River plan to address the future water needs of seventeen Western states. Passed on September 30, 1968, Public Law 90-537, 82 *Stat.* 885 created the Colorado River Basin Project and the Lower Colorado River Basin Development Fund, which authorized in turn the development of the Dixie Project in Utah and the Central Arizona Project in Arizona and New Mexico.

PROVISIONS
The Central Arizona Project was designed to move 4,000 square kilometers of water from Lake Havasu, fed by the Colorado River, to agricultural lands in Maricopa, Pima, and Pinel Counties in Arizona, and to Catron, Grant, and Hidalgo Counties in New Mexico. Because of high costs and lower-than-expected demand, however, the New Mexico portion of the project was never built. During the years of construction, the economy of Arizona began to shift from agriculture to industry, and the metropolitan areas of Phoenix, Scottsdale, and Tucson experienced rapid growth. As a result, CAP waters were reallocated, so that over time more water would be designated for municipal and industrial use, and less for agriculture.

IMPACT ON RESOURCE USE
The purpose of CAP, as it was conceived in the late 1940's, was to keep agriculture thriving without depleting groundwater supplies. By most accounts, this goal was not realized. In addition, the diversion of water from its natural course has created environmental problems downstream from Lake Havasu, including the extinction of fish and wildlife, in spite of several successful conservation efforts along the project itself. Dams along the project provide hydroelectric power, reducing the region's dependence on other forms of power generation.

Cynthia A. Bily

WEB SITES

CENTRAL ARIZONA PROJECT
http://www.cap-az.com/

U.S. DEPARTMENT OF THE INTERIOR BUREAU OF RECLAMATION
Colorado River Basin Project: Central Arizona Project
http://www.usbr.gov/dataweb/html/crbpcap.html

SEE ALSO: Hydroenergy; Los Angeles Aqueduct; Three Gorges Dam.

Ceramics

CATEGORY: Products from resources

Ceramics are inorganic, nonmetallic materials—such as naturally occurring silicates, oxides, nitrates, carbonates, chlorides, and sulfates—that are subjected to high temperatures during their manufacture and processing. Ceramic materials are high strength but brittle. As a result of modern research and development, they have multiple and varied uses.

BACKGROUND

Paradoxically, ceramic science is one of the oldest yet one of the newest technologies. Much of what is known of prehistoric humans and of the earliest civilizations has been learned from the pottery that was left behind. This longevity illustrates one of the greatest assets of ceramic materials, their durability. The fact that most of the surviving pieces are fragments gives evidence of the greatest weakness, their brittleness.

The term "ceramics" is derived from the Greek term *keramos*, which means "potter's clay." Ceramics is defined in some dictionaries as "the art of making things from baked clay." "Clay" is used in describing ceramics because it was an essential material in traditional ceramic compositions. The term "baked" is important, since high temperatures are used in most processing of ceramics. Although simple, this description of ceramics was an accurate one until the time of World War II. In the early 1940's, the field of materials science, of which ceramics is a part, experienced a push to develop new materials and processing methods. Today, a more accurate present-day description of ceramics might be "the art and science of making and using implements and other articles that are essentially composed of inorganic and nonmetallic compounds."

TRADITIONAL CERAMICS

The ceramic industries may be grouped into several divisions according to the products produced. Traditional divisions include whitewares, refractories, abrasives, structural clay products, glass, cement, and porcelain enamels. Developments in the second half of

A worker carries ceramic cylinders in Jungdezhen City, China, home to what is believed to be the oldest egg-shaped ceramics kiln in the world. (Zhang Wu/Xinhua/Landov)

the twentieth century in the fields of nuclear physics and electronics resulted in many new ceramic products, collectively known as technical ceramics.

Whitewares are materials such as clay, feldspar, whiting, and potter's flint that fire to a white color. The mineral mixtures are shaped and then partially melted at high temperatures to produce a dense hard material. The term whiteware is misleading, since products in this class are produced in a wide variety of colors, depending on the amounts of impurities in the raw materials. Common whitewares include earthenware, porcelain or other tableware products as well as casseroles and bowls, floor and wall tile, and decorative products such as vases and lamp bases. Important commercial whitewares include laboratory ware such as porcelain crucibles, combustion tubes, and grinding balls for the chemist as well as electrical porcelains such as spark plugs and insulators.

Refractories are structural materials manufactured for the purpose of withstanding corrosive high-temperature conditions in furnaces and process vessels. Refractories have high melting temperatures, good hot strength, and resistance to chemical attack and abrasion. They are made from the refractory clays, kaolin, magnesite, chrome ore, olivine, and bauxite. For more special services, refractory products are made from synthetic compositions such as carbides and borides. Among the most important users of refractories are the metallurgical industries, including the steel industry.

Glasses are ceramics that do not return to crystalline form after being melted and cooled. These noncrystalline ceramics behave as high viscosity liquids. They are essentially rigid at room temperature but gradually soften and flow as the temperature is increased. This viscosity allows glasses to be formed by processes that will not work for other ceramic materials. Glasses can be pressed into shallow shapes, drawn or rolled into tubes and sheets, blown into hollow shapes, or spun into fibers.

Most glasses are naturally transparent to visible light and are commonly used as windows, bottles, lightbulbs, lenses, and optical fibers. The basic ingredient in most glasses is silica sand, but a wide range of other materials can be added to produce glasses possessing a wide variety of tailored properties. Borosilicate glasses are resistant to both chemicals and heat, properties that make them useful both in the home and in the laboratory. Oxides of the transition metals may be added to produce glass of almost any desired color.

The porcelain enamels are glassy coatings fused onto metals to provide decoration and protection from corrosion. They are hard, rigid ceramics that are electrical and thermal insulators as well as wear-resistant and chemically inert. Available in all colors, they are found on household appliances, on structures used for food storage, in medical and hospital equipment, and in vessels used in the production of food and chemicals.

TECHNICAL CERAMICS

Research after World War II made possible a wide variety of nontraditional ceramic products based on high-purity synthetic materials processed by special techniques. A few items will illustrate the scope of this relatively new field.

Ceramics have played an essential role in the development of the computer industry. The ceramic process is used in the fabrication of the complex integrated circuits that perform the basic operations of a computer on silicon semiconductor wafers. These integrated circuits are packaged on ceramic substrate materials.

Oxides and carbides of uranium, plutonium, and thorium are ceramic materials that are used in the production of fuels for nuclear fission reactors. High-strength concrete, often containing lead, is used in shielding structures around nuclear reactors. "Hot cell" windows, made of leaded glass, maintain optical transparency when exposed to radiation. Ceramic materials are also used in virtually all segments of the aerospace industry. Refractory materials are used in building launching pads, rocket nozzles, and heat shields.

Lasers, which came into prominence in the 1960's, utilize the various quantum transitions that atoms and molecules undergo to produce intense beams of infrared, visible, or ultraviolet light. The original ruby laser used as its light-emitting medium a crystalline aluminum oxide ceramic that contained a small amount of chromium. Another important ceramic laser is the yttrium aluminum garnet doped with neodymium to emit light in the infrared region of the spectrum. As the need for more specialized materials grows, the field of ceramic science will continue to produce more and more exotic materials.

Grace A. Banks

FURTHER READING

Barsoum, M. W. *Fundamentals of Ceramics.* Rev. ed. Philadelphia: Institute of Physics, 2003.

Bormans, P. *Ceramics Are More than Clay Alone: Raw Materials, Products, Applications.* Cambridge, England: Cambridge International Science, 2003.

Carter, C. Barry, and M. Grant Norton. *Ceramic Materials: Science and Engineering.* New York: Springer, 2007.

Jones, J. T., and M. F. Berard. *Ceramics Industrial Processing and Testing.* 2d ed. Ames: Iowa State University Press, 1993.

McColm, Ian J. *Dictionary of Ceramic Science and Engineering.* 2d ed. New York: Plenum Press, 1994.

Phillips, George C. *A Concise Introduction to Ceramics.* New York: Van Nostrand Reinhold, 1991.

Sōmiya, Shigeyuki, et al., eds. *Handbook of Advanced Ceramics.* 2 vols. Boston: Elsevier/Academic Press, 2003.

SEE ALSO: Abrasives; Clays; Glass; Mica; Quartz; Sand and gravel; Silicates; Silicon.

Cesium

CATEGORY: Mineral and other nonliving resources

WHERE FOUND

The element cesium makes up only 7 parts per million of the Earth's crust. Found only in minerals, it does not occur in its free state naturally. The leading producers are in southwest Africa, the Russian republics, Sweden, and the island of Elba. In North America it is most often found in ores in South Dakota, Maine, and Manitoba, Canada. Significant reserve bases exist in Namibia and Zimbabwe as well as Canada.

PRIMARY USES

Cesium has significant applications in the manufacture of photoelectric cells and vacuum tubes. One of its isotopes, cesium 137, is used in radiation therapy. Cesium compounds have also served as antishock agents after administration of arsenic drugs. The International Atomic Energy Agency has also identified cesium 137 as one of the radioactive materials that may be used to make "dirty bombs."

TECHNICAL DEFINITION

Cesium (abbreviated Cs), atomic number 55, belongs to Group I of the periodic table of the elements and is the heaviest of the alkali metals (excluding the radioactive francium). It has twenty-two known isotopes, with masses ranging from cesium 123 to cesium 144, with an average atomic weight of 132.905. The only naturally occurring isotope is cesium 133.

DESCRIPTION, DISTRIBUTION, AND FORMS

Pure cesium is a silver-white, ductile metal that is extremely malleable. Finely divided cesium produces a blue flame and is easily oxidized by burning brightly in humid air; it may explode in the presence of water. It has a density of 1.9 grams per cubic centimeter, a melting point of 28.5° Celsius, and a boiling point of 705° Celsius.

HISTORY

Cesium was discovered and detected by spectroscopy in 1860 by the German scientists Robert Bunsen and Gustav Robert Kirchhoff, who during their analysis detected the two blue lines of cesium and named the element after the word *caesius*, Latin for "sky blue." The metal was first isolated by electrolysis in 1881. Cesium compounds are widely distributed in nature in small quantities in various ores. The greatest sources of cesium are the silicate mineral pollucite, which contains up to 34 percent cesium oxide, and camallite. Only 0.002 part per million of cesium exist, in seawater. Detectable quantities are found in plant and animal organisms, mineral waters, and soils. Cesium in conjunction with rubidium and lithium is found in several lepidolite ores in Zimbabwe and South Africa.

OBTAINING CESIUM

Cesium is obtained by applying the so-called limestone process to lepidolite ore. After treatment of the ore with limestone (known as carbonation), lithium is separated, cesium carbonate is reduced by metallic magnesium, and cesium metal is isolated by condensation of its vapors. Another process for obtaining cesium first produces cesium chloride, which upon heating with a reducing element such as calcium or lithium yields the pure metal. Cesium's low electronegativity is responsible for its vigorous reaction with oxidizing agents. It reacts readily with most ordinary compounds, such as the halogens, ammonia, nitrogen, carbon monoxide, and even organic compounds such as ethylene and acetylene.

USES OF CESIUM

Cesium metal is used in photoelectric cells and in the optical and detecting devices of many analytical instruments. Cesium compounds are used in glass and ceramic production plants, and cesium chloride is used to remove small quantities of oxygen and water during the manufacture of vacuum tubes. Cesium 137 is often used in radiation therapy treatments.

Some of the isotopes of cesium are toxic. Cesium 137 is a radioactive beta-emitter whose ions migrate to the same places in the body that sodium ions go. One of the worst radiation accidents in history occurred in

Goiânia, Brazil, in 1987. An abandoned radiotherapy clinic was visited by scavenging inhabitants of the area. They discovered a cesium 137 machine and opened the tube, thus exposing themselves to the harmful rays. Several people died, and about 250 more were contaminated. In February, 2008, the National Research Council mandated the U.S. government to seek alternatives to replace cesium 137.

Soraya Ghayourmanesh

WEB SITE

WEBELEMENTS
Caesium: The Essentials
http://www.webelements.com/caesium/

SEE ALSO: Arsenic; Isotopes, radioactive; Lithium; Nuclear energy; Nuclear waste and its disposal.

Chernobyl nuclear accident

CATEGORY: Historical events and movements

The 1986 meltdown of the nuclear reactor at the Chernobyl nuclear plant in Ukraine was the most dangerous nuclear accident of the twentieth century, killing hundreds and not only compromising the long-term health of many human beings but also killing or poisoning animals, crops, and economic resources.

DEFINITION
On April 26, 1986, an accident at the Chernobyl nuclear plant in Ukraine dispersed radioactive material over much of Europe, killing several hundred people at or near the reactor and contaminating crops and animals as far away as northern Scandinavia.

OVERVIEW
Nuclear reactors produce electricity using steam produced from the heat given off in nuclear decay to turn turbines that generate electricity. In late April of 1986, operators at reactor number four of the Chernobyl nuclear plant undertook a test to determine how long the plant's turbines could produce electric power and operate the plant's safety systems after the steam was shut off. The operators made a series of errors that allowed the cooling water to drop below the critical level. Since the emergency cooling system had previously been shut down, it did not respond to the low

water level, and the temperature of the core increased. At 1:23 A.M. on April 26, the remaining water in the reactor core—where the uranium fuel decays, generating heat—expanded rapidly, producing steam. The resulting explosion destroyed the core and part of the building. A fireball appeared, and burning lumps of graphite and reactor fuel were dispersed around the site, starting fires that carried more radioactive material into the air.

Radiation poisoning resulted in the hospitalization of approximately two hundred plant workers and firefighters within thirty-six hours of the explosion. Everyone within 10 kilometers of the plant, except for crews still trying to contain the radiation release, was evacuated by the evening of April 26. On May 2 this evacuation zone was expanded to 30 kilometers. More than 100,000 people were eventually moved from the danger area.

A cloud containing radioactive material was carried away from the site by the wind. In the areas where it was raining when the cloud passed overhead, high concentrations of radioactive material accumulated on the ground. Poland, Hungary, and the Soviet Union restricted grazing by cattle, and most of the strawberry crop in Austria was discarded because of radioactive contamination. Significant levels of radiation spread as far as Sweden. Contamination near Gävle, about 240 kilometers north of Stockholm, required that 1,000 square kilometers of grass be burned. In Lapland, in northern Scandinavia, meat from fifty thousand reindeer had to be discarded.

By 1989, about 250 persons who worked at the Chernobyl plant or assisted in the cleanup had died as a result of radiation exposure. The long-term effects of the radiation release remained less certain. Ukrainian officials estimated that the Chernobyl accident would eventually be responsible for six thousand to eight thousand deaths. The British National Radiological Protection Board estimated that about one thousand people in Western Europe would eventually die of cancers induced by the Chernobyl radiation.

Public confidence in the safety of nuclear reactors was shaken by the Chernobyl accident (and by the earlier, far less serious accident at Three Mile Island in Pennsylvania). Groups opposed to the nuclear industry gained strength, forcing the abandonment of the Shoreham reactor on Long Island, New York, and speeding up plans by the Swedish government to close all commercial reactors in that country.

George J. Flynn

SEE ALSO: Health, resource exploitation and; Nuclear energy; Nuclear Regulatory Commission; Three Mile Island nuclear accident; Uranium.

Chile

CATEGORIES: Countries; government and resources

Chile is the world's leading producer of copper, which accounts for most of the total value of the nation's exports. Other primary resources that are the bases for exports include evaporites, containing several important trace minerals (iodine, lithium, and boron); marine resources for fish and fish products; agricultural land for growing fruits (especially grapes) and nuts; and forestland for wood, paper, and paper products.

THE COUNTRY

Chile is on the southwestern margin of South America. The Pacific Ocean lies to the west, and Argentina and Bolivia are to the east. The country's territory runs north to south for approximately 4,400 kilometers. Its greatest width is barely 160 kilometers. The Atacama Desert in the north is one of the world's driest. The Andes Mountains extend the length of the country and form a natural barrier between Argentina and Bolivia. Chile is slightly smaller than Texas.

Geology, climate, and nutrient-rich coastal waters are the bases for a wealth of primary resources, but mining dominates Chile's economy. It is the world's leading producer of copper, a metal of vital importance to the global economy for its use in coins, wiring, and construction. Chile has three distinct economic regions—the north, the south, and the middle—that contribute to the export-based economy. The north is one of the world's main sources of copper and related metals. The relatively high content of iodine, lithium, and boron mined from the *salars* (salt flats) of the north has global significance. The south contributes fish and timber products. The middle exports fruits, vegetables, fish, and copper. Chile had the world's forty-fifth largest economy in 2008.

COPPER ORE

Chile produces about 35 percent of the world's copper and possesses about 30 percent of the world's total identified copper-ore reserves. In 2006, the value of copper mine production was $31.5 billion, which represented about 22 percent of the country's gross domestic product. Six of the ten largest copper mines in the world are in Chile; four of the ten are in northern Chile. In that region, broad, open-pit mines operate along the western edge of the Andes Mountains, because the ore deposits are in geologic faults near the surface. The region includes the Escondida mine, the world's largest open-pit copper mine. The mine began operating in 1990 and accounts for nearly 25 percent of Chile's total production. An international consortium (Australia, the United Kingdom, and Japan) operates the mine. The government operates the Chuquicamata mine, which is the world's second largest copper mine. The deposits of copper in middle Chile are also in the Andes, but they are so deep underground that they require tunneling to extract the ore, which is more expensive than open-pit mining. Nevertheless, there are seven Andean copper mines in the region; two of them, the El Teniente and Andina mines, are among the world's top-ten producers. El Teniente holds the distinction as the world's longest underground mine.

Chile used to simply mine the copper ore, crush it, and then export it to other countries for processing. However, beginning in the early 1990's, direct investments by foreign companies helped upgrade the nation's copper mills to include the process of smelting, which involves melting the ore to remove nonmetal impurities. Shipping the resulting concentrate saves money by reducing transportation costs. The country that imports the copper concentrate finishes the refining process by melting it into copper slabs. The leading importers of Chilean copper have been China, Japan, and the United States. Chilean companies are not likely to build their own refineries, as the high costs of importing fossil fuels to generate electricity make installing additional refining capacity less profitable than continuing to ship ores and concentrates abroad. The government could increase the reservoir capacity of hydroelectric dams in the Andes Mountains in order to help fill the shortfall in energy needs. However, it has been reluctant to do so because the dams are in environmentally sensitive areas.

IODINE

The origin of iodine is a mystery, but it is believed to have come from organic films on the sea surface or from gases and sublimates associated with Andean volcanism. Either way, the iodine is believed to have en-

Chile: Resources at a Glance

PERU
BOLIVIA
CHILE
Santiago
ARGENTINA
Pacific Ocean
Atlantic Ocean

Official name: Republic of Chile
Government: Republic
Capital city: Santiago
Area: 291,954 mi²; 756,102 km²
Population (2009 est.): 16,601,707
Language: Spanish
Monetary unit: Chilean peso (CLP)

ECONOMIC SUMMARY:

GDP composition by sector (2008 est.): agriculture, 4.8%; industry, 50.5%; services, 44.7%
Natural resources: copper, timber, iron ore, nitrates, precious metals, molybdenum, hydropower
Land use (2005): arable land, 2.62%; permanent crops, 0.43%; other, 96.95%
Industries: copper, other minerals, foodstuffs, fish processing, iron and steel, wood and wood products, transport equipment, cement, textiles
Agricultural products: grapes, apples, pears, onions, wheat, corn, oats, peaches, garlic, asparagus, beans, beef, poultry, wool, fish, timber
Exports (2008 est.): $66.46 billion
Commodities exported: copper, fruit, fish products, paper and pulp, chemicals, iodine, lithium, boron, wine
Imports (2008 est.): $57.61 billion
Commodities imported: petroleum and petroleum products, chemicals, electrical and telecommunications equipment, industrial machinery, vehicles, natural gas
Labor force (2008 est.): 7.267 million
Labor force by occupation (2005): agriculture, 13.2%; industry, 23%; services, 63.9%

ENERGY RESOURCES:

Electricity production (2006 est.): 50.37 billion kWh
Electricity consumption (2006 est.): 45.52 billion kWh
Electricity exports (2007 est.): 0 kWh
Electricity imports (2007 est.): 1.628 billion kWh

Natural gas production (2007 est.): 1.8 billion m³
Natural gas consumption (2007 est.): 4.2 billion m³
Natural gas exports (2007 est.): 0 m³
Natural gas imports (2007 est.): 2.4 billion m³
Natural gas proved reserves (Jan. 2008 est.): 97.97 billion m³

Oil production (2007 est.): 11,610 bbl/day
Oil imports (2006 est.): 222,900 bbl/day
Oil proved reserves (Jan. 2008 est.): 150 million bbl

Source: Data from *The World Factbook 2009.* Washington, D.C.: Central Intelligence Agency, 2009.
Notes: Data are the most recent tracked by the CIA. Values are given in U.S. dollars. Abbreviations: bbl/day = barrels per day; GDP = gross domestic product; km² = square kilometers; kWh = kilowatt-hours; m³ = cubic meters; mi² = square miles.

tered the atmosphere, and then surface and groundwater absorbed and transported it into the northern Chile's Atacama Desert, where it was oxidized to iodate and mineralized with nitrates in the caliche deposits. At first, Chile's iodine production was a by-product of the production of sodium nitrate fertilizer from the caliche deposits. Now, however, it is extracted from abandoned nitrate ores and tailings that remain from earlier nitrate mining. The caliche ores and tailings are mainly in the northern section of Chile's Central Valley, in Tarapacá and Antofagasta Provinces. The crushed caliche and tailings are leached in evaporation ponds to produce a solution containing sodium nitrate and calcium iodate. After the sodium nitrate precipitates in the ponds, the remaining liquid is stripped of iodine. About 60 percent of global reserves of iodine are in northern Chile. Chile accounts for 60 percent of the global production, making it the world's leading exporter of the mineral. Japan is a distant second, followed by China. Chile's production of iodine is significant, because iodine deficiency causes an increase in child mortality, mental retardation, and miscarriages. Some governments now require food manufacturers to include iodine in certain food products as a means of preventing maladies associated with iodine deficiency.

LITHIUM

Most of the world's lithium is mined in Chile. Lithium is a rare metallic element that is concentrated naturally in two main settings. It mineralizes in an igneous environment during the formation of silicic and pegmatite rocks and it appears in salt compounds as lithium carbonate and lithium chloride in dry lake beds of deserts. Thus, mining lithium involves hard-rock mining or salt-mining in ancient lake beds. Both forms of lithium concentration are rare geographically, but the lithium in lake-bed salts (or brines) is much easier to mine. Hard-rock mining was the primary source of lithium until miners discovered that certain lake beds in northern Chile had significant deposits of the metal. The first Chilean mine started producing lithium in 1986. In 1997, Chile replaced hard-rock mining operations in the United States, where most of the world production of lithium was taking place, and became the world's leading exporter of lithium. Chile provides about 40 percent of global supply, outpacing Australia, which was the second largest producer in 2008. Chile has three-fourths of the world's reserves of lithium. The mineral is mined

from the brines in *salars* in northern Chile's Atacama Desert. The deposits there are in a series of basins. The Chilean company Sociedad Química y Minera (SQM) mines the Salar de Atacama, which contributes more than 50 percent of the world's lithium. The SQM operation also produces potassium sulfate as a by-product. Two processing plants in Antofagasta, a seaport in northern Chile, refine and package the lithium for shipment overseas. Among other uses, lithium has become important in the manufacture of rechargeable batteries for hybrid cars, laptop computers, and cell phones.

BORON

Chile accounts for about 10 percent of the global production of boron. In 2006, it ranked fourth in world production behind Turkey, the United States, and Argentina, in descending order. Chile's borate deposits are in high-desert basins in the Puna region of the Andes Mountains, which overlaps the borders of Chile, Argentina, and Bolivia. In Chile, borate deposits are found in two formations, *salar* and caliche. Both formations are at about the same depth below the surface. *Salar* deposits are what remain after lake water evaporates. Chile has a large number of dry lake beds, but only six (Ascotan, Aguas Calientes Sur, Atacama, Quisquiro, Pajonales, and Surire) contain commercial borate. The borate is in layers that average between 1 to 2 meters below the surface and range from 1 centimeter to 1 meter thick. The second source of borate is caliche, a puzzling layer of sodium nitrate in the Atacama Desert, Chile's northern coastal desert. No one knows for sure how the caliche formed. The most common theory is that rocks in the moist Andes experienced underground weathering that produced nitrate salts, which contained borate compounds, and then groundwater seepage transported the salts to the lower valleys of the Atacama Desert. The nitrates accumulated near the surface there through a process driven by surface evaporation and hygroscopic and capillary activity. The resulting ore grade nitrates accumulated from 1 to 5 meters below the surface in a vast, almost continuous deposit that stretches north-south for 700 kilometers and east-west for a distance of 10 to 150 kilometers.

There are two large boron mining operations in the northern desert. The largest producer of borate is Quiborax. The company has mining operations at Salar de Surire near the Bolivian border. It has smaller operations on Salars Ascotan and Pajonales, and it operates a boric acid plant in the northern seaport town of Antofagasta. The second company is SQM, which produces boric acid as a by-product of its lithium mining operation on Salar de Atacama. Chilean boric acid and other boron-based products are exported to the United States, Brazil, and several countries in Asia. In addition to boric acid, boron-based compounds are used in the manufacture of such items as cosmetics, soaps and detergents, flame retardants, glazes on ceramics, and fiberglass.

FORESTS

Forestry is the most important economic activity of southern Chile. Large, privately owned sawmills dot the landscape. Band saws cut straight-trunk logs of fir and araucaria pine into narrow slabs of quality lumber for export. Each mill has a wood chipper that makes chips from low-grade wood. Pulp mills turn the chips into an oatmeal-like pulp. The mills then process the pulp into paper, cardboard, and particleboard products. The chemical industry also uses the pulp. Chile's forestry industry specializes in making wood pulp; only Canada, the United States, Brazil, and Sweden produce more. Chile has been the world's sixth largest exporter of wood chips, pulp, and waste paper. China and Italy are the main trading partners for the Chilean exports.

In order to conserve natural forest areas, the pulp industry depends heavily on fast-growing, commercially planted trees, such as eucalyptus (from Australia) and radiata pine (from Austria). About one-half of Chile's pulp production comes from such trees. Southern Chile's west coast marine climate is most conducive to the fastest tree growth, making Puerto Montt and the Chiloé Island the main pulp and lumber centers. Wood chips, pulp, lumber, and other wood products are the region's most valuable export. Japan, the United States, and Germany import most of these products.

A massive mining truck rolls past Chile's Andina copper mine, one of the largest in the world. (Ivan Alvarado/Reuters/Landov)

FISH

The nutrient-rich waters of the Humboldt Current are the main basis of Chile's large fishing industry. The nation ranks in the top five in the world production. Northern Chile contributes a great deal to this status. The catch includes anchovy, jack mackerel, and pilchard. Iquique, in the north, is one of the world's principal ports for its huge fishmeal exports. Fishmeal is ground-up dried fish. Anchovies, in particular, make up this product. Fishmeal is high in protein and therefore an excellent livestock food supplement. Fish oil, a by-product of fishmeal production, is an additive for the manufacture of many items, ranging from margarine to inedible varnishes and waterproofing agents. Every three to seven years, El Niño warming events cause declines in fish populations in northern Chilean coastal waters, which hurt the economy of the region. Anchovy populations, in particular, decline during these events.

Fishing for export is also a chief income source in southern Chile; Puerto Aisén is the area's main fishing port. This region is known for its salmon farming, which involves raising salmon in enormous floating cages tied to the seabed. Beginning in 1990, fish farming grew steadily and became increasingly important to Chile's total exports. Chilean salmon has become known for its boneless salmon filets and delicate smoked sliced salmon. However, the industry has been plagued by a parasitic bacterium, *rickettsia*, carried by sea lice, which causes infection-prone lesions. Nevertheless, Chile is the second largest exporter of salmon after Norway, thanks largely to Aisén's contribution of caught and farmed salmon. In value of exports, fishing ranks second behind forestry in southern Chile.

AGRICULTURAL LAND

Due in part to a favorable environment, middle Chile is a major center for agricultural exports. The area has more than 50 percent of the country's total agricultural landholdings. Most of the production takes place in the Central Valley section. Because of the fertile soils, reliable water supply, and mild climate of the valley, the country's annual export earnings from fruits and nuts alone are between $1 and $2 billion per year. The country consistently ranks in the top ten for fruit exportation. Vineyards for table grapes and wine-making take up more land than any other fruit crop in the Central Valley. The production is for the international market. Each summer, the area's table grapes, as well as strawberries and raspberries, are the first in Chile to ripen and the first to hit U.S. supermarkets, usually around Christmas. The Central Valley is responsible for the nation's high world ranking in exports of wine as well as table grapes. Grains are also widespread in the middle Chile region, particularly wheat, which occupies more than half the cropland. Fruit trees occupy much of the remaining land. The Mediterranean climate of middle Chile also allows the planting of commercial orchards of apples and avocados, which are extensive in hilly sections of the region. Other tree crops include lemons, oranges, nectarines, kiwifruits, and cherries.

OTHER RESOURCES

Chile accounts for a wide range of other industrial minerals. It accounts for approximately 7 percent of the global supply of gold, 6 percent of selenium, 3 percent of sulfur, 2.6 percent of phosphate rock, 2.5 percent of silver, 2.5 percent of salt, and between 2 percent of both diatomite and potash. The country's copper mines produce some of the silver, gold, selenium, and molybdenum, as the same geologic environment forms these minerals. Chile ranks relatively high in world production of each metal.

Richard A. Crooker

FURTHER READING

Anyadike, Nnamdi. *Copper: A Material for the New Millennium.* Cambridge, Cambridgeshire, England: Woodhead, 2002.

Central Intelligence Agency. *CIA Fact Book.* New York: Skyhorse, 2007.

Crooker, Richard A. *Chile.* Edgemont, Pa.: Chelsea House, 2004.

Garrett, Donald E. *Borates: Handbook of Deposits, Processing, Properties, and Use.* San Diego, Calif.: Academic Press, 1998.

Kogel, Jessica Elzea, et al., eds. *Industrial Minerals and Rocks: Commodities, Markets, and Uses.* 7th ed. Littleton, Colo.: U.S. Society for Mining, Metallurgy, and Exploration, 2006.

Moreno, Teresa, and Wes Gibbons, eds. *The Geology of Chile.* London: Geological Society of London, 2007.

Neira, Eduardo, Hernán Verscheure, and Carmen Revenga. *Chile's Frontier Forests: Conserving a Global Treasure.* Washington, D.C.: Global Forest Watch and World Resources Institute, 2002.

Rector, John Lawrence. *The History of Chile.* Westport, Conn.: Greenwood Press, 2005.

WEB SITES

CENTRAL INTELLIGENCE AGENCY
The World Fact Book
https://www.cia.gov/library/publications/the-
world-factbook/index.html

INTERNATIONAL COPPER STUDY GROUP
http://www.icsg.org/

INTERNATIONAL TRADE CENTRE
Countries
http://www.intracen.org/menus/countries.htm

U.S. GEOLOGICAL SURVEY
Minerals Information
http://minerals.usgs.gov/minerals/

SEE ALSO: Agricultural products; Agriculture industry; Boron; Copper; Forests; Iodine; Lithium; Timber industry.

China

CATEGORIES: Countries; government and resources

China, blessed with abundant natural resources, plays a pivotal role in the global economy and the well-being of Earth. China ranks first in both human resources and hydraulic-power resources. The nation's rich human resources have resulted in the production of the most cost-effective goods, which dominate the global market. The development of its hydraulic power reserves and use of other natural resources have made China's economy one of the top in the world.

THE COUNTRY

China, a country that occupies a vast territory with a diverse climate, varied topography, and great variety of flora and fauna, is situated in East and Southeast Asia. Its land extends from longitude 73° east (in the west) to 135° east, a stretch of more than 5,100 kilometers. From north to south, it spans from latitude 53° north to 4° north, covering a distance of 5,471 kilometers. With such a vast expanse, China is rich in land, water, climate, biological, mineral, energy, and tourism resources.

China, with a total area of approximately 9.6 million square kilometers, ranks as the third or fourth (depending on the territory counted) largest nation in the world. About one-third of it is mountainous, with plateaus and high mountains dominating the west, while lower lands and plains lace the central and eastern region. As a result of this tilting topography, major rivers flow from west to east. These include the world-famous Chang (also known as Yangtze) and Huang (also known as Yellow) rivers, both of which empty into the Pacific.

The vast territory, varied climate zones, and diverse topography provide suitable habitats for a rich flora and fauna. China is considered a mega-diversity country. Overall, an estimated thirty-two thousand species of flowering plants exist in China. More than five thousand species of vertebrates spread across the land, accounting for 11 percent of the world's total. China is also the most populated country on Earth. Utilizing its available resources and a double-digit annual gross-domestic-product growth, which began in 1982, China's economy has climbed to the third in the world, closing in on Japan for second. However, that achievement comes at a price of environmental peril. Should China expect to continue growing economically, sustainability has to be the focal point for the future.

ARABLE LAND RESOURCES

China ranks third among world nations in total territory, behind Russia and Canada. However, because of its large population and vast mountain ranges in the north and west, China's per capita total land resource accounts for only one-third of the world's average. The average arable land per capita is only 0.1 hectare, ranking sixty-seventh in the world. China's forestland averages about 0.1 hectare per capita, ranking 121st in the world. There has been a steady decline in both farm and forestland because of erosions, desertification, road construction, and urbanization.

China's land resources can be divided into many soil types: red, yellow, brown, cinnamon, black, chernozem, chestnut, desert, saline-alkali, marshland, mountain, and a variety of implicit domains. These varied soil types are formed as a result of combined effects by topography, climate, and human influences. The principal uses of the land resources fall into six categories: arable land, grassland, forest, alpine desert, desert, and permanent snow and glacier area.

The 122 million hectares of arable land can be further divided into irrigated land, paddy fields, and dry land, each accounting for 22, 26, and 52 percent of the total, respectively. The arable land distribution is

China: Resources at a Glance

Official name: People's Republic of China
Government: Communist state
Capital city: Beijing
Area: 3,705,677 mi²; 9,596,961 km²
Population (2009 est.): 1,338,612,968
Language: Standard Chinese or Mandarin
Monetary unit: renminbi (CNY)

ECONOMIC SUMMARY:

GDP composition by sector (2008 est.): agriculture, 11.3%; industry, 48.6%; services, 40.1%
Natural resources: coal, iron ore, petroleum, natural gas, mercury, tin, tungsten, antimony, manganese, molybdenum, vanadium, magnetite, aluminum, lead, zinc, uranium, hydropower potential (world's largest)
Land use (2005): arable land, 14.86%; permanent crops, 1.27%; other, 83.87%
Industries: mining and ore processing, iron, steel, aluminum, and other metals, coal; machine building; armaments; textiles and apparel; petroleum; cement; chemicals; fertilizers; consumer products, including footwear, toys, and electronics; food processing; transportation equipment, including automobiles, rail cars and locomotives, ships, and aircraft; telecommunications equipment, commercial space launch vehicles, satellites
Agricultural products: rice, wheat, potatoes, corn, peanuts, tea, millet, barley, apples, cotton, oilseed, pork, fish
Exports (2008 est.): $1.435 trillion
Commodities exported: electrical and other machinery, including data processing equipment, apparel, textiles, iron and steel, optical and medical equipment
Imports (2008 est.): $1.074 trillion
Commodities imported: electrical and other machinery, oil and mineral fuels, optical and medical equipment, metal ores, plastics, organic chemicals
Labor force (2008 est.): 807.3 million
Labor force by occupation (2006 est.): agriculture, 43%; industry, 25%; services, 32%

ENERGY RESOURCES:

Electricity production (2007): 3.256 trillion kWh
Electricity consumption (2007): 3.271 trillion kWh
Electricity exports (2007 est.): 14.56 billion kWh
Electricity imports (2007 est.): 4.251 billion kWh

Natural gas production (2007 est.): 69.27 billion m³
Natural gas consumption (2007 est.): 70.51 billion m³
Natural gas exports (2007 est.): 5.36 billion m³
Natural gas imports (2007 est.): 3.871 billion m³
Natural gas proved reserves (Jan. 2008 est.): 2.265 trillion m³

Oil production (2008 est.): 3.725 million bbl/day
Oil imports (2007): 4.21 million bbl/day
Oil proved reserves (Jan. 2008 est.): 19.6 billion bbl

Source: Data from *The World Factbook 2009.* Washington, D.C.: Central Intelligence Agency, 2009.
Notes: Data are the most recent tracked by the CIA. Values are given in U.S. dollars. Abbreviations: bbl/day = barrels per day; GDP = gross domestic product; km² = square kilometers; kWh = kilowatt-hours; m³ = cubic meters; mi² = square miles.

very uneven, mostly concentrated in areas of the North China Plain, Northeast China Plain, the Chang River Plain, Sichuan basin, and the Pearl River Delta. The flat, deep soil of the North China Plain supports production of food crops, including wheat, corn, millet, sorghum, and cotton and fruit crops of apples, pears, and grapes. The black, fertile soil in the northeast is productive for wheat, corn, soybeans, flax, and sugar beets. The Chang River Plain and Sichuan basin, known as the "land of plenty," produce rice, citrus, broad beans, and freshwater fish.

Other Land Resources

The total area of grassland in China is about 400 million hectares, of which 225 million hectares are considered usable. The grassland stretches from northeast to southwest for a span of more than 3,000 kilometers and is home to many animal husbandry bases. Nei Monggol has China's largest pastureland, where the well-known Sanhe cattle, Sanhe horses, and Mongolian sheep reside. Another important natural pasture and livestock breeding and production base is situated in the north and south of Tian Shan as well as the Xinjiang Uygur autonomous region, where the famous Ili horses and Xinjiang fine-wool sheep are raised.

Forestland in China accounts for 134 million hectares. The per-capita forestland is only one-sixth of the world's average. The forestland covers only 14 percent of total land area, much lower than the world's average of 22 percent. Forest distribution is also uneven. Manchuria, a vast plain bracketed by two mountain ranges, the Da Xingan Mountains to the west and the Xiao Xingan to the east, contains China's richest and most accessible timber resources. Coniferous trees—including spruce, pine, fir, larch, and juniper—dominate the landscape. Broadleaf species include birch, aspen, willow, and mountain ash. The second largest natural forests are found in southwest China, where the main tree species include spruce, fir, Yunnan pine, camphor, mahogany, and precious teak. Using its lumber and cheap labor, China has become a major exporter of furniture, plywood, doors, cabinets, and many other wood products.

The alpine desert, occupying about 15 million hectares, mainly located in the northern Tibet plateau, supports only sporadic grazing in scattered areas. Desert accounts for 64 million hectares, of which the Gobi alone takes up 46 million hectares. The climate is arid, with extreme fluctuations of temperature between day and night. All plants and wildlife here are adapted to arid and harsh climate. Drought-adapted shrubs include the gray sparrow's saltwort, gray sagebrush, saxaul, and low grasses, such as needle grass and bridle grass. Notable animals include the Asiatic wild ass, Asiatic ibex, black-tailed gazelle, wild camel, wild horses, jerboa, Gobi wolf, golden eagle, leopard, and lizards. The Gobi bear is one of the world's most endangered animals, with a total population of less than fifty.

Water Resources

China is very rich in water resources. The total water reserve is about 2.8 trillion cubic meters, ranking fifth in the world, but the per-capita average is less than 25 percent of the world's average. In addition, the distribution of the water resources is highly uneven; they are more concentrated in the south and east, much less in the northwest. The total length of all rivers in China is 430,000 kilometers. There are more than 50,000 rivers with a drainage area of at least 100 square kilometers each, 1,580 rivers with a drainage area of 1,000 square kilometers, and 79 of them with drainage areas exceeding 10,000 square kilometers. More than 20 rivers stretch at least 1,000 kilometers, among which the Chang and Huang are the two longest.

China's river system exhibits some unique characteristics. Most of the rivers flow from west to east, emptying into the Pacific. Only a few in the southwest flow in a north-south direction. The vast majority of the drainage areas are located in the southeast of the outflow basin, with a total covered area of 612 million hectares, or almost 64 percent of the land. In addition, the upper reaches of many rivers run through canyons or run as mountain torrents. The steep gradient creates strong and rapid water currents, which have great hydropower potential. The middle and lower reaches of many rivers weave through vast, flat plains. The wide surface and slow flow ensure use of water resources for irrigation, fisheries, and transportation.

There are about 24,900 natural lakes across China, with 13 great lakes, each covering more than 100,000 hectares of surface area. Most freshwater lakes are located in the eastern region, accounting for 45 percent of the total lake surface. These include the famous Bo Yang, Dongting, Hongze, Tai, and Chao. The majority of the lagoons are distributed in the west, including the well-known Qinghai Lake. A great number of glaciers in western China are also major reserves for both surface and groundwater, covering an area of 5.8 million hectares. The total storage capacity is 2.7 trillion cubic meters, or almost equal to China's total annual runoff.

In addition to fisheries and transportation, irrigation, hydration, industrial, and numerous other uses, water resources in China are a significant energy reserve. The total hydrological power reserve is estimated at 680 million kilowatts, ranking first in the world. Of the total, 380 million kilowatts can be developed to generate 1.9 trillion kilowatt-hours of electricity, which contribute a great deal to China's economic development and the world economy.

CLIMATE RESOURCES

China's vast territory spans multiple climate zones from the south to the north, including tropical, subtropical, warm temperate, temperate, and boreal. In addition, the Qinghai-Tibet Plateau has a unique alpine region. Nevertheless, the subtropical, warm temperate, and temperate climate zones compose approximately 70 percent of the country. As diverse as the climate is, the basic characteristic is a continental monsoon climate, which exhibits three main features: substantial daily and seasonal temperature differential; uneven precipitation distribution, with a steady drop from the southeast to the northwest by a dramatic 40:1 ratio; and dramatic wind turnover between winter and summer. During the winter, cold and dry air from high latitude rises from the north. In summer, warm and humid wind comes mainly from the ocean in the southeast.

The average annual temperatures in the eastern region descend from south to north, from 25° Celsius to 5.5° Celsius. Most of the western Qinghai-Tibet Plateau has annual average temperatures below 0° Celsius, but the Tarim basin is 10° Celsius. The temperature differential in the summer between the south and north is small, only 10° Celsius. In the winter, however, the temperature difference between these two regions can be as much as 50° Celsius. The lowest temperature in the Mohe area can dip below −50° Celsius. The average annual precipitation across China is 629 millimeters, with a steady decline in annual precipitation from southeast to northwest, which is somewhat similar to the annual temperature patterns. In general, high precipitation is concentrated in the summer months. Based on the annual rainfall pattern, China's areas can be divided into 32 percent subhumid, 18 percent semihumid, 19 percent semiarid, and 31 percent arid.

The temperature and annual precipitation pattern results in a concentrated distribution of agriculture in central and southeast provinces and the Sichuan basin, areas that are the foundation of China's economy. The vast territory in the northwest is not productive and contributes little to China's agriculture.

BIOLOGICAL RESOURCES

China is blessed with rich biological resources. It has more wild animal species than any other country. Vertebrates alone account for 5,200 species, 11 percent of the world's total. Of these animals, 499 species are mammals, 1,186 are birds, 376 are reptiles, 279 are amphibians, and 2,804 are fish. This wildlife consists of many endemic species, including some of the most well-known and rare animals: the giant panda, golden-haired monkey, Chinese alligator, crested ibis, white-lipped deer, South China tiger, red-crowned crane, brown-eared pheasant, and Yangtze River dolphin (though this animal is thought to be extinct).

The diverse flora in China includes twenty-five thousand species of seed plants. From the tropical rain forests to the boreal coniferous forests, China has almost all the natural vegetation characteristic of the Northern Hemisphere. The two hundred or so species of gymnosperms account for 25 percent of the world's total. In addition, there are seven thousand species of woody plants and twenty-nine hundred species of trees. Several endemic plant species are considered as "living fossils," including ginkgo, metasequoia, and golden pine.

China has more than five thousand years of agricultural history, during which time the country has contributed many major crops important to humankind, including rice, soybeans, peaches, pears, plums, dates, grapefruit, lychees, and tea. Based on their utilization, China has one thousand plant species for timber wood, three hundred starchy plants, more than ninety vegetable species, and six hundred oil species. Its crops and germplasm continue to make vital contributions to the world's economy.

MINERAL RESOURCES

China possesses deposits of all the discovered minerals. China's total reserve of 146 mineral resources ranks the country third among world nations. Coal, with a proved reserve of 877 billion metric tons, is found mainly in northern China, including the provinces of Shaanxi, Liaoning, Nei Monggol, and Heilongjiang. Among the 250 or so petroliferous basins identified, more than half of them (130) are under development.

The identified iron-ore reserves are estimated at 41 billion metric tons and distributed in multiple regions. China also ranks among leading nations in reserves of minerals such as tungsten, tin, antimony, zinc, molybdenum, lead, and mercury. China's rare earth reserves are more than the rest of the world's total combined. In fact, China accounts for 80 percent of the world's total reserves in that category. The diverse minerals and their large reserves provide important raw materials and energy sources that will continue to power China's economic growth and development.

In 1996, China established a thorough (although not perfect) legal system for the exploration and exploitation of its minerals. This system consists of many laws, regulations, and rules promulgated by different levels of government authorities. On one hand, China has encouraged foreign investment in mineral resources exploration and new mining technologies. On the other hand, China imports minerals from other countries and invests heavily in acquiring mineral resources abroad. In 2008, China bought more than half of Australia's mineral exports. China has become the world's largest consumer of raw materials.

ENERGY RESOURCES

China is rich in energy resources, but their distribution is uneven. China ranks third among world nations in energy reserves and output, with a total energy production equivalent to 11 billion metric tons of standard coal. In 2007, China's coal output was 2.3 billion metric tons, which was top among countries; its crude oil output was 172 million metric tons, which ranked fifth; and its power generation capacity was 720 gigawatts, which was fourth. Gas production reached 76 billion cubic meters in 2007.

China relies heavily on coal for energy, but 80 percent of the coal reserves are concentrated in the north. The most economically developed eight provinces south of the Chang River account for only 2 percent of the total coal reserves. About 85 percent of the proved oil reserves are concentrated in the east region, north of the Chang. Sixty-eight percent of hydraulic power developed is in the southwest region. China has addressed the low energy reserves in the economically vibrant south through the construction of nuclear power plants.

The rapid economic growth and development that began in 1982 have created an insatiable demand for fossil fuel (oil and gas) that far exceeds China's own production capacity. Thus, China became a major importer of oil beginning in the early 1990's. China imported 162 million metric tons of crude oil in 2007. A limit to China's storage capacity is the only reason that figure is not higher. That limit will soon change as China builds more strategic oil reserve facilities in the western region. In short, China has become the world's second largest energy user, trailing only the United States. With an ever-increasing demand for oil, China is a driving force for energy consumption. This in turn will have a significant impact on the world economy and environment.

OTHER RESOURCES

China is a country rich in tourism resources. Its vast territory and complex topography provide visitors to China with year-round opportunities. The natural scenery in the north presents thousands of kilometers of glaciers and snowy land during the winter. The southern regions provide tourists with lush scenes of vegetation. China's exotic flora and fauna, found in its many national nature reserves, attract tourists of all ages. China is dotted with magnificent rivers, lakes, mountains, and canyons. Its long cultural history has produced numerous world-class attractions. In addition, the relatively low cost of travel and lodging, combined with the world's burgeoning desire to know China, has fueled the powerful tourism engine in China.

As one of the world's four ancient civilizations, China is full of historical sites and cultural relics. Some of the most famous attractions include the Great Wall, the Terracotta Army, Ming Tombs, Peking Man, and many other attractions of historical and cultural significance.

Ming Y. Zheng

FURTHER READING

Forney, Matthew. "China's Quest for Oil." *Time* (October 18, 2004).

Lew, Alan A., and Lawrence Yu. *Tourism in China: Geographic, Political, and Economic Perspectives.* Boulder, Colo.: Westview Press, 1995.

National Geographic Society. *National Geographic Atlas of China.* Washington, D.C.: Author, 2007.

Sheehan, Peter. *Implications of China's Rising Energy Use.* Singapore: World Scientific, 2008.

Xie, Jian, et al. *Addressing China's Water Scarcity: Recommendations for Selected Water Resource Management Issues.* Washington, D.C.: World Bank, 2009.

Zhang, Q., et al. "Precipitation, Temperature, and Runoff Analysis from 1950 to 2002 in the Yangtze Basin, China." *Hydrological Sciences Journal* 50, no. 1 (2005): 65-80.

WEB SITE

CIA WORLD FACTBOOK
https://www.cia.gov/library/publications/the-world-factbook/

SEE ALSO: Agricultural products; Agriculture industry; Ecozones and biogeographic realms; Energy politics; Hydrogen; Population growth; Three Gorges Dam.

Chlorites

CATEGORY: Mineral and other nonliving resources

Chlorites are most commonly found as microscopic particles in clays. They are also found in metamorphic rocks such as schists. Metamorphic chlorites are commonly found in Michigan, Norway, the United Kingdom, and Japan. Chlorites also occur in igneous rocks as a product of biopyriboles that have been transformed by heat and moisture. They may also be found in sedimentary rocks formed from pieces of older igneous or metamorphic rocks containing chlorites.

DEFINITION

The term "chlorite" (from the Greek word for "green") refers to a variety of hydrous aluminum silicates of magnesium, iron, and other metals. They are soft green minerals with a glassy luster. Chlorites are brittle and can be ground into white or pale green powder easily. Thin sheets of chlorite are flexible but not elastic.

Chlorites are a group of silicate minerals consisting of alternating layers of molecules forming two kinds of two-dimensional sheets. One layer consists of silicate groups (one silicon atom bonded to four oxygen atoms) bound to aluminum atoms, hydroxyl groups (one oxygen atom bonded to one hydrogen atom), and magnesium, iron, or other metallic atoms. The other layer consists of magnesium, iron, aluminum, or other metallic atoms bound to hydroxyl groups. If most of the metallic atoms other than aluminum are magnesium, the mineral is known as clinochlore. If

the metallic atoms are iron, it is known as chamosite. If they are nickel, it is known as nimite. If they are manganese, it is known as pennantite. These four minerals are very similar.

OVERVIEW

Chlorites are most useful in the form of clay minerals. They mix with other substances to form clays that are widely used in pottery and construction. Clay minerals are also used in drilling "muds" (thick suspensions used to lubricate rotary drills). They may also be used as catalysts in petroleum refining and to decolorize vegetable oils.

The density of chlorite ranges from 2.6 to 3.3 grams per cubic centimeter. On the Mohs scale, they have a hardness between 2 and 2.5; they are generally soft enough to be scratched with a fingernail.

Chlorite usually exists as a microscopic component of clay, along with organic material, quartz, and other minerals. Visible pieces of chlorite may be found within a variety of rocks, particularly metamorphic rocks such as the very common schists.

Chlorites are chemically similar to other clay minerals (hydrous aluminum silicates) and are often found in combination with them. They are generally more resistant to heat than other clay minerals are. This fact is used to detect chlorite within clays. A sample of the clay is heated to between 500° and 700° Celsius, which breaks down the other clay minerals. X-ray diffraction is then used to detect the layers of silicate chains that are characteristic of clay minerals. If this pattern is detected, chlorite is present in the sample. In other regards chlorites have about the same properties as other clay minerals.

Rose Secrest

SEE ALSO: Aluminum; Clays; Metamorphic processes, rocks, and mineral deposits; Silicates.

Chromium

CATEGORY: Mineral and other nonliving resources

WHERE FOUND

Chromium is a moderately abundant element that does not occur free in nature. Its principal ore is known as chromite, (Fe,Mg) $(Cr,Al)_2O_4$. The world's chromite resources are concentrated in the Eastern

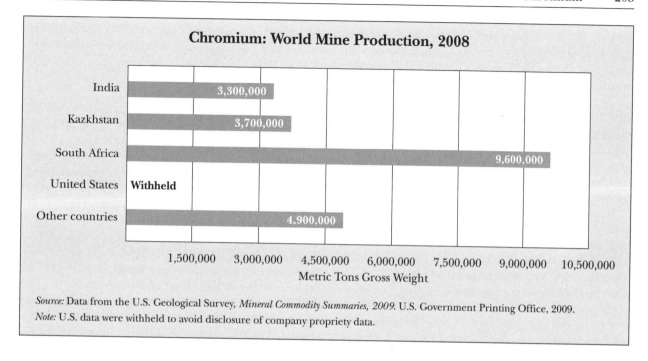

Chromium: World Mine Production, 2008

India — 3,300,000
Kazkhstan — 3,700,000
South Africa — 9,600,000
United States — **Withheld**
Other countries — 4,900,000

Metric Tons Gross Weight

Source: Data from the U.S. Geological Survey, *Mineral Commodity Summaries, 2009*. U.S. Government Printing Office, 2009.
Note: U.S. data were withheld to avoid disclosure of company propriety data.

Hemisphere, with major producers including South Africa, Kazakhstan, India, Zimbabwe, Turkey, Finland, and Brazil.

PRIMARY USES

Chromium is a strategic and critical resource used principally in the production of alloys and superalloys, stainless steel, refractory materials, pigments, and chemicals. It is used for dyeing textiles and leather tanning and as a laboratory glassware cleanser. Furthermore, chromium in its trivalent oxidation state is an essential trace nutrient for humans and other mammals.

TECHNICAL DEFINITION

Chromium (abbreviated Cr), atomic number 24, is a metallic chemical element belonging to Group VIB of the periodic table of the elements. It has four naturally occurring isotopes and an average molecular weight of 51.996. Pure chromium is silver-gray, brittle, and hard. Its specific gravity is 7.19 at 20° Celsius, its melting point is approximately 1,890° Celsius, and its boiling point is 2,200° Celsius. This lustrous metal will take a high polish and does not tarnish in air. In chemical compounds chromium may have oxidation states ranging from −2 to +6, but in most compounds it is trivalent (+3) or hexavalent (+6). The trivalent state is more common in naturally occurring compounds, while hexavalent chromium is frequently found in industrial applications.

DESCRIPTION, DISTRIBUTION, AND FORMS

Chromium is a commercially important metallic element. Forming compounds with brilliant red, yellow, and green hues, it derives its name from the Greek *chroma* (color). Its concentration in the lithosphere is 100 grams per metric ton. Total world production of chromite is about 20 million metric tons. Trivalent chromium, the form most often found in nature, is a trace element in the human body; by contrast, hexavalent chromium is a highly toxic substance whose concentrations in the environment are regulated by law.

Approximately 95 percent of the world's chromium resources are found in southern Africa, with South Africa the leading producer in the region. Other world producers include Kazakhstan, India, Turkey, Finland, Brazil, and Russia. Chromium is present in a number of minerals, but chromite is its only commercial ore. Primary deposits of chromite occur as stratiform and podiform ores found in certain types of ultrabasic (low-silica) rocks. Secondary alluvial deposits of chromite are formed by the weathering of stratiform (layered) and podiform ores.

Stratiform chromite deposits are often several meters thick, extend over large areas, have a relatively uniform composition, and frequently include platinum-bearing zones. They formed as chromite crystallized and precipitated from silicate melts. Examples include the Bushveld Igneous Complex in Transvaal, South Africa; the Great Dyke in Zimbabwe; and the Stillwater Complex in Montana. Stratiform deposits constitute more than 90 percent of the world's identified chromite reserves. All the commercially significant stratiform chromites are Precambrian in age and occur in stable cratons, portions of the Earth's crust that have experienced little deformation over a long period of geologic time.

In podiform deposits, chromite occurs as irregular pods or lenses within the host rock. Major podiform deposits are found in Kazakhstan, Albania, Greece, Turkey, Zimbabwe, Cuba, and the Philippines. Podiform chromites form along island arcs and mobile mountain belts, and most are of Paleozoic age or younger.

Chromium occurs in nature only in combination with other elements. The most important chromium ore is chromite, a brownish-black to iron-black mineral of the spinel group. It occurs as octahedral crystals, irregular masses, and alluvial deposits. Other minerals that contain chromium include the gemstones emerald and aquamarine, which owe their distinctive colors to the element.

Chromium plays a role in the body's glucose tolerance. Moderate amounts of trivalent chromium in the diet have no apparent harmful effects. Chromium metal is biologically inert and has no known toxicity.

While trivalent chromium compounds exhibit little or no toxicity, hexavalent chromium is a systemic poison and an irritant and corrosive. It can be absorbed by ingestion, inhalation, or dermal exposure. Ulcerations of the skin and mucous membranes may result from exposure. Chromate salts are suspected human carcinogens that may produce tumors of the lungs, nasal cavity, and paranasal sinuses. The 1974 Safe Drinking Water Act set the maximum allowable concentration for total chromium in drinking water in the United States at 100 micrograms per liter.

In general, chromium does not naturally occur in high concentrations in water. Elevated chromium levels in surface water or groundwater are typical because of contamination from runoff from old mining operations or improper disposal of electroplating wastes. However, in the groundwater of Paradise Valley in Maricopa County, Arizona, hexavalent chromium of natural origin is present in concentrations exceeding 200 micrograms per liter. The alkaline groundwater causes naturally occurring trivalent chromium in the soil to oxidize to soluble hexavalent chromium.

HISTORY

Chromium appears to have been unknown to ancient civilizations. It was discovered in 1797 by Louis-Nicolas Vauquelin, a French chemist, when he found that the lead in a sample of crocoite ($PbCrO_4$) from Siberia was combined with an unknown oxide mineral. Between the time of chromium's discovery and 1827, the primary source of chromite was the Ural Mountains of Russia. In 1827, the discovery of chromite in Maryland moved the United States to the forefront of world production. Large Turkish deposits were developed in the 1860's; after this time, the Eastern Hemisphere became the chief source of chromite. The chemical manufacturing industry was the main consumer of chromium until the early 1900's, when the element found increasing use in metallurgical and refractory products. During World Wars I and II, the United States increased its domestic production of the metal, and during the 1950's it stockpiled domestic ores. International political conflicts have often led to interruptions in chromium supply.

OBTAINING CHROMIUM

Sodium dichromate, from which most commercial chromium compounds are made, is produced by roasting chromite with sodium carbonate, leaching the resulting product with water, and concentrating and acidifying the leachate to cause sodium dichromate to precipitate. Ferrochromium is prepared from chromite by reducing the ore with carbon in a blast furnace. Metallic chromium is obtained by reducing chromium oxide with aluminum or carbon, or by electrolyzing a solution of ferrochromium dissolved in sulfuric acid after the iron has been removed from the solution as ferrous ammonium sulfate. Chromium metal in its purest form is produced in small quantities by vapor deposition from anhydrous chromium iodide.

USES OF CHROMIUM

The principal use of chromium is as an alloy metal, particularly in the steel industry. Combined with other metals, it imparts hardness, strength, and resistance to corrosion and heat. Chromium facilitates the hardening of steel and, if the alloy's carbon content is high, enables it to withstand extreme abrasion and wear. In ball-bearing steel, chromium improves the elastic limit and imparts an evenly distributed hardness. Chromium increases the corrosion resistance of stainless steel and is an important alloy metal in heat-resisting steels. High-chromium steel, with its high resistance to wear, is used for making items such as die blocks, press plates, chisels, hacksaw blades, and circular steel saws. Nichrome, an alloy of nickel and chromium, is used as a heating element in household appliances such as electric toasters and coffeepots. Stellite, an extremely hard alloy of cobalt, chromium, and tungsten with minor amounts of iron, silicon, and carbon, is used in metal cutting tools and wear-resistant surfaces. A similar alloy, which employs molybdenum rather than tungsten, is used in surgical tools. With its hardness and nontarnishing properties, chromium is also an ideal electroplating metal. Chromium's uses in alloys and plating make it an important strategic and critical metal.

Chromite is a valuable raw material for the manufacture of refractory materials such as refractory bricks, foundry sand, and casting items for furnaces used in metallurgy. Refractory materials are able to withstand high temperatures and contact with often corrosive gases and molten materials. Chromite is frequently used in combination with other refractory materials; for instance, mixed with the magnesium ore magnesite (magnesium carbonate) and fused in an arc furnace it is cast into refractory brick.

Various chromates and dichromates, salts of chromic acid, are used as pigments in paints and dyes, yielding vivid yellows, reds, oranges, and greens. Chromium hydroxide is used as a mordant in textile dyeing. Potassium dichromate mixed with sulfuric acid is used as a cleanser for laboratory glassware. Chromium compounds are also used in chemical manufacture and leather tanning.

Karen N. Kähler

FURTHER READING

Adriano, Domy C. "Chromium." In *Trace Elements in Terrestrial Environments: Biogeochemistry, Bioavailability, and Risks of Metals.* 2d ed. New York: Springer, 2001.

Greenwood, N. N., and A. Earnshaw. "Chromium, Molybdenum, and Tungsten." In *Chemistry of the Elements.* 2d ed. Boston: Butterworth-Heinemann, 1997.

Guertin, Jacques, et al., eds. *Chromium (VI) Handbook.* Boca Raton, Fla.: CRC Press, 2005.

Independent Environmental Technical Evaluation Group. *Chromium (VI) Handbook.* Edited by Jacques Guertin, James A. Jacobs, and Cynthia P. Avakian. Boca Raton, Fla.: CRC Press, 2005.

Katz, Sidney A., and Harry Salem. *The Biological and Environmental Chemistry of Chromium.* New York: VCH, 1994.

Kogel, Jessica Elzea, et al., eds. "Chromite." In *Industrial Minerals and Rocks: Commodities, Markets, and Uses.* 7th ed. Littleton, Colo.: Society for Mining, Metallurgy, and Exploration, 2006.

Manning, D. A. C. *Introduction to Industrial Minerals.* New York: Chapman & Hall, 1995.

Nriagu, Jerome O., and Evert Nieboer, eds. *Chromium in the Natural and Human Environments.* New York: Wiley, 1988.

Udy, Marvin J. *Chemistry of Chromium and Its Compounds.* Vol 1 of *Chromium.* New York: Reinhold, 1956.

WEB SITES

NATURAL RESOURCES CANADA
Canadian Minerals Yearbook, Mineral and Metal Commodity Reviews
http://www.nrcan-rncan.gc.ca/mms-smm/busi-indu/cmy-amc/com-eng.htm

U.S. GEOLOGICAL SURVEY
Chromium: Statistics and Information
http://minerals.usgs.gov/minerals/pubs/commodity/chromium

SEE ALSO: Alloys; Brazil; India; Kazakhstan; Metals and metallurgy; Plutonic rocks and mineral deposits; Russia; South Africa; Steel; Strategic resources; Turkey; United States.

Civilian Conservation Corps

CATEGORY: Organizations, agencies, and programs
DATE: Established 1933

The Civilian Conservation Corps, a central part of Franklin D. Roosevelt's "New Deal," was conceived as a comprehensive project which would encompass relief for the unemployed, recovery of the nation's economic health, and conservation of American natural resources.

BACKGROUND

In 1934, President Franklin D. Roosevelt noted that the United States was one of the few industrialized countries that had not established a "national policy for the development of our land and water resources." This lack was in the process of rectification when, in March, 1933, shortly after his inauguration, Roosevelt proposed the establishment of the Civilian Conservation Corps (CCC). The legislation provided for the voluntary mobilization of unemployed young men to work on various conservation projects throughout the nation.

As Congress did on most of Roosevelt's proposals during his first one hundred days in office, it acted swiftly, approving the legislation on March 31, 1933. Administered by the Labor Department, the Army, the Forestry Service, and the National Park Service, the CCC had the potential to be an administrative disaster, but disaster did not happen. By July more than 300,000 unemployed young men, aged eighteen to twenty-five and from families on relief, were already working in the CCC's thirteen hundred camps. By 1935, there were more than 500,000 men in the CCC, and before it was dismantled more than 2.5 million young men had joined, working for one dollar a day in twenty-five hundred camps.

IMPACT ON RESOURCE USE

The projects were varied, ranging from restoring battlefields of the American Revolution and Civil War to constructing trails in the High Sierra; from protecting wildlife (including stocking almost one billion fish) and building fire lookout towers to planting two billion trees—200 million as windbreaks in the Dust Bowl. Estimates indicate that of all the forests planted in the history of the United States, both public and private, more than half were planted by the so-called tree people of the CCC. From the east and west, north and south, farm boys worked alongside young men from the cities. The CCC was organized on a military basis, although participation was voluntary, and one could enter and leave when one wished. Most men stayed from several months to about one year.

Although women were excluded and African Americans were subject to a 10 percent quota and were usu-

Members of the African American Civilian Conservation Corps reconstruct gabions at the French Battery along York-Hampton Road in Yorktown, Virginia, in the mid-1930's. (National Park Service Historic Photograph Collection)

ally segregated, as a conservation organization, the CCC was an instant and lasting success. Many of America's natural resources were preserved during those few years of the 1930's in spite of the predictions by some that many of the projects were beyond the government's powers and that the CCC would be inimical to capitalism or to organized labor because of the CCC's low wages. Some feared that the CCC smacked of communist collectivism or fascist militarism. Not the least of the resources conserved were the young men themselves, whose experience developed their physical bodies as well as their intellectual and emotional capabilities. At the onset of World War II the CCC was terminated, but individual states later established their own conservation corps, such as the California Conservation Corps. John F. Kennedy's Peace Corps was also inspired in part by the CCC.

Eugene Larson

WEB SITES

CIVILIAN CONSERVATION CORPS
Civilian Conservation Corps Legacy
http://www.ccclegacy.org/

NATIONAL ARCHIVES
Records of the Civilian Conservation Corps
http://www.archives.gov/research/guide-fed-records/groups/035.html#35.4

SEE ALSO: Conservation; Dust Bowl; Forest Service, U.S.; Reforestation; Roosevelt, Franklin D.

Clays

CATEGORY: Mineral and other nonliving resources

The term "clay" may be used to describe a group of fine-grained minerals, a type of rock, or a range of particle size, generally less than four micrometers. As a rock term, clay is generally understood to mean an earthy, fine-grained material formed largely of crystalline minerals known as the clay minerals.

BACKGROUND

Clays can be found throughout the world, but economically valuable deposits are limited in extent and distribution. Major kaolin deposits in the United States are found in Georgia and South Carolina. The world's major bentonite deposits are found in Wyoming and Montana, and large fuller's earth deposits can be found in Georgia and Florida. Ball and refractory clays are abundant in Kentucky and Tennessee.

Clays are used in a number of applications requiring the incorporation of fine-grained materials that contribute to a product's physical or chemical properties. Uses include fillers in paint, paper, and plastics, additives to drilling muds, the manufacture of ceramics and brick, carriers for pesticides and insecticides, the manufacture of catalysts, and cosmetic and pharmaceutical uses.

Clays are considered "industrial minerals," a group of minerals composed of geological materials having commercial value and of a nonmetallic, nonfuel character. They may be marketed in a natural, as-mined state or as processed materials. Clays can vary widely in composition and physical characteristics. Certain similarities exist among a number of clays, however, and they can be categorized in broad terms as kaolin, bentonite or fuller's earth, ball clay, and refractory clay based on similarities in either composition or functional performance. Clays that do not fall into any of the major categories are generally referred to as common clay or shale.

MINERALOGY AND CHEMISTRY

Clays are hydrous (water-containing) aluminum silicates containing alkalies or alkaline earth elements. Magnesium or iron may substitute wholly or partially for aluminum in the clay mineral structure. Clay minerals are composed of alternating layers of two different atomic structures. The first is an aluminum-bearing octahedral sheet structure, and the second is a layer of silica tetrahedrons. The aluminum and silicon atoms are chemically bonded to oxygen in these layers, which are held to one another by weaker electrostatic bonds. Interlayer sites in many clays contain water molecules or cations such as calcium, sodium, potassium, magnesium, lithium, or hydrogen. The presence or absence of interlayer molecules affects both the physical and chemical properties of the clay.

KAOLIN

Kaolin is a clay consisting predominantly of pure kaolinite or related clay minerals. Most major depos-

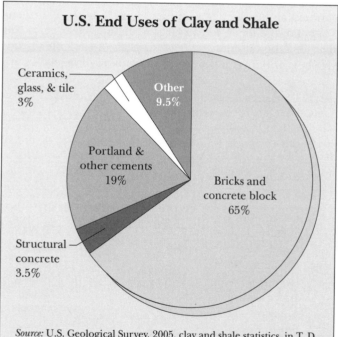

U.S. End Uses of Clay and Shale

Ceramics, glass, & tile 3%

Other 9.5%

Portland & other cements 19%

Bricks and concrete block 65%

Structural concrete 3.5%

Source: U.S. Geological Survey, 2005, clay and shale statistics, in T. D. Kelly and G. R. Matos, comps., *Historical Statistics for Mineral and Material Commodities in the United States,* U.S. Geological Survey Data Series 140. Available online at http://pubs.usgs.gov/ds/2005/140/.

Note: "Other" includes ceramics and glass, floor and wall tile, highway surfacing, other lightweight aggregates, refractories, and other heavy clay products.

its of kaolin are referred to as either primary (residual) or secondary. Primary deposits are formed in place as the weathering products of granite or other feldspar-rich rocks. Other minerals associated with deposits of this type include quartz, micas, amphiboles, tourmaline, and unweathered feldspars. Primary deposits are irregular in shape, grading downward into unaltered parent (source) rock.

Secondary deposits of kaolin are sedimentary accumulations of kaolinitic material that has been transported from its source area. Deposits of this type may contain up to 95 percent kaolinite; in contrast, primary deposits may contain as little as 10 percent. Associated minerals may include quartz, micas, other clay minerals, and a variety of high-density "heavy minerals." Secondary deposits are generally lenticular or tabular in shape, with thicknesses up to sixty meters and areal dimensions of up to about two kilometers.

Kaolin is also found as a product of hydrothermally altered rocks. Deposits of this nature are of limited size and extent. They occur as irregularly elongated pods or pipelike bodies along faults, joints, and other conduits along which hot solutions have flowed.

Kaolin is generally soft and plastic, although harder silica-bearing varieties also exist. Crystals of kaolinite are hexagonal, composed of individual platelets stacked in an accordion-like manner. There is little ionic substitution in the crystal lattice.

Kaolin has numerous industrial uses and is perhaps best known for its use in the manufacture of china and porcelain. Its chemical inertness, high brightness, white color (either naturally or resulting from processing and beneficiation), and crystal shape make it useful in other applications as well. Kaolin is used as a filler or coating in the manufacture of paper, as a filler in paint, plastics, and pharmaceuticals, and in the manufacture of rubber, tile, brick, ink, adhesives, detergents, cosmetics, pencils, pastes, and other consumer products.

BALL CLAY AND REFRACTORY CLAY

Ball clays are composed of up to 70 percent kaolin. They generally occur in secondary sedimentary deposits characterized by the presence of organic matter along with varying amounts of other clays, quartz, feldspar, calcite, and heavy minerals. Sedimentary deposits of ball clay represent accumulations of clay materials that were derived from a number of sources and that were deposited in nonmarine environments. Most deposits are lenticular, with areal dimensions of up to 850 meters and thicknesses of up to 10 or more meters.

Clay and Shale: World Mine Production, 2008

NATION	METRIC TONS		
	BENTONITE	FULLER'S EARTH	KAOLIN
Brazil (beneficiated)	240,000	—	2,490,000
Commonwealth of Independent States (crude)	750,000	—	6,200,000
Czech Republic (crude)	220,000	—	3,800,000
Germany (sales)	385,000	—	3,850,000
Greece (crude)	950,000	—	60,000
Italy (kaolinitic earth)	600,000	3,000	580,000
Mexico	435,000	100,000	960,000
South Korea (crude)	—	—	2,600,000
Spain	105,000	870,000	450,000
Turkey	930,000	—	580,000
United Kingdom	—	—	1,750,000
United States (sales)	4,870,000	2,630,000	6,750,000
Other countries	2,520,000	297,000	8,630,000

Source: Data from the U.S. Geological Survey, *Mineral Commodity Summaries, 2009.* U.S. Government Printing Office, 2009.

Ball clays are plastic or semi-plastic and are used to provide strength and malleability to ceramic bodies prior to firing. They fuse during firing, also acting as a "cement" to bind together the refractory, nonshrinking component of a ceramic body. Ball clay is used to manufacture tableware, stoneware, tiles, plumbing fixtures, and bricks. It is also used as a sealant in landfills.

Refractory clays are generally kaolin, containing only small quantities of mica or iron-bearing minerals that might combine with other materials during firing to form low-melting-point glasses. Refractory clays have a high heat resistance. Other properties that affect overall quality include shrinkage, warping, cracking, and abrasion. Refractory clays can be soft and plastic or hard like flint. They generally occur as sedimentary deposits that are lenticular or tabular in shape. They are mined for use in the manufacture of firebrick, insulating brick, and other heat-resistant clay products.

BENTONITE AND FULLER'S EARTH

"Bentonite" is generally understood to mean a clay consisting of minerals from the montmorillonite group, regardless of origin or occurrence. The most important commercial montmorillonites are the sodium and calcium varieties. Sodium montmorillonite (Wyoming or western bentonite) has high swelling capabilities when added to water. Calcium montmorillonite (southern bentonite) has a lower swelling capacity, and it generally crumbles when added to water. Other montmorillonites include those rich in lithium (hectorite), magnesium (saponite), or iron (nontronite).

Bentonite can be both physically and chemically reactive. It shrinks or swells as it releases or absorbs interstitial water or organic molecules, and it has important cation exchange and chemical sorption properties. Bentonite's physical and chemical properties account for its usefulness in modifying fluid viscosity or plasticity; it also has a variety of other uses. Bentonites can be modified through chemical treatment to enhance selected physical or chemical properties.

Wyoming bentonites are suitable for use in an as-mined condition. They are used as an additive in drilling mud to increase viscosity and aid in the removal of drillhole cuttings. The clay also helps maintain cuttings in suspension and creates an impervious coating on the wall of the drillhole to prevent fluid loss during drilling. Southern bentonites can be modified to have properties similar to Wyoming bentonites, but their use is generally restricted to other applications such as binding iron ore during pelletizing and the manufacture of catalysts and no-carbon-required (NCR) copy papers. Bentonites are also used to refine, decolor, and purify oils and beverages; to manufacture fire retardants; and as hydraulic barriers.

"Fuller's earth" refers to clays (generally bentonitic) suitable for bleaching and absorbent or other special uses. The term was first used to describe materials used for cleansing or fulling wool (removing lanolin and dirt), but it is now used more broadly to include decolorizers or purifiers in filtering applications. Fuller's earth products include cat litter, pesticide and insecticide carriers, soil conditioners, lightweight aggregate, and pharmaceuticals.

MINING AND PROCESSING

Most clay deposits are mined from open pits, although some are mined by underground methods. Open-pit mining generally involves the stripping of overburden, excavation of the clay, and transport of mined material to the processing plant. Some operations may require blasting.

The simplest operations involve excavation, transport to the plant, drying, and shipment to the customer. More complex operations may require that the mined material first be put into a slurry form for removal of grit or sand, with transport to the plant by pipeline. Clay slurries can be chemically or physically treated to remove contaminants that contribute to discoloration or poor chemical or physical performance. They can then be filtered and dried prior to packaging and shipment to the customer. Some clays are put back into slurry form prior to shipment, depending upon a customer's needs.

Kyle L. Kayler

FURTHER READING

Bergaya, Faïza, Benny K. G. Theng, and Gerhard Lagaly, eds. *Handbook of Clay Science*. New York: Elsevier, 2006.

Chatterjee, Kaulir Kisor. "Clay." In *Uses of Industrial Minerals, Rocks, and Freshwater*. New York: Nova Science, 2009.

Kogel, Jessica Elzea, et al., eds. "Clays." In *Industrial Minerals and Rocks: Commodities, Markets, and Uses*. 7th ed. Littleton, Colo.: Society for Mining, Metallurgy, and Exploration, 2006.

Manning, D. A. C. *Introduction to Industrial Minerals.* New York: Chapman & Hall, 1995.

Meunier, Alain. *Clays.* Translated by Nathalie Fradin. New York: Springer, 2005.

Murray, Haydn H. *Applied Clay Mineralogy: Occurrences, Processing, and Application of Kaolins, Bentonites, Palygorskite-Sepiolite, and Common Clays.* Boston: Elsevier, 2007.

Newman, A. C. D., ed. *Chemistry of Clays and Clay Minerals.* Harlow, England: Longman for Mineralogical Society, 1986.

WEB SITES

NATURAL RESOURCES CANADA
Canadian Minerals Yearbook, Mineral and Metal Commodity Reviews
http://www.nrcan-rncan.gc.ca/mms-smm/busi-indu/cmy-amc/com-eng.htm

U.S. GEOLOGICAL SURVEY
Clays: Statistics and Information
http://minerals.usgs.gov/minerals/pubs/commodity/clays

SEE ALSO: Ceramics; Chlorites; Open-pit mining; Paper; Residual mineral deposits; Sedimentary processes, rocks, and mineral deposits; Silicates; United States.

Clean Air Act

CATEGORIES: Laws and conventions; government and resources

DATES: 1963, rewritten in 1970, amended in later years

The Clean Air Acts of 1963 and 1970, with subsequent amendments, are intended to improve air quality in the United States, largely through mandated air quality standards.

BACKGROUND

The 1963 Clean Air Act (CAA) and its 1965 amendments attempted to improve air quality in the United States through federal support of air pollution research and aid to states in establishing air pollution control agencies. The 1970 CAA provided for national air-quality standards by specifying maximum permissible ambient air concentrations for pollutants deemed harmful to human health and the environment. The deadline for the enforcement of the primary standards was set for 1982 but was later extended.

PROVISIONS

The CAA provided that the Environmental Protection Agency (EPA), established in 1970, was to set pollution standards for new plants and that states were to create state implementation plans for enforcement.

Time Line of U.S. Clean Air Acts

YEAR	LAW	PROVISIONS
1955	Air Pollution Control Act	First U.S. law addressing air pollution and funding research into pollution prevention.
1963	Clean Air Act of 1963	First U.S. law providing for monitoring and control of air pollution.
1967	Air Quality Act	Established enforcement provisions to reduce interstate air pollution transport.
1970	Clean Air Act Extension of 1970	Established first comprehensive emission regulatory structure, including the National Ambient Air Quality Standards (NAAQS).
1977	Clean Air Act Amendment of 1977	Provided for the prevention of deterioration in air quality in areas that were in compliance with the NAAQS.
1990	Clean Air Act Amendment of 1990	Established programs to control acid precipitation, as well as 189 specific toxic pollutants.

Source: U.S. Environmental Protection Agency.

The country was divided into 247 Air Quality Control Regions for enforcement purposes. Finally, the CAA mandated pollution standards for automobiles and trucks with specified deadlines for achievement; Congress, however, repeatedly waived the deadlines. The 1970 CAA and the 1977 amendments have been successful in reducing several ambient air pollutants, most notably carbon monoxide, lead, and suspended particulates. However, ozone, nitrogen dioxide, volatile organic compounds, and sulfur dioxide remain at high levels in many areas.

The 1990 amendments to the CAA were so far-ranging as to constitute a rewriting of the act. The 1990 amendments displayed an awareness of developing problems such as acid deposition and stratospheric ozone (Titles IV and VI). Title I provided a new enforcement scheme with specific categories for cities (Los Angeles is in a category by itself) for reaching pollution standards for ozone, carbon monoxide, and particulates, with a twenty-year deadline for compliance. Title II provided specific standards for mobile source pollution with deadlines for compliance. Title III established emission limits for hazardous or toxic air pollutants with numerous deadlines for enforcement. An innovative aspect of Title IV was the establishment of a process of emissions trading whereby the most polluting utilities could acquire the excess pollution capacity of less-polluting utilities. The goal was to reduce progressively the total amount of sulfur dioxide emitted in the United States through the operation of market forces.

IMPACT ON RESOURCE USE
The CAA has been explicitly directed toward improving human health. Implicit in the CAA is a concern for the environment and the impact of air pollution on natural resources. Efforts to deal with acid deposition, for example, display a concern for the impact of sulfur dioxide on water and forest products. The implementation of automobile emission standards has had a positive effect on oil consumption.

The overall thrust of the Clean Air Act has been "technology-forcing"; in other words, industries have been forced to develop improved technologies to meet mandated standards. The results of this approach have been mixed in urban areas. Some improvement in air quality has certainly occurred. Nonetheless, costs have escalated for full achievement of the various standards of the CAA.

John M. Theilmann

SEE ALSO: Acid precipitation; Air pollution and air pollution control; Environmental Protection Agency; Ozone layer and ozone hole debate.

Clean Water Act

CATEGORIES: Laws and conventions; government and resources
DATE: Signed October 2, 1965

The Federal Water Quality Act of 1965, commonly known as the Clean Water Act, required states to set quality standards based on a waterway's usage. It proved to be a crucial step in the protection of the country's water supply.

BACKGROUND
"No one has a right to use America's rivers and America's waterways, that belong to all the people, as a sewer." With those words, President Lyndon Johnson signed the Federal Water Quality Act of 1965 and placed in motion steps to curtail pollution of the nation's water. The fight to stop water pollution began in colonial times, when local laws prohibited dumping in major waterways. However, a national water policy was lacking until passage of the 1948 Federal Water Pollution Control Act. Concerned with the health effects of water pollution, the law allowed legal intervention against polluters and provided funding for the development of sewage-treatment plants. Despite subsequent amendments furthering its cause, this act failed to provide a strong defense against polluters.

In a February 8, 1965, speech, President Johnson stated, "Every major river and waterway is now polluted," and he implored the nation to stop the destruction. Pollution stemmed from municipal waste, industrial waste, and runoff from agricultural land. Each contained a wide variety of polluting agents and contributed to a massive problem that some feared would eventually contaminate the country's entire water supply.

PROVISIONS
The Federal Water Quality Act, or Clean Water Act, provided guidelines by which states could fight water pollution. First, states were to define each waterway, in whole or in part, by its dominant usage: water supply, recreational, industrial, fish and wildlife propaga-

tion, or agricultural. Second, states were to set water quality standards based on that primary usage. If states failed to comply by June 30, 1967, or set inadequate standards, the Department of Health, Education, and Welfare (HEW) would be required to set the quality standard. The hope was to prevent pollution before it occurred. The standards could be used to support legal actions against municipal, industrial, or individual offenders. The act also created the Water Pollution Control Administration under HEW, which was to have responsibility for enforcing the act. Eventually water quality came under Environmental Protection Agency control.

IMPACT ON RESOURCE USE
In 1970, the 1948 and 1965 acts were combined to create a strong national water policy. Further amended in 1972, this policy called for stricter standards and heightened enforcement to make all navigable waters fishable and swimmable by 1983. Although that deadline was subsequently abandoned, keeping water clean enough to meet the fishable and swimmable standards remained the national goal. As water testing technology improved, the Clean Water Act (as all water quality-related acts have collectively been called beginning in 1972) strengthened the guidelines for water purity and protection. These acts were successful in reducing and eliminating contaminants in the nation's water resources.

Jennifer Davis

SEE ALSO: Clean Air Act; Environmental Protection Agency; Thermal pollution and thermal pollution control; Water pollution and water pollution control.

Clear-cutting

CATEGORY: Obtaining and using resources

At one time a standard practice in lumbering, clear-cutting has become one of the most controversial harvesting techniques used in modern logging.

DEFINITION
Clear-cutting is the practice of cutting all the trees on a tract of land at the same time. A tract that has been clear-cut will have no trees left standing. With its windrows of slash (the unmarketable portions of the tree,

such as tops and branches) and debris, a clear-cut tract of land may appear to the untrained eye as though a catastrophic event has devastated the landscape. As far as critics of clear-cutting are concerned, that is indeed what has happened.

OVERVIEW
The commercial forest industry is frequently denounced for damaging the environment through clear-cutting, particularly when clear-cutting is used to harvest timber on a large scale. Clear-cutting steep hillsides can leave the land susceptible to erosion, as the removal of all trees leaves nothing to slow the flow of rainfall. Clear-cut hillsides can lose topsoil at a rapid rate, choking nearby streams with sedimentation and killing aquatic species, such as trout and salmon. The large amounts of slash or debris left behind can pose a fire hazard. Wildlife studies have also indicated that certain species of birds and mammals are threatened when their habitats are clear cut, as they either lose their nesting area or are exposed to increased risk from predators. The northern spotted owl, for example, becomes easy prey for great horned owls when it is forced to fly across large open areas.

Representatives of the timber industry counter such criticisms by noting that, for some species of trees, selective harvesting simply does not work. Many species of trees will not regenerate in shaded areas. In addition, selective harvesting, or cutting only a limited number of trees from a stand, can also be ecologically damaging. Logging may create stress on the residual standing timber, leading to disease and die-off of the uncut trees, while the operation of mechanized equipment can be as disrupting to nesting and foraging habits of wildlife as clear-cutting the stand would have been.

Loggers further argue that criticisms of clear-cutting are often based on irrational considerations such as aesthetics—the public dislikes clear-cuts because they are ugly—rather than on sound silvicultural or ecological principles. Nonetheless, in many areas the timber industry has modified harvesting practices in response to public pressures and government concerns. Rather than clearing tracts of land in large rectangular blocks, many woods workers now cut off irregularly shaped strips that are considerably smaller in size than before. Patches of standing timber are left in clear-cut areas to provide cover for wildlife, and slash is chipped and spread as mulch to reduce the risk of brush fires. Buffer zones, or strips of uncut timber, are

A clear-cut mountainside in Canada. (©Charles Dyer/Dreamstime.com)

left along stream banks and near lakes to slow or prevent runoff from the clear-cut areas. Clear-cutting remains an appropriate harvesting method in certain situations, as in cutting even-age stands of plantation-grown trees, but modifications in its application can help prevent damage to the environment.

Nancy Farm Männikkö

SEE ALSO: Forest management; Forestry; Forests; Timber industry; Wood and timber.

Climate and resources

CATEGORIES: Ecological resources; environment, conservation, and resource management

Climate is the average of weather conditions at a place or in a region, usually recorded as both the mean (average) and the extremes of temperature, precipitation, and other relevant conditions. Resources are the factors and characteristics of the natural environment that people find useful, including climate, land, soil, water, minerals, and wild vegetation. Thus, climate is itself a natural resource, and it interacts with or affects the character or quality of other resources and their exploitation or development.

BACKGROUND

Climate can be seen as the most basic or primary of natural resources in that it affects other resources to a greater degree than it is affected by them. Perhaps the best evidence of this is in the nature and distribution of wild vegetation. (The term "wild vegetation" is preferable to "natural vegetation" because humankind has had dramatic impacts upon the character and distribution of plants.) Temperature, moisture, and solar radiation are the major factors determining the plant species that will grow in a region, and the major global vegetation types (forest, shrub, grassland, desert, and tundra) reflect climatic controls. Microclimates are in turn created within the vegetation: trees provide shade and thus a slightly cooler temperature than in the surrounding region. However, microclimates exist only in minuscule portions of the main climatic region; consequently, climate influences vegetation more than the reverse.

Solar radiation is the source of energy that drives the Earth's atmosphere and its circulation system; therefore it is the basic element in determining differences in climate. The sun's rays are vertical at some time of the year only in the tropics, between the Tropic of Cancer (23.5° north latitude) and the Tropic of Capricorn (23.5° south latitude). These lines determine where the greatest heat supply is found; regions poleward of about 40° north and south latitudes actually have a net loss of reradiation to outer space and depend upon a heat supply from the tropics, which is carried poleward by the general circulation of the atmosphere.

EQUATORIAL CLIMATES

The general circulation is the average of wind flow at the surface of the Earth and is driven by the surplus of solar radiation in the tropics. By definition, tropical climates do not experience freezing temperatures, have the least variation in length of day, and consequently experience the least "seasonality" of any latitudes. Seasons here are characterized more by precipitation contrasts—"dry" and "wet"—rather than by summer and winter temperatures. The greatest combination of heat and moisture resources on the Earth's surface, especially important in creating the conditions under which the tropical rain forest flourishes, is near the equator.

Rates of weathering of bedrock and soils are greatest in the equatorial region, because weathering is a function of the availability of heat and moisture. It follows that the depth to which rock and soils are weathered and leached (mineral plant foods dissolved and removed by groundwater flow) is greater here than elsewhere on the Earth's surface. Continuous high temperatures work against carbon storage in the soils; organic carbon storage requires recycling from wild vegetation. Oxidation of organic matter by exposure to the sun's rays follows the clearing of tropical forests. Under wild vegetation conditions, where the rain forest canopy protects soils from raindrop impact, erosion rates are not as high as one would expect from the intense rain showers. However, on sloping land, the soils become saturated and flow downslope, often catastrophically in disastrous landslides. Where wild vegetation has been removed by human activity, in farming or especially in urban centers, erosion and mass wasting (landslides) are exacerbated during rainy seasons and cause considerable loss of life and property damage.

With increasing distance from the equator, the tropics experience more pronounced seasons, particularly in moisture resources. Precipitation totals decline, and drought risk increases. Dry seasons are expected annually because of the shifting of the general circulation of the atmosphere. The timing and extent of this shift determine whether a region experiences drought (a period when significantly lower-than-average precipitation causes low levels of streamflow and increased stress on vegetation, both wild and cultivated). East and South Asia are most affected by shifting atmospheric circulation and the resultant wet and dry seasons, or "monsoons." Africa also has pronounced wet and dry seasons as a result of shifting atmospheric circulation patterns; droughts in the Sahel and East Africa are a consequence of the failure of rains to reach the region in time to support agriculture and grazing. Droughts in this part of the world result in famine: An estimated one million persons died in the Sahelian droughts of the late 1960's and 1970's. Thus climate must be defined in terms of both averages and extremes; the latter result in hazards that have dire consequences for the inhabitants of the affected region.

The probability of a drought hazard occurring increases as precipitation averages decrease (an inverse relationship) and is exacerbated by the fact that most tropical rainfall falls as intense thundershowers, which are spatially highly variable. One farm may be drenched by rain while its neighbors continue to be tormented by drought. In addition to drought risk on the margins of the tropics, the major climatic hazard is the tropical cyclone, which goes by various names, most commonly hurricane or typhoon. These cyclones, too, rarely affect the equatorial zone but frequent the tropical transition to the subtropics and midlatitudes. Movement of tropical cyclones is easterly in their early and middle stages, following the general circulation known as the trade winds.

THE SUBTROPICS

The types of climates that exist poleward of the tropics depend on the side of the continent: West sides are deserts or drylands; east sides are the humid subtropics, a transition zone with cooler temperatures and more risk of frost with greater distance from the equator. The humid subtropics are also subject to occasional easterly flow weather systems, including tropical cyclones. While they represent a serious hazard, claiming both lives and property, these easterly systems also deliver moisture and thus reduce the possibility of drought. The generally warm temperatures and moist conditions make these climates some of the most productive for crop growth, even exceeding the potential of the tropics. Leaching of soils and high erosion rates on cleared fields are nearly as great a problem as in the tropics, as is the rapid rate of organic decomposition.

The west coast drylands, which include all the world's major deserts—Sahara, Atacama, Kalahari, Australian, and North American—are a consequence of the general circulation of the atmosphere, which chooses these locations to make the swing from the prevailing westerlies of the middle latitudes to the easterly trade winds. In the process, high atmospheric pressures prevail, and winds are descending or subsiding, and therefore warming—just the opposite of the conditions required for rainfall. The drylands may extend deep into the continents, as in North America and especially in Africa and Asia; the dryness of the Sahara also blankets the Middle East and extends northward into Central Asia. Temperatures along the equatorward flank of these five major dryland zones are tropical, and where irrigation water is available, tropical plants may be grown. Most of the drylands are subtropical or midlatitude, and thus they experience frost as well as drought hazard. Weathering and erosion are appreciably less in the drylands, owing to the absence of moisture, and leaching of the soils is virtually absent. Instead, salts in the soils can build up to levels that are toxic to most plants—another climate-related hazard.

THE MIDLATITUDES

The midlatitudes extend from the subtropics to the polar climates of the Arctic and Antarctic, with temperatures following a transition from warm on the equatorward flank to too cold for agriculture nearer the poles. This is the realm of the westerlies, with extratropical cyclones delivering most of the weather. It is a zone of contrasting conditions, year-by-year and day-by-day, ranging from warmer than average to colder than average, from too humid to too dry on the inland dryland border.

Thus the hazards of extremes of temperature and precipitation often dominate life, as tropical and polar air masses converge to create the cyclones that

march from west to east. Drought risk is most important on the dryland border and results in the world's great grasslands. Summer heat may be a hazard on occasion, and nearly every winter brings storms with freezing rain, high winds, and heavy snowfalls, particularly on the eastern sides of the continents. The eastern sides are also afflicted with such intense summer storms as the tornadoes of North America (a winter phenomenon in the adjoining humid subtropics), and the tail end of hurricanes and typhoons, as these become caught up in westerly circulation and curve poleward again. The Arctic fringe of the midlatitudes is too cool for significant agriculture but yields the great subarctic forests of Canada, Scandinavia, and Russia. Polar climates are too cold for all but a few hunters and fishers and people engaged in extractive industries or scientific research.

Neil E. Salisbury

FURTHER READING

Anderson, Bruce T., and Alan Strahler. *Visualizing Weather and Climate.* Hoboken, N.J.: Wiley, in collaboration with the National Geographic Society, 2008.

Bryson, Reid A., and Thomas J. Murray. *Climates of Hunger: Mankind and the World's Changing Weather.* Madison: University of Wisconsin Press, 1977.

Grigg, D. B. *The Agricultural Systems of the World: An Evolutionary Approach.* New York: Cambridge University Press, 1974.

Le Roy Ladurie, Emmanuel. *Times of Feast, Times of Famine: A History of Climate Since the Year 1000.* Rev. and updated ed. Translated by Barbara Bray. New York: Noonday Press, 1988.

Ruddiman, William F. *Plows, Plagues, and Petroleum: How Humans Took Control of Climate.* Princeton, N.J.: Princeton University Press, 2005.

Sivakumar, Mannava V. K., and Raymond P. Motha, eds. *Managing Weather and Climate Risks in Agriculture.* New York: Springer, 2007.

Strahler, Alan H., and Arthur N. Strahler. *Introducing Physical Geography.* 4th ed. Hoboken, N.J.: J. Wiley, 2006.

Strahler, Arthur N., and Alan H. Strahler. *Elements of Physical Geography.* 4th ed. New York: Wiley, 1989.

SEE ALSO: Agriculture industry; Atmosphere; Desertification; Deserts; Drought; Dust Bowl; El Niño and La Niña; Forests; Grasslands; Monsoons; Rain forests; Weather and resources.

Climate change. *See* Greenhouse gases and global climate change

Climate Change and Sustainable Energy Act

CATEGORIES: Laws and conventions; government and resources
DATE: June 21, 2006

In the later part of the twentieth century and the early part of the twenty-first century, global temperatures have been some of the warmest ever recorded. Measures to reduce greenhouse gases and the implementation of alternative sources of renewable energy are ways of combating climate change. The United Kingdom's Climate Change and Sustainable Energy Act 2006 promotes microgeneration technologies to replace carbon-based fuel sources.

BACKGROUND

Countries in the developed world have established initiatives to reduce greenhouse gases and combat climate change. Common greenhouse gases include carbon dioxide, methane, nitrous oxide, and hydrofluorocarbons. Greenhouse gases act to absorb the Earth's infrared radiation and increase temperatures. The Kyoto Protocol, an important climate-change measure ratified by many industrialized countries, was established in 1997. Some countries establish their own greenhouse-gas emission standards. For example, the United Kingdom enacted the Sustainable Energy Act of 2003 and the Energy Act of 2004; modifications of microgeneration targets were applied to the 2006 act. The Climate Change and Sustainable Energy Act is a law that builds upon previous climate change policies.

PROVISIONS

The Climate Change and Sustainable Energy Act was enacted on June 21, 2006, in an effort to encourage microgeneration technologies aimed at reducing greenhouse-gas emissions. Microgeneration technologies include many non-carbon-fueled energy sources. Microgeneration is the generation of electricity and heat from a renewable energy source. These sources include non-fossil fuels and nonnuclear fuels, such as biomass, biofuel, wind, water-tide, solar-power, and geothermal sources. All renewable sources of fuel are useful in microgeneration. This initiative of increasing microgeneration technologies ultimately will reduce dependency on carbon-based energy emissions. The Climate Change and Sustainable Energy Act permits homes to reduce dependency on carbon-based fuel sources and increase microgeneration technologies. Building-construction regulations are also specified in this act. Each year, the ministerial authorities report to Parliament the measures taken by the government in support of this measure. Local authorities have access to the reports and ensure that these measures are followed at the local level. This act incentivizes local governments to encourage the use of microgeneration and the reduction of greenhouse-gas emissions.

IMPACT ON RESOURCE USE

A 2009 assessment by the U.S. Global Change Research Program outlined the effect of the increase in greenhouse gases. The increase of global temperatures could be as high as 6° Celsius by the year 2090, suggesting that climate change is real and has dramatic impacts. By the end of the twenty-first century, sea levels in U.S. coastal regions may rise more than 1 meter. Climate change has occurred even more rapidly in the Arctic regions, where ice is melting, and the fishing industry may experience a negative impact.

The Climate Change and Sustainable Energy Act serves as a model for other industrialized countries. For example, Germany is combating climate change with a similar law: the Renewable Energy Sources Act.

Kevin D. Weakley

WEB SITE

CLIMATE CHANGE AND SUSTAINABLE ENERGY ACT, 2006
http://www.opsi.gov.uk/acts/acts2006/pdf/ukpga_20060019_en.pdf

SEE ALSO: Agenda 21; Climate and resources; Earth Summit; Gore, Al; Greenhouse gases and global climate change; Kyoto Protocol.

Coal

CATEGORY: Energy resources

WHERE FOUND

While coal has been found on every principal continent of the Earth, regional distribution is restricted to sedimentary and metamorphosed sedimentary rock terrains of Upper Devonian age and younger (that is, the last 365 million years of geologic history). As a result of this geologic association, most of the coal reserves of the world are found in the Northern Hemisphere continents of Asia, Europe, and North America. However, there are reasonably large reserves in Australia, South Africa, and Colombia.

PRIMARY USES

Coal was historically used as a domestic fuel for the heating of homes, and more than 26 percent of the coal mined globally is a primary source of energy. Worldwide, 41 percent of coal mined is burned in power plants, principally for the generation of electricity. Another significant use is in the manufacture of coke, an improved carbon-content derivative of coal employed in the production of steel. Lesser amounts of coal are used in the direct heating of homes, for a variety of industrial purposes, and, increasingly, in liquefaction and gasification processes whereby coal is converted to liquid and gaseous forms of hydrocarbon fuels.

TECHNICAL DEFINITION

Coal is a general term encompassing a variety of combustible sedimentary and metamorphic rocks containing altered and fossilized terrestrial plant remains in excess of 50 percent by weight and more than 70 percent by volume. Categories of coal differ in relative amounts of moisture, volatile matter, fixed carbon, and degree of compaction of the original carbonaceous material. Coal is commonly termed a fossil fuel. Categories of coal include peat (a coal precursor), lignite, bituminous coal, subbituminous coal, and anthracite.

PEAT. Peat, an unconsolidated accumulation of partly decomposed plant material, has an approximate carbon content of 20 percent. In many classification schemes, peat is listed as the initial stage of coal formation. Moisture content is quite high, at least at the 75 percent level. When dry, peat has an oxygen content of about 30 percent, is flammable, and will freely but inefficiently burn slowly and steadily for months at a low-heat-content value of 5,400 British thermal units (Btus) per pound.

LIGNITE. Lignite, or brown coal, is brownish-black in color, banded and jointed, and subject to spontaneous combustion. Carbon content ranges from 25 to 35 percent. With a moisture content around 40 percent, it will readily disintegrate after drying in the open air. Because lignite has a maximum calorific value of 8,300 Btus, it is classed as a low-heating-value coal.

BITUMINOUS COAL. Deeper burial with even higher temperatures and pressures gradually transforms lignite into bituminous coal, a dense, dusty, brittle, well-jointed, dark brown to black fuel that burns readily with a smoky yellow flame. Calorific value ranges from 10,500 to 15,500 Btus per pound, and carbon content varies from 45 to 86 percent. Moisture content is as low as 5 percent, but heating value is high.

SUBBITUMINOUS COAL. The subbituminous class of coal is intermediate between lignite and bituminous and has characteristics of both. Little woody matter is visible. It splits parallel to bedding but generally lacks the jointing of bituminous coal. It burns clean but with a relatively low heating value.

ANTHRACITE. Anthracite is jet black in color, has a high luster, is very hard and dust free, and breaks with a conchoidal fracture. Carbon content ranges from 86 to 98 percent. It is slow to ignite; burns with a short blue flame without smoke; and, with a calorific value in excess of 14,000 Btus per pound, is a high heating fuel.

DESCRIPTION, DISTRIBUTION, AND FORMS

Coal is a fossil fuel found on all seven continents and is in commercial production on all but the continent of Antarctica. The top-ten producers of coal in 2008 were China, the United States, Australia, India, South Africa, Russia, Indonesia, Poland, Kazakhstan, and Colombia. In 1992, a reserve of more than 185 billion metric tons of lignite was discovered in Pakistan, but the cost of production and lack of infrastructure have prevented development or accurate analysis of the field.

The quantitative distribution of coal is more difficult to determine than its geographic distribution. Estimates indicate that total world coal resources, defined as coal reserves and other deposits that are not economically recoverable plus inferred future discoveries, are on the order of 9 trillion metric tons and exist in every country. Of this amount, estimates of world coal reserves, defined as those deposits that

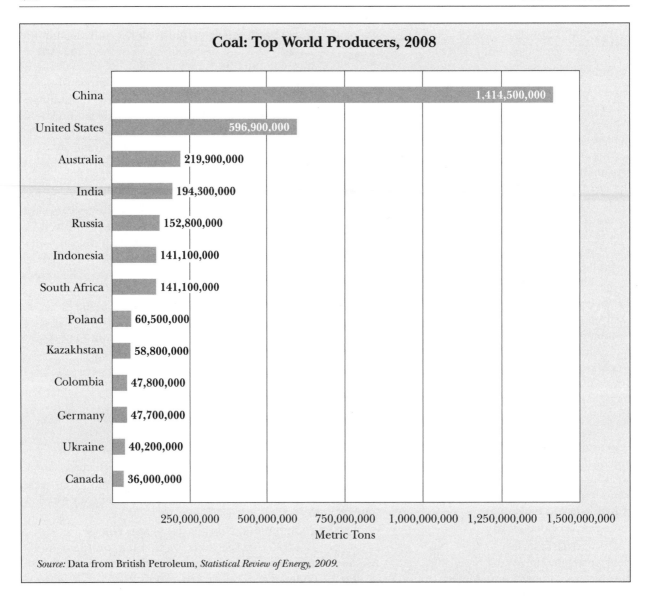

Coal: Top World Producers, 2008

Country	Metric Tons
China	1,414,500,000
United States	596,900,000
Australia	219,900,000
India	194,300,000
Russia	152,800,000
Indonesia	141,100,000
South Africa	141,100,000
Poland	60,500,000
Kazakhstan	58,800,000
Colombia	47,800,000
Germany	47,700,000
Ukraine	40,200,000
Canada	36,000,000

Source: Data from British Petroleum, *Statistical Review of Energy, 2009.*

have been measured, evaluated, and can be extracted profitably under existing technologic and economic conditions, are approximately 900 billion metric tons and are found in about seventy countries. If the latter figure is accepted as reasonable, world reserves can be divided into two categories, with about three-quarters composed of anthracite and bituminous coals and about one-quarter composed of lignite. When the lignite reserves in Pakistan can be reliably analyzed, these figures will change.

On a country-to-country comparison, the United States possesses the greatest amount of total world coal reserves. Geographic distribution in the United States is divided into five coal provinces, incorporating at least thirty-three states. These are termed the Appalachian or Eastern, the Interior, the Gulf, the Rocky Mountain, and the Northern Great Plains coal provinces.

The Eastern (Appalachian) province, stretching along the flanks of the Appalachian Mountains from northern Pennsylvania into central Georgia, contains approximately 40 percent of the bituminous coal reserves of the United States as well as the principal reserve of anthracite rank coal on the continent. Within the Interior province, bituminous coals are divided among the Michigan, Illinois, and Western Interior basins, the latter located in Iowa, Missouri, Kansas, and Oklahoma. Lignite is the chief coal found in the Gulf province, situated in Mississippi, northern Louisiana, and coastal Texas. Rocky Mountain bituminous and subbituminous deposits are scattered throughout at least five states from Wyoming south into Arizona and New Mexico. Lignite and bituminous coals constitute the Northern Great Plains province of Montana and portions of North and South Dakota.

Coal is mined in twenty-five states, but ten states alone contain 90 percent of the total U.S. reserves. These are, in order of increasing reserve tonnage, Indiana, Texas, Colorado, Ohio, Kentucky, Pennsylvania, West Virginia, Wyoming, Illinois, and Montana. Montana contains a full 25 percent of U.S. coal reserves.

Small reserves of relatively low-grade coal are known in the Pacific Northwest region. Significant amounts of coal have been discovered in Alaska, but difficulty in mining and great distance to markets cause these deposits to be classed as resources and not economic reserves.

Following the United States, the countries with the largest coal reserves are Russia, China, India, Australia, and South Africa. Estimates indicate that global coal reserves will last some 130 to 150 years at current production levels, although by some methods of calculation that period is significantly shorter.

The more common and ordinary coals are of vascular vegetable origin, formed from the compaction and induration of accumulated remains of plants that once grew in extensive swamp and coastal marsh areas. These deposits are classed as humic coals consisting of organic matter that has passed through the peat, or earliest coal formation, stage. A variety of humic coals are known.

The swamp-water environment in which humic coals form must be deficient in dissolved oxygen, the

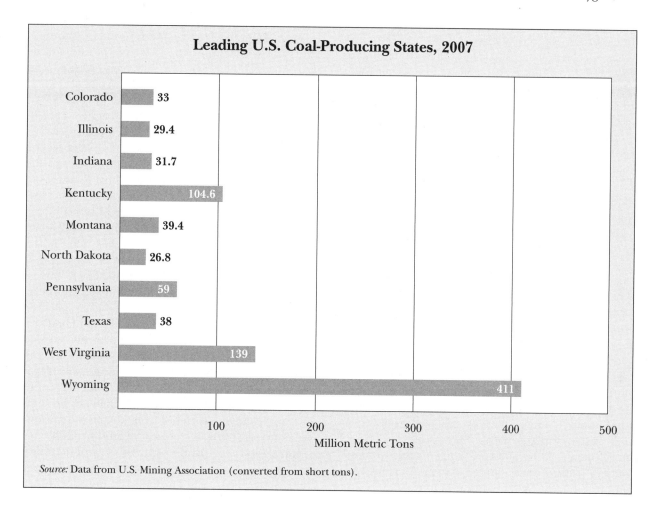

Leading U.S. Coal-Producing States, 2007

State	Million Metric Tons
Colorado	33
Illinois	29.4
Indiana	31.7
Kentucky	104.6
Montana	39.4
North Dakota	26.8
Pennsylvania	59
Texas	38
West Virginia	139
Wyoming	411

Source: Data from U.S. Mining Association (converted from short tons).

presence of which would ordinarily cause decay of the plant tissue. Under such near-stagnant conditions plant remains are preserved, while the presence of hydrogen sulfide discourages the presence of organisms that feed on dead vegetation. Analog environments under which coal is presently forming are found within the Atchafalaya swamp of coastal Louisiana and the many peat-producing regions of Ireland. A layer of peat in excess of 2 meters in thickness and covering more than 5,000 square kilometers is present in the Dismal Swamp of coastal North Carolina and Virginia.

The sapropelic class of coal, relatively uncommon in distribution and composed of fossil algae and spores, is formed through partial decomposition of organic matter by organisms within oxygen-deficient lakes and ponds. Sapropelic coals are subdivided into boghead (algae origin) and cannel (spore origin) deposits.

The vegetable origin of coal has been accepted since 1825 and is convincingly evidenced by the identification of more than three thousand freshwater plant species in coal beds of Carboniferous (360 to 286 million years ago) age. The common association of root structures and even upright stumps with layers of coal indicates that the parent plant material grew and accumulated in place.

Detailed geologic studies of rock sequences that lie immediately above and below coal deposits indicate that most coals were formed in coastal regions affected by long-term sea-level cycles characterized by transgressing (advancing) and regressing (retreating) shorelines. Such a sequence of rock deposited during a single advance and retreat of the shoreline, termed a "cyclothem," typically contains nonmarine strata separated from overlying marine strata by a single layer of coal. In sections of the Interior coal province, a minimum of fifty cyclothems have been recognized, some of which can be traced across thousands of square kilometers. Such repetition in a rock sequence is most advantageous to the economics of a coal region, creating a situation in which a vertical mine shaft could penetrate scores of layers of coal.

The formation of coal is a long-term geologic process. Coal cannot therefore be considered a renewable resource, even though it is formed from renewable resource plant matter. Studies have suggested that 1 meter of low-rank coal requires approximately ten thousand years of plant growth, accumulation, biologic reduction, and compaction to develop. Using these time lines, the 3-meter-thick Pittsburgh coal bed, underlying 39,000 square kilometers of Pennsylvania, developed over a period of thirty thousand years, while the 26-meter-thick bed of coal found at Adaville, Wyoming, required approximately one-quarter of a million years to develop.

Coal formation favors climate conditions under which plant growth is abundant and conditions for organic preservation are favorable. Such climates range from subtropical to cold, with the ideal being classed as temperate. Tropical swamps produce an abundance of plant matter but very high bacterial activity, resulting in low production of peat. Modern peats are developing in temperate to cold climate regions, such as Canada and Ireland, where abundant precipitation ensures fast plant growth while relatively cool temperatures diminish the effectiveness of decay-promoting bacteria.

The first coal provinces began to form with the evolution of cellulose-rich land plants. One of the earliest known coal deposits, of Upper Devonian age (approximately 365 million years ago), is found on Buren Island, Norway. Between the Devonian period and today every geologic period is represented by at least some coal somewhere in the world. Certain periods of time, however, are significant coal-forming ages.

During the Carboniferous and Permian periods (360 to 245 million years ago) widespread development of fern and scale tree growth set the stage for the formation of the Appalachian coal province and the coal districts of the United Kingdom, Russia, and Manchuria. Coal volumes formed during these periods of geologic time constitute approximately 65 percent of present world reserves. The remaining reserves, developed mainly over the past 200 million years, formed in swamps consisting of angiosperm (flowering) plants. The reserves of the Rocky Mountain province and those of central Europe are representative of these younger coals.

After dead land-plant matter has accumulated and slowly begun to compact, biochemical decomposition, rising temperature, and rising pressure all contribute to the lengthy process of altering visible plant debris into various ranks of coal. With the advent of the Industrial Revolution there was a need for a system of classification defining in detail the various types of coals. Up to the beginning of the nineteenth century, coal was divided into three rudimentary classes, determined by appearance: bright coal, black coal, and brown coal. Through the decades, other schemes involving various parameters were introduced, including oxygen content, percent of residue remaining after the burning of coal, ratio of carbon to volatile matter content, or analysis of fixed carbon content and calorific value (heat-generating ability).

In 1937, a classification of coal rank using fixed carbon and Btu content was adopted by the American Standards Association. Adaptations of this scheme are still in use, listing the steps of progressive increase in coal rank as lignite (brown coal), subbituminous, bituminous (soft coal), subanthracite, and anthracite (hard coal). Some classification schemes also list peat as the lowest rank of coal. (Technically speaking, peat is not a coal; rather, it is a fuel and a precursor to coal.)

Coalification is the geologic process whereby plant material is altered into differing ranks of coal by geochemical and diagenetic change. With an increase in rank, chemical changes involve an increase in carbon content accompanied by a decrease in hydrogen and oxygen. Correspondingly, diagenesis involves an increase in density and calorific value, and a progressive decrease in moisture. At all ranks, common impurities include sulfur, silt and clay particles, and silica.

U.S. reserves are found mainly in eleven northeastern counties in Pennsylvania. Subanthracite coal has characteristics intermediate between bituminous and anthracite.

Bedded and compacted coal layers are geologically considered to be rocks. Lignite and bituminous ranks are classed as organic sedimentary rocks. Anthracite, formed when bituminous beds of coal are subjected to the folding and regional deformation affiliated with mountain building processes, is listed as a metamorphic rock. Because peat is not consolidated or compacted, it is classed as an organic sediment. Graphite, a naturally occurring crystalline form of almost pure carbon, is occasionally associated with anthracite. While it can occur as the result of high-temperature alteration of anthracite, its chemical purity and common association with crystalline rock causes it to be listed as a mineral.

HISTORY

Considering the importance of coal to modern society, it is somewhat surprising that the production of this commodity played only a minor role in pre-Industrial Revolution (that is, prior to the middle eighteenth century) history. The origins of coal use date back at least several thousands of years, as evidenced by the discovery of flint axes embedded in layered coal in central England. These primitive tools have been attributed to Neolithic (New Stone Age, c. 6000-2000 B.C.E.) open-pit mining. The Chinese were acquainted early with the value of coal, using it in the making of porcelain. Coal cinders found in Roman-era walls in association with implements of similar age suggest the use of coal for heating purposes prior to the colonization of England by the Saxons.

The philosopher Theophrastus (c. 372-287 B.C.E.), noted as the academic successor to Aristotle and the author of many studies on plants, called coal *anthrax*, a Greek word later used in the naming of anthracite coal. Later, the Anglo-Saxon term *col*, probably derived from the Latin *caulis*, meaning plant stalk, evolved into "cole" prior to the emergence of the modern spelling some three centuries ago.

With the decline of forests in England by the thirteenth century, coal began to assume a significant role. The first coal-mining charter was granted the freemen of Newcastle in 1239. This early burning of coal, however, because of its propensity to befoul the atmosphere, was banned in 1306 by King Edward I. King Edward III reversed this ban and again granted the Newcastle freemen a coal-mining license, whereby this town soon became the center of the first important coal-mining district.

Coal mining was initiated in North America near Richmond, Virginia, in 1748. A decade later, coal-mining activities had moved to the rich deposits around Pittsburgh, Pennsylvania. The spread of the Industrial Revolution, invention of the iron-smelting process, and improvement of the steam engine guaranteed the classification of coal as an industrial staple. With the development of the steam-driven electric generator in the last decade of the nineteenth century, coal became the dominant fuel. A century later, world coal production exceeded 4.5 billion metric tons and constituted some 26 percent of world energy production on a Btu basis. In the early twenty-first century, with the rapid growth of the Chinese economy, China passed the United States as the top producer of coal.

OBTAINING COAL

Coal has been produced by two common methods: underground (or deep) mining and surface (or strip) mining. Underground mining requires the digging of extensive systems of tunnels and passages within and along the coal layers. These openings are connected to the surface so the coal can be removed. Prior to the development of the gigantic machinery necessary to open-pit mining, deep mining was the industry norm. This early period was characterized by labor-intensive pick-and-shovel work in cramped mine passages. Constant dangers included the collapse of ceilings and methane gas explosions.

Today, augers and drilling machinery supplement manpower to a large extent, and mine safety and health regulations have greatly reduced the annual death toll. The common method of underground extraction involves initial removal of about 50 percent of the coal, leaving a series of pillars to support the mine roof. As reserves are exhausted, the mine is gradually abandoned after removal of some or all of the pillars. Another modern underground-mining technique, with a coal removal rate approaching 100 percent, involves the use of an integrated rotary cutting machine and conveyer belt.

Surface mining of coal, accounting for about 40 percent of global production, is a multiple-step process. First, the overburden material must be removed, allowing exposure of the coal. The coal is then mined by means of various types of surface machinery, ranging from bulldozers to gigantic power shovels. Finally, after removal of all the coal, the overburden is used to fill in the excavated trench and the area is restored to its natural topography and vegetation. Economics usually determine whether underground or open-pit techniques are preferable in a given situation. Generally, if the ratio of overburden to coal thickness does not exceed twenty to one, surface mining is more profitable.

In the Appalachian coal province, coal-mining technique is closely related to geology. In tightly folded regions of West Virginia, the steeply dipping coal beds are mostly mined underground. To the northwest, folds become gentler, and both deep- and surface-mining methods are used. In the Interior province, strip mining is the most common process. In the Rocky Mountain area, where many thick coal beds lie close to the surface, strip mining again predominates, although a few underground mines are present.

With increased concern regarding the state of the natural Earth environment, and with federal passage of the Coal Mine Health and Safety Act (1969) and the Clean Air Acts (U.S.), the mining of coal in the United States has undergone both geographic and extraction-technology changes. Because the Rocky Mountain province coals, while lower grade than east-

ern coals, contain lower percentages of sulfur, the center of U.S. production has gradually shifted westward. The burning of high-sulfur coals releases sulfur dioxide into the atmosphere; it is a significant contributor to acid rain.

Western coals are often contained within layers thicker than those found in the east, are shallow in depth, and can be found under large areas—all conditions amenable to surface mining. As a result, the state of Wyoming, with a 1995 production of 240 million metric tons of low-sulfur coal that is burned in more than twenty-four states in the generation of electricity, became the leading U.S. coal producer.

Coal mining has played an integral role in the development of the industrialized world, and this role should continue well into the future. Reserve additions continue to closely equal losses due to mining, and at current levels of production estimates indicate that there is enough recoverable coal globally for some 130 to 150 years of future production.

USES OF COAL

Historically, coal has been industry's fuel of choice. Those countries in possession of sufficient coal reserves have risen commercially, while those less endowed with this resource—or lacking it altogether—have turned to agriculture or stagnated in development. The top exporters of coal are Australia, Indonesia, Russia, Colombia, South Africa, China, and the United States. The top importers are Japan, South Korea, Taiwan, India, the United Kingdom, China, and Germany.

Different ranks of coal are employed for different purposes. In the middle of the twentieth century, it was common to see separate listings of coking, gas, steam, fuel, and domestic coals. Each had its specific uses. Domestic coal could not yield excessive smoke, while coal for locomotives had to raise steam quickly and not produce too high an ash content. Immediately after World War II, fuel coal use in the United States, representing 78 percent of annual production, was divided into steam raising (29 percent), railway transportation (23 percent), domestic consumption (17 percent), electric generation (6 percent), and bunker coal (3 percent). The remaining 22 percent was employed in the production of pig iron (10 percent), steel (7 percent), and gas (5 percent). Fifty years later, more than 80 percent of the approximately 900 million metric tons of coal produced annually in the United States was used in the generation of electricity. Industrial consumption of coal, particularly in the production of coke for the steel and iron manufacturing industry, is the second most important use. Globally, 13 percent of hard coal production is used by the steel industry. Some 70 percent of global steel production depends on coal. Additional industrial groups that use coal include food processing, paper, glass, cement, and stone. Coal produces more energy than any other fuel, more than natural gas, crude oil, nuclear, and renewable fuels.

The drying of malted barley by peat fires has long been important in giving Scotch whiskey its smoky flavor. Peat has also been increasingly employed as a soil conditioner. While expensive to produce, the conversion of intermediate ranks of coal into liquid (coal oil) and gaseous (coal gas) forms of hydrocarbon fuels will become more economically viable, especially during times of increase in the value of crude oil and natural gas reserves.

New uses of coal are constantly being explored and tested. Two promising techniques are the mixing of water with powdered coal to make a slurry that can be burned as a liquid fuel and the underground extraction of coal-bed methane (firedamp). Interest in the latter by-product as an accessible and clean-burning fuel is especially high in Appalachian province localities distant from conventional gas resources.

Albert B. Dickas

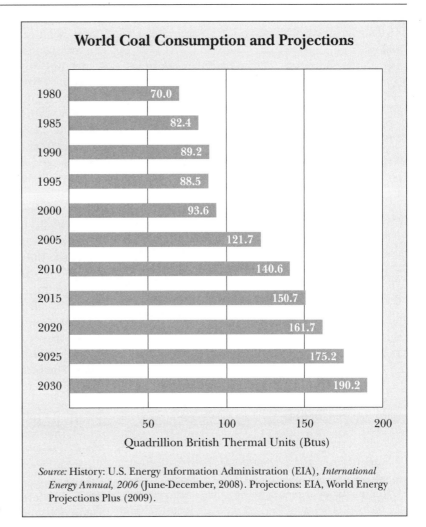

World Coal Consumption and Projections

Year	Quadrillion British Thermal Units (Btus)
1980	70.0
1985	82.4
1990	89.2
1995	88.5
2000	93.6
2005	121.7
2010	140.6
2015	150.7
2020	161.7
2025	175.2
2030	190.2

Source: History: U.S. Energy Information Administration (EIA), *International Energy Annual, 2006* (June-December, 2008). Projections: EIA, World Energy Projections Plus (2009).

FURTHER READING

Berkowitz, Norbert. *An Introduction to Coal Technology.* 2d ed. San Diego, Calif.: Academic Press, 1994.

Freese, Barbara. *Coal: A Human History.* Cambridge, Mass.: Perseus, 2003.

Goodell, Jeff. *Big Coal: The Dirty Secret Behind America's Energy Future.* Boston: Houghton Mifflin, 2006.

Schobert, Harold H. *Coal: The Energy Source of the Past and Future.* Washington, D.C.: American Chemical Society, 1987.

Speight, James G. *The Chemistry and Technology of Coal.* 2d ed., rev. and expanded. New York: M. Dekker, 1994.

Thomas, Larry. *Coal Geology.* Hoboken, N.J.: Wiley, 2002.

_____. *Handbook of Practical Coal Geology.* New York: Wiley, 1992.

WEB SITES

AMERICAN COAL FOUNDATION
All About Coal
http://www.teachcoal.org/aboutcoal/index.html

NATURAL RESOURCES CANADA
About Coal
http://www.nrcan.gc.ca/eneene/sources/coacha-eng.php

U.S. DEPARTMENT OF ENERGY
Coal
http://www.energy.gov/energysources/coal.htm

U.S. GEOLOGICAL SURVEY
Coal Resources: Over One Hundred Years of USGS
    Research
http://energy.usgs.gov/coal.html

WORLD COAL INSTITUTE
Gas and Liquids
http://www.worldcoal.org/

SEE ALSO: American Mining Congress; Asbestos; Carbon; Coal gasification and liquefaction; Environmental degradation, resource exploitation and; Industrial Revolution and industrialization; Mining safety and health issues; Mining wastes and mine reclamation; Open-pit mining; Peat; Strip mining; Surface Mining Control and Reclamation Act; Underground mining.

Coal gasification and liquefaction

CATEGORIES: Energy resources; obtaining and using resources

Synthetic fuels offer alternatives for systems, such as vehicles, designed to operate on liquid or gaseous fuels. Historically, these fuels have been used when imports of petroleum or natural gas are restricted by boycotts or warfare. The conversion of coal to synthetic fuels can reduce the amounts of sulfur and ash released into the environment, providing a cleaner fuel.

BACKGROUND

Coal is one of the most abundant fossil fuel resources in the world. The worldwide reserves of coal are likely to last substantially longer than reserves of petroleum and natural gas. Several factors can create shortages of liquid or gaseous fuels, including international trade embargoes (as occurred during the 1970's), wars, and, in the long run, the depletion of petroleum and gas reserves. Gaseous or liquid fuels are easier to handle and transport than are solids, and they are easier to treat for removal of potential pollutants, such as sulfur. Worldwide there is an immense investment in combustion devices of many kinds designed to operate on liquids or gases. A large-scale replacement of all these units, or retrofitting them to burn solid coal, is

not practically or economically feasible. Solid coal is not a practical alternative for many applications of liquid or gaseous fuels, such as automobile engines. Conversion of coal to synthetic gaseous or liquid fuels offers opportunities for providing alternative fuel supplies, for removing sulfur and ash from the fuel before combustion, and for providing strategic security against the possible interruption of imports.

COAL GASIFICATION

The simplest approach to producing gaseous fuel from coal is heating in closed vessels under conditions that would not allow combustion to occur. In such a process, the coal decomposes to a variety of products, including gases, liquids (coal tar), and a solid residue. Depending on the quality of the coal used, the gas can have excellent fuel qualities, because it is rich in hydrogen and methane and has a calorific value of about two-thirds that of natural gas. The product has a variety of names: town gas, illuminating gas, or coal gas. The process itself also has various names, including pyrolysis, destructive distillation, and carbonization.

If the primary objective is to produce a gaseous fuel, then simple carbonization is very wasteful of the coal, because only about 20 percent is converted to gas. Much of the original coal still remains a solid, and some converts to a liquid. However, if the gas is collected as a by-product, for example from the conversion of coal to metallurgical coke, then sale of the gas can provide extra revenue; it can also be used as a fuel inside the plant. Carbonization is not useful when the intent is to convert the maximum amount of coal to a gaseous fuel.

The principal method for converting coal completely to a gaseous fuel is the reaction of coal with steam. When steam is passed over a bed of red-hot coal, the product is water gas, which consists mainly of hydrogen and carbon monoxide. The reaction of steam with coal is endothermic (it requires a source of heat in order to proceed). Consequently, some portion of the coal must be burned to provide the heat to "drive" the reaction of coal with steam. This is usually accomplished by allowing the combustion reaction and the reaction with steam to proceed simultaneously in the same vessel. Initially this was accomplished by feeding coal, air, and steam together into a reactor. The heat-releasing combustion reaction effectively balances the heat-consuming reaction with steam, and the process can operate continuously.

When air is used for the combustion reaction, the product gas will inevitably be diluted with large amounts of nitrogen. Consequently, its calorific value will be very low, about 10 to 20 percent of the value of natural gas. For this reason, modern approaches to coal gasification use coal, steam, and oxygen as the feedstocks. Though this adds to the cost and complexity of separating oxygen from air for the gasification process, it is more than recompensed by a much higher quality product.

GASIFIER DESIGNS

Early designs of gasifiers were so-called moving bed gasifiers, in which a bed of solid coal slowly descended through a tall cylindrical vessel to react with a steam-oxygen (or steam-air) mixture at the bottom. Such gasifiers, such as the Lurgi gasifier, developed in Germany in the 1930's, have a disadvantage in that the heating drives out any moisture that may be in the coal and generates some liquids or tars. Some of the compounds driven out of the coal will dissolve in the water, producing a wastewater that must be treated before discharge into the environment. The tars represent a by-product for which uses must be found or which must be disposed of in environmentally acceptable ways. Despite these apparent disadvantages, the Lurgi is one of the most successful gasifier designs in the world: The gasifier is used in the synthetic fuels plants in South Africa as well as in the Dakota gasification plant in Beulah, North Dakota, the primary coal gasification facility in the United States.

Alternative approaches to gasification rely on the so-called entrained flow method, in which finely pulverized coal is blown into the gasifier or injected as a coal-water slurry. In these gasifiers, the coal is heated and reacted so rapidly that the formation of by-product tars is avoided. One such gasifier is the Koppers-Totzek, which is used in many places around the world, mainly to produce hydrogen for ammonia synthesis (for eventual production of fertilizers). The Koppers-Totzek unit uses pulverized solid coal. The Texaco gasifier injects coal in the form of a slurry.

SYNTHESIS GAS

The composition of the gas depends on the specific gasification process used. Generally, the main components are hydrogen and carbon monoxide, the mixture of which makes synthesis gas. One application of synthesis gas is the production of methane, which can then be sold as substitute for natural gas. Synthesis gas can be converted to liquid fuels, as discussed below. The gas can also be burned, particularly in gas turbines that are part of combined-cycle plants for electricity generation. Other uses include production of methanol as a liquid fuel, acetic anhydride for chemicals production, or hydrogen (by removing the carbon monoxide).

COAL LIQUEFACTION

There are two major routes for production of synthetic liquid fuels from coal. The first is called indirect liquefaction, because the coal itself is actually converted to synthesis gas by gasification. In a subsequent step, the synthesis gas is converted to liquid fuels. The dominant technology for this process was developed by Franz Fischer and Hans Tropsch in Germany in the 1920's. Synthesis gas is reacted over a catalyst at high temperatures and pressures. Depending on the specific choice of catalyst, the pressure and temperature of the reaction, and the relative amounts of hydrogen and carbon monoxide, it is possible to produce a variety of liquid fuels, ranging from gasoline to heating oils. The Fischer-Tropsch process, coupled with coal gasification, produced about 757 million liters per year of synthetic liquid fuels used by Germany during World War II. Subsequently, it was commercialized on a large scale in South Africa, which was barred from international trade in oil during the apartheid years but possesses large reserves of coal.

The alternative approach is direct liquefaction. Direct liquefaction is based on the observation that most desirable petroleum products contain about two atoms of hydrogen per atom of carbon. Coal has on average less than one hydrogen atom per carbon atom. The direct conversion of coal to synthetic petroleum-like liquids therefore requires adding hydrogen chemically to the coal. Direct liquefaction is sometimes also called coal hydrogenation. The methods for performing direct liquefaction were developed by Friedrich Bergius, who received the Nobel Prize in Chemistry in 1931. The Bergius process requires extremely high temperatures (500° Celsius) and pressures (up to 4,500 kilograms per six square centimeters), a situation which poses difficult engineering challenges for large-scale operation. Nevertheless, the Bergius process provided three billion liters of synthetic fuels per year to the German war effort in World War II. A metric ton of coal will yield approximately 150 to 170 liters of gasoline, 200 liters of diesel fuel, and 130 liters of fuel oil.

During the 1970's and 1980's, much ingenious research in chemistry and process engineering was directed toward reducing the severe conditions of the Bergius process in order to make the eventual product more economically competitive with petroleum. Despite substantial progress, a synthetic crude oil from coal is likely to cost about $30 to $40 per barrel. There are no direct liquefaction plants operating in the world, though China had plans to open one by 2007, which did not happen.

Harold H. Schobert

FURTHER READING

Berkowitz, Norbert. *An Introduction to Coal Technology.* 2d ed. San Diego, Calif.: Academic Press, 1994.

Freese, Barbara. *Coal: A Human History.* Cambridge, Mass.: Perseus, 2003.

Goodell, Jeff. *Big Coal: The Dirty Secret Behind America's Energy Future.* Boston: Houghton Mifflin, 2006.

Higman, Chris, and Maarten van der Burgt. *Gasification.* 2d ed. Boston: Elsevier/Gulf Professional, 2008.

Probstein, Ronald F., and R. Edwin Hicks. *Synthetic Fuels.* New York: McGraw-Hill, 1982.

Schobert, Harold H. *Coal: The Energy Source of the Past and Future.* Washington, D.C.: American Chemical Society, 1987.

Speight, James G. *The Chemistry and Technology of Coal.* 2d ed., rev. and expanded. New York: M. Dekker, 1994.

Thomas, Larry. *Coal Geology.* Hoboken, N.J.: Wiley, 2002.

_____. *Handbook of Practical Coal Geology.* New York: Wiley, 1992.

Williams, A., M. Pourkashanian, J. M. Jones, and N. Skorupska. *Combustion and Gasification of Coal.* New York: Taylor & Francis, 2000.

WEB SITES

AMERICAN COAL FOUNDATION
All About Coal
http://www.teachcoal.org/aboutcoal/index.html

NATURAL RESOURCES CANADA
About Coal
http://www.nrcan.gc.ca/eneene/sources/coacha-eng.php

U.S. DEPARTMENT OF ENERGY
Coal
http://www.energy.gov/energysources/coal.htm

U.S. DEPARTMENT OF ENERGY
Gasification Technology R&D (Research and Development)
http://www.fossil.energy.gov/programs/powersystems/gasification/index.html

U.S. GEOLOGICAL SURVEY
Coal Resources: Over One Hundred Years of USGS Research
http://energy.usgs.gov/coal.html

WORLD COAL INSTITUTE
Gas and Liquids
http://www.worldcoal.org/pages/content/index.asp?PageID=415

SEE ALSO: Carbon; Coal; Electrical power; energy politics; Synthetic Fuels Corporation.

Coast and Geodetic Survey, U.S.

CATEGORY: Organizations, agencies, and programs
DATE: Established as Coast Survey in 1807; reestablished in 1832; renamed Coast and Geodetic Survey in 1878; abolished in early 1970's

The Coast and Geodetic Survey, moving far beyond its original assignment of making coastal navigation charts, was a research agency that became a world leader in geodesy. It developed and refined navigation and measurement techniques and did research in hydrography and coastal geology.

BACKGROUND

The U.S. Congress created the Coast and Geodetic Survey, initially known as the Coast Survey, early in the nineteenth century to survey the Atlantic coast of the United States and develop accurate charts for navigation and shipping. Legislation in 1807, the Coast Survey Act, first provided for surveying and mapping the nation's coastline, but Congress failed to allocate adequate funding. As a result, little progress was made. In 1832, Congress authorized reestablishment of the Coast Survey. Lawmakers at the time intended for the Coast Survey to be a temporary agency: Funding would be provided only until the charts needed for safe navigation were completed, and then the Coast Survey would be dissolved. Under the leadership of its early superintendents, however, the Coast Survey expanded its mission to include basic research into hydrography, topography, cartography, meteorology, coastal geology, and a wide range of other topics relating to the physics of the Earth. By the time the Coast Survey completed charts of the Atlantic and, after the acquisition of Western territories, Pacific coastlines, the organization was so thoroughly established as a scientific agency that it became difficult for legislators to argue against continued funding. In 1878, the agency's name was changed to the Coast and Geodetic Survey.

IMPACT ON RESOURCE USE

Over the course of the more than 150 years of the Coast and Geodetic Survey's existence, the agency achieved numerous scientific and technical breakthroughs. In the process of completing its original mission of creating navigation charts, the organization evolved into a scientific research agency that became a world leader in geodesy. It developed methods for use in triangulation, arc measurement, geodetic astronomy, determining longitude and latitude, and other aspects of measuring the Earth. The Coast and Geodetic Survey improved instruments used in surveying and navigation for determining position, distance, angles, directions, and elevations, and it investigated the best methods to be used in reproducing maps. As part of its research in geodesy, the survey conducted methodical observations of solar eclipses. For the solar eclipse of August 7, 1869, for example, the survey stationed observation teams in Tennessee, Kentucky, Illinois, Iowa, and Alaska. Other astronomical observations made at various times included studying the transit of the planets Mercury and Venus. Measurements of the great arcs of the thirty-ninth parallel and the ninety-eighth meridian both provided a basis for the government surveys of the interior of the United States and suggested a more refined model of the shape of the Earth.

In addition, the Coast and Geodetic Survey pioneered research in tidal flows, hydrography, and oceanography. The organization determined the best sites for lighthouses and navigation buoys and researched the history of names of prominent geographic features for use on maps and charts. Minor functions of the Coast and Geodetic Survey included

serving as the keeper of the nation's standard weights and measures.

Though the Coast and Geodetic Survey was eventually dismantled, its research traditions continued in other agencies, such as the National Oceanic and Atmospheric Administration (NOAA), a scientific agency created as part of President Richard Nixon's reorganization of the Department of Commerce in 1970. NOAA's National Ocean Service, for example, prepares charts and monitors tidal activity.

Nancy Farm Männikkö

WEB SITES

U.S. COAST AND GEODETIC SURVEY
National Geodetic Survey
http://www.ngs.noaa.gov/

U.S. COAST AND GEODETIC SURVEY
Office of Coast Survey
http://www.nauticalcharts.noaa.gov/

SEE ALSO: Landsat satellites and satellite technologies; National Oceanic and Atmospheric Administration; U.S. Geological Survey.

Coastal engineering

CATEGORY: Environment, conservation, and resource management

Coastal engineering is the discipline that studies the natural and human-induced changes of the geomorphology of the coastal zone. It also develops methods and techniques for protecting and enhancing the coastal environment.

DEFINITION

Coastal engineering focuses on the special engineering needs of the coastal environment. The discipline studies both natural and anthropogenic effects (those caused by human activity) on the geometry and other physical characteristics of the coastal zone, which includes riverine deltas, inlets, estuaries, bays, and lagoons. In the offshore direction, the activities of the coastal engineer are limited to the relatively shallow waters of the continental shelf.

One aspect of coastal engineering is the development and protection of coastal environments like this beach at Point Lobos, California. (©Joseph Salonis/Dreamstime.com)

OVERVIEW

Since the coastline serves as the boundary between the land and the ocean, the coastal engineer must understand the dynamic interaction between water and sediments. Water dynamics involves the action of astronomical tides, tsunamis, storm surges, wind waves, and longshore currents. Water forces continuously change the shape of the coastline through sediment erosion and deposition. Episodic events such as hurricanes may have a significant effect on the stability and integrity of a coastal system. Coastal engineers are mostly interested in sandy or muddy beaches, which are readily subject to sediment erosion. The weathering of rocky beaches to wave action is a slow process and is not of direct interest to coastal engineers.

The coastline is an extremely dynamic system, subject to short-term and long-term changes. Spatially these changes may be localized or may extend for great distances. Generally, if left undisturbed, the coast tends to develop its own defense systems against wave action through barrier islands and sand dunes. Any attempts by humans to regulate the shape of the coastline at a particular site may have adverse effects on another site on the same coastline. Coastal engineers investigate wave and current forces and their impact on the shape of the coastline. For that purpose, coastal engineers collect and analyze field data and use physical models (applying deterministic or probabilistic analytical techniques) and computer models to simulate the wave and current climate. These procedures can lead to predictions of the amount and fate of the transported sediments that cause accretion or erosion of the coastline.

Coastal engineers also investigate techniques for protecting residential and industrial developments along the coast, maintaining recreational facilities and beaches, and providing safe navigation through inlets and coastal waterways. Therefore, constructing structures such as jetties, breakwaters, groins, bulkheads, marinas, and harbors falls within the domain of the coastal engineer. Beach nourishment and inlet dredging are also projects undertaken by coastal engineers.

In order to assess the prevailing hydrodynamic and sedimentological conditions of the coastal zone efficiently and effectively, engineers develop equipment and instrumentation for data collection of wave and current characteristics, suspended and bottom sediments, and other supplementary information such as salinity and temperature of the ambient water. Coastal engineers are also involved in the environmental aspects of coastal waters. Estimation of the spread of an oil spill; the flashing capacity of a lagoon, finger canals, or any other protected water body; dissolved contaminant advection and dispersion; and sediment contamination are all topics of interest to the coastal engineer.

Panagiotis D. Scarlatos

SEE ALSO: Coastal Zone Management Act; Deltas; Ocean current energy; Ocean wave energy; Oceans; Salt; Sand and gravel; Tidal energy.

Coastal Zone Management Act

CATEGORIES: Laws and conventions; government and resources
DATE: Enacted October 27, 1972

The Coastal Zone Management Act provides a framework for protecting and developing the U.S. coastal zones. Achieving both protection and development depends on land management accompanied by land-use planning and land-use regulation and control.

BACKGROUND
The Coastal Zone Management Act of 1972 was passed by Congress in order to establish "a national policy and develop a national program for the management, beneficial use, protection, and development of the land and water resources of the nation's coastal zones, and for other purposes." The coastal zones included in the act are those of the Atlantic and Pacific Oceans, the Gulf of Mexico, and the Great Lakes. The length

of coastline involved is about 153,000 kilometers. The extensive nature of the coastal area of the United States means that thirty states and four territories—Puerto Rico, the Virgin Islands, Guam, and American Samoa—are eligible for coastal zone management assistance.

The Coastal Zone Management Act was passed as a result of concern for the vulnerable nature of the coastal zones and their exposure to intensive development pressures. These pressures include recreation, fishing, agriculture, housing, transportation, and industrial development. With more than half of the U.S. population living within eighty kilometers of a coastal area, the pressures are considerable. The act is administered by the National Oceanic and Atmospheric Administration's Office of Coastal Zone Management. The federal role consists of providing assistance to states as they develop programs to manage the coast in a manner sufficient to deal with the problems arising from competing land uses.

PROVISIONS
Federal assistance takes the form of both financial and technical aid. Paragraph (h) of section 302 of the act emphasizes the importance of a state's role in exercising its authority over the land and water resources of the coastal zone. Especially important in this exercise of authority is the encouragement of citizen involvement in the overall planning process. From the state perspective, such citizen participation has helped in the development of land-use planning guidelines relating to designation of the coastal zone areas, determination of land uses within the coastal zone, the identification of areas of particular concern, the identification of the ways by which the state will control land and water uses, and guidelines for establishing the priority of uses.

IMPACT ON RESOURCE USE
Over the years, the Coastal Zone Management Act has been amended several times. In 1976, the states were given additional time and money for program development. Energy-related coastal development, provisions for access to public beaches, and increased agency cooperation were also part of the 1976 amendments. According to the *Congressional Quarterly Almanac* (1985), the reauthorization of the Coastal Zone Management Act in 1985 lowered the federal share of costs to be paid. Changes in 1990 gave the states more say over federal activities in offshore areas, espe-

cially regarding oil and gas production. The 1990 reauthorization established coastal nonpoint source pollution control plans and required the Environmental Protection Agency to establish uniform national guidelines for controlling nonpoint source pollution in coastal areas. The act was further amended in 1996, 1998, and 2004 to regulate aquaculture facilities and to research the effects of algal blooms and hypoxia.

Jerry E. Green

SEE ALSO: Coastal engineering; Land management; Land-use planning; Land-use regulation and control; National Oceanic and Atmospheric Administration; Population growth.

Cobalt

CATEGORY: Mineral and other nonliving resources

WHERE FOUND

Cobalt is widely distributed in the Earth's crust in many ores, but only a few are of commercial value; the most important of these are arsenides and sulfides. The world's major sources are in the Democratic Republic of the Congo, Australia, Canada, Zambia, Russia, and Cuba.

PRIMARY USES

The largest use of cobalt is in superalloys, alloys designed to resist stress and corrosion at high temperatures. Other important uses are in magnetic alloys for motors, meters, and electronics and as a binder in cemented carbides and diamond tools.

TECHNICAL DEFINITION

Cobalt (abbreviated Co), atomic number 27, belongs to Group VIII of the transition elements of the periodic table and resembles iron and nickel in many chemical and physical properties. It has one naturally occurring isotope, with an atomic weight of 58.194. Cobalt as a metal is lustrous and silvery with a bluish tinge. It has an allotropic form that is stable only above 417° Celsius. Its density is 8.90 grams per cubic centimeter; it has a melting point of 1,495° Celsius and a boiling point of 3,100° Celsius. Cobalt is known to exist in more than two hundred ores. These are invariably associated with nickel and often also with copper and lead. Cobalt is tougher, stronger, and harder than nickel and iron although less hard than iridium and rhodium. It is ferromagnetic at less than 1,000° Celsius. Like other transition elements, it has multiple oxidation states (II and III are most common), forms coordination complexes, and produces several colorful compounds and solutions.

DESCRIPTION, DISTRIBUTION, AND FORMS

Cobalt is about 29 parts per million of the Earth's crust, making it the thirtieth element in order of abundance. It is less abundant than the other first-row transition elements except scandium. Other than the reserves of cobalt in Africa and Canada, there are smaller reserves in Australia and in Russia. In 2006, for example, the leading producers of cobalt ore were the Democratic Republic of the Congo (41 percent), Zambia (12 percent), Australia (11 percent), Canada (10 percent), Russia (8 percent), Cuba (6 percent), and China (3 percent). Total world production was about 67,500 metric tons.

Studies have shown that land with a cobalt deficiency will cause ruminant animals to lose their appetite, lose weight, and finally die; the disease is essentially a vitamin B_{12} deficiency. Vitamin B_{12} is necessary in ruminants for metabolism. In other animals cobalt does not seem to be essential. However, humans do need vitamin B_{12}, also called cyanocobalamine; in humans a B_{12} deficiency causes megaloblastic anemia.

Cobalt appears in many materials, including soils and water. There is evidence that minute quantities can be harmful to higher plant life. It can also be harmful to animals; for example, sheep are harmed if they consume more than 160 milligrams of cobalt per 45 kilograms of weight. There is no evidence that the normal human level of exposure to cobalt is harmful.

HISTORY

Egyptian pottery from 2600 B.C.E., Iranian glass from 2250 B.C.E., and Egyptian and Babylonian blue glass from 1400 B.C.E. owe their blue color to cobalt. Apparently, however, the art of making blue glass from cobalt ores disappeared until the end of the fifteenth century, when Christoph Schürer used cobalt ores to impart a deep blue color to glass. Cobalt ores were used not only to color glass but also as a blue paint for glass vessels and on canvas. In 1735, Swedish chemist Georg Brandt recognized the source of the color and is considered the discoverer of cobalt. In 1780, Torbern Olaf Bergman showed it to be a new element.

Although the name is close to the Greek *cobalos*, for mine, the word cobalt is thought to come from the German word *Kobald*, for goblin or evil spirit. Miners called certain ores kobald because they did not produce copper but did produce arsenic compounds that were harmful to those near the smelting process.

OBTAINING COBALT

Cobalt is usually produced as a by-product of copper, nickel, or lead, and the extraction method depends on the main product. In general, the ore is roasted to remove gangue material as slag and produce a mixture of metals and oxides. The copper is removed with sulfuric acid. The iron is precipitated with lime, and sodium hypochlorite precipitates the cobalt as a hydroxide, which is reduced to metal by heating with charcoal.

USES OF COBALT

In the United States, superalloys account for 45 percent of cobalt use. Other uses include magnetic alloys, cemented carbides, catalysts, driers in paint, pigments, steel, welding materials, and other alloys. One isotope, cobalt 60, is important as a source of gamma rays. It is used in the medical field to treat malignant growths. The steel alnico, which also contains aluminum and nickel, is used to make permanent magnets that are twenty-five times as strong as ordinary steel magnets. In the ceramics industry, cobalt is used as a pigment to produce a better white by counterbalancing the yellow tint caused by iron impurities.

C. Alton Hassell

FURTHER READING

Greenwood, N. N., and A. Earnshaw. "Cobalt, Rhodium, and Iridium." In *Chemistry of the Elements*. 2d ed. Boston: Butterworth-Heinemann, 1997.

Hampel, Clifford A., ed. *The Encyclopedia of the Chemical Elements*. New York: Reinhold, 1968.

Kim, James H., Herman J. Gibb, and Paul D. Howe. *Cobalt and Inorganic Cobalt Compounds*. Geneva, Switzerland: World Health Organization, 2006.

Leopold, Ellen. "The Rise of Radioactive Cobalt." In *Under the Radar: Cancer and the Cold War*. New Brunswick, N.J.: Rutgers University Press, 2009.

Mertz, Walter, ed. *Trace Elements in Human and Animal Nutrition*. 5th ed. 2 vols. Orlando, Fla.: Academic Press, 1986-1987.

Ochiai, Ei-ichiro. *General Principles of Biochemistry of the Elements*. Vol. 7 in *Biochemistry of the Elements*. New York: Plenum Press, 1987.

Silva, J. J. R. Fraústo da, and R. J. P. Williams. "Nickel and Cobalt: Remnants of Life?" In *The Biological Chemistry of the Elements: The Inorganic Chemistry of Life*. 2d ed. New York: Oxford University Press, 2001.

Syracuse Research Corporation. *Toxicological Profile for Cobalt*. Atlanta, Ga.: U.S. Dept. of Health and Human Services, Public Health Service, Agency for Toxic Substances and Disease Registry, 2004.

Weeks, Mary Elvira. *Discovery of the Elements*. 7th ed. New material added by Henry M. Leicester. Easton, Pa.: Journal of Chemical Education, 1968.

WEB SITES

NATURAL RESOURCES CANADA
Canadian Minerals Yearbook, Mineral and Metal Commodity Reviews
http://www.nrcan-rncan.gc.ca/mms-smm/busi-indu/cmy-amc/com-eng.htm

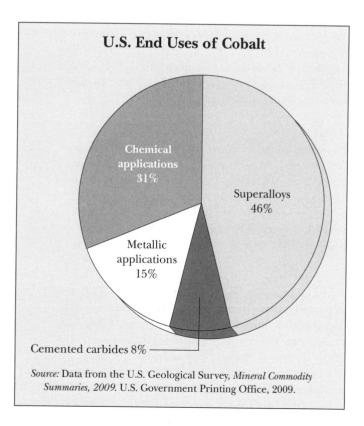

U.S. End Uses of Cobalt

Chemical applications 31%

Superalloys 46%

Metallic applications 15%

Cemented carbides 8%

Source: Data from the U.S. Geological Survey, *Mineral Commodity Summaries, 2009.* U.S. Government Printing Office, 2009.

U.S. GEOLOGICAL SURVEY
Cobalt: Statistics and Information
http://minerals.usgs.gov/minerals/pubs/
    commodity/cobalt

SEE ALSO: Alloys; Canada; Ceramics; Congo, Democratic Republic of the; Magnetic materials; Metals and metallurgy; Russia; Steel.

Cogeneration

CATEGORY: Energy resources

Cogeneration is the productive use of waste heat from industrial processes or from electrical power generation. Heat from cogeneration may be used to produce electricity or in manufacturing.

DEFINITION

Cogeneration refers to methods of producing electrical power from heat that would otherwise be wasted as well as other ways of using waste heat productively. Cogeneration results in energy savings and, particularly when it can be made economically feasible enough to be applied widely, in the conservation of nonrenewable energy resources. A considerable amount of heat—and therefore energy—is wasted in the production of electrical power and in many manufacturing operations.

OVERVIEW

The generation of electricity from fossil fuels involves the use of heat to transform the chemical energy stored in the fuels into high-pressure, high-temperature steam. The steam drives turbogenerators, which in turn produce electricity. A waste product from this operation is low-temperature steam, which must be cooled by large amounts of water before it can be recycled back in liquid form to the plant's boiler. One goal of cogeneration is harnessing this low-pressure steam.

Water must undergo a phase change—that is, it must be heated enough to be turned from liquid to steam—in order to produce electricity. Producing steam is an energy-intensive process because of the physical nature of water. Once water in its liquid phase reaches a temperature of 100° Celsius, its temperature stabilizes and remains the same for the amount of time it takes to turn the water to steam. The heat re-

quired for this phase change is called latent heat. Latent heat cannot be measured in the same way that sensible heat (heat that raises the temperature of a material) can be. Utilities have generally been unable to use this latent heat, and capturing this energy is a major point of cogeneration.

Cogeneration can be achieved in two different cycles, the topping cycle and the bottoming cycle. Power utilities use only the topping cycle, which uses energy input to generate electricity and uses the waste heat for a practical purpose. A number of other industries use this cycle as well. The bottoming cycle, which applies the energy input to process heat and uses the waste to produce electricity, is not as common. One example of its use is in the paper industry. Waste heat from the kraft chemical recovery process is captured in a series of water-filled tubes, and the resultant steam is used to generate electricity and process heat. Efficiencies can reach 85 percent at integrated pulp and paper mills, since exhaust steam from the powerhouse can help dry the paper. A modern mill can produce 75 percent or more of the electrical power and steam that it needs. There have been cases where paper mills have been able to supply electricity to local areas that have lost power because of natural disasters.

The implementation of cogeneration depends on its economic feasibility. Some proposed projects are not put into operation because of the significant capital expenditures involved. Perhaps the most sensible approach involves cooperative agreements between users and producers of electricity. Substantial energy savings are possible. The European Union garners more than 10 percent of its total energy from cogeneration.

Vincent M. D. Lopez

SEE ALSO: Electrical power; Energy economics; Steam and steam turbines.

Commoner, Barry

CATEGORY: People
BORN: May 28, 1917; Brooklyn, New York

Commoner, a research biologist, has been referred to as "Dr. Ecology," "the Paul Revere of ecology," and an "elder of America's environmental movement."

BIOGRAPHICAL BACKGROUND

Barry Commoner grew up on the streets of Brooklyn with an unusual interest in and zeal for the outdoors. Fascinated by nature, he spent weekends exploring parks for specimens to study under the microscope. His interest in biology was spurred at James Madison High School and Columbia University. Following completion of his bachelor's degree he entered Harvard University and earned a doctoral degree in cellular physiology. He remained an academic scholar with the exception of a stint in the Navy during World War II and a year as associate editor of *Science Illustrated* in 1946. His teaching career started at Queens College, and he later returned there following thirty-four years at Washington University. He left Washington University to enter politics as the presidential candidate of the Citizens Party in 1980. He headed the Center for the Biology of Natural Systems at Queens College until leaving the post in 2000. Into his tenth decade, he remained a revered voice in the field of ecology.

IMPACT ON RESOURCE USE

As a research scientist, Commoner contributed considerably to knowledge of viral function and to cellular research with implications for cancer diagnosis. As an environmental activist, he was vital in educating the public that in the Earth environment "everything is connected to everything else." A prolific author, Commoner wrote numerous books about the environment, including *Science and Survival* (1966), *Making Peace with the Planet* (1992), and *Zeroing out Dioxin in the Great Lakes: Within Our Reach* (1996).

As an "eco-socialist," Commoner rejected the environmental degradation caused by capitalism and advocated ecological priorities over economic ones in a system of communal ownership. To this end, Commoner has emphasized nature over technology, holding that the interconnectedness of nature and humankind makes it impossible to escape the consequences of our treatment of the planet. In the second of his "Four Laws of Ecology," Commoner states that "Everything must go somewhere. There is no 'waste' in nature and there is no 'away' to which things can be thrown." Hence, resources must be used both sustainably and with full responsibility for the impact of their use on the system as a whole.

Kenneth H. Brown

SEE ALSO: Biosphere; Conservation; Ecosystems; Energy politics; Environmental degradation, resource exploitation and; Environmental ethics; Environmental movement; Renewable and nonrenewable resources; Sustainable development.

Composting

CATEGORIES: Environment, conservation, and resource management; plant and animal resources

Composting is a way for gardeners and farmers to enrich and otherwise improve the soil while reducing the flow of household waste to landfills. Essentially the slow natural decay of dead plants and animals, composting is a natural form of recycling in which living organisms decompose organic matter.

BACKGROUND

The decay of dead plants and animals starts when microorganisms in the soil feed on dead matter, breaking it down into smaller compounds usable by plants. Collectively, the breakdown product is called humus, a dark brown, spongy, crumbly substance. Adding humus to soil increases its fertility. Compost may be defined in various ways. The *Oxford English Dictionary* defines it (as a noun) as a mixture of ingredients for fertilizing or enriching land, a prepared manure or mold; *Webster's New World Dictionary* defines it (as a verb) as the making of compost and the treatment of soil with it. Compost and composting derive from the Old French *composter*, "to manure" or "to dung."

HISTORY

The origins of human composting activities are buried in prehistory. Early farmers undoubtedly discovered the benefits of compost, probably from animal manure deposited on or mixed with soil. In North America, American Indians and then Europeans used compost in their gardens. Public accounts of the use of stable manure in composting date back to the eighteenth century. Many New England farmers also found it economical to use fish in their compost heaps.

While living in India from 1905 to 1934, British agronomist Sir Albert Howard developed today's home composting methods. Howard found that the best compost pile consists of three parts plant matter to one part manure. He devised the Indore method of composting, alternating layers of plant debris, manure, and soil to create a pile. Later, during the composting process, he turned the pile or mixed in earthworms.

How Composting Works

Composting is a natural form of recycling that takes from six months to two years to complete. Bacteria are the most efficient decomposers of organic matter. Fungi and protozoans later join the process, followed by centipedes, millipedes, beetles, and earthworms. By manipulating the composition and environment of a compost pile, gardeners and farmers can reduce composting time to three to four months. Important factors to consider are the makeup of the pile, the surface area, the volume, the moisture, the aeration, and the temperature of the compost pile.

Yard waste such as fallen leaves, grass clippings, some weeds, and the remains of garden plants make excellent compost. Other good additions to a home compost pile include sawdust, wood ash, and kitchen scraps, including vegetable peelings, egg shells, and coffee grounds. Microorganisms digest organic matter faster when they have more surface area to work on. Gardeners can speed the composting process by chopping kitchen or garden waste with a shovel or running it through a shredding machine or lawn mower.

The volume of the compost pile is important because a large compost pile insulates itself, holding in the heat of microbial activity. A properly made heap will reach temperatures of about 60° Celsius in four or five days. Then the pile will settle, a sign that is working properly. Piles 0.76 cubic meter or smaller cannot hold enough heat, while piles 3.5 cubic meters or larger do not allow enough air to reach the microbes in the center of the pile. These portions are important only if the goal is fast composting. Slower composting requires no exact proportions.

Moisture and air are essential for life. Microbes function best when the compost heap has many air passages and is about as moist as a wrung-out sponge. Microorganisms living in the compost pile use the carbon and nitrogen contained in dead matter for food and energy. While breaking down the carbon and nitrogen molecules in dead plants and animals, they also release nutrients that higher organisms such as plants can use.

The ratio of carbon to nitrogen found in kitchen and garden waste varies from 15 to 1 in food waste to 700 to 1 in wood. A carbon-to-nitrogen ratio of 30 to 1 is optimum for microbial decomposers. This balance can be achieved by mixing two parts grass clippings (carbon-to-nitrogen ratio, 19:1) and one part fallen leaves (carbon-to-nitrogen ratio, 60:1). This combination is the backbone of most home composting systems.

Modern Uses and Practice

Composting remains an important practice. Yard and kitchen wastes use valuable space in our landfills. These materials compose about 20 to 30 percent of all household waste in the United States. Composting household waste reduces the volume of municipal solid waste and provides a nutrient-rich soil additive. Compost or organic matter added to soil improves

A woman mixes her indoor composting box that contains worms that convert household waste into compost. (Beth Balbierz/MCT/ Landov)

soil structure, texture, aeration, and water retention. It improves plant growth by loosening heavy clay soils, allowing better root penetration. It improves the water-holding and nutrient-holding capacity of sandy soils and increases the essential nutrients of all soils. Mixing compost with soil also contributes to erosion control and proper soil pH balance.

Some cities collect and compost leaves and other garden waste and then make it available to city residents for little or no charge. Some cities also compost sewage sludge or human waste, which is high in nitrogen and makes a rich fertilizer. Properly composted sewage sludge that reaches an internal temperature of 60° Celsius contains no dangerous disease-causing organisms. One possible hazard, however, is that it may contain high levels of toxic heavy metals, including zinc, copper, nickel, and cadmium.

The basic principles of composting used by home gardeners also are used by municipalities composting sewage sludge and garbage, by farmers composting animal and plant waste, and by some industries composting organic waste. Food and fiber industries, for example, compost waste products from canning, meat processing, dairy, and paper processing.

Judith J. Bradshaw-Rouse

FURTHER READING

Bem, Robyn. *Everyone's Guide to Home Composting*. New York: Van Nostrand Reinhold, 1978.

Campbell, Stu. *Let It Rot! The Gardener's Guide to Composting*. 3d ed. Pownal, Vt.: Storey Communications, 1998.

Jenkins, Joseph C. *The Humanure Handbook: A Guide to Composting Human Manure*. 3d ed. White River Junction, Vt.: Chelsea Green, 2005.

Martin, Deborah L., and Grace Gershuny, eds. *The Rodale Book of Composting*. New, rev. ed. Emmaus, Pa.: Rodale Press, 1992.

Simons, Margaret. *Resurrection in a Bucket: The Rich and Fertile Story of Compost*. Crows Nest, N.S.W.: Allen & Unwin, 2004.

WEB SITES

CORNELL WASTE MANAGEMENT INSTITUTE, DEPARTMENT OF CROP AND SOIL SCIENCES, CORNELL UNIVERSITY
Cornell Composting
http://www.css.cornell.edu/compost/ Composting_Homepage.html

U.S. ENVIRONMENTAL PROTECTION AGENCY
Composting
http://www.epa.gov/wastes/conserve/rrr/ composting/index.htm

SEE ALSO: Conservation; Erosion and erosion control; Incineration of wastes; Landfills; Recycling; Soil degradation; Soil management; Waste management and sewage disposal.

Comprehensive Environmental Response, Compensation, and Liability Act. *See* Superfund legislation and cleanup activities

Concrete. *See* Cement and concrete

Congo, Democratic Republic of the

CATEGORIES: Countries; government and resources

Beginning in the late nineteenth century, the Congo (now Democratic Republic of the Congo), then a Belgian colony, was recognized as a potentially rich source for raw materials. By the time of Congolese independence in 1960, certain provincial regions, particularly the former colonial province of Katanga, had become the center for the mining and transport, by foreign companies, of a number of major mineral resources, including copper, cobalt, zinc, cadmium, germanium, tin, manganese, and coal.

THE COUNTRY

The Democratic Republic of the Congo (DRC) is located in west-central Africa, with its westernmost limit running along the Atlantic coast. The country is separated from the Republic of the Congo by the Congo River. Its other neighbors are the Central African Republic, Sudan, Uganda, Rwanda, Burundi, Tanzania, Zambia, and Angola. Although not all areas of the country receive the massive amounts of rainfall characteristic of the interior Congo basin zone, there is an extensive zone that is heavily forested.

Democratic Republic of the Congo: Resources at a Glance

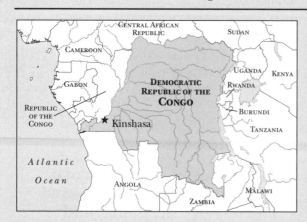

Official name: Democratic Republic of the Congo
Government: Republic
Capital city: Kinshasa
Area: 905,420 mi²; 2,344,858 km²
Population (2009 est.): 68,692,542
Language: French
Monetary unit: Congolese franc (CDF)

ECONOMIC SUMMARY:

GDP composition by sector (2000 est.): agriculture, 55%; industry, 11%; services, 34%
Natural resources: cobalt, copper, niobium, tantalum, petroleum, industrial and gem diamonds, gold, silver, zinc, manganese, tin, uranium, coal, hydropower, timber
Land use (2005): arable land, 2.86%; permanent crops, 0.47%; other, 96.67%
Industries: mining (diamonds, gold, copper, cobalt, coltan, zinc), mineral processing, consumer products (including textiles, footwear, cigarettes, processed foods and beverages), cement, commercial ship repair
Agricultural products: coffee, sugar, palm oil, rubber, tea, quinine, cassava (tapioca), palm oil, bananas, root crops, corn, fruit, wood products
Exports (2007): $6.1 billion
Commodities exported: diamonds, gold, copper, cobalt, wood products, crude oil, coffee
Imports (2007) $5.2 billion
Commodities imported: foodstuffs, mining and other machinery, transport equipment, fuels
Labor force (2007 est.): 23.53 million
Labor force by occupation (1991 est.): agriculture, 65%; industry, 16%; services, 19%

ENERGY RESOURCES:

Electricity production (2006 est.): 7.243 billion kWh
Electricity consumption (2006 est.): 5.158 billion kWh
Electricity exports (2006 est.): 1.799 billion kWh
Electricity imports (2006 est.): 6 million kWh

Natural gas production (2007 est.): 0 m³
Natural gas consumption (2007 est.): 0 m³
Natural gas exports and imports (2007 est.): 0 m³
Natural gas proved reserves (Jan. 2008 est.): 991.1 million m³

Oil production (2007 est.): 22,160 bbl/day
Oil imports (2006 est.): 8,220 bbl/day
Oil proved reserves (Jan. 2008 est.): 180 million bbl

Source: Data from *The World Factbook 2009.* Washington, D.C.: Central Intelligence Agency, 2009.
Notes: Data are the most recent tracked by the CIA. Values are given in U.S. dollars. Abbreviations: bbl/day = barrels per day; GDP = gross domestic product; km² = square kilometers; kWh = kilowatt-hours; m³ = cubic meters; mi² = square miles. Current labor force occupational data are unavailable.

Traditionally the world-famous Congo River served as the main artery of access to the interior. Development of modern alternative modes of transport, especially railways, has been gradual and not altogether successful.

The potential global impact of DRC mineral production has been reduced by the country's chronic political instability, much of which has been concentrated in mineral-rich areas of the country. Another problem affecting the global status of exports from the Democratic Republic of the Congo is the predominance of foreign investors (in the form of multinational concessionaires) in the mining sector. This seems to be less a problem of antiforeign sentiment than a result of "shifting" foreign involvement. Many foreign operations have been hampered by unstable conditions, while others have actually withdrawn entirely from development commitments signed with the government in Kinshasa, the country's capital.

COPPER

The large southern area of the Democratic Republic of the Congo, formerly the Shaba (1971-1997) or Katanga (1960-1971, 1997-2009) Province but in 2009 divided into four provinces—Haut-Katanga, Tanganyika, Lualaba, and Haut-Lomami—is part of an enormous metallogenic zone running from Angola in West Africa to Zambia. The area is commonly called the "Copperbelt" of Africa, although other minerals, especially cobalt, are mined in the same area. It is estimated that 10 percent of the world's copper reserves (approximately 50 million metric tons) are located within the Democratic Republic of the Congo. Before the year 2000, the country's copper was mined primarily by the state-run firm Gécamines (Générale des Carrières et des Mines). About a decade after the country gained independence, Gécamines received world attention for the relatively low cost of its copper, but this advantage was lost in stages as various disruptive factors reversed the situation, making Congolese copper much more expensive on the world market.

Copper production by Gécamines was still relatively high at the beginning of the twenty-first century (about 19,000 metric tons) but fell by about 1,000 metric tons, largely because of an inability to operate many existing mines at full capacity; some mines were completely inactive. A marked example of declining productivity was the Society for Congolese Industrial and Mining Development (Sodimco), a minor "counterpart" to Gécamines, whose output in 2001 was less than 550 metric tons of copper. Sodimco extracted the copper from the Musoshi and Kinsenda mines, whose copper reserves have been estimated to be more than 220 million metric tons.

In an effort to obtain a more competitive global position for DRC copper, the Kinshasha government concluded a partnership between Gécamines and the Finnish-run Outokumpu Mining Group to exploit both copper and cobalt reserves. The trend of seeking collaborative operations with foreign mining firms increased over the next few years. In 2002, Anvil Mining, an Australian firm with operations in Canada, obtained a concession for operating the Dikulushi copper and silver mine in the traditional Katanga mining zone. Results were encouraging: Mining yielded almost 13,000 metric tons of copper in 2003, which was followed by announcement of plans to expand the Dikulushi mine.

Another foreign concern, International Panorama Resources (IPR) of Canada, joined (at 51 percent participation) with Gécamines to use high-tech methods to reprocess copper- and cobalt-bearing tailings from mines located at Kambove and Kakanda. The initial level of IPR's involvement, like that of other foreign companies concerned about declining public security in the areas of their concessions, was cut back despite signs that copper prices were returning to reasonably attractive levels.

In fact, the 1999 price of $0.27 per kilogram of copper recovered to $1.70 by 2006. However, in the period between 2006 and 2009, the price fluctuated considerably, and available stockpiles during the 2008 onset of the global financial and economic crisis suggested that decreasing demand would push prices down again, below $1.50 or even lower.

Despite recurring technical, financial, and political difficulties in mining copper, the DRC continued to receive bids from foreign firms interested in either mining or processing the country's copper deposits. In 2004, for example, the South African mining company Metorex agreed to mine and process ore (including cobalt) in the region near Lubumbashi (specifically the Ruashi and Etoile mines).

Specialized information services on the Web (such as MBendi Information) list specific ongoing mining projects and companies, both foreign and national, involved in the Congolese copper sector. The total of at least one dozen active firms and projects suggests that the DRC is dedicated to maintaining copper mining as a priority.

COBALT

The DRC is one of ten sub-Saharan countries in Africa with substantial reserves of cobalt (the DRC and Zambia are the most important). The cobalt is frequently found in veins bearing copper and, along with nickel, is separated out as a by-product of copper mining.

The DRC's location across the central African Copperbelt means that the country has a substantial share, almost 35 percent, of the world's cobalt. In modern times the metallic element colbalt (Co) is used to make strong alloys and is essential as a radio-isotope (Cobalt 60) in producing gamma rays.

Specialized importers' demand, therefore, is relatively high. Although government-run Gécamines suffered cobalt production setbacks, because of under-utilization of partially exploited mining locations, in the years after 2000, the company continued to enter into joint exploitation contracts with foreign firms interested in particularly promising special projects. Perhaps the most outstanding of these projects was the 2004 acquisition, by the London-based Adastra Minerals, of full rights to process massive tailings sites at the Kolwezi location. This ambitious project set as its aim reclaiming major amounts of both copper (more than 40,000 metric tons annually) and cobalt (more than 6,000 metric tons annually) from more than 100 million metric tons of oxide tailings at Kolwezi.

PETROLEUM AND NATURAL GAS

The limited (22-kilometer) stretch of the DRC's Atlantic coast (running between northern Angola and the oil-rich enclave of Cabinda) was the scene of oil exploration activities as early as the 1960's, but production was not significant until offshore wells in the same region began production in 1976. The Mibale offshore field, eventually estimated to hold almost 50 percent of the coastal basin's reserves, was discovered in 1973 by Chevron. More than forty wells had been drilled, most offshore, by the mid-1980's, yielding five working oil fields and one natural gas field.

Exploration of inland areas, especially along the eastern border of the DRC and in the central Congo basin, produced less promising results. Some hope for exploitation of proven reserves in the region bordering Uganda was registered, but not effectively pursued. Natural gas reserves in regions close to the Rwanda border await efficient exploitation. In the case of natural gas, not only infrastructural problems, such as the remoteness of the region and lack of ef-fective transport, but also recurrent political instability and regional violence have continued to hamper follow-up to exploratory soundings.

As for the DRC's more promising offshore petroleum sector, a series of arrangements and rearrangements of foreign oil companies' involvement in consortium agreements with the Kinshasha government have been made. The most important consortium arrangement involved participation at 50 percent holdings by Congo Gulf Oil (Chevron), 32 percent by Congo Petroleum Company (Teikoku Oil of Japan), and 18 percent by Union Oil of California.

GOLD

Mining for gold in the area around Namoya (some 250 kilometers from Bukavu, on the edge of forested areas leading eastward to the Rwandan and Ugandan borders), first by alluvial methods in the 1930's, and then by open-pit mining in the 1950's, was interrupted during the early years of Congolese independence. Although production was restored gradually, periodic outbreaks of civil violence in key ore-producing sub-zones (Namoya, Twangiza, Kamituga, and Lugushwa) have hampered efforts to effectively exploit gold mining in the northeastern provincial region. Anti-government rebel forces occupied, abandoned, then reoccupied the key population centers during the entire first decade after 2000.

These disruptive conditions have not prevented key foreign mining concerns from seeking contractual agreements for concessions from the Kinshasha government.

DIAMONDS

Although the DRC, and specifically the Kasai-Oriental Province, is potentially the largest producer of diamonds in Africa, it has fallen far short of fulfilling this potential. Despite the existence of a formal commercial diamond concession, Minière de Bakwanga (MIBA)—a joint operation involving the Belgian company Sibeka and the government of the DRC—only about a third of the country's diamonds are exported by MIBA. Knowing the origin and channels pursued by many "informal" dealers to commercialize the majority of diamonds mined in the DRC is nearly impossible. A major cause for this comes, again, from extremely unsettled political conditions and recurring outbreaks of violence. Conditions of disorder lend themselves to the possibility of illicit dealings in the diamond market. Fear of involvement in criminal diamond dealings (known in West and central Africa as the "blood diamond" trade) caused the major South African diamond importer Kimberley Process to blacklist the DRC in 2004. This stopped officially recognized export processes but did not stop "private" intermediaries from conducting smuggling operations. Some estimates of the Congolese government's losses because of diamond smuggling have been as high as a one-half billion dollars annually.

In the same year that Kimberley denounced diamond operations in the DRC, De Beers arranged a confidentiality-covered diamond concession agreement, committing more than $200 million to conduct much needed improvements.

MANGANESE

The DRC produced upwards of 45,000 metric tons of manganese ore annually in the early 1970's, most of which was transported by rail from the Lulua basin to export facilities at Benguela on the Angolan coast. The principal, if not the only, firm involved in these operations, the Kisenge Manganese Mining Enterprise, experienced dramatic declines in exports (down to a little more than 27,000 metric tons in the late 1980's) during the long period of civil war in Angola. In 1993, production came to a de facto end. Kisenge, in its efforts to regain a section of the manganese market by introducing high-tech dry-cell modes to process high-grade electrolytic manganese dioxide, has encountered difficulty, given the fact that several of its African neighbors also produce manganese at attractive prices.

TANTALUM AND NIOBIUM

The DRC possesses a number of coltan (tantalum-ore) producing mines in the Lake Kivu region. The primary mining operation there is Anvil Mining (with home offices in Australia and Canada), a firm which is heavily involved in DRC copper mining. Tantalum, along with a similar metal always found alongside tantalum, is a highly corrosion-resistant element used widely as a component in metal alloy processes. Although tantalum could be an increasingly significant DRC export, two factors may limit such development (beyond the fact that Australia produces most of the tantalum for the world market): Almost all the central African neighbors of the DRC—including Rwanda, Tanzania, Uganda, Zambia, and Gabon—also produce tantalaum for export; and, after Anvil Mining launched its major mining operations in the first few

years of the twenty-first century, controversy over the ecological impact such mining might have, both for surrounding forests and for animal life in the region, has come to the forefront.

OTHER RESOURCES

Given the extensive forested area of the Congo River basin, the DRC is in a position to export a variety of rare hardwoods and some industrially attractive common lumber. This sector has yet to develop to its full potential because of the lucrative, if risky, mineral industry.

Byron D. Cannon

FURTHER READING

Nest, Michael Wallace, François Grignon, and Emizet F. Kisangani. *The Democratic Republic of Congo: Economic Dimensions of War and Peace.* Boulder, Colo.: Lynne Reinner, 2006.

Renner, Michael, and Thomas Prugh. *The Anatomy of Resource Wars.* Washington, D.C.: Worldwatch Institute, 2002.

Renton, Dave, David Seddon, and Leo Zellig. *The Congo: Plunder and Resistance.* New York: Zed Books, 2007.

Wolfire, Deanna, Jake Brunner, and Nigel Sizer. *Forests and the Democratic Republic of Congo: Opportunity in a Time of Crisis.* Washington, D.C.: World Resources Institute, 1998.

SEE ALSO: Belgium; Cobalt; Copper; Diamond; Gold; Oil and natural gas distribution.

Conservation

CATEGORY: Environment, conservation, and resource management

Humanity's footprint is being felt around the world. As the global population continues to increase, the natural resources necessary to sustain life continue to decline. Fresh water, fossil fuels, and arable land are just a few of the natural resources that must be properly managed to sustain a global population that may reach 9.1 billion by the year 2050, as predicted by the United Nations.

BACKGROUND

The planet Earth may be unable to support future increases in population unless, on a worldwide scale, humans begin to conserve and reduce their rates of consumption and increase efforts to recycle resources for new uses. Moreover, the current global economy is no longer sustainable and is destroying the environment and providing little to support the globally impoverished. Internationally, governments and social activists have begun to work together to establish policies that protect the environment and the sustainability of life while concomitantly fostering harmonious economic growth.

"Conservation" generally refers to the use of resources found in the natural environment in such a way that the resources will serve humans effectively and will be available to humans for as long as possible. Therefore, it does not refer to the indefinite "preservation" of resources in their natural state. Quantitatively, effective conservation could be said to involve obtaining the maximum use for the maximum number of people.

The Earth can be viewed as a life-support system composed of four major subsystems through which energy flows and matter cycles. The subsystems are the atmosphere, biosphere, lithosphere, and hydrosphere, referring to gases, life systems, rock and mineral materials, and water, respectively. As energy flows and matter cycles within and among these subsystems, they interact as component parts to compose the Earth's ecosystem (an ecosystem may be defined as a community of plants, animals, and other organisms interacting in an environment). Humans alter the natural cycling of energy and flow of matter in the Earth's ecosystem. We extract things from natural systems, convert them into what we perceive as more useful products, and then return them to the natural environment in different forms and physical states. In order to achieve more desirable energy conversions, we also use energy from the environment. Natural resources are all of the things that humans take from the environment to help satisfy their needs and wants.

RESOURCES AND RESERVES

All the matter and energy on Earth make up its "stock." Natural resources are subsets of this stock that help humans meet their energy and material needs. Those natural resources that are available in a usable form and at an affordable price under prevailing technology and socioeconomic conditions make up "reserves." For example, uranium was not a part of human energy reserves until the technology to capture and control the flow of nuclear energy was developed. Agrofuels produced from plant resources and biofuels developed from recently lifeless plant and animal materials are other examples of the marriage between natural resources and technology to meet energy demands for such uses as powering vehicles and heating buildings.

Natural resources may be classified as renewable, nonrenewable, and perpetual. Renewable resources are those that can be reproduced at a rate equal to or greater than the rate of consumption. Renewable resources are replenished through natural, physical, and biogeochemical cycles. Examples of renewable resources are forest and soil. They are conserved when they are used and reused at a rate, and in such a way, that does not destroy their sustainability. This does not mean that they cannot be depleted; it means that the rate of consumption does not exceed the rate at which they are replenished over an extended period.

Nonrenewable resources, on the other hand, are those for which the rate of consumption exceeds the rate of renewal. They are exhaustible, cannot be replenished, and exist in fixed amounts. Nonrenewable resources, such as minerals and fossil fuels, are conserved by more thorough exploitation of their deposits and more efficient use. Some can be recycled or reused. Recycling involves collecting and reprocessing a resource, while reuse involves using a resource again in the same form. The reprocessing of used aluminum cans into new cans is an example of recycling. Washing beverage bottles before using them again is an example of reuse. Other nonrenewable resources, such as coal and oil, are gone forever once they are used.

Perpetual resources, such as water, wind, tides, and solar energy, continue to flow throughout the Earth's ecosystem whether humans use them or not. Therefore, they are sometimes called flow resources. Even when their quality is altered they generally continue to flow within the Earth's ecosystem, making them inexhaustible. However, man is affecting the flow of some of these resources, such as water, and the recent harnessing of wind resources to produce energy is leading some scientists to suggest that altering the flow of wind with multiple, large turbines may lead to climate change.

CONSERVATION VS. PRESERVATION

"Conservation" of natural resources means using things found in the natural environment wisely. In a more quantitative sense, it means sustainability of the natural resources by obtaining the maximum use for the maximum number of people without compromising future needs. It does not imply that resources should be entirely preserved for use later; rather, it means that they should be employed in a way that serves humans as well and as long as possible. Although preservation is closely associated with some aspects of conservation, the two approaches are different, as "preservation" means the complete protection of natural resources from human disturbance. It is true that to conserve some resources is to preserve them: We conserve natural resources such as ecosystems, for example, by restricting their use and protecting them from being altered, because their value is diminished if they are not retained in their original state. However, we conserve most resources when we use them in a certain way, not when we leave them idle.

HISTORICAL PERSPECTIVE

Not until technology developed significantly, and the world's human population reached a certain size, did human exploitation of the environment begin to have significant effects. Until that time, conservation of resources was simply not an issue. For most of humankind's existence, people lived a simple hunter-gatherer existence, obtaining just enough food to survive. Most people lived in small groups—fifty or fewer people—that had little effect on resources or the environment. They made simple tools and weapons. Many groups were nomadic, migrating with the seasons and following game animals. The shift from a hunting-and-gathering society to a sedentary one began about ten thousand years ago. People began breeding animals and cultivating wild plants, thereby having a greater impact on the environment. Slash-and-burn cultivation involved cutting down trees and other vegetation, leaving the cut vegetation on the ground to dry, and then burning it to enrich the soil.

A primary concern of the modern environmental movement is the abandonment of polluting fuels. In 2009, these protesters called for the plant that provides power to the U.S. Capitol to cease its practice of burning coal for electricity. (Roger L. Wollenberg/UPI/Landov)

Farmers were "subsistence farmers," producing only enough to feed their families.

With the invention of the metal plow about seven thousand years ago, agriculture could be practiced on a larger scale. Animals were used to pull the plows, increasing crop productivity and making the cultivation of new soils possible. Forests were cut and grasslands were plowed—soil erosion and degradation of wildlife habitats inevitably began to follow on a small scale. Occasional food surpluses were produced for sale or storage. Surpluses allowed the development of urban cultures by releasing people from the farm. By the nineteenth century, urbanization and the Industrial Revolution were having profound impacts on the environment and the rate of resource consumption.

HISTORY OF THE CONSERVATION MOVEMENT

In 1864, George Perkins Marsh published *Man and Nature: Or, Physical Geography as Modified by Human Actions*. Marsh's book, which claimed that humanity could no longer afford to continue wastefully exploiting natural resources, is thought by some to mark the beginning of the conservation movement. However, American Indians must also be given credit as one of the first peoples to practice sustainable natural resource use. In 1878, John Wesley Powell completed *A Report on the Lands of the Arid Region of the United States*. Powell's study of the geomorphology and arid landscape transformations in the Colorado River basin was grounded in scientific methodology and called for the creation of a federal agency to survey and map all U.S. lands. In 1879, the United States Geological Survey was created for this purpose. At the beginning of the twentieth century there was growing concern that resource mismanagement could have tragic future consequences. These concerns were based on scientific findings associated with the exploitation and depletion of timber. In 1907, the Inland Waterways Commission, headed by U.S. Forest Service chief Gifford Pinchot, reported that the use and control of water would have an impact on other resources, including timber, soil, wildlife, and minerals. Pinchot's views on resource management greatly influenced forest and water management policies in the United States.

During the Great Depression of the 1930's, the Franklin Delano Roosevelt administration instituted a number of programs in the United States that addressed natural resource problems and helped create employment. In the wake of the severe drought and wind erosion in the Dust Bowl, the Public Works Administration initiated the Prairie States Forestry Project. Its goal was to establish a shelter belt of trees and shrubs from the Texas panhandle to the Canadian border in North Dakota. This project was designed to reduce wind erosion on rangeland and cropland. Other efforts included the creation of the Tennessee Valley Authority (TVA) and the Civilian Conservation Corps (CCC). The TVA was an innovative water resource management program that involved comprehensive regional planning. Though confined to the Tennessee River and its tributaries, it provided a model for total resource management. The aim of the CCC was to provide employment while repairing some of the damage that had resulted from past exploitation of natural resources and neglect of the environment. Workers constructed bridges, roads, and fire lanes for the development of recreational facilities; conducted tree-planting programs; instituted soil- and water-erosion control projects; made lake and stream improvements; and participated in flood control projects.

Many of these early conservation practices in the United States spread to other countries and, over time, several international conservation organizations were formed, including the United Nations Environment Programme, the International Union for the Conservation of Nature, and the World Wildlife Fund. After World War II, nations focused on resource-related problems, many times creating agencies to assess the impact that the war had on forest and natural resources. Moreover, the use of atomic bombs in the war—and the widespread nuclear testing that occurred in the 1950's—exposed ecosystems to significant levels of radiation. This situation marked the beginning of the modern conservation movement.

THE MODERN CONSERVATION MOVEMENT

Although the United States is credited as the frontrunner of the early conservation movement through its linking of ecology with conservation and resource management practices on public lands, during the modern conservation movement, especially in the 1980's, the United States focused on economic growth and deregulation, sacrificing conservation. Nevertheless, the efforts of the Worldwatch Institute and older organizations such as the Sierra Club, the Audubon Society, and Friends of the Earth kept the general citizenry aware of environmental and resource-related issues and their consequences.

In 1962, Rachel Carson, in her book *Silent Spring*, cautioned the public against the indiscriminate use of chemical pesticides. She argued that persistent substances released into the environment move throughout the food chain, concentrating over time, while pests may develop a resistance to the poisons. By the 1960's, pollution from industrial and vehicular sources was beginning to be recognized as a global issue, as industrialized nations increased their spoliation and depletion of natural resources. In the United States, President John F. Kennedy introduced a number of natural resource initiatives aimed at preserving wilderness areas, developing marine resources, reserving shorelines for public use, expanding outdoor recreation, formulating plans for developing water resources and developing actions against water pollution, and encouraging the development of substitutes for resources in short supply. Also, he organized the Youth Conservation Corps to provide a workforce to implement the program. By the 1970's, during the administration of President Richard M. Nixon, the United States had begun to adopt environmental laws such as the Clean Air Act and created the Environmental Protection Agency as its enforcement agency. The first Earth Day to celebrate sustainable use of natural resources was in 1970.

The international community came together to discuss the environment for the first time in 1972. The United Nations held the Conference on the Human Environment in Stockholm, Sweden. This conference, which came to be known as the Stockholm Convention, resulted in the creation of the United Nations Environment Programme. The 1987 publication of the Brundtland Report (also known as the *Our Common Future*) by the United Nations World Commission on Environment and Development was one of the first documents to take on the issue of sustainable global development in modern times in a manner similar to that espoused by Pinchot in earlier times. The goal of the Brundtland Report was to foster global economic development that is conservation-oriented and economically balanced.

In 1980, another international organization became active in conservation. The International Union for Conservation of Nature (IUCN) published *World Conservation Strategy*. The purpose of this publication, and one of the ongoing goals of the IUCN, was to assist developing nations in conservation planning to protect and maintain natural resources: air, water, soil, forests, and animals.

Since 1992, the international community and world leaders have continued to come together regularly to discuss global environmental problems. At the 1992 United Nations Conference on Environment and Development held in Rio de Janeiro, Brazil, much of the discussion concerned the Brundtland Report. This conference, which came to be known as the "Rio Earth Summit," focused on dire predictions concerning global warming, climate change, the ozone hole; concerns about the depletion of natural resources, loss of habitats, and biodiversity; and continued concerns with resource pollution and depletion, especially forests and marine resources. Some experts at the Rio Summit suggested that society had to choose between economic development and conserving the environment. Although governments have been unwilling to make an either/or choice, one outcome of the Rio Earth Summit was the ratification by many nations of various international agreements to resolve some of the issues discussed at the Summit. For example, the Summit led to the ratification of the 1987 Montreal Protocol, which concerns depletion of ozone by man-made chemicals, and the 1992 Kyoto Protocol, to limit industrial emissions that may be affecting global climate change.

Sustainable development became the main topic of discussion at the U.N. 2002 Earth Summit held in Johannesburg, South Africa. Many world leaders came together to promulgate international regulations to address such environmental problems as improving air and water quality; improving food access, agricultural productivity, and sanitation in developing countries; and developing strategies and economic incentives to cope with international environmental issues related to war, poverty, and disease.

Although the United States has not been a signatory to some of the latter-day environmental protocols, environmental conservation organizations, including the Sierra Club, and individuals, such as former U.S. vice president Al Gore, alert the public to environmental issues. Gore won the 2007 Nobel Peace Prize together with the U.N. Intergovernmental Panel on Climate Change for their efforts in getting out the conservation message on global climate change. International organizations continued the conservation movement in preparation for the 2012 Earth Summit.

POPULATION AND RESOURCE CONSUMPTION
Population growth is a major factor when considering the time it will take to deplete the Earth's nonrenewable resources. A resource is considered economically depleted after 80 percent of its known reserves have been exploited, because at that point the resource becomes too expensive for wide use. As the world's population grows, the rate of resource exploitation grows. More production is necessary to satisfy the needs and wants of larger populations: More materials are needed, more energy is consumed, and more pollution is created.

Ecologists have come to realize that the Earth is a huge ecosystem with a definite carrying capacity. That is, there is a limit to the number of people that can be supported by the Earth. The rate of resource depletion is a function both of the rate of population growth and of the rate of consumption of resources per person. More resources are consumed per individual in wealthy countries than in poor countries. As poor countries strive to develop, greater pressures are placed on the Earth to provide resources and to assimilate wastes. Overpopulation occurs when there are too many people for the available resources or when population growth exceeds economic growth; such conditions ultimately begin to cause damage to the Earth's life-support system.

WATER RESOURCES: THE NEXT GREAT CONFLICT

The availability and purity of water may be the next great natural resource issue facing the world, and control of water resources could lead to serious conflict. Water not only is necessary to sustain life and health but also is needed for food production and various industrial uses. Water resources continue to be polluted; rivers have dried up and have been dammed, thus reducing downriver flows to wetlands and floodplains; underground water supplies from aquifers have been used faster than they are replenished with rainfall; and development is destroying wetlands and other water resources and converting them, in some cases, to deserts. Because the global society has always relied on water as a renewable resource, it has continued using management policies that are no longer viable. In order to maintain human and wildlife populations, habitats, and health, and in order to ensure that there are sufficient water resources to sustain food production, water resource management policies must change.

OTHER NATURAL RESOURCE ISSUES

Other global natural-resource issues concern extractions from the Earth: minerals, precious metals, and gems such as diamonds; oil and gas drilling; and coal mining. Some of the methods used for these extractions and the consequences of accidents and spills have raised the global consciousness about their impact on the environment. A search for renewable resources to replace many of these nonrenewable resources is under way within the global community.

Also controversial is the negative environmental impact of outdated rangeland management techniques, uncontrolled timber harvesting, forest destruction, and mismanaged disposal and dumping.

Mammoth Hot Springs in Yellowstone National Park. (Photo courtesy PDPhoto.org)

Many developed nations suffer from wasteful consumerism and overuse of natural resources, such as those that provide energy. Government structures to foster conservation are lacking in most developing countries, and in many industrialized nations government leaders and the public are unwilling to make genuine efforts to conserve vital and dwindling natural resources, especially if they negatively impact economic growth. Scientists predict that these abuses of the environment and overuse of natural resources can no longer continue at their present rate if we want to preserve the future of humanity.

ECONOMICS AND CONSERVATION

Economics plays an important part in the balancing of resource conservation and resource exploitation. Continued growth in the use of a nonrenewable resource can occur only for a number of years before the resource is depleted. As a resource becomes scarce, the price increases, making it less affordable and reducing the rate of consumption. This is a self-regulating process that makes conservation more practical as resources become more scarce in a market-driven system.

Effective conservation programs often require governmental influence, regulation, or incentives. Since most resources are associated with property, governmental agencies that regulate land, businesses, and private citizens all make decisions that affect resource consumption. The general aim of many decision makers is to maximize the return on investments; conservation must therefore be profitable within a reasonable time for people to practice it voluntarily. In a free enterprise system, resource exploitation produces income from the land and provides much of the incentive for land ownership. Thus, resource exploitation is likely to win out over conservation if there are no incentives to conserve.

Conservation practices must be congruent with economics. Conservation programs are not effectively executed when economic necessity or opportunity intervenes. For the most part, conservation is good for the economy over the long term, because it improves the efficiency of production systems. However, because modern economic growth has not been balanced and has not conserved natural resources, more drastic measures may be necessary to control future growth.

One of the more controversial proposals to combat economic growth issues facing the environment are taxes on carbon-related energy sources. Another highly debated policy recommendation is over emission trading, or cap-and-trade. Controlled ownership of resources through vehicles such as trusts to avoid depletion of natural resources—mostly nonrenewable resources—is another proposal being debated. Those involved in national and global political and social debate must become serious in reaching a consensus for resolving the many environmental issues facing the world and recommend sustainable policies that bring together economists and environmentalists in working for the same achievable goals regarding future growth. However, no matter what policies are eventually adopted, one of the main goals of balancing economic growth with conservation must be continued public awareness. The public and organizations are more likely to become supportive partners for sustainable economic growth if they are provided with not only information on economic growth and its effect on the environment, but also feasible, market-driven solutions.

ASSESSING THE FUTURE

Experts attempting to assess the future of natural resources are divided in their opinions. Positions range from optimistic to direly pessimistic to somewhere between the two extremes. Those who believe that technology can and will solve human problems have reason to be optimistic, and, to a great extent, history supports this view. Whenever humans experience shortages, they turn to technology for solutions—either developing more efficient ways of finding, ex-

tracting, and using resources or finding substitutes for them.

On the other hand, technology may not be able to continue solving all humankind's problems—at least not in a timely enough manner to avoid a crisis. The primary basis for the pessimistic argument is that increases in resource consumption rates, coupled with an increase in population, may not allow enough time to find technological solutions to resource shortages. Furthermore, the heavy modern dependence on nonrenewable resources is certain to cause resource shortages.

A more moderate view of the resource future suggests that, although there is good reason for concern, humankind has sufficient time to avoid a major crisis if we begin moving toward a sustainable society now. A sustainable society is one that allows humanity to meet its needs today without compromising its environment and future needs. Sustainability almost certainly requires that people in developed countries begin to live a lifestyle that includes more conservation and recycling, a greater dependence on renewable and perpetual resources than on nonrenewable resources, population control, and more self-discipline. This view embraces the ecological approach to resource management and employs the multiple-use concept. For example, forest conservation not only provides timber but also preserves a habitat for plants and animals; it can serve to help manage water resources, prevent flooding and soil erosion, and provide recreational areas. When we reach sustainability, most of humankind's material and energy needs will be provided by renewable and perpetual resources that should last indefinitely if properly managed.

The ecological approach is holistic. Based on the philosophy that all things in the natural environment are interlaced through a complex system of feedback loops, it implies that the whole is functionally greater than the sum of its parts. This approach to resource management requires an understanding and anticipation of the consequences of human actions throughout the ecosystem.

Jasper L. Harris, updated by Carol A. Rolf

FURTHER READING

Castillon, David A. *Conservation of Natural Resources: A Resource Management Approach.* 2d ed. Madison, Wis.: Brown & Benchmark, 1996.

Chiras, Daniel D., and John P. Reganold. *Natural Resource Conservation: Management for a Sustainable*

Future. 10th ed. Upper Saddle River, N.J.: Pearson Prentice Hall, 2009.

Degregori, Thomas R. *The Environment, Our Natural Resources, and Modern Technology.* New York: John Wiley & Sons, 2008.

Freyfogle, Eric T. *Why Conservation Is Failing and How It Can Regain Ground.* New Haven, Conn.: Yale University Press, 2006.

Greenland, David. *Guidelines for Modern Resource Management: Soil, Land, Water, Air.* Columbus, Ohio: C. E. Merrill, 1983.

Greiner, Alfred, and Will Semmler. *The Global Environment, Natural Resources, and Economic Growth.* New York: Oxford University Press, 2008.

Harper, Charles L. *Environment and Society: Human Perspectives on Environmental Issues.* 4th ed. Upper Saddle River, N.J.: Pearson/Prentice Hall, 2008.

Jakab, Cheryl. *Natural Resources (Global Issues).* North Mankato, Minn.: Smart Apple Media, 2008.

Knight, Richard L., and Courtney White, eds. *Conservation for a New Generation: Redefining Natural Resources Management.* Washington, D.C.: Island Press, 2009.

Krupp, Fred, and Miriam Horn. *Earth: The Sequel— The Race to Reinvent Energy and Stop Global Warming.* New York: W. W. Norton, 2008.

Loeffe, Christian V., ed. *Conservation and Recycling of Resources: New Research.* New York: Nova Science, 2006.

Miller, G. Tyler, Jr. *Resource Conservation and Management.* Belmont, Calif.: Wadsworth, 1990.

Parson, Ruben L. *Conserving American Resources.* 3d ed. Englewood Cliffs, N.J.: Prentice-Hall, 1972.

Raven, Peter H., Linda R. Berg, and David M. Hassenzahl. *Environment.* 6th ed. Hoboken, N.J.: Wiley, 2008.

Scott, Nicky. *Reduce, Reuse, Recycle: An Easy Household Guide.* White River Junction, Vt.: Chelsea Green, 2007.

WEB SITES

CONSERVATION INTERNATIONAL
http://www.conservation.org/Pages/default.aspx

INTERNATIONAL UNION FOR CONSERVATION OF NATURE
http://www.iucn.org/

THE NATURE CONSERVANCY
http://www.nature.org/

UNITED NATIONS ENVIRONMENT PROGRAMME
http://www.unep.org/

WORLD RESOURCES INSTITUTE
http://www.wri.org/

WORLD WILDLIFE FUND
http://www.panda.org/

WORLDWATCH INSTITUTE
http://www.worldwatch.org/

SEE ALSO: Capitalism and resource exploitation; Civilian Conservation Corps; Conservation International; Developing countries; Endangered species; Environmental degradation, resource exploitation and; Environmental movement; International Union for Conservation of Nature; Population growth; Renewable and nonrenewable resources; Sustainable development; United States; World Wide Fund for Nature.

Conservation biology

CATEGORIES: Environment, conservation, and resource management; scientific disciplines

Biological scientists throughout the world are interested and involved in conservation biology as a means of preserving biodiversity. Evolutionary biologists, botanists, ecologists, and geneticists, as well as those in applied-science management fields such as wildlife management, fisheries, and forestry, all play important roles in the broad context of conservation biology.

BACKGROUND

Conservation biology is a multidisciplinary field that incorporates the knowledge base and skill sets of all of the biological sciences in order to design and implement methods that will attempt to ensure the long-term continuation of species, ecosystems, and ecological processes.

HISTORICAL PERSPECTIVE

Conservation biology as a scientific discipline has its roots in the conservation movement of the early twentieth century. Wildlife scientists such as Aldo Leopold, foresters such as Gifford Pinchot, and progressive politicians such as Theodore Roosevelt wielded tremendous influence in both conservation and preservation efforts. In the 1960's and 1970's, there was phenomenal growth of community ecology data and important ecological theories, such as island biogeography, promoted by Robert H. MacArthur, Edward O. Wilson, and Daniel Simberloff. Social trends of this time period also contributed to the development of this field, as many people embraced the environmental movement, and, accordingly, a number of significant pieces of environmental legislation were passed. As more and more species either neared extinction or became extinct, the movement to "save the planet" became ever more insistent.

Consequently, much of the focus of conservation biology since the 1970's has been on saving endangered and threatened species. The United States Fish and Wildlife Service (USFWS) defines an endangered species as one that is in danger of extinction throughout all or a significant portion of its range. A threatened species is likely to become endangered in the foreseeable future. The USFWS tracks the numbers of endangered and threatened species both within the United States and around the world. In 2009, the number of endangered animal species within the United States was 410, with 163 listed as threatened. Bird, fish, mammal, and clam species topped the endangered animal list. The endangered plant species total was 600; 146 plant species were threatened. Throughout the remainder of the world, 527 animal species were endangered and 44 were threatened; 1 plant species was listed as endangered and 2 were threatened. Obviously, these numbers vary from year to year; nevertheless, the data support the need for worldwide conservation efforts.

MINIMUM VIABLE POPULATIONS

In the past in Europe and North America, most extinctions or local extirpations of species occurred because of overhunting. Examples of this in North America include bison, cougar (in the eastern U.S., with the exception of the remnant Florida panther population), red wolf, and passenger pigeon. In Europe, the wolf, wild boar, goshawk, and capercaillie were gone by the nineteenth century.

Although overhunting is still a reason for species decline in some parts of the world, today the primary cause for the large number of endangered and threatened species is habitat fragmentation. This occurs when a large area of habitat is divided into a number of smaller patches comprising a smaller total area. Often these smaller patches are unsuitable for species of the original habitat, and thus dispersal of species into

the "new" habitat can be low. Conservation biologists face the challenge of preserving as many individuals of the endangered or threatened species as possible within suitable habitat, thereby enabling genetic diversity within the species to continue. As a result of fragmentation, conservation biologists are often trying to discover a minimum viable population (MVP) number for each imperiled species. Although the number of five hundred individuals has often been used as a base guideline for MVP, many scientists argue that the specific number of individuals needed to ensure genetic diversity varies by species and that no set number applies to all species.

If the MVP becomes too low, serious genetic problems within the population may occur, as the number of individuals is simply too low to prevent inbreeding. Probably the best known example of this is the cheetah, a species in which almost all of the individuals are now related to one another. Biologists have noted deleterious genetic effects such as sperm malformation and high infant mortality within the cheetah population. With species that have greatly reduced population numbers, conservation biologists are faced with the management challenge of reducing inbreeding, encouraging outbreeding if enough individuals remain, and seeking to enable members of the species to migrate, if possible.

RESERVES

Along with determining MVPs for endangered and threatened species, biologists seek to meet the management goals mentioned above by creating or maintaining suitable reserve sites. As with deciding on MVP, determining the necessary size and shape of a reserve can be extremely difficult and is again species dependent. Based on their research, several conservation biologists have suggested that a circular shape for reserves is best in order to minimize dispersal distances and to minimize the amount of edge habitat. Within both temperate and tropical forest areas, negative edge effects include temperature and humidity changes, wind exposure, tree mortality, and penetration of light into formerly shaded areas.

Many researchers recommend single large reserve areas for large herbivores, large carnivores, and birds, rather than a number of small reserves, unless an extensive corridor of suitable habitat can connect the small reserves. The efforts of national conservation organizations are often necessary to establish and maintain large nature reserves, whereas regional and even local groups may be able to keep smaller reserves going for species that do not require large expanses of habitat in which to survive.

Active management of reserves is usually necessary in order to provide continued suitable habitat for endangered and threatened species. Often exotic vegetation must be removed from reserves, or a certain successional stage of vegetation must be maintained. Elimination of exotic animal species, such as wild boars or brown-headed cowbirds, may be needed. Once land has been set aside for the preservation of imperiled species, conservation biologists must be vigilant in its management in order to preserve the biodiversity of the area.

Lenela Glass-Godwin

FURTHER READING

Groom, Martha J., Gary K. Meffe, and C. Ronald Carroll. *Principles of Conservation Biology*. Sunderland, Mass.: Sinauer Associates, 2006.

Pullin, Andrew S. *Conservation Biology*. New York: Cambridge University Press, 2002.

Soulé, Michael E., and Gordon H. Orians. *Conservation Biology: Research Priorities for the Next Decade*. Washington, D.C.: Island Press, 2001.

WEB SITE

WORLD RESOURCES INSTITUTE
Global Forest Watch: Frequently Asked Questions
http://www.globalforestwatch.org/english/about/faqs.htm

SEE ALSO: Biodiversity; Biological invasions; Biomes; Biosphere; Biosphere reserves; Conservation; Endangered species; Endangered Species Act; Genetic diversity; Species loss; Sustainable development; Wildlife biology.

Conservation International

CATEGORY: Organizations, agencies, and programs
DATE: Established 1987

Conservation International initiates projects and secures funding to promote biodiversity and protect endangered animal and plant species and vulnerable ecosystems, both terrestrial and aquatic, by sponsoring scientific research, educational programs, and publi-cations. This nonprofit organization urges indigenous peoples, governments, and businesses to incorporate environmentally compatible actions when interacting with natural resources.

BACKGROUND

In February, 1987, several Nature Conservancy leaders, including Peter A. Seligmann, decided to establish Conservation International (CI) to introduce innovative conservation programs based on scientific investigations that concentrated on biodiversity. In 1989, Seligmann became CI's chief financial officer, and Russell A. Mittermeier succeeded him as president, remaining in that position into the twenty-first century. CI's headquarters are located in Arlington, Virginia.

IMPACT ON RESOURCE USE

Protecting biodiversity shapes all CI's endeavors. CI emphasizes that nature is essential to humans but that economic and political agendas often cause imbalances in nature and destruction of natural resources. CI's Rapid Assessment Program (RAP) involves scientific teams surveying a specific country's ecosystems. Their reports assist each country's government leaders, conservationists, and researchers to determine how to protect vulnerable natural resources. RAP work has aided in creation of national parks and has helped officials stop unlawful oil drilling. With projects in approximately forty-five countries, CI maintains field offices in five divisions: South America, Africa and Madagascar, East and Southeast Asia, Mexico and Central America, and Indonesia-Pacific.

CI scientists identify sites that CI refers to as "biodiversity hot spots" because those places are endangered by damaging situations, depleted resources, and threatened unique species. By 2008, CI had designated thirty-four hot spots, noting that those places represented 2.3 percent of the Earth. CI created Conservation Priority-Setting Workshops to devise effective conservation strategies to advance biodiversity in hot-spot communities. CI's Debt-for-Nature program secures rights to protect endangered natural resource sites in trade for financial assistance. By 2008, CI estimated it had protected a total of approximately 1.2 million square kilometers.

CI's Center for Applied Biodiversity Science (CABS) and Tropical Ecology Assessment and Monitoring (TEAM) Network endeavor to save valuable ecosystems from destruction by human activities. CI scientists conducted pioneering biodiversity studies of coral reefs and reptiles in 2007. They discovered previously unknown species of plants, frogs, geckos, and jumping spiders. In 2008, CI scientists participated in a global mammal survey that determined that more than one-half of primates are at risk of extinction.

CI recognizes that climate change threatens biodiversity and therefore implements programs, such as tree planting, to counter deforestation. CI estimates this work decreases greenhouse-gas emissions by about 1 to 2 billion metric tons annually. The Mantadia Conservation Carbon Project in Madagascar protects 450,000 rain forest hectares, which absorb 9 million metric tons of carbon dioxide emissions.

By providing educational opportunities and employment incentives, CI encourages indigenous people living in fragile ecosystems to practice conservation. CI helped Kayapó Indians in Brazil protect more than 11 million hectares from loggers. CI also endorses ecotourism to generate income and biodiversity awareness.

CI publications include the *RAP Bulletin of Biological Assessment*, volumes in the CI Tropical Field Guide series, and pocket guides. Significant CI-sponsored books are *Megadiversity: Earth's Biologically Wealthiest Nations* (1997), *Hotspots: Earth's Biologically Richest and Most Endangered Terrestrial Ecoregions* (1999), *Wilderness: Earth's Last Wild Places* (2002), and *Hotspots Revisited* (2004).

Elizabeth D. Schafer

WEB SITE

CONSERVATION INTERNATIONAL
http://www.conservation.org

SEE ALSO: Biosphere reserves; Conservation; Conservation biology; Endangered species; Endangered Species Act; Wilderness.

Consultative Group on International Agricultural Research

CATEGORY: Organizations, agencies, and programs
DATE: Established 1971

The focus of the Consultative Group on International Agricultural Research is on agricultural productivity, profitability, and sustainability. The organization's cross-cutting research focuses on reducing poverty, protecting the environment, promoting the sustainable use of the natural resources, and fostering human well-being and equality in terms of access to food.

BACKGROUND
The Consultative Group on International Agricultural Research (CGIAR) was established in 1971 in response to the international community's concern about famine in many parts of the world, especially in Africa and Asia. The creation of the CGIAR was the result of efforts that started in Mexico City between Mexico and the Rockefeller Foundation. These efforts eventually led to the Bellagio Conference, where Rockefeller and Ford Foundation representatives convinced the heads of multilateral and bilateral agencies of the importance of agricultural research and its positive impact on food production around the world.

The CGIAR is composed of fifty-six public- and private-sector members whose goal is to support fifteen international agricultural research centers located in strategic regions around the world. The goal of the fifteen international agricultural research centers is to address the issues of food production, livestock, forestry, economics, water, and natural resources. The CGIAR governance structure is composed of the consultative group executive council, which includes the chairman of CGIAR, the co-sponsors, and other members; the CGIAR secretariat; the CGIAR committees; the fifteen international research centers; and the center committees.

IMPACT ON RESOURCE USE
The CGIAR's mission is to promote sustainable agricultural development in order to provide food security, alleviate poverty through research, and support natural resources management in developing countries. The CGIAR research program implemented by the fifteen research centers covers food crops, forestry, livestock, irrigation management, aquatic resources, environment, and policy. In addition, the research centers provide support and services to developing countries' national agricultural research programs.

The CGIAR is involved in many resource protection programs, such as the Challenge Program on Water and Food, from a research perspective. This program is a multi-institutions initiative with the objective of creating and disseminating information geared toward improving the water productivity in river basins. The emphasis of the program is to create synergies and partnerships among the stakeholders in ways that are pro-poor, gender equitable, and environmentally sustainable.

Since the 1970's, climate change has been a research area of interest to CGIAR scientists. They have been working on the effects of climate change on natural resources, including water resources, and developing crop varieties that can continue to provide the needed food to an ever-growing world population. The scientists have also been active in identifying policies and new approaches for communities to deal with climate change and its consequences. All these years of research have led to the release of improved crop varieties, new farming techniques and crop production methods, and the development of policies to help rural populations, especially in developing countries, manage natural resources in a sustainable way.

Lakhdar Boukerrou

WEB SITE

CONSULTATIVE GROUP ON INTERNATIONAL
    AGRICULTURAL RESEARCH
http://www.cgiar.org

SEE ALSO: Agriculture industry; Agronomy; Greenhouse gases and global climate change; Land Institute; Land-use planning.

Copper

CATEGORY: Mineral and other nonliving resources

WHERE FOUND
Copper deposits are found in several types of geologic environments. Most common are the porphyry copper ore deposits that formed in magmatic arcs associated with subduction zones. These types of ores are found in Canada, the western United States, Mexico, Peru, and Chile. Other important copper deposits were formed by different processes and are found in central Europe, southern Africa, Cyprus, Indonesia, and Japan.

PRIMARY USES
The major uses of copper are in the electrical industry because of the substance's ability to conduct electric-

ity efficiently. Copper is also utilized extensively in the construction industry especially for plumbing. Most of the remaining copper is alloyed with other metals to make bronze (with tin), brass (with zinc), and nickel silver (with zinc and nickel, not silver).

TECHNICAL DEFINITION
Copper (chemical symbol Cu) is a reddish mineral that belongs to Group IB of the periodic table. Copper has an atomic number of 29 and an atomic weight of 63.546, and it is composed of two stable isotopes, copper 63 (69.17 percent) and copper 65 (30.83 percent). Pure copper has a face-centered cubic crystalline structure with a density of 8.96 grams per cubic centimeter at 20° Celsius. The melting point of copper is 1,083° Celsius, and the boiling point is 2,567° Celsius.

DESCRIPTION, DISTRIBUTION, AND FORMS
Copper is a ductile metal and a good conductor of heat and electricity. It is not especially hard or strong, but these properties can be increased by cold working of the metal.

Copper is a relatively rare element, making up only 50 parts per billion in the Earth's crustal rocks. It occurs in nature both in elemental form and incorporated into many different minerals. The primary minerals are the sulfides (chalcopyrite, bornite, covellite, and others), oxides (cuprite and others), and carbonates (malachite and azurite). Copper has two valences (degrees of combining power), +1 and +2, and important industrial compounds have been synthesized using both oxidation states. The most useful industrial +1 (cuprous, or Cu I) compounds are cuprous oxide (Cu_2O), cuprous sulfide (Cu_2S), and cuprous chloride (Cu_2Cl_2). Important +2 (cupric, or Cu II) compounds used by industry are cupric oxide (CuO), cupric sulfate ($CuSO_4$), and cupric chloride ($CuCl_2$).

Although copper is relatively rare in the crust of the Earth, it has been concentrated into ore deposits by geologic processes. There are four major types of copper ore deposits, each formed by a different set of geologic events.

Most of the copper mined is taken from porphyry copper deposits. These deposits are composed of copper minerals disseminated fairly evenly throughout porphyritic granitic rocks and associated hydrothermal veins. The primary ore mineral is chalcopyrite, a copper/iron sulfide. Porphyry copper ore deposits are generally located in rocks that have been formed near convergent plate boundaries where the granites have been produced from magma generated during the subduction of an oceanic plate beneath a continental plate. This tectonic regime has existed along the western coasts of North America and South America for more than 200 million years; consequently, giant porphyry copper deposits are found in western Canada, the western United States, Mexico, Peru, and Chile. The world's two largest producers of copper are Chile and the United States, and the largest copper ore deposit in the world is located in Chile. Other porphyry copper deposits are found in Australia, New Guinea, Serbia, the Philippines, and Mongolia.

A second kind of copper ore deposit is commonly called a Kupferschiefer type because of the large quantity of copper found in the Kupferschiefer shale of central Europe. The copper occurs in a marine shale that is associated with evaporites and nonmarine sedimentary rocks. The origin of the copper in these ores is still debated. The Zambian-Democratic Republic of the Congo copper belt of southern Africa contains more than 10 percent of the world's copper reserves.

Copper is also found in massive sulfide deposits in volcanic rocks, ophiolites, greenstone belts, and fumarolic deposits. Copper-bearing massive sulfide ores are found in Canada, Cyprus, and Japan.

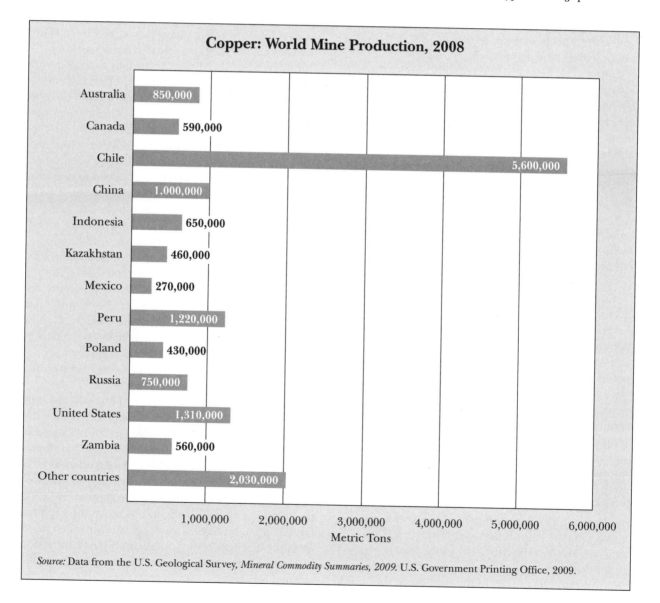

Copper: World Mine Production, 2008

Country	Metric Tons
Australia	850,000
Canada	590,000
Chile	5,600,000
China	1,000,000
Indonesia	650,000
Kazakhstan	460,000
Mexico	270,000
Peru	1,220,000
Poland	430,000
Russia	750,000
United States	1,310,000
Zambia	560,000
Other countries	2,030,000

Source: Data from the U.S. Geological Survey, *Mineral Commodity Summaries, 2009.* U.S. Government Printing Office, 2009.

A fourth type of copper deposit is found on the deep-ocean floors, where manganese nodules have formed very slowly in areas of unusually slow sedimentation. These nodules contain not only manganese but also copper, cobalt, and nickel in economically important concentrations. Since these nodules generally form in water depths of 900 to 2,000 meters, they are difficult to mine. They do, however, represent an important potential source of copper for the future.

Copper is an essential trace element of life and is found in various concentrations within plants and animals. For example, copper is found in many blue-blooded mollusks and crustaceans because it is the central element in hemocyanin, a molecule that transports oxygen in the organisms. It is found in lesser concentrations in many other organisms, such as seaweeds, corals, and arthropods.

Copper can be found in most soils, and its absence or unavailability to plants will cause the soil to be relatively infertile. For example, many muck soils that are very rich in organic material cannot sustain plant life because the copper is bound to the organic matter and is therefore not available to plants.

Some soils have suffered from copper pollution attributable to the excess of copper-bearing fertilizers and the application of copper-rich fungicides or sewage wastes to the land. Research has shown that the accumulations of copper in these soils will not be effectively leached from the land for decades or even centuries because the copper has an affinity for soil colloids that can tightly bind the copper.

Copper is distributed throughout the Earth's lithosphere, hydrosphere, atmosphere, and pedosphere in various concentrations. About 5 percent of the copper content of the lithosphere is found in sedimentary rocks, particularly shale, and only about 0.00004 percent in soils. Only about 0.001 percent of the copper of the lithosphere is in exploitable concentrations, and some of these deposits have been mined for centuries. The total production of copper by mining is approximately 300 million metric tons, of which about 80 percent was mined in the twentieth century. Almost 30 percent of the entire world's historic production of copper was mined in the 1980's. The total copper mined amounts to about twice the total copper in the upper 2 centimeters of soil worldwide and nearly ten times the total copper found in all living organisms. Much of the copper produced has been used and then disposed of on land or wasted in water or the atmosphere. The impact of the transfer of this much

copper from the deposits of the crust to the surface of the Earth is not yet well understood.

The total amount of copper released into the atmosphere has been estimated to be almost three times the amount of carbon in the atmosphere today. The residence time of copper in the atmosphere is quite short, and there probably has not been a significant buildup of copper over time, but the atmosphere does act as a medium for transferring copper around the globe. Copper pollution of many local ecosystems has been well documented in areas near smelters and copper mines. Although it is clear that copper concentrates in the soils and waters near the areas, the impact of copper pollution is often hard to separate from the environmental effects resulting from increased levels of other heavy metals and from sulfur dioxides and other gases released from smelters.

Research has also shown that urban areas generally have much higher levels of copper in the soils and air than are found in rural areas. In many cases the copper concentration in urban soils is more than ten times that of nearby rural areas. In addition, it is well established that the dumping of sewage into rivers, lakes, and the ocean can raise the concentrations of copper in the sediments by factors of two to one hundred times the background levels in unpolluted areas. However, distinguishing the environmental impact of copper from the effects of the associated metals found in sewage effluent is difficult.

Copper is an essential element in the human diet. It is found in several oxidative enzymes, such as cytochromes a and a3, ferroxidase, and dopamine hydroxylase. The copper is used by enzymes in the oxidation and absorption of iron and vitamin C. The level of copper in the body is primarily controlled by the excretion of the element in bile. Absorbed copper is probably stored internally by some intracellular proteins.

Generally, copper deficiencies in humans are rare. There are two known genetic diseases, Wilson's disease and Menkes disease, that disrupt copper metabolism. In Wilson's disease, an unknown mechanism restricts the excretion of copper in bile, and as a result copper builds up in various tissues in the body. Once diagnosed, Wilson's disease can be treated by giving the patient a chelating agent to remove the accumulated copper. Menkes disease, commonly called steely or kinky hair syndrome, causes inefficient utilization of copper in the body. This lack of copper affects the normal formation of connective tissue and the loss of some widespread enzymatic activity. Death generally occurs within the first three years.

HISTORY

Copper was one of the first metals mined and used by humans. It, along with gold and silver, occurs naturally as a free elemental metal and thus can be extracted and used without smelting or refining. Neolithic humans probably learned that this unusual metal could be shaped by hammering with stone tools and that the copper tools could be hardened by continued cold working. The first use of copper probably predated 8000 B.C.E. By 6000 B.C.E. it was known that copper could be melted in crude furnaces and poured into casts to elaborate weapons and ornaments.

A worker in a Chinese factory guides a forklift loaded with rolls of copper tubes. (AP/ Wide World Photos)

Egyptian copper artifacts are dated as far back as 5000 B.C.E., and ancient Egyptians appear to have been the first to alloy copper with tin to make bronze. The earliest record of a bronze artifact dates to about 3700 B.C.E. Bronze makes better weapons and ornaments because it is much harder and tougher than pure copper. As a result, the bronze technology spread throughout the Middle East and into Asia. Bronze items at least as old as 2500 B.C.E. have been found in China, but the alloy may have been used earlier.

Bronze was superseded by iron as the metal of choice for weapons and for structural uses. This technological advance occurred after furnaces were developed that could obtain temperatures high enough to smelt iron from its ores. After the introduction of iron and later steel into common use, copper and its alloys were used primarily for ornaments, utensils, pipes for plumbing, and coinage. Because of its natural resistance to most corrosion caused by air and seawater, copper was commonly utilized for purposes requiring such protection. The discovery of electricity and the invention of the incandescent lightbulb and electric motors led to the extensive use of copper for the transmission of electricity. This became the most common and most important use of copper.

OBTAINING COPPER

Copper is mined in fifty to sixty countries worldwide, with Chile accounting for about 35 percent of the production in 2008. The primary ore minerals of copper are chalcopyrite (copper-iron sulfide), chalcocite (copper sulfide), covellite (copper sulfide), azurite (copper carbonate), and malachite (copper carbonate). Other ore minerals of lesser importance are native copper, bornite, enargite, tetrahedrite, cuprite, tenorite, chalcanthite, and chrysocolla.

The copper sulfide minerals are found in porphyry, massive sulfide, and Kupferschiefer type deposits, and the copper carbonates and copper oxides are commonly found in the upper zones of such deposits that have been exposed to weathering and groundwater action.

Much of the copper of the world is extracted from open-pit mines that expose the ore deposits. The overburden of surrounding rock or soil covering the ore is physically removed, and the ore extracted by drilling and detonating explosives to loosen the ore. Underground mining is done using standard techniques of tunneling and blasting. The ore from either underground mines or open-pit mines is then gathered and hauled to ore processing plants, where the ore is crushed and the copper and other metals are concentrated. The concentrated ore usually measures 20 to 30 percent copper, and it is then either smelted or leached to produce a relatively high concentration of copper, which still contains some impurities. This smelted copper is then electrolytically refined to a purity of more than 99 percent.

USES OF COPPER

Copper was one of the first metals used by humans because it can be found in nature as pure metal and can be worked easily by hand. Pure copper was probably first mined and used by humans around 8000 B.C.E. Through the ensuing ages, copper has remained an important metal and a component of such important materials as pewter, brass, and other bronzes. After the Industrial Revolution, copper became the second most used metal in the industrial world behind only iron. However, the discovery of aluminum, its properties, and its general availability made aluminum more useful in modern society.

Copper is one of the most commonly used metals in the world, and, because of its special qualities of high ductility and electrical conductivity, it is used extensively in the electrical industries. Copper that has been refined electrolytically is up to 99.62 percent pure; the primary remaining material is oxygen. The oxygen helps to increase the density and conductivity of copper wire. The wire can be produced in large quantities by rolling the copper into rods, which are then drawn through tungsten carbide or diamond dies to form the wire.

Copper is also produced in sheets or smaller strips by initially rolling hot copper, with later rollings done with cold copper. The resultant strips or sheets are generally of even thickness and uniform surface appearance. This strip copper can be cut or pressed to be used in the electrical or construction industries.

One of the earliest uses of copper was in the production of bronze. The early bronzes were copper/arsenic alloys; later, tin was added at various concentrations. Modern bronzes are alloys of copper and tin, and they are used primarily for ornaments, bells, and musical instruments. The bronze used in making bells and musical instruments usually contains up to 20 percent tin to impart the proper tonal qualities to the sounds produced from these instruments. Another traditional use for copper is in the production of pewter, which is an alloy of copper and lead. Since lead is highly toxic, the use of pewter has been re-

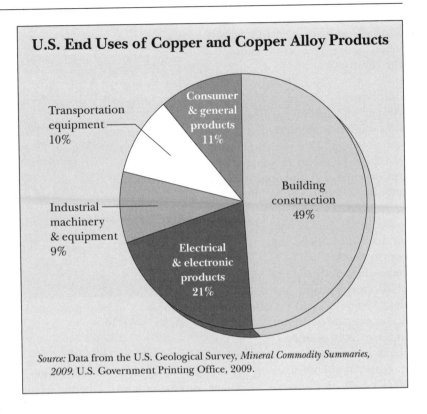

U.S. End Uses of Copper and Copper Alloy Products

Transportation equipment 10%

Consumer & general products 11%

Industrial machinery & equipment 9%

Electrical & electronic products 21%

Building construction 49%

Source: Data from the U.S. Geological Survey, *Mineral Commodity Summaries, 2009.* U.S. Government Printing Office, 2009.

stricted in recent times and is generally reserved for ornamental pieces.

Brass is a widely used alloy of copper and zinc. Although the copper content of brass can range from less than 5 percent to more than 95 percent, only brasses of at least 55 percent copper can be worked and used industrially. White brasses contain more than 45 percent zinc and are not at all malleable and thus are not useful for industrial purposes. The various relative concentrations of copper and zinc produce brasses of widely varying physical properties of hardness, ductility, and malleability. Many brasses can be drawn into wire, rolled into sheets, or formed into rods.

Copper and nickel are completely miscible and therefore can be mixed in any relative concentration. The various mixtures produce alloys with various physical properties and different industrial uses. The alloys using 2 percent to 45 percent nickel produce a material with a much higher hardness than pure copper, and the mixture of about 20 percent nickel produces an extremely ductile alloy that can be cold worked without annealing. This makes this mixture useful for drop forging, cold stamping, and pressing. Industrially this alloy is commonly used for fittings in the automobile industry and for bullet sheathing. Copper and nickel occur together in some ores and can be smelted to produce a natural alloy called Monel metal. The natural ores usually also contain some manganese, which, with other impurities, is incorporated in the alloy. It is also produced artificially by mixing the appropriate levels of nickel, copper, and manganese. Monel metal is extremely strong at normal and high temperatures and thus has many engineering applications.

Copper can also be alloyed with various metals to form other types of bronzes. It can be mixed with 9 percent aluminum to form aluminum bronzes, which are corrosion-resistant metals. Manganese bronzes, which are high-strength alloys, usually contain copper, zinc, aluminum, and 2 to 5 percent manganese. The addition of 1 to 3 percent silicon and 1 percent manganese to copper produces the silicon bronzes, which have good welding and casting qualities. A very strong alloy of copper and about 2 percent beryllium can be strengthened by heat working and will produce a metal with a hardness equal to that of many of the harder steels.

Many copper-containing compounds are used for industrial purposes. Cuprous oxide is used as an antifouling agent in some paints and to give some glass a red color. A green color can be imparted to glass by cupric oxide, and cupric chloride is used in the manufacture of some pigments. Copper sulfate is commonly used as a desiccant and in the production of electrolytically refined copper. Like many other copper compounds, copper carbonates impart strong blue or green colors to solutions and are used in the production of many pigments. Copper can also be combined with arsenic; these compounds are used as insecticides.

Jay R. Yett

FURTHER READING

Adriano, Domy C. "Copper." In *Trace Elements in Terrestrial Environments: Biogeochemistry, Bioavailability, and Risks of Metals*. 2d ed. New York: Springer, 2001.

Brookins, Douglas G. *Mineral and Energy Resources: Occurrence, Exploitation, and Environmental Impact*. Columbus, Ohio: Merrill, 1990.

Greenwood, N. N., and A. Earnshaw. "Copper, Silver, and Gold." In *Chemistry of the Elements*. 2d ed. Boston: Butterworth-Heinemann, 1997.

Joseph, Günter. *Copper: Its Trade, Manufacture, Use, and Environmental Status*. Edited by Konrad J. A. Kundig. Materials Park, Ohio: ASM International, 1999.

Krebs, Robert E. *The History and Use of Our Earth's Chemical Elements: A Reference Guide*. Illustrations by Rae Déjur. 2d ed. Westport, Conn.: Greenwood Press, 2006.

Linder, Maria C. *Biochemistry of Copper*. Vol. 10 in *Biochemistry of the Elements*. New York: Plenum Press, 1991.

National Research Council. *Copper in Drinking Water*. Washington, D.C.: National Academy Press, 2000.

Nriagu, Jerome O., ed. *Copper in the Environment*. 2 vols. New York: Wiley, 1979.

WEB SITES

COPPER DEVELOPMENT ASSOCIATION, INC.
Copper.org: The Ultimate Source for Information on Copper and Copper Alloys
http://www.copper.org

NATURAL RESOURCES CANADA
Canadian Minerals Yearbook, Mineral and Metal Commodity Reviews
http://www.nrcan-rncan.gc.ca/mms-smm/busi-indu/cmy-amc/com-eng.htm

U.S. GEOLOGICAL SURVEY
Copper: Statistics and Information
http://minerals.usgs.gov/minerals/pubs/commodity/copper

SEE ALSO: Alloys; Bronze; Metals and metallurgy; Mining wastes and mine reclamation; Plate tectonics; Plutonic rocks and mineral deposits; Secondary enrichment of mineral deposits.

Coral reefs

CATEGORIES: Ecological resources; plant and animal resources

WHERE FOUND
Typical coral reefs occur in shallow water ecosystems of the Indo-Pacific and Western Atlantic regions. Lesser known cold-water reefs are found at depths between 40 and 3,000 meters along continental shelves, continental slopes, seamounts, and fjords worldwide.

PRIMARY USES
Reefs protect shorelines from wave action and storm damage. Historically, coral has been used in bricks and for mortar. Other uses include souvenirs, aquarium specimens, and even human bone grafts.

The diverse array of plants, invertebrate animals, and vertebrate life that a reef supports are used by humans as food, living and preserved displays, and traditional medicine. Bioprospecting has identified a promising chronic-pain treatment from a reef mollusk. Two possible cancer drugs and an anti-asthma compound have been isolated from reef sponges.

Technical Definition

Corals are animals in the phylum Cnidaria, kin to jellyfish. As members of the class Anthozoa, they are closely related to sea anemones. Reef-building corals secrete calcium carbonate ($CaCO_3$) skeletons that surround the individual soft-bodied organisms comprising the colony. The living layer mounts itself on layer upon layer of the unoccupied skeletons of its ancestors.

Corals are carnivorous, capturing and stinging zooplankton with tentacles surrounding the single opening that serves as mouth and anus. Corals derive a greater amount of nourishment from photosynthetic algae living within cells lining their digestive cavity. Bleaching refers to the loss of these endosymbionts, called zooanthellae, from the coral host or loss of pigment from the algae. Coral may or may not recover from a bleaching episode.

Description, Distribution, and Forms

According to the Global Coral Reef Monitoring Network, 20 percent of reefs have been lost, 24 percent risk imminent collapse because of human pressure, and 26 percent are threatened with collapse over time. Threats to this diverse, productive, complex, and fragile ecosystem are wide-ranging. Some of the damage originates from imbalances on land. Nutrient excesses run off farms and end up in the oceans, feeding explosive reproduction of bacteria. The bacteria use up the available oxygen, creating uninhabitable "dead zones." Another chain reaction begins with deforestation. Increased erosion washes large amounts of

This coral reef in Bonaire, the Netherlands Antilles, was badly damaged by a 2008 hurricane. (Roger L. Wollenberg/UPI/Landov)

soil into the waterway, increasing water turbidity, which blocks light to the coral's zooanthellae. Particulate matter also settles onto the corals, smothering them. Pollution from the construction and operation of marinas, prawn farms, desalination plants, sewage treatment works, and hotels further degrades the reefs. Ship grounding, channel dredging, deep-water trawling, oil and gas exploration, laying of communication cable, dynamite and cyanide fishing, and tourism each take a toll.

Environmental stress renders corals more susceptible to disease. Disproportionate changes in herbivores and predators further disrupt life on the reef. Reduced herbivory by sea urchins or parrot fish allows algae to replace corals. When tritons, large predatory snails, are harvested for their showy shells, population explosions of the crown-of-thorns starfish can decimate reefs.

Storms, such as the 2004 tsunami in the Indian Ocean, shatter and smother large numbers of corals. Climate change will likely expose the reefs to intolerable temperature fluctuations. Low temperatures in 1968, high temperatures in 1987, and major El Niño and La Niña events in 1998 each caused wide-ranging bleaching. Rising levels of carbon dioxide, combined with warmer seawater, inhibit formation of the corals' skeletons.

Designating marine protected areas (MPAs), of which the United States has two hundred, is intended to enhance the management and monitoring of unique ocean ecosystems such as coral reefs. However, fishing and resource extraction are allowed to continue in MPAs, so reef conservation requires stronger protection, such as "no-take areas."

Australia's Global Coral Reef Monitoring Network publishes the *Status of Coral Reefs of the World* biannually. It includes recommendations for reef conservation from more than eighty countries. Nearly one-half of the coral reef countries and states have populations under 1 million. Roughly half of those have less than 100,000 inhabitants. It stands to reason that with less international political clout, banding together advances protection of the reefs.

An area equal to 1 percent of the world's oceans, 190 million kilometers, is covered by coral reefs. Indonesia has the largest area of warm-water (18°-32° Celsius) reefs. Norway is estimated to have the most cold-water (4°-13° Celsius) coral reefs. Cold-water reefs occupy depths below light penetration. Rather than relying on photosynthetic algae, cold-water reefs are supplied particulate and dissolved organic matter and zooplankton by currents. Species diversity of coral and associated organisms is lower, and the reefs grow more slowly than their tropical counterparts.

Individual corals are measured in millimeters. Together, billions of these animals form reef structures as imposing as Australia's Great Barrier Reef, which is 2,000 kilometers long and 145 kilometers wide. This is even more impressive when one realizes that a reef may grow as little as 1 meter in one thousand years.

Dependent upon coral species and physical environment, reefs can be branching, massive, lobed, or folded. On a larger scale, reefs are fringing, barrier, atoll, or platform. Fringing reefs extend from the shoreline. Barrier reefs run parallel to the coast, separated from shore by a lagoon. An atoll is a living reef around a central lagoon. Platform reefs lie far offshore, in calm waters; they are flat-topped with shallow lagoons.

HISTORY

Coral reef history stretches back hundreds of millions of years. Coral larvae that gave rise to modern-day reefs settled on limestone during the Holocene epoch, ten thousand years ago. Humans have been exploiting reef resources for the past one thousand years. Atlantic warm-water reefs are less diverse than those of the Pacific. Reasons for this disparity include lower temperatures, younger geologic age of the ocean, and lower sea levels during the Ice Age in the Atlantic than in the Pacific.

Charles Darwin published *The Structure and Distribution of Coral Reefs* in 1842. One hundred years ago, the world's reefs were healthy. Pollution and sedimentation had not emerged as problems, and natural fish populations were harvested sustainably.

In the 1950's, the geology of reef formation, reef zonation and productivity, and the role of disturbance were areas of study advanced considerably with the widespread use of scuba gear. During the 1980's, research shifted to human impact and decline of coral reefs and how to conserve and restore reefs.

The study of cold-water reefs awaited necessary instrumentation and deep submersibles, available only since the late 1990's. Within the same time frame, the Kyoto Protocol limited carbon emissions, one-third of the Great Barrier Reef was designated a no-take area, and sea urchins returned the balance to Caribbean reefs, each a measure that promises to improve the health of coral reefs.

OBTAINING REEF RESOURCES

Coral reefs support the marine aquarium trade and luxury live food markets. Fishes and reef organisms are captured by hand, hook and line, spear, nets, and trawl nets. Overfishing has led to reliance on methods with indiscriminate by-catch and habitat destruction via dynamite and cyanide fishing. Handling and transfer mortality drive extraction rates even higher in order to meet global demand.

USES OF REEF RESOURCES

The main uses of coral reefs are their in situ ecosystem services. The vivid interdependency of the diversity they support rivals that of tropical rain forests. Hundreds of species of coral support thousands of other organisms, including, but not limited to, algae, seagrass, plankton, sponges, polychaete worms, mollusks, crustaceans, echinoderms, and fish. More than onehalf of all marine fish species are found on coral reefs and reef-associated habitats. Larger predators, such as sharks and moray eels, feed on the fish. The extensive coral reef food web cycles nutrients in oligotrophic (nutrient-poor) tropical waters.

Over millennia, coral reefs have formed landmasses rising up from the sea. The Maldives, Tuvalu, the Marshall Islands, and Kiribati are atoll countries sitting atop coral islands. The Florida keys are well-known coral islands.

Calcification in corals, mollusks, and others sequesters one-third of human-induced CO_2 emissions. Loss of this carbon sink would exacerbate the effects of climate change. The value of that cannot be measured. Tourism, fishing, and ecosystem services are valued at hundreds of billions of dollars annually. Used in traditional medicine for centuries, reef organisms continue to be studied for use in Western medicine. Antiviral, antifungal, and anticancer products; inflammatory response mediators; and even sunblock are under development, some of which have already been administered to patients. Marine biotechnology is a multibillion-dollar industry, with strong growth potential. Ultimately, the health of humanity is tied to the health of the reefs.

Sarah A. Vordtriede

FURTHER READING

Brennan, Scott R., and Jay Withgott. *Environment: The Science Behind the Stories*. San Francisco: Benjamin Cummings, 2005.
Côté, Isabelle M., and John D. Reynolds, eds. *Coral Reef Conservation*. New York: Cambridge University Press, 2006.
Feely, R. A., et al. "Impact of Anthropogenic CO_2 on the $CaCO_3$ System in the Oceans." *Science* 305, no. 5682 (July 16, 2004): 362-366.
Hare, Tony. *Habitats*. New York: Macmillan, 1994.
Kricher, John C. *A Neotropical Companion: An Introduction to the Animals, Plants, and Ecosystems of the New World Tropics*. Princeton, N.J.: Princeton University Press, 1997.
Lalli, Carol M., and Timothy Richard Parsons. *Biological Oceanography*. Oxford, Oxfordshire, England: Butterworth Heinemann, 1997.
Moyle, Peter B., and Joseph J. Cech, Jr. *Fishes: An Introduction to Ichthyology*. 2d ed. Englewood Cliffs, N.J.: Prentice-Hall, 1988.
Pechenik, Jan A. *Biology of the Invertebrates*. 6th ed. New York: McGraw-Hill, 2010.
Tunnell, John Wesley, Ernesto A. Chávez, and Kim Withers. *Coral Reefs of the Southern Gulf of Mexico*. College Station: Texas A&M University Press, 2007.

WEB SITES

CORAL REEF ALLIANCE
http://www.coral.org/

U.S. ENVIRONMENTAL PROTECTION AGENCY
Habitat Protection: Coral Reef Protection
http://www.epa.gov/OWOW/oceans/coral/

SEE ALSO: Animals as a medical resource; Australia; Biotechnology; Calcium compounds; Clean Water Act; Coastal Zone Management Act; Ecosystems; El Niño and La Niña; Environmental degradation, resource exploitation and; Fisheries; Monsoons; Oceanography; Oceans.

Corn

CATEGORY: Plant and animal resources

WHERE FOUND

Corn grows as far north as Canada and Siberia (roughly 58° north latitude) and as far south as Argentina and New Zealand (40° south). Although adaptable to a wide range of conditions, corn does best with at least 50 centimeters of rainfall (corn is often irrigated in drier regions) and daytime temperatures between 21° and 26° Celsius. Much of the United States meets these criteria, hence its ranking as the top corn-producing country in the world.

PRIMARY USES

Corn is the most important cereal in the Western Hemisphere. It is used as human food, as livestock feed, and for industrial purposes.

TECHNICAL DEFINITION

Corn (*Zea mays*) is a coarse, annual plant of the grass family. It ranges in height from 1 to 5 meters, has a solid, jointed stalk, and grows long, narrow leaves. A stalk usually bears one to three cobs, which develop kernels of corn when fertilized.

DESCRIPTION, DISTRIBUTION, AND FORMS

Corn no longer grows in the wild; it requires human help in removing and planting the kernels to ensure reproduction. In the United States and Canada, "corn" is the common name for this cereal, but in Europe, "corn" refers to any of the small-seeded cereals, such as barley, wheat, and rye. "Maize" (or its translation) is the term used for *Zea mays* in Europe and Latin America.

HISTORY

Christopher Columbus took corn back to Europe with him in 1493, and within one hundred years it had spread through Europe, Asia, and Africa. Reportedly, a corn crop is harvested somewhere in the world each month.

Corn's exact origins remain uncertain, but most scholars agree that it is closely linked to a grass called *teosinte*, which is native to Mexico. Through unknown means a wild corn evolved with tiny, eight-rowed "ears" of corn about 2 centimeters long. Corncobs and plant fragments from this wild corn have been

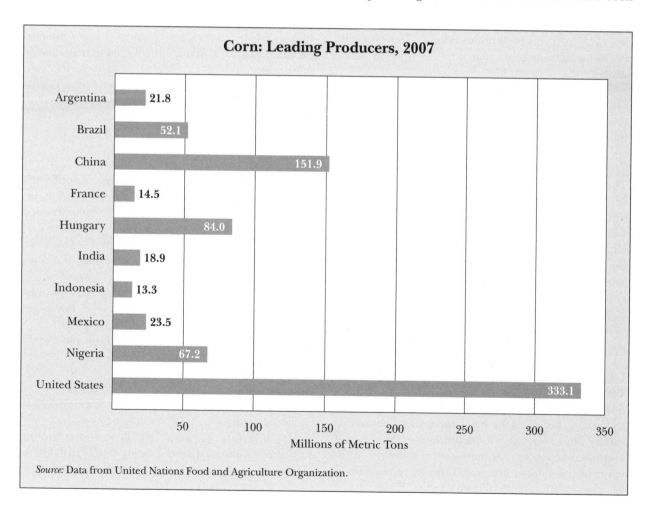

Corn: Leading Producers, 2007

Country	Millions of Metric Tons
Argentina	21.8
Brazil	52.1
China	151.9
France	14.5
Hungary	84.0
India	18.9
Indonesia	13.3
Mexico	23.5
Nigeria	67.2
United States	333.1

Source: Data from United Nations Food and Agriculture Organization.

dated to 5200 B.C.E. By 3400 B.C.E., the fossil record shows a marked change in corn, notably increased cob and kernel size, indicating greater domestication. Fully domesticated corn (which could not survive without human help) had replaced the wild and other early types of corn by 700 C.E.

Extensive attempts at hybridization began in the late nineteenth century, but the increase in yield was usually a disappointing 10 percent or so. By 1920, researchers had turned to inbreeding hybridization programs. In these, corn is self-fertilized, rather than being allowed to cross-pollinate naturally. Following a complex sequence of crossing and testing different varieties, the lines with the most desirable traits were put into commercial use, and they often produced 25 to 30 percent gains in yield. Although these early hybrids focused on increasing the yield, researchers later began to look for insect-resistant and disease-resistant qualities as well. One of the hybridizers of the 1920's was Henry A. Wallace, founder of Pioneer Seed Company (the world's largest seed company) and later U.S. vice president under Franklin D. Roosevelt. By the 1950's, hybrid corn varieties were in widespread use.

OBTAINING CORN

Corn processing takes place in one of three ways: wet milling, dry milling, or fermentation. In wet milling, corn is soaked in a weak sulfurous acid solution, ground to break apart the kernel, and then separated. The resulting by-products are found nearly everywhere. Dry milling is a simpler process, involving the separation of the hull from the endosperm (the food storage organ, which is primarily starch in most corn) and the germ (the plant embryo) by repeated grinding and sieving. Fermentation of corn changes the starch to sugar, which is then converted by yeast to alcohol. The process eventually results in ethyl alcohol, or ethanol (which is blended with gasoline to reduce carbon monoxide emissions), acetone, and other substances.

USES OF CORN

The types of corn still in use are dent, flint, flour, pop, and sweet. Dent corn, characterized by a "dent" in the top of each kernel, is the most important commercial variety. Flint corn tends to be resistant to the rots and blights known to attack other types; it is also more tolerant of low temperatures and therefore appears at the geographical edge of corn's range. Flour corn is known for its soft kernel, making it easier to grind into flour and thus popular for hand-grinding. A mainstay at American movie theaters and as a snack food, popcorn will, with an optimum moisture content of about 13 percent, explode to as much as thirty times its original volume when heated. Also popular in the United States and eaten fresh, sweet corn is so named because, unlike other types, most of the sugars in the kernel are not converted to starch.

Commercially, corn is used mostly for livestock feed and industrial processing. It is high in energy and low in crude fiber but requires supplements to make a truly good feed. Industrial processing creates a great variety of products found in everyday life—underscoring the importance of corn to the world's economy.

The cornstarch from wet milling supplies corn syrup (it is sweeter than sugar and less expensive, and billions of dollars' worth is produced for soft drink manufacturers each year), starches used in the textile industry, ingredients for certain candies, and substances used in adhesives, to name a few. Other byproducts provide cooking oil; oil used in mayonnaise, margarine, and salad dressing; soap powders; and livestock feed. Dry milling produces hominy, grits, meal, and flour, all of which are used for human consumption.

Brian J. Nichelson

FURTHER READING

Fussell, Betty. *The Story of Corn.* New York: Knopf, 1992.

Mangelsdorf, Paul C. *Corn: Its Origin, Evolution, and Improvement.* Cambridge, Mass.: Belknap Press of Harvard University Press, 1974.

Pollan, Michael. "Industrial Corn." In *The Omnivore's Dilemma: A Natural History of Four Meals.* New York: Penguin Press, 2006.

Smith, C. Wayne, Javier Betrán, and E. C. A. Runge. *Corn: Origin, History, Technology, and Production.* Hoboken, N.J.: John Wiley, 2004.

Sprague, G. F., and J. W. Dudley, eds. *Corn and Corn Improvement.* 3d ed. Madison, Wis.: American Society of Agronomy, 1988.

Wallace, Henry A., and William L. Brown. *Corn and Its Early Fathers.* Rev. ed. Ames: Iowa State University Press, 1988.

Warman, Arturo. *Corn and Capitalism: How a Botanical Bastard Grew to Global Dominance.* Translated by Nancy L. Westrate. Chapel Hill: University of North Carolina Press, 2003.

White, Pamela J., and Lawrence A. Johnson, eds. *Corn: Chemistry and Technology*. St. Paul, Minn.: American Association of Cereal Chemists, 2003.

WEB SITES

U.S. DEPARTMENT OF AGRICULTURE, ECONOMIC RESEARCH SERVICE
Corn
http://www.ers.usda.gov/Briefing/Corn

U.S. DEPARTMENT OF AGRICULTURE, ECONOMIC RESEARCH SERVICE
Feed Grains Database
http://www.ers.usda.gov/Data/FeedGrains

SEE ALSO: Agricultural products; Agriculture industry; Biofuels; Ethanol; Horticulture; Plant domestication and breeding.

Corundum and emery

CATEGORY: Mineral and other nonliving resources

WHERE FOUND
Corundum occurs in a number of geological environments. The most important of these are contact metamorphic zones, silica-poor igneous rocks, pegmatites, and placers. The principal producer of corundum is South Africa, but commercial deposits also exist in Canada, India, Madagascar, and Russia. Minor deposits are found in North Carolina and Georgia. The finest rubies and sapphires have always been mined in Asia: rubies from Burma, India, and Thailand; sapphires from Sri Lanka, India, and Thailand.

Turkey is the world's leading producer of emery, with other significant deposits found on the Greek island of Naxos and in the Ural Mountains of Russia. In the United States, the most important emery deposits are around Peekskill, New York. The United States exports no emery and imports most of what it consumes from Turkey and Greece.

PRIMARY USES
Corundum and emery are used as abrasives. In addition, the transparent, colored varieties of corundum, ruby and sapphire, have long been prized as gems because of their rarity and beauty.

TECHNICAL DEFINITION
Corundum, another name for aluminum oxide (Al_2O_3), is the second-hardest natural substance. It occurs as an opaque material and as transparent gems. Emery is a natural mixture of corundum and magnetite.

DESCRIPTION, DISTRIBUTION, AND FORMS
Corundum, or aluminum oxide, can be categorized in two ways: as an abrasive and as a gem mineral. Both uses result from corundum's extreme hardness (nine on the Mohs scale). Corundum as an abrasive has been largely replaced by alumina.

Emery, named for Cape Emeri in Greece, is a natural gray to black mixture of corundum and magnetite, usually with lesser amounts of spinel and hematite. The hardness of emery ranges from seven to nine, and its usefulness as an abrasive increases with the corundum content. Like corundum, emery has largely been replaced, but in this case by synthetic materials.

HISTORY
The gem varieties of corundum, ruby and sapphire, have a long history of use. Ruby attains its red color from the presence of chromic oxide. Sapphires occur in a variety of colors, but those most prized as gems are colored deep blue by the presence of iron and titanium oxides. Beginning in the early twentieth century, both rubies and sapphires were synthesized. Even the prized "star" varieties can be manufactured, and the synthetic gems are virtually indistinguishable from their natural counterparts.

OBTAINING CORUNDUM AND EMERY
Both corundum and emery are obtained through mining, the later of which has been mined in Greece for more than two thousand years. However, most corundum and emery are now obtained synthetically.

USES OF CORUNDUM AND EMERY
Corundum has limited use as crushed grit or powder for polishing and finishing optical lenses and metals and is used on paper, cloth, and abrasive wheels. As corundum wears, small pieces constantly flake off to form fresh edges, enhancing its ability to cut. In addition to their value as gems, synthetic rubies are used in industrial and medical lasers.

Emery finds some applications on coated abrasive sheets (emery cloth), as grains and flour for polishing glass and metal surfaces, on grinding wheels, and on nonskid pavements and stair treads. Emery forms principally by contact metamorphism in limestones.

Donald J. Thompson

WEB SITE

CORUNDUM
http://www.minerals.net/mineral/oxides/
corundum/corundum.htm

SEE ALSO: Abrasives; Gems; Metamorphic processes, rocks, and mineral deposits; Mohs hardness scale; Placer deposits.

Cotton

CATEGORY: Plant and animal resources

WHERE FOUND

Cotton (genus *Gossypium*) is grown within the tropical and subtropical regions of the world in areas that have adequate amounts of sunshine and fertile soil. In general, areas that receive 600 to 1,200 millimeters of rainfall annually are best suited for cotton production because the plant requires a large amount of water in order to grow well. However, dryland cotton farming occurs in areas with lower rainfall totals with the help of irrigation.

Within the United States, most of the cotton crop is grown in Alabama, Arizona, Arkansas, California, Georgia, Florida, Kansas, Louisiana, Mississippi, Missouri, New Mexico, North Carolina, Oklahoma, South Carolina, Tennessee, Texas, and Virginia. Cotton is also commercially produced in China, India, Pakistan, Uzbekistan, Brazil, Australia, Egypt, Argentina, and Turkey.

PRIMARY USES

Cotton fibers are primarily used in the textile industry for the manufacture of clothing. Smaller amounts of cotton are used to produce fishing nets, cotton paper, tents, and gunpowder. In some parts of the world, cotton is still used to make mattresses. Refined cottonseed oil is used as a vegetable oil in many foods, such as baked goods. Cottonseed hulls are often mixed in with other plant materials to form a roughage ration for cattle.

TECHNICAL DEFINITION

Cotton is a plant in the mallow family, Malvaceae. This botanical group is a large family containing a number of plants important to horticulture, including the hibiscus. Cotton plants may grow to a height of 3 meters, but most commercial varieties have been bred to be shorter for easier harvesting. The plant has leaves with three to seven lobes; the ovary of the cotton flower is a capsule or boll, which, when ripe, opens along the dark brown carpels to reveal the usually white inner fibers. Longer fibers are known as staples, while shorter fibers are called linters. When separated from one another by a process known as ginning, the fibers can be woven into cotton yarn and used for textile manufacturing.

DESCRIPTION, DISTRIBUTION, AND FORMS

Four species of cotton—*Gossypium hirsutum, G. barbadense, G. arboreum,* and *G. herbaceum*—are commercially produced, with *G. hirsutum* accounting for about 90 percent of the world's production. Approximately 8 percent of the world's cotton is produced from *G. barbadense,* and the remaining 2 percent comes from *G. arboreum* and *G. herbaceum. G. hirsutum,* upland cotton, is native to Florida, the Caribbean, Mexico, and Central America and is the cotton with which most Americans are familiar. *G. barbadense* is a plant of tropical South America and is known commercially as pima cotton. Tree cotton, *G. arboreum,* is native to India and Pakistan, while the last commercially important species, *G. herbaceum,* is found in the Arabian Peninsula and southern Africa and is known as levant cotton.

In addition to the four commonly cultivated species of cotton, five noncommercial species of this genus are found in tropical and subtropical areas of the world. These include *G. australe* and *G. sturtianum,* both found in Australia; *G. darwinii,* which grows in the Galápagos Islands; *G. thurberi,* a plant of northern Mexico and Arizona; and *G. tomentosum,* a Hawaiian Island endemic.

Cotton is one of the most pesticide-intensive of all cultivated crops. Genetically modified cotton was developed in the twentieth century in an attempt to alleviate some of the cotton farmer's dependence upon pesticide use. The bacterium *Bacillus thuringiensis* produces a natural pesticide that is toxic to a number of insects, most notably members of the insect orders Coleoptera (beetles) and Lepidoptera (butterflies and moths). By inserting within cotton tissues the

B. thuringiensis gene that codes for this specific toxicity, geneticists were able to develop cotton varieties that were resistant to some of the important pests, such as boll weevils and bollworms. In recent years, some of this cotton has been found to be no longer resistant to pests.

A small percentage of commercially grown cotton is produced with organic methods. No insecticides are used on organically grown cotton, and crop rotation is a technique used in an attempt to keep the soil fertile and to discourage pests.

HISTORY

Cotton has been cultivated by a number of cultures for at least six thousand years. The ancient peoples of India, China, Egypt, and Mexico all grew and made use of cotton in weaving textiles. The fiber has been extensively traded throughout both the Old and New Worlds for the past two thousand years. During the first century C.E., traders from the Middle East brought fabrics such as calico and muslin to markets in southern Europe. Great Britain's famous East India Company brought cotton cloth from India during the seventeenth century. Raw cotton was imported from the American colonies in the 1700's, and this import spurred a need for the development of machinery that could process and spin the cotton. Advances such as the spinning jenny, developed in 1764, and Sir Richard Arkwright's spinning frame, developed in 1769, enabled Britain to produce cotton yarn and cloth with increased speed and efficiency. American Eli Whitney's well-known 1793 invention of the cotton gin allowed cotton seeds to be easily stripped from the fibers.

During the American Civil War, Britain could not obtain cotton from the United States and so bargained with Egypt for its supply. After the war, however, Britain turned again to buying its cotton from the United States, and the resulting loss of trade was a severe blow to the Egyptian economy. Cotton continued to be a staple crop for the southern United States throughout the 1800's and 1900's and remains a primary export crop for the country.

OBTAINING COTTON

In traditional cotton farming, cotton fields are cleared of old plants from the previous growing season and thoroughly plowed into rows. The farmer may clear fields in the winter or wait until early spring before planting. Cotton seeds are planted mechani-

A woman in India brings a bundle of organic cotton to the town center to be ginned. (AP/Wide World Photos)

cally in the spring, when the soil is warm enough for seeds to germinate. Germination occurs in five to ten days if adequate soil moisture is available; a full stand of cotton is generally present in eleven days if germination is successful. Within five to seven weeks "squares" (cotton flower buds) open to produce a creamy yellow flower that self-pollinates within three days. As the flower matures it changes color from light yellow to pink to darker red before falling off the plant to reveal the tiny "boll." Approximately forty-five to eighty days after the bolls form, they split along the carpels of the fruit to reveal white fibers. A boll may contain as many as 500,000 of these fibers, which are called staples. Staple length varies among the different cotton species, with upland cotton having staple lengths of 0.81 inch to 1.25 inches and pima cotton having lengths of 1.31 inches to 1.5 inches.

If the cotton is to be mechanically picked, it must

first be defoliated, so that leaves will not be picked along with the cotton bolls. After completing the defoliation, cotton pickers can drive through the fields and pick the cotton as long as it is dry. Moisture, from either dew or rain, damages the cotton fibers once the bolls have opened, so farmers hope for dry weather during harvesting.

Picked cotton is formed into bales weighing 218 kilograms each; thirteen to fifteen bales may then be formed into modules and transported to the cotton gin. The ginning process fluffs the cotton and cleans it of dirt, plant trash, and seeds. Cleaned cotton is compressed again into bales, which are inspected; if cleared for sale, the bales are stored in a temperature- and moisture-controlled warehouse until being moved to a processing facility.

Worldwide, 31.3 million hectares of cotton were planted in 2008, with 112.9 million 218-kilogram bales produced. China leads the world in cotton production, with 25.3 million bales produced in 2007. India, the United States, Pakistan, and Brazil complete the list of the top five cotton-producing countries.

USES OF COTTON

Cotton's primary use is in the manufacture of textiles. Although there are many different types of cotton fabric, some of the best known include terrycloth, a soft fabric used to make bath cloths, towels, and robes; denim, used in jean manufacture, which can be dyed a variety of colors but usually is dyed blue; chambray, a soft, blue cloth from which work shirts are made; and corduroy and twill, from which heavier, sturdier items of clothing are made. Cotton yarn is used in quilt making. Egyptian cotton is often used to produce bedsheets and pillowcases.

After cotton seeds are removed from raw cotton during the ginning process, cottonseed oil can be refined and used as a vegetable oil in cooking. It is also used in shortening and salad dressing and is a common component of baked goods such as crackers and cookies. Cottonseed meal and cottonseed hulls are fed to ruminant livestock such as cattle and goats, and the meal can be fed to fish and poultry. Nonruminant mammals are unable to eat cottonseed products because of a toxic chemical, gossypol, which will sicken and possibly kill these animals.

Strong fishnets and tents can be made from cotton fibers. When exposed to nitric acid, cotton can be used to form "guncotton" or "smokeless powder," a type of explosive that is safer to use than black powder.

Cotton fibers have been used for many years in the production of paper and as binding for books. Cotton paper is stronger than wood-pulp-based paper and retains ink better. Therefore, it is often used to produce paper money and archival copies of important books and documents.

Lenela Glass-Godwin

FURTHER READING

Hake, S. Johnson, T. A. Kerby, and K. D. Hake. *Cotton Production Manual*. Oakland: University of California, Division of Agriculture and Natural Resources, 1996.

Smith, C. Wayne. *Crop Production: Evolution, History, and Technology*. New York: John Wiley and Sons, 1995.

Smith, C. Wayne, and Joe Tom Cothren. *Cotton: Origin, History, Technology, and Production*. New York: John Wiley and Sons, 1999.

Tripp, Robert Burnet. *Biotechnology and Agricultural Development: Transgenic Cotton, Rural Institutions, and Resource-Poor Farmers*. New York: Routledge, 2009.

WEB SITES

NATIONAL COTTON COUNCIL OF AMERICA
http://www.cotton.org/

SUSTAINABLE COTTON PROJECT
http://www.sustainablecotton.org/

SEE ALSO: Agricultural products; Agriculture industry; Agronomy; American Forest and Paper Association; Botany; Farmland; Flax; Hemp; Irrigation; Paper; Paper, alternative sources of; Plant fibers; Renewable and nonrenewable resources; Textiles and fabrics.

Council of Energy Resource Tribes

CATEGORY: Organizations, agencies, and programs
DATE: Established 1975

The Council of Energy Resource Tribes (CERT) seeks fair payment for resources pumped or mined on American Indian reservation land and advises tribes regarding conservation, lease arrangements, royalties, and economic development.

BACKGROUND

The Council of Energy Resource Tribes was founded by a group of tribal leaders seeking to monitor and receive appropriate payment for energy resources on American Indian land. Historically, tribes had been underpaid, sometimes scandalously, for mineral resources obtained on their lands. The leasing policies of the U.S. Bureau of Indian Affairs (BIA) engendered considerable controversy and resentment; the BIA frequently allowed corporations to obtain oil, coal, and other resources from American Indian land for prices well under market value. Moreover, leasing royalties sometimes were underpaid or went unpaid altogether.

Estimates indicate that energy resources contained on American Indian land account for 10 percent of the U.S. total. One of the founders of CERT, Peter MacDonald, a Navajo who was CERT's first elected chair, referred to these resources as wealth "so vast it has not yet been measured." CERT set out to inventory the resources of the tribes of the West and found that they controlled one-third of U.S. coal and uranium resources and large supplies of petroleum and natural gas. CERT began to demand higher royalties for coal, oil, and uranium mined on American Indian lands and worked to integrate various aspects of reservation energy development.

IMPACT ON RESOURCE USE

The founders of CERT had noted the activities of the Organization of Petroleum Exporting Countries (OPEC) as an influential international energy resource organization, and they hoped to achieve similar influence over tribal resources as they entered the domestic market. CERT helps tribes negotiate contracts regarding resources found on reservation lands. It provides on-site technical assistance and advice in the areas of conservation, resource management, and economic development. CERT was founded by leaders from twenty-five tribes; by the end of the first decade of the twenty-first century, it had more than sixty tribal members. The organization's headquarters are in Denver, Colorado.

Vincent M. D. Lopez

WEB SITE

COUNCIL OF ENERGY RESOURCE TRIBES
http://www.certredearth.com/

SEE ALSO: Coal; Oil and natural gas distribution; Oil embargo and energy crises of 1973 and 1979; Oil industry; Organization of Petroleum Exporting Countries; Uranium.

Cropland. *See* Farmland

Crystals

CATEGORY: Mineral and other nonliving resources

Crystals are composed of regularly repeating three-dimensional patterns of atoms or ions; a crystal is therefore a highly ordered structure. Crystals have a number of electronic and scientific applications, including uses in optics and in radio transmitters (piezoelectric quartz crystals). Well-formed crystals are also prized by collectors, and crystals of gem minerals are cut into jewelry.

BACKGROUND

Crystals are solids that naturally display smooth planar exterior surfaces called "faces," which form during the growth of the solid. These faces collectively produce a regular geometric form that mimics the orderly internal atomic arrangement of the elements present in the solid. Some scientists use the term "crystal" to refer to any solid having an ordered internal atomic structure regardless of whether the solid displays faces. However, most scientists use the word "crystalline" for such solids when no faces are present. Many solids display a cleavage, a flat planar surface formed when the solid is broken; cleavage fragments are sometimes mistaken for crystals.

Crystals are described and classified according to the symmetrical relationship existing between the faces. The fundamental way of describing a crystal is to list the "forms" that it displays. Scientists recognize a total of forty-eight different forms, many designated by common geometric terms such as cube, octahedron, tetrahedron, pyramid, and prism. Most crystals display multiple forms. For example, quartz crystals display one prism and at least two sets of pyramids. Considering every possible symmetrical arrangement of faces, every crystal can be placed into one

Amethyst crystals are purple in color and are often used as gemstones. (©iStockphoto.com)

of thirty-two groupings called crystal classes. These classes are further grouped into six crystal systems based on similar symmetry characteristics. The names of the six systems, from most to least symmetrical, are isometric, hexagonal, tetragonal, orthorhombic, monoclinic, and triclinic.

WHERE CRYSTALS ARE FORMED

Large crystals can develop when the faces growing in a melt, solution, or gas are unimpeded by other surrounding solids. This situation commonly occurs where open cracks and cavities exist in rock and the liquid or vapor from which the crystal is growing has free access to the open space. The largest crystals are found in igneous pegmatites. The Etta pegmatite in the Black Hills of South Dakota contained a 12-meter crystal weighing more than 18 metric tons. The largest known crystal was a single feldspar from a pegmatite in Karelia, Russia, that weighed several thousand metric tons. Crystals are also found along fault planes, in hot springs areas, around vents for volcanic gases, and in cavities within igneous and sedimentary rocks where underground water is circulating. Another mechanism for the growth of crystals occurs during

the process of metamorphism. Preexisting rocks that are subjected to elevated temperatures and pressures within the Earth can recrystallize while still solid. During this metamorphism some of the new minerals that form have a strong surface energy and will develop faces even while in contact with other growing minerals.

The growth conditions discussed above are so common within the Earth that crystals can be found in almost every state in the United States and every country in the world. It is impossible to specify all the important occurrences of large, well-formed crystals. Some of the more notable classic localities in the United States include quartz in Hot Springs, Arkansas, and Herkimer County, New York; galena in the tristate district of Missouri, Kansas, and Oklahoma; zinc-bearing minerals in Franklin, New Jersey; garnets at Gore Mountain, New York; iron oxides in the upper peninsula of Michigan; and fluorite and celestite at Clay Center, Ohio.

USES OF CRYSTALS

Particularly well-formed crystals are highly prized by collectors and museums. Most crystals, however, are more valuable for their chemistry or as crystalline solids. Many crystals are crushed during the processing of ore minerals. It was a common practice for miners to save the larger, better-formed crystals from the crushing mill because they were worth more as specimens for collectors than they were worth as ore material. Most crystals of gem minerals are cut and faceted to make jewelry. A large diamond crystal, for example, is worth more as a well-faceted gemstone than as a crystal specimen.

There are a growing number of technological uses of "crystalline solids" where the systematic internal arrangement of atoms can produce a variety of desirable physical phenomena useful in the fields of electronics and optics. As an example, very pure untwinned quartz is called "optical grade crystal" even though it lacks faces. Quartz crystal is cut, ground, and made into lenses and prisms for optical instruments and is also used in radio oscillators, timing devices, and pressure gauges in the electronics industry.

CRYSTAL DEFECTS AND GROWTH RATES

Crystal defects occur naturally as crystals are formed; they are also sometimes introduced artificially, as they have useful electrical, mechanical, and optical qualities. A growing crystal typically requires the proper placement of trillions of atoms per hour. About one atom in every one hundred thousand is misplaced to form a defect. These defects can be point disorders, or they can geometrically be combined to form line, plane, or three-dimensional disorders. The Schottky defect is a point disorder in which an atom is missing from the spot it should occupy, leaving a hole in the pattern. The Schottky defect results when a second layer of atoms is quickly deposited before all the positions can be filled in the first layer. The Frenkel defect occurs when an atom is out of its proper position and can be found nearby, inappropriately stuck between other atoms. The impurity defect is yet another point disorder, occurring when an atom of a foreign element (an impurity) either substitutes for the normal atom or is stuffed between the proper atoms of the structure.

Coloration can be caused by various point defects. When an electron is captured by the hole of a Frenkel defect it will absorb energy from passing light and become what is known as a "color center." An abundance of Frenkel color centers in fluorite will give the crystal a purple color. An impurity defect can be accompanied by a shift in electrons, also causing a color

center. Smoky quartz is caused by color centers resulting from impurity defects. The electron shifts are either induced by low levels of radiation in the Earth over geological time or by artificial exposure to an intense X-ray or gamma-ray beam for a few minutes. A significant number of the smoky quartz crystals on the market began as natural colorless quartz that has been irradiated.

Line disorders are linear defects and are commonly called "dislocations" because they create an offset within the crystal. The most common is an edge dislocation resulting when an entire plane of atoms is pinched out and terminated as adjacent planes on either side begin to bond directly together. When crystals are stressed they will often deform by slipping along linear disorders.

Crystals can also become deformed or malformed because of variations in the growth rates of different faces or different parts of the crystal. When the chemistry of the growing solution begins to lack the atoms needed by the crystal, then the faces can stop growing while the edges where faces meet will continue to grow. In extreme instances the resulting malformed crystal has a skeletal look, showing a network of edges without any faces, yet all the symmetrical forms are still evident, allowing proper classification of the crystal.

TWINNING

During formation, a solid may produce a symmetrical intergrowth of two or more crystals. When the intergrowth is crystallographically controlled, the resulting composite is called a twinned crystal. The individual crystals within the twinned aggregate are related to one another by a different symmetrical element—one that is not seen in any of the individual parts. This often results in a symmetrical, exotically shaped aggregate that does not appear to belong to any single crystal class. Crystals displaying exceptional twins can be more valuable for their twinning than as mineral specimens.

HISTORY OF CRYSTALS

Crystals have a history that reaches back into the realm of legends and myths. An important early work that combined legend with the first sound science was the thirty-seven-volume *Historia Naturalis*, written by Pliny the Elder in the first century. Pliny described many real as well as nonexistent crystals, which he stated were formed by such exotic processes as "the light of the moon" or "the purge from the sea."

Nicolaus Steno established the first law of crystallography in 1669, known as the law of constancy of interfacial angles. The law holds that for all crystals of a given mineral the angles measured between similar faces are always exactly the same. This law allows for the positive identification of deformed or malformed crystals simply by measuring the angles between existing faces. In 1781, René-Just Haüy was the first to recognize that a crystal is composed of a large number of smaller particles arranged in a regular geometric order such that it fills space without gaps. This was a remarkable advance, considering that it preceded the concept of the atom in chemistry by more than twenty years. In 1830, based on graphical and mathematical considerations, Johann Hessel predicted the existence of thirty-two classes of symmetry corresponding to modern crystal classes. In the 1920's, two crystallographers, C. H. Hermann and Charles-Victor Mauguin, developed the notation that is used to designate the symmetrical arrangement of faces found on any crystal.

Dion C. Stewart

FURTHER READING

De Graef, Marc, and Michael E. McHenry. *Structure of Materials: An Introduction to Crystallography, Diffraction, and Symmetry.* Cambridge, England: Cambridge University Press, 2007.

Klein, Cornelis, and Barbara Dutrow. *The Twenty-third Edition of the Manual of Mineral Science.* 23d ed. Hoboken, N.J.: J. Wiley, 2008.

Read, P. G. *Gemmology.* 3d ed. Boston: Elsevier/Butterworth-Heinemann, 2005.

Smyth, Joseph R., and David L. Bish. *Crystal Structures and Cation Sites of the Rock-Forming Minerals.* Boston: Allen & Unwin, 1987.

Tilley, Richard J. D. *Crystals and Crystal Structures.* Hoboken, N.J.: John Wiley, 2006.

Wenk, Hans-Rudolf, and Andrei Bulakh. *Minerals: Their Constitution and Origin.* New York: Cambridge University Press, 2004.

SEE ALSO: Gems; Geodes; Hydrothermal solutions and mineralization; Minerals, structure and physical properties of; Pegmatites; Quartz.

D

Daly, Marcus

CATEGORY: People

BORN: December 5, 1841; Derrylea, County Cavan, Ireland

DIED: November 12, 1900; New York, New York

Marcus Daly, an Irishman with few job skills and little education, immigrated to the United States and became, in one-quarter of a century, one of three "copper kings" in the United States. After he discovered that his silver mine at Anaconda in Montana contained a large copper vein beneath the silver, he successfully exploited the copper and virtually made "Anaconda" a household word in the United States.

BIOGRAPHICAL BACKGROUND

The youngest of eleven children in an Irish family in County Caven, Ireland, Marcus Daly was born December 5, 1841. Five years after immigrating to the United States at the age of fifteen, Daly sailed to San Francisco, then worked at a silver mine of the Comstock Lode in Virginia City, Nevada. By 1871, he was a foreman in Ophir, Utah, for the Walker Brothers mining syndicate. There he met and married Margaret Evans; they had three daughters and a son. When Daly was sent to the Montana Territory to acquire a silver mine for Walker Brothers, he kept a one-fifth interest for himself. He sold that interest in 1876 and, with additional backing, purchased the Anaconda claim.

In addition to his mining career, Daly was a horse owner and breeder and the founder of the influential *Anaconda Standard* newspaper. He died at the Netherlands Hotel in New York City at age fifty-eight. His remains are in a mausoleum in Greenwood Cemetery in Brooklyn, New York.

IMPACT ON RESOURCE USE

The Anaconda mine was principally a silver mine until Daly discovered a copper vein about 91 meters deep and 30 meters wide beneath the silver vein. By this time, copper was coming into use for electricity and telegraph wire. While the price of copper in the early 1880's was only around $0.35 to $0.45 per kilogram, smelting costs were high because the ore had to

be shipped to Swansea, Wales, to be smelted. Daly was determined to reduce those costs and realize a profit. With financial backing, he built the town of Anaconda, Montana, where he built his own smelter and connected it by rail to nearby Butte. By 1890, the Butte copper mines saw an annual production of copper valued at more than $17 million. Daly bought coal mines and forests to supply the fuel and timber he needed and built his own power plants.

From 1895 to 1980, the Anaconda smelter was a major employer. It closed because of a labor strike; one-quarter of Anaconda's workforce became unemployed, an economic blow from which the town did not recover. Standard Oil bought the Anaconda Company in 1899 and had a major impact on the economy of that area until the 1970's. From the 1950's to the 1970's the Anaconda Copper Mining Company engaged in open-pit mining until copper prices collapsed, at which time the Atlantic Richfield Company (ARCO) bought the company. However, ARCO ceased its mining operations in Butte in 1982, bringing to a close what Daly had begun almost one century earlier and leaving a pit containing heavy metals and dangerous chemicals. A plan to solve the groundwater problem was instigated during the 1990's.

Victoria Price

SEE ALSO: Copper; Mining safety and health issues; Mining wastes and mine reclamation; National Park Service; Smelting.

Dams

CATEGORY: Obtaining and using resources

Dams are designed for a number of purposes, including conservation and irrigation, flood control, hydroelectric power generation, navigation, and recreation; most major dams have been constructed to serve more than one of these purposes.

BACKGROUND

A dam is an artificial facility that is constructed in the path of a flowing stream or river for the purpose of storing water. Historically, dams are the oldest means of controlling the flow of water in a stream. The primary function of most dams is to smooth out or regulate flows downstream of the dam. Generally dams are permanent structures. In some cases, however, temporary structures may be constructed to divert flows, as from a construction site. Cofferdams are used in this regard—not to store water but to keep a construction area free of water. Such temporary structures are designed with a higher assumed risk than are permanent dams. Dams date (in recorded history) to about 2600 to 2900 B.C.E.

USES OF DAMS

Dams are primarily used for four purposes: conservation, navigation, flood control, and generation of hydroelectric power. A fifth but somewhat less important use is recreation. Conservation purposes include water supply (including irrigation) and low-flow augmentation (to achieve wastewater dilution requirements). Flood-control objectives dictate that a dam's reservoir be as empty as possible so that any excess water from the watershed (the area upstream of the dam that sheds water to it) can be detained or retained in the reservoir to reduce any potential flood-related damage of property and/or loss of life. A single dam can be used for all the foregoing purposes. In that case, the reservoir is called a multipurpose reservoir. Rarely can the cost of a major dam be justified for one purpose.

TYPES OF DAMS

Dams are classified according to the type of material used in their construction and/or the structural principles applied in their design (for structural integrity and stability). Generally, dams are constructed with concrete or earthen materials readily available at the construction site. In some cases the nature of the construction site with regard to underlying rock formation, climate, topography, and sometimes the width and load-carrying capacity of the valley in which the dam is constructed significantly influences the type of dam selected. Common types include earthfill or earthen dams, rockfill dams, and concrete dams, which include gravity dams (their structural stability depends on the weight of the concrete), arch dams, and buttress dams. Buttress dams are further categorized as flat-slab (also called Ambursen dams after Nils Ambursen, who built the first of this kind in the United States in 1903), multiple-arch, and massive-

head dams. Arch dams are designed to take advantage of the load-bearing abutments in the valley or gorge where the dam is constructed. The structure is designed so that all the loading is transmitted to the abutments. Therefore these abutments must be rock of high structural integrity and strength capable of sustaining substantial thrust loading with little displacement. Arch dams are typically thinner than gravity dams and are constructed from reinforced concrete. Arch dams (as the name implies) are curved to ensure that compressive stresses are maintained throughout the dam. The basic buttress dam consists of a sloping slab supported by buttresses at intervals over the length of the reservoir. Earthen (or earthfill) dams are constructed as earth embankments. To avoid the destructive effects of seepage through the dam (especially "piping," a slow leak that develops into destructive erosion through the core of the dam), an impervious core is constructed to prevent seepage. For example, the use of compacted clay core is common. Rockfill dams are like earthfill dams but use crushed rock as fill material. The impermeable core is usually constructed using concrete.

Dams can be further classified as major (with a storage capacity of more than 60 million cubic meters), intermediate (with a storage capacity between 1 and 60 million cubic meters), and minor (with a storage capacity of less than 1 million cubic meters). Major dams are designed to handle the probable maximum precipitation (PMP). PMP is the estimated maximum precipitation depth for a given duration which is possible over a particular geographical region at a certain time of year. Intermediate dams are designed to withstand the flood from the most extreme rainfall event considered to be characteristic of its watershed or basin. Floods that occur every fifty to one hundred years are used in the design of minor dams.

Dams associated with hydropower plants can be categorized by the height of the water surface at the plant intake above the tailwater (the water surface at the discharge end of the hydropower plant). This vertical difference in height is called the "head." Three categories exist: low (head between 2 and 20 meters), medium (head between 20 and 150 meters), and high (head above 150 meters).

SIZING OF DAMS

The useful or service storage volume of dams is determined by an analysis of streamflows occurring at the proposed dam site and of the expected average releases or demand flows from the reservoir. Several methods have been developed, ranging from the Rippl method (attributed to Wenzel Rippl in 1883, also called the stretched-thread method) to optimal reservoir sizing schemes which employ more sophisticated operations research techniques. Rippl's method is simply a mass diagram analysis technique. Another less cumbersome method for estimating the active (service) storage of a dam is the sequent peak method. Reservoir storage can be divided into three components: flood storage capacity for flood damage mitigation, dead storage needed for sediment storage, and the active storage for the regulation of streamflow and water supply.

RESERVOIR BENEFITS AND COST

The construction of a dam can be justified only if it is cost-effective. That is, the total benefits resulting from its construction must be greater than the direct or in-direct costs incurred in its construction and operation. Benefits accrue from hydropower sales, water supply and flow augmentation, recreation activities, and flood damage mitigation. Costs (or disbenefits) include net loss of streamflow because of evaporation, loss of water to seepage, the inundation of areas upstream from the dam, destruction of aquatic habitat, and the prevention of migration of fish in the stream, to mention a few.

SILTATION

One of the factors that can shorten the useful life of a dam is the unavoidable siltation that will occur during the projected life (service period) of a reservoir. In the design of any reservoir, the portion of the reservoir earmarked or set aside for reservoir siltation is the part of the reservoir storage referred to as dead storage. Siltation occurs in the reservoir as the sediment load carried by flow entering the reservoir is

The Glen Canyon Dam, opened in 1966, dammed a portion of the Colorado River in Arizona, creating Lake Powell. (Tami Heilemann/ UPI/Landov)

trapped in the reservoir because of decreased flow velocities within the reservoir. This siltation can lead to other problems, especially if organic debris is carried in the sediment load. Because organic material will degrade, typically resulting in the depletion of dissolved oxygen in the stored water, water quality can easily be affected by such loads. In addition, because the sediment load in the water discharged from a reservoir may be decreased because of siltation, unnaturally clarified water in the channel downstream may lead to above-normal erosion of the downstream streambed. Further, sediment deposition and buildup in a dam can submerge and choke benthic communities (bottom animal and plant life), thereby changing the character of reservoir bottom plants. In order to control the level of siltation in the reservoir, it may be necessary to undertake programs to reduce bank erosion. Activities which lead to increased sediment load, including construction activities, must be minimized and their effects carefully monitored. Bank stabilization schemes are very important first-line defense measures against the reduction of reservoir capacity by siltation.

HYDROPOWER PRODUCTION

Hydroelectricity is produced when flow from a reservoir is passed through a turbine. A turbine is the direct reverse of a pump. In the case of a pump, mechanical energy is converted to fluid energy. For example, in a typical pumping station, a pump is supplied with electric power that is converted to mechanical energy—usually to turn a motor. The mechanical energy is then converted to energy which is imparted to the fluid being pumped, resulting in increased fluid energy. A turbine is used to generate hydroelectricity in a directly opposite manner. In this case, water from the reservoir travels through special piping called penstocks and impinges on the turbine wheels (which can be rather large—up to 5 meters in diameter), causing them to spin at very high rotational speeds. A significant proportion of hydropower installations are used for "peaking." Peaking is the practice of using hydropower plants to supply additional electric power during peak load periods. Because hydropower plants can be easily brought online in an electric power grid (in contrast to fossil-fuel powered plants), they are often used in this manner. Hence hydropower plants are used in most cases as part of an overall power supply grid.

There are two types of hydropower plants: storage and pumped storage. In a storage hydropower plant water flows only in one direction. In contrast, in a pumped-storage plant, water flow is bidirectional. In pumped-storage facilities, power is generated during peak load periods, and during off-peak (low load) periods water flow direction is reversed—water is pumped from the tailwater pool (downstream) to the headwater pool (the upstream reservoir). This is economically feasible only because the price of energy is elastic and time dependent. During peak load periods, energy is relatively expensive, so the use of a hydropower plant to meet demand requirements is cost-effective. During off-peak periods, it is economical to pump water upstream, and water is stored (or re-stored) as potential energy. The amount of hydroelectricity generated for a unit flow of water is directly proportional to the volumetric rate of flow, the hydraulic head (approximately the difference between the surface water elevation at the headwater pool and the surface water elevation at the tailwater pool), and the mechanical efficiency of the hydropower plant (turbines).

Researchers continue to explore the most cost-effective way to incorporate hydropower production in the operation of multipurpose reservoir systems. Many operational research techniques have been reported in the literature. In general, mathematical formulations (models) that describe important interactions and constraints necessary to model and evaluate operational objectives are developed and solved by efficient methods. The value of such work lies in the fact that substantial benefits could be reaped from efficient use of existing reservoirs (dams) in contrast to the capital-intensive construction of new ones.

Hydropower production is a nonconsumptive use of water. This means that the water that passes through the turbines can be used (without undergoing any treatment) for other purposes. This nonconsumptive nature is one of the most attractive aspects of hydropower production; hydropower generation does not result in the significant degradation of water quality. However, problems with hydropower production do exist, most notably dissolved oxygen reduction and the adverse effects on aquatic life sensitive to changes in dissolved oxygen. Highly sensitive marine species which require a relatively stable aquatic system may suffer shock and undue stress from the drawdown of reservoir pool levels. Furthermore, pool elevation changes (swings) to sustain hydropower production may result in the significant reduction of recreational benefits. On the other hand, smaller downstream flows (during reservoir filling times and low water-demand periods) may cause water quality to degrade by increasing the temperature of water and pollutant concentrations. Significant temperature increases can be devastating to some species. For example, it is known that even slight temperature increases affect trout and salmon. The optimum temperature range for salmonids is about 6° to 13° Celsius. Adult fish will die when the water temperature exceeds 28° Celsius, while the juveniles will die when the temperature exceeds 22° Celsius. Unfavorable thermal conditions may discourage fish migration and cause the death of marine life because increasing temperatures delay or postpone the migration of adult fish, encouraging or promoting the development of fungus and other disease organisms. Eventually the balance of the ecosystem is modified, since predator or competitive species are favored, adversely affecting the salmon or trout population.

OTHER ECOLOGICAL EFFECTS

With the construction of a dam, several permanent or temporary changes may occur to an ecosystem. These include changes attributable to the pool of water behind the dam, such as temperature increases because the water is relatively stagnant. In addition, salts and hydrogen sulfide could accumulate. These altered conditions could lead to the decimation of sensitive stream-type organisms, stressed marine life, diseases or disablement, and displacement of native marine and aquatic organisms. Increased temperature of the reservoir pool could also lead to increased evaporation and other ecological problems. In delta areas, the lowering of the rate of river flow (and volume) by upstream dams may result in saltwater intrusion.

Emmanuel U. Nzewi

FURTHER READING

Fritz, Jack J., ed. *Small and Mini Hydropower Systems: Resource Assessment and Project Feasibility.* New York: McGraw-Hill, 1984.

Henry, J. Glynn, and Gary W. Heinke. *Environmental Science and Engineering.* 2d ed. Upper Saddle River, N.J.: Prentice Hall, 1996.

Jansen, Robert B., ed. *Advanced Dam Engineering for Design, Construction, and Rehabilitation.* New York: Van Nostrand Reinhold, 1988.

Jobin, William R. *Sustainable Management for Dams and Waters.* Boca Raton, Fla.: Lewis, 1998.

Leslie, Jacques. *Deep Water: The Epic Struggle over Dams, Displaced People, and the Environment.* New York: Farrar, Straus and Giroux, 2005.

Linsley, Ray K., et al. *Water Resources Engineering.* 4th ed. New York: McGraw-Hill, 1992.

McCully, Patrick. *Silenced Rivers: The Ecology and Politics of Large Dams.* Enlarged and updated ed. New York: Zed Books, 2001.

Mays, Larry W. *Water Resources Engineering.* Hoboken, N.J.: John Wiley & Sons, 2005.

Scudder, Thayer. *The Future of Large Dams: Dealing with Social, Environmental, Institutional, and Political Costs.* London: Earthscan, 2005.

Vischer, D. L., and W. H. Hager. *Dam Hydraulics.* New York: Wiley, 1998.

SEE ALSO: Electrical power; Floods and flood control; Hydroenergy; Hydrology and the hydrologic cycle; Irrigation; Water supply systems.

Deep drilling projects

CATEGORY: Obtaining and using resources

Deep drilling projects are ambitious attempts to investigate the origins and structure of the Earth; another aspect of the projects is the location of resources that may someday be feasible to exploit. Among the important early deep drilling projects were the ill-fated American Mohole Project of the early 1960's and the Russian drilling project on the Kola peninsula, begun in 1970.

BACKGROUND

Most of the Earth is hidden from human view. Of its 13,000-kilometer diameter, we see only a thin rind. The deepest gold mines are slightly more than 3 kilometers deep; tunneling deeper meets heat greater than miners can stand, and increasing pressure causes frequent tunnel collapses. Drilling can go much deeper than tunneling because the narrow bore holes can better resist pressure. Also, drilling keeps people away from the heat, and the smaller amount of rock moved means considerably less cost to reach a given depth.

The central limitation to the usefulness of drilling is that bore holes are much smaller than mine shafts, and materials brought up can be no larger than the size of the hole. A drill hole provides cheap samples, but moving major amounts of material becomes expensive unless the material flows. However, even with that limitation, bore holes sample a vast world that cannot be found at the surface. For the geological and biological sciences, the surface holds the present, but the subsurface holds the previous millions of years. For mining, there seems to be tremendous ore potential at depths about two and a half times the maximum depth to which tunnel mines can reach. As far as tapping heat sources, the potential is many times greater than that available near the surface.

HISTORY

When prices of whale oil rose in the 1850's, Edwin Drake began mining for rock oil—petroleum. He dug at the location of a natural petroleum seep. When water flooded his digging pit, he drove a pipe down toward the expected oil. Along the way, he noted what materials were shoved up by his operation.

Generations of drillers continued such well logs of cuttings coming up from each depth, such as sandstone, shale, and limestone. Geologists used those logs to map the rise and fall of certain distinctive rock layers (strata), which showed bending and folding of the rocks. They in turn researched marker fossils that allowed the cuttings to show more precise dating and thus to show connections among the rock layers. Those connections allowed mapping of underground layers, making oil drilling more successful. More complex geological drilling methods were developed to obtain actual core samples (tubes containing rock just as drilled, rather than as cuttings). The cores allow detailed scientific studies, and for conventional mining they provide a comparatively cheap method of surveying ore bodies before tunneling.

THE MOHOLE PROJECT—A GLORIOUS FAILURE

Nothing better illustrates the connections of geology to mining than the Mohole Project. Andrija Mohorovičić analyzed seismic waves from earthquakes and concluded that rock of the Earth's crust changes significantly about 16 to 40 kilometers below the surface

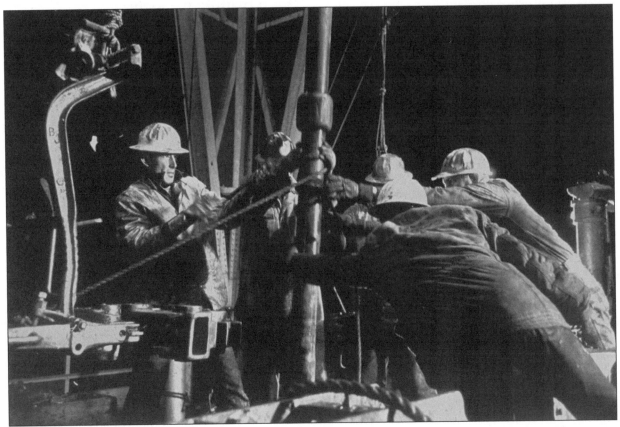

A crew of workers steady machinery on the Project Mohole ship in 1961. (Time & Life Pictures/Getty Images)

as it changes to partially melted mantle. There was considerable speculation as to how rocks might be different at this Mohorovičić discontinuity, or "Moho," and in the 1950's, researchers in a variety of fields from a number of countries discussed proposals about drilling to the Moho for samples. Such a project, it was understood from the outset, would be very expensive.

In the United States, the National Academy of Sciences proposed a government-funded drilling project in 1958; it was nicknamed the "Mohole." Ocean drilling was to be undertaken because the crust is much thinner under the ocean floor. However, drilling into the ocean floor required three major innovations. First, the locations with a shallower Moho in the rocks were in deep water, so the drilling platform had to be an oceangoing vessel rather than a tower resting on the bottom or a simple barge. Second, because anchoring in those depths would be difficult, the drilling vessel had to actively maintain its position. Third, while out of sight of land, the drilling vessel crew had to navigate within a circle of a few tens of meters and return exactly to the drill hole after pulling out of the hole for any reason. This last, most difficult innovation, was managed by satellite position-finding and acoustic beacons on the seafloor.

The project did not attain its goal of reaching the Moho, and some observers considered the attempt an embarrassment to U.S. science. Sufficient funding was not provided, and indeed the project began costing far more than anticipated. However, the project could be considered successful in that technologies developed were subsequently used for drilling throughout the oceans of the world. Oceangoing rigs allowed exploratory drilling in deep areas of the continental shelf before companies made multibillion-dollar investments in production platforms. Thus Mohole Project technology was a major factor in opening many offshore oil fields.

DEEP DRILLING AFTER MOHOLE

To explore geology, the Joint Oceanographic Institutions for Deep Earth Sampling sent the Glomar Challenger on ninety-six voyages, drilling cores in the oceans. (The work continues as the internationally funded Ocean Drilling Program.) Some of the revolutionary discoveries that these cores contributed to were: similarities in rock on both sides of the Atlantic Ocean, lending credence to the concept of ocean spreading as part of continental drift; the fact that

turbidites, deposits from undersea landslides and mudflows, cover large areas of the ocean floor; salt deposits in parts of the Mediterranean Sea from when sea levels were low enough to make the Straits of Gibraltar dry land and the Mediterranean a salty inland sea; few areas of geologically very old ocean floor, suggesting that much of the ocean floor has sunk back under other tectonic plates as other areas expanded; evidence that the dinosaur extinction may have been caused by a comet or asteroid striking the Earth; oil and natural gas deposits extending down the continental slope and perhaps out to the ocean floor, with vast economic implications; and indications of methane hydrate (natural gas frozen together with water) on much of the ocean floor, possibly holding more energy than all other fossil fuels combined.

Drilling on land has also yielded discoveries. The "ultradeep" drill hole in the Kola Peninsula of Russia (east of Norway) reached 12,261 meters despite steadily increasing problems of heat, pressure on the borehole, and logistics of moving samples up from such great depths. Cores from Kola confirmed that metal ores continue deep into the Earth. Also, changes in the returning drilling mud suggested that water and hydrocarbons might continue to those depths.

In 1994, a German hole in Bavaria drilled to 9,100 meters confirmed abundant fluids at those depths. Applying advanced instruments, German scientists found brines with calcium and sodium salts twice as concentrated as those in the ocean. Furthermore, they found channels in the rock large enough for the fluids to move. Thus, brines can deposit hydrothermal metal ores at these depths, and the rocks are permeable enough to hold hydrocarbon reserves. Both these findings changed the previous belief that pressures below several kilometers squeeze the rock too tightly for fluids to exist.

Drilling around the Chicxulub depression, a buried crater in Mexico, has provided evidence that it was the place where a meteor hit the Earth, which may have contributed to climate changes that led to the extinction of the dinosaurs. Drilling has also been used to map major faults, such as the San Andreas in California. One of the prime objects of land drilling, particularly in Hawaii, is finding intrusions of molten rock (magma) near the surface. Their presence helps forecast where and when such rock may escape as lava. In areas such as the Salton Sea in the southeast of California, drilling has helped map hot water deposits for possible energy production.

Ultimately, energy might be the greatest resource from deep drilling. Theoretically, one can tap the heat of radioactive decay in the Earth's core by digging deeply enough from any spot on the surface. The Iceland Deep Drilling Project attempts to tap naturally occurring geothermal steam or hot water, which occurs much closer to the surface. Research programs have attempted to inject fluids, such as water, to return heat to the surface. A limitation on this technology is the cost of drilling to the required depths compared with prices of competing energy sources. Cheaper drilling methods could lead to greater use of this energy source. Likewise, improvements in drilling technology could increase the amount and variety of minerals extracted by drilling.

Roger V. Carlson

FURTHER READING

Crotogino, Fritz. "Reference Value Developed for Mechanical Integrity of Storage Caverns." *Oil and Gas Journal* 94, no. 44 (October 28, 1996): 76.

Gunther, Judith Anne. "Frozen Fuel." *Popular Science* 250, no. 4 (April, 1997): 62.

Harms, Ulrich, Christian Koeberl, and Mark D. Zoback, eds. *Continental Scientific Drilling: A Decade of Progress and Challenges for the Future.* New York: Springer, 2007.

Headden, Susan. "Drilling Deep for Dollars." *U.S. News and World Report* 119, no. 2 (July 10, 1995): 40.

National Research Council. *Drilling and Excavation Technologies for the Future.* Washington, D.C.: National Academy Press, 1994.

WEB SITES

SCIENCE DAILY
Geothermal Energy Exploration: Deep Drilling for "Black Smoker" Clues
http://www.sciencedaily.com/releases/2007/11/071108092749.htm

U.S. DEPARTMENT OF ENERGY
"Deep Trek" and Other Drilling R&D (Research and Development)
http://www.fossil.energy.gov/programs/oilgas/drilling/index.html

SEE ALSO: Geothermal and hydrothermal energy; Integrated Ocean Drilling Program; Oceans; Oil and natural gas exploration; Oil and natural gas reservoirs; Oil shale and tar sands.

Deep ecology

CATEGORY: Environment, conservation, and resource management

Deep ecology is a philosophy centered on the interaction of humans with the natural environment and the rights of the natural world. Deep ecology challenges dominant paradigms concerning the role of humans in the natural world and provides the basis for some of the more radical environmental activist agendas.

DEFINITION

Deep ecology is an ecocentric philosophy that argues for the recognition of the intrinsic value of nonhuman entities and their right to exist and flourish. It calls for a more balanced and egalitarian interaction between humans and nature as opposed to the relationship of human dominance over nature.

OVERVIEW

In 1973, Arne Naess, a Norwegian philosopher, coined the term "deep ecology" as a philosophy distinct from "shallow ecology," which he saw the environmental movement as embodying. Naess defined shallow ecology as that which was concerned with the protection of nature only as it contributed to the well-being of people. Deep ecology, he argued, is guided by many principles that contradict a belief in human domination of the natural world. Rather than prioritizing the needs of man in the natural world, deep ecology takes a more holistic view of nature and man's relationship with it. A reasonable view of natural egalitarianism exists within the deep ecology philosophy, which recognizes that exploitation is necessary for survival but extends rights to nonhuman entities. Those rights are based on a philosophy that nonhumans do not exist solely to serve the needs of humans. Deep ecology recognizes the importance of diversity and denounces competitive Darwinian notions of "only the strong survive" in favor of a more cooperative view of natural systems and relationships. Deep ecology supports classless structures in which there is less domination of humans over other humans, particularly in terms of the peoples of developed and developing nations. These principles are pursued through an appreciation for complexity in human and natural systems rather than efforts to diminish the natural world into categorical parts. Deep ecologists argue that their philosophy can best be realized through "local autonomy and decentralization."

Deep ecology has been used by activist organizations like Earth First! to justify eco-sabotage of industrial development. This vein of deep ecology is more radical and calls for a reversal of roles in which the rights of the natural world take precedence over the rights of humans. This antihuman view has caused controversy and resistance to the basic normative premises of deep ecology, especially because of its deprioritization of economic and technological growth. Deep ecology is also the philosophy behind the bioregionalism movement, an effort to pursue decentralized social organizations that are based on a respect for ecosystem needs and their role in human spiritual development.

In sum, deep ecology recognizes that the natural world has intrinsic value beyond the services it provides for human systems. It rejects notions of human superiority to nature. It questions unfettered economic growth and technological progress. It extends its nondominance tenet to human-to-human relations, particularly those between developed and developing countries. It rejects ideas that human nature is inherently wicked and competitive, thus justifying continued exploitation of underprivileged humans and nonhuman life. Furthermore, deep ecology argues that the foregoing principles should guide environmental policies.

Katrina Taylor

SEE ALSO: Animals as a medical resource; Carson, Rachel; Commoner, Barry; Developing countries; Earth First!; Ecology; Endangered species; Endangered Species Act; Environmental degradation, resource exploitation and; Greenpeace; Leopold, Aldo; Sierra Club; Species loss.

Deforestation

CATEGORY: Geological processes and formations

Deforestation, the removal of forests without adequate replacement, is an increasingly serious problem worldwide, contributing to timber scarcity and soil depletion and contributing to global warming.

BACKGROUND

Humans have long been cutting down forests for lumber, to clear land for agricultural use, or to make room for settlements. For much of human history forests were feared as places of danger, so clearing was often seen as part of a civilizing process. Not until the latter part of the twentieth century were large numbers of people disturbed by the continued process of deforestation and its implications. By the late twentieth century, the clearing of tropical rain forests had become the major focus of the deforestation issue. This depletion of plant life may be contributing to global warming. Using remote sensing surveys, scientists estimate that 1 percent of tropical forests are cleared or severely degraded every year.

CAUSES OF DEFORESTATION

By the late twentieth century, there were three primary causes of deforestation worldwide: cattle ranching, commercial logging, and subsistence agriculture. Other causes include gathering fuel wood, clearing for roads and settlements, and clearing as part of mining operations. In a few cases acid precipitation has also played a role in loss of forest cover. In some less-industrialized countries (especially in Africa) fuel-wood gathering along forest verges helps to gradually push back forest boundaries, and, in the past, wood was a major industrial fuel. In the Middle Ages, clearing for settlements and related agricultural use helped to deforest much of northern Europe. In the nineteenth and early twentieth centuries, many forested areas in the United States were clear-cut to obtain lumber, and this practice remains a cause of deforestation in parts of Asia and South America. Mining operations (especially strip mines) have reduced forests in some areas, and mining wastes make reforestation difficult.

Underlying causes of deforestation are complex, but the most important component is population pressure. Rapidly increasing populations demand increased arable land to feed the population and to exploit for economic purposes. Forestland is often the last source of arable land once other land is utilized. Technological advances such as chain saws, trucks, and bulldozers have made removing forests easier, which has sped up the process of deforestation. In developed nations, such as the United States and those of Western Europe, reforestation still occurs but not at the rate it occurs in developing countries, especially in the tropics. In those areas forest clearing occurs at a

A boy sits near a woodpile in the Aceh Province of Indonesia. The practice of burning wood for fuel has been a significant cause of deforestation in Indonesia and other developing countries. (Tarmizy Harva/Reuters/Landov)

rate that is not sustainable. By the late twentieth century, most deforestation was occurring in tropical parts of South America, Asia, and Africa.

Clearing forests for commercial agriculture, both for cropland and for cattle raising, accounts for approximately 12 percent of tropical forest destruction. Some of the land may be allocated to plantation agriculture, which may be sustainable provided there is extensive use of fertilizers. Because most of the nutrients found in tropical forests are in the living plants and decomposing matter on the forest floor, clearing removes these nutrients and the land soon becomes unproductive even with fertilization. Cleared rain forest land is suitable for cattle grazing for a period of six to ten years. Thereafter the land reverts to scrub savanna.

Commercial logging has always been a cause of deforestation. Considerable forest area in the northeastern and southern United States had been logged by the early twentieth century. Beginning in 1920, much

of this land was reforested: There was more forested land in the United States in the late twentieth century than there was in 1920. Most timber companies in the United States follow a policy of clear-cutting and then replanting, although generally the replanted land is not the varied type of forest that existed before.

Little deforestation occurred in Asia, South America, and Africa before the nineteenth century. Even by 1900 most areas of the tropics, except India and Brazil, had lost little forest cover. This situation changed in the twentieth century. Tropical rain forests are harvested for export, especially in Southeast Asia, and this accounts for 21 percent of tropical rain forest deforestation. Much of this logging occurs at a rate much faster than can be sustained. In parts of Malaysia logging occurs at twice the sustainable rate. Industrialized countries have limited the impact of deforestation on their own countries, but their increasing demand for forest products, especially timber, has led to the continuing deforestation of tropical countries.

Subsistence agriculture is the most important cause of tropical rain forest deforestation, accounting for 60 percent of the destruction of tropical rain forests. Clearing for agriculture has always been an important cause of deforestation, but the increased population pressure in many developing countries is contributing to an increasingly rapid rate of deforestation. Many subsistence farmers in these countries have been displaced from traditional agricultural lands. These farmers generally follow a program of slash-and-burn agriculture in which trees are cut, allowed to dry, and burned, and then crops are immediately planted. The yield for the first crops is usually quite high because the nutrients that were in the burned trees transfer to the soil. However, soil productivity rapidly drops off, and the subsistence farmer must soon move to another area to start the process over again. The land may then be suitable for cattle ranching for a few years. If practiced on a small scale with a long period between cycles, slash-and-burn agriculture is sustainable, but it is not on its present scale.

All of these causes of deforestation often interact, leading to further deforestation. For example, in order to obtain access to a forest to be harvested for timber a logging company often cuts a road through the forest. Villages grow up around tropical mining and logging sites, and as they do, more trees are cut to make way for settlement. In some cases governmental policies contribute to deforestation, especially in Asia where state-owned agricultural and timber plantations contribute to deforestation.

Finally, the demand for goods by industrialized countries is often a driver of deforestation. In nineteenth century Brazil large areas were deforested in order to plant coffee to be sold in the world marketplace. In this case, only the economically elite landowners benefited. Japanese consumption of timber has led to the rapid deforestation of Malaysia and parts of Indonesia. The consumption of beef throughout the industrial world leads to additional land clearing for ranching in South America. Although the industrialized countries have largely halted the loss of

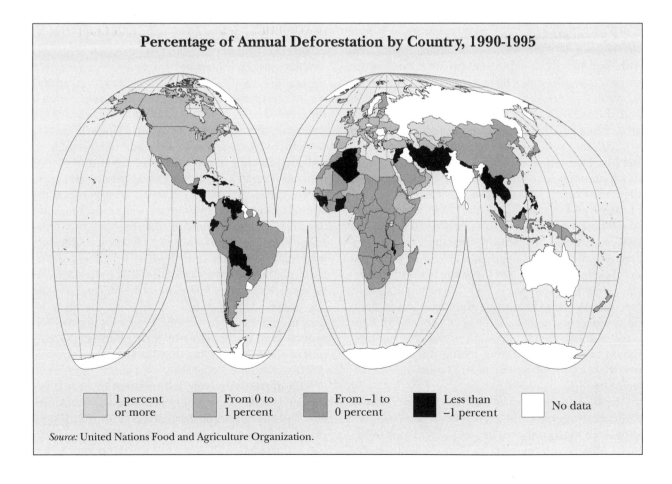

Percentage of Annual Deforestation by Country, 1990-1995

1 percent or more	From 0 to 1 percent	From −1 to 0 percent	Less than −1 percent	No data

Source: United Nations Food and Agriculture Organization.

their forests, their consumption patterns have led to the continuing deforestation of the tropics.

IMPACT OF DEFORESTATION

Deforestation has several directly observable impacts on and long-term consequences for the environment. Clearing of forests without suitable replanting decreases timber supplies, often leads to potential degradation of the soil and water, reduces species diversity, and may contribute to long-term climatic change. In addition there are often negative impacts on indigenous populations who are forced to move or subsist on substandard land.

Because of reforestation projects, forest cover in the United States and Western Europe began growing in 1990, in spite of population pressure. However, in the tropics, the rate of deforestation began accelerating in 1990. The United Nations Food and Agriculture Organization reports that Brazil, for example, lost 423,033 square kilometers of Amazonian forest (roughly the size of California) from 1990 to 2005. Although the rate of decrease had slowed dramatically by 2007, the deforestation rate in Amazonia increased by 3.8 percent from August, 2007, to July, 2008, as Brazil deforested 11,968 square kilometers of the area. Although Brazil has deforested the most land, other tropical countries also have deforested large areas, most notably Indonesia, Sudan, Burma, Côte d'Ivoire, and the Democratic Republic of the Congo. Total area deforested is one means of measuring deforestation; another is percentage of forested land cleared. Because Brazil has such a large total of forested land, its situation does not appear as bad by this measure. Eighteen tropical countries cleared at least 20 percent of their forests between 1990 and 2005. Comoros, an island nation near Madagascar, cleared 60 percent of its forests during the period; Burundi cleared 47 percent of its forests; and Togo, Mauritania, and Honduras also cleared significant forestland during this period. Haiti and Madagascar had cleared much of their forestland before 1990 but continued to clear what little forested land remained. The countries with high rates of deforestation have cleared land for a combination of reasons, including selling the wood products to foreign firms and producing more land for agriculture.

Much of the logging of the past was carried out without any regard to the availability of future timber supplies, and this remains the case in areas such as Malaysia. Most recent commercial logging operations engage in clear-cutting of an area rather than selective cutting of some trees.

When trees are replanted and allowed to mature in clear-cut areas, it is possible to achieve a sustainable yield. However, the original forest often consisted of a variety of trees, while newly planted forests generally consist of only one or two types of trees, often pines. In areas in which no replanting is done after the timber is harvested, a variety of negative impacts occur, such as erosion and the subsequent silting up of neighboring streams.

Some cleared forestland remains suitable for agriculture for a long period of time. Tropical rain forest land, however, is not always suitable for agriculture. Once exposed to the direct impact of rain and sunlight, this land quickly becomes degraded through erosion, oxidation, and laterization. After only a few years of agricultural productivity, the former rain forest land is often abandoned with scant hope of regeneration.

Forested land slows runoff from rains, preventing erosion and floods downstream. When tropical rain forests are cleared, runoff increases, leading to pollution of streams and, eventually, to the silting up of reservoirs downstream and the loss of topsoil. This process spreads the impact of deforestation to areas that are not directly affected by the forest clearing and may create substantial costs as the useful life of reservoirs is reduced.

The impact of forest clearing on species diversity is twofold. Even when forests are replanted by commercial loggers they are generally monoculture forests with only one species of tree, reducing local species diversity. Clear-cutting, in particular, often forces some animals and birds to migrate from the area, often not to return. Estimates indicate that the 7 percent of the Earth's surface that is covered by tropical rain forests is home to 47 percent of the Earth's species of animals, plants, and other organisms. The dramatic deforestation of tropical rain forests that occurred in the late twentieth century has caused some species to be destroyed even before they have been cataloged. This reduction in species diversity through direct destruction or the loss of habitat may lead to the loss of various organisms of great value.

The impact of global deforestation in producing climate change is gradually becoming known. A variety of studies indicate that deforestation can have a substantial long-term regional and global impact in increasing carbon dioxide and methane, two greenhouse gases. Some researchers indicate that diminished biomass leads to a decrease in the absorption of carbon dioxide and resulting global warming. In addition, deforestation can lead to greater climatic extremes within a particular region. Brazil, which is not an industrial country, is now viewed as the fourth largest contributor to global warming because of the impact of deforestation, especially in terms of forest fires that occur when timber is cut in some areas.

In some tropical countries the indigenous forest populations have come under intense pressure from companies and individuals who want to clear the forests for profit. The situation is most troubling in the Amazon basin in Brazil, where native people such as the Bororo have been attacked and killed in efforts to force them out of the forest so that it can be cleared. In other areas native people may not be attacked but are forced to subsist without their usual habitat or move elsewhere. Although the Brazilian government has taken some measures to alleviate the abuses in Amazonia, timber cutters still threaten the native people.

Prospects for the Future

Many of the industrialized nations are no longer clearing forestland for agriculture and engage in controlled harvesting of timber so that sustainable yields can be achieved. In some cases, for example in the eastern United States, substantial reforestation began occurring in the early twentieth century. Nevertheless, threats to the forests of industrialized countries remain, most notably through acid precipitation, which has caused substantial damage to forests, such as Germany's Black Forest, in some regions.

In developing countries, particularly those with tropical forests, deforestation is a significant problem. In some cases the rates of deforestation are continuing to increase. Without efforts to deal with population and economic pressures, slowing the rate of forest loss will be difficult. Some developing countries are trying to preserve their forests as future reserves or as present economic assets by having them serve as attractions for foreign tourists. Costa Rica, for example, has lost much of its forest but has instituted a program of setting aside extensive forest reserves as a method of preservation. Designating parkland is not always effective, however. In some countries, people, often driven by poverty, continue to cut timber in parks. An example of this behavior has occurred in the Bom Futuro National Reserve in Brazil, which lost nearly one-quarter of its forest cover (64,800 hectares) from 2002 to 2007.

Some international environmental groups have offered economic incentives to developing nations to preserve their forests. The Nature Conservancy, for example, engages in a program of buying up parts of a nation's debt in return for guarantees that the country will preserve some of its forests. The Brazilian government is taking measures to strengthen local land ownership rules, setting aside forest reserves and limiting tax credits for firms that do not comply with environmental rules governing deforestation. However, overcoming local logging that is driven by economic necessity is difficult. Selective logging is used in Bolivia so that local communities can achieve some economic gain and preserve large forest tracts rather than indigenous people having to sell large tracts to timber companies to raise money. Elsewhere, governments continue to pursue economic development at all costs, leading to further deforestation. Extensive work by all nations working together to prevent further deforestation is necessary.

John M. Theilmann

Further Reading

Benhin, James K. A. "Agriculture and Deforestation in the Tropics: A Critical, Theoretical, and Empirical Review." *Ambio* 35, no. 1 (February, 2006): 9-16.

Chew, Sing C. *World Ecological Degradation: Accumulation, Urbanization, and Deforestation, 3000 B.C.-A.D. 2000.* Walnut Creek, Calif.: AltaMira Press, 2001.

Geist, Helmut J., and Eric F. Lambin. "Proximate Causes and Underlying Driving Forces of Tropical Deforestation." *BioScience* 52, no. 2 (2002): 143-150.

Humphreys, David. *Logjam: Deforestation and the Crisis of Global Governance.* London: Earthscan, 2006.

Jensen, Derrick, and George Draffan. *Strangely Like War: The Global Assault on Forests.* White River Junction, Vt.: Chelsea Green, 2003.

Laarman, Jan G., and Roger A. Sedjo. *Global Forests: Issues for Six Billion People.* New York: McGraw-Hill, 1992.

May, Elizabeth. *At the Cutting Edge: The Crisis in Canada's Forests.* Rev. ed. Toronto: Key Porter Books, 2005.

Moran, Emilio F., and Elinor Ostrom, eds. *Seeing the Forest and the Trees: Human-Environment Interactions in Forest Ecosystems.* Cambridge, Mass.: MIT Press, 2005.

Nagendra, Harini. "Do Parks Work? Impact of Protected Areas on Land Cover Clearing." *Ambio* 37, no. 5 (July, 2008): 330-337.

Palo, Matti, and Heidi Vanhanen, eds. *World Forests from Deforestation to Transition?* Boston: Kluwer Academic, 2000.

Raven, Peter H., Linda R. Berg, and David M. Hassenzahl. *Environment.* 6th ed. Hoboken, N.J.: Wiley, 2008.

Russell, Emily Wyndham Barnett. *People and the Land Through Time.* New Haven: Yale University Press, 1997.

Vajpeyi, Dhirendrea K., ed. *Deforestation, Environment, and Sustainable Development: A Comparative Analysis.* Westport, Conn.: Praeger, 2001.

Williams, Michael. *Deforesting the Earth: From Prehistory to Global Crisis.* Chicago: University of Chicago Press, 2003.

Woodwell, George M. *Forests in a Full World.* New Haven: Yale University Press, 2001.

SEE ALSO: Acid precipitation; Agenda 21; Brazil; Clear-cutting; Climate and resources; Forestry; Forests; Genetic diversity; Plants as a medical resource; Rain forests; Reforestation; Slash-and-burn agriculture; Wood and timber.

Deltas

CATEGORY: Geological processes and formations

A delta is a deposit of sediments, composed primarily of clay, gravel, and sand, at the mouth of a river. Deltas are sometimes highly valued as agricultural lands. The sandstones formed at the front of a delta are often good reservoir rocks for oil and gas deposits.

DEFINITION

Deltas are triangular-shaped bodies formed when rivers flow into large bodies of standing water; they form where the river's speed and ability to carry sediments are suddenly reduced. The formation of deltas is affected mainly by climate, seasonal fluctuations of marine and river forces, geological features (the shape of existing coastline and of the seafloor), and river size and flooding patterns. The shape and internal structure of deltas can be explained by the nature and interaction of two forces: the sediment-carrying stream from a river and the current and wave action of the water body in which the delta is being built. This interaction ranges from complete dominance of the sediment-carrying stream (still-water deltas) to complete dominance of currents and waves, resulting in redistribution of the sediment over a wide area (no deltas).

OVERVIEW

Through progressive outbuilding, the delta can become overextended with long river courses. Eventually shorter, steeper, less-resistant paths to the sea will be developed and the existing delta will be abandoned in favor of a shorter course. The Mississippi Delta is a good example, where seven different deltas have been built over the past five thousand years. Abandoned deltas gradually submerge and become eroded by wave action. The presently active Mississippi Delta would be abandoned for a new one off the Atchafalaya River if artificial control did not keep the flow in check.

While dozens of major deltas exist today, not all rivers, or even all major ones, have deltas. This situation is the result of a rise in sea level following the last glacial period, which produced deep bodies of water along many coastlines around the world that have not yet been filled. Delta thicknesses vary widely. The Nile Delta is 15 meters thick in a shallow embayment, whereas the Mississippi Delta is more than 100 meters thick, building out into deep water.

Deltas have fertile soil that makes them excellent agricultural areas. The rich land of the Mississippi Delta in Louisiana produces fruits, vegetables, and other crops. The Nile Delta has been farmed since ancient times, while the Irrawaddy Delta in Burma and the Mekong Delta in Vietnam support large rice fields. The Netherlands (with its Rhine and Maas Deltas) is an example of what can be done toward land reclamation when population is great.

Over time, because of pressure on the underlying beds, a delta is buried deeper and deeper. Since the sandstones formed at the front of a delta often have good porosity (pore spaces) and permeability (channels connecting the pores), if there is a source of petroleum, then old, deeply buried deltas can develop into good oil reservoirs. An excellent example is the Bell Creek oil field in the Powder River Basin, extending from southeastern Montana into northeastern Wyoming.

Alvin K. Benson

SEE ALSO: Agricultural products; Land-use planning; Oil and natural gas reservoirs; Rice; Sedimentary processes, rocks, and mineral deposits; Streams and rivers.

Denmark

CATEGORIES: Countries; government and resources

Denmark is the leading exporter of fish in Europe. The country is also the leader in wind-energy use and technological advances and the production of wind turbines. Chalk and limestone cover a majority of the landscape. The chalk cliffs of Møn Island and several limestone caves are key tourist sites. The energy surplus that allows the export of natural gas and oil brings billions of dollars into Denmark's economy each year.

THE COUNTRY

Denmark became a state during the tenth century and a constitutional monarchy in 1849. Its citizens often rank as the happiest in the world in global surveys, and the country is the second most peaceful in the world. Denmark is located on the Jutland Peninsula in northern Europe. It borders the Baltic and North Seas and Germany to the south. Sweden is located to the northeast. The country also includes the islands of Fyn, Sjælland, and several other smaller ones. Its position gives it control of the Danish Straits, which link the Baltic and North Seas. Denmark is a low-lying nation, prone to flooding, that is protected from the sea by a series of dikes. The elevation of the country ranges from 171 meters above sea level to 7 meters below sea level. Denmark is a pioneer in harnessing energy from wind power, combating the country's air pollution problem. Approximately one-quarter of the population lives in the capital city of Copenhagen. Denmark joined the European Union in 1973 but did not adopt the euro as its currency. Denmark's standard of living and per-capita gross national product are among the world's highest. The country is also a welfare state, leading the world in income equality. Among Denmark's top resources are limestone, chalk, natural gas, petroleum, and salt.

FISH

Surrounded by water, Denmark has a long history with the fishing industry. A wide range of fish are found off the shores of Denmark, including haddock, mackerel, cod, and trout. The town of Skagen, in the northern tip of Denmark, is famous for its sea fishing. A local museum is dedicated to the history of the town and the fishing industry. Pike and trout are found in the country's rivers, lakes, and estuaries. Organic fish farms can be found throughout the country and are highly regulated by the Danish government. The organic fish farms cannot use feed containing genetically modified organisms or colorants, cannot treat fish with medicine more than once in their lives, and cannot harm predatory animals that might affect the fish population. In order to protect the fish from attackers, the farms are usually enclosed using a fine mesh or bird nets.

Denmark is Europe's largest exporter of industrial fish. The country has a number of fish-processing companies, but those exports are not as high. Most processed fish is made with herring, mackerel, or cod.

Denmark's economy is reliant on the country's fishing industry. In this 1956 photo, a Danish fisherman prepares his catch for market. (Hulton Archive/ Getty Images)

Denmark: Resources at a Glance

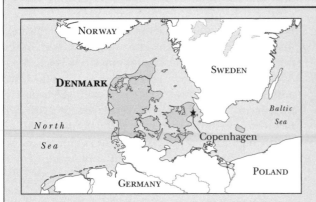

Official name: Kingdom of Denmark
Government: Constitutional monarchy
Capital city: Copenhagen
Area: 16,640 mi^2; 43,094 km^2
Population (2009 est.): 5,500,510
Language: Danish
Monetary unit: Danish krone (DKK)

ECONOMIC SUMMARY:

GDP composition by sector (2008 est.): agriculture, 1.3%; industry, 26.1%; services, 72.6%
Natural resources: petroleum, natural gas, fish, salt, limestone, chalk, stone, gravel and sand
Land use (2005): arable land, 52.59%; permanent crops, 0.19%; other, 47.22%
Industries: iron, steel, nonferrous metals, chemicals, food processing, machinery and transportation equipment, textiles and clothing, electronics, construction, furniture and other wood products, shipbuilding and refurbishment, windmills, pharmaceuticals, medical equipment
Agricultural products: barley, wheat, potatoes, sugar beets, pork, dairy products, fish
Exports (2008 est.): $114.9 billion
Commodities exported: machinery and instruments, meat and meat products, dairy products, fish, pharmaceuticals, furniture, windmills
Imports (2008 est.): $116.4 billion
Commodities imported: machinery and equipment, raw materials and semimanufactures for industry, chemicals, grain and foodstuffs, consumer goods
Labor force (2008 est.): 2.88 million
Labor force by occupation (2005 est.): agriculture, 2.9%; industry, 23.8%; services, 72.7%

ENERGY RESOURCES:

Electricity production (2007 est.): 36.99 billion kWh
Electricity consumption (2006 est.): 34.68 billion kWh
Electricity exports (2007 est.): 11.38 billion kWh
Electricity imports (2007 est.): 10.43 billion kWh

Natural gas production (2007 est.): 9.223 billion m^3
Natural gas consumption (2007 est.): 4.555 billion m^3
Natural gas exports (2007 est.): 4.517 billion m^3
Natural gas imports (2007 est.): 0 m^3
Natural gas proved reserves (Jan. 2008 est.): 70.51 billion m^3

Oil production (2007 est.): 313,800 bbl/day
Oil imports (2006 est.): 164,000 bbl/day
Oil proved reserves (Jan. 2008 est.): 1.188 billion bbl

Source: Data from *The World Factbook 2009.* Washington, D.C.: Central Intelligence Agency, 2009.
Notes: Data are the most recent tracked by the CIA. Values are given in U.S. dollars. Abbreviations: bbl/day = barrels per day; GDP = gross domestic product; km^2 = square kilometers; kWh = kilowatt-hours; m^3 = cubic meters; mi^2 = square miles.

These products are made with both imported and domestically caught fish. Only 5 percent of the processed fish products remain in Denmark. Between 1983 and 1998 the amount of fresh fish and fillets exported from Denmark doubled. Because of this large increase, the processed fish industry has relied more heavily on imports. The four main imports are herring (from Norway), trout, salmon, and shrimp. The industry produces a wide variety of products that are frozen, canned (mostly herring, mackerel, and blue mussels), smoked, pickled, and marinated. Most meat and oil processing is done in the northern and western portions of the country, with mackerel and herring mainly processed in the north. Amanda Seafood, established in 1916, was among the first makers of Danish canned fish. During the mid-1950's the company introduced a line of pressed cod roe in cans. The Lykkeberg company was founded by Peter Lykkeberg in 1899 to produce "semi-preserved" herring. The company remains in business and is known globally for the quality of its herring. Fish and seafood exports account for roughly 3.5 percent of Denmark's exports. In the fifteen years following 1983, exports increased from 634,900 metric tons to more than 1 million metric tons. By 2002, Denmark was exporting 1.03 million metric tons of fish. Danish fishermen caught 1.32 million metric tons of fish that year.

Natural Gas

Following the discovery of natural gas in Denmark's region of the North Sea, the Danish government passed the Natural Gas Supply Planning Act in 1979. The first gas was pumped to shore five years later. The gas supply continued to grow until it was available nationwide by early in the 1990's. In 2002, natural gas accounted for 23 percent of Denmark's energy consumption. At that time, the reserves in the North Sea were estimated to be enough to last for eighteen years. Between 2006 and 2007, Danish exports of natural gas rose by 60 percent to more than 4.5 billion cubic meters, ranking the country twenty-fourth in that category worldwide. Exports dropped 9 percent by 2008. Denmark has considered building a pipeline to Poland to import natural gas when its reserves in the North Sea begin to decline. Denmark's increasing reliance on wind power has helped increase the number of years the country can be energy self-sufficient. Denmark first had a surplus of oil and gas in 1995. In 2007, exports of natural gas and oil amounted to 28.3 billion Danish kroner (about $5.4 billion). In January,

2009, Denmark's estimated reserves for natural gas were 107 billion cubic meters.

Oil

In 1973, Denmark relied on oil for 88.7 percent of its energy needs. By 2001, the country had lowered that to 45.8 percent. Oil production began in 1972, in the coastal waters surrounding the country. There are nineteen active oil-producing fields in Denmark. In January, 2008, Denmark's oil reserves were estimated to be 1.188 billion barrels, ranking it forty-seventh in that category worldwide. At the beginning of 2009, the country's oil reserves had dropped. At its 2009 rate of production, accounting for its estimated reserves, Denmark was expected to exhaust its oil in 2018 and its natural gas in 2020. However, with improved technology and the discovery of additional oil sources, Denmark could extend its domestic oil use to 2029.

A study published in 2009 may lead to increased Danish oil production. A group of researchers from the Nano-Science Center at the University of Copenhagen have been studying the rocks on the floor of the North Sea. The rocks are mainly composed of chalk, which no study has previously investigated in this capacity. They found that the areas that contained oil displayed drastically different surface qualities from those expected. The chalk was expected to repel the oil; instead the scientists found that the oil stuck to it. These findings may lead to a new or better method of extracting oil from the North Sea and increased oil production.

Limestone

Much of Denmark is limestone. The Mønsted mine and quarry west of Viborg is the largest limestone mine in the world. The mine shut down in 1953 after one thousand years of mining. Limestone was initially of little use to the Danes, but this changed after the country converted to Christianity. Many churches were built using limestone, more than two thousand in two hundred years, greatly boosting the area's economy. An underground furnace was also built to burn limestone; the result was used as a mortar. There are around 60 kilometers of underground caves of varying sizes and depths. Two kilometers of the mines are equipped with electricity and are open to the public. The mines include two underground lakes. There is a multimedia presentation that explains the history of limestone and the mines. Concerts are also held in some of the larger caves. The limestone caverns are the winter home to more than five thousand bats. The cool, steady conditions allow the Mønsted caves to be used to age 180 metric tons of cheese made by a local dairy.

The Daugbjerg mine is located 3 kilometers from the Mønsted mine. This mine is also open to the public, with candlelight tours giving tourists an idea about the working conditions of miners. These caves are where the legendary Jens Olesen, a Robin Hood-type criminal from the 1620's, hid from authorities. The mine also ages cheese and stores sausages and wines, all of which can be purchased on site. The Daugbjerg mine is home to the largest collection of bats, more than twelve thousand, in Denmark.

The Thingbæk mine was owned by Anders Bundgaard, a sculptor by trade. In 1936, the caves were converted into a sculptural museum. Limestone was mined there for generations, but the mine was not highly profitable. Most of the exhibits were Bundgaard's own works of art, including plaster models of famous foreign pieces. He created the Emigration Cave, which features a number of reliefs that tell the story of those who moved to the United States. In 1969, plaster works of another artist, C. J. Bonnesen, were donated to the museum.

The rocky island of Bornholm in the Baltic Sea also has a number of limestone caves, caverns, mines, and quarries. The largest cavern is 70 meters long and is located in the northern section of the island. Several other mines and quarries can be found throughout the country. Through the end of the twentieth century, Denmark still produced almost 1 million metric tons of agricultural and industrial limestone.

CHALK

Møns Klint, the cliffs of Møn, are a major tourist attraction along the eastern coast of the island of Møn in the Baltic Sea. The cliffs are bright white and composed of chalk. They cover 8 kilometers along the coast of the island. Some of the cliffs have a steep drop of 120 meters from the top to sea level. The cliffs and surrounding land are protected as part of a natural reserve. Tourists who visit the cliffs enjoy walking and cycling along the many marked trails throughout the nature reserve. In 2007, a museum was opened near the top of the cliffs that focuses on the geological history of Denmark and the formation of the chalk cliffs.

The chalk formed from the shells of millions of microscopic sea creatures that were more than seventy million years old. Layers of chalk strata covered the seabed as the creatures died. Glaciers crossed Denmark during the last ice age, about sixteen thousand years ago. The glaciers moved westward across the area, putting the seabed under great pressure. The chalk strata were compacted and pushed upward in front of the slow-moving glacier. When the glacier retreated, the chalk cliffs of Møns remained. The cliffs of Rügen, Germany, across the Baltic, formed at the same time from the same deposits. The area is abundant with fossils of shellfish. The soil in the region is very chalky, which has led to the growth of a variety of rare plants, including several orchids. The soil conditions also give beech trees at the top of the cliffs a light-green hue, which the trees keep throughout the summer.

Because of the steepness of the cliffs and the qualities of chalk, landslides are a possibility. In 1952, at Røde Udfald a landslide created a peninsula that stretches 450 meters out into the ocean. In 1988, at Møns Klint, one of the landmark cliffs slid into the ocean. Several other landslides and rock slides have occurred. The worst landslide in fifty years on Møn was in 2007. Store Taleren (the big speaker)—417,200 metric tons of chalk, clay, and sand—fell into the ocean. The landslide created a peninsula that reached 300 meters into the Eastern Sea. A smaller rockslide that formed a peninsula 100 meters long occurred to the south less than six weeks later.

WIND ENERGY

Following the oil crisis of 1973 many Danes began to rally for cheaper, cleaner energy, other than nuclear power, which they felt was unsafe. The Nordic Folkecenter for Renewable Energy, the leader in developing commercial applications of wind and renewable energy sources, was founded in 1983. By the mid-1980's, the grassroots movement finally convinced the government to focus on non-oil energy sources. In 1988, the government set a goal of lowering carbon emissions by 22 percent by 2005. Typical wind speeds measured at 10 meters inland are 4.9-5.6 meters per second. Highest values are found in the western region of the country and on islands to the east. However, Denmark's offshore regions have the highest wind speed capacities in Europe: 8.5-9 meters per second measured at an elevation of 50 meters.

In 1996, the Danish government began offering tax credits to citizens who either invested in wind-turbine collectives or purchased their own turbines. In 2004, reports showed that 86 percent of Danes were in favor of wind energy. The first offshore wind farm worldwide, Vindeby, was built by Denmark in 1991. The Middelgrunden offshore wind farm was the largest in the world when it was built in 2000. The farm consists of twenty turbines off the coast of Copenhagen. In 2009, Denmark had approximately six thousand wind turbines in operation, with more scheduled to follow. A larger wind farm, off the island of Anholt, was expected to be operational by 2012. The existing wind farms produce a growing amount of Denmark's electricity supply, rising from 12.1 percent in 2001 to 19.7 percent in 2007. Denmark is the world leader in manufacturing wind turbines, exporting approximately 90 percent of those produced. In 2003, 38 percent of the global wind-turbine industry was Danish companies.

Despite the high approval rating of wind energy among Danes, and the world's growing desire to end its dependence on coal and oil, wind energy has a number of critics. Wind farms worldwide have killed tens of thousands of birds and bats, including many rare and endangered species. Other critics argue that the wind farms are actually doing more harm than good. Denmark had not shut down any of its fossil fuel power plants as of 2009. Some scientists argue that the wind farms actually increase carbon emissions because a growing number of power plants are needed to back up the turbines in case of diminished wind speeds. Electricity produced by wind is the highest priced of renewable energies.

OTHER RESOURCES

The production of salt is sometimes referred to as Denmark's first industry. The island of Laesø has an abundance of salt, which was first produced there hundreds of years ago. Now the island is a popular tourist site. The Salt Center, the only salt-themed museum in Scandinavia, offers a variety of activities and exhibits. The center features the history of salt and the salt industry, a science lab for hands-on salt experiments, and a "Dead Sea" indoor pool where visitors can experience weightlessness.

Denmark also has a number of farming cooperatives and one of the world's leading free-trade economies. The country produces barley, wheat, potatoes, and sugar beets. The Danish diet consists of fish, pork, and cheese and other dairy products. Most of Denmark's agricultural trading partners are fellow European Union countries.

Jennifer L. Campbell

FURTHER READING

"Denmark: Wind Power." *BusinessWeek* (September 15, 2003): 22.

Fielding, Andrew, and Annelise Fielding. *The Salt Industry.* Westminster, Md.: Shire, 2008.

Jensen, Jørgen. *The Prehistory of Denmark.* London: Routledge, 2000.

Jespersen, Knud. *A History of Denmark.* New York: Palgrave Macmillan, 2004.

Jones, Gwyn. *A History of the Vikings.* 2d ed. New York: Oxford University Press, 2001.

Van Est, Rinie. *Winds of Change: A Comparative Study on the Politics of Wind Energy Innovation in California and Denmark.* Utrecht, Netherlands: International Books, 2000.

SEE ALSO: Fisheries; Limestone; Renewable and nonrenewable resources; Wind energy.

Department of Agriculture, U.S.

CATEGORY: Organizations, agencies, and programs
DATE: Established 1862

The U.S. Department of Agriculture is known for its stewardship of natural resources, research to ensure a safe and abundant food supply, inspection of agricultural products, and provision of loans in rural communities.

BACKGROUND

President Abraham Lincoln founded the U.S. Department of Agriculture (USDA) to help farmers improve their yield. This service is one of many now provided by the agencies within the USDA. Many USDA programs assist farmers. The USDA Consolidated Farm Service Agency (CFSA) administers programs to improve the economic stability of agriculture. Farmers are helped to adjust production to meet demand through acreage reductions. Federal crop insurance guards against losses from unavoidable causes.

IMPACT ON RESOURCE USE

USDA researchers provide objective statistical information to food producers to enable them to produce high-quality food without damaging the environment. For a rural population struggling with job losses, emigration, and declining living standards, the USDA will fund projects that create jobs, services, and housing. For the general population, the USDA acts as a bridge between farmer and consumer by advocating nutrition. Most nutrition programs are directed at low-income Americans; such programs include soup kitchens and food banks, nutrition programs for the elderly, and the food stamp and national school lunch programs.

The USDA keeps track of what Americans eat, where they eat it, and how much they spend on food. Statistics are also gathered on farm income, employment, and the poverty rate in rural areas of the United States. Ensuring that food is safe to eat is a prime concern of the USDA. Inspection teams stamp their ap-

proval on meat and poultry, and tools to aid in the detection of bacteria are continually developed by USDA's Food Safety and Inspection Service. A water-quality program protects the nation's waters from contamination by agricultural chemicals and provides financial assistance to address environmental concerns.

As a steward of the land, the USDA manages federal lands through the U.S. Forest Service and the Natural Resources Conservation Service (NRCS, formerly the Soil Conservation Service). About 78 million of the 300 million hectares of forestland in the United States are in the Forest Service system. The Forest Service strives to sustain ecosystems by ensuring their health, diversity, and productivity. Lands are

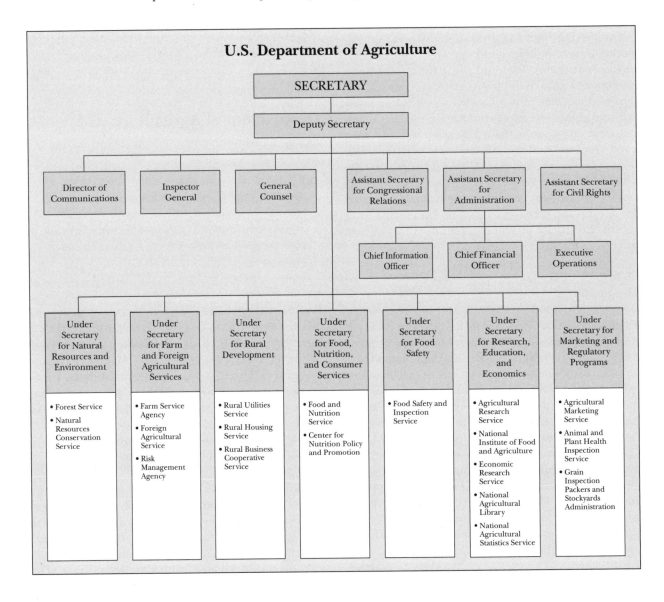

protected from wildfire, epidemics of disease and insect pests, erosion, floods, and air and water pollution. Advocating the policy of multiple use, the Forest Service encourages public recreation in national forests. Rangelands are managed to provide food for both livestock and wildlife; they also serve as watersheds and recreational sites.

The NRCS provides landowners with technical assistance for developing and implementing conservation plans. Its field staff also collect data from more than twelve hundred mountain sites to provide vital information on water supplies; its Plant Materials Centers develop plant strains to increase propagation for mass production. The passing of the Federal Crop Insurance Reform and Department of Agriculture Reorganization Act in 1994 resulted in substantial reorganization of the USDA with the goals of improving coordination among its agencies and cutting costs to taxpayers.

Jill A. Cooper

WEB SITE

U.S. DEPARTMENT OF AGRICULTURE
http://www.usda.gov/wps/portal/usdahome

SEE ALSO: Agriculture industry; Agronomy; Forest Service, U.S.; Natural Resources Conservation Service; Public lands.

Department of Energy, U.S.

CATEGORY: Organizations, agencies, and programs
DATE: Established 1977

The Department of Energy is the primary developer and manager of U.S. energy resources. Energy is an area crucial to the U.S. economy and subject to political debate. The Department of Energy oversees the nation's massive energy needs while also trying to conserve its precious resources.

BACKGROUND
The Department of Energy is part of the executive branch of the U.S. government. The secretary of energy is a member of the president's cabinet, confirmed by the Senate. James Schlesinger was the first energy secretary. Established by Congress on October 1, 1977, the Department of Energy assumed responsi-

bilities that numerous federal agencies had previously had in managing the nation's natural resources. The Department of Energy assumed duties long exercised by the Department of the Interior and three federal agencies—the Federal Power Commission, the Federal Energy Administration, and the Energy Research and Development Administration (ERDA). The Department of Energy also oversees the nation's nuclear energy and weapons programs.

IMPACT ON RESOURCE USE
The Department of Energy was established during the administration of President Jimmy Carter in reaction to the oil crisis of the 1970's. Its roots, however, go deeper in history. The federal government had always played a role in developing and managing the nation's water, timber, mineral, coal, oil, and other energy resources. With the Manhattan Project of the 1940's and the Atomic Energy Commission of the 1950's (eventually incorporated into the ERDA), the federal government exercised exclusive control over the creation of atomic weapons and energy. The Department of Energy assumed these responsibilities by way of the October 1, 1977, Department of Energy Organization Act. The United States has always enjoyed an abundance of energy through its vast natural resources and unparalleled industrial development. However, in the 1970's, the nation had to reassess its energy situation when the major oil-producing countries declared oil embargoes. The response was the creation of the Department of Energy, whose mandate was to foster energy research, development, and production to meet domestic and international challenges. In line with Carter's energy policies, the Department of Energy began programs to increase use of solar energy and to conserve fossil-fuel resources. The administration of President Ronald Reagan emphasized increased production of energy by reducing federal regulation of the energy supply. In response to threatened oil embargoes, the Department of Energy built up petroleum reserves, reaching 250 million barrels in 1982. The Department of Energy also began well-publicized programs to dispose of by-products of energy development. For example, in 1983, the Department of Energy created a Civilian Radioactive Waste Department. It also started a program to develop "clean" (less-polluting) coal-burning facilities. In 1989, the Department of Energy created an office of Environmental Restoration and Waste Management.

U.S. Department of Energy

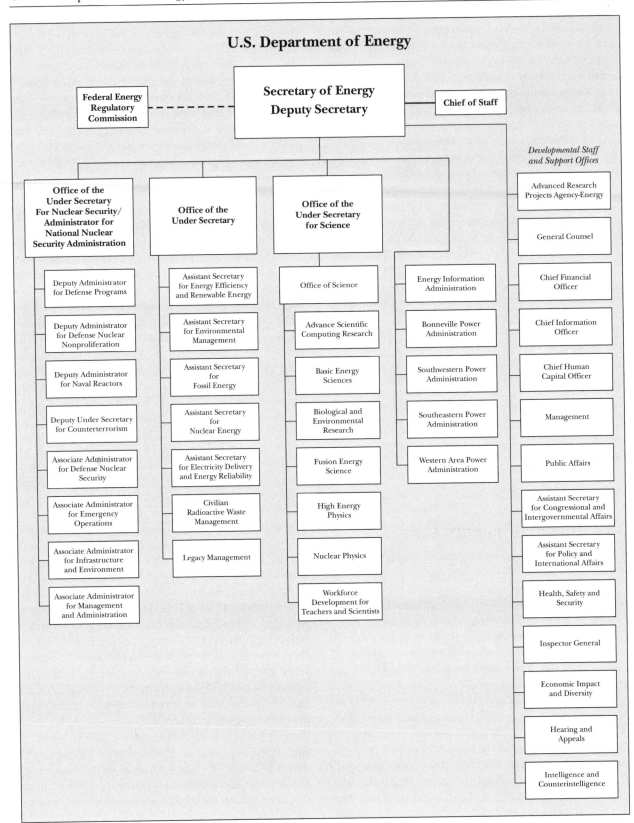

Federal Energy Regulatory Commission

Secretary of Energy
Deputy Secretary

Chief of Staff

Developmental Staff and Support Offices

Office of the Under Secretary For Nuclear Security/ Administrator for National Nuclear Security Administration

Office of the Under Secretary

Office of the Under Secretary for Science

Advanced Research Projects Agency-Energy

General Counsel

Deputy Administrator for Defense Programs

Assistant Secretary for Energy Efficiency and Renewable Energy

Office of Science

Energy Information Administration

Chief Financial Officer

Deputy Administrator for Defense Nuclear Nonproliferation

Assistant Secretary for Environmental Management

Advance Scientific Computing Research

Bonneville Power Administration

Chief Information Officer

Deputy Administrator for Naval Reactors

Assistant Secretary for Fossil Energy

Basic Energy Sciences

Southwestern Power Administration

Chief Human Capital Officer

Deputy Under Secretary for Counterterrorism

Assistant Secretary for Nuclear Energy

Biological and Environmental Research

Southeastern Power Administration

Management

Associate Administrator for Defense Nuclear Security

Assistant Secretary for Electricity Delivery and Energy Reliability

Fusion Energy Science

Western Area Power Administration

Public Affairs

Associate Administrator for Emergency Operations

Civilian Radioactive Waste Management

High Energy Physics

Assistant Secretary for Congressional and Intergovernmental Affairs

Associate Administrator for Infrastructure and Environment

Legacy Management

Nuclear Physics

Assistant Secretary for Policy and International Affairs

Associate Administrator for Management and Administration

Workforce Development for Teachers and Scientists

Health, Safety and Security

Inspector General

Economic Impact and Diversity

Hearing and Appeals

Intelligence and Counterintelligence

After the end of the Cold War in 1990, the Department of Energy deemphasized production of new nuclear weapons and shifted some support to theoretical research: particle acceleration experiments at the Department of Energy's Fermi National Accelerator Laboratory, SLAC National Accelerator Laboratory, and other national laboratories. During the Bill Clinton administration, the Department of Energy proposed numerous regulations for disposal of hazardous wastes (such as plutonium). Under the free market ideology of President George W. Bush, the Department of Energy promoted extraction of oil and nonrenewable energy resources from federal lands in the West and in Alaska.

Howard Bromberg

WEB SITE

U.S. DEPARTMENT OF ENERGY
http://www.energy.gov/

SEE ALSO: American Mining Congress; American Petroleum Institute; Atomic Energy Acts; Atomic Energy Commission; Biofuels; Biotechnology; Department of Agriculture, U.S.; Department of the Interior, U.S.; Department of Transportation, U.S.; Energy economics; Energy politics; Energy storage; Gasoline and other petroleum fuels; Manufacturing, energy use in; Nuclear Energy Institute; Oil embargo and energy crises of 1973 and 1979; Organization of Arab Petroleum Exporting Countries; Organization of Petroleum Exporting Countries; Solar energy.

Department of the Interior, U.S.

CATEGORY: Organizations, agencies, and programs
DATE: Established 1849

The U.S. Department of the Interior is the federal agency entrusted with conserving much of the nation's natural resources. These resources include federal forests and grazing land; national parks; water and irrigation; oil, gas, and coal; American Indian lands; and fish and wildlife.

BACKGROUND
The Department of the Interior is part of the executive branch of the U.S. government. The secretary of the interior is a member of the president's cabinet,

confirmed by the Senate. The three original executive departments of the federal government established in 1789 were Foreign Affairs, War, and Treasury. Given the limited role intended for the federal government in internal affairs, there was no executive department to handle general domestic management. As the range of federal responsibilities emerged, Congress established the Department of the Interior on March 3, 1849, to assume various domestic duties of the federal government.

IMPACT ON RESOURCE USE
In the second half of the nineteenth century, the Department of the Interior conducted a wide range of domestic activities, such as controlling American Indian affairs, managing federal lands, paying federal pensions, granting patents, conducting the census, constructing the infrastructure for the District of Columbia, surveying the Western territories, and overseeing federal monetary and land grants to hospitals and colleges. As a result, the Department of the Interior received the unofficial title of "Department of Everything Else." As Congress created additional departments to assume these manifold tasks, the chief purpose of the Department of the Interior came into view: to manage and conserve the natural resources of the nation.

The principal work of the modern Department of the Interior is performed by eight bureaus. Perhaps the best way to understand the crucial role the Department of the Interior plays in administering the nation's resources is to outline the functions of its major divisions. The Bureau of Land Management manages more than 100 million hectares of federal lands, much of which is leased for cattle grazing and ranching, lumber logging, coal and mineral mining, and oil and gas drilling. These leases raise as much as $23 billion annually for the federal government and account for about 30 percent of the nation's energy production. The National Park Service manages 33 million hectares, comprising 391 federal parks, monuments, and cultural sites. The Fish and Wildlife Service manages about 40 million hectares of wildlife refuges to conserve and foster marine and animal life. The Bureau of Indian Affairs manages 27 million hectares of American Indian tribal and reservation lands. The Bureau of Reclamation manages 479 dams and 348 reservoirs, which provide water to much of the West. The U.S. Geological Survey conducts geological and topographical research.

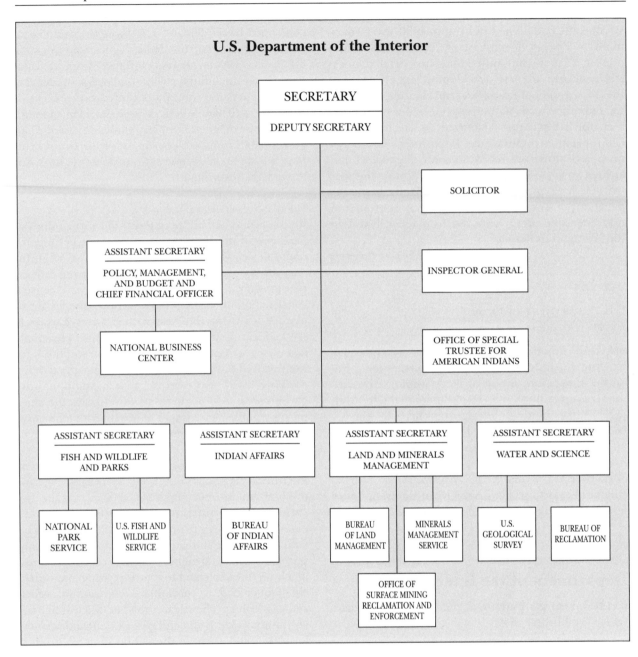

U.S. Department of the Interior

SECRETARY

DEPUTY SECRETARY

SOLICITOR

ASSISTANT SECRETARY

POLICY, MANAGEMENT, AND BUDGET AND CHIEF FINANCIAL OFFICER

INSPECTOR GENERAL

NATIONAL BUSINESS CENTER

OFFICE OF SPECIAL TRUSTEE FOR AMERICAN INDIANS

ASSISTANT SECRETARY

FISH AND WILDLIFE AND PARKS

ASSISTANT SECRETARY

INDIAN AFFAIRS

ASSISTANT SECRETARY

LAND AND MINERALS MANAGEMENT

ASSISTANT SECRETARY

WATER AND SCIENCE

NATIONAL PARK SERVICE

U.S. FISH AND WILDLIFE SERVICE

BUREAU OF INDIAN AFFAIRS

BUREAU OF LAND MANAGEMENT

MINERALS MANAGEMENT SERVICE

U.S. GEOLOGICAL SURVEY

BUREAU OF RECLAMATION

OFFICE OF SURFACE MINING RECLAMATION AND ENFORCEMENT

In total, the Department of the Interior plays a crucial role in conserving federal lands, forests, and parks; irrigating and supplying fresh water; protecting marine and land wildlife; and leasing lands for material, mineral, and energy production. With jurisdiction over such a wealth of resources, the Department of the Interior has been prone to scandal. In 1929, Department of the Interior secretary Albert Falls was convicted of bribery in the Teapot Dome scandal. In the administration of President George W. Bush, Department of the Interior officials often seemed ambivalent about the natural treasures that they were obliged to protect. In a December, 2008, report, Department of the Interior inspector general Earl Devaney found unethical, wasteful, and corrupt behavior in the Minerals Management Service and other divisions of the Bush administration's Department of the Interior.

Howard Bromberg

WEB SITE

U.S. DEPARTMENT OF THE INTERIOR
http://www.doi.gov/

SEE ALSO: Bureau of Land Management, U.S.; Bureau of Mines, U.S.; Bureau of Reclamation, U.S.; Department of Agriculture, U.S.; Department of Energy, U.S.; Department of Transportation, U.S.; Forest Service, U.S.; National Park Service; National Parks Act, Canadian; Public lands; U.S. Geological Survey.

Department of Transportation, U.S.

CATEGORY: Organizations, agencies, and programs
DATE: Established 1966

The Department of Transportation works to provide efficient, economic, safe, and environmentally sound national transportation systems on land, in the air, over U.S. waters, and through underground pipelines. In this role, it regulates the transport of resources throughout the country. It is one of the departments of the federal government that reports directly to the president of the United States.

BACKGROUND

On March 2, 1966, President Lyndon B. Johnson proposed the structure for a new executive department pertaining to federal aspects of transportation. On October 15, 1966, Congress established the Department of Transportation. More than thirty existing agencies with some ninety thousand employees were brought together in creating the Department of Transportation.

IMPACT ON RESOURCE USE

The transportation systems of the nation are intricately linked to the resources of the nation and the world. Most physical resources—anything from timber to gasoline to crushed stone—are transported from producer to consumer through parts of the national transportation system. The transportation industry is itself a major consumer of many resources, and the Department of Transportation assists in efforts to reduce pollution and destruction of natural ecosystems and to increase the efficiency of the industry's use of resources.

Environmental issues that are researched through funding from the Department of Transportation include the safe packaging and transportation of hazardous materials and the effects of airline and automobile emissions on air quality. Also studied are the water quality in rivers and oceans (particularly as affected by merchant shipping and inland barge transportation) and how best to preserve wetlands or wildlife habitats during the construction of highways, airports, and urban transit systems. The Department of Transportation conducts research on the feasibility of electric transportation regarding both automobiles and mass transit.

The department is the main force in the federal government for developing and coordinating a national transportation system and developing a national policy regarding transportation. Its responsibilities include the development and enforcement of transportation safety improvements, the development of international transportation agreements, and the smooth running of accessible transportation for the general public. It coordinates transportation issues with states and cities and provides technical assistance to other levels of government. The department acquires equipment and services and disburses federal funding to state and municipal authorities for transportation purposes.

The Department of Transportation has a number of operating divisions. Each is headed by an administrator who answers directly to the secretary of the Department of Transportation, who heads the department and serves on the president's cabinet. The divisions are the Federal Motor Carrier Safety Administration, Federal Railroad Administration, Federal Transit Administration, the Pipeline and Hazardous Materials Safety Administration, the Surface Transportation Board, the Federal Aviation Administration, the Federal Highway Administration, the Saint Lawrence Seaway Development Corporation, the National Highway Traffic Safety Administration, the Maritime Administration, and the Research and Special Programs Administration.

In 2003, the Department of Transportation underwent a slight restructuring when two of its divisions, the United States Coast Guard and the Transportation Security Administration, became parts of the Department of Homeland Security. Each of the eleven divisions is involved in specific aspects of resource and environmental management. The National Highway Traffic Safety Administration, for example, assists in the development and enforcement of national fuel economy standards. The Federal Aviation Administration assists in studies related to changes in the ozone layer as a result of airline emissions.

Dion C. Stewart

WEB SITE

U.S. DEPARTMENT OF TRANSPORTATION
http://www.dot.gov/new/index.htm

SEE ALSO: National Oceanic and Atmospheric Administration; Transportation, energy use in.

Desalination plants and technology

CATEGORY: Obtaining and using resources

Seawater and other salt-containing waters are converted into potable water by distillation, reverse osmosis, and other processes experimentally, and increasingly practically, in regions where water resources are limited or expensive.

BACKGROUND

For many years, large ships at sea have used distillation processes to convert seawater into usable water for passengers and crews because it is more economical than carrying enormous quantities of fresh water for drinking, cooking, and cleaning. In desert regions and some areas that have limited suitable fresh water available, distillation and, more recently, membrane processes have been introduced for the conversion of brackish water, industrial effluents, wastewater, and seawater. Large-scale pilot processes have been rare. One notable example is a plant that was built in San Diego in the 1950's and later shipped to the U.S. naval base at Guantánamo Bay in Cuba. It can produce 13 million liters of distilled water per day.

Because brackish water and various wastewaters contain between 500 and 5,000 parts per million of dissolved solids, and seawater and geothermally produced brines contain up to 50,000 or more, a number of different processing methods have been developed. In addition, the end use of the water may dictate the superiority of one method above the others. For many agricultural purposes, water containing a few thousand parts per million can be used, whereas U.S. drinking water standards are set at a maximum of 500 (in actuality, many U.S. cities' water supplies exceed this standard).

DISTILLATION METHODS

Distillation methods were first described by Aristotle, but they had their first practical use aboard English naval vessels in the 1600's. Since then they have become much more complex, but they still involve a high-cost, energy-intensive boiling process, and subsequently a cooling process for liquefaction of the steam generated. The original processes required submerged tubes, which became encrusted with chemical deposits. Multistage flash process plants are currently used in which the latent heat of evaporation of the water is captured and reused, and the scaling is diminished by adding chemicals or removing the ions causing the deposits. Newer variations of these processes are being investigated. Some attempts have been made to couple power generation plants with distillation units, which may provide more desirable economy of operation.

Various versions of the multistage flash process are used in many parts of the Middle East and in more than three-quarters of the currently operating systems. Other designs for distillation plants have been proposed, and some have been built. Most of these have used horizontal tube processes with a design that permits multiple stages with vacuum distillation and a gradual reduction of saline content by incorporating steam with the brine. Large installations are currently incorporating this design. Smaller plants have employed a vapor compression procedure for industrial plants and resort hotels, but these are gradually being replaced by reverse osmosis facilities.

Solar distillation procedures would appear to offer great future alternatives in the very regions where water is in short supply. If solar energy could be more cheaply and efficiently obtained, and the land area needed made available, the saline water conversion problem would be solved relatively easily.

MEMBRANE METHODS

Although reverse osmosis has been most heavily promoted, there is actually a large group of related procedures that utilize membrane separations to purify water. In ordinary osmosis, such as occurs through cell walls, a semipermeable membrane (one through which only the solvent can flow) allows water to flow from a less concentrated solution into a more concentrated one (thus exhibiting an "osmotic pressure"). In reverse osmosis, pressure is exerted on the more concentrated solution, overcoming the osmotic pressure and reversing the flow. After the brine (saline water) has been concentrated in this manner, the process is repeated with fresh brine.

Among the membranes that have been utilized, most are polyamides and polyimides, which closely resemble protein structures. Reverse osmosis has been most effective with brackish waters, which do not have the high osmotic pressure of seawater to overcome. However, improved membrane systems have permitted construction of larger seawater charged reverse osmosis plants in the 13-million-liters-a-day range. A procedure known as electrodialysis permits an electric field to assist in directing ion flow through membranes, which are permeable to either cations or anions; some success in using this method with brackish water has been achieved. Pressurization cycles with ion exchange resins or membranes have been successful with low energy requirements, but experiments have failed to find the high-strength materials required to survive the high pressures needed.

ION EXCHANGE METHODS

Utilizing ion exchange resins in a normal flow-by mode is very reasonable for purifying slightly brackish water. In fact, it is used to soften water in many communities with hard-water supplies. Resins that replace metallic ions with positive hydrogen ions, and nonmetal ions with negative hydroxide ions, can readily accomplish that limited task, but they are not adequate for seawater conversion. The necessity of regenerating the exhausted resins with acid or base make designing a continuous process more difficult.

FREEZING AND SOLVENT EXTRACTION METHODS

When a solution freezes under equilibrium conditions, the solid formed is pure solvent. Therefore, when an iceberg forms, it contains very pure water. It has been proposed that icebergs could be towed to water-short regions. However, mechanical problems, such as providing appropriate freezing chambers and removing brine from the ice surface have prevented these methods from being seriously explored. Solvent extraction procedures have been tried experimentally, but solvent use and removal are costly.

William J. Wasserman

FURTHER READING

Khan, Arshad Hassan. *Desalination Processes and Multistage Flash Distillation Practice.* New York: Elsevier, 1986.

Lauer, William C., ed. *Desalination of Seawater and Brackish Water.* Denver, Colo.: American Water Works Association, 2006.

National Research Council of the National Academies. *Desalination: A National Perspective.* Washington, D.C.: National Academies Press, 2008.

Simon, Paul. *Tapped Out: The Coming World Crisis in Water and What We Can Do About It.* New York: Welcome Rain, 1998.

Spiegler, K. S., and A. D. K. Laird, eds. *Principles of Desalination.* 2d ed. New York: Academic Press, 1980.

WEB SITE

NATIONAL ACADEMIES PRESS
Desalination: A National Perspective
http://books.nap.edu/
openbook.php?record_id=12184&page=R1

SEE ALSO: Oceans; Salt; Solar energy; Water.

Desertification

CATEGORY: Geological processes and formations

Desertification is the degradation of semiarid lands and includes the reduction in the biological diversity of the ecosystem, the reduction in soil nutrients, and soil erosion.

BACKGROUND

Desertification occurs over a period of years, with numerous factors interacting to stress the environment. Desertification results when social, political, and economic forces cause agricultural exploitation beyond the carrying capacity of marginal arid lands. Airborne and waterborne erosion strip vulnerable topsoil, rendering the land less productive over time. People living in areas undergoing desertification have poor harvests and are increasingly unable to feed themselves.

Although desertification can result from natural causes over eons, it can occur in relatively short periods of time, notably as a result of improper land-use management—usually a combination of deforestation and overgrazing on semiarid grasslands. Nonnative cash crops and monoculture plantations quickly deplete soils, impoverishing the ecosystem and accelerating desertification. In developed countries, boom and bust agricultural practices in arid lands cause overexpansion during favorable climatic conditions, followed by drought. People living on marginal lands in less developed countries depend on subsistence agricultural production. Drought causes these people severe hardships, as their crops fail and animal herds die. Sustainable development of semi-arid lands in less developed countries would benefit many impoverished people worldwide.

DESERTIFICATION IN THE WESTERN HEMISPHERE

In 1806, Zebulon Pike characterized the southern plains as a sandy wasteland, an area later called the "Great American Desert" on maps. Following the Homestead Act of 1862, 65 hectares of shortgrass could be claimed by settlers living and working on the land, and some people thought that to be sufficient incentive to migrate there. Amish and Mennonite settlers found the 65 hectares sufficient for their type of agriculture, but the concept of large commercial ranches and farms, coupled with the introduction of machinery, prompted the passage of the Enlarged Homestead Act of 1909, resulting in a land rush.

By the time World War I began, wheat was the favored crop in the Great Plains. Previously uncultivated land throughout Kansas, Colorado, New Mexico, Oklahoma, and Texas was plowed and planted with wheat by residents and absentee farmer-speculators between the end of World War I and 1930. When a lengthy drought began in 1931, precipitation was spotty, and wheat crops began failing. Fields were abandoned, and the airborne soil erosion which characterized the Dust Bowl began.

Within the United States, elimination of homesteading, massive purchase of marginal land, large public works projects, and agricultural subsidies helped reclaim marginal desert lands throughout the Great Plains and Southwest. The "New Deal" of President Franklin Delano Roosevelt began land reclamation using the Soil Conservation Service and the Civilian Conservation Corps throughout the Dust Bowl region, sowing sorghum and planting shelterbelts of trees in an effort to limit soil erosion. The introduction of contour plowing limited some of the worst disk-plowing problems for agriculture.

THE SAHEL: SOUTHERN ENCROACHMENT OF THE SAHARAN DESERT

The African region known as the Sahel, which roughly follows the 15° north parallel, is an example of dry woodland and dry wooded grassland undergoing desertification. Its northern border with the Sahara Desert receives 150 millimeters of annual rainfall; its southern border receives 600 millimeters of rain yearly.

Between 1931 and 1960 the Sahel experienced greater than normal levels of precipitation, coupled with a doubling in population. During this time, a large part of the Sahel was populated by nomadic peoples herding small livestock flocks and practicing subsistence agriculture. In 1970, a period of decades-long drought began. This drought signaled a period of overgrazing by livestock and deforestation to feed cooking fires, two key factors in accelerating desertification. Starting in 1968, the Sahel began to move southward from its 1931-1960 boundaries. Warmer ocean waters changed rainfall patterns, resulting in less precipitation in the northern Sahel in the late twentieth century. More than 60 percent of foreign aid in the region was expended on road construction, which consumed valuable water resources. Development of large-scale dams in the Senegal River Valley during the 1980's caused population displacement because much of the irrigated land was taken over by large plantations growing cash crops of peanuts, rice, and cotton. Deforestation to expand plantations was widespread in Senegal.

Annual rainfall began to increase in the mid-1990's. Satellite data show that vegetative growth in the Sahel increased beyond what would be expected from observed rainfall. In Niger, where felling of nitrogen-fixing gao acacia trees has stopped, an estimated 49,000 square kilometers of savanna showed increased vegetation by 2008.

In 2008, the population of the Sahel was estimated at fifty million. Emigration via the port of Dakar to Europe, or overland to North Africa, continues to reduce the population, as does continuing warfare in the Darfur region of Sudan, which claimed an estimated 200,000 lives between 2003 and 2008. Deforestation has been rapid around Darfur refugee camps, as trees have been cut to fuel refugee cooking fires and brick kilns for houses for United Nations aid workers.

MITIGATION OF DESERTIFICATION

Identification of the problems caused by desertification by national governments and international agencies led to concerted efforts to halt and reverse the process during the late twentieth and early twenty-first centuries. Developed nations, including the

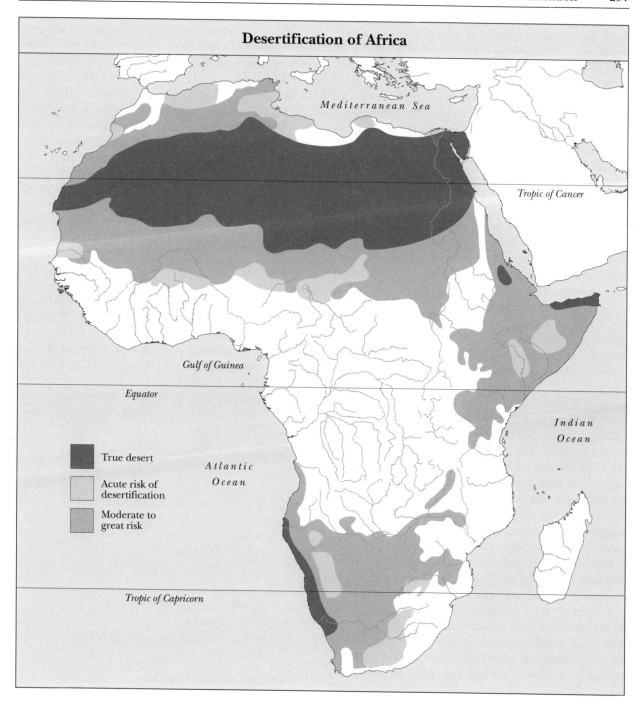

Desertification of Africa

True desert

Acute risk of
desertification

Moderate to
great risk

United States and Australia, have relied heavily on technology to combat desertification. Ranchers have formed effective organizations to lobby the central governments for aid. Drilling wells, building dams, installing irrigation canals, using chemical fertilizers on depleted soil, using crop-dusting airplanes to limit pest damage, and implementing large-scale reforestation and revegetation programs are some of the methods used to combat desertification.

In Australia, ranchers of large areas import feed in drought years and move herds of cattle and sheep out of desert environments to more productive grazing land. Government-sponsored selective breeding programs produced special cattle breeds—the Belmont Red and the Australian Milking Zebu—better suited to production in arid lands.

Less developed countries rarely have the resources to purchase technology. International aid efforts focused on building dams have been found to result in dislocation of hundreds of thousands of people while worsening public health problems like schistosomiasis and malaria. Because of these problems, beginning in the 1990's, international aid organizations increasingly emphasized the need for introducing low technology to combat desertification and permit sustainable development. Important initial steps included involvement of the local populace to establish sustainable land-use policies and then to teach agricultural techniques to reclaim land. Natural revegetation, the self-seeding by plants remaining in the area, is encouraged, as is the use of direct seeding of crops and planting of trees to limit erosion. Where overgrazing by livestock is removing most of the sparse natural vegetative covering, reducing and limiting herd size is important. Concentration of landownership accelerates growth of unsustainably large herds and encourages overgrazing. Farmers at the subsistence level own few animals, using them mainly for milk production.

Minimizing the use of wood for cooking fuel through the introduction of more efficient cooking stoves and solar cookers has lessened desertification in the Sahel. Other successful low-technology methods include digging shallow basins for planting in eastern Mali and stone line construction to retain water and limit erosion in Burkina Faso. In 1984, after stone lines were completed in Yatenga Province in Burkina Faso, crop yields doubled.

In less developed countries where a few landowners control large, semiarid plantations utilized for nonsustainable cash crops, such as peanuts and cotton, land redistribution to smaller, privately owned farms growing drought-resistant crops for local consumption is ideal. However, the World Bank underwent a paradigm shift in the 1980's that favored commercial farmers over small farmers. This accelerated desertification in many arid regions of less developed countries, especially in Africa. Large farmers raise unsustainable large herds and force poor people onto marginal land.

Mitigation of desertification becomes difficult when severe periodic droughts occur. Expansion of agriculture above subsistence levels is inevitable during good times when crop yields increase. When drought struck the U.S. Great Plains from 1954 to 1957 and again from 1974 to 1977, airborne erosion identical to the 1930's Dust Bowl occurred, with dramatic economic consequences. Deep-well irrigation was introduced, lessening the apparent risks of large-scale monocrop agriculture in the region. Technology has become essential to maintaining agriculture in the Great Plains.

Anita Baker-Blocker

FURTHER READING

Hazell, Peter, and Stanley Wood. "Drivers of Change in Global Agriculture." *Philosophical Transactions of the Royal Society of London* 363, no. 1491 (February 12, 2008): 495-515.

Liebesman, Lawrence R., and Rafe Petersen. *Endangered Species Deskbook.* Washington, D.C.: Environmental Law Institute, 2003.

Worster, Donald. *Dust Bowl: The Southern Plains in the 1930's.* 25th anniversary ed. New York: Oxford University Press, 2004.

WEB SITES

ENVIRONMENT CANADA: CANADIAN WILDLIFE SERVICE
Species at Risk
http://www.cws-scf.ec.gc.ca/
theme.cfm?lang=e&category=12

NOAA FISHERIES SERVICE: OFFICE OF PROTECTED RESOURCES
Endangered Species Act
http://www.nmfs.noaa.gov/pr/laws/esa

U.S. FISH AND WILDLIFE SERVICE
Endangered Species Program
http://www.fws.gov/endangered

SEE ALSO: Climate and resources; Deserts; Drought; Erosion and erosion control; Food shortages; Irrigation; Overgrazing; Soil management; United Nations Convention to Combat Desertification; World Bank.

Deserts

CATEGORY: Ecological resources

Deserts are regions defined by the scarcity of a crucial resource, water. They are unique ecosystems with their own types of plant and animal life; a number of desert plants have been used by humans for thousands of years. Mining for minerals and petroleum also occurs in desert regions around the world.

BACKGROUND

Although deserts are characterized by general aridity, there is no universal definition of a desert. Webster's dictionary defines a desert as an "arid land with usually sparse vegetation; especially such land having a very warm climate and receiving less than 25 centimeters of sporadic rainfall annually." Deserts are generally thought of as hot and dry, but heat is not necessarily a requisite of most definitions of a desert. Low precipitation does not, alone, characterize a desert. Arctic tundra landscapes often receive scant precipitation, yet tundra soils are often saturated from low evaporation and restrictive permafrost below a narrow active thawed layer during the summer. The common perception of a desert is a trackless expanse of sand such as the Sahara or the Arabian Desert. In reality, however, deserts are often fairly well vegetated. The characteristic that all deserts have in common is aridity. Aridity refers to a general dryness, not to short drought periods.

CHARACTERISTICS OF DESERTS

Deserts are located on all continents; Antarctica is considered a desert. They occur on a variety of substrates but often are characterized by historical erosion patterns leaving alluvial fans on the foothills of small mountains or hills and isolated islands of more resistant material. These remnants are called buttes in the western United States. Sandy soils are common, but wind-blown soils and ash deposits from volcanoes are also prevalent in many deserts. Desert soils often lack structural aggregation and are subject to erosion. They often have surface crusts from raindrop impact and deposits from sediments that are left as water infiltrates into the soil.

Camels are led through the Sahara Desert, the largest hot desert on the planet. (Fei Xuan/Xinhua/Landov)

In the United States, cool deserts (sagebrush grass and salt-desert shrub types) occur in old lake beds. Ancient Lake Bonneville in northern Utah and Lake Lahontan in Nevada once occupied much larger areas and dominated the landscape. These deserts are also influenced by the Sierra Nevada and Cascade Mountain ranges, which cast a rain shadow effect on their eastern valleys. Intermittent drainages (wadis or arroyos) often cut across desert landscapes; they contain running water only during or immediately after a rainfall event. These drainages support unique vegetation and serve as important habitats for birds and other animals.

Another major feature of deserts is that nutrients are often limiting. Soil nitrogen and organic matter are especially low in these ecosystems. Free-living and symbiotic nitrogen-fixing bacteria are scarce in deserts. Research indicates that lichens and algae, forming crusts on desert soils, may be the major source of soil nitrogen for plant growth.

DESERT ADAPTATIONS

Rainfall events occur infrequently in deserts. Both plants and animals must have adaptations to take advantage of these episodic periods of available water to survive in these harsh environments. Thus one sees flushes of desert flowers during spring and summer months, especially in years when rainfall is abundant. These same flowers may not be seen again for several years. Desert plants exhibit several adaptations that allow them to exist successfully under these stressful conditions. Some plants, such as mesquite, have deep root systems that allow access to deep sources of water. They do not have to rely on rainfall during the growing season. Some plants have dense, shallow root systems that allow them to tap soil water in the soil surface from light showers. Some plants have both types of root systems. Cactus and other succulents have the ability to store water in their tissues for use during periods of low rainfall. Some plants, such as the creosote bush, shed many leaves to reduce transpirational requirements. Others have few stomata on their leaf surfaces, thereby reducing transpirational stress. These stomata tend to close and restrict transpiration. Desert soils are often high in salt content from surface evaporation of rainfall that does not penetrate far into the soil, and plants growing on saline soils have special adaptations for coping with these conditions.

Animals also have many adaptations to desert conditions. Some desert animals can live in dormant stages during unfavorable periods. Many exhibit no definite breeding season and can breed whenever conditions are favorable. Some, including birds, can conserve water by reducing loss through concentrated urine. Some desert animals obtain most of their water through the food they eat. Many are nocturnal, thereby avoiding the high temperatures of the day. Intermediate-sized and small mammals often burrow to escape the heat and find more favorable conditions.

CONSERVATION AND PREVENTION ISSUES

Desert plants and animals are frequently under threat from a variety of natural and human-related activities. Since water resources are so scarce, any external factor that changes the water cycle or the availability of water at critical times may threaten organisms. In some cases the existence of desert plants and animals is not obvious, and adequate information on their status is lacking.

Many desert landscapes were formed by erosion, but changes may be very slow and difficult to ascertain. For example, there has been much concern over the increase in desert areas in the world. The word "desertification" has been used to describe the degradation of arid and semiarid areas into desertlike environments. For some time nearly all observers believed that the Sahara Desert was expanding, but this has become a subject of debate. Detailed remote sensing analyses have suggested that the Sahara Desert may expand and contract, perhaps in response to climatic cycles. In many areas in Africa, such as the Sahel, livestock populations are increasing to support the expanding human population. During the dry season, woody plants supply needed high-quality forage for these animals. These same woody plant resources are also heavily exploited for fuel wood despite restrictions placed on their harvest. Depletion of these valuable woody plant resources could have serious consequences for these delicate ecosystems. Other examples of resource problems in desert areas include overhunting of native ungulates for animal products such as tusks.

NATURAL RESOURCES

Deserts of the world hold most of the reserves of oil, natural gas, and coal, and they therefore serve as a source of natural wealth for many countries in the Middle East. These resources remained sufficient to supply energy needs into the twenty-first century, but with escalating costs, alternative energy sources will become more important. Deserts also provide other minerals, such as silver, lead, diamonds (in southern Africa), and copper, but many deserts such as the Sahara are not important for mineral resources.

Desert plants are also used as food by many native people. In the southwestern United States, American Indians used cactus fruits as a staple food. In the Sahel in northern Africa, the following types of foods were available in substantial quantities: rhizomes and fleshy stems, the seeds of forbs, grass seeds, fruits, edible gums, and mannas. Fibers from desert plants are also used for basket weaving in many countries, and plant pigments are used as natural dyes.

VEGETATIONAL DYNAMICS

In desert regions of the United States and elsewhere, shrubby plants are increasing at the expense of grassland. Reasons for this change are not clear, but several factors are probably important. Some workers have suggested that climatic changes have favored a shift from grasses to shrubs. Increased carbon dioxide concentration of the atmosphere from burning fossil fuels is one hypothesis. Others insist that the introduction of domestic livestock beginning in 1850 disrupted the ecological balance in favor of shrubs. Lack of fire to restrict development of shrubs in grassland has also been advanced as a possible cause. Several studies in southwestern deserts in the United States have shown that native mammals and rabbits can exert considerable influence on vegetation and can reduce grass cover and abundance. It is possible that all these factors, and probably others not considered, have together been responsible for changes in desert vegetation.

Increases in shrubs, such as mesquite in the United States, eventually alter nutrient distribution patterns. In relatively uniform grasslands, soil nutrients are distributed fairly evenly. As shrubs such as mesquite increase at the expense of grasses, however, the shrubs are able to take up nutrients from a much larger volume of soil. These nutrients then tend to become concentrated around the individual mesquite trees and to form islands of nutrient concentration. Interdune areas often suffer soil loss through wind erosion, and the soil accumulates around individual mesquite plants. If the soil is deep enough, mesquite dunes eventually form. Interdune areas with little surface soil are deficient in nutrients, especially nitrogen, and lack water-holding capacity. These changes also affect animal life. Some animals, such as bannertailed kan-

garoo rats and pronghorn antelope, utilize grassland habitat and are favored by grassland. Others, such as those that feed on mesquite (insects and arthropods), are favored by the mesquite dunelands.

Mining for coal and other minerals often disturbs desert ecosystems. Mines are limited in size and in the area affected, but they can leave conspicuous scars on the landscape, especially with deep open-pit mines. The area disturbed by the mines can be restored, but restoration is difficult and expensive.

Rex D. Pieper

FURTHER READING

Evenari, Michael, Imanuel Noy-Meir, and David W. Goodall, eds. *Hot Deserts and Arid Shrublands.* New York: Elsevier, 1985.

Goudie, Andrew. *Great Warm Deserts of the World: Landscapes and Evolution.* New York: Oxford University Press, 2002.

Laity, Julie. *Deserts and Desert Environments.* Hoboken, N.J.: Wiley-Blackwell, 2008.

Quinn, Joyce Ann. *Desert Biomes.* Westport, Conn.: Greenwood Press, 2009.

Sowell, John. *Desert Ecology: An Introduction to Life in the Arid Southwest.* Salt Lake City: University of Utah Press, 2001.

Ward, David. *The Biology of Deserts.* New York: Oxford University Press, 2009.

West, Neil E., eds. *Temperate Deserts and Semi-Deserts.* New York: Elsevier Scientific, 1983.

WEB SITE

U.S. GEOLOGICAL SURVEY
Deserts: Geology and Resources
http://pubs.usgs.gov/gip/deserts

SEE ALSO: Conservation; Desertification; Ecology; Ecosystems; Farmland; Geochemical cycles; Irrigation; Rangeland; Soil.

Developing countries

CATEGORIES: Countries; social, economic, and political issues

Developing countries' resources have helped to feed and fuel the world's developed countries. As the developing countries themselves industrialize, and as their

populations grow, the demands on these resources in-crease, and the issues of resource constraints and envi-ronmental degradation rise on the political agenda.

BACKGROUND

Developing countries are a diverse group, with tre-mendous variety in size, income, and industrial devel-opment. China and Singapore reflect the size dispari-ties, with the former measuring about 9.6 million square kilometers and the latter approximately 1,000 square kilometers. Of the 210 countries the World Bank categorizes as high, middle, or low income, 70 percent are classified as developing countries. Of these, 30 percent are categorized as low-income coun-tries (with per capita earnings equivalent to $975 or less). These include Bangladesh, Chad, and Ethiopia. The Bahamas, Cyprus, Kuwait, and Qatar are among the 31 percent in the high-income category. Although many of these countries are still very dependent on primary goods, a small number, including South Ko-rea and Venezuela, have undergone significant indus-trialization.

Resource use in developing countries is condi-tioned by a web of global, national, and local factors. The nature of their economies and their relative lack of economic power combine to determine their pat-tern of resource use. This pattern is closely associated with the asymmetric economic relations between de-veloping countries and industrialized countries. Con-sumption patterns in industrialized countries high-light the variety of goods and services associated with a consumer culture; conversely, in most developing countries the focus is on basic needs. Industrialized countries are far greater consumers of commercial energy resources such as oil, natural gas, and coal. De-veloping countries, however, consume more wood and wood products, primarily as fuel wood and char-coal, and clear more of their forests, primarily for agri-culture. Resource use patterns change over time: In the past, industrialized countries engaged in substan-tial deforestation, and as developing countries indus-trialize during the twenty-first century, their use of commercial energy sources will increase significantly.

In their efforts to satisfy both the interests of the in-dustrialized countries' capital and their own needs, some developing countries extend the boundaries of their economies by exhausting soils, removing old-growth forests, or overexploiting fisheries. A combi-nation of forces operate at the global, national, and local levels to shape policies regarding development, trade, and investment—often with disastrous conse-quences for the environment.

LOCAL FACTORS

Inequalities within the societies of developing coun-tries result in skewed patterns of access to land and other assets, with elites benefiting disproportionately. For example, in South American countries, 17 per-cent of the landowners control 90 percent of the land. Short-term needs can force landless families to farm fragile mountain slopes and torch rain forests in or-der to plant foods. In Brazil, poor people clear the for-ests to farm. Because of the fragility of the soils, in a short time yields diminish, and farmers must move on to other areas of rain forest. Similar practices result in the depletion and degradation of freshwater re-sources, soils, forests, and habitats.

The poor are both agents and victims of environ-mental degradation, whether it is a result of their own actions or a consequence of consumption by higher-income groups. The poor have few or no alternatives when the environmental resources on which they depend are degraded. Dwindling food supplies, un-safe drinking water, polluted air, and unsanitary conditions contribute significantly to reduced life ex-pectancy and high child mortality. Moreover, long-standing traditional social and economic patterns encourage poor Third World people to have many children. The result is a vicious cycle: A large popula-tion leads to more poverty and increasingly threatens the renewable resources on which local populations depend.

Thus, development and environment are inextri-cably linked: Development that alleviates poverty is essential if renewable resources are to be preserved in developing nations, and material redistribution is necessary. For sustainable use of natural resources to be feasible, people need to have some measure of con-trol of, and access to, resources. Case studies indicate that small holders who own their land tend to take care of it, unlike squatters and tenant farmers, who tend to deplete soils, forests, and water resources more rapidly because they assume or fear they will lose access to them.

NATIONAL FACTORS

Problems at the local level are often reinforced by national policies that neglect or discriminate against the poorer members of society, with negative conse-quences for the environment. For example, tax laws may favor the rich, or the structure of development investment may favor urban areas. Sometimes farmland near cities is taxed at its development value rather than as agricultural land. As a consequence, poor farmers who cannot afford the higher taxes are forced off the land. In addition, government enactments intended to manage common property resources can have negative effects on both the poor and the environment. For example, in a number of West African countries, colonial and subsequent governments claimed all the trees as their own. Farmers could cut them only after a laborious permit process, and certain species could not be cut at all. While this slowed the process of deforestation, it also dissuaded farmers from planting trees. Recently, this practice has been reversed, and countries such as Burkina Faso, Mali, and Niger are encouraging farmers to mix trees and crops, an ancient farming practice in West Africa.

Governments have also been slow to implement adequate land-planning policies and environmental impact assessment. In many Caribbean states, environmental legislation is fragmented into several disparate regulations, and responsibility for its administration is distributed among various departments. As a consequence, developing countries are repeating some of the environmental problems associated with the industrialized countries, such as air and water pollution, toxic emissions, and waste disposal problems.

GLOBAL FACTORS

Global factors combine with local and national factors to exacerbate unsustainable resource-use patterns. At the global level, developing countries' options are constrained by a number of interrelated forces, such as declining terms of trade, oppressive debt burdens, and inappropriate investment strategies. These forces have significant consequences for resource consumption.

With their dependence on primary products, developing countries are often among the losers when trading systems are liberalized. The market prices of primary products have fallen rapidly, while the prices of the manufactured goods that they import have risen significantly. In the effort to make up such financial shortfalls, developing countries may feel forced to tap their natural resources more extensively.

One result of a focus on free trade, with its emphasis on growth, is the exploitation of natural resources for short-term profit. This exploitation may mean the clearing of rain forests for cattle ranching or the shifting of agricultural land from domestic food production to export crops. In addition, environmental standards and resource regulations can be challenged as barriers to trade. Regulations produced by the North American Free Trade Agreement (NAFTA) and the General Agreement on Tariffs and Trade (GATT) are illustrative. Under NAFTA, each country has to provide other parties with the same access to its resources that it provides to its own citizens and other domestic parties. The Uruguay Round of GATT resulted in some provisions with direct implications for environmental regulations. One of GATT's objectives is to limit most restrictions on trade: Therefore GATT can be used to challenge the rights of nations to use import and export controls to conserve threatened resources such as forests and fisheries. The new trade provisions also discourage the use of strong environmental provisions by states, because these could be judged as being in violation of GATT rules. These regulations work against the concept and practice of sustainable use of resources.

International institutions, such as the World Bank and the International Monetary Fund (IMF), encourage export-led development as a priority, but this export-led strategy has reduced many countries' capacity to address their environmental problems. The World Bank, as the principal single source of funding for Third World development, can have a profound impact on environmental policy in developing countries. Its development model has emphasized large-scale schemes dealing with water management, power generation, and transport infrastructure. Many of these projects have resulted in serious disruptions of local ecosystems, in environmental stress, and in the displacement of thousands of people. The World Bank, and the other multilateral development banks, such as the InterAmerican Development Bank, the Asian Development Bank, and the African Development Bank, allocate more than one-half of their project loans to areas that can have marked effects on the environment, including agriculture, rural development, dams, and irrigation schemes. Oversight of the projects' environmental consequences is inadequate.

IMF policy has also had significant environmental consequences for developing countries. The IMF has responded to the Third World debt problem by requiring the countries to adopt structural adjustment programs. These programs include a wide range of policy measures intended to restore creditworthiness:

cuts in government expenditures, reduction or elimination of subsidies, currency devaluation, and reduction of trade barriers. The intent of these programs is to increase foreign exchange earnings so that the countries can make debt payments. However, structural adjustment can have disastrous impacts on the environment. The emphasis on boosting exports to earn foreign exchange can result in the destruction of natural resources such as forests, wetlands, and mangroves and in the excessive development of ecologically damaging industries such as mining. The pressure for countries to reduce government expenditures drastically can cause the elimination or postponement of programs to manage wildlife or enforce environmental laws. Additionally, structural adjustment programs that hurt the poor will often also hurt the environment: As a last resort, unemployed people might farm fragile hillsides or engage in slash-and-burn agriculture in forest areas.

In recent decades, some developing countries have experienced more rapid economic growth than industrialized countries have. In part, their growth reflects an increasing transfer of basic production to developing countries and the expansion of manufacturing there. These shifts create additional economic value and employment, but they also increase the environmental burden. Corporations are shifting complete industrial operations to the Third World. The end products are then shipped back to the developed country, where consumers get the benefit of the product while shifting the environmental costs of production to others. For example, there has been a significant shift of plant investment for organochloride manufacture to the developing world. In the 1980's and 1990's, U.S. companies relocated more than two thousand factories to Mexico, where enforcement of environmental laws is minimal.

Transnational corporations play a major role in this industrial transition. These corporations are the principal beneficiaries of a liberalized trading system. Because they control the bulk of world trade and investment, they are major environmental actors. They can affect the environment in Third World countries, both directly and indirectly. In order to attract investment from these corporations, a Third World country might adopt inadequate environmental regulations or might choose not to enforce existing laws. Virtually all commercial enterprises have direct environmental consequences because of process and product pollution. The former includes pollution generated by the chemical, iron and steel, petroleum, and paper industries. The latter variety is found in agriculture.

Because agriculture is the primary economic sector for many developing countries, examining transnational agribusiness is important. Agribusiness interests have made alliances with research institutes, agricultural colleges, regulatory agencies, government ministries, and aid agencies. These relationships enable them to shape agricultural practices and policies significantly. Their practices usually reflect a cost-benefit analysis that marginalizes environmental costs.

Corporate policy can have negative consequences for resources such as land, forests, and water. Transnationals control 80 percent of the land used for export crops worldwide. This fact is reflected in land-use patterns in countries such as Brazil and India. In Brazil, corporations own more land than is owned by all the peasants combined, and in India, some of the more wealthy farmers grow maize and sunflowers for Cargill and tomatoes and potatoes for Pepsi. Corporations specialize in monoculture, with heavy use of chemical fertilizers and pesticides. With the focus on production for export, developing countries become dependent on food imports. This focus has also aided in the destruction of tropical rain forests. More than one-quarter of Central America's rain forest has been turned to grass for cattle ranching. Almost all the beef raised has been exported. In the 1970's, beef production in Latin America attracted more than $10 billion from the World Bank and the InterAmerican Development Bank. In Africa and Asia, corporations are also at work in the forests, but for timber rather than beef. These activities have meant the destruction of ecosystems and a decrease in biodiversity.

PROSPECTS FOR SUSTAINABLE DEVELOPMENT
Sustainable development was a major agenda item at the 1992 Earth Summit in Rio de Janeiro. Agenda 21, which was adopted at the conference, emphasized sustainable development and the provision of basic needs for the poor. As global awareness of resource limits and environmental damage grow, developing countries are under increasing pressure to adjust rapidly to environmental circumstances. Developed countries have been the major contributors to common property problems, such as ozone depletion and climate change, but they cannot address these problems adequately without the cooperation of developing countries. As a result, developing countries are being pressed to minimize their use of the processes and

commodities that enriched the industrialized countries.

During negotiations over environmental management regimes, developing countries have been able to bargain for some financial assistance to help them make the transition to more sustainable processes. Still, this small fund will not have a major impact on their transition to a more sustainable consumption pattern. Developing countries need to protect their endangered renewable-resource base. Accomplishing this will require reorienting development to alleviate poverty and enable poor people to meet their basic needs in ways that do not degrade water, soil, and forest resources or reduce biodiversity. This task will be extremely difficult as long as large amounts of their natural resources are owned or controlled by foreign entities. In the present global economic context, many developing countries recognize only two viable economic options: exploiting their natural resources to the point of exhaustion or importing "dirty industries." Consequently, the structural inequities that distort global and national societies and economies jeopardize the transition to sustainable development. If these inequities are not addressed, sustainable resource use will be an ever-receding mirage.

Marian A. L. Miller

FURTHER READING

Ascher, William, and Robert Healy. *Natural Resource Policymaking in Developing Countries: Environment, Economic Growth, and Income Distribution.* Durham, N.C.: Duke University Press, 1990.

Barbier, Edward B. *Natural Resources and Economic Development.* New York: Cambridge University Press, 2005.

Bonfiglioli, Angelo. *Lands of the Poor: Local Environmental Governance and the Decentralized Management of Natural Resources.* New York: United Nations Capital Development Fund, 2004.

Dellink, Rob B., and Arjan Ruijs, eds. *Economics of Poverty, Environment, and Natural-Resource Use.* New York: Springer, 2008.

Durning, Alan Thein. *Poverty and the Environment: Reversing the Downward Spiral.* Washington, D.C.: Worldwatch Institute, 1989.

Elliott, Jennifer A. *An Introduction to Sustainable Development.* 3d ed. New York: Routledge, 2006.

French, Hilary F. *Costly Tradeoffs: Reconciling Trade and the Environment.* Edited by Ed Ayres. Washington, D.C.: Worldwatch Institute, 1993.

Gupta, Avijit. *Ecology and Development in the Third World.* 2d ed. New York: Routledge, 1998.

Miller, Marian A. L. *The Third World in Global Environmental Politics.* Boulder, Colo.: Lynne Rienner, 1995.

World Bank. *Poverty and the Environment: Understanding Linkages at the Household Level.* Washington, D.C.: World Bank, 2008.

WEB SITE

WORLD RESOURCES INSTITUTE
World Resources 2008: Roots of Resilience—Growing the Wealth of the Poor
http://www.wri.org/publication/world-resources-2008-roots-of-resilience

SEE ALSO: Agenda 21; Brazil; Capitalism and resource exploitation; China; Deforestation; Earth Summit; India; Indonesia; Land ethic; Monoculture agriculture; Population growth; Rain forests; Resources as a source of international conflict; Slash-and-burn agriculture; South Korea; World Bank; World Commission on Environment and Development.

Diamond

CATEGORY: Mineral and other nonliving resources

Diamond is one of the world's most important minerals and gemstones; it is the element carbon (C) crystallized in the isometric system.

BACKGROUND

Diamond is the hardest known substance, natural or artificial, and is number 10 on the Mohs hardness scale. The close-packed cubic arrangement of the atoms gives diamond its unique hardness. It also has the highest thermal conductivity of any known substance.

Historical records of diamonds date back to 3000 B.C.E. In recent centuries, Golconda diamonds of India dominated diamond production until the early eighteenth century. In 1725, Brazilian diamond mines gained prominence. South Africa's "great diamond rush" began in 1867, and in 1890, the De Beers company consolidated dozens of mining communities in Africa. Diamond derives its name from the Greek word *adamas*, which means "unconquerable."

Almost all of the world's diamond production comes from Africa, most notably South Africa. Other diamond-producing countries include Angola, Borneo, Ghana, Guyana, Namibia, Sierra Leone, Tanzania, Venezuela, Congo, Brazil, and Russia (Siberia). In the United States diamonds have been found in Arizona, Arkansas, Montana, and Nevada.

TECHNICAL DEFINITION

The atomic number of carbon is 6, and its atomic weight is 12.011. It belongs to Group IVA of the periodic table of elements. Gem diamonds have a density of 3.52, although "black diamonds" have a density of about 3.15. Diamond slowly burns to carbon dioxide at a very low temperature (900° Celsius).

Diamond's high refractive index (2.417) and strong dispersion property (0.058) guarantee its supremacy as a gemstone. However, only about one-fifth of all the diamonds mined qualify as gems. Most of the remaining uncut diamonds are used by industry. Tunnel boring and oil-well drilling equipment uses diamond-studded rotary bits. Carbide grinding wheels, abrasion-resistant cutting tools, and glass-etching and glass-cutting equipment use industrial-quality diamonds. Some dentists and surgeons use diamond-headed scalpels to cut delicate bones and tissue. Diamond coatings are used in integrated circuits, prosthetic devices, and biosensors. Diamond is the most important industrial abrasive, and industry uses about 80 percent (by weight) of all diamonds produced. However, this represents only about 30 percent by value.

CREATION AND PROPERTIES OF DIAMOND

About 30 meters inside the Earth, exceedingly high pressures and temperatures (more than 1,400° Celsius) cause magnesium-rich rock melts to crystallize, resulting in the formation of diamonds. Samples of deep mantle material contain diamonds as a natural component. The reaction of groundwater with hot, magnesium-rich, deep mantle material aided by carbon dioxide leads to the formation of a rock called kimberlite. Kimberlite is an igneous rock that is ultrabasic and contains very little silica. Kimberlite is the world's principal source of diamonds. Explosive eruptions create craters filled with deep mantle rock formations and permit diamond-containing rocks to surface through cracks. These are known as diamond pipes (sometimes incorrectly called "volcanic necks").

In addition to being the hardest substance, diamond is an excellent conductor of heat. Because dia-

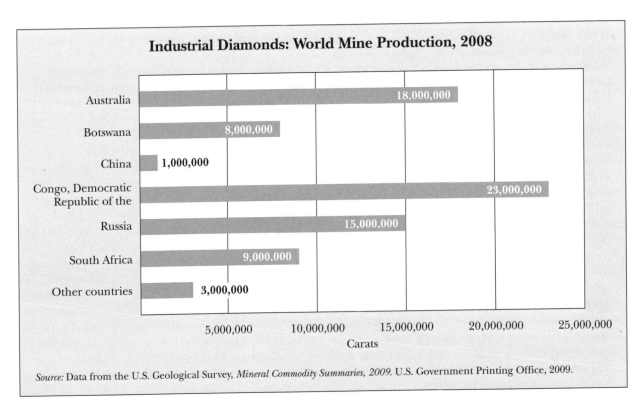

Industrial Diamonds: World Mine Production, 2008

Country	Carats
Australia	18,000,000
Botswana	8,000,000
China	1,000,000
Congo, Democratic Republic of the	23,000,000
Russia	15,000,000
South Africa	9,000,000
Other countries	3,000,000

Source: Data from the U.S. Geological Survey, *Mineral Commodity Summaries, 2009.* U.S. Government Printing Office, 2009.

These miners, photographed around 1905, and others worked the dozens of South African mines owned by Cecil Rhodes's De Beers Consolidated Mines. Until 1891 the company controlled 90 percent of the world's diamond production. (Library of Congress)

monds possess the highest thermal conductivity of any known substance, industrial-quality diamonds are used in abrasion-resistant cutting tools. Almost all diamonds are nonconductors of electricity. However, some diamonds permit the passage of electric current when bombarded with radiation. Diamond crystals form as octahedrons, dodecahedrons, and cubes. A well cut gem can reflect almost all the light that it receives. This quality is called "luster." In addition, it can disperse or separate the colors of the spectrum while reflecting the incident light. This quality is called "fire."

OCCURRENCE OF DIAMOND
Mining experts have discovered hundreds of diamond-containing dikes and pipes in Transvaal, Kimberley

District, and Free State (formerly Orange Free State), South Africa; Yakutsk, Siberia; Shinyanga, Tanzania; Mbuji-Mayi, Democratic Republic of the Congo; Yengema, Sierra Leone; Murfreesboro, Arkansas; and several other locations. However, it is not economically feasible to carry out "mine-at-depth" procedures in most of these pipe mines. Unless new pipes are discovered, natural diamonds may be exhausted relatively soon.

The erosion of diamond pipes over millions of years has resulted in secondary deposits called alluvial or placer deposits. These deposits contribute significantly to the world's total diamond production. Most alluvial diamonds are recovered from stream gravel, but beach gravel is also a good source. Diamond-containing beach gravel extends to the depths of

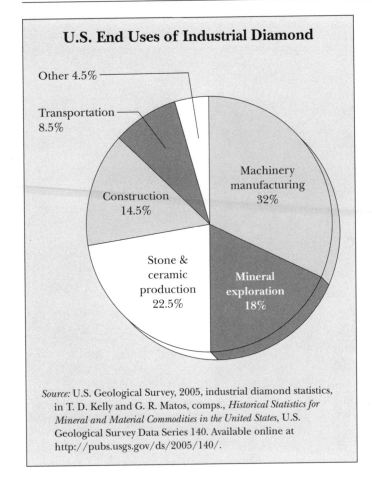

U.S. End Uses of Industrial Diamond

Other 4.5%

Transportation 8.5%

Construction 14.5%

Machinery manufacturing 32%

Stone & ceramic production 22.5%

Mineral exploration 18%

Source: U.S. Geological Survey, 2005, industrial diamond statistics, in T. D. Kelly and G. R. Matos, comps., *Historical Statistics for Mineral and Material Commodities in the United States*, U.S. Geological Survey Data Series 140. Available online at http://pubs.usgs.gov/ds/2005/140/.

the ocean floor, although there is no economical means of recovering diamonds from ocean depths. Diamonds are also found in glacial tills. Minute quantities of microscopic diamonds have been found in meteorites as well.

SYNTHETIC DIAMONDS

On February, 15, 1955, the General Electric Company announced its success in creating a synthetic diamond. Since then synthetic diamonds have become widely used in grinding wheels and a number of other applications. They are normally single crystals, usually octahedral in shape. Since they have several cutting edges, they are preferred over natural diamonds for industrial purposes. To make them, graphite (another form of crystalline carbon) is subjected to very high temperatures and pressures. Extreme pressures as high as 296,076 atmospheres (about 30 billion pascals) and temperatures as high as 3,037° Celsius (water boils at 100° Celsius) have been used, depending

upon the actual process. Two common procedures are shock conversion and static conversion. Synthetic diamonds are also manufactured by the static crystallization of certain alloys and molten metals.

Synthetic diamonds, normally black in color, are produced in grain sizes that are about one-hundredths of a centimeter in diameter. It is possible to "grow" larger, gem-quality synthetic diamonds, but the process is too costly to be feasible. Synthetic diamonds are chemically and crystallographically identical to the naturally occurring diamond gemstone. "Imitation diamonds," on the other hand, are completely different from either synthetic or genuine diamonds. Imitation diamonds do not possess either the hardness or the crystallographic structure of the genuine diamond; they are chemically different. They are made of glass or other material and are simply intended to imitate the appearance of a diamond.

CUTTING DIAMOND

After mining and recovery, gem-quality diamonds are separated from industrial-quality ones. A rough, uncut diamond looks like a dull piece of glass. Precise cutting, artful grinding, and skillful polishing of the diamonds yield outstanding gems, and some have attained historic fame. Diamond cutting began in India and was later perfected in Italy. Only a diamond can cut a diamond: Diamond crystals are cut, cleaved, shaped, and polished by "diamond dust on a lap." World-famous diamond cutting establishments are concentrated in Antwerp, Belgium, and in Amsterdam, the Netherlands. India and Israel have also emerged as world leaders in diamond cutting. The most popular cut is the "brilliant cut," which has a round shape with fifty-eight facets. Gem-quality diamonds are classified according to their weight, clarity, color, and absence of flaws. The weight of a diamond is measured in carats; a carat equals 0.2 gram, or about 0.00704 ounce. Transparent, colorless, and light blue diamonds are extremely rare and are considered to be highly valuable gems. There are red, pink, blue, and green diamonds. Diamonds with a yellow tint are more common. As the tint becomes increasingly yellowish, the value decreases. Industrial-quality diamonds are gray, brown, or black and are almost opaque. They are gems of poor quality.

FAMOUS DIAMONDS

The largest diamond ever found, the Cullinan, was found in 1905 in the Premier Mine, Transvaal, South Africa, and weighed 3,106 carats. This stone was cut and polished into several gems, two of them world famous: The 530-carat Star of Africa and the 309-carat Star of Africa II are among the British crown jewels, housed in the Tower of London. These are the world's largest cut diamonds. The cutting of the Cullinan also resulted in another seven large gems and ninety smaller ones.

The 109-carat Koh-i-Noor ("mountain of light"), set in the British crown itself, is the oldest diamond gemstone known to historians; its history has been traced back to 1304. This diamond had its origin in India, and it originally weighed 186 carats before Queen Victoria had it recut in 1852. Many believe that the largest blue diamond, the 44.5-carat Hope diamond, presently in the Smithsonian Institution, adorned the eye of an Indian god. Other world-famous diamonds India has contributed include the Regent or Pitt (140 carats, presently in the Louvre, France); the Orlov (200 carats, presently in Russia); the Florentine (137 carats, location unknown); and the Great Mogul (280 carats, location also unknown).

Mysore Narayanan

FURTHER READING

Balfour, Ian. *Famous Diamonds.* 4th ed. London: Christie's, 2000.

Chatterjee, Kaulir Kisor. "Diamond." In *Uses of Industrial Minerals, Rocks, and Freshwater.* New York: Nova Science, 2009.

Green, Timothy. *The World of Diamonds.* New York: Morrow, 1981.

Hart, Matthew. *Diamond: A Journey to the Heart of an Obsession.* New York: Walker, 2001.

Hazen, Robert M. *The Diamond Makers.* New York: Cambridge University Press, 1999.

Maillard, Robert, Ronne Peltsman, and Neil Grant, eds. *Diamonds, Myth, Magic, and Reality.* New rev. ed. New York: Bonanza Books, 1984.

Nazaré, M. H., and A. J. Neves, eds. *Properties, Growth, and Applications of Diamond.* London: IEE, 2001.

O'Donaghue, Michael. *Gems: Their Sources, Descriptions, and Identification.* 6th ed. Oxford, England: Butterworth-Heinemann, 2006.

Prelas, Mark A., Galina Popovici, and Louis K. Bigelow, eds. *Handbook of Industrial Diamonds and Diamond Films.* New York: Marcel Dekker, 1998.

Zoellner, Tom. *The Heartless Stone: A Journey Through the World of Diamonds, Deceit, and Desire.* New York: St. Martin's Press, 2006.

WEB SITES

AMERICAN MUSEUM OF NATURAL HISTORY
The Nature of Diamonds
http://www.amnh.org/exhibitions/diamonds

NATURAL RESOURCES CANADA
Canadian Minerals Yearbook, Mineral and Metal Commodity Reviews
http://www.nrcan-rncan.gc.ca/mms-smm/busi-indu/cmy-amc/com-eng.htm

U.S. GEOLOGICAL SURVEY
Industrial Diamonds: Statistics and Information
http://minerals.usgs.gov/minerals/pubs/commodity/diamond

SEE ALSO: Abrasives; Carbon; Gems; Graphite; Mohs hardness scale; Rhodes, Cecil.

Diatomite

CATEGORY: Mineral and other nonliving resources

WHERE FOUND

Diatomite is found in deposits near present-day or ancient bodies of water, because it is composed of the silica shells of water-dwelling diatoms. Diatomite deposits are found throughout the world; major producers include the United States, China, Denmark, and Japan. The United States is the main producer of diatomite, accounting for at least 50 percent of the world's diatom exports every year.

PRIMARY USES

Uses for diatomite fall into four main categories: for filtering, for insulating and building, as a filler material, and as a mild abrasive. Diatomite is commonly used to filter a wide variety of substances, ranging from oils to drinking water. As an abrasive, it is used in toothpastes and metal polishes. Many products, ranging from ceramics to paints, use diatomite as a filler to add volume.

TECHNICAL DEFINITION

Chemically, diatomite consists primarily of silica with trace amounts of magnesium, sodium, iron, and other elements, although exact proportions vary. Purified diatomite is essentially silica (SiO_2), with an average molecular mass of 60.8. Diatomite has a melting point of 1,710° Celsius and a density of 2.3 grams per cubic centimeter. Heating it to high temperatures forms crystalline silica.

Diatomite is usually white (if pure), buff, gray, and rarely black. In situ, it is generally found as a soft sedimentary rock or as powder. Raw diatomite is typically processed by a series of crushing, drying, size-reduction, and calcining procedures to produce different grades of diatomite for different specialized applications.

DESCRIPTION, DISTRIBUTION, AND FORMS

Diatomite is a soft, chalklike, fine-grained sedimentary rock composed primarily of the fossilized silica shells of microscopic algae called diatoms. It is finely porous, is low in density, and has low thermal conductivity. Diatom frustules are composed of two symmetrical silica valves, which can be elaborately ornamented with tiny holes and protrusions. These tiny holes are what make diatoms an ideal material for filtration. The word "diatom" comes from Greek *diatomos*, meaning "cut in half," because of the two valves.

Diatoms live in a wide range of moist environments, although most abundantly in marine (oceanic) and lacustrine (freshwater) environments. Three main types of diatomite deposits are recognized in the United States: marine rocks near continental margins, lacustrine rocks formed in ancient lakes or marshes, and sedimentary rocks in modern lakes, marshes, and bogs. Another commonly used term for diatomite, diatomaceous earth, more properly refers to unconsolidated or less lithified forms of diatomite.

One of the most important marine diatomite deposits is near Lompoc, California, reported to be the world's largest producing district by volume. Economically important lacustrine deposits in the United States are found in Nevada, Oregon, Washington, and eastern California. In 2007, the United States produced 33 percent of the world's diatomite. Other leading producers were China (20 percent), Denmark (11 percent; all moler diatomite, containing 30 weight percent clay), Japan (6 percent), and France (4 percent).

HISTORY

Some of the earliest references to diatomite are to the ancient Greeks' probable use of it to form lightweight bricks for building; they also used diatomite as an abrasive. In 535 C.E., the Roman Emperor Justinian I used diatomite bricks in building the church of St. Sofia in Constantinople (now Istanbul).

Diatomite use became industrially important to Western Europe after 1867, when Alfred Nobel invented dynamite. Pulverized diatomite was commonly used to absorb and stabilize the nitroglycerine used to make dynamite. By the late 1800's, the United States had become the primary producer of diatomite. By 1900, diatomite's uses had expanded to include many of its present-day uses, including beer filtration and building materials.

During the 1920's, techniques for calcining (thermally treating) and grading diatomite enabled a wider variety of uses for this resource. By World War II, the U.S. Army and Navy made wide use of diatomite to purify drinking water, to remove oil from boiler and engine water, and to create low-light-reflectance paints for ships.

OBTAINING DIATOMITE

Because of its abundance and usual occurrence near the surface in the United States, most diatomite produced is obtained from open-pit mines. The diatomite is excavated by machine after the overburden is removed. Outside the United States—particularly in China, Chile, and France—underground diatomite mining is fairly common. These mines are usually pit-and-pillar mines excavated by machine, although some small mines are excavated using hand tools. In Iceland, diatomaceous mud is dredged from Lake Myvatn. Diatomite is often dried in the open air near the mine before processing.

Diatomite processing is often carried out near the mine from which it is extracted. Raw diatomite may contain up to 65 percent water and is expensive to transport. Primary crushing of ore is usually done with spiked rolls and hammer mills, reducing the ore to 1.25-centimeter pieces while limiting damage to the diatom structure.

Passage through heated air, milling fans, and air cyclones further dries the diatomite and begins to classify for size as well as remove impurities of different density. Processing aims to separate individual diatom valves without destroying their structure, which is key to filtration uses.

Calcining, which increases filtration rate, specific gravity, and particle hardness, as well as oxidizing iron, is usually done with rotary kilns. Calcining is particularly important for filter grades.

USES OF DIATOMITE

Diatomite is primarily used as a filtration medium but also is used for insulation, as a filler and absorbent, and as a mild abrasive, in addition to some specialized medical uses. The most common use of diatomite is in filtration, because of its finely porous nature. These uses include water purification, beer and wine filtering, and the removal of oils from water. As a water filtration element, diatomaceous earth usually is used as a layer on a filter element or septum (a permeable cover over interior collection channels), called pre-coat filtration. Diatomite water filtration systems are

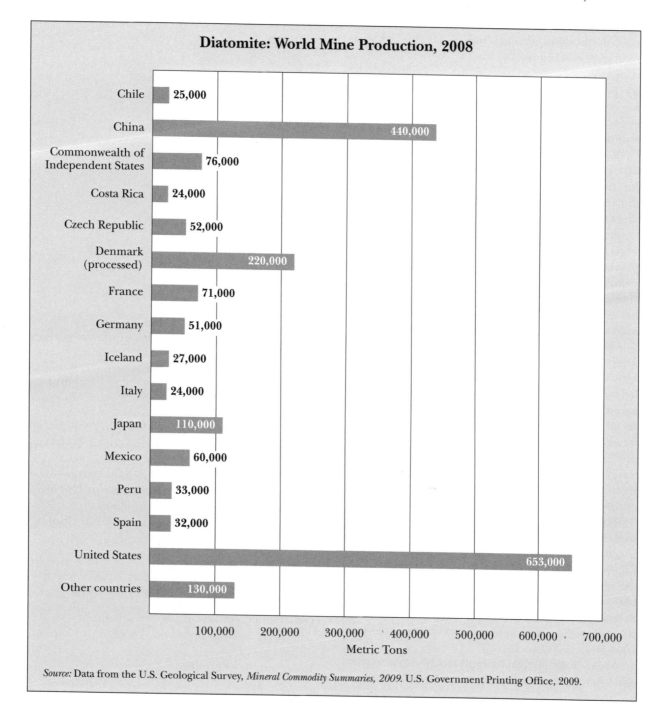

Diatomite: World Mine Production, 2008

Country	Metric Tons
Chile	25,000
China	440,000
Commonwealth of Independent States	76,000
Costa Rica	24,000
Czech Republic	52,000
Denmark (processed)	220,000
France	71,000
Germany	51,000
Iceland	27,000
Italy	24,000
Japan	110,000
Mexico	60,000
Peru	33,000
Spain	32,000
United States	653,000
Other countries	130,000

Source: Data from the U.S. Geological Survey, *Mineral Commodity Summaries, 2009.* U.S. Government Printing Office, 2009.

lightweight, cheap, and simple and can remove bacteria and protozoans as well as cysts, algae, and asbestos. This usage of diatomite first became important during World War II, when the U.S. Army needed a water filter suitable for mobile military operations. The first municipal diatomaceous-earth water filtration system was set up in 1948, and more than two hundred operate presently in the United States. Diatomite is also used to filter nonpotable water, such as that which is used in swimming pools.

Diatomite began to be used after Prohibition to filter beer and wine in the United States, replacing wood pulp in filters. It is also used to filter liquid sweeteners, oils and fats, petroleum and other chemicals, and pharmaceuticals.

Another major use of diatomite is in building, where it is used for lightweight blocks and bricks and for thermal insulation (high clay-content Danish moler in particular). Diatomite is also a frequent cement additive; diatomite for cement requires less processing.

As a filler, diatomite has many uses. In addition to providing bulk, diatomite can reduce reflectivity in paints, reduce caking in granular mixtures, and provide a variety of effects in plastics, including preventing film sticking. Diatomite is absorbent and often used for cleaning industrial spills and in cat litter.

As an insecticide, diatomite is less toxic than chemical pesticides, as it works by absorbing lipids from insects' exoskeletons, causing dehydration. However, it harms beneficial insects as well as pests. Diatomite also is used as a growing medium for hydroponics and an additive in various types of potting soil, because it retains water and nutrients while draining quickly, similar to vermiculite. Medical-grade diatomite is sometimes used for deworming, as the sharp edges of the frustules are thought to kill parasites, but the efficacy of this is questionable.

Diatomite is also used in cosmetics—for example, in facial masks to absorb oil—and as a minor abrasive in jewelry polishes and toothpastes. Some processes for extracting and purifying DNA use diatomite, which will remove DNA but not RNA or proteins. Diatomite and a highly concentrated denaturing agent are used to remove DNA, and then a slightly alkaline, low ionic strength buffer (such as water) can be used to extract DNA from the diatomite.

While diatomite can be replaced by other materials—such as silica sand, perlite, talc, ground lime, ground mica, and clay—for most of its applications,

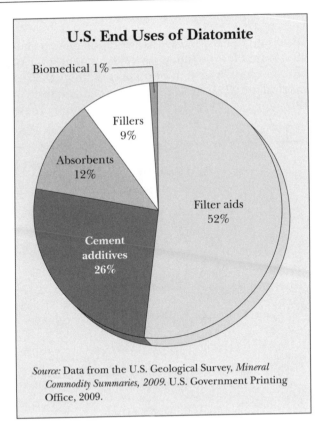

U.S. End Uses of Diatomite

Biomedical 1%
Fillers 9%
Absorbents 12%
Cement additives 26%
Filter aids 52%

Source: Data from the U.S. Geological Survey, *Mineral Commodity Summaries, 2009.* U.S. Government Printing Office, 2009.

its abundance, availability, and low cost make it a popular and heavily used resource.

Melissa A. Barton

FURTHER READING

Fulton, George P. *Diatomaceous Earth Filtration for Safe Drinking Water.* Reston, Va.: American Society of Civil Engineers, 2000.

Stoermer, Eugene F., and John P. Smol, eds. *The Diatoms: Applications for the Environmental and Earth Sciences.* New York: Cambridge University Press, 1999.

U.S. Geological Survey. *Minerals Yearbook.* Washington, D.C.: Author, 2008.

WEB SITE

U.S. GEOLOGICAL SURVEY
History and Overview of the U.S. Diatomite Mining Industry, with Emphasis on the Western United States
http://pubs.usgs.gov/bul/b2209-e/

SEE ALSO: Clays; Lime; Silicates; Water.

Dimension stone

CATEGORY: Mineral and other nonliving resources

WHERE FOUND

Dimension stone, or natural stone, is mined in quarries around the world. The largest concentrations are found in China, India, Italy, Canada, and Spain. In the United States, a country that produces less than 15 percent of the worldwide supply (although it is the dominant market for the stone), quarries are found in thirty-five states, principally (in order of percentage) Indiana, Vermont, Georgia, Wisconsin, and Massachusetts.

PRIMARY USES

Dimension stone is used primarily for domestic decorating and home improvements in upscale housing. It also provides massive block foundation support for large-scale engineering projects, as well as material for monuments, memorial stones, and walkways.

TECHNICAL DEFINITION

Dimension stone is any natural rock—igneous, metamorphic, or sedimentary—precisely cut from a quarry to a specific size (in blocks or slabs) for a specific function (as opposed to crushed stone, which is fractured rubble blasted from quarries to facilitate its removal). Commercially, granite is the most widely used (about one-third of the dimension stone quarried), followed by limestone, marble, sandstone, and, to a much lesser extent, slate and travertine. The decision about which class of dimension stone is to be used is based on color and texture as well as appearance and durability.

DESCRIPTION, DISTRIBUTION, AND FORMS

Because dimension stone requires precise mining, must maintain a usable appearance throughout the excavation process, and has a comparatively high expense in transportation, it accounts for roughly only 2 percent of the total rock mined annually. In the United States, for instance, approximately 1.4 million metric tons of dimension stone are mined annually. Dimension stone can be either rough block (for heavy construction and residential foundations) or dressed block (for statuary, paving stones, and domestic decoration), with its distinctive luster. In fact, finish also is used to classify types of dimension stone. In addition to being reflective, surfaces can be pitted, nonreflective (both smooth and rough), and patterned (often produced by hand).

The four principal types of dimension stone—granite, limestone, marble, and sandstone—are graded by color, grain, texture, mineral patterns and swirls, natural surface finish, durability, strength, and mineral makeup. For instance, dimension granite, an igneous rock, is valued for its relative availability; its durability in the face of weathering and environmental pollution, specifically acid rain, because it is most often used for exterior construction projects; its uniform texture; its hardness; and its variety of colors. Dimension limestone, a sedimentary rock composed largely of calcite, is easy to cut into massive blocks and, although not impervious to acid rain, is remarkably durable (the Pyramids at Giza are made of dimension limestone). However, because of dimension limestone's enormous weight, it is used primarily for foundations and smaller buildings. Dimension marble is a metamorphic rock that is both durable and strong. With its exquisitely smooth, polished surface, marble can be cut into large blocks (up to 63 metric tons) and used to create spectacular public buildings (for instance, the Taj Mahal and the Lincoln Memorial). Dimension sandstone, a sedimentary rock, is most often light gray or yellowish-brown; however, its tendency to streak because of weathering creates striking, aesthetically appealing striation effects. Its surface is coarse and finely grained. It is particularly fragile, susceptible to weathering, and has to be replaced; thus it is limited in its uses.

HISTORY

Using carefully cut, ponderous blocks of durable rock for major engineering undertakings dates to antiquity in both the Far East, predominantly China, and the Mediterranean basin, most notably the stunning pyramid constructions in Egypt, the marble temples around Athens, and the mosques of Turkey. By the Renaissance, rich mineral deposits of marble and granite in Italy and Spain were being utilized to construct great cathedrals and a wide variety of public buildings, courthouses, and palaces. Because of the precise method for cutting the stone, as well as the often extraordinary cost of transporting a massive amount of chiseled rock without damaging its integrity, dimension stone was used almost exclusively for public projects financed by monarchies, the Catholic Church, or wealthy aristocrats.

Large deposits of granite, limestone, and marble found in New England and in the Middle Atlantic states, most notably Tennessee and Indiana, made dimension stone affordable in the New World. Dimension stone played an enormous role in shaping the look of (and providing the architectural support for) many public edifices and private residences across the United States. By the mid-twentieth century, however, newer building materials—reinforced concrete, aluminum, and steel—eclipsed dimension stone. That changed dramatically when environmental concerns about the pollution created by the production of those construction materials returned attention to all-natural dimension stone. In addition, the home building boom in the United States during the 1990's created a market of upscale consumers interested in using natural stone to decorate their custom-built homes. In the same decade, interest in dimension stone was bolstered by large-scale public construction projects, most notably the Denver International Airport, the Korean War Veterans Memorial, the National World War II Memorial, and the Franklin Delano Roosevelt Memorial (the latter three are located in Washington, D.C.).

OBTAINING DIMENSION STONE

The process of obtaining dimension stone—drilling, extracting, cutting, shaping, and polishing—is usually tailored to follow a specific mining order; dimension stone is seldom mined without a contract for a particular project. Since the 1960's, extracting dimension stone has been enhanced, and made comparatively easy, by significant developments in engineering tools. Unlike the excavation of crushed stone, which relies on indiscriminate detonations and heavy machinery, the recovery of usable dimension stone requires care. Each type of dimension stone requires its own methodology depending on the needs of the construction project, the depth of the mineral deposit, and the mining operation's financial resources. The methodology is further impacted by the location of the vein—whether cutting into a hill (called a bench quarry) or digging into the flat ground, operations that can go to 90 meters.

Obtaining dimension stone begins with limited blasting. Then jet piercers, which use a high-velocity jet flame—a concentrated, highly combustible blast of oxygen and fuel oil shot through a nozzle under enormous pressure—channel into the quarry face. In the case of marble, limestone, and sandstone, safer

electrical drilling machines with steel chisels that chop channels into the walls and cut away the desired blocks are frequently used; this method is more time-consuming. In the case of granite and marble, once channels are created, large blocks are pried from the quarry face or extracted from the quarry mine and cut on site into usable shapes (ranging from 0.3 to 18 meters long and 4 meters thick), called mill blocks. Each block is then removed from the quarry area with derricks. In turn, these blocks are processed for their specific project, that is, given the appropriate shape, size, dimension, and finish by certified masons who use a variety of precision saws. Diamond saws are used most often because of their hardness and their ability to cut intricately and carefully.

USES OF DIMENSION STONE

Despite the availability of less expensive substitute building materials, the extraordinary expense of such precisely cut stone, and the care needed during its transportation, dimension stone has maintained its position within the engineering and architectural fields for close to three millennia. Slabs of cut stone, most often granite or sandstone, provide a reliable,

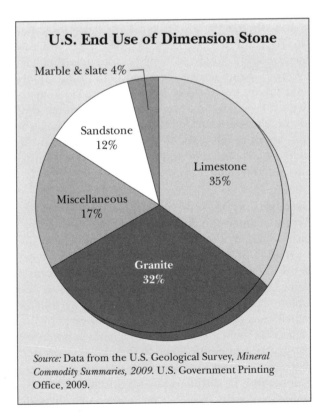

U.S. End Use of Dimension Stone

Marble & slate 4%
Sandstone 12%
Miscellaneous 17%
Limestone 35%
Granite 32%

Source: Data from the U.S. Geological Survey, *Mineral Commodity Summaries, 2009.* U.S. Government Printing Office, 2009.

durable, and attractive foundation for both buildings and residences. However, the use of the stone for spectacular building projects is the use most often recognized by people. Dimension stone such as granite and marble is most associated with grand public spaces and with important monuments dedicated to historically significant people and events, public buildings (like banks and government facilities), cathedrals, grand private homes, upscale hotels, cemetery headstone markers, and elegant mausoleums. In addition, thinner cuts of dimension marble are used for cladding, the outer skin of stone applied to buildings to protect the foundation stone and to give the building an aesthetic quality.

Dimension stone creates an elegant, tasteful, and earthy feel to home interiors. It provides tops for kitchen counters and bathroom vanities as well as material used for staircases and ornamental arches in homes where owners are interested in creating distinctive—and expensive—custom-designed interior effects. Because no two slabs of dimension stone are exactly alike, interior effects can be both striking and individual. Because of the wide variety of textures and colors in natural stone, homeowners can complete virtually whatever decorating motif they conceive by using cut stones for floor tiles, walkways, flagstones, ornamental statuary, and roofing shingles.

Joseph Dewey

FURTHER READING

Adams, Heather, and Earl G. Adams. *Stone: Designing Kitchens, Baths, and Interiors with Natural Stone.* New York: Stewart, Tabori & Chang, 2003.

Bell, Ron. *Early History of Indiana Limestone.* Bloomington, Ind.: AuthorHouse, 2008.

Dupré, Judith. *Monuments: America's History in Art and Memory.* New York: Random House, 2007.

Greenhalgh, Michael. *Marble Past, Monumental Present: Building with Antiquities in the Mediaeval Mediterranean.* Boston: Brill, 2008.

Isler, Martin. *Sticks, Stones, and Shadows: Building the Pyramids.* Norman: University of Oklahoma, 2001.

WEB SITE

U.S. GEOLOGICAL SURVEY
Minerals Information: Dimension Stone Statistics and Information
http://minerals.usgs.gov/minerals/pubs/ commodity/stone_dimension/

SEE ALSO: Diamond; Granite; Igneous processes, rocks, and mineral deposits; Limestone; Marble; Open-pit mining; Sand and gravel; Sandstone; Sedimentary processes, rocks, and mineral deposits.

Dow, Herbert H.

CATEGORY: People
BORN: February 26, 1866; Belleville, Ontario, Canada
DIED: October 15, 1930; Rochester, Minnesota

Herbert H. Dow's main discovery was that underground liquid brine from prehistoric saltwater oceans contained many chemicals. He sought a way to extract these chemicals from the Earth and was initially successful in extracting bromine. He later discovered ways to extract other chemicals from the brine, including magnesium, sodium, calcium, and chlorine. His later research led to more efficient methods of extraction.

BIOGRAPHICAL BACKGROUND

Although born in Canada, Herbert H. Dow lived in that country for about only six weeks. His American parents returned to Derby, Connecticut, where his father worked as a mechanical engineer. In 1878, his father's company, the Derby Shovel Manufacturing Company, moved to Cleveland, Ohio, and the family moved too. In 1884, Dow entered the Case School of Applied Science in Cleveland (now Case Western Reserve University), where he studied chemistry. While still a student at Case, Dow realized the importance of subterranean brine as a source of chemicals. His first successful extraction process was for bromine, a chemical used in sleep medicines and by photographers. Upon graduation from Case, Dow became a professor of chemistry at Huron Street Hospital College in Cleveland and continued to work on his research to develop a cost-effective method of extracting bromine.

In 1890, with the assistance of several associates, Dow established the Midland Chemical Company in Midland, Michigan. Midland was selected for the company's location because of the high-quality bromine in the subterranean waters underneath that city. A short time later, because of differences of opinion between Dow and his backers, Dow left Midland and returned to Cleveland, where he founded the Dow

Process Company. After developing methods to extract chemicals such as chlorine and sodium, Dow became wealthy. He moved his company to Midland, where it became Dow Chemical Company in 1896. By 1900, he had taken over the Midland Chemical Company.

IMPACT ON RESOURCE USE

By 1891, Dow had perfected the electrolysis process of extracting bromine that became known as the "Dow process." Many of Dow's patents were for efficient means of extracting chemicals from other substances. Thus, he was able to lower the cost of chemical products and produce those chemicals more efficiently and effectively. For example, in the early 1900's, Germany was the center of the chemical industry, but Dow was selling bromine for less than 75 percent of the price charged in Europe. Dow expanded during World War I by producing chemicals used in explosives. Following the war, the company became active in supplying chemicals to the automobile industry. Dow also improved the quality of gasoline. By the time of his death at the Mayo Clinic in 1930, Dow had received more than ninety patents for processes for extracting chemicals.

Although Dow's research dealt with how to mine chemicals from ancient oceans, his ideas and technology have had broader uses. The same methods can be used to mine modern seas. Thus, shortly after Dow's death, his company opened its first seawater processing plant. Dow was one of the founders of the modern chemical industry. He took halogen science from theory to reality.

Dale L. Flesher

SEE ALSO: Bromine; Calcium compounds; Chlorites; Magnesium; Marine mining.

Drought

CATEGORY: Environment, conservation, and resource management

Drought is a shortage of precipitation that results in a water deficit for some activity. Droughts occur in both arid and humid regions. Traditional and modern societies have evolved methods of adjusting to the drought hazard.

BACKGROUND

In order to analyze and assess the impacts of drought, as well as delimit drought areas, the characteristics of "drought" must be defined. Conditions considered a drought by a farmer whose crops have withered during the summer may not be seen as a drought by a city planner. There are many types of drought: agricultural, hydrological, economic, and meteorological. The Palmer Drought Severity Index is the best known of a number of indexes that attempt to standardize the measurement of drought magnitude. Nevertheless, there remains much confusion and uncertainty on what defines a drought.

Roger Graham Barry and Richard J. Chorley, in *Atmosphere, Weather, and Climate* (1992), noted that drought conditions tend to be associated with one or more of four factors: increases in extent and persistence of subtropical high-pressure cells; changes in the summer monsoonal circulation patterns that can cause a postponement or failure of the incursion of wet maritime tropical air onto the land; lower ocean surface temperatures resulting from changes in ocean currents or increased upwelling of cold waters; and displacement of midlatitude storm tracks by drier air.

EFFECTS OF DROUGHT

Drought can have wide-ranging impacts on the environment, communities, and farmers. Most plants and animals in arid regions have adapted to dealing with drought, either behaviorally or through specialized physical adaptations. Humans, however, are often unprepared or overwhelmed by the consequences of drought. Farmers experience decreased incomes from crop failure. Low rainfall frequently increases a crop's susceptibility to disease and pests. Drought can particularly hurt small rural communities, especially local business people who are dependent on purchases from farmers and ranchers.

Drought is a natural element of climate, and no region is immune to the drought hazard. Farmers in more humid areas grow crops that are less drought resistant. In developing countries the effects of drought can include malnutrition and famine. A prolonged drought struck the Sahel zone of Africa from 1968 through 1974. Nearly 5 million cattle died during the drought, and more than 100,000 people died from malnutrition-related diseases during just one year of the drought.

Subsistence and traditional societies can be very resilient in the face of drought. American Indians either stored food for poor years or migrated to wetter areas. The !Kung Bushmen of southern Africa learned to change their diet, find alternate water sources, and generally adapt to the fluctuation of seasons and climate in the Kalahari Desert.

More than any other event, the Dust Bowl years of the 1930's influenced Americans' perceptions and knowledge of drought. Stories of dust storms that turned day into night, fences covered by drifting soil, and the migration of destitute farmers from the Great Plains to California captured public and government attention. The enormous topsoil loss to wind erosion, continuous crop failures, and widespread bankruptcies suggested that the United States had in some way failed to adapt to the drought hazard.

FEDERAL DROUGHT RESPONSE IN THE UNITED STATES

Beginning in the 1930's, the federal government took an increasing role in drought management and relief. In 1933, the federal government created the Soil Erosion Service, known today as the Natural Resources Conservation Service. No other single federal program or organization has had a greater impact on farmers' abilities to manage the drought hazard. President Franklin D. Roosevelt's Prairie States Forestry Project (1934-1942) planted more than 93,078 hectares of shelterbelts in the plains states for wind erosion control. The federal government purchased approximately 400,000 hectares of marginal farmland for replanting into grass. Federal agencies constructed water resource and irrigation projects.

Post-Dust Bowl droughts still caused hardships, but the brunt of the environmental, economic, and social consequences of drought were considerably lessened. Fewer dust storms ravaged the plains. New crop varieties and better farming practices decreased crop losses during drought years. Government programs and better knowledge have enabled families and communities to better cope with drought.

COPING WITH FUTURE DROUGHTS

Numerous attempts have been made to predict droughts, especially in terms of cycles. However, attempts to predict droughts one or more years into the future have generally been unsuccessful. The shorter the prediction interval, the more accurate the prediction. Nevertheless,

progress has been made in estimating drought occurrence and timing. For example, the El Niño/Southern Oscillation may be a precursor to drought in some areas. Possibly with time the physical mechanics of climate and drought will be understood adequately for long-term predictions to have value.

Perhaps of greater value is the current capacity to detect and monitor drought in its early stages (usually meaning within one to twelve months). Early recognition of potential drought conditions can give policy makers and resource managers the extra time needed to adjust their management strategies. Information on soil moisture conditions aids farmers with planting and crop selection, seeding, fertilization, irrigation rates, and harvest decisions. Communities that have a few months' warning of impending drought can increase water storage, implement water conservation measures, and obtain outside sources of water.

The progress made in the world's developed countries has not always been available to the developing nations. Overpopulation and overuse of agricultural lands have resulted in regional problems of desertifi-

A drought results from a lack of precipitation that causes massive water shortages, affecting entire populations of people. (©Galyna Andrushko/ Dreamstime.com)

cation and have impeded the ability of developing nations to respond. Monitoring equipment can be costly. Furthermore, drought adjustments used in the United States may not be applicable to other countries' drought situations.

David M. Diggs

FURTHER READING

Allaby, Michael. *Droughts.* Illustrations by Richard Garratt. Rev. ed. New York: Facts On File, 2003.

Barry, Roger G., and Richard J. Chorley. *Atmosphere, Weather, and Climate.* 6th ed. New York: Methuen, 1992.

Brichieri-Colombi, Stephen. *The World Water Crisis: The Failures of Resource Management.* New York: I. B. Tauris, 2009.

Collier, Michael, and Robert H. Webb. *Floods, Droughts, and Climate Change.* Tucson: University of Arizona Press, 2002.

Hewitt, Ken, ed. *Interpretations of Calamity from the Viewpoint of Human Ecology.* Boston: Allen & Unwin, 1983.

Riebsame, William E., Stanley A. Changnon, Jr., and Thomas R. Karl. *Drought and Natural Resources Management in the United States: Impacts and Implications of the 1987-89 Drought.* Boulder, Colo.: Westview Press, 1991.

Wilhite, Donald A., ed. *Drought: A Global Assessment.* New York: Routledge, 2000.

_____. *Drought and Water Crises: Science, Technology, and Management Issues.* Boca Raton, Fla.: Taylor & Francis, 2005.

_____. *Drought Assessment, Management, and Planning: Theory and Case Studies.* Boston: Kluwer Academic, 1993.

Worster, Donald. *Dust Bowl: The Southern Plains in the 1930's.* 25th anniversary ed. New York: Oxford University Press, 2004.

WEB SITES

AGRICULTURE AND AGRI-FOOD CANADA
Drought Watch
http://www.agr.gc.ca/pfra/drought/mapscc_e.htm

NATIONAL INTEGRATED DROUGHT INFORMATION SYSTEM
U.S. Drought Portal
http://www.drought.gov/portal/server.pt/community/drought_gov/202

NATIONAL OCEANIC AND ATMOSPHERIC ADMINISTRATION
Drought Information Center
http://www.drought.noaa.gov

SEE ALSO: Atmosphere; Climate and resources; Desertification; Dust Bowl; Erosion and erosion control; Irrigation; Weather and resources.

Dust Bowl

CATEGORY: Historical events and movements
DATE: 1930's

The environmental catastrophe called the "Dust Bowl" was centered in the southern Great Plains of the United States and was caused by a combination of extended drought and human misuse of the land.

DEFINITION
The Dust Bowl represents one of the most salient examples of environmental maladaptation in modern history. The region called the "Dust Bowl" included a swath of territory stretching 480 kilometers east-west and 800 kilometers north-south in the Great Plains. The Dust Bowl was centered in the panhandles of Texas and Oklahoma, southeastern Colorado, northeastern New Mexico, and western Kansas. High rates of soil erosion and recurring dust storms characterized the Dust Bowl region. The term "Dust Bowl" was used in an article by an Associated Press reporter in 1935; the phrase stuck and quickly came to refer to the entire region of the Great Plains during the 1930's.

OVERVIEW
Relatively wet climatic conditions and good grain prices had stimulated extensive settlement of agriculturally marginal areas of the Great Plains during the 1910's and 1920's. Government policies and Great Plains boosters had encouraged thousands of people to settle in areas that often averaged less than 40 centimeters of precipitation annually. Compounding the problem, farmers practiced agricultural techniques that made the soil highly susceptible to wind and water erosion.

In many parts of the United States and most areas of the Great Plains, the period between 1930 and 1941 represents some of the driest years on record. Annual

A Dust Bowl farmer uses a tractor to clear sand covering his cropland in 1937. (AP/Wide World Photos)

rainfall in the Dust Bowl region dropped to single digits. A combination of low rainfall, exposed soil, and high winds resulted in extensive dust storms. The U.S. Soil Conservation Service kept a record of dust storms of "regional" extent: There were fourteen in 1932, thirty-eight in 1933, twenty-two in 1934, forty in 1935, sixty-eight in 1936, seventy-two in 1937, sixty-one in 1938, thirty in 1939, and seventeen each in both 1940 and 1941. Some of these huge dust storms made their way east, where they deposited dust on ships 480 kilometers out in the Atlantic Ocean.

Dust Bowl conditions and the Great Depression of the 1930's caused widespread farm foreclosures and a mass migration from the region. Penniless, the migrants moved to major urban areas or to other agricultural areas, such as California. The plight of these "Okies" was immortalized in John Steinbeck's novel *The Grapes of Wrath.*

The Dust Bowl experience forced the region's residents and the federal government to find ways to better adapt to the area's marginal climate. New and more effective tillage techniques were used to conserve moisture and minimize erosion. Summer fallowing became a widespread practice after the Dust Bowl experience. Surface and subsurface water resources were exploited for irrigation use. A direct outgrowth of the Dust Bowl years was a plethora of government programs to protect the land and farmers during periods of drought. For example, the Soil Erosion Service, a part of Franklin D. Roosevelt's New Deal program, was established as a temporary agency in 1933 to aid Great Plains farmers. It became permanent in 1935, and its name changed to the Soil Conservation Service (later the Natural Resources Conservation Service). The effort to adjust to the Great Plains environment paid off when major periods of drought occurred in the region during the 1950's, the mid-1970's, and the late 1980's. More vegetative cover on the land, federal crop insurance, and more knowledgeable farmers resulted in fewer dust storms, less erosion, and less financial strain on farmers.

David M. Diggs

SEE ALSO: Civilian Conservation Corps; Desertification; Drought; Erosion and erosion control; Natural Resources Conservation Service; Soil management; Weather and resources.

Dynamite

CATEGORY: Obtaining and using resources

The invention of dynamite has had an effect on the procuring of coal, silver, gold, and any other materials which are mined by tunneling.

DEFINITION

Many different formulations are called dynamite, but all are stabilized forms of nitroglycerine. Dynamite is an explosive that is highly dense so that a large explosive power is available from a small volume of material.

OVERVIEW

Explosives have been a part of underground mining ever since their discovery. Until the mid-1800's the only explosive available was black powder, which was lacking in power and created flames that constituted a fire or dust explosion hazard in mines. Nitroglycerine was discovered by an Italian chemist, Ascanio Sobrero, in 1847. It is an oily organic liquid that is a highly powerful explosive—and an extremely unstable chemical. Temperature increases or mechanical shock readily detonate nitroglycerine. Although it did find use in the mining industry, the hazard of premature explosions was extreme, and the industry searched for an alternative.

The material known as dynamite was discovered by Swedish inventor Alfred Nobel in 1867. After several years of experiments aimed at stabilizing nitroglycerine, Nobel found that when the liquid was absorbed by diatomaceous earth the mixture was safe to handle and did not explode unless a blasting cap was used to initiate the reaction. Nobel went on to commercialize the production of dynamite by building manufacturing facilities on a worldwide basis and thereby accumulating a large fortune. Upon Nobel's death, his will left a considerable portion of his fortune to establish the Nobel Prizes.

Modern dynamite is a dry granular material that is fundamentally stabilized nitroglycerine. It finds its greatest application in underground mining, where its high explosive power per volume is a desired quality. Other chemicals are mixed with the basic ingredients to improve certain aspects of its performance. Some particular formulations are designed to reduce the level of carbon monoxide and nitrogen dioxide that are produced in the explosion so that they do not create a hazard for miners. Another form is of particular use when high explosive power is needed at low operating temperatures.

When packaged for use, the solid is packed into paper cylinders ranging from 2 to 20 centimeters in diameter and from 20 to 100 centimeters in length. These sticks are placed in boreholes in the mine face, tamped into place, and fitted with an electrical detonator. In coal mining a dynamite form that produces a slow shock wave is used so that the pieces of coal dislodged are relatively large. For other deep mining purposes a form producing a fast shock wave is used to fragment the rock more thoroughly into smaller rock pieces that can be more easily processed. Dynamite also finds a role in strip mining or pit mining, where its highly dense explosive power is not needed. In these instances, it is used as a primer to detonate other, lower-cost, blasting agents.

Kenneth H. Brown

SEE ALSO: Coal; Diatomite; Quarrying; Strip mining; Underground mining.

E

Earth First!

CATEGORY: Organizations, agencies, and programs
DATE: Established 1979

Earth First! comprises a group of activists from around the world who employ radical, sometimes illegal tactics to oppose environmental exploitation and are dedicated to defending "Mother Earth." The movement is a network of autonomous groups with no central office, paid officers, or decision-making boards. Members are motivated by a belief in biocentrism or deep ecology.

BACKGROUND

Earth First! was founded in the United States by David Foreman. Calling itself a movement rather than an organization, it is active in several countries. Its tools include grassroots organizing, litigation, civil disobedience, and "monkeywrenching." Earth First! activists criticize the corporate structures and image-consciousness of many environmental groups. They are committed to saving the wilderness and use the slogan, "No compromise in the defense of Mother Earth."

Earth First! activists have adopted a variety of militant tactics, including drilling steel spikes into trees (to make it impossible to cut them with mechanized saws), adding sugar to the fuel tanks of bulldozers, and chaining themselves to tree crushers. The organization also uses theatrical demonstrations to keep the public aware of environmental issues. The *Earth First!* journal, published six times per year, chronicles the activities of the radical environmental movement.

IMPACT ON RESOURCE USE

One of Earth First!'s visions for the future is the development of a 290-million-hectare wilderness system. In this area, priority would be given to the preservation of indigenous species and ecosystems. Stringent guidelines would mandate no human habitation except for those indigenous to the area and living a traditional lifestyle; no mechanized equipment; no roads, buildings, or power lines; no logging, mining, industry, agricultural development, or livestock graz-

ing; and the reintroduction of indigenous species and removal of all species not native to the area.

Marian A. L. Miller

WEB SITE

EARTH FIRST!
Earth First! Worldwide
http://www.earthfirst.org/

SEE ALSO: Environmental movement; Friends of the Earth International; Greenpeace; Sea Shepherd Conservation Society.

Earth Summit

CATEGORIES: Laws and conventions; historical events and movements
DATE: June 3-14, 1992

The United Nations Conference on Environment and Development in Rio de Janeiro, Brazil, also known as the Earth Summit, focused on the environment and sustainable development. Delegates from participating countries signed several documents—including Agenda 21, the Rio Declaration on Environment and Development, the Statement of Forest Principles, the United Nations Framework Convention on Climate Change, and the United Nations Convention on Biological Diversity—regarding the management of global resources.

BACKGROUND

In the 1960's, the issue of environmental protection was gaining prominence in the United States and in other developed countries. As part of this political climate, the United Nations held the 1972 U.N. Conference on the Human Environment in Stockholm, Sweden. At the conference, 114 countries adopted a declaration on the management of global resources. The United Nations Environment Programme was created after the conference to facilitate coordinated international action. In the 1970's and 1980's, global

Brazilian president Fernando Collor de Mello signs the United Nations Convention on Climate Change at the 1992 Earth Summit, while U.N. secretary general Boutros Boutros-Ghali, right, and other diplomats applaud. (AP/Wide World Photos)

environmental problems such as overpopulation, over-consumption, ozone depletion, and transboundary air pollution increased. These problems were connected to other issues in world politics, including globalization, the liberalization of world trade, relations between developed and developing countries, and international resource production and use. This resulted in the creation of the World Commission on Environment and Development in 1983, chaired by former prime minister of Norway, Gro Harlem Brundtland, to develop an international strategy to address global environmental and resource problems. The Brundtland Commission's efforts resulted in the 1987 report *Our Common Future,* which established the discourse of sustainable development. The report led the United Nations to organize the Earth Summit in 1992.

PROVISIONS
Delegates from participating countries signed several global provisions, such as Agenda 21, at the Earth

Summit. Agenda 21 is a nonbinding plan of action to pursue international sustainable development, addressing specific environmental issues and domestic policies. The Rio Declaration on Environment and Development is a nonbinding set of twenty-seven principles to direct sustainable development efforts throughout the world. Its main concern is sustainable development, but it recognizes the importance of healthy, functioning ecosystems. The Statement of Forest Principles, another nonbinding statement adopted at the Earth Summit, pertains to the management of global forest resources and indicates a recognition of the differential obligations of developed and developing countries for the protection of the environment. Also, signed at the Earth Summit was the United Nations Framework Convention on Climate Change, an international treaty to address the issue of global greenhouse-gas emissions. Also signed was the United Nations Convention on Biological Diversity, the first treaty to address the issue and importance of the preservation of biodiversity through the protection of ecosystems rather than through the protection of independent species.

IMPACT ON RESOURCE USE

The impact of the Earth Summit is related mainly to the documents discussed above. Agenda 21 impacted resource use by providing recommendations for specific resource management policies, including a call for the repeal of subsidies incongruent with sustainable development. It also requires countries to include environmental factors in their statistical accounting. The United Nations Framework Convention on Climate Change did not in itself establish limits to greenhouse-gas emissions, but it required the subsequent adoption of limits like those in the 1997 Kyoto Protocol. The Convention on Biological Diversity led to the subsequent adoption of the Cartagena Protocol on Biosafety, which allows for the regulation of genetically modified organisms.

Katrina Taylor

SEE ALSO: Agenda 21; Biodiversity; Greenhouse gases and global climate change; Kyoto Protocol; United Nations climate change conferences; United Nations Environment Programme; United Nations Framework Convention on Climate Change.

Earthquakes

CATEGORY: Geological processes and formations

Earthquakes result from fractures within the Earth which are produced by a buildup of stress in brittle rock. When the frictional forces holding blocks of rock together are overcome, the Earth moves and produces cracks which can infill with minerals.

DEFINITION

Earthquakes occur following the rapid release of energy stored in rocks. Rocks beneath the Earth's surface are continually subjected to forces in all directions. When the forces exceed the limits which the rocks can sustain, they respond by either folding or breaking. If the forces are relatively rapid and the rocks are brittle, then the rocks actually break. The result is a shaking of the ground. This shaking is most prominent on the Earth's surface.

OVERVIEW

An earthquake first originates at a point called the focus, which is beneath the Earth's surface. This fracture, which begins at a point, grows from a microscopic crack into a large fault which can extend for many kilometers. However, as mentioned, this fracture will be propagated only through brittle material. In other words, faults will not extend indefinitely into the Earth's subsurface. Nor will they extend indefinitely through brittle material, because there will be a point where there is insufficient energy remaining to break rock far removed from the initial source of a fracture. Focal depths of earthquakes occur over a range of depths, extending from just below the Earth's surface to a depth of approximately 700 kilometers. Below this great depth rocks are no longer brittle and thus cannot break.

In addition to the more obvious effects of seismic activity on the surface, earthquakes cause a considerable amount of subsurface activity. Seismic energy passing through brittle rock produces faults and cracks of varying sizes throughout the rock. These fissures serve as conduits for fluids, which can move through the rock much more readily than they could before the rock was broken. If the fluids contain dissolved minerals, these will be deposited in concentrated amounts. Such is the case when molten rock rises below the surface and is injected into cracks. Concentrated deposits of gold, silver, and other valuable metals are commonly found filling cracks that were produced by earthquakes that occurred in the recent geologic past.

Large-scale faulting can move massive blocks of rock closer to the Earth's surface. If these blocks are later exposed by erosion of the overlying material, new minerals are exposed. Layers containing coal, limestone, and gravels become available for mining.

David M. Best

SEE ALSO: Lithosphere; Pegmatites; Plate tectonics; Seismographic technology and resource exploitation.

Earth's crust

CATEGORY: Geological processes and formations

The earth's crust is the outer hard layer of the planet. The crust overlies the Earth's mantle and is separated from it by the Mohorovičič discontinuity, or Moho. There are two great classes of crust on Earth, oceanic and continental, which differ in thickness, composition, density, age, mode of formation, and significance for mineral resources.

BACKGROUND

The earth consists of a nested set of spheres of different composition and of decreasing density with distance from the center of the Earth. The crust is the outermost and lowest-density hard shell, significantly less dense (2.7 to 3.0 grams per cubic centimeter) than the underlying mantle (3.3 grams per cubic centimeter). The earth's two distinct types of crust—continental and oceanic—differ in five fundamental aspects: thickness, density, composition, age, and mode of formation.

CONTINENTAL AND OCEANIC CRUST

Continental crust is generally found beneath the exposed parts of the Earth's surface known as continents. In addition, continental crust is submerged and makes up the continental shelves and submerged continental platforms. Correspondingly, a larger proportion of the Earth's surface is composed of continental crust (40 percent) than is exposed above sea

level as continents (25 percent). Oceanic crust makes up the floor of the oceans; in rare cases it rises above sea level, such as in Iceland and Ethiopia. Our store of nonrenewable natural resources is produced and kept in the crust. Hydrothermal systems associated with oceanic crust formation at mid-ocean ridges produce metal deposits. Nearly all economic ore deposits are extracted from the continental crust. Basins in the continental crust and along the continental margins are the principal sites for the formation and storage of oil and gas deposits.

Typical continental crust is about 40 kilometers thick, has a density of about 2.7 grams per cubic centimeter, and has a bulk composition similar to the volcanic rock andesite; it is about 60 percent silicon dioxide (SiO_2). Continental crust as old as 4 billion years has been found, and 2.5 billion-year-old continental crust is common. The earth is about 4.5 billion years old, and continental crust from the Earth's first 500 million years has not been preserved. This contrasts with the situation for Earth's moon, where the lunar highlands preserve crust that formed shortly after the moon itself. Oceanic crust is about 6 kilometers thick, has a density of about 3.0 grams per cubic centimeter, and has a bulk composition similar to the volcanic rock basalt (about 50 percent SiO_2). Although ophiolites may be much older, the oldest in situ oceanic crust is about 170 million years old.

The large difference in age between oceanic and continental crust reflects the greater density of the former, which allows it to slide back into the mantle along subduction zones. In contrast, buoyant continental crust is difficult to subduct. The formation of oceanic and continental crusts is fundamentally different as well: Oceanic crust forms by seafloor spreading at mid-ocean ridges, whereas continental crust forms at island arcs lying above subduction zones (such as Japan or the Mariana Islands in the western Pacific). Although the area of oceanic crust is much larger than that of continental crust (60 percent versus 40 percent of the Earth's surface), the volume of continental crust is much larger than that of oceanic crust (80 percent versus 20 percent).

METAL AND HYDROCARBON DEPOSITS

The two types of crust play different roles in the formation of nonrenewable natural resources such as metallic ores and hydrocarbons. Metallic ores are predominantly produced at diver-

Chemical Composition of Earth's Crust

ELEMENT	WEIGHT (%)	VOLUME (%)
Oxygen (O)	46.59	94.24
Silicon (Si)	27.72	0.51
Aluminum (Al)	8.13	0.44
Iron (Fe)	5.01	0.37
Calcium (Ca)	3.63	1.04
Sodium (Na)	2.85	1.21
Potassium (K)	2.60	1.88
Magnesium (Mg)	2.09	0.28
Titanium (Ti)	0.62	0.03
Hydrogen (H)	0.14	—

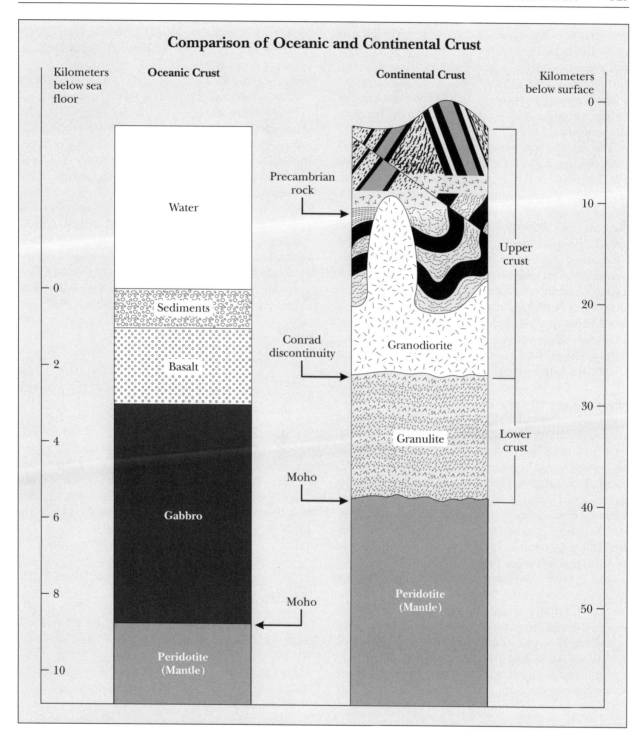

Comparison of Oceanic and Continental Crust

Oceanic Crust

Kilometers below sea floor

Water

Sediments

Basalt

Gabbro

Peridotite (Mantle)

Moho

0

2

4

6

8

10

Continental Crust

Kilometers below surface

Precambrian rock

Conrad discontinuity

Granodiorite

Granulite

Moho

Peridotite (Mantle)

Upper crust

Lower crust

0

10

20

30

40

50

gent or convergent plate boundaries—that is, where oceanic crust is either produced or destroyed. Vast deposits of manganese and cobalt exist on the deep-sea floor in the form of manganese nodules. Hydrocar-

bon deposits form principally in basins on continental crust or beneath continental margins, at the boundary between oceanic and continental crust. The configuration of continents may also be important for controlling oil and gas deposits, because it can cause the formation of restricted basins where oxygen-poor waters allow organic matter to be preserved and buried. The relatively thin sedimentary sequences typically deposited on oceanic crust are not conducive to formation and preservation of hydrocarbon deposits.

The distribution of mineral and hydrocarbon resources is strongly controlled by the age of the crust and the sedimentary basins that these harbor. In spite of the fact that the oceanic crust is the principal factory for generating ore deposits, a minuscule proportion of these are presently exploited, largely for economic reasons. Because of its age and mode of formation, the continental crust acts as a warehouse for ore deposits produced over Earth's history, especially those deposits produced at convergent plate boundaries. Particularly rich ores are preserved in crust produced in the first 2 billion years of Earth history, and those nations which have large tracts of such ancient crust (among them are Australia, Canada, Russia, and South Africa) are blessed with especially rich metal deposits.

RESOURCE FRONTIERS

A wide range of mineral and hydrocarbon resources are sought on all continents except Antarctica. This search benefits increasingly from abundant technological resources, including satellite remote sensing, geophysical surveys, geochemical studies, and traditional field mapping, and from the tremendous increase in computing power available to process large and complex data sets. These nonrenewable resources are likely to be depleted in the future, leading to a rise in prices that will reward exploitation of "frontier" deposits. Resource frontiers pertaining to the Earth's crust include mining and drilling for oil deeper below the continental surface, drilling for oil in deeper water offshore, the mining of deep-sea resources, and exploiting geothermal and hydrothermal resources for energy, including the tremendous heat energy stored in the deep continental crust and vented from hydrothermal sites along the midocean ridges.

Robert J. Stern

FURTHER READING

Brown, Michael, and Tracy Rushmer, eds. *Evolution and Differentiation of the Continental Crust.* New York: Cambridge University Press, 2006.

Condie, Kent C. *Earth as an Evolving Planetary System.* Boston: Elsevier Academic Press, 2005.

Davis, Earl E., and Harry Elderfield, eds. *Hydrogeology of the Ocean Lithosphere.* New York: Cambridge University Press, 2004.

Fowler, C. M. R. *The Solid Earth: An Introduction to Global Geophysics.* 2d ed. New York: Cambridge University Press, 2005.

Grotzinger, John P., et al. *Understanding Earth.* 5th ed. New York: W. H. Freeman, 2007.

Mathez, Edmond A., and James D. Webster. *The Earth Machine: The Science of a Dynamic Planet.* New York: Columbia University Press, 2004.

Rogers, John J. W., and M. Santosh. *Continents and Supercontinents.* New York: Oxford University Press, 2004.

Taylor, Stuart Ross, and Scott M. McLennan. *The Continental Crust: Its Composition and Evolution, an Examination of the Geochemical Record Preserved in Sedimentary Rocks.* Boston: Blackwell Scientific, 1985.

WEB SITE

U.S. GEOLOGICAL SURVEY
The Earth's Crust
http://earthquake.usgs.gov/research/structure/crust/index.php

SEE ALSO: Deep drilling projects; Geothermal and hydrothermal energy; Hydrothermal solutions and mineralization; Igneous processes, rocks, and mineral deposits; Lithosphere; Marine vents; Oil and natural gas distribution; Oil and natural gas reservoirs; Ophiolites; Plate tectonics; Plutonic rocks and mineral deposits; Seafloor spreading; Volcanoes.

Earthwatch Institute

CATEGORY: Organizations, agencies, and programs
DATE: Established 1971

Earthwatch is an international nonprofit organization that advocates research and scientific literacy to help resolve environmental issues such as sustainable resource management. Earthwatch supports scientific research projects and assigns volunteers to those projects; builds networks to share expedition-based curriculums and lessons; collaborates with other conservation and environmental organizations; and solicits corporate partners and private individuals to help promote a sustainable environment.

BACKGROUND

Founded in 1971, in Boston, Massachusetts, Earthwatch Institute began with four Smithsonian scientists and small teams of volunteers. Earthwatch was established as government funds for scientific research decreased. The organization sought a funding model that would bridge research with action to increase public scientific literacy and involvement.

Earthwatch Institute is the world's largest environmental volunteer nonprofit organization. The mission of Earthwatch is to engage people worldwide in scientific field research and education to promote the understanding and action necessary for a sustainable environment. The Earthwatch community includes research scientists, educators, students, global members, volunteers, collaborating conservation organizations, and corporate partners.

Earthwatch Institute is a public charity under the U.S. Internal Revenue Code. The organization has headquarters in Australia, Belize, Costa Rica, England, Japan, Kenya, and the United States.

IMPACT ON RESOURCE USE

Earthwatch prioritizes and supports effective scientific research that focuses on sustainable resource management, climate change, oceans, and sustainable cultures. Such projects include data on species, habitats, and protected areas. Scientific results are published worldwide in scholarly journals and shared with partner organizations, government agencies, and policy makers.

Earthwatch research results have confirmed that sustainable resource management is crucial not only to social and economic development but also to understanding ecosystem complexities. Such studies include the Amazon Riverboat Exploration, which found that since local communities have been actively involved in the management of the Pacaya-Samiria National Reserve in the Peruvian Amazon there has been a decrease in hunting and an increase in populations of certain wildlife species.

Other Earthwatch research focuses on ways that various species are affected by climate change and may suggest ways to mitigate negative impacts, such as those caused by human activities. In 2006, James Crabbe received an award for his outstanding research on coral reefs in Jamaica and Belize. He uses a remotely operated vehicle (ROV) to obtain digital images and measure growth of coral at depths that are difficult or impossible to reach by diving. His research results include findings that the rising Jamaican water temperature has caused a measurable decline in coral cover.

Earthwatch supports research on the stability and productivity of life in oceans and coastal regions. In 2007, Earthwatch completed the first baseline survey of species inhabiting the subtidal and intertidal zones of the Seychelles. The study had the support of the Mitsubishi Corporation. Research data, including photographic documentation, were shared with the Seychelles government, local communities, and conservation groups. With assistance from project scientists, teacher volunteers in the Seychelles and United Kingdom have developed ecology curriculum resources for educational use.

An Earthwatch focus on both current and past sustainable cultures contributes to a better understanding of human interaction with the environment. Research on ancient civilizations, such as that which inhabited the Rapa Nui, or Easter Island, provides assessments on behavioral change, attitudes, and adaptation. Chris Stevenson has led the project for approximately two decades. Research findings include information linking climatic changes with changes in farming that may be helpful in analyzing modern environmental problems.

June Lundy Gastón

WEB SITE

EARTHWATCH
http://www.earthwatch.org

SEE ALSO: Biodiversity; Biotechnology; Resources for the Future; Sustainable development.

Ecology

CATEGORY: Scientific disciplines

Ecology is the scientific study of the interrelationships among organisms—including their habitats, distribution, and abundance—and the relationships of these organisms with their environment, known as bionomics. From a global perspective, ecology concerns many issues that affect the interaction and connections between living and nonliving environments, and, hence, the availability, distribution, and use of global resources.

BACKGROUND

In the 1860's, Ernst Haeckel, a German scientist, coined the word "ecology" based on the Greek word *oikos*, which means "house." The terminology is apt, because ecology focuses on the complex environmental conditions that form organisms' habitats. Historically, ecology was rooted in natural history, which in the 1800's sought to describe the diversity of life and evolutionary adaptations to the environment. In modern usage, ecology includes the study of the interactions among organisms—such as humans, animals, insects, microbes, and plants—and their physical or abiotic environment. The abiotic environment concerns factors such as climate (air and temperature), hydrology (water), geological substrate (soil), light, and natural disasters that affect the environment. The abiotic factors are essential for sustaining the life of organisms.

Ecology also involves the study of biotic environmental components that influence habitats and the distribution and abundance of species of organisms in geographic space and time. The interaction between living organisms and the nonliving environment in a self-contained area is known as an ecosystem. Ecologists study processes such as how energy and matter move though interrelated ecosystems like ponds, forest glades, or rocks with moss growing on them. Maintaining an ecosystem requires the proper balance of air, water, soil, sunlight, minerals, and nutrients.

ECOLOGICAL LEVELS

Modern ecology is interdisciplinary and is based on multiple classifications. Descriptive unit classifications based on the study of organisms and processes start with the simplest and build to the most complex, from individuals to populations, species, communities, ecosystems, and biomes.

- Physiological ecology, the simplest classification, concerns the interaction of individual organisms with their life-sustaining abiotic environment and the impact of biotic components on their habitats.
- Population ecology is the study of the interaction of individuals of different species (whether bacterium, plant, or animal) that occupy the same location and are genetically different from other such groups.
- Community ecologists analyze the interaction of interdependent species populations living within a given habitat or area, known as an ecological community.
- Ecosystem ecology includes the nonliving environment and concerns decomposition of living organisms and intake of inorganic materials into living organisms. In other words, ecosystem ecologists study the flow of energy and the cycling of nutrients through the abiotic and biotic environments of interacting ecological communities.
- The interaction of multiple ecosystems with one another is known as a biome. Some familiar biomes include coniferous forests, rain forests, tundra regions, deserts, coral reefs, and oceans.
- Finally, scientists involved in biosphere ecology study the interaction of all matter and living organisms on the planet.

ECOLOGICAL SUBFIELDS

The terminology used for other ecological classifications emphasizes the interdisciplinary nature of ecology. Paleoecology, for example, involves archaeology in the study of ancient remains and fossils in order to analyze the interrelationships of historic organisms and reconstruct ancient ecosystems. Using evolutionary theory, behavioral ecologists consider the roles of behavior in enabling organisms to adapt to new and changed environments. In systems ecology, scientists use systems theory to manage energy flows and biogeochemical cycles in ecosystems. With some basis in anthropology, political ecologists seek equilibrium in political, economic, and social decision making that impacts the environment. Landscape ecologists conduct spatial analyses and examine processes and interrelationships of ecosystems over large, regional geographic areas. Global ecology is the study of interrelationships between organisms and their environment on a global scale.

GENETIC ECOLOGY

Two emerging specialty subfields of ecology are genetic and evolutionary ecology. In genetic ecology, scientists study genetic variations in species that lead to the evolution of new species or to the adaptation of existing species to new or changed environments. These new or changed environments may be the result of many factors, including abiotic changes, such as an increase or decrease in temperature; increased predation of a species, including overhunting or overfishing; or an unsustainable increase in population. When the environment changes or ecosystems are disturbed, species must adapt or face extinction. Genetic ecology considers genetic factors that allow some species to adapt to and survive environmental changes more easily. In some recent studies of plant species scientists used genetic ecology to analyze how quickly specific plants migrate and adapt to new habitats in response to climate change. Although earlier predictions indicated that plant migration would keep up with environmental change, recent studies indicate that migration will be slower than originally believed. Genetic ecology is also an important tool in studying animal species as well as managing wild and captive animal populations and improving population health.

Genetic ecologists are involved in genetic engineering in order to assess the relationship between genetics of a species and the ecosystem that supports the survival of that species. One argument is that an organism's genetic structure fits exactly with the external ecosystem that supports its survival, especially the external and life-sustaining oxygen-carbon dioxide system. The concern is that interspecies genetic engineering will upset the delicate ecological balance that allows a species to maintain its existence within a specific ecosystem and will adversely affect the continuous and systematic reproduction of ecosystems supported by symbiotic relationships, such as an organism's energy production and processing systems. Unless an organism is able to evolve by adapting its genetic structures to changes in an ecosystem, it is unlikely to survive. An example of genetic engineering that may adversely affect the environment and other living organisms involves pest-resistant corn. Pollen of some corn genetically modified to code for *Bacillus thuringiensis* was initially thought to threaten monarch butterflies. Later studies showed this not to be the case, but a greater concern emerged: So-called Bt corn may encourage the development of resistant pests, which could then threaten corn crops. Until the emergence of a better understanding of the relationships between genetic structures of all living organisms and the relationships of organisms to ecosystems, genetic engineering may present serious dangers.

EVOLUTIONARY ECOLOGY

Evolutionary ecology brings together ecology, biology, and evolution. Evolutionary ecologists look at the

The Blue Ridge Mountains, part of the Appalachian Mountains in the eastern United States, represent both biological and political issues that concern the modern ecologist. (AP/Wide World Photos)

evolutionary history, developmental processes, and behavioral adaptations and interactions of organisms from all over the world for the purpose of studying biodiversity. This type of study operates mainly at the levels of population, species, and communities and utilizes many subsets of ecology. Scientists employ paleoecology to establish historic patterns of biodiversity; genetic ecology, especially DNA techniques, to study variation and to make genealogical connections among organisms; telemetry and satellites to study patterns in distribution of various species; and computer simulations and field experimentation to test out hypotheses. Both genetic and evolutionary ecology are important for the conservation of biodiversity and for developing applications to solve biological problems.

APPLIED ECOLOGY

Ecology also involves many aspects of applied science in which the results of scientific study are applied to real-life situations, from natural resource management to urban planning. Biotic natural resources have been managed at the individual and population levels since the agricultural revolution occurred eight thousand to ten thousand years ago. Until the 1960's, forestry, fish, and wildlife management techniques were aimed at increasing the productivity of single species—usually game species, such as quail and trout, or commercial tree species, such as loblolly pine. As community ecology and ecosystem ecology matured, and as popular concern for the loss of species arose in the 1960's, natural resource management agencies began to look at the effects of single-species management techniques on the entire community. Range management has always taken the community ecology perspective in managing native grass and shrub communities for livestock forage production. However, range conservationists also manage forage production for wildlife as well as for livestock. Conservation biology applies the understanding of all ecological levels in the attempt to prevent species extinction, to maintain species genetic diversity, and to restore self-sustaining populations of rare species or entire communities.

Population ecology remains the core of these applied ecological disciplines. Population ecology mainly deals with mortality rates, birthrates, and migration into and out of local populations. These are the biotic factors that influence population size and productivity. The goal of consumptive natural resource man-

agement is the harvesting of population or community productivity. The goal of nonconsumptive natural resource management is to manage for natural aesthetic beauty, for the maintenance of diverse communities, for the stability of communities and ecosystems, and for a global environment that retains regional biotic processes.

ISSUES IN ECOLOGY

Among the applications of ecological studies are some of the following:

- climate change; and global warming;
- loss of species populations and concomitant loss of biodiversity, including threatened species and endangered species (such as the collapse of bee colonies important for pollination) and the introduction of exotic invasive species into unnatural habitats;
- changes in global ocean currents and their effect on terrestrial biomes such as forests and deserts;
- human activities, including the release of pollutants and their impact on the food chain and animal species, and global resource consumption levels and their impact on ecosystems, land conversion and habitat loss, infrastructure development, and overexploitation;
- blockage of solar energy and holes in the ozone layer; and
- the potential impact of space debris on the global environment.

Internationally, environmental scientists and others are entering into treaties, conducting serious discussions at global conferences, and collaborating on solutions to resolve these and many other issues—including the availability of food and other resources—that may affect future survival. Making humans aware of the many ecological concerns and gaining their support in protecting, conserving, and preserving the environment and global resources for future generations, thus enhancing the health of the Earth, may be the most important goal of the study of ecology.

James F. Fowler, updated by Carol A. Rolf

FURTHER READING

Bertorelle, Giorgio, et al. *Population Genetics for Animal Conservation.* New York: Cambridge University Press, 2009.

Cain, Michael L., William D. Bowman, and Sally D. Hacker. *Ecology*. Sunderland, Mass.: Sinauer Associates, 2008.

Morin, Peter Jay. *Community Ecology*. 2d ed. Oxford, Oxfordshire, England: Blackwell, 2008.

Sherratt, Thomas N., and David M. Wilkinson. *Big Questions in Ecology and Evolution*. New York: Oxford University Press, 2009.

Weisman, Alan. *The World Without Us*. New York: Picador, 2008.

WEB SITES

CELL PRESS
Trends in Ecology and Evolution
http://www.trends.com/tree/default.htm

ECOLOGY GLOBAL NETWORK
http://ecology.com/index.php

THE GLOBAL EDUCATION PROJECT
http://www.theglobaleducationproject.org/earth/global-ecology.php

SEE ALSO: Aggregates; Conservation biology; Deep ecology; Ecosystems; Ecozones and biogeographic realms; Fisheries; Food chain; Forest management; Overgrazing; Species loss; Wildlife; Wildlife biology.

Ecosystem services

CATEGORY: Ecological resources

Ecosystem services are the means by which societal benefits and support are provided by ecosystems. Such benefits and support are also known as natural capital. They include climate regulation, water availability, the maintenance of wildlife and their habitats, fodder, and the production of raw materials such as wood, fiber, medicines, and a range of foods. All are fundamental components in people-environment relationships, given their necessity for human well-being, and all contribute to the provision and/or maintenance of global resources.

BACKGROUND

Ecosystem services are closely linked with biogeochemical cycles and energy transfer. In biogeochemical cycles nutrients are continuously transferred between the constituent parts of the Earth's surface: rocks, soils, water (freshwater and marine), plants, animals, and the atmosphere. These processes are vital in energy transfers within food chains and webs. The spatial and temporal distribution of these processes is determined to a large extent by climatic characteristics but also influences global climate via the carbon cycle. Such processes affect the quality of the "commons" (air, water, oceans), the maintenance of which is essential to human well-being. These processes also control the natural capital that accrues within all ecosystems and that is used for society's needs. Ecosystem services underpin all human activity through the continuous generation of resources and the environmental processes that are essential to that generation. Inevitably, ecosystem services are complex, are under pressure from a growing global population, and require careful management. The *Millennium Ecosystem Assessment* (*MEA*), compiled as a collaborative effort by 1,360 scientists worldwide between 2001 and 2005, summarizes the state of and major trends in global ecosystems and their services under the four headings used below.

SUPPORTING SERVICES

The primary supporting services are nutrient cycling, soil formation, and primary production. Nutrient, or biogeochemical, cycling involves the transfer of elements and compounds within and between the biosphere (organisms and their environment), atmosphere, and pedosphere (soils). They consist of pools or stores between which fluxes occur. For example, in the carbon cycle the major pools are living organisms, dead organic matter, the oceans, and the atmosphere. Fluxes occur between these pools at rates that vary according to factors such as climate. Nutrient cycles also link the inorganic and organic components of the environment and operate at various spatial and temporal scales. For example, photosynthesis, respiration, and decomposition link microbes, plants, and animals with water, soils, and the atmosphere through carbon, hydrogen, nitrogen, phosphorus, and many other elemental cycles. Most major nutrients—carbon is the most obvious example—have a pool in the atmosphere and are thus an influence on climate. These are gaseous biogeochemical cycles. Those nutrients without an atmospheric pool—for example, phosphorus, iron, and calcium—are sedimentary biogeochemical cycles.

Soil formation involves the breakdown of solid bedrock into small particles by biological, chemical, and physical processes known collectively as weathering. Dead organic matter from microbes, insects, and pioneer plants is mixed with the particles to create new habitats for organisms; this aids water retention, which continues the weathering process and contributes to the release of nutrients for use by plants. Many factors—the most important being climate—influence the processes and rates of soil formation, water availability, and degree of acidity or alkalinity.

Primary production is the amount of organic matter produced per unit area per unit time by organisms that can photosynthesize (green plants on land and algae in the oceans). These organisms have the ability to absorb solar energy and convert it to chemical energy through the generation of complex organic compounds such as sugars and carbohydrates. Although less than 1 percent of the solar energy that reaches Earth is used in photosynthesis, this small amount fuels the biosphere. Primary production is the first stage in energy transfer through ecosystems and is thus the basis of all food chains and webs. All animals, including humans, depend on primary production for survival—not only for food and shelter but also for a wide range of goods, including fiber, wood, and medicine. Rates of primary production (primary productivity) are influenced by environmental factors such as water availability, annual temperature regimes, soil types, and nutrient availability. Nutrient cycling, soil formation, and primary production are vital for the ecosystem services described below.

PROVISIONING SERVICES

Provisioning services encompass food, wood, fiber, genetic resources, fuel, and fresh water. Primary production on land and in the oceans underpins the generation and replenishment of many resources on which humanity depends. Apart from fossil fuels, these are all renewable resources and are all organic or biological in origin. The provision of fresh water is renewable but is inorganic in essence, though influenced by ecosystem (biological) characteristics.

Global food production is a vast enterprise that essentially processes carbon and is a major generator of wealth. It involves crop and animal agriculture at various scales (subsistent or commercial); may have a fossil-fuel subsidy, as in the case of "industrialized" agriculture; and requires a reliable supply of fresh water. An indication of the magnitude of this production is reflected in the Food and Agriculture Organization's (FAO's) 2006 data for the major staple crops: 695 million metric tons of maize, 634 million metric tons of rice, and 605 million metric tons of wheat. A proportion of this is used as animal feed to create secondary productivity such as meat and milk products. These and other crops, including cotton fiber, are produced on about 15 million square kilometers of cropland.

An increasing proportion of crop production—notably that of corn, soybean, and canola—is used to generate biofuels, while several crops are grown specifically as biofuels. However, the value of growing materials to use as biofuels is controversial because the crops take up land that could be used for food production. An additional roughly 28 million square kilometers of pasture support a large proportion of the world's cattle and sheep. Cotton is the world's major fiber; about 25 million metric tons were produced in 2005.

Fish derived from inland and marine waters form an important component of human diets. According to FAO statistics, some 141.4 million metric tons of fish were produced in 2005, about 35 percent of which was from inland waters, where aquaculture predominates, and about 65 percent of which was from marine waters, where the harvesting of wild populations is predominant. Some 97 percent of this is consumed directly by humans; the remainder is processed for animal feed. However, the global fishing industry is facing problems because fish stocks have been seriously depleted. The reduction or loss of this service illustrates the difficulties that arise when conservation and management are inadequate: Marine ecosystems are altered and social consequences arise.

The world's natural forests and plantations are another major resource with a host of uses, the most important of which are as materials for construction, furniture, fencing, pulp and paper, garden products, and fuel. Forests are also a source of nonwood resources, including nuts, berries, fodder, and game. In 2007, about 3.6 billion cubic meters of roundwood was produced globally. The chief producers were India, China, the United States, Brazil, and Canada. The proportion removed for wood fuel is unknown. However, the loss of forest cover because of agriculture, logging, and poor management reduces the capacity of the terrestrial biosphere to store carbon. FAO indicates that between 1990 and 2005 carbon stocks in forest biomass decreased by 1.1 billion metric tons of carbon annually; this reflects impairment of an ecosystem service.

The organisms in the world's ecosystems contain a

wealth of genetic resources with vast potential. Biodiversity prospecting is the term given to programs designed to tap this resource by identifying species and screening them for useful properties such as crop protection chemicals and pharmaceuticals. About 25 percent of prescription medicines are plant based, including the widely used aspirin, while the bacterium *Bacillus thuringiensis* is the basis of insect pest control in a range of crops. The bacterium itself is produced as a commercial spray, but the gene component responsible for insect mortality has been identified and inserted into a number of crops, notably cotton and maize, so that these genetically modified varieties produce their own insecticide. As further advances in biotechnology and genetic modification ensue, further opportunities to harness genetic resources will arise.

Fossil fuels are also generated through primary productivity but relate to geological eras many millions of years in the past, when the carbon cycle involved the storage or sequestration of huge volumes of plant-based carbon in reservoirs that eventually became rocks. For example, coal formed in wetlands, and limestone formed in the oceans. These processes continue to operate but at such slow rates that fossil fuels cannot be considered renewable.

Fresh water, a vital resource for human well-being, is renewable. It is a component of the hydrological cycle, a fundamental facilitating factor in ecosystem and society functioning. Water from precipitation reaches the Earth's surface and its subsequent passage depends largely on how evaporation, recharge of groundwater reservoirs, and runoff are affected by the ecosystems through which it passes. Forest and mountain ecosystems are especially important in this context, accounting for about 85 percent of total runoff, which supports approximately 4 billion of the world's estimated 6.7 billion people. Cultivated land accounts for most of the remainder. Wetlands are also important as water stores and hydrological regulators.

REGULATING SERVICES

Climate, flood, and disease regulation, water purification, and pollination are major regulating services. Climate and the Earth's ecosystems have been interdependent throughout geologic time; the major link between the two is the global carbon cycle, though other biogeochemical cycles are also involved. This mutual development has manifested in various ways but is especially significant in terms of global temperature regimes and atmospheric composition.

The Earth and its atmosphere form a closed system, or nearly so, in terms of chemical constitution. The redistribution of atoms and molecules between the Earth's core, lithosphere, biosphere, and atmosphere has been, and continues to be, mediated by life-forms on land and in the oceans. Overall, this relationship has maintained life in the biosphere and helped to spur evolution. It also has caused major shifts in the carbon cycle as carbon is removed from the atmosphere into the biosphere and, eventually, the lithosphere. The evolution of photosynthesis, for example, was particularly important because it not only fixed carbon from the atmosphere but also released oxygen, paving the way for the evolution of mammals, including humans.

Beginning with the Industrial Revolution, humans began to alter the carbon cycle profoundly through fossil-fuel consumption and deforestation. Evidence indicates that these may contribute to global warming. The speed of the alteration in the carbon cycle is more rapid than the gradual processes that characterize the geological past; thus, concerns about serious consequences for human well-being seem to be justified.

Flood regulation is a function of all ecosystems but is most important in forests, grasslands, and wetlands. Following receipt of high rainfall or snowfall such ecosystems store water in the vegetation and soils and temper its release to groundwater, streams, and rivers. This reduces the impact of floodwaters on ecosystems and society in built-up areas like river valleys, estuaries, and deltas. Degradation of upstream ecosystems can impair this capacity and imperils millions of people. Erosion control is also linked with the preservation of an adequate vegetation cover in river catchments and safeguards downstream land use and settlements. The passage of water through ecosystems—in which vegetation, microorganisms, and soils act as filters—contributes to water purification. Pollutants such as metals, excess nutrients such as nitrogen, and sediments are removed, which improves conditions for downstream ecosystems and land use.

Many diseases experienced by crops and animals (including humans) are influenced by ecosystem diversity; pest and disease outbreaks are not likely in biodiverse regions because the passage of viruses is made difficult by the buffering capacity of non-host species. The natural control of vectors is also enhanced with high biodiversity.

Pollination is another vital ecosystem service. It facilitates the sexual reproduction of many plants, including crops, with genetically diverse offspring as a result. Without such fertilization, fruiting would not occur. Many animal species—bats, birds, and insects such as bees, butterflies, flies, moths, and beetles—are involved in pollination. About 33 percent of human food production depends on these wild pollinators; thus, the service is of economic importance.

CULTURAL SERVICES

Cultural services—aesthetic, spiritual, educational, and recreational—do not provide immediately tangible resources akin to food, for example, but they contribute to human well-being in many ways. Furthermore, in the context of education, they may improve understanding of ecosystem form and function and contribute to sustainable management strategies. Distinct types of ecosystem provide a sense of place, influence culture, inspire art forms, and are important in many religions. Wealth generation—through the value of landscape, wildlife, and recreation—is another cultural ecosystem service. Other forms of employment, such as forestry, conservation, and management, also contribute to wealth generation.

FUTURE CONTEXT

Global population is estimated to increase to 8 billion by 2030. This will compound pressure on already stretched ecosystem services and require an increase in food production by at least 25 percent. According to the *MEA*, humans have altered global ecosystems more substantially since the mid-twentieth century than at any other time in history. This happened because of a threefold growth in population, rapid conversion of forests and grasslands to agricultural land, technologies such as automobiles requiring fossil fuels, and rising standards of living that encompass increased resource use. More than half of the services provided are being degraded mostly at the expense of the poorest people. One aspect of this degradation is the high rate of plant and animal extinction such as the loss of genetic resources, a process that, unlike many other environmental problems, is irreversible. Unsustainable practices and resulting inequity require immediate attention from local, national, and international political and environmental institutions. Each requires the inventory and valuation of ecosystem services, monitoring, investment in management, education programs, and cooperation at all scales.

A. M. Mannion

FURTHER READING

Botkin, Daniel B., and Edward A. Keller. *Environmental Science: Earth as a Living Planet.* 7th ed. New York: John Wiley & Sons, 2009.

Mannion, Antoinette M. *Carbon and Its Domestication.* Dordrecht, Netherlands: Springer, 2006.

Melillo, Jerry, and Osvaldo Sala. "Ecosystem Services." In *Sustaining Life: How Human Health Depends on Biodiversity*, edited by Eric Chivian and Aaron Bernstein. New York: Oxford University Press, 2008.

Ninan, K. N., ed. *Conserving and Valuing Ecosystem Services and Biodiversity: Economic, Institutional and Social Challenges.* Sterling, Va.: Earthscan, 2008.

WEB SITES

FOOD AND AGRICULTURE ORGANIZATION OF THE
    UNITED NATIONS
FAOSTAT
http://faostat.fao.org/default.aspx

MILLENNIUM ECOSYSTEM ASSESSMENT
Millennium Assessment 2009
http://www.millenniumassessment.org/en/
    index.aspx

SEE ALSO: Agriculture industry; Biosphere; Carbon cycle; Ecology; Ecosystems; Ecozones and biogeographic realms; Fisheries; Geochemical cycles; Greenhouse gases and global climate change; Hydrology and the hydrologic cycle; Natural capital; Nitrogen cycle; Phosphorus cycle.

Ecosystems

CATEGORY: Ecological resources

An ecosystem is formed by the complex interactions of a community of individual organisms of different species with one another and with their abiotic (nonliving) environment.

BACKGROUND

A biological community consists of a mixture of populations of individual species; a population consists of potentially interbreeding members of a species. Individual organisms interact with members of their own species as well as with other species. An ecosystem is

Taiga, featuring coniferous forests and located in the northern portion of the Northern Hemisphere, is one type of ecosystem. (©Irina Bekulova/Dreamstime.com)

formed by this web of interactions among species along with the physical, chemical, and climatic conditions of the area.

Abiotic environmental conditions include temperature, water availability, soil nutrient content, and many other factors that depend on the climate, soil, and geology of an area. Living organisms can alter their environment to some degree. A canopy formed by large forest trees, for example, will change the light, temperature, and moisture available to herbaceous plants growing near the forest floor. The environmental conditions in a particular area can also be affected by the conditions of neighboring areas; the disturbance of a stream bank can lead to erosion, which will affect aquatic habitat for a considerable distance downstream. It can be difficult to anticipate the wide-ranging affects of ecosystem disturbance.

Species and individuals within an ecosystem may interact directly with one another through the exchange of energy and material. Predators, for exam-

ple, obtain their energy and nutritional needs through consumption of prey species. Organisms also interact indirectly through modification of their surrounding environment. Earthworms modify soil structure physically, affecting aeration and the transport of water through the soil. In turn, these alterations of the physical environment affect root growth and development as well as the ability of plants to secure nutrients.

Ecosystems are not closed systems: Energy and material are transferred to and from neighboring systems. The flow of energy or material between the components of an ecosystem, and exchanges with neighboring ecosystems, are governed by functions of the abiotic and biotic ecosystem components. These ecological processes operate simultaneously at many different temporal and spatial scales. At the same time that a microorganism is consuming a fallen leaf, the process of soil formation is occurring through chemical and physical weathering of parent material; plants are competing with one another for light, water, and nutrients; and weather may be changing—a storm front, for example, may be approaching.

Ecosystem Boundaries and Temporal Scales

Because of the exchange of energy and material, it is not possible to draw clear boundaries around an ecosystem. A watershed is formed by topographic conditions forming physical barriers guiding the gravitational flow of water, yet wind carries seeds and pollen over these barriers, and animals can still move from watershed to watershed. The strength of the interactions among neighboring systems is the basis on which humans delineate ecosystem boundaries. In truth, all ecosystems around the world interact with one another to some degree or another.

Ecological processes operate at many different timescales. Some operate over such long timescales that they are almost imperceptible to human observa-

tion. The process of soil formation occurs over many human life spans. Other processes operate over extremely short time intervals. The reproduction of soil bacteria, the response of leaves to changing temperature over the length of a day, and the time required for chemical reactions in the soil are all very short when compared to a human life span. Usually the timescale of a process is related to its spatial scale; processes that operate at short timescales also tend to operate over short distances.

Ecosystem Disturbance

Ecosystems are subject to disturbance, or perturbation, when one or more ecosystem processes are interrupted. Disturbance is a natural ecological process, and the character of many ecosystems is shaped by natural disturbance patterns. The successful reproduction of many prairie species may be dependent on

Gazelles graze on an African savanna, one type of ecosystem. (©Birute Vijeikiene/Dreamstime.com)

periodic fire. Suppression of fire as a means of protecting an ecosystem may lead to the local extinction of small plants, which depend on periodic fires to increase light availability by removing larger grasses and providing nutrients to the soil. The formation of sandbars in streams may be controlled by periodic flood events that remove great amounts of sediment from stream banks. Protection of existing ecosystems can depend on the protection or simulation of natural disturbances. This is even true of old-growth forests; the natural disturbance interval due to fire or windstorm may be centuries, and yet interruption of the natural disturbance pattern may lead to shifts in species composition or productivity.

Increasing the frequency of disturbance can also affect ecosystem structure and function. Repeated vegetation removal will favor species that take advantage of early-successional conditions at the expense of species that are more adapted to late-successional conditions. In order to ensure continued functioning of ecosystem processes and the survival of all species, it is necessary to have a mix of systems in early-successional and late-successional stages in a landscape. Human resource utilization must be managed within this context in order to ensure the long-term sustainability of all ecosystem components and to reduce the chances of extinction of some species because of human alteration of natural disturbance intervals.

ECOSYSTEM STABILITY

A system is stable if it can return to its previous condition at some time after disturbance. The length of time required to return to the original condition is the recovery time. Stability is an important property of ecosystems that are utilized by humans. The recovery of fish populations, the reestablishment of a forest following harvesting, and the renewed production of forage following grazing all depend on the inherent stability of the affected ecosystem. The stability of an ecosystem is dependent on its components and their interrelationships. Disturbance may primarily affect one component of an ecosystem, as with salmon fishing in the Pacific Ocean. The ability of the entire ecosystem to adjust to this disturbance depends on the complexities of the interrelationships between the salmon, their predators and prey, and their competitors.

The length of the recovery time varies with the type of system, the natural disturbance interval, and the severity of the disturbance. The population of algae

along the bottom of a streambed may be severely disturbed by spring flooding, yet may be resilient and return to its pre-disturbance condition in a short time. A forest containing one-thousand-year-old mature trees may be extremely resilient and able eventually to reestablish itself following a windstorm or harvesting, but the recovery time extends over many human lifetimes.

There are species that require disturbance in order to regenerate themselves. These species may be present in great abundance following a disturbance. Their abundance then decreases over time, and if there is no disturbance to renew the population, they will eventually die out and no longer be present in the ecosystem.

A system is usually stable only within some bounds. If disturbed beyond these recovery limits the system may not return to its previous state but may settle into a new equilibrium. There are examples in the Mediterranean region of systems that were overgrazed in ancient times and that have never returned to their previous species composition and productivity. Forest managers, farmers, fishermen, and others must understand the natural resiliency of the systems within which they work and stay within the bounds of stability in order to ensure sustainable resource utilization into the future.

MATTER AND ENERGY CYCLES

Ecological processes work through the cycling of matter and energy within the system. Nutrient cycling consists of the uptake of nutrients from the soil and the transfer of these nutrients through plants, herbivores, and predators until their eventual return to the soil to begin the cycle anew. Interruption of these cycles can have far-reaching consequences in the survival of different ecosystem components. These cycles also govern the transport and fate of toxic substances within a system. It took many years before it was realized that persistent pesticides such as dichloro-diphenyl-trichloroethane (DDT) would eventually be concentrated in top predators, such as raptors. The decline in populations of birds of prey because of reproductive failure caused by DDT was a consequence of the transport of the chemical through ecosystem food webs. Likewise, radionucleides from the disaster at the Chernobyl nuclear reactor have become concentrated in certain components of the ecosystems where they were deposited. This is particularly true of fungi, which take radionucleides and heavy metals from their food sources but do not shed the substances. Humans eating mushrooms from these forests can receive larger than expected doses of radiation, since the concentration in the fungi is much greater than in the surrounding system.

A basic understanding of ecosystem properties and processes is critical in designing management methods to allow continued human utilization of systems while sustaining ecosystem structure and function. With increasing human population and advancing living standards, more and more natural ecosystems have been pushed to near their limits of stability. It is therefore critical for humans to understand how ecosystems are structured and function in order to ensure their sustainability in the face of continued, and often increasing, utilization.

David D. Reed

FURTHER READING

Aber, John D., and Jerry M. Melillo. *Terrestrial Ecosystems.* 2d ed. San Diego, Calif.: Harcourt Academic Press, 2001.

Allen, T. F. H., and Thomas W. Hoekstra. *Toward a Unified Ecology.* New York: Columbia University Press, 1992.

Bormann, F. Herbert, and Gene E. Likens. *Pattern and Process in a Forested Ecosystem: Disturbance, Development, and the Steady State Based on the Hubbard Brook Ecosystem Study.* New York: Springer, 1979.

Dickinson, Gordon, and Kevin Murphy. *Ecosystems.* 2d ed. New York: Routledge, 2007.

Golley, Frank Benjamin. *A History of the Ecosystem Concept in Ecology: More than the Sum of the Parts.* New Haven, Conn.: Yale University Press, 1993.

H. John Heinz III Center for Science, Economics, and the Environment. *The State of the Nation's Ecosystems 2008: Measuring the Lands, Waters, and Living Resources of the United States.* Washington, D.C.: Island Press, 2008.

Hobbs, Richard J., and Katharine N. Suding, eds. *New Models for Ecosystem Dynamics and Restoration.* Washington, D.C.: Island Press, 2009.

Schilthuizen, Menno. *The Loom of Life: Unravelling Ecosystems.* Berlin: Springer, 2008.

Trudgill, Stephen. *The Terrestrial Biosphere: Environmental Change, Ecosystem Science, Attitudes, and Values.* New York: Prentice Hall, 2001.

Williams, R. J. P., and J. J. R. Fraústo da Silva. *The Chemistry of Evolution: The Development of Our Ecosystem.* Boston: Elsevier, 2006.

SEE ALSO: Biodiversity; Biosphere; Carbon cycle; Conservation; Ecology; Ecosystem services; Ecozones and biogeographic realms; Endangered Species Act; Nitrogen cycle; Species loss; Sustainable development.

Ecozones and biogeographic realms

CATEGORIES: Ecological resources; environment, conservation, and resource management; plant and animal resources

Ecozones and biogeographic realms are large-scale classifications that help scientists assess population sizes, histories, and locations of plant and animal species worldwide. The information aids the management and conservation of biological resources and is used to guide the choices of natural United Nations Educational, Scientific and Cultural Organization (UNESCO) World Heritage sites. It also provides clues to how species evolved.

BACKGROUND

Biogeography is the study of the distribution of living organisms in the world, past and present. "Ecozone" (short for "ecological zone"), "biogeographic realm," "life zone," and "biogeographic zone" are broadly synonymous terms for the major physical demarcations in this distribution. These terms are similar to the concept of the biome. However, whereas a biome is generally held to be a major community defined by principal vegetation and animal groups adapted to a particular environment, the ecozone takes into account the geological and evolutionary history of a region.

The idea for dividing the biosphere into distinct regions based on biological criteria dates to scientist-explorers of the eighteenth and early nineteenth centuries. In 1778, after sailing around the world with Captain James Cook, the English scientist J. R. Forster claimed that the world was composed of belts of similar vegetation, each fostered by a distinct climate. In 1804, German scientist Alexander von Humboldt, considered by many to be the father of biogeography, built upon Forster's conclusions to demonstrate that vegetation varied regularly in accordance with altitude just as it did with distance from the equator.

BIOGEOGRAPHIC REALMS

Miklos D. F. Udvardy proposed the modern biogeographic realm schema in a 1975 paper, "A Classification of the Biogeographic Provinces of the World." He defined a biogeographic realm as a continental or subcontinent region with unifying features of geography and plant and animal life. Each realm could be further divided into subrealms, or biogeographic provinces, and these into subprovinces, districts, and subdistricts, in order to define more precisely local variations in species types and distribution.

Udvardy recognized eight major biogeographic realms. Each represents a region in which life-forms have adapted as a community to climatic conditions. The realms draw upon the established five classes of biomes to identify vegetation-climate interrelations: tropical humid rain forests, subtropical and temperate rain forests, temperate needle-leaf forests, tropical dry or deciduous forests, and temperate broad-leaf forests and subpolar deciduous thickets. The Nearctic Realm, comprising 22.9 million square kilometers of the Earth's surface, includes most of North America. The Palearctic Realm, comprising 54.1 million square kilometers, covers most of Eurasia and North Africa. The Afrotropical Realm, comprising 22.1 million square kilometers, contains sub-Saharan Africa. The Indomalayan Realm, comprising 7.5 million square kilometers, includes Afghanistan-Pakistan, South Asia, and Southeast Asia. The Oceanic Realm, comprising 1 million square kilometers, groups together Polynesia, Fiji, and Micronesia. The Australian Realm, which is 7.7 million square kilometers, similarly groups together Australia, New Guinea, and associated islands. The Antarctic Realm, 0.3 million square kilometers, comprises the continent Antarctica. Finally, the Neotropical Realm, 19 million square kilometers, includes South America and the Caribbean.

ECOZONES

Although the terms "ecozone" and "ecological zone" are used with varying meanings by others, Jürgen Schultz supplied the definitive treatment of the concept. In *The Ecozones of the World* (2005), he defines an ecozone as a large region of land where physical characteristics, such as climate, soil type, landscape, and geology, create a distinctive environment that supports a mixture of plant life that in turn supports a mixture of animal species. As do other classification schemes, Schultz's recognizes that vegetation is the salient feature of a region, and he organizes the ecozones spatially by relating vegetation to climate and (as some classification schemes do not) seasonal variations in climate. Schultz emphasizes that no strict borders separate the ecozones; rather, they are concentrations of highly uniform life and landscape.

Shultz recognizes nine ecozones. The polar subpolar zone includes the areas between the North and South Poles and their respective polar tree lines, 22 million square kilometers. All of it lies within the area of permafrost; some parts are ice-covered (polar deserts), and some are tundra or bare rock. It is quite barren, characterized by very low average temperature, precipitation, and biological production; a short growing season; and low total biomass.

The boreal zone, found only in the Northern Hemisphere, covers 20 million square kilometers and generally extends from the polar tree line to the central steppes (grassy plains). It is best known as a region of coniferous forests.

Most of the temperate midlatitudes zone also is located in the Northern Hemisphere—in eastern and western Eurasia and North America—although there are small areas of it in South America, Australia, and New Zealand. It includes 14.5 million square kilometers in narrow corridors between boreal evergreen forests and steppes. It is moderate in most of its characteristics, such as average temperature, precipitation, growing season, and total biomass.

The dry midlatitudes zone occupies small areas of North America, large swaths of east-central Eurasia, the eastern part of Patagonia in South America, and part of New Zealand, for a total area of 16.5 million square kilometers. Although this zone has various subdivisions, it is arid, with at most five months of plant growth and widely dispersed plants, such as cactus, adapted to dry, salty soils.

The subtropics with winter rain zone includes 2.5 million square kilometers, most of it along the Mediterranean coasts of Europe and western North Africa, but it also includes areas in southern Australia. Because the Euro-African and the Australia areas are so far apart, their plant and animal life vary considerably.

The subtropics with year-round rain zone includes 6 million square kilometers total; parts of it occur in the south of the United States, southern China, southeastern South America, eastern South Africa, and eastern Australia. The zone sees high average temperature and precipitation, a long growing season, and very large biomass.

The dry tropics and subtropics zone is the largest:

31 million square kilometers, which is nearly 21 percent of the entire world landmass. Deserts, semideserts, thorn savanna, and thorn steppe lie within it.

The tropics with summer rain zone constitutes, approximately, bands of moist and dry savannas north and south of the equator, 25 million square kilometers, in northern and eastern South America, central and southern Africa, India, Southeast Asia, and northern Australia and nearby islands. Areas of it lie in Central America as well.

The last zone, tropics with year-round rain, is primarily equatorial: northern South America, central Africa, Indonesia, and Malaysia. This zone comprises tropical rain forests in its 12.5 million square kilometers and has highest values in all categories of ecozone messurement—for example, the highest average temperature, precipitation, length of growing season, and biomass.

HUMAN IMPACT

In comparison with Earth's landmass, the planet's oceans are not yet thoroughly studied for classification into biological regions. The difficulty of exploration and the flowing, changing nature of oceans make it difficult to distinguish boundaries underwater. However, in order to identify and protect at-risk ecosystems and to estimate exploitable resources, scientists have proposed various marine ecozones for coastal areas, which are the best understood. They also have the greatest human presence and use, including fishing, waste disposal, recreation, and transportation. These zones include beaches, coral reefs, kelp forests, human-made structures such as docks and pilings, mangrove swamps, mudflats, rocky shores, and salt marshes. (Deep-sea ecosystems may eventually be construed to compose ecozones, such as the ecosystems around underwater volcanic vents.)

On land, logging, farming, grazing domestic animals, and construction of cities account for the greatest modifications to ecozones. Because of these, the original vegetation cover in many temperate and tropical zones has been removed, wholly or partly. Schultz contends that agriculture and grazing represent the optimal expression of biological production within the physical environment of an ecozone.

Roger Smith

FURTHER READING

Dickinson, Gordon, and Kevin Murphy. *Ecosystems.* 2d ed. New York: Routledge, 2007.

MacDonald, Glen Michael. *Biogeography: Space, Time, and Life.* New York: John Wiley & Sons, 2003.

Moles, Manuel C., Jr. *Ecology: Concepts and Applications.* 5th ed. Boston: McGraw Hill Higher Education, 2010.

Pickett, Steward T. A., Jurek Kolasa, and Clive G. Jones. *Ecological Understanding: The Nature of Theory and the Theory of Nature.* 2d ed. Boston: Academic Press, 2007.

Schultz, Jürgen. *The Ecozones of the World: The Ecological Divisions of the Geosphere.* 2d ed. New York: Springer, 2005.

WEB SITES

ECOLOGICAL SOCIETY OF AMERICA
http://www.esa.org

ENVIRONMENTAL INFORMATION COALITION
The Encyclopedia of Earth
http://www.eoearth.org

SEE ALSO: Deep ecology; Deserts; Ecology; Ecosystem services; Ecosystems; Forests; Grasslands; Rangeland; Wetlands.

Edison, Thomas

CATEGORY: People
BORN: February 11, 1847; Milan, Ohio
DIED: October 18, 1931; West Orange, New Jersey

Edison, whose inventions include the modern form of incandescent light, typified the age of technology-driven innovation, which demanded the widespread availability of electrical power.

BIOGRAPHICAL BACKGROUND

Thomas Edison spent his early years selling newspapers on a railroad and working as a telegraph operator in Boston. Familiarity with electrical equipment led him to a number of early inventions, one of which, an improved stock ticker, he was able to sell for $40,000, a sum he spent in setting up his own workshop at the age of twenty-three.

IMPACT ON RESOURCE USE

In 1876, he established a research laboratory in Menlo Park, New Jersey, and he turned his attention to developing a system of electric lighting in 1878. Electrical arc lighting had been demonstrated in 1808 by British scientist Sir Humphry Davy, but it required high currents and was very dangerous. In the search for a more practical electric light, Edison joined a field of other eager inventors. Joseph W. Swan, an English chemist, had limited success before abandoning the idea in 1860. Edison's approach was to seek a low-power lightbulb so that several could be used together to illuminate a room. After an exhaustive search for a filament material that would provide moderate illumination for many hours without burning out, he settled on a carbonized thread. Edison also tackled the problem of electric power distribution, opening the first distribution station, the Pearl Street Station, in New York in 1882.

Donald R. Franceschetti

SEE ALSO: Electrical power; Hydroenergy.

Thomas Edison's numerous inventions, which included the electric lightbulb, helped propel humanity into the modern age. (Library of Congress)

Edison Electric Institute

CATEGORY: Organizations, agencies, and programs
DATE: Established 1933

The Edison Electric Institute is an association of investor-owned electric utility companies operating all over the world. Member companies generate 79 percent of the power produced in the United States and service 70 percent of the nation's electricity consumers.

BACKGROUND

The Edison Electric Institute was formed when public investors realized that their companies needed a collective regulatory policy regarding assignment of service territories (franchises) so as to eliminate the duplication of service and equipment and become more economically efficient. The Edison Electric Institute assumed the promotional responsibilities of the National Electric Light Association, the forerunner to the Edison Electric Institute. The institute continued to grow by absorbing the Electric Energy Association in 1975 and the National Association of Electric Companies in 1978.

IMPACT ON RESOURCE USE

The Edison Electric Institute represents the interests of the shareholder-owned electric power industry. Millions of small investors collectively own most electric utilities, either by the direct purchase of stock or indirectly through life insurance policies, retirement funds, and mutual funds. Electric utilities that are Edison Electric Institute members market some of their electricity at wholesale rates to other electricity-producing entities. These other entities include more than two thousand municipality-owned systems, some federally owned hydroelectric projects, and many of the one thousand rural electric cooperatives.

The Edison Electric Institute also functions as an information center by educating the general public, communicating with government agencies on topics of public interest, and serving as a forum for the interchange of ideas and information with its member companies and their personnel. The Edison Electric Institute conducts numerous surveys and studies that provide information to its members on utility operations, regulations, sales, revenues, environmental practices, and marketing opportunities.

Dion C. Stewart

WEB SITE

EDISON ELECTRIC INSTITUTE
http://www.eei.org/Pages/default.aspx

SEE ALSO: Edison, Thomas; Electrical power; Energy
politics; Tennessee Valley Authority.

El Niño and La Niña

CATEGORY: Geological processes and formations

*The replacement of normal near-surface Pacific Ocean
temperatures by either warmer waters off the Peruvian
coast (El Niño) or colder waters in the eastern Pacific
(La Niña) causes significant changes in climate that
lead to agricultural losses or surpluses, outbreaks of
disease, unexpected losses or increases in wildlife, and
floods or droughts. El Niño also has affected the rate of
the Earth's rotation.*

DEFINITION

El Niño is signaled by a warm current
of water off the Peruvian coast in
contrast to the normally cold waters
that rise to the surface. This change
alters the circulation pattern of the
Pacific Ocean, which in turn causes
changes in climate. La Niña creates
an opposite effect by extending and
deepening the impact of the normal
circulation pattern in the Pacific because of colder water than normal in
the eastern Pacific.

OVERVIEW

Peruvian and Ecuadorian fishermen
have long noted that for a few weeks
in December the waters off their
coasts grow warmer, an effect they
called El Niño ("the boy child") because of the event's proximity to
Christmas. In some years this warming is more significant in both its
temperature and its duration and can
have worldwide impact.

Sir Gilbert Walker, in his study of
Asian monsoons, was the first to document the normal pattern of Pacific

Ocean circulation. Walker realized there was a yearly
cyclical variation in the atmosphere over the southwest Pacific Ocean, which he termed the "Southern
Oscillation." The Pacific Ocean is normally characterized by strong equatorial currents and trade winds
driven by rising cool water off the coast of Peru that
moves toward the equator and heads westward, setting up a circulation cell effect. This Southern Oscillation circulation results in warm water and an area of
low pressure producing wet conditions in the South
Pacific and correspondingly relatively dry conditions
on the west coasts of the Americas. The rising cool
water off Peru also brings nutrients to the surface that
attract plankton, which in turn sustain an anchovy
population that proves a stable food source for many
marine creatures, birds, and humans. The birds fur-
nish a steady supply of guano, a source for fertilizer.

El Niño entirely reverses this circulation model
within the Pacific Ocean with dramatic consequences
during years of its occurrence. With El Niño there are

*El Niño, shown in this 2006 satellite image as it passes across the Pacific Ocean, is a con-
dition occurring every three to eight years that causes numerous worldwide atmospheric
changes. (NASA)*

dry conditions in the South Pacific and wet conditions on the western coasts of North and South America. Fishing off the coasts of Peru and Ecuador becomes a futile endeavor, stormy weather is common, and the fertilizer industry collapses. Droughts are triggered in various parts of the globe, including Australia, New Zealand, Southeast Asia, India, the Philippines, Mexico, and southeast Africa. Excessive beach erosion occurs in California. Huge floods strike Cuba, Louisiana, and Mississippi. Coral reefs in the Pacific Ocean experience massive death.

La Niña ("the girl child") is an oceanic and atmospheric phenomenon that is the opposite of El Niño, as surface waters in the eastern Pacific become much colder than normal. A La Niña winter produces colder than normal air over the Pacific Northwest and the northern Great Plains and warms much of the rest of the United States. It results in increased precipitation in the Pacific Northwest and also increases hurricane activity in the Caribbean and Gulf of Mexico, perhaps twenty times higher than during El Niño years.

Dennis W. Cheek

SEE ALSO: Erosion and erosion control; Floods and flood control; Geothermal and hydrothermal energy; Guano; Monsoons; Ocean thermal energy conversion; Ocean wave energy; Oceanography; Oceans; Weather and resources.

Electrical power

CATEGORIES: Obtaining and using resources; energy resources

Electrical power is so convenient that $350 billion worth of it was sold by utility companies in the United States alone in 2008. However, a need for greater efficiency and environmental care will probably slow growth in sales, and it is possible that in the future power distribution methods and the mix of power sources will change radically.

BACKGROUND

People have always feared the power of lightning. Ancient peoples undoubtedly knew of static electricity (as in making sparks by walking across wool rugs). Some archaeologists believe that certain ancient Mes-

opotamian and Egyptian pots might have been batteries, perhaps for creating metal plating on jewelry or weapons. However, nothing lasting was developed until electricity had a scientific basis. Benjamin Franklin's famous experiment—flying a kite in the thunderstorm—proved that lightning is essentially the same phenomenon as static electricity. Besides leading to lightning rods to protect from lightning, the discovery encouraged other researchers to seek the power of lightning.

DEVELOPMENT OF ELECTRICAL POWER

In 1800, Alessandro Volta demonstrated that two different metals, connected by a wire and placed in an acid solution, could generate electricity—just as millions of lead-acid car batteries have done in the twentieth century. In 1801, Sir Humphry Davy demonstrated an arc lamp, which got some use. In 1832, both Michael Faraday and Joseph Henry demonstrated generators, although these were only laboratory-scale machines.

Batteries were still the major power source in 1837, when the first electrical appliance arrived: the telegraph. This device revolutionized communications. A telegraph operator could instantly send a coded message through a wire by using a "key" to connect and disconnect electrical power. Hundreds or thousands of kilometers away, the message was received when the bursts of transmitted electricity moved a tiny electromagnet in a pattern that could be decoded by the operator at that end.

Then Thomas Edison, the towering figure in electrical power, invented the incandescent lightbulb in 1870 (the same year that Joseph Wilson Swan also developed one in England). When Edison tried to sell lights, there were few buyers because batteries were too expensive. In a desperate race with creditors, Edison's company built improved industrial-sized generators, strung wires, and discovered vital refinements, including fuses and switches. Edison invented the electric utility, which allowed thousands of electrical inventions to follow.

Edison's direct current, however, could not be increased in voltage to go more than a few kilometers. Nikola Tesla's invention of the alternating current (AC) motor allowed electricity to increase in voltage to press through resistance in the wires and then decrease in voltage at the using site. AC electrical grids began to serve customers tens, hundreds, then thousands of kilometers away. Mass production and im-

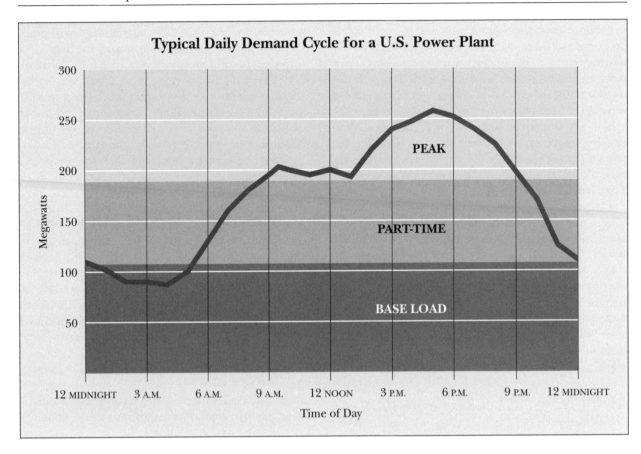

Typical Daily Demand Cycle for a U.S. Power Plant

Megawatts

300

250

200

150

100

50

PEAK

PART-TIME

BASE LOAD

12 MIDNIGHT   3 A.M.   6 A.M.   9 A.M.   12 NOON   3 P.M.   6 P.M.   9 P.M.   12 MIDNIGHT

Time of Day

provements in technology allowed the price per kilowatt of electricity to drop from dollars to mere cents.

POWER FROM COAL

Anything with chemical energy, motion, or a difference in temperature has the potential to generate electrical power. Combustion of fossil fuels has been the greatest energy source, and coal is the most heavily used fossil fuel. Its abundance (particularly in the United States and China) makes it cheap, and some estimate that coal could provide most of the world's total energy by itself for more than a century.

Most coal-fired generators boil water to steam, which flows through turbine blades similar to those of jet engines. Such plants cause complaints because they also release soot and sulfur dioxide (from sulfur impurities in the coal) through their smokestacks. Also, they only transform one-third of the coal energy into electricity, the balance being lost as "waste heat."

For older plants in rich countries, low-sulfur coal is burned or various scrubbing technologies are used to clean the exhaust gas. Filters or electrostatic plates

may be used to catch exhaust dust. Calcium carbonate ($CaCO_3$) dust in the combustion chamber turns the sulfur dioxide into sodium sulfate, which can be caught as dust. Coal can also be cleaned of sulfur and metals before being burned. However, poorer countries that cannot afford to implement such technologies often simply must suffer with dirty, unhealthful air.

More advanced coal-fired plants avoid generating pollutants that must be cleaned from the exhaust gases. Combined-cycle plants heat a water-coal mixture, so hydrogen and oxygen in the water (H_2O) generate hydrogen sulfide (H_2S, which can be easily stripped out), methane (CH_4), and carbon monoxide (CO). Burning the latter two gases shoots hot gases through a turbine. Gases leaving the turbine "topping cycle" make steam in a boiler, just as in the old plants. Combining the two cycles yields efficiencies greater than 50 percent.

Another advanced method, fluidized-bed combustion, uses a hot bed of sand with coal, air, and calcium carbonate flowing up through the sand. Slag at the top contains calcium sulfate, so air cleaning is easier. Fluidized-bed systems often increase efficiency with a liquid-metal topping cycle. Molten metals, such as sodium or potassium, can stand hotter temperatures than steam, so one of these metals is circulated through pipes in the fluidized bed and out to a turbine. Waste heat from that topping cycle then powers a steam boiler.

Coal-fired plants can be clean and efficient, but the required equipment generally involves large, expensive plants, with the equipment cost being a major part of the electricity cost. Hence, coal-fired plants must run nearly continuously to pay for themselves. As such, they are "base-load" plants.

POWER FROM OIL, HYDROENERGY, AND FUEL CELLS

Plants burning oil or natural gas (CH_4) use the same gas and steam turbines as coal-fired plants. They can be built much more cheaply because the fuel can be easily cleaned of sulfur, they have more concentrated energy, and pumping fluids is easier than moving solids. However, these fuels are more expensive. Thus, oil- and gas-fired electricity is more expensive than coal-fired, and it is cheaper for the owners not to run them all the time. Consequently, oil- and gas-fired plants are often "peaking plants," switched on when electrical demand is highest and off when demand drops.

Hydroelectric power (hydroenergy) is the modern version of ancient waterwheels. Water from a dammed river flows down through a turbine. Hydroenergy is cheap and is available on a few minutes' notice. The limitation is that most good sites in the developed countries already have dams. Likewise, tidal power, as in the Bay of Fundy and the Rance River delta, has limited sites.

Fuel cells are also more efficient and less polluting. They operate as batteries do, except that fossil fuels become carbon dioxide and water at the electrodes. Fuel cells yield efficiencies as high as 70 percent; if the catalysts can be made cheaply enough, fuel cells may eventually dominate the market. Some researchers have even suggested the development of sugar-powered fuel cells, based on the principle that all life is powered by biological sugar fuel cells.

POWER FROM NUCLEAR REACTORS

Nuclear fission (splitting atoms) is another way to get heat to spin turbines. Heavy metals (uranium and heavier elements) are less stable than other elements.

Certain isotopes (versions of an element with more or less neutrons) are radioactive because they naturally fission into lighter elements, emitting heat and radiation in the process. When a critical mass of fissionable material is brought together, neutrons released from radioactive decay trigger fissions of enough other atoms to cause a self-sustaining nuclear chain reaction.

A secret Allied World War II project culminated in two fission bombs being dropped on Japan in 1945, ending the war. It was predicted that this awesome technology would supplant other energy sources and produce "electricity too cheap to meter." Breeder reactors were designed both to produce power and to bombard slightly radioactive material to transmute it into fuel.

Fission energy has not achieved prices lower than coal-fired electricity, and there are long-term costs of protecting spent (but still radioactive) fuel from accidental release or diversion into bombs. The most important immediate cost factor is that a power plant, as opposed to a bomb, must operate for years without killing people or damaging the equipment. This protection involves great expense, because a fission reactor produces intense radiation. Personnel must be shielded by massive amounts of lead and concrete, and much of the structure of a reactor can be weakened by neutron embrittlement during years of operation. Worse, an out-of-control fission reactor can overheat, explode (although not as powerfully as a bomb), and release highly poisonous radioactive materials. Consequently, fission reactors must have complex redundant safety features and containment domes to protect against radioactive leaks. Breeder reactors, with their massive neutron fluxes, are the most likely reactors to have serious accidents.

High-temperature gas reactors could operate at higher temperatures, could have greater safety margins, and could have continuously replaced spherical fuel elements. However, the 1986 Chernobyl reactor disaster (in what was then the Soviet Union) and the earlier accident at Three Mile Island, Pennsylvania, in 1979, have caused the public to have a negative view of fission, so research into gas reactors has not received sufficient funding.

Nuclear fusion (combining lighter atoms into heavier ones) is being researched, but it is an unlikely competitor. In the Sun, four hydrogen atoms are fused into one helium atom. A reactor on Earth making a similar reaction could not achieve the pressure of the

Sun, so it would have to compensate with higher temperature (held in by a magnetic field) and heavier isotopes of hydrogen (deuterium and tritium). Advantages to fusion would be that hydrogen isotope fuels are essentially inexhaustible and that a fusion reactor with mechanical problems would simply stop rather than going out of control. The problems would be that fusion, with its heavier hydrogen isotopes, generates neutron fluxes comparable to those of a fission breeder, which would soon damage the complex magnetic containment system. Worse, fusion reactor heat flux per unit volume is less than that of fission reactors, so costs per kilowatt would be high.

POWER FROM WIND, PHOTOVOLTAIC CELLS, AND GEOTHERMAL SOURCES

Wind power was reborn in the energy crisis of the 1970's. Tax incentives given during the energy crisis allowed "wind farms" in high-wind areas to approach profitability. Eventually, these machines evolved into more cost-effective systems. Then gears were developed to accommodate a range of wind speeds. Today, wind systems produce power at prices comparable to coal-fired plants, and wind systems can operate profitably in areas with less than maximum wind. However, wind power is variable. An electrical grid cannot count on receiving more than 20 percent of its power from wind lest a calm day cause a power failure.

Photovoltaic (solar) cells are large transistors that produce electricity when struck by sunlight. Prices of photovoltaic power dropped from hundreds of times that of grid power in the 1960's to three times that of coal-fired power in the mid-1990's. Further price drops from lower production cost, higher cell efficiencies, and the integration of cells into building construction could allow photovoltaics to produce many times the electricity presently used. (Production peaks during afternoon peak demand, but production stops after dark.) Even if prices do not decline, photovoltaics are competitive for small and distant sites (such as roadside phones and railroad signals) because they do not require large installations and they have no moving parts.

Geothermal energy taps hot steam underground to run turbines. Advanced systems can use hot water, and future systems may pump fluids (such as water or helium) into areas of hot rock so the fluids can carry heat back up to a power plant. If drilling costs could be reduced sufficiently, geothermal energy could grow into a major source of electricity.

OCEAN ENERGIES, EFFICIENCY, AND COGENERATION

If the foregoing systems do not provide enough power, more exotic methods may conceivably be used in the future. Ocean waves and currents could supply a major fraction of energy used. The difference between hot tropical ocean waters and the near-freezing deep water has powered experimental power plants, and this ocean thermal energy conversion (OTEC) could theoretically supply many times the world's electrical use. However, many practical problems remain to be solved.

Finally, increased efficiency of electrical use would have the same effect as more generators, perhaps as much as 75 percent more, and at costs cheaper than building new power plants. There are hundreds of ways to increase the efficiency of electrical use, including more efficient electric motors, compact fluorescent lights, greater use of light-emitting diodes (LEDs), more insulation, smart windows, and solid state displays instead of picture tubes in televisions and computer monitors. (The last item alone could retire the equivalent of several nuclear power plants.)

A similar increase in efficiency comes from cogeneration, the use of "waste heat" from power plants for other uses, such as district heating or chemical processing. Because most power plants are far less than 50 percent efficient, full cogeneration would effectively double energy from electric utilities. Many industrial plants are adding cogeneration to existing heating operations. Ultimately, fuel cells might be made small enough to combine water heating and space heating with electrical generation, making houses tiny power plants.

ISSUES FOR ELECTRIC UTILITIES

The electric power industry is one of the largest in the world, generating power and maintaining cables linking generators and power uses. Such networks entail technology and management issues affecting trillions of dollars. First, the power sources must be chosen.

Second, storing electricity is expensive, so generated power must be used when generated. Consequently, generating capacity must be enough to cover the highest use "peaks" in early afternoon (notably air-conditioning), morning, and early evening. Generators are not fully used at other times. Consequently, utilities increasingly charge extra for peak times, charge less for off-peak hours, and offer bonuses for appliances that switch off on command.

Likewise, some areas have seasonal variations in

supply and demand. Pacific Northwest power dams have maximum water flow during spring and summer, when the Southwest has the greatest air-conditioning load. In the winter, water flow is low, but the Southwest has less demand then. High voltage lines allow the two regions to exchange power. A world grid has been suggested for much greater savings.

Batteries for vehicles and portable appliances are a growing part of electricity use. Dry cells cost the equivalent of dollars per kilowatt hour. Liquid-cell batteries, such as the lead-sulfuric acid batteries for cars, are cheaper, but they are still expensive and heavy. Furthermore, as much as one-third of energy is lost. Increasing battery performance and lowering costs are key to practical electric-driven cars. Such cars would decrease pollution (one big plant cleans emissions better than thousands of car engines), and energy efficiency would increase (gasoline engines have low efficiency). They would vastly increase power plant construction, and nightly charging would help balance the day peak.

Finally, electrical utilities are large enough to be a major factor in possible greenhouse warming caused by increased carbon dioxide in the atmosphere. If greenhouse warming continues at its present rate, there will be a greater push toward efficiency and away from fossil fuels.

Roger V. Carlson

Electrical power lines demarcate much of the American landscape. (©Alexfiodorov/Dreamstime.com)

FURTHER READING

Bodanis, David. *Electric Universe: How Electricity Switched on the Modern World.* London: Little, Brown, 2005.

Breeze, Paul. *Power Generation Technologies.* Burlington, Mass.: Elsevier/Newnes, 2005.

Casazza, J. A., and Frank Delea. *Understanding Electric Power Systems.* New York: Wiley, 2003.

Flavin, Christopher, and Nicholas Lenssen. *Powering the Future: Blueprint for a Sustainable Electricity Industry.* Washington, D.C.: Worldwatch Institute, 1994.

Gabriel, Mark A. *Visions for a Sustainable Energy Future.* Lilburn, Ga.: Fairmont Press, 2008.

Grigsby, Leonard Lee, ed. *Electric Power Generation, Transmission, and Distribution.* Boca Raton, Fla.: CRC Press, 2007.

Grubb, Michael, Tooraj Jamasb, and Michael G. Pollitt. *Delivering a Low-Carbon Electricity System: Technologies, Economics, and Policy.* New York: Cambridge University Press, 2008.

Kutz, Myer, ed. *Environmentally Conscious Alternative Energy Production.* Hoboken, N.J.: John Wiley, 2007.

Shively, Bob, and John Ferrare. *Understanding Today's Electricity Business.* San Francisco: Enerdynamics, 2007.

Warkentin-Glenn, Denise. *Electric Power Industry in Nontechnical Language.* 2d ed. Tulsa, Okla.: Penn-Well Books, 2006.

WEB SITE

U.S. ENVIRONMENTAL PROTECTION AGENCY
Electric Power
http://www.energy.gov/energysources/
electricpower.htm

SEE ALSO: Biofuels; Coal; Cogeneration; Department of Energy, U.S.; Energy economics; Energy Policy Act; Energy storage; Fuel cells; Geothermal and hydrothermal energy; Greenhouse gases and global climate change; Hydroenergy; International Atomic Energy Agency; Nuclear energy; Ocean current energy; Ocean thermal energy conversion; Ocean wave energy; Photovoltaic cells; Solar energy; Wind energy.

Emery. *See* Corundum and emery

Eminent domain. *See* Takings law and eminent domain

Endangered species

CATEGORY: Plant and animal resources

Because endangered plants and animals constitute a large and growing proportion of all organisms on Earth, their loss would mean a devastating decline of proven and potential resources for agriculture, medicine, and the global economy. Their vanishing would also result in the deprivation of less tangible but also important ecological and aesthetic benefits.

BACKGROUND

Although countless species have passed from an endangered condition to extinction throughout the history of life on Earth, the concept of "endangered species" is a human creation. After humans emigrated from their birthplace in Africa and populated large areas of Europe and Asia, they began imperiling the habitats and lives of their fellow earthlings, often to the point of extinction. With the growth of advanced industrialized societies, this rate of extinction increased. For example, during this period such creatures as the dodo, great auk, and passenger pigeon ceased to exist. Some people, such as George Perkins Marsh in his *Man and Nature* (1864), protested against humanity's mindless assault on wild flora and fauna, but other scientists became enthusiastically involved in locating and exploiting the Earth's natural resources. Conservation efforts did begin in Africa, India, and North America in the late nineteenth and early twentieth centuries, but not until the develop-

ment of the modern environmental movement in the second half of the twentieth century did large numbers of people, scientists as well as laypersons, recognize the dire status of endangered species and begin to become actively engaged in their preservation.

NATURE, QUANTITY, AND VARIETY OF ENDANGERED SPECIES RESOURCES

Lawyers, landowners, businesspeople, and environmentalists have understood the term "endangered species" from their distinctive viewpoints, but scientists, striving for objectivity, have defined endangered species as undomesticated plants and animals with so few interbreeding individuals that the species faces imminent extinction in all or most of its habitat. The numbers can range from single individuals—such as "Lonesome George," the last member of a species of Galápagos tortoise—to fewer than twenty whooping cranes in the late 1940's, to thousands of such whale species as the blue, bowhead, humpback, and gray. When wild species have abundant but declining numbers in their ecological niches, they are often described as "threatened." Some scientists classify species as safe, vulnerable, endangered, or critical in quantitative terms, depending on the probability of a species' declining by a certain percentage over the subsequent fifty years. With the growth of legislation to protect threatened and endangered species, such as the Endangered Species Act (1973) in the United States, lawmakers discovered that, to save these species, they also had to protect their habitats, because they needed not only food, water, air, and light but also sites for breeding, reproduction, and rearing offspring.

Uncertainty exists about how many different life-forms now exist on Earth. Estimates range from 1.5 million to as high as 30 or even 100 million. Further uncertainty exists about the precise numbers of endangered species. Based on samples of species numbers that scientists of the International Union for Conservation of Nature (IUCN) had evaluated through 2006, the percentage of endangered species might be as high as 40 percent of all life-forms, which would mean 600,000 to 12 million endangered species, depending on whether one accepts low or high evaluations for total species numbers. When scientifically counted rather than estimated numbers are proffered, as they are in IUCN's Red List of Endangered Species, the figures are considerably smaller: In 2007, the list stated that more than 40,000 species were at "heightened risk," with 16,306 at an "extreme risk" of extinction. In May, 2007, the numbers given by the U.S. Environmental Protection Agency were 1,351 endangered American invertebrates, plants, and animals. Because of the continuing discoveries of both safe and endangered species, these numbers must be viewed as tentative.

AGRICULTURE AND ENDANGERED SPECIES RESOURCES

Some scientists estimate that more than 80,000 plant species are edible, but, throughout history, humans have utilized only about 10 percent of these for food. In advanced industrialized societies, the number of species employed in commercialized agriculture was considerably smaller, about 150, and by the twenty-first century, an even smaller number, fewer then 20, had become the source of 95 percent of the world's food. Nonedible plants also serve humankind, by purifying water, enhancing soil fertility, and moderating climate changes. Other species—such as bees, birds, and bats—have had a pivotal influence in pollinating the world's crops. However, declines among various species of these pollinators have led scientists to search for causes and induced governments to protect the most seriously threatened. The extinctions of some species of pollinators have already caused reduced harvests of certain fruits and vegetables. Because of the mixture of wild and domesticated pollinators, placing a monetary value on these resources

is difficult, though some have ventured an estimate as high as $200 million. Doubt also exists about precisely how many of the more than 100,000 pollinators are endangered, but even domesticated bee species have undergone an alarming drop in numbers that has created concern among agriculturalists. These pollinators are sometimes called keystone species because they serve an ecological role much greater than their numbers by directly and indirectly influencing the kinds and quantities of many other species. Just as in architecture the removal of a keystone leads to the collapse of an arch, the extinction of these species will result in the extinctions of many other species and the collapse of entire communities of life-forms.

Another role for endangered plants in agriculture is in breeding programs. When an endangered plant becomes extinct, an irreplaceable store of genetic information is lost for humanity. Some of these genes may contain information on how to resist disease, counteract insects, or survive droughts. Plant geneticists have pointed out that massive monocultures, which rely on a restricted variety of plants, pose great dangers, because disease, drought, and insect infestations can quickly destroy millions of hectares. By using species of wild plants, botanists have been able to create crops that are pest-, disease-, and drought-resistant. Because many of these plants are threatened or endangered, various countries are collecting, organizing, stockpiling, and preserving seeds of these species in "seed banks," to be drawn on for breeding

Endangered and Threatened and Species, 2008

	MAM-MALS	BIRDS	REP-TILES	AMPHIB-IANS	FISHES	SNAILS	CLAMS	CRUSTA-CEANS	INSECTS	ARACH-NIDS	PLANTS
Total listings	**357**	**275**	**119**	**32**	**151**	**76**	**72**	**22**	**61**	**12**	**747**
Endangered species	325	254	79	21	85	65	64	19	51	12	599
United States	69	75	13	13	74	64	62	19	47	12	598
Other countries	256	179	66	8	11	1	2	—	4	—	1
Threatened species	32	21	40	11	66	11	8	3	10	—	148
United States	12	15	24	10	65	11	8	3	10	—	146
Other countries	20	6	16	1	1	—	—	—	—	—	2

Source: Data from U.S. Department of Commerce, *Statistical Abstract of the United States, 2009,* 2009.
Note: Numbers reflect species listed by U.S. government as "threatened" or "endangered"; actual worldwide totals of species that could be considered threatened or endangered are unknown but are believed to be higher.

purposes when new diseases, pests, and weather conditions cause serious reductions of those plants upon which human health and life depend. An example of such a seed bank in the United States is the National Plant Germplasm System in Colorado, under the aegis of the Department of Agriculture.

ENDANGERED SPECIES AND MEDICINE

Throughout their history on Earth human beings have used nature as a kind of pharmacopoeia, utilizing plant and animal products to alleviate sickness and cure various diseases. For example, the bark of a willow tree was the source of a substance that reduced fever and pain (this substance later resulted in the commercial drug aspirin). Even though researchers, especially those active during and since the chemical revolution of the eighteenth century, have developed a growing number of artificial drugs that have proved increasingly effective in treating certain infectious

and degenerative diseases, modern medicine continues to depend on plants and animals to provide substances that treat, and even cure, diseases directly or that serve as precursors to creating drugs that can treat or cure a variety of human ills. In the late twentieth and early twenty-first centuries, some scientists estimated that one-fourth to one-half of all medicines prescribed by doctors derive in some way from natural sources. For example, more than three million Americans who suffer from heart disease rely on digitalis, a drug derived from the purple foxglove plant. Even recent drugs often have their source in nature. Between 1998 and 2002 more than 70 percent of small-molecule drugs licensed by the U.S. Food and Drug Administration could be traced to natural sources. According to the World Health Organization, many people in developing countries depend on natural remedies for more than three-quarters of their medical needs. While many of the plant and animal species

The proboscis monkey, whose name is taken from its prominent nose, is an endangered species native to Borneo. Scientists estimate that only one thousand such monkeys remain. (AP/Wide World Photos)

on which the developed and developing worlds depend are abundant, an increasing number of these are threatened or endangered.

What is worrisome is that only a small portion of the world's flora and fauna have been studied for possible medical benefits, and these species are disappearing at an accelerated rate. Plants, animals, and even microbes on land and in fresh and salt water possess vast numbers of chemical compounds with potential benefits for medicine that have barely begun to be analyzed. This is particularly true of species in tropical rain forests. The National Cancer Institute has estimated that two to three thousand tropical plants contain cancer-fighting chemicals. Other plants have been the source of drugs that have proven effective in treating malaria, high blood pressure, and other diseases. Nevertheless, these rain forests continue to be cut down and burned at such a high rate that, within fifty years, 20 to 30 percent of the Amazon, for example, will be converted into savanna. Only about 1,000 of the more than 125,000 flowering plant species in these tropical forests have been studied for their potential medicinal benefits. If the present rate of destruction continues, many of the endangered species will become extinct before scientists can examine them.

COMMERCIAL USES OF ENDANGERED PLANT AND ANIMAL SPECIES

To certain environmentalists the commercial use of endangered species is something that, for all times and under all circumstances, should be condemned. These environmentalists believe that the historical evidence is clear: Commercial overexploitation of many plant and animal species has led to their extinctions. On the other hand, certain economists point out that endangered species exist in a world of humans, whose needs for food, clothing, shelter, and work have to be taken into consideration. In such an analysis, trade-offs are inevitable. However, calculating a dollar value for endangered species has proved difficult. In general, biodiversity serves humanity in many ways, because healthy ecosystems provide the clean air and water and useful plants and animals that ultimately make human life possible. Because many plants and animals have limited commercial benefits, their ecological services tend to be undervalued. Some scientists have tried to measure the value of biodiversity quantitatively, but because of the complex interactions within ecosystems and the complex ways in which humans interact with these ecosystems, the estimates that have been made have had only limited usefulness for policy analysts.

In contrast, concrete evidence does exist about the negative effects of commercialization on endangered species. For example, passenger pigeons, despite their immense numbers in the United States in the early nineteenth century, were overhunted for food and sport, leading to their total extinction in the early twentieth century. In developing countries the need for food, shelter, and an improved way of life has led to the destruction of the habitats of many plants and animals. In Madagascar, for instance, a periwinkle that is the source of alkaloids important in the treatment of certain cancers is close to disappearing in the wild. The unsustainable hunting of various land mammals in Central Africa has created the so-called "bushmeat crisis," in which several species, including primates, have been declared critically endangered. The global trade in endangered species is big business, with a value, according to some studies, of more than $10 billion. Smuggling endangered species has become, next to the drug trade, the world's second most profitable illegal business.

Some countries have allowed the commercial or recreational exploitation of such endangered species as salmon, whales, and elephants, as long as these practices maintain or increase the numbers of the threatened species. Lawmakers and political leaders who are responsible for these practices argue that the value of endangered species often has to be balanced by the human requirements of food and an opportunity for economic betterment. In the United States, lawmakers have discovered that they have to come to terms with landowners on whose properties 90 percent of endangered species reside. This situation has resulted in policies rewarding those owners who practice sustainability for endangered species and their habitats. Even though these practices have resulted in job creation and substantial economic benefits, many environmentalists have been extremely critical of these attempts to balance conservation and commercialization. Since 1975, the Convention on International Trade in Endangered Species of Wild Fauna and Flora (CITES) has fostered global cooperation in preventing the overexploitation of endangered species. Although this treaty has more than 150 signatory states, critics point out that illegal trade continues and endangered species continue to disappear from the Earth.

AESTHETIC, TOURISTIC, AND SPIRITUAL BENEFITS OF ENDANGERED SPECIES

Many conservation biologists and ecologists insist that the real values of endangered species are not extrinsic (economic or instrumental) but intrinsic (scientific, aesthetic, and spiritual). John Muir, the naturalist who once said that the best way to protect American forests was to station a soldier by every tree, felt that species protection was a deeply moral issue. Like the human species, plants and animals have the right to exist on Earth. Certain pure scientists, who believe in knowledge for knowledge's sake, lament the disappearance of so many plants and animals before their chemical composition, structure, and functioning could be understood. Based on the knowledge gained from a selection of endangered species, the extinction of many species has resulted in the permanent loss of much valuable scientific knowledge.

More difficult to measure are the aesthetic and spiritual values of endangered species. Nevertheless, many human beings experience aesthetic pleasure in observing and taking photographs of various plants and animals. The Audubon Society and BirdLife International have as their principal purposes the conservation of all bird species, whether endangered or plentiful. Professional wildlife photographers and filmmakers often try to educate the public about the beauty of all kinds of species, both those with immediate emotional appeal and those whose strangeness requires understanding before appreciation can follow. Environmentalists influenced by religious ideas believe that it is contrary to God's will when human selfishness and greed cause the extinction of endangered species, because, in the biblical book of Genesis, God called all these creatures good.

Some believe that ecotourism offers private and public landowners a profitable way to use endangered species, while maintaining or increasing their numbers. When travelers visit wildlife parks or preserves to view rare plants and animals, they promote personal development, conservation, and the local economy. Costa Rica, for example, has created several "mega reserves" in an attempt to conserve its more than 500,000 plant and animal species. Core areas are kept pristine while surrounding buffer zones are places that ecotourists can visit. The withdrawal of all this land by the state has been compensated for by a billion-dollar-a-year tourism business. Similarly, in Africa conservation biologists have calculated that lions, gorillas, and elephants generate much more money from tourists than if these creatures were killed and their skins and tusks sold illegally. On the other hand, some preservationists warn that this expanding industry can damage sensitive ecosystems with consequent habitat destruction, resulting in the loss of the very species that ecotourists have traveled so far to see.

CONTEXT

Endangered species do not exhibit the easily grasped benefits of domesticated plants and animals. Nevertheless, based on the many national and international laws that have been promulgated for their protection, endangered species constitute an important resource. Conservationists have found it relatively easy to garner public support for such charismatic megafauna as whales and grizzly bears as well as such symbolic birds as bald eagles and peregrine falcons. However, public opinion is less supportive when it comes to gray wolves, who stray from their preserves to prey on livestock, or such microflora as a rock lichen, whose ecosystem services escape most people. Endangered species have become a bone of contention between environmentalists and developers. From the perspective of environmentalists, biodiversity is a necessary condition for the health of the planet and human development. They have tried to convince businesspeople that if ecosystems fail, businesses will fail also. Furthermore, unless humans find ways to live cooperatively and sustainably with other life-forms, they will soon find themselves becoming yet another endangered species.

Robert J. Paradowski

FURTHER READING

Burgess, Bonnie B. *Fate of the Wild: The Endangered Species Act and the Future of Biodiversity.* Athens: University of Georgia Press, 2001.

Chivian, Eric, and Aaron Bernstein, eds. *Sustaining Life: How Human Health Depends on Biodiversity.* New York: Oxford University Press, 2008.

Cothran, Helen, ed. *Endangered Species.* San Diego, Calif.: Greenhaven Press, 2001.

Dobson, Andrew P. *Conservation and Biodiversity.* New York: Scientific American Library, 1996.

Foreman, Paul, ed. *Endangered Species: Issues and Analyses.* New York: Nova Science, 2002.

Littell, Richard. *Endangered and Other Protected Species: Federal Law and Regulation.* Washington, D.C.: Bureau of National Affairs, 1992.

MacKay, Richard. *The Penguin Atlas of Endangered Spe-

cies: A Worldwide Guide to Plants and Animals. New York: Penguin Books, 2002.

Mann, Charles C. *Noah's Choice: The Future of Endangered Species.* New York: Knopf, 1995.

Petersen, Shannon. *Acting for Endangered Species: The Statutory Ark.* Lawrence: University Press of Kansas, 2002.

Wilson, Edward O. *The Future of Life.* New York: Vintage Books, 2003.

WEB SITES

INTERNATIONAL UNION FOR CONSERVATION OF NATURE
http://www.iucn.org/

U.S. ENVIRONMENTAL PROTECTION AGENCY
http://www.epa.gov/

U.S. FISH AND WILDLIFE SERVICE
Endangered Species Program
http://www.fws.gov/endangered/wildlife.html

SEE ALSO: Animals as a medical resource; Biodiversity; Botany; Conservation; Conservation biology; Conservation International; Ecosystems; Endangered Species Act; Environmental degradation, resource exploitation and; Environmental Protection Agency; Food chain; Global Strategy for Plant Conservation; International Union for Conservation of Nature; Plants as a medical resource; Species loss; United Nations Convention on Biological Diversity; United Nations Convention on International Trade in Endangered Species of Wild Fauna and Flora.

Endangered Species Act

CATEGORIES: Laws and conventions; government and resources
DATE: Signed into law December 28, 1973

The Endangered Species Act has been successful in saving and increasing the populations of some endangered species and ecosystems. There is disagreement, however, as to how far the U.S. government should go in its protection of species and their habitats.

BACKGROUND
The first law to authorize federal government action to preserve wildlife was the Lacey Act of 1900. Using

the federal power to regulate interstate commerce, the Lacey Act authorized federal enforcement of state wildlife regulatory laws and allowed the U.S. secretary of agriculture to preserve and restore bird species. In 1920, the U.S. Supreme Court used federal treaty-making authority to override state law and uphold the constitutionality of the Migratory Bird Treaty Act of 1918. The federal government further asserted its authority in the Migratory Bird Conservation Act of 1929 and the Fish and Wildlife Coordination Act of 1934.

In 1939, the management of wildlife was brought under the control of the Department of the Interior as a natural resource. In 1964, the department established the Committee on Rare and Endangered Wildlife Species, which published the "Red Book," the first government listing of fish and wildlife threatened by extinction. Public interest in protecting species from extinction increased during the 1960's, and the first comprehensive federal law in this regard was passed in 1966; the Endangered Species Preservation Act created broad policy without providing enforcement power. Federal agencies were to preserve, to the extent "practicable and consistent" with the primary purposes of the agencies, the habitats of native vertebrate species that the Department of the Interior declared in danger of extinction. The National Wildlife Refuge System was created to allow the department to buy and protect the habitats of endangered species.

In 1969, the Endangered Species Conservation Act extended the Lacey Act to cover interstate commerce in illegally taken reptiles, amphibians, and selected invertebrates. Commercial interests strongly influenced the final act. By 1970 Congress was reconsidering its position on endangered species. In a February 8, 1972, environmental message, President Richard Nixon stated that existing legislation did not provide the tools needed to save disappearing species and that legislation should be passed that would allow a species to be restored before it reached the critical stage. In 1972, the Marine Mammal Protection Act was passed to protect "depleted" marine populations as well as those threatened with extinction.

PROVISIONS
Endangered species legislation that was introduced into Congress in 1972 expanded federal power into areas formerly under state authority. It lowered the endangerment threshold, thereby covering species in a large part of their range. Federal agencies could use

their authority to protect listed species, and private citizens would be allowed to bring suit in court.

With environmental concerns high, there was little controversy when the Endangered Species Act (ESA) was finalized and signed into law. As the Supreme Court stated in *Tennessee Valley Authority v. Hill* (1978), when it upheld stopping construction of the Tellico Dam in order to protect a tiny fish called the snail darter, "the plain language of the Act, buttressed by its legislative history, shows clearly that Congress viewed the value of endangered species as 'incalculable.'" Critics have said that in the environmental furor of the early 1970's, Congress passed the ESA without fully considering the economic effects of the law.

Under the ESA, species in need of protection may be listed by the Fish and Wildlife Service and the National Marine Fisheries Service as either "threatened" or "endangered." Section 7 requires that the activities of federal agencies—including those involved with federal land and resource management plans (LRMPs)—not jeopardize listed species or their habitats. Section 9 has been particularly contentious. One argument concerns whether modification of habitat on private lands consists of a "taking" of an endangered or threatened species that is punishable under law. This was the issue in *Sweet Home Chapter for a Greater Oregon v. Babbitt* (1992), in which the Court upheld the Fish and Wildlife Service's reading of the ESA.

AMENDMENTS AND SUGGESTED CHANGES

The 1978 amendments to the ESA required that designation of the "critical" habitat of a species accompany the listing of the species, and they permitted consideration of the economic impact of the listing. These changes almost stopped the listing of additional species. Amendments to Section 4 required the secretary of the interior to prepare "recovery plans" for all listed species in order to bring the population of a species to a healthy level.

Amendments in 1982 loosened the connection between the listing of a species and its critical habitat designation by requiring concurrent listing of the habitat only to the "maximum extent prudent and determinable." A new approach was instituted to ease enforcement of the act. Called the habitat conservation plan (HCP), it allows "incidental takes" of an endangered species as its habitat is being developed as long as there are plans to minimize the loss of the species and to offset potential future losses. An executive committee consisting of local governments, landowners, developers, and environmentalists directs an HCP, with the Fish and Wildlife Service supervising and approving the plan. Scientific guidelines are laid down by a biological advisory team, which creates population viability analyses (PVAs) to estimate the survival chances for a species.

The 1988 amendments added to the listing procedure by requiring that the Department of the Interior monitor the listing status of a candidate species. They stated that an invertebrate is not to be passed over for a mammal nor an obscure species for a well-known one, and they protected plants on private land. Public input into the recovery planning process was formalized.

Congress began heated debate on reauthorization of the Endangered Species Act in 1992. In 1995, some members of Congress pushed for a repeal or a major overhaul of the ESA, and in April of that year, a congressional moratorium halted the listing of additional species. There were proposals to give the Department of the Interior the power to permit a listed species to become extinct and to remove mandatory protection for endangered species. A rider to a fiscal-year 1997 bill exempted certain flood control activities from review under the act. In the 1997 *Bennett v. Spear* decision, the Supreme Court upheld the right of citizens to sue the government for overenforcement of the ESA if enforcement results in harm to their business.

A number of suggestions were put forward to make the Endangered Species Act more acceptable to all parties while still protecting threatened and endangered species. In 1996, an Endangered Natural Heritage Act was proposed in order to cover loopholes in the ESA and to ensure that listed species recover. Its approach was to have federal agencies "prevent the need of listing species in the future" by conserving depleting species. Another suggestion was to protect ecosystems, or "biologically rich landscapes," rather than concentrating on individual species.

IMPACT ON RESOURCE USE

In the late twentieth century, a contentious debate, involving laypersons as well as scholars, occurred on whether the ESA had been a success or failure. The crux of the disagreements was how to achieve a balance between human needs and those of threatened or endangered species of plants and animals. Some scientists pointed out that the ESA may have saved a few species but its policies actually resulted in the ex-

President Bill Clinton announces the 1999 removal of the bald eagle from the endangered species list, a proclamation that highlighted the success of the Endangered Species Act. (AP/Wide World Photos)

1996, participants at a forum at the University of Wyoming debated the contentious issue of species protection on private and public lands. This debate was not purely academic; ranchers and environmentalists had clashed over the success or failure of the reintroduction of wolves into Yellowstone Park.

Because of these and other critiques of the ESA, two bills for possible amendments were introduced in 1997, one in the House of Representatives, the other in the Senate. Both bills centered on the increasingly critical problem of habitat destruction. It had become clear to both scientists and politicians that all species are part of certain ecosystems, and when species decline, something is wrong with the ecosystem. Thus, the solution to declining numbers lies in fostering viable ecosystems. The Supreme Court had already upheld a Fish and Wildlife Service regulation that defined harm to an endangered species to include habitat destruction. Both bills also included incentives to encourage landowners to preserve species and habitats. In the late 1990's and early 2000's, legal actions led the Fish and Wildlife Service and other agencies to protect many critical habitats in such states as Hawaii and California. In 2001, the law was extended to include not only species in danger of extinction but also distinct populations in particular regions. For example, while certain species of salmon are not in danger of extinction in the Pacific Northwest, some salmon populations are in danger of vanishing from particular areas. These latter populations have been listed as threatened or endangered.

At the start of the twenty-first century many members of the administration of President George W. Bush sided with those who believed that the ESA was inefficient and wasteful of taxpayer dollars and that the law was too onerous, especially for landowners. Certain administrators stopped adding endangered species and critical habitats to the list, unless forced to do so by court order. Environmentalists interpreted these and other actions of the Bush administration as bureaucratic obstacles that resulted in reduced num-

tinction of many more. Furthermore, attempts to preserve every species run counter to evolutionary laws. Libertarians insisted that administering the act often led to the violation of landowners' rights, even prompting some to destroy habitats and eliminate species to prevent government interference.

On the other hand, environmentalists have argued that the ESA has either stabilized or improved the numbers of listed endangered species, with only a small number becoming extinct. Furthermore, administrative faults have been seen as the result of inadequate funding from Congress. In order to resolve the deadlock over what to do with the ESA, discussions have taken place at various venues. For example, in bers of protected species and habitats. In 2003, members of the administration proposed removing the protection of foreign species to permit hunters to kill, circuses to capture, and the pet industry to import animals that are endangered in other countries. As expected, environmentalists reacted negatively to this proposal.

In 2004, an amendment to a defense act exempted military lands from critical habitat designation, if the secretary of defense deemed that protecting these habitats would weaken national security. In 2006, the ESA was further threatened by attempts to remove the protection of critical habitats from the law. Republicans also attacked the $1.6 billion ESA budget, claiming the agency cost much more than it was worth. By the summer of 2008, administrators had succeeded in delisting more than forty species previously designated as endangered, and more than twenty were down-listed from endangered to threatened. Furthermore, President Bush decided that federal officials were not required to consult with scientists when questions arose about whether logging or mining in a particular area might harm an endangered species. In fact, just before leaving office, President Bush put into effect rules that gave federal agencies wide leverage in removing species from the endangered list, without any checks and balances by the Fish and Wildlife Service or the National Oceanic and Atmospheric Administration.

Soon after Barack Obama became U.S. president in January, 2009, he restored rules requiring agencies to consult with relevant government scientists to make sure that endangered species would continue to be protected. Congress then passed a bill to enable the Obama administration to overturn the "eleventh-hour" Bush regulations that had weakened the ESA. Obama insisted that his policy would be to find ways to strengthen the act, not weaken it. The 2009 budget for the ESA was $146 billion, and the secretary of the interior, Ken Salazar, took the side of environmentalists in several controversial issues. For example, he affirmed the success of the reintroduction of the gray wolf to the continental United States by removing it from the endangered-species list. In March, 2009, the Fish and Wildlife Service announced that a rare Hawaiian plant, *Phyllostegia hispida*, would become the first species to be protected by the Obama administration, and environmentalists expressed the hope that newly appointed officials would move expeditiously to protect the more than 250 endangered-species candidates whose protection had been stalled by various bureaucratic procedures during the Bush administration.

Colleen M. Driscoll, updated by Robert J. Paradowski

FURTHER READING

Baur, Donald C., and William Robert Irvin, eds. *Endangered Species Act: Law, Policy, and Perspectives*. Chicago: Section of Environment, Energy, and Resources, American Bar Association, 2002.

Burgess, Bonnie B. *Fate of the Wild: The Endangered Species Act and the Future of Biodiversity*. Athens: University of Georgia Press, 2001.

Czech, Brian, and Paul R. Krausman. *The Endangered Species Act: History, Conservation Biology, and Public Policy*. Baltimore: Johns Hopkins University Press, 2001.

Foreman, Paul, ed. *Endangered Species: Issues and Analyses*. New York: Nova Science, 2002.

Goble, Dale D., J. Michael Scott, and Frank W. Davis, eds. *The Endangered Species Act at Thirty: Renewing the Conservation Promise*. Washington, D.C.: Island Press, 2006.

Liebesman, Lawrence R., and Rafe Petersen. *Endangered Species Deskbook*. Washington, D.C.: Environmental Law Institute, 2003.

Littell, Richard. *Endangered and Other Protected Species: Federal Law and Regulation*. Washington, D.C.: Bureau of National Affairs, 1992.

Mann, Charles C. *Noah's Choice: The Future of Endangered Species*. New York: Knopf, 1995.

Petersen, Shannon. *Acting for Endangered Species: The Statutory Ark*. Lawrence: University Press of Kansas, 2002.

Rohlf, Daniel J. *The Endangered Species Act: A Guide to Its Protections and Implementation*. Stanford, Calif.: Stanford Environmental Law Society, 1989.

Scott, J. Michael, Dale D. Goble, and Frank W. Davis, eds. *Conserving Biodiversity in Human-Dominated Landscapes*. Vol. 2 in *The Endangered Species Act at Thirty*. Washington, D.C.: Island Press, 2006.

Sullins, Tony A. *ESA: Endangered Species Act*. Chicago: American Bar Association, 2001.

Vega, Evelyn T., ed. *Endangered Species Act Update and Impact*. New York: Nova Science, 2008.

WEB SITE

U.S. FISH AND WILDLIFE SERVICE
Endangered Species Program
http://www.fws.gov/endangered/wildlife.html

SEE ALSO: Biodiversity; Department of the Interior, U.S.; Ecozones and biogeographic realms; Endangered species; Environmental Protection Agency; Fish and Wildlife Service, U.S.; National parks and nature reserves; Species loss.

Energy crises. *See* Oil embargo and energy crises of 1973 and 1979

Energy economics

CATEGORIES: Energy resources; social, economic, and political issues

Energy is needed by modern society to refine ores, manufacture products, transport people and goods, heat buildings, and power appliances. Various forms of energy, from simple combustion to nuclear and solar power, all have economic advantages and disadvantages, and changes in energy economics, society, and international politics are interrelated.

BACKGROUND

The manufacture of any product requires energy inputs. Producing a book, for example, requires sawing and trucking lumber; pulping and processing the pulp into paper; transporting the paper; composing, printing, and delivering the book; and finally, providing lighting and space conditioning in the buildings in which it is written, made, and sold.

The economics of energy influence decisions in a wide range of industries. Rising petroleum prices in the 1970's caused tens of billions of dollars to be invested in more efficient automobiles, thicker walls, more insulation, and better furnaces. They also led to increases in coal mining and research in other energy technologies. Increased natural gas prices caused farmers to increase their use of nitrogen-fixing crops (such as alfalfa and soybeans) in attempts to reduce reliance on synthetic nitrogen fertilizer. Energy choices help shape societies. Although many energy technologies have been used through time, the dynamics of the changes have remained the same, and those dynamics will continue to determine future energy changes.

ELASTICITY OF ENERGY DEMAND

Economists agree that, normally, increasing price causes people to buy less of a product and eventually to find substitutes. During much of the twentieth century, however, it was believed that market forces did not apply to energy: Energy use, it was thought, would rise or fall in a straight line with the economy. Real energy prices drifted downward until the early 1970's, and demand did move according to the strength of the economy, including a drop during the Great Depression in the 1930's. Then, during the Arab-Israeli War (the Yom Kippur War) in 1973, Arab petroleum-exporting countries declared an oil embargo against governments supporting Israel. Besides not selling directly to targeted countries, participating producers lowered production to agreed-upon quota levels so that large supplies of petroleum would not be available for resale to target countries.

This action demonstrated the market power available to a production cartel of dominant producers. The Organization of Petroleum Exporting Countries (OPEC), of which Arab producers are a part, used that power to increase petroleum prices from $2.90 per barrel in mid-1973 to $11.65 by December of that year. Six years later, the 1979 Islamic Revolution in Iran disrupted production and pushed prices toward $39 per barrel. However, all cartels plant the seeds of their own destruction. Energy users sought cheaper, more reliable energy sources. The high oil prices spurred drilling in new areas, which eventually generated competing production. More important, consumers used more coal; drove less; bought smaller, more efficient cars; lowered thermostats; and built more efficient houses. They even used less electricity (with baneful effects for the nuclear fission industry).

As demand began to slip below production capacity, Saudi Arabia reduced production to maintain low supplies. By 1985, however, Saudi sales were moving rapidly toward zero, while other OPEC members were producing more than their quotas and being enriched. Finally, Saudi Arabia increased its oil production, and the cost per barrel plummeted to nearly $10 before drifting upward again over several years to a market-set range of the high teens to low twenties. With inflation factored in, petroleum prices had returned to the levels of the mid-twentieth century.

By the summer of 2008, oil prices had risen to $147 a barrel, driven up by world events, concern over shrinking reserves, and lack of stability in the Middle East. The recession of 2008 caused consumption and, therefore, prices to decline. While developed countries encouraged substitution of oil consumption with renewable energy sources, developing countries such as China and India increased their demand for oil.

Another energy industry, the uranium industry, had a shorter but more painful cartel experience in the 1970's and 1980's. Price increases caused by an unofficial cartel of producer governments helped cripple plans for reactor construction, causing prices—and the unofficial cartel—to collapse.

COMBUSTION AND ENERGY EFFICIENCY

A basic rule is that the simplest and cheapest energy sources are the first to be exploited. Slavery and animal power were the prime movers for ancient industry. Only declining population near the end of the Roman Empire contributed to an increased use of waterwheels for grinding grain. Once such mechanisms were developed, they proved more cost-effective than intensive human or animal labor because waterwheels do not have to be fed, as animals and human workers do. However, centuries had passed before society was driven to experiment with waterwheels and mills.

Likewise, combustion energy came into use long before nuclear energy or solar energy from photovoltaic cells because it was easier to develop. In the industrialized world the age of wood fuel has passed, but there are still large reserves of coal, petroleum, and natural gas to be exploited. Therefore, competition from new reserves and better mining techniques may keep nonfossil energy sources minor for decades or even centuries to come. Sources of petroleum and natural gas that have yet to be exploited include deposits beneath deep ocean waters. Considerable investment has been made in tapping the oil found in tar sands in Canada, and coal use continues to increase—including the manufacture of synthetic liquid fuels from coal. Finally, according to some theorists, methane hydrates (methane frozen together with ice) may prove to contain more energy than all other fossil fuels combined.

The advantages of combustion energy can be seen in the differences between heating a house with oil and heating with an electric heat pump. Installing an oil furnace is not a major part of the house construction, and oil may be bought as needed. A heat pump (warming the indoors by cooling air from outside the house) may deliver more heat than even an extremely efficient burner. However, a heat pump is more complex than a furnace, so it costs more to buy and maintain. Moreover, electricity from a power plant is usually only about one-third efficient, with two-thirds lost as waste heat, so a heat pump must produce three times the heat of the burner just to equal the burner's heat efficiency. Electrical resistance heating uses three times the fuel of a furnace.

Amory Lovins used this reasoning in his *Soft Energy Paths: Toward a Durable Peace* (1977) to argue that most tasks using only low-grade heat could be best served by combustion. He continued the argument by saying that if efficiency could be improved, energy use could decrease. People do not need energy per se: They need the services that energy provides. Thus, if end-use efficiency can be doubled, energy production can be cut in half. Improved energy efficiency can produce the same results as new mines, oil wells, and electric utilities, and energy conservation is often much cheaper than obtaining new energy.

However, improving efficiency presents a number of difficulties. Rather than several major solutions, energy conservation involves hundreds of minor "fixes." The companies developing and marketing technology for such relatively small tasks are often small companies with less access to expertise and capital than the large energy-producing companies and utilities. End users, especially individuals, have even fewer resources available. Finally, the many minor (and often obscure) improvements in energy efficiency are often too complex and too diffuse for their developers to build a political constituency that could lobby for government subsidies. For all these reasons, only a fraction of the vast potential savings available from increased energy efficiency has been realized.

The comparisons of combustion with more exotic technologies also apply at the level of generating electrical power. Natural gas (mostly methane, CH_4) is expensive fuel compared with coal, but it burns cleanly in a simple burner. Oil burns almost as cleanly, and as a liquid fuel, it is convenient to store and use. Coal is cheapest, but as a solid it is inconvenient, and it has dirty waste products.

NUCLEAR ENERGY ECONOMICS

Nuclear fission offers vast amounts of energy. However, nuclear reactors require expensive materials and safeguards. Moreover, reactors cannot sustain the temperatures of combustion chambers. Lower temperatures mean lower efficiency, so a reactor must use proportionately more energy; it also emits more waste heat per unit of electricity generated than other sources. Finally, radiation eventually damages the structure, so reactors have a limited service life. These factors result in a high overall cost, even with subsidized fuel production and government-provided disposal of nuclear wastes.

Meanwhile, combustion plants have options not available to nuclear plants for increasing efficiency and thus decreasing costs. Waste heat from natural-gas-fired turbines can run a steam turbine "bottoming cycle" to approach efficiencies of 50 percent and more. Coal-fired plants can pretreat the coal with heat and steam to generate methane and carbon monoxide (CO) for burning in a gas turbine. Spent steam from steam turbines can be used for industrial heating (a process known as cogeneration). Fission reactors, although they produce steam, miss this opportunity because they are usually sited away from other facilities for security and safety reasons. Lacking these options, fission reactor designers increased the size of plants in the 1970's to improve efficiency. However, costs, complexity, and risk increased more than proportionately. The accident involving a partial meltdown at the Three Mile Island, Pennsylvania, nuclear plant in 1979 demonstrated the hazards involved.

More important, the complexity and perceived risk of fission reactors caused financial meltdowns. A number of utilities had contracted for construction of fission reactors in the 1960's and 1970's to fill projected electrical needs. When rising prices slowed growth in electrical demand in the 1980's, many generator projects under construction had insufficient markets and were abandoned. Reactor projects that had stretched over many years were particularly expensive to abandon. Billions of dollars were lost, and plans to build fission reactors in the United States virtually came to a halt. Globally, the construction of nuclear power plants continues to decline.

SOLAR ENERGY ECONOMICS
Solar energy has economic problems as well. The resource is vast and free, but it is thinly spread energy, and the equipment to capture it is expensive. As with nuclear fission, most of the cost comes "up front," before power—and revenue—are received. However, with increased investment in solar technology and a commitment by many states and countries to increase generation of energy from renewable sources, the cost of solar energy will become competitive with that of combustion generated energy. However, solar energy stops at night and is undependable because of clouds. The use of solar energy close to the point where it is captured—especially in solar water heaters—can be economically effective. It appears that the cost of solar-generated energy on a larger scale will become competitive with combustion-generated electricity in regions with optimal solar conditions in the next decade. Commitments in California and Hawaii, as well as Germany and Spain, are driving innovation in the solar-energy industry. An interesting historical footnote is that a budding solar-engine industry at the beginning of the twentieth century was destroyed by competition from combustion engines.

The production of electricity by arrays of photovoltaic cells cannot compete economically in areas served by the "electrical grid," which has cheaper power cabled from large generating plants. However, photovoltaics are cheaper at the fringes of the grids (where power costs include electricity plus extensive cabling and poles) and for some small uses. They are also useful in isolated areas not served by utilities. These somewhat limited markets allow photovoltaic production to continue. Continued production allows photovoltaic producers to move down the "learning curve" toward lower costs that may yet allow photovoltaics to work in from the fringe toward the center of the grid.

Photovoltaic prices started in the thousands of dollars per installed watt for spacecraft in the 1960's. As with other electronic devices, prices have dropped steeply. However, as opposed to most electronics, photovoltaic cells must be large so as to cover a large sunlight-collecting area. Even if photovoltaic prices drop to inconsequential levels, the underlying structure supporting the cells will still keep photovoltaic arrays expensive. Thus, for solar energy to compete as a major part of electrical supply, cell efficiency must increase or the arrays must be integrated into other structures, such as roofs and exterior walls of buildings.

TRANSPORTATION ECONOMICS
In the transportation industry, the advantages of simplicity and cost are multiplied for certain fossil fuels. Hydrocarbons, such as gasoline and some slightly heavier petroleum fuels, have more energy by both weight and volume than coal does. For this reason, ships, which used coal-fired boilers at the beginning of the twentieth century, were being powered by oil-fired boilers by the second half of the century. For

smaller vehicles, another crucial advantage of liquid hydrocarbons is that they can be simply and easily pumped into an engine. The complexity of feeding coal to a boiler adds to the cost of running a steam railroad locomotive and is prohibitively expensive for automobiles and trucks.

When hydrocarbon fuels from petroleum eventually become very expensive because of diminishing reserves, there will undoubtedly be replacement fuels, but all potential replacements currently known have expensive disadvantages. Synthetic fuels produced from coal have proved economically unfeasible except in emergencies. Production of ethyl alcohol from agricultural products involves energy losses from farming, from energy used by yeasts to make alcohol, and from the energy required to concentrate the alcohol. Electric automobiles involve the two-thirds waste from electrical generating plants plus the cost of buying and moving massive batteries. A revolution in battery technology is changing those economics.

An electric car charges its battery in Essen, Germany. By 2020, Germany hopes to have one million electric cars on the road, a development that was made possible by an economic stimulus package that stressed the need for alternative forms of energy. (AP/Wide World Photos)

ENERGY RESOURCE BELL CURVES AND ENERGY CRISES

Geologist Marion King Hubbert noted a bell-shaped curve in the use of resources, now commonly called the "Hubbert curve" and often used in estimates of resource use and reserves. (Hubbert first applied his curve to petroleum in the late 1940's and subsequently reviewed and amended his prediction a number of times.) According to the Hubbert curve, a resource is used experimentally at first. Then, use increases rapidly until the resource begins nearing a point of half exhaustion. At that point, difficulty in obtaining the diminishing supplies begins driving up costs, so demand growth begins to slow. As prices continue rising, competing energy sources emerge, and production of them increases. Use of the first resource declines in a mirror image of its earlier rise, and it gradually fades away. Hubbert noticed this pattern in the production of onshore petroleum in the forty-eight contiguous states of the United States. In 1948, he correctly predicted that production in this

region would peak in the early 1970's. He noted that such energy curves had already occurred for other major energy sources in the United States, including firewood, whale oil, anthracite coal, and bituminous coal. Extension of such analyses to world energy production suggested that there would be a worldwide energy crisis after production of oil and gas peaked. Worries about such a crisis encouraged price increases, stockpiling, and government actions that helped create the energy crises of the 1970's.

The discovery of new reserves and the development of new energy sources can cause different kinds of crises that are as damaging economically as shortages are. In the 1930's, a Texas oil boom combined with the Great Depression to reduce petroleum prices to ten cents a barrel, nearly bankrupting the industry. The response was a group of state oil regulatory commissions that limited petroleum production.

Energy economics can have a wide range of ramifications. A by-product of the cheap energy of the mid-twentieth century was the growing problem of waste materials, from junked automobiles to tin cans and, later, aluminum and plastic containers. The seriousness of the problem was recognized in the 1960's, but not until the rise in energy prices of the 1970's was recycling of materials widely adopted, slowly reducing the volume of waste. Perhaps most notably, energy-intensive aluminum was recycled, and waste cans grew more scarce.

The 1970's energy crises resulted in two major economic reforms that will help ameliorate future crises. First, as noted, price increases led to increased efficiency. Second, a major energy source was reborn when the price of natural gas was released from government price controls. At twenty cents per 5.7 cubic meters, gas had been so cheap that it was often not even reported in drilling logs, so supplies were vastly underrated. The possibility exists that in the twenty-first century more energy will come from gas than from petroleum. In addition, those crises spurred research that may eventually yield viable new energy solutions.

In the 1970's, some observers saw the energy crises as an indication that petroleum reserves would be imminently sliding down the diminishing side of Hubbert's bell-shaped curve. Such predictions were premature, but his analyses nevertheless show that energy production must continue evolving. As noted earlier, combustion processes will probably be cheaper than other energy sources for some time, at least in the United States. Nonetheless, if history is an indication, fossil fuels may eventually be supplanted. In 1850, "rock oil" (petroleum) was used only in small amounts, natural gas was a curiosity, and nuclear reactions and the electronic interactions that make solar cells work were entirely unknown. Nonetheless, all these have become important energy sources.

Roger V. Carlson

FURTHER READING

Banks, Ferdinand E. *The Political Economy of World Energy: An Introductory Textbook.* Hackensack, N.J.: World Scientific, 2007.

Craddock, David. *Renewable Energy Made Easy: Free Energy from Solar, Wind, Hydropower, and Other Alternative Energy Sources.* Ocala, Fla.: Atlantic, 2008.

Dumaine, Brian. *The Plot to Save the Planet: How Visionary Entrepreneurs and Corporate Titans Are Creating Real Solutions to Global Warming.* New York: Crown Business, 2008.

Flavin, Christopher, and Nicholas Lenssen. *Power Surge: Guide to the Coming Energy Revolution.* New York: W. W. Norton, 1994.

Lovins, Amory B., et al. *The Energy Controversy: Soft Path Questions and Answers.* Edited by Hugh Nash. San Francisco: Friends of the Earth, 1979.

Pernick, Ron, and Clint Wilder. *The Clean Tech Revolution: The Next Big Growth and Investment Opportunity.* New York: Collins, 2007.

Ridgeway, James. *Powering Civilization: The Complete Energy Reader.* New York: Pantheon Books, 1982.

Shojai, Siamack, ed. *The New Global Oil Market: Understanding Energy Issues in the World Economy.* Westport, Conn.: Praeger, 1995.

Stobaugh, Robert, and Daniel Yergin, eds. *Energy Future: Report of the Energy Project at the Harvard Business School.* New York: Vintage Books, 1980.

Yergin, Daniel. *The Prize: The Epic Quest for Oil, Money, and Power.* New York: The Free Press, 2008.

SEE ALSO: Animal power; Biofuels; Buildings and appliances, energy-efficient; Coal gasification and liquefaction; Cogeneration; Department of Energy, U.S.; Energy Policy Act; Energy politics; Energy storage; Ford, Henry; Fuel cells; Manufacturing, energy use in; Oil embargo and energy crises of 1973 and 1979; Oil industry; Peak oil; Photovoltaic cells; Synthetic Fuels Corporation; Transportation, energy use in.

Energy Policy Act

CATEGORIES: Laws and conventions; government and resources

DATE: Final passage July 29, 2005; signed into law August 8, 2005

The U.S. Energy Policy Act of 2005 authorized government subsidies, loan guarantees, and tax breaks for producers of both conventional and alternative energy as well as a variety of conservation measures. Although its true impact upon resource use has been a source of debate, the act has resulted in changes in U.S. energy policy and raised numerous issues regarding its future.

BACKGROUND

Introduced as the debate over future U.S. energy policy was escalating, in light of supply disruptions and price fluctuations, the Energy Policy Act of 2005 was intended to address concerns about scarcity of energy resources by encouraging increased production of both conventional and unconventional energy resources. Provisions calling for revision of auto emissions standards and permitting drilling for oil in the

Arctic National Wildlife Refuge were stricken from the bill prior to passage. It was introduced in the House of Representatives on April 18, 2005, and passed the final vote of both houses on July 28 and 29. President George W. Bush signed the bill into law on August 8, 2005.

PROVISIONS

The act authorized loan guarantees for energy production methods that minimize or avoid creation of greenhouse gases, such as nuclear energy, "clean coal" technology, and renewable energy sources such as wind, solar, geothermal, and tidal power. The act also increased the amount of ethanol required in gasoline sold in the United States, provided tax breaks for property owners installing energy-efficient features to homes and commercial buildings, offered tax incentives to purchasers of hybrid automobiles, and extended the duration of daylight savings time. Some provisions of the act—such as tax breaks for producers of fossil fuels, emphasis upon expanding coal mining, tax incentives for oil companies drilling in the Gulf of Mexico, research into the potential effects of shale oil extraction on public lands, and making gas and oil companies exempt from portions of the Safe Drinking Water Act—sparked controversy and prompted accusations that the act favored fossil-fuel producers and failed to provide sufficient environmental protections.

IMPACT ON RESOURCE USE

Despite the broad scope of the Energy Policy Act of 2005, many of its provisions had not been implemented as of fiscal year 2008-2009, as Congress had not appropriated much of the money required to implement the provisions. Other provisions were rapidly implemented but produced lukewarm or unintended results; the mandated increase in the ethanol content of gasoline created short-term disruptions in gasoline supplies as refineries struggled to accommodate the changes and contributed to sharp global increases in the price of corn and other cereal grains, exacerbating problems with hunger in some developing countries. Other provisions, such as incentives for purchases of hybrid automobiles, realized modest short-term success as purchases of these automobiles increased and escalating competition among automobile manufacturers resulted in a wider variety of hybrid automobiles entering the marketplace. Still other provisions, such as incentives to make homes and commercial buildings more energy-efficient, appeared to incentivize changes in behavioral patterns.

Michael H. Burchett

WEB SITE

U.S. DEPARTMENT OF ENERGY
Energy Policy Act
http://www.energy.gov/about/EPAct.htm

SEE ALSO: Biofuels; Buildings and appliances, energy-efficient; Climate Change and Sustainable Energy Act; Department of Energy, U.S.; Electrical power; Energy economics; Energy politics; Ethanol; Hydroenergy; United States; Wind energy.

Energy politics

CATEGORY: Social, economic, and political issues

Energy systems affect politics, social mobility, and economic performance. Although wood and human labor continue to be important sources of energy in many countries, modern industrial civilizations have been shaped by access to fossil fuels—principally coal and, more recently, petroleum and natural gas—and they depend on these fuels to function. Energy resources thus are inevitably a concern of governments and a subject of fundamental importance in the making of both domestic and foreign policy. Sometimes those decisions involve issues of war or peace.

BACKGROUND

Historically, civilizations have rested on their energy base. Those that controlled slaves when human labor was the principal source of energy erected pyramids and temples thousands of years ago. Civilizations that did not possess that energy source are buried in the past, often surfacing only as footnotes in ancient history texts.

Modern history can be similarly written. In 1800, nearly a score of countries—including Spain, Portugal, Austria, and Holland—of roughly equal power contended for influence. A century later, those capable of significantly influencing world affairs numbered approximately one-half dozen, some of which were not included in the earlier listing. The winnowing process revolved around coal, the essential fuel for full participation in the Industrial Revolution.

Among the Northern Hemisphere powers, only the United States, Britain, the newly formed Germany, Russia, and Japan possessed it in abundance. Fifty years later, this number had been reduced to the two superpowers of the postwar era: the United States and the Soviet Union. These were two industrialized countries with large indigenous sources of oil: the most efficient, utilized, and strategically important source of energy in the twentieth century. Lacking it, Adolf Hitler planned Germany's World War II strategy around an early acquisition of the oil fields of western Russia and North Africa. Similarly, to maintain access to oil, the United States and a grand alliance composed predominantly of industrialized, oil-importing states fought a war in 1991 to eliminate the threat Iraq posed to the vastly important Saudi Arabian fields in the Persian Gulf, the Earth's late twentieth century geopolitical heartland.

Pre-1973 Energy Politics in United States

Perhaps because of its vast energy resources, the United States did not have a definitive domestic energy policy prior to the oil crisis of 1973. It did have, as David Howard Davis notes in his *Energy Politics* (1982), fuel policies for each of the three fossil fuels it held in abundance (coal, gas, and oil) as well as for the nuclear power industry, whose development the government encouraged after World War II. These policies often differed widely from one another, reflecting the different physical properties and periods of origin of each of the four fuels. An overall energy policy did not exist. Moreover, much of the time, the individual fuel policies were by-products of other policy concerns; for example, the attention given to oil in the United States in the postwar era was related to the importance of oil to postwar economic growth, whereas environmental considerations led to a 1970 freeze on the construction of the Alaska oil pipeline.

Energy in general and oil in particular were much more direct concerns of the makers of American foreign policy, especially after the U.S. Navy converted from coal to oil in the early twentieth century. To secure a supply of oil for refueling the fleet, the government encouraged American oil companies to go abroad. Although the U.S. government never created its own public oil company to seek a secure oil supply, it frequently used its political, economic, and diplomatic power to assist the American-based multinational corporations that developed that oil. Thus, after World War I, antitrust laws were never applied to

the cooperative activities of the principal U.S. oil firms, much less to the international activities of the five great, American-based multinational oil companies (Exxon, Texaco, Gulf, Mobil, and Standard Oil of California) that collaborated with Royal Dutch Shell and British Petroleum in the "Seven Sisters" cartel that effectively controlled the world oil market between 1926 and 1966. To the contrary, Congress rewrote U.S. tax codes after World War II to benefit those American oil companies in the Arabian Peninsula that suddenly had to share their profits with Persian Gulf governments. Likewise, President Dwight Eisenhower pressured Britain into including American firms when it reopened the British Petroleum venture in Iran after covert American operatives toppled the Iranian government, which had nationalized Iran's oil industry, in 1954. Prior to 1973, foreign policy required attention to energy far more than domestic policy did, and in the international arena, energy politics was oil politics.

Oil Crises of the 1970's and Energy Politics in the Energy Importing World

Events beginning with the 1973 Arab embargo on the United States and other countries friendly to Israel during the October, 1973, Yom Kippur War vastly intensified the importance of energy as a policy issue. To be sure, Arab embargoes had been threatened during both the 1956 and 1967 Arab-Israeli wars; however, on those occasions the threat had little meaning. Most Western countries either were still producing most of the energy they consumed or were able to procure ample imported oil in an international buyer's market where supply often exceeded demand.

By 1973, imported oil had become essential to the economy of much of the developed world. Even the United States, although still one of the world's major petroleum producers, was importing nearly 30 percent of the oil it required to maintain the high living standard of American consumers. In Japan and Western Europe, where postwar economic recovery had been based on oil rather than on indigenous coal supplies, and where imported petroleum accounted for 60 to 80 percent of all energy being used, petroleum imports had become essential to life itself. The oil embargo thus came as a terrifying shock to the industrialized world. Western civilization, or at least the materially rich lifestyle associated with it, had become dependent on an energy source that the Western, oil-importing countries did not control and for which there was no immediately available energy substitute.

Vulnerability of this nature is normally exploited in the amoral world of international politics, and so it was in 1973. In the aftermath of the Yom Kippur War, the U.S. allies were pressured—by the threat of losing their shipments of Arab oil—into endorsing the United Nations resolution calling for Israel to return the Arab land it acquired during the 1967 Arab-Israeli war. The same states also bid, almost hysterically, against one another for available oil supplies. By the end of October of that year, the Organization of Petroleum Exporting Countries (OPEC) had exploited this situation, taken over the control of oil production from the Seven Sisters, and established the official price of OPEC oil at four times its prior cost. In its turn, this sudden jump in the price of oil to nearly twelve dollars per barrel ignited a global recession. The recession had barely ended before the fall of the shah of Iran in January, 1979. The outbreak of war between Iraq and Iran in the fall of that year significantly reduced the supply of exportable oil, producing a second oil crisis in which the price of OPEC oil catapulted to more than thirty-six dollars per barrel.

The oil crises of 1973 and 1979 made energy the key policy issue throughout the developed, energy-importing world for several years. The crises triggered double-digit inflation and unemployment figures in most Western countries and collectively cost the Western world as much as $1 trillion in lost gross national product. Lest OPEC oil again become available only in limited amounts and/or at prohibitive costs, countries sought a mix of energy sources capable of minimizing their dependency on imported petroleum. Toward that end, most states without domestic oil or natural gas options gravitated toward a "co-co-nuk" strategy of enhanced conservation efforts, a greater use of coal, and more reliance on nuclear power in their national energy systems. As a result of these efforts, and of economies reshaping around the service sector and less energy-intensive industries, Japan and most industrialized states in Western Europe subsequently reduced the pro-

portion of imported energy in their overall energy profiles—even after recovering from their oil-crises-induced recessions. However, in most instances they also still remained dependent on oil imports for one-half or more than one-half of their total energy needs. Like the United States, these countries have had difficulty reconciling their continued dependency on oil and use of coal with the commitments that they have made to reducing fossil fuel emissions under the environment-related agreements negotiated during the 1990's.

Energy Politics and U.S. Foreign Policy from 1979 to September 11, 2001

The United States has had less success than other industrialized states in lowering oil imports. A number of factors have combined to preclude an easy shift from petroleum to other energy sources. Among these causes are the declining productivity of U.S. domestic oil fields, political opposition to nuclear power following the 1979 accident at the Three Mile Island nuclear power plant, and the high economic and environmental costs of such alternatives to imported oil, such as coal liquefaction. Lifestyle decisions made during the era of cheap energy (such as single-family suburban homes remote from work sites and a reliance on the automobile for transportation) also

Anticipating the gas and oil shortage that would result from the energy crisis of 1973, Austrian motorists wait in line to fill up their gas tanks. Issues related to oil and gas dominated energy politics in the latter half of the twentieth century. (Rue des Archives/The Granger Collection, New York)

have made the shift difficult. Consequently, oil imports have accounted for one-half or more of the oil that the United States consumes each year. Meanwhile, even with imports at this level, the country's domestic oil reserves have steadily declined, from more than 45 billion barrels of oil in 1973 to fewer than 25 billion by the mid-1990's, and to fewer than 10 billion in 2009.

For the United States, securing oil at a stable price for itself and its import-dependent allies became a central foreign policy objective following the oil crises of the 1970's. The focus has been on the Persian Gulf, where three factors have shaped U.S. policies: longstanding U.S. relationships with the oil-exporting states in the region, the geopolitical importance of this oil-rich area, and the special relationship the United States has with Israel.

The U.S. government has supported and cultivated the friendship of governments in the Persian Gulf area for a long time. A little-noted feature of the U.S. lend-lease deal with Britain before U.S. entry into World War II involved London paying millions of dollars to the king of Saudi Arabia to assure continued access to Saudi oil. More publicized was the successful U.S. effort to restore the shah of Iran to power in 1954 and its extensive arming of the shah during the 1970's to enable Iran to serve as America's "policeman" in the Persian Gulf. Most visible of all were the deployment of U.S. warships to the Persian Gulf during the latter stages of the 1980-1988 war between Iraq and Iran in order to protect oil shipments and U.S. efforts to organize an international force to restore the Kuwaiti monarchy after Iraq's 1990 occupation of that country. Both ventures dramatized the growing importance, in both U.S. foreign policy and the world energy market, of the oil-rich states along the Arabian Peninsula's Persian Gulf.

The overthrow of pro-Western governments in the oil-producing states of Iraq, Algeria, and Libya during the 1950's and 1960's and the fall of the shah of Iran in 1979 intensified the importance of the oil-rich states of the Arabian Peninsula: Kuwait, Saudi Arabia, the United Arab Emirates, Bahrain, Qatar, and Oman. The vast majority of all known petroleum reserves is located in a very small percentage of the known pools of oil, and the richest of these pools lie under the lands of Iraq, Iran, Saudi Arabia, Kuwait, and the smaller Arabian states in the area. In fact, approximately three-quarters of the total proven oil reserves of petroleum-exporting states and more than 60 per-

cent of the known oil reserves in the world lie in this region.

Saudi Arabia is the linchpin, with not only the largest reserves (conservatively estimated at more than 200 billion barrels in the mid-1990's) but also the ability to produce more than one-third of the oil imported by the Western world during the 1990's and early twenty-first century. Maintaining the stability of Saudi Arabia's government and access to its oil have thus become central objectives of U.S. foreign policy. The protection of Saudi Arabia was the first goal for the United States in deploying its troops to the Persian Gulf following Iraq's occupation of Kuwait in August, 1990. Energy concerns similarly explain why, following the war against Iraq and the liberation of Kuwait, the United States chose to retain a large military presence in the area in order to keep Iraq in check and better defend the Saudi fields should the need arise to do so.

UNITED STATES AS MEDIATOR

Petroleum politics after the Yom Kippur War also explain in part the mediator role that the United States assumed following that war in trying to negotiate an overall settlement of the Arab-Palestinian-Israeli conflict. Keeping friendly governments in power and maintaining access to Middle East oil for itself and its allies have been two of the enduring goals of U.S. policy in the Middle East. Ensuring the survival of Israel has been a third. Prior to 1973, support of Israel was arguably the highest priority of the three goals. This was true despite the fact that pursuing it frequently handicapped U.S. pursuit of the other two goals, because Arab states found it difficult to be publicly close to the strongest ally (the United States) of their worst enemy (Israel).

The Organization of Arab Petroleum Exporting Countries' (OAPEC's) oil embargo during the Yom Kippur War effectively linked access to oil to the Arab-Israeli conflict. After the war, the United States adopted a more evenhanded approach to the Arab-Israeli conflict and accepted the long-term role as mediator. The 1978 Camp David Accords—in which Egypt recognized Israel in exchange for Israel returning the Sinai Peninsula to Egypt—and the 1990's agreements between Israeli, Palestinian, and Arab leaders—which led to Palestinian home rule zones in Gaza and the West Bank being created—were more than just significant U.S. foreign policy accomplishments. To the extent that they helped avert future

Top Energy-Consuming Countries, 2005

	TOTAL (QUADRILLION BTUS)	PER CAPITA (MILLION BTUS)
Canada	14.3	436.2
China	67.1	51.4
France	11.4	181.5
Germany	14.5	176.0
India	16.2	14.8
Japan	22.6	177.0
Russia	30.3	212.2
United Kingdom	10.0	165.7
United States	100.7	340.0
World	462.8	71.8

Source: Data from U.S. Energy Information Administration, *International Energy Annual, 2005.*

Note: Values are in British thermal units (Btus). Totals are in quadrillions; hence U.S. consumption of 100.7 is 100,700,000,000,000,000. Per capita consumption is in millions; hence U.S. per capita consumption of 340.0 is 340,000,000.

Arab-Israeli wars, they also represented successes in U.S. international energy policy.

ENERGY POLITICS IN THE EARLY YEARS OF THE NEW MILLENNIUM

During both the era of low oil prices in the 1990's and the era of high oil prices between 2005 and 2008, Western governments struggled to reconcile their desire to create a cleaner environment with their continued dependency on fossil fuels. During the first of these two periods, the low cost of imported energy simultaneously deflected their attention away from developing alternatives to imported sources of energy and encouraged consideration of environmentally friendly legislation, even if it increased energy costs. Not surprisingly the latter proposals were invariably opposed, frequently successfully so, by lobbyists for the energy industries in those societies. The environmentalists, however, also scored their victories. In the United States, for example, the efforts of the oil companies to acquire exploration and drilling rights in the Arctic reserve were consistently beaten back by environmentalists, and European environmentalists have had some success in getting major European oil companies to endorse, verbally at least, environmentally friendly energy plans.

The terrorist attacks on the United States on September 11, 2001, reshaped the energy debate, and subsequent developments quickly made energy politics a mainstay of international relations between 2001 and 2008. In a world with a tightening oil market resulting from the increased demand for oil by India and China, both of whom accelerated development projects of relatively inexpensive imported oil, pursuing policies deemed offensive by oil-exporting states suddenly became more difficult for the United States. Thus, U.S. efforts after 9/11 to track down and cut off the funding of terrorist groups supported by Saudi religious organizations floundered when the U.S. government was, under the changed economic and political conditions, unwilling or unable to lean heavily on the Saudi government to crack down of such bodies. Similarly, U.S. efforts to isolate Iraq, a country seemingly bent on acquiring nuclear weapons, came to little when Western U.S. allies proved to be unwilling to antagonize Iran, Iraq's eastern neighbor, in a time when Iranian oil exports were important to the world's economic health. Perhaps most important, the U.S. invasion of Iraq in 2003 radically altered the world oil market and produced both a series of foreign policy problems for the United States and aggressive foreign policy actors on the world stage.

A collateral consequence of the U.S. decision to remove Iraqi president Saddam Hussein from power was that it eliminated a central element that had encouraged OPEC to keep its prices in the moderate range throughout the 1990's. Iraq was operating under U.N. sanctions and was only permitted to export a small amount of its production capacity; however, it was within the power of the U.N. to remove those sanctions at any time. The threat of substantial Iraqi oil exports suddenly being unleashed on the world market in response to irresponsible OPEC pricing action influenced OPEC's decision makers for more than a decade, encouraging them to keep their price increases modest. The disruption of Iraq's oil production capacity as a result of the U.S. invasion, and the subsequent turmoil in Iraq, removed that factor. When the growing demand for oil subsequently coincided with the political uncertainties surrounding its availability from other suppliers such as Iran and Nigeria (whose oil-producing region is hotly contested by several tribal groups), the result was a stratospheric rise in the price of oil from the $35-per-barrel range that existed prior to the invasion to $150-per-barrel by 2008. By that point the governments of the developed oil-importing world had already begun reconsidering energy alternatives—this time of a "green" variety—and the global demand for oil was contracting. Between 2003 and 2008, however, the high prices made the leaders of oil-exporting countries such as Iran, Venezuela, and Russia aggressive in the realm of foreign policy.

Joseph R. Rudolph, Jr.

FURTHER READING

Anderson, Irvine H. *Aramco, the United States, and Saudi Arabia: A Study in the Dynamics of Foreign Oil Policy, 1933-1950*. Princeton, N.J.: Princeton University Press, 1981.

Baev, Pavel. *Russian Energy Policy and Military Power: Putin's Quest for Greatness*. New York: Routledge, 2008.

Beaubouef, Bruce Andre. *The Strategic Petroleum Reserve: U.S. Energy Security and Oil Politics, 1975-2005*. College Station: Texas A & M University Press, 2007.

Campbell, Kurt M., and Jonathon Price, eds. *The Global Politics of Energy*. Washington, D.C.: The Aspen Institute, 2008.

Davis, David Howard. *Energy Politics*. 4th ed. New York: St. Martin's Press, 1993.

Deece, David A., and Joseph S. Nye, eds. *Energy and Security*. Cambridge, Mass.: Ballinger, 1981.

Falola, Toyin, and Ann Genova. *The Politics of the Global Oil Industry: An Introduction*. Westport, Conn.: Praeger, 2005.

Gallagher, Kelly Sims, ed. *Acting in Time on Energy Policy*. Washington, D.C.: Brookings Institution Press, 2009.

Goldman, Marshall I. *Petrostate: Putin, Power, and the New Russia*. New York: Oxford University Press, 2008.

Klare, Michael T. *Blood and Oil: The Dangers and Consequences of America's Growing Dependency on Imported Petroleum*. New York: Henry Holt, 2005.

_____. *Rising Powers, Shrinking Planet: The New Geopolitics of Energy*. New York: Metropolitan Books, 2008.

Mattson, Kevin. *"What the Heck Are You up to, Mr. President?" Jimmy Carter, America's "Malaise," and the Speech That Should Have Changed the Country*. New York: Bloomsbury, 2009.

Morris, Paul M., ed. *National Energy Policy: Major Federal Energy Programs and Status*. New York: Novinka Books, 2006.

Roberts, Paul. *The End of Oil: On the Edge of a Perilous New World*. Boston: Houghton Mifflin, 2005.

Rosenbaum, Walter A. *Environmental Politics and Policy*. 7th ed. Washington, D.C.: CQ Press, 2008.

Shaffer, Brenda. *Energy Politics*. Philadelphia: University of Pennsylvania Press, 2009.

Standlea, David M. *Oil, Globalization, and the War for the Arctic Refuge*. Albany: State University of New York Press, 2006.

Stoff, Michael B. *Oil, War, and American Security: The Search for a National Policy on Foreign Oil, 1941-1947*. New Haven, Conn.: Yale University Press, 1980.

Yergin, Daniel. *The Prize: The Epic Quest for Oil, Money, and Power*. New ed. New York: The Free Press, 2008.

SEE ALSO: Alaska pipeline; Coal; Coal gasification and liquefaction; Department of Energy, U.S.; Energy economics; Energy Policy Act; Iran; Oil and natural gas distribution; Oil embargo and energy crises of 1973 and 1979; Oil industry; Resources as a source of international conflict; Russia; Saudi Arabia; United States; Venezuela.

Energy storage

CATEGORIES: Energy resources; obtaining and using resources

When more energy is available than is needed at a given time, the excess energy can be stored for later use in a number of ways, including electrochemical cells, pumped storage, and solar heat storage.

BACKGROUND

Energy storage is important for utility load leveling, electrical vehicles, solar energy systems, uninterrupted power supply, and energy systems at remote locations. Two important parameters to consider when discussing energy storage are the duration of storage and the amount of energy stored per unit weight or volume. Duration of energy storage may vary from a fraction of one second to many years. In a nuclear

Specific Energy Storage Capacities of Various Materials

Uranium-235 (fission reaction)	7.0×10^{10}	Glauber's salt (at 32.4°C)	251
Reactor fuel (2.5% enriched UO$_2$)	1.5×10^9	Calcium chloride hexahydrate (at 29.6°C)	191
Natural uranium	5.0×10^8	Water (temperature change = 40°C)	167
Hydrogen (LHV)	1.2×10^5	Sodium acetate trihydrate (at 58°C)	180
Methane (LHV)	5.0×10^4	Cross-linked high density poly- ethylene (at 126°C)	180
Gasoline (LHV)	4.4×10^4		
Lithium hydride (at 700°C)	3.8×10^3	Lead-acid battery	119
Falling water (altitude change = 100m)	9.8×10^2	Flywheel (uniformly stressed disc)	79
		Coil spring	0.16
Draw salt (220-540°C)	4.9×10^2	Capacitor	0.016

Note: All values are in kilojoules per kilogram. LHV stands for "lower heating value," indicating that the nonuseful energy given off in steam has been subtracted from the figure.

power plant, nuclear fuel is stored within a reactor for a year. Coal piles, gas and oil storage tanks, and pumped hydro (hydroelectric power) are maintained by power utilities for several days' use, depending on the need. Similarly, for a solar energy system, energy storage may be required on an hourly, daily, or weekly basis. The amounts of energy stored per unit weight (specific energy) and per unit volume (energy density) are critical in determining the size of a storage system.

Other factors of importance in the design of a storage system include the time rates at which energy can be stored (charging) or removed (discharging) and the number of useful cycles of charging and discharging. Depending on the nature of available energy, it can be stored as mechanical, thermal, chemical, electrical, or magnetic energy. Electrical energy can be either stored as chemical energy in batteries, called electrochemical cells, or stored as mechanical energy by pumping water from a lower elevation to a higher elevation (pumped hydro). Electrical energy can also be converted to thermal energy and then stored as thermal energy.

ELECTROCHEMICAL CELLS

An electrochemical cell consists of an anode, a cathode, and an electrolyte. When a cell is connected to a load, electrons flow from the anode to the cathode. In this operation, oxidation (loss of electrons) takes

place at the anode, and reduction (gain of electrons) occurs at the cathode. The cell chemistry of the well-known lead-acid battery is as follows: The anode is lead (Pb), the cathode is lead oxide (PbO$_2$), and the electrolyte is sulfuric acid (H$_2$SO$_4$). The overall cell reaction is as follows:

$$\underset{\text{Cathode}}{\text{PbO}_2} + 2\,\text{H}_2\text{SO}_4 + \underset{\text{Anode}}{\text{Pb}} \underset{\text{Charge}}{\overset{\text{Discharge}}{\rightleftharpoons}} \underset{\text{Cathode}}{\text{PbSO}_4} + 2\text{H}_2\text{O} + \underset{\text{Anode}}{\text{PbSO}_4}$$

The forward reaction represents the change during discharge when the cell is connected to a load, and the backward reaction represents the change that occurs when electric energy is stored. The theoretical voltage and capacity of a cell are functions of the anode and cathode materials. The theoretical voltage can be calculated from the standard electrode potentials of the materials. The capacity of a cell is expressed as the total quantity of electricity involved in the electrochemical reaction and is defined in terms of coulombs or ampere-hours. Theoretically, one gram-equivalent weight of a material will deliver 96,487 coulombs or 26.8 ampere-hours. A battery consists of one or more cells connected in series, parallel, or both depending on the desired output voltage and capacity.

Electrochemical energy storage is more commonly known as battery storage. Batteries are classified as primary and secondary batteries. Only secondary batteries are rechargeable and are therefore suitable for energy storage applications. Lead-acid and nickel-cadmium are well-known rechargeable batteries and are the most commonly used. Lead-acid batteries have been used for more than a century and are still the most popular batteries. An example is the automobile battery. Large numbers of electrochemical cells have been identified that can be used for storing electricity; a few of these are nickel-cadmium, nickel metal hydride, and lithium-iron sulfide. Electric storage in batteries has shown great potential in applications such as cell phones, laptop computers, tools, and electric vehicles and as a means of storing electricity for load-leveling purposes in power plants. The growing interest in electric vehicles is driving innovation in the battery industry. The automobile industry is looking for a better-performing, lower-cost battery.

The current favorite, the lithium-ion battery, has led to research into lithium-air and lithium-sulfur batteries, which have much higher energy capacity and lower weight.

PUMPED STORAGE

Another means of storing electricity is to pump water from a lower reservoir (which can be a lake or a river) to a higher reservoir. The potential energy stored in water by virtue of its elevation can be used later to generate electricity when needed by using hydraulic turbines. The motors that drive the pumps are reversible and act as electrical generators when water falls from the upper reservoir to drive the turbines. The main components of a pumped storage plant are the upper reservoir, waterway passage, power house, and lower reservoir.

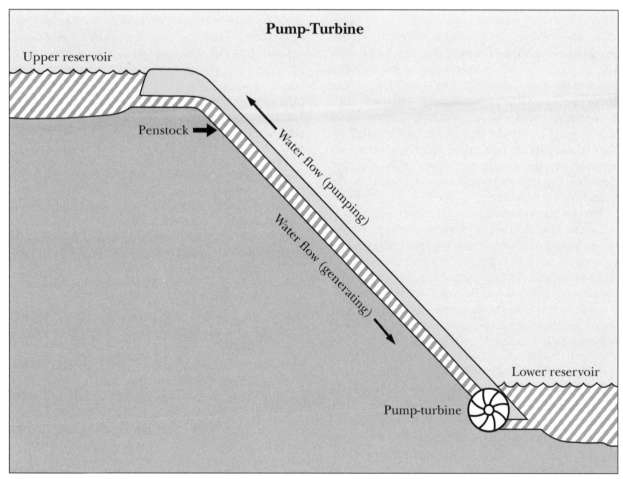

The development of the reversible pump-turbine, which acts as a motor and pump when rotating in one direction and as a turbine and generator when rotating in the other, has made pumped storage more practical.

Advantages of pumped hydro units include simple operation, high reliability, low maintenance, long life, quick start from a standstill, and economic generation of peaking electrical energy. Several such systems are in operation in the United States. Power-generating capacities of these systems vary between 5 megawatts and 2,000 megawatts or higher. The overall efficiencies of these power plants vary between 65 and 90 percent (these figures include the efficiencies of pumps, hydraulic turbines, and generators, and losses from the upper reservoir). In spite of the technical and economic viability of pumped hydro, the requirement of a specific type of topography and some environmental concerns limit its application. To overcome these problems, underground pumped hydro storage can be used. In this case a large cavern or an aquifer can be used as the lower reservoir.

Solar Heat Storage

When converted into heat, solar energy can be stored in the form of sensible heat and latent heat. Sensible heat is stored in a material by raising its temperature. The amount of sensible heat stored in a material is equal to the product of the mass, specific heat, and the temperature rise of the material. The most common sensible heat storage materials include water, propylene glycol, rocks, and molten salts. Water has the highest specific heat value. The higher the temperature rise, the greater the amount of heat stored. However, the highest temperature is limited by the properties of the material.

Thermal energy can also be stored as latent heat in a material when it changes phase, as from solid to liquid or liquid to vapor. Some materials also change phase from solid to vapor directly or from one solid phase to another. The amount of latent heat stored in a material is equal to the product of the mass of the material and its latent heat. Because materials change phase at a constant temperature, latent heat is stored and retrieved at a fixed temperature known as the transition temperature. Some common phase change materials (PCMs) used for heat storage are paraffin waxes, Glauber's salt (sodium sulfate decahydrate), calcium chloride hexahydrate, sodium acetate trihydrate, and cross-linked high-density polyethylene.

Solar heat storage has major applications in space heating, crop drying, cooking, electric power generation, and industrial process heat. Heat storage in water is the most economical and well-developed technology. Hot water is stored in tanks made of glass- or stone-lined steel, fiberglass, reinforced polymer (plastic), concrete with plastic liner, and wood. The storage tanks may be located above or below ground. In North America and China, aquifers have been used for long-term storage of hot water. Molten nitrate salt (50 percent sodium nitrate, 50 percent potassium nitrate), also known as Draw salt, which has a melting point of 222° Celsius, has been used as a storage material for a solar thermal power system in an experiment in Albuquerque, New Mexico. This was the first commercial demonstration of generating power from storage. Solar Two, a 10-megawatt solar thermal power demonstration project in Barstow, California, also was designed to use this molten salt to store solar energy. It led to the development of Solar Tres Power Tower near Seville, Spain.

PCMs encapsulated in tubes, trays, rods, panels, balls, canisters, and tiles have been used for solar space-heating applications. The most common PCMs used are hydrated salts of sodium sulfate, sodium thiosulfate, sodium acetate, barium hydroxide, magnesium chloride, and magnesium nitrate. For building space-heating applications, PCM can be encapsulated in the building components themselves. They can be incorporated in the ceiling, wall, or floor of the building. For example, paraffin wax mixtures have been used for heat storage in wallboards.

D. Yogi Goswami and Chand K. Jotshi

Further Reading

Baxter, Richard. *Energy Storage: A Nontechnical Guide.* Tulsa, Okla.: PennWell Books, 2006.

Dell, Ronald M., and David A. J. Rand. *Understanding Batteries.* Cambridge, England: Royal Society of Chemistry, 2001.

Harper, Gavin D. J. *Fuel Cell Projects for the Evil Genius.* New York: McGraw-Hill, 2008.

Kreith, Frank, and D. Yogi Goswami, eds. *Handbook of Energy Efficiency and Renewable Energy.* Boca Raton, Fla.: CRC Press, 2007.

Lane, George A., ed. *Solar Heat Storage: Latent Heat Materials.* 2 vols. Boca Baton, Fla.: CRC Press, 1983.

Linden, David, and Thomas B. Reddy, eds. *Handbook of Batteries.* 3d ed. New York: McGraw-Hill, 2001.

O'Hayre, Ryan, Suk-Won Cha, Whitney Colella, and Fritz B. Prinz. *Fuel Cell Fundamentals.* 2d ed. Hoboken, N.J.: John Wiley & Sons, 2009.

See also: Electrical power; Fuel cells; Hydroenergy; Photovoltaic cells; Solar energy.